Rogn Fjeld
October, 1989

W9-CRB-932

Exploring American Religion

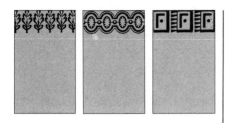

Exploring American Religion

Denise Lardner Carmody

John Tully Carmody

UNIVERSITY OF TULSA

MAYFIELD PUBLISHING COMPANY

Mountain View, California

Copyright © 1990 by Mayfield Publishing Company

All rights reserved. No portion of this book may be reproduced in
any form or by any means without written permission of the publisher.

Library of Congress Cataloging-in-Publication Data

Carmody, Denise Lardner.
    Exploring American religion / Denise Lardner Carmody, John Tully
Carmody.
       p.   cm.
    Bibliography: p.
    Includes index.
    ISBN 0−87484−750−8
      1. United States—Religion.   I. Carmody, John.
  II. Title.
    BL2525.C36   1990
    291'.0973—dc20   89−34098
               CIP

Manufactured in the United States of America

9 8 7 6 5 4 3 2 1

Mayfield Publishing Company
1240 Villa Street
Mountain View, California 94041

Sponsoring editor, James Bull; managing editor, Linda Toy; production
editor, Sondra Glider; manuscript editor, Loralee Windsor; text and
cover designer, Al Burkhardt. The text was set in 10/12 Meridien by
Graphic Typesetting Service and printed on 50# Finch Opaque by
Banta Company.

Cover painting: *Sierra Nevada Morning*, by Albert Bierstadt. Courtesy
The Thomas Gilcrease Institute of American History and Art, Tulsa,
Oklahoma.

Contents

Preface

This book is an introductory survey of American religion. It contains three parts, each of which leads students into central features of American religious life. Part One, a succinct history of American religion, offers a sense of the chronological unfolding. Part Two discusses the American religious worldview, considering what Americans have thought about important religious problems and theological options. Part Three deals with contemporary trends and identifies the challenges now facing American religion.

The chapters in each part combine discussions of major religious patterns with analyses of representative personalities and texts. Thus Chapter 4, in Part One, examines Revolutionary and Republican religion by discussing three main patterns ("Later Colonial Trends and the Great Awakening," "Enlightened Religion," and "Independence and Constitution"), then exploring the significance of Thomas Jefferson, and finally analyzing James Madison's "A Memorial and a Remonstrance." Similarly, Chapter 11, in Part Two, focuses on the American sense of peoplehood by discussing three main features ("A Demographic Sketch of

America," "Ethnicity in American Piety," and "The Lively Experiment [in Pluralism]"), then considering the significance of Abraham Lincoln, and finally analyzing Alexis de Tocqueville's *Democracy in America.*

Our hope has been that by approaching American religion from several different angles of inquiry, we might suggest its complexity and diversity. By offering portraits of leading men and women from diverse backgrounds, we hope to engage students' interest and help them relate to the dramatic character of their heritage. The analyses of representative writings enable teachers to add readings from primary sources and ensure that students have at least some acquaintance with classics of American religious literature.

We have taken a broad view of "religion," letting the term include sentiments as well as institutions, rituals as well as ethical standards. Without overlooking instances of religious bigotry and repression, we take a positive view, locating the center of the American religious enterprise in human beings' struggles with the mysteriousness of their condition.

Our thanks to Jim Bull and Sondra Glider

of Mayfield Publishing Company, to our colleagues in the Faculty of Religion at the University of Tulsa, and to the following scholars who read the prospectus or manuscript and offered helpful criticisms: Gary Alexander, University of Wisconsin, Stevens Point; Henry Levinson, University of North Carolina, Greensboro; Edward Linenthal, University of Wisconsin, Oshkosh; Robert Mullin, North Carolina State University; Amanda Porterfield, Syracuse University; Mary Schneider, Michigan State University; and Timothy Wadkins, San Jose State University.

For Sally and Tom Kitch

Exploring
American
Religion

PART One

A History of American Religion

In being so bold as to write a text on American religion, the authors have tried to be guided by what student readers, most of whom will be young Americans, most want and need to know. The assumption has been that readers deserve a twofold exposition, corresponding to what might be called the outside and the inside of religion. On the one hand, there is the story of how various groups, all of whom were guided by religious assumptions, contributed to the creation of the United States or American culture. On the other hand, there are the worldviews, the metaphysical statements, implicit in such a historical process. This first part of the text provides a historical sketch of what religion has meant in the region now known as the United States.

This history devotes two chapters to the antecedents of American religion and seven chapters to what developed from the period of colonization to the end of the Second World War. The antecedents studied here are the Native American religions that existed long before whites came to America and the European traditions on which the early settlers drew. The seven historical periods surveyed are the era of the European colonies, the time of the revolution and founding of the new nation, the period of renewed

Gilbert Stuart's famous portrait of Washington inevitably suggests the unfinished character of the venture Washington spearheaded. (Courtesy Museum of Fine Arts, Boston; jointly owned by the Museum of Fine Arts, Boston, and the National Portrait Gallery, Smithsonian Institution, Washington, D.C.)

1

evangelical fervor, the era of renewed European immigration, the Civil War era, the period from reconstruction to 1914, and the era of the two world wars. Each chapter sketches how religious developments unfolded and studies both representative personalities and representative texts.

C H A P T E R 1

Before the Whites

An Overview of Native American History

The currently predominating theory of Native American origins has it that as much as 60,000 years ago Paleolithic hunters came to North America by way of what is now the Bering Strait but was then a land bridge. (Even now the strait averages only 98 to 164 feet in depth and at its narrowest is about 53 miles wide, separating the Seward Peninsula of Alaska from the easternmost portion of the USSR.) The hypothesis is that the glaciers of the Ice Age had absorbed the sea waters, leaving a narrow corridor through which the hunters could follow their prey into Alaska. They would have been people of what ethnologists call North Asiatic, proto-Mongoloid stock. Ecological conditions being similar on both sides of the Bering Strait, the small groups that migrated could have continued their cultural traditions with little thought of entering a new era or land.

This northern (arctic or subarctic) origin of Native Americans explains many of the cultural features found not only in the far North, where the Inuit (Eskimos) continued to battle severe conditions, but even in more temperate areas. Among such widely dispersed cultural features one may count veneration of a high god, of the

Much American art has romanticized Native Americans, but many artists who worked when the western territories were only recently opened were clearly impressed by the dignity and simplicity of Native American life. (Crow Encampment, A. J. Miller; Gilcrease Museum, Tulsa, Oklahoma)

thunderbird, and of mother earth; rituals honoring the bear; taboos surrounding hunting; sweat lodges for purification; shamanic ceremonies (geared to ecstatic healing, intercession with the spiritual world, and guidance of the souls of the dead to their places of rest); and myths concerning creation, the origin of death, and many features of the human condition. Those comparing religions locate such features in the Paleolithic hunting cultures of Eurasia and so think of Native American cultures as offshoots of a parent Eurasian cultural matrix.

Complicating this simple view, however, are such factors as the weak impress of such a Paleolithic hunting culture in recent eastern Siberia, perhaps due to the influx of tribes from southern Asia during the last millennium, and the more intense form of **shamanism** one finds in Siberia, perhaps due to Tibetan influences. Among Native Americans intense shamanism is pronounced only among the Inuit and tribes of the Northwest, although both South American and South Asian tribes manifest less-dramatic forms of shamanic ecstasy. A third complication is linguistic, since the American tribes display a bewildering variety of languages, most of which show no obvious relationship to languages of the Old (Asian) World. On the other hand, the majority of the American Indian languages have a common structure and so many be genetically related among themselves.

Before about 10,000 B.C.E. (Before the Christian or Common Era), the picture of Native American cultures (and so religions) is conjectural. After 10,000 B.C.E., there are increasingly clear traces of a hunting culture in the process of adapting to new or changing habitats. In eastern North America big game such as the mammoth, the camel, the giant bison, and the three-toed horse were the major prizes, no doubt supplemented by plants, nuts, berries, and roots. The sorts of ceremonies one finds in ancient Asia for killing and eating large animals probably flourished in eastern North America,

perhaps along with such Asian notions as paying homage to a "master" of the animals, who freed or confined them as he (or she) wished. Between 8000 and 4000 B.C.E. the big game died out, perhaps due to a combination of climatic conditions and human killing. Only the bear survived and continued to command special rites. (Bear rituals have been found in Scandinavia, northern Japan, the American Northeast and Northwest, and even in the American Southwest among the Pueblo.) That Asian influences continued to shape American tribes during this period is suggested by the presence of such Asian myths as that of the earth diver (a hero who brings mud from the bottom of the sea to form the earth).

From about 7000 to 5000 B.C.E. the common Paleolithic hunting culture fragmented into several different regional variations. The sorts of game, fish, or plants afforded by the particular area into which a group of tribes had wandered stimulated an adaptation of their ceremonies and myths. For example, tribes moving into such desert areas as the Southwest, the Great Basin, and parts of California became less dependent on animals and more dependent on wild plants, seeds, and nuts. They also developed basket weaving and discovered plants with hallucinogenic properties (such as peyote). Maize (Indian corn) and tobacco, the cultivation of which probably began in Central America, were taken over by tribes of eastern North America. The cultivation of maize led to significant cultural changes, because it fostered a settled village life and enhanced the status of women, who had much to do with its cultivation. Both religious ideas and religious rituals followed in the train of such cultural changes, shifting to a sharper focus on fertility and bloody sacrifices. (Why is not certain; perhaps to restore blood, the coin of life, to Mother Earth, who was spending her substance in producing crops).

By 3000 to 2000 B.C.E. maize was being cultivated in the American Southwest. This led to the predominance of village cultures by 500 C.E.

The Southwest was also influenced by other aspects of Central American culture. For example, the Hohokam culture of southern Arizona, which flourished from about 500 to 1200 C.E., seems to have risen and fallen in tandem with the Toltec empire in Central America. From the Toltecs came such innovations as irrigation canals, courts for ritual ball games, and large mounds of earth or adobe that served as platforms for temples. The traditional Hopi and Pueblo cultures retained this influence in their pottery and their mask *(kachina)* ceremonies. From about 1000 B.C.E. to 700 C.E. cultures featuring burial mounds flourished in the Southeast. The last of these, called the Hopewell, had ceremonies shaped by the cultivation of maize.

After 700 C.E., the so-called Mississippi tradition promoted huge rectangular mounds used as platforms for temples, as intensive agriculture flourished in the lower Mississippi Valley and the Southeast. The Natchez of the lower Mississippi had not only giant temples but also sacred kings, a hierarchy of social classes, and elaborate religious ceremonies aimed at promoting agricultural fertility. Eventually aspects of such agriculturally based religious complexes penetrated the woodland tribes of the Northeast and the tribes of the central plains, both of whose cultures had previously been shaped by hunting.

Just before the advent of the Europeans, then, the North American tribes were diversified into numerous geographical areas, each supporting a religious culture geared to obtaining food and housing in that locale. In the Arctic the necessity for hunting and the fierce weather conditions led to veneration of the land and sea animals pursued for food and the pursuit of shamanic ecstasy for contact with the spiritual powers controlling the people's destiny. Hunting also predominated in the Subarctic; moose and caribou were especially important and so predominated in hunting ceremonies. Shamanic **divination** was important in the Sub-

arctic, and sweat baths were employed for ritual purity. The woodlands of the Northeast housed both hunters and agriculturalists; the Iroquois, for example, celebrated rites for the three "sisters": maize, squash, and beans. In the woodlands of the Southeast agriculture predominated, priests and curing ceremonies stood out, and tribes were regularly organized along the maternal line of descent. The prairies welcomed the first eastern woodlands tribes displaced by the whites and lay open to exploration by horseback. Because both hunting and agricultural practices prevailed, the buffalo and maize were both important (and so featured in religious ceremonies). Modern Native Americans have often considered the plains religious culture, which involved such ceremonies as the Sun Dance and the ritual smoking of a pipe (both of which we consider later), the best model for a latter-day pantribal religion.

Fishing predominated along the Pacific Northwest coast, and totem poles, canoes, plank houses, and Asian-looking conical hats distinguished the tribes from those of the other continental areas. Fishing also predominated over hunting and agriculture in the plateau of the area known as the Great Basin between the coastal ranges and the Rocky Mountains. Plateau tribes regularly sought visions and were ruled by hereditary chiefs. The people of the Great Basin were probably the most impoverished of the continent's tribes, living on seeds, nuts, and rodents in the dryness of the semidesert. The California tribes were influenced by the coastal, basin, and southwestern cultures adjacent to them to the north, east, and south. In the central valleys and coastal regions they enjoyed a fairly easy life in a mild climate that provided many edible wild plants, as well as animals and fish. The California tribes stood out for their lofty concepts of the Supreme Being and their initiation of youths into religious societies.

By 1500 C.E. the Southwest was populated by both farming and hunting peoples; the native

Pueblo and Hopi practiced agriculture, while tribes recently arrived from the East, such as the Apache and Navaho, stressed hunting. The Pueblo had an elaborate ceremonial system, the major purpose of which was to try to create harmony between the tribe and the powers of rain and fertility that rules the agricultural year.[1]

Common Religious Themes

Since colonial times white observers have tended either to denigrate Native American culture as benighted or to make Native Americans exemplars of the "noble savage." Roger Williams, founder of Rhode Island, chose the second option and maintained that the Native American was by birth as good as an Englishman. William Penn, founder of Pennsylvania, showed a kindly inclination to the first option: "These poor people are under a dark night in things relating to religion, to be sure, the tradition of it."[2] Yet Penn admired the Native Americans' belief in a great king who made human beings and dwelt in a land to the southwest, where he would welcome the souls of the good. He also admired the ceremonies he observed, which included sacrifices of the first fruits of the hunt by laying them on a fire and the round dances, complete with choral singing, that occurred at such festivals as the corn harvest.

In a broader historical perspective, outstanding themes include the Native Americans' dedication to place; the nonliterate character of their culture; and their focus on sacred objects and actions, ceremonies for passing through the life cycle, and ceremonies geared to sustaining an economy indebted to plants and animals.

The sacred significance of place comes through in the songs the Navaho sang as they built their dwellings (hogans). The songs recalled the building of the first hogan, where the human race began. They expressed the Navaho conviction that building the hogan was the first necessary step if any later planning and execution were to be successful. Latent in this conviction was the idea that all planning requires a solid base, a fulcrum from which to move other things to their appointed spaces and times. Without a hogan one had no fixity and was adrift on the surface of things. Before they had hogans, the people were confused. They had nothing and could do nothing. Only when they made hogans did they have places where they could come together, sit down, and plan their future. Indeed the Navaho word for "leader" reflects this background. Where the whites speak of their leaders as kings, presidents, or dictators, the Navaho speak of "planners."

The importance of place emerges even in the myths and traditions of the hunting peoples who migrated to follow the game. Not only was the portable teepee invested with special significance, the tribe traveled a well-known route in an established seasonal cycle. Beneath the obvious need to adapt to their given ecological niche (for example, by devising suitable clothing), the tribe had to support inclinations to become intimate with the land and learn all the shadings of its geological layout, the kinds and traits of its birds, and the properties of its plants and berries. Native Americans were at one with nature. Little of our modern technology, which both keeps nature at bay and bends it to our will, mediated between the earliest Americans and the land. So the place where they lived and roamed formed their psyches more directly and obviously than our cities or states form our psyches today. Certain places were sacred as hunting or burial grounds. Certain other places were weird and dangerous, perhaps because the destructive powers of nature had lashed out at a given river that flooded or a given slope down which had rumbled an avalanche.

The earliest Americans had oral, nonwriting cultures, and in a technical sense were prehistoric. It is not immediately apparent how much that separates their cultures from ours. Writing is another way of placing something between

*The beauty and vastness of the land were the major
influences in Native American culture, nurturing a
spirit sensitive to the divine presence in every striking
locale.* (*Multnomah Falls*, Albert Bierstadt; Gilcrease
Museum, Tulsa, Oklahoma)

oneself and nature or other people. It is a mediator, another way of taming experience and avoiding some of the shock of spontaneous encounters. It can also distance people from their words. Thus the first Native Americans who had to negotiate with whites were suspicious from the outset: What was the worth of words written on paper, words a person did not have to speak face to face and stand behind as expressions of his or her own honor?[3]

In their poems, prayers, songs, and charms Native Americans came alive, externalizing their hopes and fears. Perhaps for that reason, many tribes worried about loose speech. Only words and prayers that came from a quiet recollected spirit and a decisive mind were likely to bring good. Only words expressing thoughts purified by sacrifice, fasting, and solitude were likely to please the pure spirits responsible for everything good in the world. Finally there was the matter of memory and tradition—what tribal elders stored as the wisdom learned through many generations. When history is oral—composed of memories not committed to paper but kept alive in people's hearts—it is more personal but more fragile. One has to hear it told regularly, let it pierce one's spirit in song, and feel it extend into one's feet as the stuff of ritual dance if it is to make present moments pregnant with the best possibilities of the past. Indeed it must become myth—time past packed into stories—if it is to become a sacred tale of how one's people first discerned and established their proper identity.

Sensitivity to the significance of place and the formative powers of language account for many of the cultural emphases shared by Native American peoples. Those comparing cultures note, however, that virtually all tribes sponsored religious art as another way of externalizing their needs and beliefs. Thus healers might draw in sand the impression they had received of a patient's illness, just as they might sing to rouse the curative powers. Baskets and blankets carried designs that were miniature charts of the cosmos. The northern shaman about to go into ecstatic trance through dancing and singing donned distinctive garb, each part of his costume reminding both him and those looking on of the pole he had to descend to the underworld or the bird he would become to fly to the heavens. The costumes of ritual dancers performing at the harvest festival or ceremonies for the new year were also symbolic. The totem poles carved with spirit faces, the masks for the kachina dance, and the animals the Inuit carved on ivory or stone were more than decoration. Because spirits moved everywhere—in animals as well as in human sickness or feats of bravery—everything might bear a spiritual message. So the polar bear carved with one paw poised to strike and a mouth ready to devour might be a symbol of death, reminding Inuit hunters about the need for caution and everyone else about the perils of living off other creatures.

Messages such as these sounded different depending on one's station on the track from birth to death. Like most other nonliterate peoples, Native Americans created ceremonies designed to bring the traditional wisdom home with special force several times during the life cycle. At birth there were ceremonies and traditions for naming the child and purifying both the child and the mother. Often the child was named for a recently deceased relative whose qualities were desirable or whose spirit had been restless, seeking a new embodiment. (Many tribes believed in reincarnation.) Blood was always a potent sight, so birth as well as injury and death required special precautions. Indeed, many tribes surrounded menstruation with special taboos, secluding women each month and making much of the menarche (first menstrual period). Generally the notion was that women's power of bearing life had to be segregated from men's power of bringing death through hunting or warfare. Nature was a delicate system of counterbalancing powers, and if men and women came into contact at the wrong times—when the power of fertility was strong in women or men had just returned from the kill—everything could be thrown out of kilter. Young people learned about all this in connection with their preparation for puberty. What was expected of them as mature women or men became the subject matter of painful ordeals, vision quests, songs, and dances that got the message into every nerve ending.

Finally Native Americans commonly ritualized the work that provided the tribe its food and clothing. Thus the buffalo that furnished the plains Indians everything from supper to moccasins and tents was praised, petitioned, and held in mind constantly, as was the seal that was equally important in the economy of coastal Inuit. The corn that many tribes raised as their staple food stimulated parallel rituals. The shift from hunting to agriculture drew more attention to Mother Earth and feminine powers, but the significance of the fertilizing sun and rain also grew. Each of these economic foci, as well as other important Indian works, tended to be set against a mythic template. What was being done now had been done for generations, indeed had been prescribed at the foundations of the present world order, when culture heroes or first ancestors had set the basic pattern. So work, no less than giving birth, marrying, and dying, moved to rhythms and patterns established by superhuman powers. Their meaning depended on nothing so fragile as human convention. They were part of the way things were, with nature and human beings coordinated elements of a single living and sacred whole.

The Legacy Offered

Historically, considerations of Native American culture have seldom presented a balanced appreciation that discerned both spiritual riches and technological poverty (poverty compared to European technology, that is). In terms of tools adapted to their habitat and simple lifestyle, Native American "technology" could be extremely efficient; witness the Inuit snow knife, with which an experienced worker could construct an igloo in half an hour. This section considers the spiritual riches, probing the inside of the cultures that white incursions so frequently destroyed.

Joseph Epes Brown, perhaps the dean of recent scholars of Native American religion, has drawn from his studies of Lakota and other tribal cultures an arresting summary of the legacy that white culture has rarely appreciated or even considered seriously. A single example, the use of the sweat lodge, suggests the psychosomatic and symbolic genius that lay waiting to be tapped:

During the four periods of sweating within the [darkened] lodge, prayers are recited, sacred songs are sung, and a pipe is ceremonially smoked four times by the circle of people. At the conclusion of the fourth and last period the door is opened so that "the light enters into the darkness, that we may see not only with our two eyes, but with the one eye which is of the heart, and with which we see and know all that is true and good." Going forth into the light from the house of darkness, in which all impurities have been left behind, represents human liberation from ignorance, from the ego, and from the cosmos. The person is now a renewed being entering symbolically into the world of light or wisdom.[4]

Clearly the sweating is as much spiritual as physical. Indeed Native Americans were loathe to separate the spiritual from the physical, insisting that the human being is a unity of body and soul. Sweating in the dark, feeling the moisture of the steam released by pouring water over hot stones, the participants might think they were back in the womb, waiting to be reborn and start afresh. Saying their prayers and singing their songs, they could relate themselves to the holy powers of the four directions; to the spirits of the animals that helped them; and to the Great Spirit, their Father, who had given them so much. They could also relate themselves to the long file of ancestors who had prayed, sung, and sweated just like this. The smoke from the pipe carried their prayers to the heavens, and as they passed the pipe around the circle, they could feel their sharing of the same traditions, the same human condition. If the people could remain a circle, a holy hoop, it could resist all the forces threatening destruction.

It is of course wrong to romanticize the legacy of the Native American tribes. They could be devious, furious, and murderous, especially to outsiders. They could slaughter game beyond all tribal need and degrade the land carelessly. Not every Native American habitat was an ecological paradise, and many Native Americans took to drink and noisy machinery with a shocking rapidity. Still these negative aspects of the cultural portrait should receive less emphasis than the positive aspects, for at least two reasons:

1. On the whole most American tribes seem to have been disciplined, creative, and spiritually gifted, and the major horror stories about depravity come from tribes whose traditional cultures had already been grievously wounded.

2. In dealing with "legacies" it is always wise to accent the positive in appraising what remains of permanent worth. Thus in reflecting on the legacy of Italian culture it would be foolish to place more emphasis on the Mafia than on Dante and Vivaldi. Similarly in reflecting on the legacy of Irish culture it would be foolish to place more emphasis on alcoholism than on Yeats and Joyce. Crime and vice are certainly features of the cultural landscape. But crime

and vice are nothing seriously to compare with the potential benefits of purifications in the sweat lodge or visions at coming of age.

As a last suggestion of the legacy to be found in the Native American traditions consider Joseph Epes Brown again, this time on the Native American sense of humanity itself. Native Americans certainly distinguished between themselves and animals, but not with the sense of superiority common in modern Western assumptions about human nature (which is probably endemic to the present ecological crisis created by modern Western technology):

> In the multiple expressions of Native American lore, in myths and folktales, in rites, ceremonies, art forms, music, and dances, there is the constant implication of, indeed direct references to, the understanding that animal beings are not lower, that is, inferior to humans, but rather, because they were here first in the order of creation, and with the respect always due to age in these cultures, the animal beings are looked to as guides and teachers of human beings—indeed, in a sense their superiors.[5]

Compare this attitude with modern Western anthropocentrism and acquisitiveness. Don't assume that all right is on either side, but let the Native American and modern Western views share, discuss, and challenge one another as equals. People in both cultures are mortal. None of them has ever mastered the divine mystery of creation and none knows the end of the world. Each is forced to live by faith and has to struggle to get nature, society, the self, and divinity into perspective. Is the Native American respect for animals as elder creatures merely a quaint remnant of a worldview obviously passé? Is the modern Western instinct to fill the earth and subdue it the parent of great feats of scientific understanding and technological mastery that any culture ought to consider imitating? "No

A teepee reconstructed at Fruitlands in Harvard, Massachusetts, as part of a museum of New England Americana. A symbolist might consider the teepee the housing of the original spirit of American religion. (Photo by J. T. Carmody)

and yes, yes and no," many respondents will find themselves saying. As they do, they will also be saying that it has been tragic that what existed on the continent before the whites has so largely passed from the scene.[6]

Black Elk on the Traditional Rites of the Lakota

Perhaps the best known and most influential of the reminiscences or interpretations of traditional Indian life is associated with Black Elk, a Lakota (Oglala Sioux) who died in 1950. Con-

fiding first in John Neihardt and then in Joseph Epes Brown, Black Elk gave accounts of both his own life and the Lakota ceremonial system.[7]

The latter account is the focus here. According to Black Elk (whom some commentators have regarded as untrustworthy because he converted to Christianity, but who always thought of himself as still being a Lakota visionary), his people had long celebrated seven ceremonial rites, most of them given by a lovely lady, the Buffalo Maiden, generations back. In addition to these seven rites, the sacred pipe was used on many solemn occasions as a way of sending the people's thoughts and prayers to the Great Spirit. The rites included a ceremony for purifying the souls of the dead, the sweat lodge ceremony for purification (discussed previously), a ceremony for crying for a vision to direct one's life, the sun dance ceremony, a ceremony for making friendly acquaintances relatives, a ceremony to prepare a girl for womanhood, and a ceremonial ball game. About purifying the souls of the dead Black Elk said:

> By keeping a soul according to the proper rites, as given to us by the White Buffalo Cow Woman . . . one so purifies it that it and the Spirit become one, and it is thus able to return to the "place" where it was born—*Wakan-tanka*—and need not wander about the earth as is the case with the souls of bad people; further, the keeping of a soul helps us to remember death and also *Wakan-tanka*, who is above all dying.[8] [*Wakan-tanka* refers to the holy ultimate, the Great Spirit or God.]

The sun dance is perhaps the most famous Lakota rite revived in recent days, and Black Elk's story of its origin shows it was considered an instrument of spiritual reform. It arose when the people once were camped in a good place, assembled in a circle, their customary pattern and a sign of their unity. The old men were holding a council when they noticed that one of their number, named Kablaya, had dropped his robe to his waist and was dancing with his hands raised to the sky. When they sent a man to investigate, he too began dancing with his robe dropped and his hands upraised. Kablaya explained that he had had a vision from *Wakan-tanka* instructing him in this new mode of praying. Long ago *Wakan-tanka* had given them the pipe as the mode of their prayer, but they had grown lax and now needed a new ritual. When this revelation was taken to the keeper of the pipe, he approved, noting that according to tradition they were eventually to have seven ways of praying, and that this dance seemed an appropriate addition.

Kablaya then gave all the specific instructions that had come in his vision, setting the pattern for the sun dance. There were many particulars, including prayers to helping animals, tobacco for offerings, purifications in a ceremonial lodge, preparation of a cottonwood tree to be the center of the ritual, smoking of the pipe, and vows by the dancers. But the most dramatic instruction certainly was that the men should consummate their dancing by fixing leather thongs to both the cottonwood tree and their own chests and finally so dance that the thongs ripped out of their chests. This was to be an offering of pain and endurance to the Great Spirit and a symbol of everything dark or untoward ripping out of their hearts.

The origin of the rite to make friends (or former enemies) into relatives lay in an exchange of corn and tobacco. The Ree, who had been at war with the Lakota, prized corn, while the Lakota, to whom corn was not native, prized tobacco and their sacred pipe. A Lakota visionary found some corn without realizing it belonged to the Ree and thought it a great benefit. The Ree mourned the loss of their corn and asked for it back, sending the Lakota gifts of tobacco. Out of the reconciliation effected by this ancient exchange came the Lakota rite for making relatives.

The equipment traditionally considered necessary for this rite is typical of other Lakota ceremonies and shows how nature was always assumed as both the context and the source of many ingredients of their rituals: a pipe, tobacco, four stalks of corn with ears, one stalk without ears, dried buffalo meat, red and dark blue paint, eagle plumes, a knife, a buffalo skull, three sticks (to make a rack), sweet grass, and a dried buffalo bladder. Purifying the ingredients by smoking them on the rack, the ritual leader would pray to *Wakan-tanka* and the directions of the compass. The bundle containing the sacred ingredients was shown to the Ree and offered to *Wakan-tanka*, with prayers using such holy things as the buffalo bladder to consummate the peacemaking between the two peoples.

On another day of the ceremony, representatives of the Ree received back the corn that had been in question. Ree prayed over Lakota and Lakota prayed over Ree. Lakota painted Ree and Ree painted Lakota. In several different ways, therefore, the two peoples mixed their sacred symbols, their prayers, and their hopes that they would live in peace, blessed by the Great Spirit who cared for both of them.

The sacred ball game symbolized the course of human life. The object of the game (which apparently resembled a simplified form of lacrosse) was possession of the ball. To Black Elk the ball represented *Wakan-tanka*, whom human beings ought to spend their lives striving to find. In latter times the game had become a team sport, with little individual opportunity to get the ball (or score). But originally all participants had a chance. The greater odds against scoring in the format of the recent game suggested to Black Elk the greater ignorance of modern times.

In the vision traditionally held responsible for the original game, offerings of elements such as sweet grass and smoke from the pipe comprised a lengthy prelude. Clearly the game was not a worldly sport but a sacred occasion. At one point the visionary saw a little girl, who then became a buffalo calf, then was a mature buffalo cow, and then returned to human form. No doubt this symbolized the oneness of the Lakota with the buffalo that was crucial to their economy. When the visionary saw the little girl with the ball (made of buffalo hair covered with buffalo skin), she

tossed the ball to the place where the sun goes down, and all the people scrambled for it and returned it to the center. In the same manner, the girl tossed the ball towards the place where the Giant lives, towards the place where the sun comes up, and then to the place towards which we always face; each time the ball was returned to the girl at the center. The last time the little girl threw the ball straight up, and immediately they all turned

back into buffalo, and, of course, none of them were able to catch the ball, for the buffalo people do not have hands as we do. The little girl, who was now a buffalo calf again, took the ball and nudged it towards me, and the leader of the buffalo people then said to me: "This universe really belongs to the two-leggeds, for we four-legged buffalo people cannot play with a ball; you should therefore take this and return to your people and explain to them that which we have taught you here."[9]

Through this system of seven traditional rites, the Lakota dealt with such human problems as reconciling enemies and preparing young people for adult responsibilities. They tried to pacify the souls of the dead and the souls of the living who mourned and worried. The sweat lodge provided the chance for a regular cleansing of body and spirit, while the sun dance provided a chance to do penance and rededicate oneself to a life worthy of the Great Spirit. The sacred ball game reminded the people of their orientation in the universe, how all the directions made sense only when the common good stood at the center and how the goal of all the people's striving—in work and play, in war and peace—ought to be to find *Wakan-tanka*. Running through most of the ritual prayers as a leitmotiv was the smoke of the sacred pipe. As the smoke rose toward the heavens, and passed around the circle to unite the people, so the spirits of the Lakota were to rise toward *Wakan-tanka*, and their hearts were to feel they were one—a single unbroken hoop.

Key Terms

Divination: efforts to discern the future, find the will of the holy powers, or determine a cause of sickness. Most tribal peoples have developed religious functionaries who carry out divination by going into trance, being taken over by a helping spirit, or reading the signs of such "systems" as cracks in a tortoise shell, the flight of birds in the sky, the pattern of chits shaken out of a basket, or the entrails of animals. Divination sometimes became a protoscience, attributing order to natural elements and seeking the correlation between this order and human affairs. Usually diviners were shrewd about the psychosomatic causes of illness and the psychosocial causes of disputes, aberrant behavior, and other problems that brought families or tribes into crisis (times for reconsideration and decision).

Shamanism: archaic techniques for gaining ecstasy. This definition, which owes much to Mircea Eliade, one of the pioneer students of the phenomenon of shamanism across many different religious complexes, points to both the mechanics of shamans and some of their motivation. By dancing, ingesting tobacco or hallucinogens, staring hypnotically at a skull, fasting, retreating into solitude, letting themselves be mesmerized by the beating of a drum, singing, and other preparatory and suggestive techniques, shamans gained the ability to inhabit two different realms of consciousness. In addition to normal consciousness, they could "travel" to a realm in which they encountered the gods or spirits responsible for crucial factors in the life of their people (the movement of the game, for example). They could also speak with animals, guide the souls of the dead, or fight with the malignant spirits responsible for an illness. The shamanic tribes relied on their visionaries to heal a community dispute; find where the absent game had gone; cure illnesses; determine where the tribe ought to travel; and placate the spirits responsible for disease, flood, or famine—that is, to deal with all crises requiring communications with the powers holding their fate. In

time, the ecstatic experience itself moved many shamans to sing or dance as a personal need. They had become positively addicted to their flights and enraptured by the expanded consciousness to which their shamanizing took them.

Discussion Questions

1. What are the main reasons for postulating a north Asian origin for Native Americans?
2. How did agriculture tend to change cultures traditionally based on hunting?
3. What were the major consequences of nonliteracy?
4. How did Native American art express basic religious convictions?
5. What are some of the major implications of the Native American regard of animals as elder fellow creatures?
6. How did light and sweat function in the Lakota sense of purification?
7. How could a ball game become a sacred ritual?
8. What were the main symbolisms of the sacred pipe?

Notes

1. See Ake Hultkrantz, "North American Religions: An Overview," in *The Encyclopedia of Religion*, vol. 10, ed. Mircea Eliade (New York: Macmillan, 1987), pp. 530–535; see also the same author's *The Religions of the American Indians* (Berkeley: University of California Press, 1979).

2. See Sam Gill, *Native American Religions: Sources and Interpretations* (Belmont CA: Wadsworth, 1983), p. 9. Pages 5–11 suggest the range of the first white views of Native Americans.

3. See Sam Gill, "Nonliterate Traditions and Holy Books," in *The Holy Book in Comparative Perspective,* ed. Frederick M. Denny and Rodney L. Taylor (Columbia: University of South Carolina Press, 1985), pp. 224–239.

4. Joseph Epes Brown, *The Spiritual Legacy of the American Indian* (New York: Crossroad, 1982), p. 43.

5. Ibid., p. 124.

6. See the novels of N. Scott Momaday, which join a Native American heritage and sensibility with the gifts of a fine storyteller.

7. See John Neihardt, *Black Elk Speaks* (Lincoln: University of Nebraska Press, 1961); and Joseph Epes Brown, *The Sacred Pipe* (Baltimore: Penguin, 1971).

8. Brown, *The Sacred Pipe*, p. 11.

9. Ibid., p. 135.

2

The European Background

Catholic Christianity

The word *catholic* means "according to the whole." *Universal* is a fair synonym. When followers of Christ were trying to clarify their faith in the early Christian centuries, an important criterion became what the whole Church, the universal tradition, had held. Of course looking at the early Church from a modern vantage point, few beliefs or practices seem to have been held uniformly. But the ideal was that the Church should be not only one (united), holy (reflective of God's own life), and apostolic (faithful to the witness of the first followers of Jesus), but also catholic—recognizably the same everywhere.

In fact "catholic" Christianity came to full self-consciousness only through its third-, fourth-, and fifth-century battles with dissidents. When the dissidents lost the doctrinal wars at such early Christian councils of bishops as those at Nicaea (325) and Chalcedon (451), they became known as heretics (those who had chosen against the mainstream). The victors called themselves the orthodox (those adhering to right opinion and right praise of God) and Catholics (those associated with the healthy whole, unlike the separatists).

17

Catholic Christianity was always troubled by protests and dissension, from the early centuries when the Church fathers set the tone to the middle ages, when various **millennialist** sects and **Gnostic** reformers proclaimed the end of history or the need for sweeping change. Only in the schism of Eastern and Western Christianity in 1054, however, did the Church suffer a wound so grievous and serious that its catholicity was in question ever after. The Protestant Reformation of the 16th century further sundered both the reality and the image of Catholic Christianity. Nonetheless Catholic Christians clung to the ideal of representing a universal faith, tradition, and Church. Both Eastern Christians (who often referred to themselves as Orthodox) and Protestant Christians represented splits from the trunk of the ecclesiastical tree. Reunification was a consummation devoutly to be wished, but Catholics thought reunion required a return to the Catholic fold.

What were the main characteristics of the Catholic fold and faith when Catholic missionaries were establishing the first outposts of European religion in the New World? High on most scholars' lists would be the centrality of the pope, the bishop of Rome and successor of the apostle Peter. Catholic Christianity also stressed a system of sacramental rituals, the seven most important being

1. Baptism (the washing through which one entered the Church and started divine life)
2. Confirmation (a rite for coming of age)
3. Matrimony (the solemnization of marriage)
4. Orders (consecration to official service in the Church)
5. Penance (a rite for reconciliation with God and the community after sin)
6. Anointing (preparation for death)
7. The eucharist (a rite commemorating the death and resurrection of Christ and offering communion with Christ through reception of bread and wine believed to be Christ's body and blood).

Any Catholic theologian, whether of the 16th century or of the present day, would demand much greater nuance in describing the crux of the sacramental system, but for present purposes this sketch will do.

The majority of Catholic Christians believed that to gain salvation (healing from God that would lead to forgiveness and the eternal enjoyment of God in heaven) one had to participate in this sacramental system. In extraordinary circumstances salvation could come outside it, but it was the ordinary means that God had established. The Church, led and represented by those in orders, had the duty and right to administer this sacramental system. At the top of the entire ecclesiastical pyramid the pope had the greatest duties, rights, and powers, but any priest was a representative of Christ and shared in the Petrine power (Matthew 16:19) to loose people from the sins that would bring them damnation or keep them bound by Satan. Catholic Christians believed in the mercy of God, and they consoled themselves with prayers to the many saints whom they regarded as intercessors on their behalf. Above all they consoled themselves with prayers to the Virgin Mary, Christ's mother, to whom they believed Christ could refuse nothing. Faith in the mercy of God and the efficacy of Christ's sacrificial death were certainly necessary, but the upshot of this faith frequently was a demand to believe in the Church and follow its precepts.

The first Catholic missionaries to the Americas came from the leading men's religious orders. These were groups of priests and brothers (laymen who had consecrated themselves to serve God and the Church) living under vows of poverty, chastity, and obedience. As their religious superiors directed, they went out to spread the gospel (the "glad tidings" of Christ) in the New World. Other groups were going out to India and East Asia in the same spirit. The Franciscans, Jesuits, and Dominicans were the most important sources of missionaries, and most of them came from Spain or France.

The Franciscans owed their origin to Francis of Assisi (1182–1226), a saint much beloved for his joy, intimacy with nature, and gifts of living in extreme poverty and bearing the *stigmata* (wounds) of Christ. The Franciscan ideal was a simple life dedicated to showing the freedom that love of Christ could bring. The Jesuits, founded by Ignatius of Loyola (1491–1556), had a special vow of obedience to the Pope and established a reputation as excellent schoolmasters. Ignatius had been a soldier, so much of the Jesuit spirituality had a military turn: discipline, obedience, self-reliance. The Dominicans derived from the Castilian priest Dominic (1170–1221), who had obtained permission to found an order to preach against medieval heretics. The greatest Catholic theologian, Thomas Aquinas (1225–1274), was a Dominican, and the Dominicans were closely involved in the Inquisition established by the Catholic church to crack down on heretics during the late medieval and early Reformation period.

All of these religious orders went out to the New World, just as they went to India and Asia, with the conviction that it was crucially important for them to preach and bring the sacraments to people who had not heard of Christ. Without such preaching and sacramental ministry, pagans would be on the straight road to hell. Spanish missionaries went to Puerto Rico at the end of the 15th century (1493) and shortly thereafter worked in Florida. Later they worked in what is now Louisiana, the Southwest, and California. Their regular practice was to form mission stations or *reductions*, where Indians could receive religious instruction and work and live under direction. This was their pattern in Central and South America as well.

The French missionaries, who also had influence in Louisiana but made most of their mark in northeastern and north central America traveled with the hunting tribes when they could. Both Spanish and French missionaries were handicapped by the bad example if not outright rapacity of their fellow countrymen,

who often exploited the natives, and both lost many men as martyrs to the cause of conversion. On the whole the results of both groups were mixed. Some Native Americans certainly became Catholic Christians (and have remained so to this day). But many others disliked the regimentation the missionaries tried to impose; identified the missionaries with the other whites seeking to profit from them; or resented the attacks on their traditional ways of life, including their religious ways. Many Native Americans succumbed to white venereal disease and alcoholism. Often the conversions were few in number or dubious in depth, and the white influence as a whole seemed as much bad as good.[1]

Protestant Christianity

Medieval Christianity was rocked from time to time with reform movements. During the 14th century the papacy was at its lowest ebb; the popes generally lived in Avignon, France rather than Rome; and there were several claimants to the papal throne. Not surprisingly, therefore, such reformers as the Englishman John Wycliffe (about 1325–1384) and his Czech disciple John Huss (about 1369–1415) preached an emendation of morals and a correction of doctrinal abuses. Many Christians viewed the Black Death (bubonic plague) of the 14th century as a judgment on the sinfulness of the Church, and by the end of the century the movement known as the *devotio moderna* (modern devotion) was under way in the Netherlands. The classic writing representing this movement is the *Imitatio Christi* attributed to Thomas à Kempis (about 1380–1471). The piety of the *Imitatio* is warm and personal but tinged with tears. Thomas laments the sinfulness of the world and urges the constant remembrance of death, which can sweep down like a flash flood.

Grünewald represents a European Christian faith at the border of the medieval and reformed eras, when the suffering of Christ and the sinfulness of human beings were predominant themes. (The Small Crucifixion, Matthias Grünewald; National Gallery of Art, Washington, D.C., Samuel H. Kress Collection)

Other factors certainly led up to the Protestant Reformation sparked by the preaching of Martin Luther in 1517, but the basic cause was the desire to clean up the Church and furnish the common people better spiritual fare. Luther was an Augustinian monk, well schooled in the Catholic sacramental system. Although he stressed the Bible and wanted individuals to take more responsibility for their own consciences, his first instinct was not to tear down the sacramental system. Instead he wanted to reform the sacraments and the theology and politics of the Catholic church to make them better fit his own sense that justification (standing right in the sight of God) came entirely from faith on the human side and grace on the divine side. Luther and representatives of Catholicism were not able to work out their initially rather minor differences, and the often-delayed official response of the Catholic church at the Council of Trent (1545–1563) offered the Protestants little room to maneuver.

The result was that 50 years after Luther's initial challenge Western Christendom was deeply divided. Luther had translated the Bible into the vernacular. He himself had left the monastery to marry, and thousands had followed his example. Political squabbles among the German princes had led them to choose their religious sides in terms of political expediency, while the response from Rome had tended to be thunderous threats and postponed action on the substance of Protestant's criticisms. Eventually the Council of Trent did produce what some historians have called the Counter-Reformation, as the Jesuits and others offered the clergy new vigor, better learning, and a mobile spirituality suited for the adventurous age. But during the decades when it most counted (the 30 years from 1517 to 1547), the will to peace, reconciliation, or even simply shrewd dealing seems to have left both sides.

Martin Luther, John Calvin, and the other leading thinkers of the Protestant Reformation were proposing a new set of emphases rather than a wholesale sacking of the Church. Until their own thought became rigid, they were mainly interested in reforming Christian morals (by disciplining a clergy often lax and ignorant) and faith (by purging what they took to be excesses and superstitions). For example, they wanted to trim the influence of saints and the Blessed Virgin because they felt that the uniqueness and centrality of Christ had been compromised. They also wanted to trim the power of the pope, the bishops, and the clergy because they felt that the common people had become like sheep to be led or bilked as the clergy saw fit. In the place of this clericalist church they wanted to develop a laity who could themselves aspire to sanctity. The pattern for these new emphases, the Reformers thought, lay ready to hand in the Old and New Testaments. There all believers were urged to think of themselves as "a chosen race, a royal priesthood, a holy nation, God's own people, that you may declare the wonderful deeds of him who called you out of darkness into his marvelous light" (1 Peter 2:9).

Luther and Calvin surely did not envision congregations acting democratically, let alone anarchically, as they later did. The first reformers were neither so naive nor so unpatriarchal as to think that when the Holy Spirit was loosed in the common people's hearts they would immediately become saints in every feature. In fact when the peasants became agitated, Luther panicked and let loose with venomous tirades against their unruly movement. Calvin's Geneva seldom saw such impropriety precisely because Calvin took care from the outset to make the city a **theocracy** with full discipline and oversight.

Prior to the debates kindled by the Protestant Reformation virtually all Christians had held generally that human beings both require divine grace (help, life) for salvation and must cooperate with such grace. Early in the fifth century Augustine of Hippo and a British or Irish monk named Pelagius had squared off on this matter, although how antagonistic their positions actually were is debatable. The traditional stereotype draws Augustine as the great defender of divine grace and Pelagius as a heretic over-stressing human freedom. Those who have read Augustine's *Confessions* know that he came to Christian faith only as an adult, having first lived what he later took to be a life of foul carnal sin. After his conversion Augustine praised the complete freedom with which God had saved him and distrusted his own flesh (to put it mildly). Indeed Augustine judged as inevitably sinful all sexual intercourse, even that pursued within marriage. Only children legitimated marital sex, and the ideal would have been to beget children with neither desire nor pleasure.

Augustine bequeathed this rather pessimistic view of human nature to subsequent Christendom, while other leading teachers tended to soften it. For example, the Greek Fathers tended to speak more of grace as lifting people up to God's life than as remedying human sin, although they did not neglect sin. However, Luther was an Augustinian, so he got a solid dose of the master's stress on the gratuity of salvation and the wretchedness of human nature or effort apart from God. Calvin trained as a lawyer, developing a fine mind for controlling both practical and theoretical problems. When he became converted to the new reforming wave, Augustine became his great mentor, too. From this threefold heritage—Augustine, Luther, Calvin—the Reformation was virtually doomed to think badly of human nature, well of God's grace, and confusedly about precisely how to put the two together. Luther had been galvanized by reading Paul's letter to the Romans, and gradually he developed the notion that Paul speaks there (Romans 8:29) of a double predestination, that is, of some people to heaven and others to hell. This view is especially associated with Calvin, although he usually stressed God's fore-choosing people to "life" rather than "death." Nonetheless his Puritan followers frequently felt that human nature was so weak or wicked that it could do nothing on its own, and that for his own good reasons God had elected some to receive grace and go to heaven, but not all. We shall see some of the further consequences of this feeling later.

The main reason for the further splintering of Protestantism into a great variety of churches lay in the Reformers' principle that individual conscience was the primary law in religious life. What the individual found in the Bible could be interpreted as God's direct will, somewhat bypassing either the rest of the Christian Church or past **tradition.** Certainly neither Luther nor Calvin meant to give such a simple-minded or individualistic impression, but many groups split and split again because they could not find a way to establish an institutional authority. Whether they vested it in elders (presbyters), the congregation as a whole, or some other locus (bishops or their equivalents), the Protestants were loathe to make this power strong enough to overbalance the power of individualism. Obviously many groups of individuals cooperated sufficiently to remain in existence as churches, and one can still speak meaningfully of churches that go back to Luther and Calvin. But along the way great numbers moved out to form new churches, as the statistics on church membership in the United States now suggest: about 8 million Lutherans and 3.5 million Presbyterians (the latter probably the most direct descendants of Calvinist theology), compared to about 25 million Baptists (a family of churches with a complicated dependence on both the Church of England and the Puritans).

The Missionary and Colonizing Impulse

Whether they came from Catholic or Protestant countries, the whites who went out to the New World regularly had a twofold motivation. They wanted to gain territory, and so wealth, for the crown they represented, and they wanted to spread their own brand of Christian culture, which implied establishing their religion among the Native Americans.

The economic and political overtones of exploration were clearly understood from the time of Columbus. In his papal bull *Inter Caetera*, issued on May 4, 1493, Alexander VI tried to mediate incipient territorial disputes between Spain and Portugal due to the discoveries of Columbus. The 1494 treaty of Tordesillas, for which Alexander VI was also responsible, established a line dividing the zones of Spain and Portugal and led to the Portuguese presence in what is now Brazil. By 1508, however, Pope Julius II had granted Spain universal patronage over all ecclesiastical benefices in the New World. Clearly, therefore, the beginnings of the Catholic exploratory and missionary enterprise expressed the Church's desire to work harmoniously with Catholic sovereigns, particularly the king of Spain.

However, the priests who went in the wake of the Spanish explorers were sensitive to the religious implications of dealing with the Native Americans. In opposition to the view of some of the explorers that the Indians were no better than dumb beasts, the priests regularly protested that they were subjects of God's plan of salvation. In 1537 Paul III issued the papal bull *Sublimis Deus*, which still makes interesting reading:

> The sublime God so loved the human race that He created man in such wise that he might participate, not only in the good that other creatures enjoy, but endowed him with capacity to attain to the inaccessible and invisible Supreme Good and behold it face to face; and since man, according to the testimony of the sacred scriptures, has been created to enjoy eternal life and happiness, which none may obtain save through faith in our Lord Jesus Christ, it is necessary that he should possess the nature and faculties enabling him to

receive that faith, and that whoever is thus endowed should be capable of receiving that same faith. Nor is it credible that any one should possess so little understanding as to desire the faith and yet be destitute of the most necessary faculty to enable him to receive it. Hence Christ, who is the Truth itself, that has never failed and can never fail, said to the preachers of the faith whom He chose for that office "Go ye and teach all nations." He said all, without exception, for all are capable of receiving the doctrines of the faith.

> The enemy of the human race, who opposes all good deeds in order to bring men to destruction, beholding and envying this, invented a means never heard of before, by which he might hinder the preaching of God's word of Salvation to the people: he inspired his satellites who, to please him, have not hesitated to publish abroad that the Indians of the West and the South, and other people of whom We have recent knowledge should be treated as dumb brutes created for our service, pretending that they are incapable of receiving the Catholic Faith.[2]

About five years later, probably in 1542 and around what is now southern Kansas, a Franciscan priest named Juan de Padilla became the first martyr to this vision. Padilla had accompanied the Spanish explorer Coronado through what is now Mexico and much of the American Southwest for more than two years. When Coronado turned back in frustration, Padilla and at least two of his brother Franciscans stayed behind to evangelize the Native Americans. Shortly thereafter he was killed.

The details of Padilla's death are sketchy, but it may be useful to imagine some of the circumstances. He had gone out from Spain in great hope, perhaps fired by an ambition for spiritual conquest or service, parallel to the ambition that drove the Spanish soldiers in search of gold. For more than two years he had accompanied a military expedition, no doubt ministering to the needs of the soldiers and trying as occasion offered to evangelize the natives. Perhaps it was completely foolhardy for him to remain after the soldiers decided to turn back, but on the other hand perhaps his group had met friendly natives and interested some in Christianity.

By whatever calculation, Padilla and the others judged it worth risking their lives. The chance to spread the gospel and life of Christ weighed heavier than the pain or even death they might suffer. What might Padilla have been thinking the night before he died? Was it evident that the Indians had no more use for them? Or were they killed in a fluke bit of rage, some Indian lashing out at a foreign face that on a better day might have seemed intriguing? As with the stories of many other missionaries and colonists, it is impossible to know. But Padilla calls to mind a faith that now seems otherworldly, until we remember what has been happening recently in Latin America.

Like the Catholic expeditionaries, the colonists who arrived at Jamestown and Plymouth early in the 17th century had both economic and religious hopes. They wanted to establish an English realm on new soil, bring a good return to the investors who had supported them, and provide a prosperous living for their own families. For many it was equally important to make a new start in a place where they would be free to worship as they wished.

The Puritans, who began as a movement to reform Anglican Christianity under Elizabeth I (1558–1603), had suffered under James I (1603–1625), who followed Elizabeth in keeping control of national religious policy. The radical Puritan thinker Robert Browne called for separating from the corrupt religious establishment and gathering independent "congregational" churches that would be run by Puritan believers without outside interference. Having emigrated to Holland in search of more congenial surroundings, a group of Browne's followers calling themselves Pilgrims made their way to Plymouth (Massachusetts) in 1620. The Pilgrims and other separatists horrified many other Puritans, who wanted to reform the English church from within. As Rosemary

Haughton has shown, the separatists had difficulty imagining the balance between secular and sacred occupations. In their drive to fill all of life with the saintliness held out in the Bible, they often found ordinary, unconverted people intolerable and so tended to live an ingrown life on the margins of society.[3]

The colony established at Virginia in 1607 was not separatist, but it certainly had religious overtones. Alexander Whitaker, writing "Good News from Virginia," petitioned those from whom he sought financial help with arguments to the effect that God had guided the Virginia enterprise in its first years. Whitaker's work was published in London in 1613, and he surely wished all hearts to be moved by the plight of the native heathen, whose conversion to Christianity would more than justify the colonial expenditures.

Note the similarities and differences from the views of Pope Paul III given earlier:

Secondly, let the miserable condition of these naked slaves of the divell move you to compassion toward them. They acknowledge that there is a great good God, but know him not, having the eyes of their understanding as yet blinded: wherefore they serve the divell for feare, after a most base manner, sacrificing sometimes (as I have heere heard) their own Children to him. I have sent one Image of their god to the Counsell in England, which is painted upon one side of a toadstoole, much like unto a deformed monster. Their priests (whom they call *Quiokosoughs*) are no other but such as our English Witches are. They lie naked in bodie, as if their shame of their sinne deserved no covering: their names are as naked as their bodie: they esteem it a vertue to lie, deceive and steal as their master the divell teacheth them. . . . If this bee their life, what thinke you shall become of them after death? but to be partakers with the divell and his angels in hell forevermore.[4]

Therefore, Whitaker pleads, those reading his lines should dig deep for funds to help save the heathen from hellfire. It would be stretching things to say that most of the early colonists shared with the earlier Spanish missionaries a primary concern for converting the natives, but it would also distort the colonial enterprise not to note that at the beginning saving the heathen from hellfire seemed a good work and obvious service of God.

Oliver Cromwell

Oliver Cromwell (1599–1658) is probably the most dramatic figure in whom to read the lessons of the Puritan revolt that quickened 17th century England and provided essential parts of the background for American colonial thought. As a leading opponent of King Charles I in the English civil war, and then the leading officeholder in the Puritan-dominated Commonwealth, Cromwell summarized in his person most of the victorious military, political, and religious currents of his day.

Cromwell was born in eastern England, the only son of a landlord, justice of the peace, and member of one of the parliaments of Queen Elizabeth. His parents were long-standing Protestants and their families had profited from the dissolution of the English monastic holdings under King Henry VIII. Cromwell's schooling occurred under strongly Calvinist masters, who taught that although the sins of human beings could be punished on earth, God would guide the elect to righteousness.

From early adulthood Cromwell seems to have been a responsible son to his widowed mother and a solid husband, father, and citizen of his native fens. Shortly before he was 30 he apparently experienced a religious conversion, which seemed like passing from darkness into light. Whereas previously he had felt himself the worst of sinners, afterward he was convinced he was one of God's chosen.

By the time he was 40 an inheritance from his mother's brother had made him financially secure, and in 1628 he was elected to Parliament under Charles I. But Cromwell's political star began to ascend only when he was elected from the town of Cambridge to first the Short and then the Long Parliament of 1640. There he made friends highly critical of the monarchy. Since his first years in Parliament Cromwell had made fiery speeches against the English bishops, criticizing especially their support of elaborate ritual and episcopal authority. His own conviction was that the individual could contact God directly and did not need an elaborate church structure. Individuals should be free to choose their own clergy, whose principal duty would be to inspire the laity by their preaching. Cromwell himself had supported itinerant preachers who were at odds with the English bishops. *The Book of Common Prayer,* the official prayerbook of the English church, offended him; like the episcopate and the English liturgical ritual, it pretended to mediate the individual's relationship with God. So while Cromwell agreed with many of his fellow members of parliament that taxes, monopolies granted by the king, and other political burdens were serious injustices, he had longer been known for his religious opposition to the established order that linked church and crown.

In 1641 Cromwell and his friends succeeded in sending through Parliament a "Grand Remonstrance" of more than 200 clauses expressing their many grievances. One of these clauses censured the bishops and the corrupt clergy who cherished a formality and superstition that supported their own ecclesiastical tyranny. However, the king would not accept the Remonstrance, which only widened the gap between him and his parliamentary critics.

In 1642 the parliamentary and royalist parties moved toward civil war as the king left London to raise an army. Cromwell showed himself full of practical gifts in helping to organize a parliamentary army. He began with his own political constituency in Cambridge and served as a captain in the forces of Parliament for the first major battles of the civil war. By February of 1643 Cromwell was a colonel and well on his way to recruiting a first-rate cavalry regiment. He treated his men well but demanded strict discipline. Troopers who swore were fined; troopers who got drunk were thrown in the stocks. Men could be thrown out of the army for calling one another "roundheads"—the name the king's supporters called them because of their close-cropped heads—and deserters were whipped. All this discipline paid off in combat, for the key to Cromwell's great success (often with smaller numbers of troops than his opponents) was his ability to check his men as they charged into battle and get them to regroup into more advantageous formations.

The parliamentary forces fared well, but Cromwell was displeased with the leisurely attitude of the commanders, whom he criticized as not really wanting victory. When Sir Thomas Fairfax took over the parliamentary forces things went more as Cromwell had hoped, and he soon had the problem of what to do with a victorious army that distrusted Parliament. Cromwell tried to mediate between the two groups, since he belonged to both, but what he took to be unfair treatment of the army finally caused him to side with it against Parliament.

Now quite powerful, Cromwell tried to persuade the much weakened king to accept a constitutional settlement, which Parliament would approve. He also tried to placate the army, which trusted neither the king nor Parliament. By the end of 1647 it was becoming clear that no solution could be found. On January 3, 1648, Cromwell told Parliament that God had hardened the king's heart. Encouraged by the king's agreement with the Scots, the royalists took up arms again, and the second civil war ensued. Cromwell fought successfully in Wales and the north of England, all the while corresponding with the governor of the Isle of Wight, where the king had fled. Negotiations with the king broke down, and at the end of 1648 Cromwell ceased his hesitation and as a commissioner of the High Court of Justice agreed first to put the king on trial and then, when the king would not plead, to sign the king's death warrant.

When the British Isles were then declared a republic named the Commonwealth, Cromwell served as the first chairman of the council of state, which was the executive branch of a one-house parliament. For the first three years of his tenure he was principally engaged in campaigns against the royalists in Ireland and Scotland. The massacre at the Drogheda garrison near Dublin in September of 1649 made Cromwell's name infamous in Irish history. Cromwell returned the hatred, thinking the Irish superstitious savages. He also led the army against the Scots who had rallied to Charles II, but as fellow Puritans they were less objectionable to him than the Catholic Irish. In 1650 and 1651 Cromwell won significant victories against the Scots, although his own health was failing and his troops were outnumbered.

The battle at Worcester against the Scots in 1651 ended the second civil war. Tensions remained high between the army and Parliament, and eventually Parliament was dissolved in 1653. Cromwell had hoped to establish an amnesty that would allow matters to return to normal, but mutual distrust between the army and Parliament had delayed that goal. Cromwell hoped the Little Parliament of the summer of 1653 would be the assembly of saints long needed to establish a Puritan republic. However, where previous parliaments had proven slow and indecisive, the saints proved so rash that he reproved himself for experimenting with rule by the elect.

In 1654 Cromwell was in full charge of the country as the Lord Protector. The more than 80 ordinances he and his Council of State passed aimed to reform the law, set up a Puritan church, establish religious toleration outside the church, advance education, and decentralize government. Cromwell sought a humane administration of the criminal law and high ethical standards for clergy and schoolmasters. Despite his

The thistle atop this Edinburgh church was a symbol of the Scottish crown and cause. Scots such as Adam Smith and David Hume furnished much of the rationale for the fusion of capitalism, industrialization, hard work, and material prosperity that proved immensely influential in the United States. (Photo by J. T. Carmody)

considerable power, he had his own difficulties with Parliament. It seemed bent on changing the basic nature of traditional English society, while he wanted to conserve much of the inherited order. For example, an influential group in Parliament wanted to level differences between tenants and landlords, which Cromwell thought would bring chaos. Some even rejected the "four fundamentals" of the new constitution: government by a single person and Parliament, regular summoning of parliaments, liberty of conscience, and control of the army divided between the protector and Parliament. Eventually Cromwell won allegiance to this platform and an oath of loyalty to the protector from all but 100 convinced republicans.

In his last years Cromwell continued to battle with Parliament to uphold his own authority. He died in London of malaria in 1658, having a second time dissolved a parliament he could not control. His body was buried in Westminster Abbey, but in 1661, after the restoration of King Charles II, his remains were dug up and his head hung on a pole on top of Westminster Hall.

The career of Oliver Cromwell shows the power of several forces during the 1640s and 1650s. Both king and established church were ripe for overthrow because many of the middle class and the lower nobility had economic or religious grievances. Religiously Cromwell seems to have been content to abolish bishops and establish a congregational form of church polity. Christians outside the established church could practice their own faith, as long as they did not create unrest. Radical religious groups such as the Quakers might run afoul of sedition laws, but Cromwell tended to defend their religious liberty. If one accepted the Puritan rule, then one could pray and preach largely as one wished. On the other hand, the blood shed by the Puritans in battles against the Scots and the Irish Catholics and in widespread witch-hunts had entered the historical record as more evidence that religious zealotry was likely to produce considerable suffering. Some American colonists following events back home in England might rejoice that their Calvinist convictions were coming into power, but the more sober among them had to realize that government by saints probably would turn out to be as vexatious as government by kings.[5] (As the English witch-hunts showed the problems with religious zeal on the Continent, so the witch-hunts in New England showed the problems with American Puritanism.)

Bartolomé de las Casas on the Rights of Natives

The Spanish historian and priest Bartolomé de las Casas (1474–1566) provides our last indication of the background to the American venture in colonial and then republican religion. De las Casas wrote voluminously about the missions of Central and northern South America, and he had the distinction of being the first Catholic priest ordained in the New World (1510). But he has gained most renown and figures in our account because he was the first to realize the implications of the European subjugation of Native Americans and to protest the injustices the Indians were suffering.

No chapter of American history has lacked prophetic personalities willing to point out the wrongs that some were inflicting on others. But the racist overtones of the Europeans' expeditions arguably soured the entire American venture from the outset. This will not be a major theme in our history, although it will certainly return when we consider slavery, the Civil War, and Black religion. But that is all the more reason to pause at the outset and remember that history tends to be written by the conquerers and people whom destiny favored. The conquered are silenced and kept on the margins; they get little attention and can easily fade from sight.

De las Casas began his career in the New World as a soldier, venturing to the West Indies in 1502. As a result of his good services, especially during the conquest of Cuba in 1513, he received an *encomienda,* a grant of land from the Spanish crown. The natives located on the land came with the grant. From the outset de las Casas felt responsible for instructing his natives in the Christian faith. In his eyes they were much like the serfs who came with a European estate.

Working as a priest de las Casas began to be troubled by the arrangements made for the natives. In 1514 he returned his serfs to the governor of the Caribbean area, and in 1515 he returned to Spain to argue at the royal court for better treatment of the natives. Gaining the ear of Francisco Cisneros, the powerful archbishop of Toledo, he advanced a plan to reform the administration of the Indies. Appointed priest-procurator of the Indies and named to a commission to investigate the status of the natives, he returned to America at the end of 1516.

After this visit de las Casas returned to Spain to work on the legal problems of overhauling the *encomienda* system and establishing a peaceful method of colonizing the New World. The crux of his plan was to bring farmers to establish agricultural settlements. He defended the Indians whenever possible in Spain and at the end of 1519 impressed King Charles I (also known as Emperor Charles V) with a moving speech to the Spanish parliament. The king therefore accepted de las Casas's proposal to establish towns of free natives. In these towns Spaniards and natives would join in communities and create a new American civilization.

A group sailed from Spain at the end of 1520 to launch the experiment in what today is northern Venezuela. However, there were few agriculturalists in the group and the landholders in Santo Domingo, not wanting to give up their *encomiendas*, opposed the whole idea. An attack by some natives proved the final straw, and by early 1522 the experiment had ended disastrously. Back in Santo Domingo de las Casas decided to intensify his religious commitment and distance himself from the world by entering the Dominican order. By 1527 he was the prior of a Dominican house in Santo Domingo and had decided to write an apologetic account of what had happened in the Indies. This developed into a significant work in its own right, but perhaps more importantly it led to a full history of the Indies, which was de las Casas's masterpiece. His approach was to offer a prophetic interpretation of all that he had learned about the Indies, exposing the domination, injustice, oppression—the sin—the Europeans had inflicted on the natives. His intuition was that Spain would soon have to suffer for having acted so wrongly.

Working steadily on his project, de las Casas broke off only to send to colonial governors in Madrid three long letters detailing the individuals and institutions that had maltreated the natives. The burden of his attack in these letters, as in most of his analyses, was the sinfulness of the *encomienda* system. Both his writings and his activities in Central America regularly brought

him into conflict with the Spanish secular authorities, but he seldom backed down. In 1537 he wrote another work that became well known, *De Unico Modo* (The Only Way), in which he argued that only a peaceful evangelization of the Indians befit the gospel and might succeed. In fact de las Casas and other Dominicans tried their new approach (in contrast to the military approach previously favored by the Spanish) in a previously unconquered part of what is now Costa Rica. The approach worked quite well, so de las Casas set out for Spain to report their success and try to gain support for such a new policy.

While in Spain he wrote a short account of the destruction of the Indies (published in 1542) that attributed the Christians' massacres of natives to their desire for gold. King Charles signed a new series of laws limiting the *encomiendas* to a single generation, which meant they could not be passed on as an inheritance. The laws also stipulated that after one generation the owners had to set the natives free. In 1545 de las Casas returned to Central America as bishop of what is now Guatemala, empowered to enforce these new laws. Soon he instructed his priests not to grant absolution to any Spanish landholders not obeying the new laws. This and his other adamant policies caused such an uproar that by 1547 he was recalled to Spain, having alienated the landholders beyond reconciliation.

In Spain de las Casas became an influential figure at the imperial court. He also became embroiled in a controversy with Juan de Sepulveda, who had written in defense of waging war against the Native Americans. The basis of Sepulveda's arguments was the Aristotelian view that some beings are by nature inferior to others: children to adults, women to men, natives to whites. The two antagonists locked horns at the Spanish church council of Vallodolid in 1550, and their dispute polarized the Spanish church. Although de las Casas has emerged from his-

tory as the enlightened party, in fact Sepulveda's views dominated practical policy: The natives
were treated as inferior beings who should have
been glad to serve the Spaniards. But de las
Casas continued to write, wield what influence
he could at court, and champion the natives'
cause. He finished his history of the Indies, once
more predicting that Spain would reap terrible
punishments for its sins against the natives. He
died at the age of 92, having done more than
any man of his time to make the Spanish consider the motives and effects of their colonial
venture. His influence waned during the 17th
and 18th centuries, but Latin American liberation movements of the 19th and 20th centuries revived his name, finding in his writings a
precursor of many of their own judgments that
the Spanish colonial empire had been poisoned
from the beginning.

The papal bull of Paul III, *Sublimis Deus*, which
defended the humanity of the natives, was
inspired by de las Casas. In his own writings,
however, he went beyond what the pope had
taught, castigating specific defects of the
Spaniards:

> In God's name, consider . . . what sort of deeds
> are these [acts of murder and torture], and whether
> they do not surpass every imaginable cruelty and
> injustice, and whether it squares well with such
> Christians as these to call them devils; and whether
> it could be worse to give the Indians into the charge
> of the devils of hell rather than to the Christians
> of the Indies.[6]

Key Terms

Gnostic: one who claims secret, privileged
knowledge, usually purporting to bring
salvation. One of the earliest doctrinal battles the early Christian church fought was
with various Gnostic groups, most of whom
downplayed the centrality of faith in Christ
for salvation and condemned works of the
flesh—eating, procreating, and celebrating—as the main ways people were trapped
apart from God. More broadly Gnostics have
been those elitist groups that claimed to
possess a superior insight or spiritual regime
not available to the hoi polloi and exempted
themselves from the ordinary laws of
Christian morality. Because of this they have
generally been repudiated by both church
authorities and the Christian "sense of the
faithful," which has confessed the narrow
way of Christ to be the only sure way to
salvation.

Millennialist: one who expects the millennium, the thousand-year reign of Christ.
Millennialists come in different garbs and
with different subtheories, but common to
them all is an expectation that history will
soon stop (often at the end of a thousand-
year period) and God will intervene to set
things right. Millennialism draws on the
more orthodox notion of Christ's second
coming to render judgment and bring the
saved to heaven. It has ties with both gnosticism and apocalyptic literature (that
claiming to have been disclosed by God
because Christ will soon return) and
throughout Christian history it has spiced
many reform movements. In the United
States such groups as the Seventh Day
Adventists and the Jehovah's Witnesses have
been shaped by millennialism.

Theocracy: political rule by religious leaders.
Theocracies usually deny much separation
between civil and religious realms, arguing
that God is Lord of all creation. Most traditional religions have been theocratic.
Classical Hindu, Buddhist, Moslem, Christian, and Jewish cultures all were holistic
fusions of what we now call secular and
sacred concerns. The advantages of theocratic regimes include the possibility of a
holistic culture and the probability that
religious and ethical questions will be considered very important for civic life. The

disadvantages of theocracies include the probability that the religious leaders will shortchange secular competencies and that they will try to regulate the morals of other citizens.

Tradition: past practice and understanding of a culture or faith that is considered a living mentor. Etymologically tradition is what is "handed on." It holds the danger of becoming merely a sterile repetition of what was done in the past, but it is also inevitable: No age starts completely anew; every age is bound to be shaped by prior ages, even when it rebels against them. Church officials often argue about who should guide and clarify tradition and how tradition should be shaped. In periods when individual conscience came into clear focus, tradition could be set against private interpretation, whether concerning the Bible or Christian doctrine and morality. Every new cultural era has the difficult task of trying to translate tradition afresh, for study soon shows that one cannot simply repeat past formulas or practices. To do so in changed circumstances would not hand on the original message but cause it to miscarry.

Discussion Questions

1. What is the ideal embedded in the notion "catholic?"
2. What was the relation between the Catholic sacramental system and the Catholic missionary ventures?
3. How did the Protestant Reformation spotlight individual conscience?
4. How did their Augustinian heritage lead many Protestants toward separatism?
5. In what ways were the European missions and colonies morally ambiguous ventures from the outset?

6. How did the Devil figure in the early European estimates of the Native Americans?
7. What were Cromwell's main objections to the Church of England?
8. Explain the main failings of Oliver Cromwell the soldier saint.
9. What argument did the Spaniards use to justify subjugating the natives as part of the *encomienda* grants?
10. Why did Bartolomé de las Casas expect the Spaniards' maltreatment of the Indians to bring disaster?

Notes

1. See John Tracy Ellis, ed., *Documents of American Catholic History,* vol. 1 (Wilmington DE: Michael Glazier, 1987); James Hennessey, S. J., *American Catholics* (New York: Oxford University Press, 1981), pp. 9–35; Jay P. Dolan, *The American Catholic Experience* (Garden City NY: Doubleday, 1985), pp. 15–68; and Sidney E. Ahlstrom, *A Religious History of the American People* (New Haven CT: Yale University Press, 1972), pp. 18–69.
2. Ellis, ibid., pp. 7–8. See Ellis for the other documents referred to as well.
3. See Rosemary Haughton, *The Transformation of Man* (Springfield IL: Templegate, 1967).
4. Alexander Whitaker, "Good Newes from Virginia," in *God's New Israel,* ed. Conrad Cherry (Englewood Cliffs NJ: Prentice-Hall, 1971), p. 33.
5. See "Oliver Cromwell," in *The New Encyclopedia Britannica,* vol. 16 (Chicago: Encyclopedia Britannica, 1987), pp. 875–879.
6. Available in Edward Gaustaud, ed., *A Documentary History of Religion in America,* vol. 1 (Grand Rapids MI: Eerdmans, 1983), p. 64. See also "Las Casas, Bartolomé de," in *The New Encyclopedia Britannica,* vol. 7 (Chicago: Encyclopedia Britannica, 1987), pp. 168—169.

The Colonial Era

New England

Until recently New England and Virginia dominated discussions of colonial history. In the current decade, however, some historians have argued that America has always been more diverse than the orthodoxy established by such a colonial axis suggests.[1] Nonetheless it remains standard to configure American religious history as primarily a Protestant story and to make the New Englanders (who were the busiest chroniclers) the fountainhead of the Protestant mainstream. There will be ample opportunity to show the religious diversity that the American population came to house, so at the outset this book follows the standard emphasis on New England.

As the name implies, this area of the New World was settled by people from Britain. Whereas New Spain to the far south and west and New France to the north and west had a Catholic cast, New England represented a Protestantism nurtured for some generations in Britain. In fact, however, the predominant religious outlook in New England was a minority position in the motherland, since many of the New England settlers had separated from the established Church of England. The Church of

From the time the United States achieved stability and a measure of material prosperity, American religion sought to bless domestic comforts as bulwarks of religious virtue. (Drawing Room, 1754; The Nelson-Atkins Museum of Art, Kansas City, Missouri [Nelson Fund])

England continued to be a major reference point, but the Calvinist theology of the New England **Puritans** was more influential.

In New Netherlands, which centered on Manhattan Island, Dutch Calvinism prevailed, while the short-lived New Sweden, centered on what is now Wilmington, Delaware, brought Swedish Lutheran traditions to the New World. Of the original 13 colonies only Maryland had Roman Catholic origins, while in the 1680s Quakers seized the opportunity to establish a foundation in what became Pennsylvania.

Despite some difficulties, Virginia became an Anglican establishment, so Massachusetts and Connecticut carried the Puritan ball. (Rhode Island became a refuge for exiles from Puritan orthodoxy.) Massachusetts owes its religious distinction to the steady line of theologians and educators who fashioned that Puritan orthodoxy. The congregationalism they established faced much opposition, but the victories of Cromwell in England strengthened their power.

In speaking of the Puritan spirit that characterized Massachusetts, historian Sydney

Ahlstrom reaches back to the prophet Amos, for a good illustration of the perennial fight against luxury that the Puritans thought they were conducting:

> Woe to those who are at ease in Zion, and to those who feel secure on the mountain of Samaria. . . . Woe to those who lie upon beds of ivory, and stretch themselves upon their couches, and eat lambs from the flock, and calves from the midst of the stall; who sing idle songs to the sound of the harp, and like David invent for themselves instruments of music; who drink wine in bowls, and anoint themselves with finest oils, but are not grieved over the ruin of Joseph! (Amos 6:1, 4–6)

Among the Christian reformers who worked in this spirit, opposing luxury and thinking true piety would never stray far from lamenting one's sins, Ahlstrom numbers Augustine, Bernard of Clairvaux, and Hugh Latimer, an early leader of the Reformation in England. Insofar as they brooded over religious experience with something of the apostle Paul's stimulus from conversion and something of Augustine's intensity and introspection, the Puritans can be considered quite orthodox. Thus the Puritans were not simply a dissident branch of the Protestant Reformation but the carriers to the New World of a thirst for purification that had long animated many Christians.

The New England Puritans inherited from their English forebears the conviction that the way to establish a purified religious body and realm was to insist on strict discipline. They believed this had to begin with the reformation of personal character, so that by reading the Scriptures and examining their consciences Puritans might fashion people who had no time for idle recreations or displays of vanity but concentrated vigorously on attaining a sober, obedient godliness.[2] The Puritan ideal in civil matters was orderliness and respect for English legal tradition, as long as that proved compatible with efforts to obey God's laws. Whatever resistance the Puritans offered to the established (monar-chical) order was necessary, in their eyes, to oppose the blasphemous efforts of the Church of England to impose clerical overlords (bishops) and pomp in religious ceremonies, which they found incompatible with simple, straightforward Christian faith. So Puritan wrath tended to flame at such adornments as giving a ring in the wedding ceremony or wearing a surplice (a flimsy, decorative liturgical garment), and they distinguished themselves from other Christians by keeping the Sabbath with exceptional rigor.

The Puritans who arrived in 1620 to establish the Plymouth Plantation looked forward to creating a realm in which saintliness, as they conceived it, might flourish. Sobered but undaunted by the wilderness they encountered, they were hard at work on Christmas day, erecting their common storage building in deliberate defiance of the "popish" custom of celebrating Christmas as a holiday (holy day). Just before disembarking from their ship, the Mayflower, they had signed a compact, meant in part to put down the grumblings of some on board and unite the fledgling community. Note the conjunction of religious piety with a call for civil obedience and discipline.

> In the name of God, Amen. We whose names are underwritten, the loyal subjects of our dread sovereign lord, King James, by the grace of God, of Great Britain, France, and Ireland, King, Defender of the Faith, etc. Having undertaken for the glory of God, and advancement of the Christian faith and honor of our king and country, a voyage to plant the first colony in the northern parts of Virginia [where they thought they were], do by these present, solemnly and mutually, in the presence of God and one another, covenant and combine ourselves into a civil body politic, for our better ordering and preservation and furtherance of the ends aforesaid; and by virtue hereof to enact, constitute, and frame such just and equal laws, ordinances, acts, constitutions, offices from time to time as shall be thought most meet and convenient for the general good of the colony; unto which we promise all due submission and obedience. . . .[3]

From 1620 to 1650, the Plymouth colony grew from about 100 to about 1000. The original members had come from Holland, hoping to find in Virginia a freedom they thought unavailable in England and the adventure of founding a religious realm that Holland seemed unlikely to allow. The first winter nearly half the original settlement died, many of them from scurvy. But according to Ahlstrom the very difficulties of the beginning won the Plymouth colony "a secure place in American hearts. From the viewpoint of church history, moreover, its symbolic significance is great, for it remains the classic instance in America of congregational Separatism."[4]

Although the colony had few intellectuals, no public school for 50 years, and no church for 10, it saw its history as a providential work and found sufficient sustenance in the double dose of scriptural instruction offered by a lay leader each Sabbath to see it through. Eventually Plymouth agreed to the demands of other Massachusetts settlers that members of the Massachusetts Bay Colony be converted churchgoers, but in the beginning it enjoyed the freedom to fashion its own political body, which became a fertile seed of the New England tradition of rule by the local congregation. Under Governor William Bradford, who was elected annually for 30 years, Plymouth showed other establishments to the north, such as Salem, a good **congregationalist** example.

Puritan Theology

The Plymouth Pilgrims eventually gave way to the New England colony chartered in 1629. This colony developed around Boston a Puritanism less separatist than that of the group at Plymouth. Indeed the Bostonians applied and developed a fuller, more political and national notion of the covenant between God and his saints that allowed them to identify civil and religious duties quite closely. Not all New Englanders liked the political or disciplinary consequences of the fuller notion of covenant, but it prevailed nonetheless. Neither a theocracy nor a democracy, Puritan government offered religious freedom only with sizable restrictions.

One interesting study of the relation between biblical and political convictions in colonial New England stresses the significance of the different translations of the Bible used by the Puritans. A translation produced in 1560 by Puritan exiles in Geneva had won the day early in the Puritan movement. Aimed at ordinary lay people, it contained commentary that stressed the believer's personal relationship to Christ (whom it found prefigured throughout the Old Testament as Luther had). The Genevan Bible pounded home the central Reformation theme of justification by faith in Christ alone, stressing all the prophetic promises that Christ had fulfilled. The notion of a covenant between God and his chosen people (an entire social group) received little attention.

According to Harry Stout, however,

as the Puritan movement continued to grow, and as the prospect of New World settlement began to dawn, questions of national policy and social order increasingly received attention from the learned divines. Taking seriously their own insistence that Scripture speaks to all of life completely and infallibly, the ministers found it increasingly necessary to apply biblical doctrines to questions of a temporal and political nature. The changed social situation together with numerous advances in biblical scholarship since 1560 convinced many of the need for a new vernacular edition of the Bible better suited to the needs of the new century. The resultant Authorized [King James] Version of 1611 was soon adopted by most Puritan clergymen and inaugurated a new era in Puritan history.[5]

In addition to the better scholarship behind its translation, the Authorized Version had the advantage of possessing no marginal notes that narrowed the reader's attention to the private significance of the scriptural message. Theological currents in Puritan circles had come to speak of a special national covenant between God and the saintly people.

Nowhere was the movement beyond the Geneva Bible more evident than in the Puritan-sponsored migration to Massachusetts Bay in 1630. This migration had as its overarching mission nothing less than the carving out of a new world order solely according to biblical precept. Theirs would be a society governed in every detail according to the Word of God as interpreted by his ministers. Elements of the population could, and no doubt did, demur from this official policy privately, but they could not introduce their grievances publicly. In public settings, the only allowable voice was the Word of God as channeled through his personal ambassadors, the clergy.[6]

The first to implement the new emphasis on the national covenant was the governor of the Massachusetts colony, John Winthrop, who preached a landmark sermon on the flagship *Arabella* before the colonists disembarked. Winthrop developed the biblical metaphor of a "city upon a hill," whose task it would be to show the world a model of Christian charity. The colonists' success in carrying out this venture would determine whether they would prosper in the new land or be "consumed out of it." As Winthrop came to his peroration, he made the official ideology of the new enterprise very plain: The colonists were entering on a covenant with God. The colonial effort would be a joint, divine-human work. In the background of this language stood the covenant between Israel and the Lord struck on Mount Sinai. Strict obedience to the articles of the Massachusetts covenant would be the best way to ensure the success of the colonial venture (much as the prevailing biblical view of the bond between God and Israel had been that keeping the covenant laws was the way to prosperity). Winthrop is rather spiritual in his understanding of what the covenant entails, using the words

of the prophet Micah (6:8) about doing justice, loving mercy, and walking humbly with God. Those with extra ought to share with those in want. The two ways sketched by Moses in Deuteronomy 30 lie before the colonists. The way of life is to love God and one's neighbor. Remarkably enough, Winthrop exhorted the Massachusetts colonists to begin the undertaking that would shape so much subsequent conviction about America's special destiny not by speaking of defending the free world but by urging his fellow colonists to share everything communally, in a spirit of love.[7] Needless to say, this spiritual ideal proved hard to realize, as can be seen most dramatically in the cases of dissidents such as Anne Hutchinson and Roger Williams.

To conclude this brief indication of the foundation Puritan theology gave the colonial experience in New England, consider the founding of Harvard College in 1636. The Reformation's stress on the Bible, combined with the translation of the Bible into the vernacular and the Puritan desire to build a commonwealth on biblical principles, had been a great stimulus to literacy. Some scholars have even claimed that the New Englanders became the most literate people in the world of their day (their males attained virtually 100-percent literacy).[8] Harvard College was founded to train the new generation of ministers who would lead the Massachusetts colony in its mission to be the city on a hill. By 1650 the college had made sufficient progress to be granted a formal charter by the General Court of Massachusetts. The charter was to incorporate a college that had already shown itself conducive to the education of both the English and Indian youth of the country "in knowledge and godliness." The council of seven overseers (a president, five fellows, and a treasurer) were all "inhabitants in the Bay," and they had the power to purchase or acquire lands, tenements, or inheritances within the jurisdiction of Massachusetts (not exceeding 500 pounds per year) and to receive limitless amounts for the direct use of the president, fellows, and scholars of the college.

The language is that of a legal document, precise and formal, but one would scarcely think it could be launching what is now an educational enterprise with finances reaching several billions. No doubt many different motives had gotten up steam by 1650, but we should not underestimate the original desire to develop a learned clergy. From its beginnings in England Puritanism had made the preaching of the clergy the principal means for instructing the faithful (and so shaping their social behavior).

> Preaching as the centerpiece of worship was the visible result of Puritanism's emphasis on edification to the neglect of the sacramental aspects of religion. The Puritan clergy regarded preaching as an ordinary means of salvation from which the godly learned about spiritual freedom and the comforts of *renewing* grace. It was also a way to instruct the unregenerate about God's provision of *restraining* grace so that social order might continue. Strictly speaking, the doctrines of renewing and restraining grace were to be taught to all, because one's religious status was, in theory, independent of one's worldly estate. In practice, however, the clerical reformers, in their reflections on the social utility of preaching, tended to fuse religious and political concerns, so that lessons applicable to the unregenerate became targeted on England's unruly lower classes.[9]

In New England preaching was hardly less theoretical or practical.

The Middle and Southern Colonies[10]

In 1644 at least 18 different languages were spoken on Manhattan Island, then under Dutch control. Since 1626 New Netherlands had been a significant colonial enterprise, but French and English establishments had been at work close by even before then. The English especially resented the Dutch presence and secured the surrender of New Amsterdam in 1664. The Duke of York became the nominal head of the English colony, having received from the Crown a grant of property that ran from the Delaware River to Maine. The Dutch Reformed Church had been the religious power in New Netherlands, and in Europe that church had distinguished itself as a haven for religious refugees (such as the Pilgrims who emigrated to Plymouth). The English takeover entailed efforts to establish the Church of England in what had become New York, though only in 1692 did Anglicanism become the official religion (in four of the ten counties of the area), and as late as 1695 80 percent of the population of New York was still Calvinist. As the Church of England took over, however, many of the Dutch took their faith into New Jersey, which became the flowering point of the Dutch Reformed Church in the 19th century.

In the middle of the 17th century, however, New Jersey was something of a wilderness between the Hudson and Delaware rivers. Governor Peter Stuyvesant of New Netherlands conquered New Sweden in 1655, but there was no immediate imposition of Dutch influence. In 1666 strict Puritans from New Haven set up a "New Ark" community in New Jersey, the first of several developments that made that area a religious sanctuary. Between 1674 and 1676 Quakers led by William Penn came into possession of what was called "West Jersey," while "East Jersey," centered on Newark, became a predominantly Puritan enclave. Puritans, Baptists, and Quakers were much on the move in those years, fleeing persecution in England, where the Crown had been restored. Eventually this area largely adopted a Presbyterian form of church government, giving more power to elders than to the congregation conceived as a democratic body. West Jersey developed as a predominantly Quaker zone of influence, with meeting houses organized at each settlement.

In 1702 Queen Anne of England unified New Jersey and New York, but the instructions accompanying this action provided for liberty of religious conscience, in recognition of the diversity of churches in the area. All but "papists" were to be free to worship as they wished.

In Pennsylvania William Penn and his Quaker followers deliberately launched an experiment in statehood. Quakers had existed in New England, the southern colonies, and Jersey, but Pennsylvania became their showpiece. The creative force behind Quakerism was the mysticism of George Fox (1624–1691), an English radical Puritan whose experiences of exultation brought him to speak of a new age of the spirit. Penn himself was a well-rounded man, both spiritually sensitive and adept in practical governance. The pacifist son of a naval war hero, Penn was the friend of kings and eminent philosophers as well as of George Fox, an aristocrat by birth who advocated a radical democracy. After the modest Quaker successes in West Jersey, Penn secured a grant of land west of the Delaware.

Arriving in 1682, Penn immediately organized a government and within a year had laid out what was to be the city of Philadelphia. The Quakers (or Society of Friends) became a religious force in the colonies second only to the New England Puritans, and by 1700 immigrants had created more than 40 Quaker meetings. The colony went through both political and religious turmoil, however, the latter stemming largely from charges of laxity and heresy.

Penn's own sons became Anglicans, and the problem of bringing up a second generation in the spiritual fervor of the first proved more than the colony could handle. The perfectionist rigor that had helped the Quakers organize their venture with dispatch and began to succeed in business simply couldn't inspire the full gamut of human affairs. By the mid-18th century Quaker critics were calling for a relinquishment of the large landholdings and great prosperity enjoyed by the offspring of the leading founders. The result was the loss of some Quakers to other traditions and the withdrawal of those who heeded the call to a rather mystical, separatist mentality.

In 1632 the Calvert family secured from the English crown permission to establish a colony in the New World. Lord George Calvert, Baron of Baltimore, had become a Catholic convert in 1625, and one of his principal aims for the new colony was to offer his fellow Catholics a refuge from the hostility and anti-Catholic laws prevailing in England. Baltimore had tried to establish Catholic settlements in Newfoundland and Virginia, without success. But from the execution of his plan by Calvert's son Cecilius in 1632 until the takeover by Puritans in 1654, Maryland preserved religious tolerance for all Christians, offering Catholics a temporary refuge, where they might begin life in the New World. Although they often suffered discrimination under Protestant leadership, a sturdy if small community continued in Maryland, its most prominent families distinguishing themselves in government and agriculture.

In 1634 three English Jesuits established a Catholic mission in southern Maryland. Unlike the Spanish and French missionaries, they had to support themselves like ordinary gentlemen of the colony. Moreover, within 20 years they came under penal restrictions making them liable to criminal sanctions for any proselytizing. English Jesuits had vivid memories of brothers such as Edward Campion and Robert Southwell martyred in England 50 years previously and therefore worked circumspectly. Originally they had hoped to missionize local Native Americans, but the hostility of both the natives and the Puritans in neighboring Virginia limited that prospect.

Indeed in 1642 Virginia passed an act against Catholics and priests, requiring all suspected of being such to swear an oath of religious allegiance to the English crown. In England 11 priests were put to death from 1641 to 1642, which increased the anti-Catholic mood in Virginia. (Massachusetts Bay also passed an anti-priest law in 1647.)

Virginia, Maryland, and the Carolinas, which usually count as southern colonies, were the strongholds of the Church of England, although without the usual Anglican bishops. All the other colonies together counted only about a dozen self-sufficient parishes before 1700. Although the Virginia colony (named for Elizabeth the Virgin Queen) began in 1607, it did not have the religious intensity of the colonies founded slightly later by Puritans, Quakers, and others seeking freedom from the Anglican establishment. Virginia began as a frankly commercial enterprise. Spanish tales of gold inflamed the imaginations of some investors. Whatever religious fervor worked in others ran mainly to opposing the popery of the Spanish competition and evangelizing the natives into Protestant rather than Catholic Christianity. Administrative incompetence and native uprisings delayed the progress of the colony in the early years, and the carving of Maryland from the original Virginia grant for the Catholic Calverts created violent resentment. Things appeared to be settling in 1642 when William Berkeley became governor, but a massacre by natives in 1644, along with the beginnings of what became civil war in England, complicated the position of the governor, who as a royal appointee was loyal to both the crown and the established church.

While the Puritans were in control in England, Virginia Anglicans moved toward a more austere faith, and even after the Stuart restoration their Anglicanism had a flinty flavor. Nonetheless, many religious commentators attacked the colony as lax and immoral. Although the Puritan doctrine of vocation encouraged hard work, the early introduction of tobacco, which was increasingly maintained by African labor, tainted its purity. Owners throve on slave labor, however, and their self-interest led the Virginia legislature to declare in 1667 that baptism did not alter a person's bondage or freedom. For Blacks to become Christians was fine, as long as they continued to be slaves. In a more enlightened vein Anglicans did establish (in 1693) William and Mary College, which was destined to exert considerable influence.

In the Carolinas religious motives played an even smaller role in the early colonization. Although Anglicanism was the predominant faith of the original eight proprietors, they offered liberty of conscience to all willing to settle in their wild territory. The official establishment of the Church of England in North Carolina, which the assembly passed in 1701, did not take hold until 1741. In South Carolina Anglicanism had things easier; its official establishment of 1704 held despite some resistance of clergy who disliked its grant of supervisory powers to laity. In many parts of the Carolinas, however, dissenters—mainly Quakers and Puritans—were in the majority. Some of them were refugees from Virginia, where nonconformity was a serious offense. The main problem in these southern colonies tended to be the lack of trained clergy, for apart from Maryland's Jesuits most of the ministry had only mediocre religious education or talent.

Georgia, the last of the Southern colonies, came on the scene only in 1732, as a buffer against Spanish Florida and an experiment in humanitarianism. Anglicanism was the official tradition, but Georgia welcomed dissidents, including many Moravians and Lutherans. However, apart from the fact that Charles and John Wesley struggled briefly in Georgia (gaining experience that shaped their later Methodist reform of Anglicanism), the general story was of a clergy both sparse and undistinguished. The great exception was George Whitefield, who filled the churches to overflowing both in Georgia and throughout the middle colonies.

Religious Freedom

Many historians of American culture have argued that its greatest accomplishment was creating a pluralistic framework in which people of different religious and national backgrounds could live alongside one another in relative peace. By the time it came to fashioning a constitution for the postrevolutionary nation, the colonies had enjoyed or suffered more than a century and a half of experimentation with various solutions to the problem of pluralism. We sometimes forget that while the Pilgrims and many other immigrant groups came to the New World in search of religious liberty for themselves, they were little inclined to grant such liberty to others. Certainly there were official exceptions to the general policy of establishing a church that would live hand in glove with the political power of the colony—Maryland and Rhode Island come to mind—but the prevailing mentality continued to be that church and state were but two different expressions of one commonweal and ought to be united by a common set of values.

Massachusetts and Connecticut held out the longest against arguments for a full religious liberty that would remove discrimination against any citizen on the basis of faith. Only when the philosophers of the European **Enlightenment** had developed powerful arguments for tolerance and nondiscrimination (based on their experience of the evils of established religions in Europe) did the makers of the American Republic decide to separate church and state. Probably the contentiousness of the different colonial church groups weighed more heavily than the possibility of convincing the population that it was desirable to have many different religious traditions contributing to one civil culture.

Sidney Mead, one of the ablest exponents of the American experiment in religious liberty, makes it plain that the mainstream of the Protestant Reformation actually agreed with the Catholic desire for religious uniformity:

By the time English colonization got underway in the 17th century, the Reformation movement had shattered the once tangible unity of European Christendom. The spiritual reformation of the church was concurrent with the rising self-consciousness of the emerging nations. Quite naturally the reformation of the church found diverse expressions in the several countries—Lutheranism in the realms of the German princes and in the Scandinavian countries, Anglicanism in England, Reformed in Geneva and Scotland. In general these right-wing Protestant groups agreed with Roman Catholics on the necessity for enforcing religious uniformity in doctrine and practice within a civil commonwealth. This view of many centuries' standing in Christendom the new churches accepted without question. Meanwhile, in the social crevices created by universal upheaval, certain sects or left-wing groups were emerging as blades of grass spring up through the cracks once a cement sidewalk is broken. Throughout Europe, Catholics and Protestants alike tried to suppress these groups by force, branding them as heretics and schismatics who constituted a threat to the whole structure of Christian civilization. All of the first settlements on that part of the continent that was to become the United States were made under the religious aegis of right-wing groups with the exception of Plymouth where a handful of separatists "made a small, bustling noise in an empty land."[11]

The bigger noises were made by establishmentarians such as the Anglicans in Virginia, the Dutch Reformed in New Netherlands, the Lutherans in New Sweden, and the Puritans in Massachusetts. But even the Pilgrims expected religious uniformity within their domain at Plymouth, passing laws against the Quakers and others they considered heretics. In all these cases religious unanimity was supposed to be the basis for colonial unity and prosperity.

The few cases of positive appreciations of religious liberty tend more to confirm this general characterization than greatly to weaken it. In Maryland Protestants went along with the religious freedom initially extended by the founding Catholics only until they could grasp control for themselves, at which point they passed harsh laws against those who deviated from their own Puritanism. (For their part, the Catholic founders were probably influenced as much by the practical realities of their being a small group as by any positive commitment to religious liberty as an inalienable right of the human conscience. Little in traditional Catholic theology supported such a commitment.)

The colony that Roger Williams founded at Providence as an asylum for those unhappy and unwelcome in the Massachusetts Bay theocracy did consider pluralism a positive virtue. But Massachusetts took a very dim view of the colony, considered it a sewer, and tolerated it only because it seemed impossible to suppress. Mead thinks that the plaudits offered William Penn and the Quakers for their tolerance in the Jerseys and Pennsylvania should also be restrained because by then the example of the neighboring colonies had shown that enforced religious uniformity was not likely to work. Moreover, parent England itself had experimented with toleration during the Puritan era of 1648–1660 under Cromwell (in a rather limited form and largely as a matter of political expediency). Overall, then, colonial America had a very limited view of religious liberty. Religious liberty was simply the right to establish one's own sort of church and then strive mightily to keep those who did not want to belong to it out of one's geographical area.

This is not to say that Colonial America was not religiously diverse. It was very diverse by the standards of its own day. By the standards of our day, of course, most of the colonists could be grouped within the Protestant third of Christianity. There were relatively few Catholics or Orthodox, and Jews were but tiny populations (of largely Sephardic immigrants from Brazil)

in New Amsterdam and Newport (Rhode Island). Jews did not have a burial ground in Newport until 1677 nor their first synagogue (in New York) until 1692. All other major religions had virtually no representation.

Black Americans possessed of African traditions were on the American scene from 1619 and forged their own spiritual way in reaction to their condition of slavery and the Christianity of the whites who owned them. It is useless to speak of religious liberty in their case—although they often made sincere commitments to Christian faith—because the white version of such faith usually did not recognize their simple humanity.

Between 1607 and 1787, therefore, Americans painfully came to realize that the diversity of their population made it imperative to constitute any conjoint national enterprise on the basis of a fuller religious freedom than what most of their long-standing churches had traditionally favored. The ebbs and flows of religious enthusiasm, witchcraft trials, interactions with Native Americans, slavery, plantation life, and dealings with both the British motherland and other European countries had shown that America had no religious uniformity. All Christian groups lacked at least two of the traditional marks of the true Church, unity and catholicity, so none actually had much claim to be the established national religion.

Roger Williams and Anne Hutchinson

Roger Williams (about 1603–1683) was a graduate of Cambridge University in England who emigrated to the Massachusetts Bay Colony in 1631. Although he was a Puritan, he had strong views about freedom to separate from a Puritan body when one found it insufficiently pure. When he expressed these opinions in Massachusetts, the authorities found him a threat to their self-conception as a model community with a divine errand in the wilderness. Williams opposed not only the quality of communal life he found in Massachusetts but also this theocratic point of view. To his mind there was no justification for the enforcement of religious uniformity by civil authorities. He also repudiated the taking of civil oaths, and, as a final inflammatory indignity, he attacked the Massachusetts colony for having expropriated native land.

Williams served briefly as a pastor at both Plymouth and Salem, taking the latter post in defiance of the Massachusetts General Court. In 1635 he was tried and convicted of sedition. The relatively mild punishment (in view of the hanging of four Quakers in Boston 25 years later) was banishment from the Massachusetts territories. In 1635 Williams purchased land from local natives and founded Providence, which became the capital of an area under his inspiration called Rhode Island. His foundation stressed religious liberty and welcomed people rejected in other places for their unorthodox religious views. As the next stage in his own religious evolution, Williams became a **Baptist,** in view of which he mounted strong attacks on the Massachusetts practice of infant baptism. He also continued to attack the intrusion of civil authority into religion.

Williams gradually won a reputation as one of America's leading defenders of religious liberty. A pamphlet he wrote in 1644 entitled *The Bloody Tenet of Persecution* was much admired, and some opponents saw him as a freethinker. In fact, however, he remained quite Puritan (Calvinist) in his basic theology, adding his own view that the Bible gave no basis for religious persecution. Both the civil and religious realms came from God, but neither had the right to intrude in the affairs of the other. The civil realm owed obedience to God the Creator, while the ecclesiastical realm owed obedience to God the Redeemer. This led, logically enough, to his arguing for the separation of church and state.

His thought also entailed a democratic view of civil government, because God had placed the source of all civil power in the people as a whole.

In 1651 Massachusetts arrested three Baptists for their views on infant baptism and the limits of civil authority and had one of them publicly whipped. Williams wrote an indignant letter to the Massachusetts governor, John Endicott, instructing him in the noblest of virtues, freedom of conscience. Williams described conscience as a persuasion fixed in the mind and heart that forces one to such and such a judgment. Conscience is a universal faculty, found in all people, he said, regardless of their religious persuasion (Jews, Turks, Protestants, and Papists must all follow conscience). People like the governor trample on this faculty in their broadsided hatred of those they consider heretics. Heretics deserve to be hanged, they believe (because heretics would sunder orthodox faith, without which people go to hellfire). Williams tried to turn this argument against Endicott by citing its similarity to the rationale of the Catholic persecutors who had flamed against Protestant "heretics" a century earlier. Then mimicking the charge that Christ made against Saul, Williams had the persecuted accuse Endicott of trying to afflict the Body of Christ subsisting in them.

In Williams' view all of this was folly because it is impossible to maintain Christian faith by the sword. In fact to fight against another person's sincere conscience is to fight against the God resident in that conscience. His concluding counsel to the governor was that he pray for better enlightenment, so that he might see the significance of the consciences he moved against.

Anne Hutchinson (1591–1643) emigrated to the Massachusetts Bay Colony in 1634, following her minister John Cotton. She soon showed herself an outspoken person of initiative, holding meetings in her home to discuss the sermons she and her friends were hearing. Gradually she became more forthcoming about her own views, which called for much greater freedom and individual inspiration than the Massachusetts orthodoxy allowed. At first her views had the support of Cotton and other eminent religious teachers, but when she went on to claim special revelations they abandoned her. In 1637 she was excommunicated from the Massachusetts colony and fled to Rhode Island. She then moved on to New York, where she was killed by natives. Like Roger Williams she was perceived as a threat to the solidarity of the community in Massachusetts. There was no room for dissent in the city on the hill, no tolerance for those who imperiled the errand in the wilderness. What the Massachusetts orthodoxy saw as the national covenant implied in the impulse to purify all of life and subject it to God, Anne Hutchinson saw as an effort to gain justification by works. Perhaps significantly, the Bible from which she quoted long passages during her trial was not the Authorized Version used by her accusers but the Genevan Bible. That older translation focused on the individual's need to find justification by personal faith in Christ. Her judges did not so much refute her arguments as simply write them off as obviously a wrongful interpretation of Scripture, while her claims to have received special revelations from God greatly diminished her credibility.

Nonetheless several eminent historians of American religion have been charmed by Anne Hutchinson. Edward Gaustad thinks her main problem was that she stepped outside what was thought seemly for a woman. She knew and talked too much, and her trial verged on being a farce.[12] Martin Marty, responding to an invitation to write on a moment in American history when he wished he'd been there, chose the trial of Anne Hutchinson:

> The amazingly scrupulous records we have of Anne Hutchinson's trial in early November of 1637 tantalize me into wishing I could have been there. Hers was a religious culture and ours is pluralist and secular, but the troubling issues from back then have analogies now. In facing state (John Winthrop) and church (John Cotton), she represented dissent against establishment. As so often since, neither side looked good, and, from other angles, both sides made a case. They fought over the covenant of grace and the covenant of works, ideas almost incomprehensible to many today. Yet they are signal issues about liberty and license versus law and responsibility, and remain alive today.
>
> Why go to Europe for Joan of Arc when in America someone on trial also claimed to have heard voices? That is, instead of sticking to the letter of the text, she claimed the spirit spoke directly. What are claims of authority even now? How much do we, must we, live by the book? And there are classic woman-man issues here. Without question, her accusers-prosecutors-judges-sentencers, who were one and the same persons, and who banished her, were harder on her because she was a woman, not a mere dissenter or heretic.
>
> The personalities draw me: Anne Hutchinson—gifted, charismatic, often wild, destined to be killed in an Indian massacre. John Winthrop—judgmental yet enthralled. John Cotton—half leaning toward Hutchinson but not daring to be caught there. Here was a combat of minds and spirits more interesting than massacres or wars; it still haunts.[13]

As background for this case, Rosemary Skinner Keller cites the Puritan conviction that keeping women in their socially prescribed place was essential to the maintenance of order. While most women apparently accepted this, some read the Pauline scriptures and applied to themselves such texts as Galatians 3:28 (where there is neither male nor female in Christ—apparently a vision of sexual equality); Titus 2:3–4 (approving older women teaching younger women); and I Corinthians 11:3–5 (indirectly allowing women to prophesy). So Anne Hutchinson had some ammunition on her side. Keller notes among Hutchinson's other powerful arguments her attack on the Massachusetts demand for works (obedience to precepts of the national covenant) as in conflict with justification by faith, and her insistence that grace is given to individuals as God wishes (and not just to clergy).

Colonial women such as Anne Hutchinson were expected to make hearth and home their principal interest, though they were allowed considerable scope for cultural refinement. (Kitchen, 17th century; The Nelson-Atkins Museum of Art, Kansas City, Missouri [Nelson Fund])

Keller also notes that Hutchinson and two of her followers were further stigmatized as witches. They had worked as midwives and in one case had been present at the birth of a stillborn, deformed fetus. Gossip had it that the fetus was hideous and the bed had shaken two hours before its birth—manifest signs of the devil. The banishment of Hutchinson and her friends was part of a pattern women suffered in Massachusetts, where insubordination to male religious authorities was virtually certain to get them in deep trouble.[14]

Massachusetts certainly was not all of colonial America, but by virtue of its intellectual influence in the first American centuries the fate of two of its early dissenters is worth noting. Such later Massachusetts luminaries as Jonathan Edwards, Ralph Waldo Emerson, and William James (the three thinkers historian William Clebsch has considered most representative of American religious thought) all carved out their niches against the backdrop of the early struggles to establish what religious freedom Massachusetts would permit.

The Cambridge Platform

The Cambridge Platform of 1648 is a good illustration of the Puritan mentality that has colored our sense of colonial religion.[15] The General Court in Massachusetts had been petitioned for more religious tolerance by members of the colony chafing under the clerical rule of John Winthrop and his allies. In 1646 the conservatives managed to delay any firm resolution of the problem of where to vest religious and political authority because they feared that the more liberal attitudes prevailing in England would relax the firm discipline they favored. By 1648 Cromwell and the Puritans had seized power in England, which made the climate right for a reassertion of the conservative position on clerical control. The Cambridge Platform dealt with such matters as the power of the church, the standards for admitting members into the church, excommunication, the relations among individual congregations, and the powers of civil magistrates in ecclesiastical matters.

Concerning the power of the church, the platform first noted that supreme power over all the churches belonged only to Jesus Christ, whom it described as King and Head of the church. The government rested on his shoulders and he had all power in heaven and earth to carry it out. Next the document reasons that the church must possess sufficient power to preserve itself. Third, one might call the government of the church mixed, since it is a monarchy respecting the Kingship of Christ, but a democracy respecting the common body of believers, and an aristocracy respecting the **presbytery.** The church expresses its power by choosing its own officers and admitting or expelling members. Of special interest is the case where a member is to be admonished. Members have the right to admonish fellow members they have found offending against the virtue expected of a Christian, and if the offenders remain unrepentant the church may excommunicate them.

Specifically the elders have the duty to examine candidates for admission and pronounce upon offenders sentences that express the will of God. Still there ought to be sweet harmony between this power of the elders and the powers of the community at large.

Three important features of the platform should be noted at this point:

1. All of the language refers to brothers, not because women could not be censured (witness the case of Anne Hutchinson), but because only men held power.
2. The stress on reprimands and offenses is remarkable, as though the central business of the church (the reason God had given it power over its affairs) were dealing with backsliders.
3. Positing a democratic power among the common members and an aristocratic power among the elders and saying that these two powers should coexist in sweet agreement seems extremely naive. The situation seems to have conflict bred in its bones. Even though one might agree that the Spirit of God can bring sweet harmony, one expects wise legislators to minimize the chances for sour conflict.

In its comments on the procedures for admitting new members into the church, the platform begins by warning that the doors of the churches of Christ do not stand so wide open that all sorts of people may walk in as they wish. One of the key requirements of the proper admission procedure is that individuals make a public confession of the way God has worked in their souls. In other words, they have to claim that they have had religious experiences warranting their admission into the company of church members. Children of church members also have to make such a confession when they come of age and desire admission to the Lord's Supper. Such children may have been baptized as infants or minors, but if they wish to function as fully adult members of the church they must confess God's appropriate working in their souls. Baptism has set them in covenant with God, but they lack **regeneration** and should be kept under watch, admonished, and censured for any failings, that they may be healed.

Other points of interest in the platform include the stipulation that members cannot move from one community to another without church approval because such liberty would tend to weaken the church body. The purpose of censures is to prevent, remove, and heal offenses in the church. Censures also prevent the tainted leaven from infecting the whole mass of dough and keep away the wrath of God likely to fall on a church that has tolerated notorious offenders. Censures should be neither too harsh nor too mild: Some will be saved by compassion, others by fear. Those excommunicated should be kept at a distance, minimizing both spiritual and civil contacts. Specifically, church members should not eat or drink with excommunicates. On the other hand, the excommunicate does not incur civil liabilities, may still come to church to hear the Word of God, and should be considered not an enemy but a sibling needing admonition. Civil magistrates ought not meddle in church affairs, and church members owe civil magistrates obedience in civil matters. Still civil authority ought to restrain and punish idolatry, blasphemy, heresy, the venting of corrupt opinions, contempt for preaching, profanation of the Lord's Day, and disturbance of worship.

Despite the language about the distinction of the civil and ecclesiastical realms, the platform does not teach a separation of church and state like that later established by the Constitution. The assumption is still of a monolithic rather than a pluralistic society. Indeed when civil authority has the duty to banish idolatry, blasphemy, and heresy and to make sure the Lord's Day is not profaned, one finds it reaching well into the religious realm. The platform does not

spell out what constitutes idolatry, blasphemy, heresy, or profanation of the Lord's Day. Such judgments would fall to church elders, who would no doubt choose strict interpretations of doctrine, liturgy, and morals. Those who had argued for greater liberty of conscience in Massachusetts could see their hopes withering on the vine. Beneath the cool, detached language of the platform lay a firm mind and a will to impose strict discipline on all.

Key Terms

Baptist: pertaining to churches that arose out of English Congregationalism in the 17th century. The first Baptists were Puritan congregations that had withdrawn from the Church of England to achieve a purer church life free of civil control. Their leader was John Smyth, a clergyman who had left the Anglican church about 1606 to minister to a separatist congregation at Gainsborough on Trent. This congregation emigrated to Amsterdam in 1608 to escape persecution. In Amsterdam Smyth rejected infant baptism as unscriptural and a hinderance to forming a pure church. The influence for this position may have come from the Mennonites he encountered in Amsterdam. Other early Baptists then backed away from joining with the Mennonites, returned to England, and established a church opposed to infant baptism. Another group of Baptists emerged in England in 1638. This group established baptism by immersion. Baptists grew in numbers in the mid-17th century, when Puritanism was gaining power, but after the restoration of the crown they were subject to discrimination. In the United States Roger Williams founded the first Baptist church in Rhode Island in 1639.

Congregationalist: In 16-century English terminology *congregationalist* was often synonymous with *separatist,* because most of the churches separating from the established Church of England favored a political order in which power was vested democratically in the congregation as a whole. The congregation as a whole had a covenant with God, who had gathered (congregated) them as his people. Calvinist theology generally prevailed in the Congregational churches. In American terminology, both the Plymouth Pilgrims and the Massachusetts Puritans were congregationalists; they stressed a Calvinist theology of covenant, stood separate from the Anglican church, and made the community as a whole the locus of church power.

Enlightenment: a European movement of the 17th and 18th centuries that urged people to cast aside traditional religious authority, including that of the Bible, and think for themselves. Enlightenment thinkers such as Hume, Voltaire, and Kant doubted the reality of miracles, distrusted ecclesiastical influences, and were repulsed by religious wars and bigotries. They considered humanity sufficiently mature to manage its own affairs without outside, "supernatural" influences, and they especially prized the autonomy of the individual conscience.

Presbytery: the council of elders charged with running a church. Presbyterian churches tend to deny the distinction of bishops from elders that Episcopalian churches find in the New Testament. Their elders are of two main kinds: teachers (ministers) and rulers elected by the congregations. Presbyterian churches claim Calvinist roots, their system of government having first been developed in Calvin's Geneva. The Scottish church, under John Knox, stressed presbyterianism and exported it to the New World. Although the 17th century Massachusetts Puritan churches spoke of elders, they are usually considered to have been more congregational than presbyterian. Insofar as any congregation elects presbyters and has some rights over the presbyterian council, however, the distinction between the two forms of church government can be narrow.

Puritans: The current connotations of prudishness and repression of sensuality distort the historical reality of the groups who first carried this name. The origins of these groups lay in objection to the adornment of worship, which was promoted by the Book of Common Prayer issued under Queen Elizabeth I. Those who so objected were called Puritans because they wanted a simpler form of worship, closer to what they thought was the spirit of the Bible (as interpreted by the Protestant Reformers, especially Calvin). Other Puritans opposed the appointment of bishops in the English church because they felt that such a move was contrary to the pure biblical faith they hoped the English Reformation would achieve. The Puritan movement stressed conversion, a strict moral code, austerity, and hard work, for all of which it usually assumed scriptural foundations.

Regeneration: a term meaning rebirth, mentioned by such New Testament texts as Titus 3:5, John 3:5, and Matthew 19:28. In early Christian theological reflection, a question arose about the relation between the rebirth accomplished in baptism and the need for Christians to pray for forgiveness: Is not the work of the Holy Spirit in baptism, where the person is reborn to divine life, sufficient to grant forgiveness? Augustine distinguished between the washing away of sins in baptism and the need for the regenerate person to resist the infirmity that leads to sin. By the time of John Wesley and the Methodist reform this distinction had broadened. Wesley denied that baptism was more than an external work and argued that true or full rebirth would be an internal work. Other Protestant groups thinking this way demanded a confession of rebirth or a testimony to God's action in the person's soul as a condition for adult participation in church life. Some churches equated regeneration with a vivid, adult experience of the Holy Spirit that usually included striking gifts such as the ability to speak in tongues.

Discussion Questions

1. Why can one consider Puritanism a perennial strain in Christian tradition?
2. How did Puritan separatism relate to congregationalism?
3. Why did Puritanism develop the notion of a national covenant?
4. What is the significance of the fact that America's first college was founded to educate clergy?
5. Where did Anglicans and Separatists have their main influences in the Middle and Southern Colonies?
6. How did the Quaker and Roman Catholic colonial communities develop?
7. In what sense was the granting of religious freedom in colonial America reluctant?
8. What are the main arguments for and against religious freedom?
9. Why did Roger Williams want to separate the religious and civil spheres?
10. What was the link between Anne Hutchinson's expulsion from Massachusetts and her being suspected of witchcraft?
11. How was the Cambridge Platform a victory for the conservative and clerical party?
12. Why was the platform so concerned about punishing offenders and regulating excommunication?

Notes

1. See, for example, Catherine L. Albanese, *America: Religions and Religion* (Belmont CA: Wadsworth, 1981) and R. Laurence Moore, *Religious Outsiders and the Making of Americans* (New York: Oxford University Press, 1986).
2. See Sydney E. Ahlstrom, *A Religious History of the American People* (New Haven CT: Yale, 1972), pp. 129–130.
3. Mortimer J. Adler, ed., *The Annals of America*, vol. 1 (Chicago: Encyclopedia Britannica, 1976), p. 64.
4. Ahlstrom, op. cit., p. 138.
5. Harry S. Stout, "Word and Order in Colonial New England," in *The Bible in America*, ed. Nathan O. Hatch and Mark A. Knoll (New York: Oxford University Press, 1982), p. 25.
6. Ibid., p. 26. For further background, see David Zaret, *The Heavenly Contract* (Chicago: University of Chicago Press, 1985).
7. For the text see Conrad Cherry, ed., *God's New Israel* (Englewood Cliffs NJ: Prentice-Hall, 1971), pp. 39–43; Adler, op. cit., pp. 109–115; Edwin S. Gaustad, ed., *A Documentary History of American Religion*, vol. 1 (Grand Rapids MI: Eerdmans, 1982), pp. 106–107.
8. See Kenneth A. Lockridge, *Literacy in Colonial New England* (New York, 1974), pp. 72–101.
9. Zaret, op. cit., pp. 62–63.
10. This section is based on Ahlstrom, op. cit., pp. 184–213.
11. Sidney E. Mead, *The Lively Experiment* (New York: Harper & Row, 1976), pp. 16–17.
12. Gaustad, op. cit., p. 132.

13. Martin E. Marty, "Anne Hutchinson on Trial," in *A Sense of History,* ed. Byron Dobell (New York: American Heritage, 1985), pp. 3–4.

14. See Rosemary Skinner Keller, "New England Women: Ideology and Experience in First-Generation Puritanism (1630–1650)," in *Women & Religion in America,* ed. Rosemary Radford Ruether and Rosemary Skinner Keller, vol. 2 (San Francisco: Harper & Row, 1983), pp. 139–144.

15. See Adler, op. cit., pp. 190–194.

Revolutionary and Republican Religion

Later Colonial Trends and the Great Awakening

The Puritans continued to furnish much of the intellectual energy during the middle and end of the colonial period. But as conflict with Britain came closer, the leaders of Virginia and New York furnished most of the political vision.

A good representative of the second generation of New England Puritans was Increase Mather (1639–1723). The son of a pastor in Dorchester, Massachusetts, he studied at Harvard, and then in England and Ireland, where he received an M.A. from Trinity College, Dublin, in 1658. Mather was starting a successful ministerial career in England when the Restoration closed all prospects for Puritans. Returning to Boston in 1661 he married the daughter of John Cotton, became influential in church politics, and in 1685 accepted the presidency of Harvard College. He renegotiated his colony's charter in a successful mission to England and became so powerful in Massachusetts that he nominated the governor and slate of magistrates in 1692. Unfortunately his later years were less glorious. He was forced out of the presidency of Harvard; suffered a strong rivalry from Solomon Stoddard of Northhampton, who dominated the western part of the colony; and was held responsible for the miscarriages of justice wrought by the Salem witchcraft trials, even though he and his son Cotton (a luminary of the third Puritan generation) gave the court good advice it did not take. Toward the end of his life he supported such progressive causes as inoculation against smallpox and peace between Puritans and Baptists.

Increase Mather was a voluminous theological writer and a good representative of the best of the Puritan preaching style: learned and orderly. An excerpt from a sermon preached on the occasion of the drowning of two Harvard undergraduates and published in 1697 illustrates what Puritan religion had become by the turn of the century.

> We proceed to Enquire 3. Whence is it that men know not their Time. Answ. It is from God. He will have them be kept in ignorance and uncertainties about their Time: And this for wise & holy Ends. e.g. 1. That so his Children might live by Faith. That so they might live a life of holy dependence upon God continually. They must not know their Times, that so they might Trust in the Lord at all times. God would not have his Children to be anxiously solicitous about future Events, but to leave themselves and theirs with the Heavenly Father, to dispose of all their Concernments, as He in his Infinite Wisdom and Faithfulness shall see good. 2. That their obedience may be tried. That they may follow the Lord, as it were blindfold, withersoever He shall lead them, though they do not see one step of their way before them, as Abraham did. Heb. 11.8 . . .[1]

Sermons such as these went on much longer than today's twenty-five-minute exercises. People were expected to sit up straight, pay attention, and ponder the implications for their own sorry souls. Indeed from about 1650 much Puritan literature lamented the failures of New England to keep her special covenant with God. Godliness was thought to be declining, and ministers regularly saw such phenomena as conflicts in local congregations, crop failures, droughts, and epidemics as negative judgments of God. Perhaps the most famous early specimen of this line of thought was a poem by Michael Wigglesworth entitled *God's Controversy with New England,* published in 1662. After rehearsing the glorious beginnings of the colony, the poet laments the recent backsliding. Instead of holiness, God now finds carnality. Instead of burning zeal, there is lukewarm indifference. Where temperance used to prevail, now there is excess in meat, drink, and clothing. On and on the verses plow, like a farmer determined to turn over each row of arid, disappointing earth. Readers of Wigglesworth came away with little reason for boasting, though he does assure them at the end that New England will still be the site of God's delight.[2]

Less scrupulous observers of colonial religion in the decades after the founding Puritans have seen no indication that the people had become morally bankrupt, although their ardor for their errand in the wilderness seems to have waned. As they tamed the land, they found it hard to think in terms of biblical imagery of the desert or the desolate wastes. There were difficulties, however, including the loss of the colony's charter in 1684 and conflicts with Quaker and Baptist settlers. But during the 1740s the founding ardor returned with vigor, as Jonathan Edwards, America's first great theologian, led what became known as the Great Awakening. Edwards dared to hope that the stirrings begun in western Massachusetts might be the start of a spiritual renewal for all humankind. At the least they showed that God still had great purposes for New England.

In 1742 Edwards published a book on this theme, using a **typological exegesis** of Scripture to find the recent religious revival prophetically foretold. Although some years later Edwards and many others lamented some of the results of the Great Awakening (theological controversy, division in denominations, and sometimes uncontrolled emotionalism), at the outset the signs all seemed exhilarating. Edwards used such texts as Isaiah 40:9 to set the background: God's planned use of America, the far-away isles waiting and ripe. Europe, the old continent, was a less likely candidate, its isles not having borne the fruits of renewal required by biblical prophecy. And so it went with other prophecies, leading Edwards to conclude that America, indeed New England, was the area where the latter day glory, God's blazing final manifestation, was probably to begin.

> And if we may suppose that this glorious work of God shall begin in any part of America, I think, if we consider the circumstances of the settlement in New England, it must needs appear the most likely, of all American colonies, to be the place whence this work shall principally take its rise. And, if these things be so, it gives us more abundant reason to hope that what is now seen in America, and especially in New England, may prove the dawn of that glorious day; and the very uncommon and wonderful circumstances and events of this work, seem to me strongly to argue that God intends it as the beginning or forerunner of something vastly great.[3]

Note the continuance of the theme of providence struck more than 100 years previously, when John Winthrop had preached about the mission to be a city on a hill and the errand in the wilderness. The Great Awakening roused more than religious spirit. It revived the original colonial conviction that the New World offered the chance to create a people worthily covenanted with God: a New Israel. Edwards, Wigglesworth, and Increase Mather were all shaped by a sense of destiny hard to credit now but quite alive until very recently. In the 19th and 20th centuries the United States continued to consider itself a place of special opportunities. Indeed it came to consider itself the leader of the free world, the defender of liberty and human rights, a nation born with the manifest destiny of a land blessed by God for righteous global leadership.

Enlightened Religion

The Puritan religion that shaped American colonialism had a complex relationship with the European Enlightenment. On the one hand, the Puritans' stress on the affections and God's work in the soul and their dependence on biblical texts distanced them from the rationalism and independence of religious authorities that Enlightenment thinkers were advocating. On the other hand, no less a Puritan giant than Jonathan Edwards was delighted by the writings of John Locke on the workings of human reason. The framers of the Declaration of Independence and the American Constitution no doubt owed more to Locke and other Enlightenment figures than to Edwards and the Puritans, but the Puritans' own intellectualism kept the gap between reason and religion less threatening than it might have been.

Locke's *Essay Concerning Human Understanding* (1690) treated in passing the difference between the light enthusiasts claimed to have received through divine revelation and the light (to his mind much surer) that came from solid reasoning:

> Immediate revelation being a much easier way for men to establish their opinions and regulate their conduct, than the tedious and not always successful labour of strict reasoning, it is no wonder that some have been very apt to pretend to revelation, and to persuade themselves that they are under the peculiar guidance of heaven in their actions and opinions, especially in those of them which they cannot account for by the ordinary methods of knowledge and principles of reason. Hence we see, that, in all ages, men in whom melancholy has mixed with devotion, or whose conceit of themselves has raised them into an opinion of greater familiarity with God, and a nearer admittance to his favour than is afforded to others, have often flattered themselves with a persuasion of an immediate intercourse with the Deity, and frequent communications from the Divine Spirit. . . . St. Paul himself believed he did

well, and that he had a call to it, when he persecuted the Christians, whom he confidently thought in the wrong; but yet it was he, and not they, who were mistaken. Good men are men still liable to mistakes, and are sometimes warmly engaged in errors, which they take for divine truths, shining in their minds with the clearest light.

Light, true light, in the mind is, or can be, nothing else but the evidence of the truth of any proposition; and if it be not a self-evident proposition, all the light it has, or can have, is from the clearness and validity of those proofs upon which it is received. To talk of any other light in the understanding is to put ourselves in the dark, or in the power of the Prince of Darkness, and, by our own consent, to give ourselves up to delusion to believe a lie.[4]

The more that religious people disputed, even went to war, on the basis of their supposed revelations and inspired interpretations of human events, the better Locke's reliance on sober reason sounded. Those schooled in such a philosophy and those who admired the natural philosophy of Isaac Newton (Edwards among them) were bound to think American culture would be better served by principles admitting rational debate than by emotional claims to election, inspiration, or even a providential national covenant.

Both Newton and Locke had thought of their work as forwarding the Christian cause, the one by clarifying the laws by which God ran the material world and the other by clarifying the common sense required for political sanity (and a reasonable faith). More radical in their religious implications were the writings of the Scottish philosopher David Hume (1711–1776), whose empiricism made him highly critical of proofs for the existence of God, arguments from natural law, and miracles, to say nothing of claims for biblical revelation. In response to such challenges as Hume's, British Christian defenders such as Joseph Butler, William Paley, and Thomas Reid sought to establish a middle way, in which Christian faith could seem reasonable but not rationalistic. All of these advocates of reason had great influence among educated Americans.

One of the most influential results of the Enlightenment in religion was the largely British movement called Deism, which began in the 17th century and flourished in the 18th century. The Deists applied the Enlightenment focus on reason to traditional Christian faith, asking what from the traditional corpus of faith might be defended as actually reasonable to believe about God. They concluded that such matters as the Incarnation, the Trinity, immortality, revelation, miracles, the authority of the Bible, and the authority of the priesthood or ministry were highly dubious. It was better to stress "natural religion" (what reason could conclude about God and human nature apart from biblical revelation or church teaching). It was also better to develop a political situation in which people tolerated one another's religious opinions and practices than to promote an established church and discriminate against sects or separatists. Some historians place Locke among the Deists, and virtually all include the French writer Voltaire (1694–1778). For the United States one has only to mention the names Franklin, Jefferson, and Washington to suggest how influential those persuaded by deistic views proved to be, while Thomas Paine (1737–1809) showed the radical "free thinking" to which Deism might lead.

Sidney Mead, writing about "Christendom, Enlightenment and the Revolution," has focused on the establishment of religious liberty as the spiritual core of the Revolution itself. Taking his cue from a letter of John Adams written in 1815, which says, "The Revolution was in the minds and hearts of the people; a change in their religious sentiments of their duties and obligations," Mead stresses the separation of church and state that came with the establishment of a legal religious freedom.

The many portraits of Washington suggest the deep impact he made on both his contemporaries and later generations. Here the presidential statesman prevails over the revolutionary general. (George Washington, Rembrandt Peale; Gilcrease Museum, Tulsa, Oklahoma)

When the American Revolution was completed, let us say with John Adams by around 1815, not only had the Established Church of England been rejected, but, more important, the very idea of Establishment had been discarded in principle by the new Constitution. For the first time in Christendom there was legal *religious freedom* as distinct from toleration in a commonwealth. Church and state could no longer be seen as coextensive functional institutionalized authorities—as merely two ways of looking at the same society. A church became a voluntary association within the commonwealth, in competition with perhaps hundreds of others. Loyalty to God, symbol of the highest ideals and standards (cultural system), could now

be distinguished from loyalty to the monarch or state, symbols of nation (social system), and it was possible to conceive that the two might be in conflict. This development is what John Adams meant by "the Revolution"—the change that took place "in the minds and hearts of the people" which he described as "a change in their religious sentiments of their duties and obligations."[5]

Thomas Jefferson, in his "Notes on Religion" written around 1782, had thoughts similar to those of Adams. In particular he judged that the American revolutionary enterprise had gone beyond the tolerance envisioned by Locke.

Locke denies tolerance to those who entertain opinions contrary to those moral rules necessary for the preservation of society, as for instance, that faith is not to be kept with those of another persuasion, that Kings excommunicated forfeit their crowns, that dominion is founded in grace, or that obedience is due some foreign prince; or who will not own and teach the duty of tolerating all men in matters of religion; or who deny the existence of a god (it was a great thing to go so far—as he himself says of the parliament which framed the act of toleration—but where he stopped short we may go on).[6]

Thus enlightened religion American style came to mean principles that first had proven useful in throwing off the claims of the British crown (which had argued that its authority came from God). These principles took on a life of their own, based on the logic of extending to the citizens of the new Republic the full implications of the liberty of conscience and disestablishment of both monarchical and ecclesiastical authority at the heart of the spiritual revolution.

Independence and Constitution

The Revolution lodged in liberty of conscience began with the Declaration of Independence familiar to most American schoolchildren. Notice the explicit reliance of the Declaration on the enlightened, if not deistic, principles just discussed:

> When, in the Course of human events, it becomes necessary for one people to dissolve the political bands which have connected them with another, and to assume, among the Powers of the earth, the separate and equal station to which the Laws of Nature and of Nature's God entitle them, a decent respect to the opinions of mankind requires that they should declare the causes which compel them to separation.
>
> We hold these truths to be self-evident, that all men are created equal, that they are endowed by their Creator with certain inalienable Rights, that among these are Life, Liberty, and the pursuit of Happiness . . . We, therefore, the Representatives of the United States of America, in General Congress, appealing to the Supreme Judge of the World for the rectitude of our intentions . . . with a firm reliance on the protection of divine Providence . . . mutually pledge to each other our Lives, our Fortunes, and our sacred Honour.[7]

The first reference to religious principles reveals the naturalistic bent of the writers: "the Laws of Nature and of Nature's God." Divinity here is not the biblical Lord revealing the divine will through the pages of Scripture. Divinity is the deity who has made the world according to orderly designs that human reason may penetrate. When people grasp the laws of nature, they perceive the divine intentions. The God sanctioning the plan of the writers to dissolve their political ties to England is the vague divinity standing behind what they are confident has been encoded in nature.

The self-evident truths that elaborate the foundations of the political freedom the writers are claiming are rights attributed to the Creator of humankind. Precisely what being "endowed" with these rights means is not clear from the text, but the likeliest inference is that such rights are legislations of Nature's God. The writers do not explain their understanding of creation either. It is not clear whether they thought God fashioned each human soul or functioned more distantly as the original source of the material world. Of course they precede Darwin and evolutionary theory by nearly a century, but deistic thought had already made the Creator much less immediately involved in either nature or human affairs than biblical or earlier Christian faith had assumed. Life, liberty, and the pursuit of happiness are similarly distant from faith, hope, and charity or from the instruments of salvation, such as right preaching and right administration of the sacraments, which earlier Christian ages might have nominated as the prime "rights" people might have expected their rulers to nurture.

The appeal to divinity as a judge upholding the rectitude of the intentions driving the writers, and as a protecting Providence, is as enlightened as the other religious references in the declaration. The writers may well have believed in divine Judgment and Providence quite sincerely, even passionately, but the language they chose deliberately avoided scriptural references, **apocalyptic** imagery, and the other appurtenances of biblical religion. Moreover no Christ or Holy Spirit gives authority to the declaration. From its beginnings, therefore, the United States was not a Puritan commonwealth, not a biblical covenant, but a venture in rational politics.

This is not to say that Puritan theology had completely died. Abigail Adams, writing to her husband John in 1776, was seriously playful in what analysis suggests was a Puritan as well as an enlightened frame of mind:

> I long to hear that you have declared an Independancy—and by the way in the new Code of Laws which I suppose it will be necessary for you to make I desire you would Remember the Ladies, and be more generous and favourable to them than your ancestors. Do not put such unlimited power into the hands of the Husbands. Remem-

ber all Men would be tyrants if they could. If perticuliar care and attention is not paid to the Laidies we are determined to foment a Rebelion, and will not hold ourselves bound by any Laws in which we have no voice, or Representation.

That your Sex are Naturally Tyrannical is a Truth so thoroughly established as to admit of no dispute, but such of you as wish to be happy willingly give up the harsh title of Master for the more tender and endearing one of Friend. Why, then, not put it out of the power of the vicious and the Lawless to use us with cruelty and indignity with impunity. Men of Sense in all Ages abhor those customs which treat us only as the vassals of your Sex. Regard us then as Being placed by providence under your protection and in immitation of the Supreme Being make use of that power only for our happiness.[8]

The enlightened or deistic strain of this letter is clearest in the passing reference to providence and the Supreme Being. These, one may assume, undergird Adams's sense that women, like the colonists in their controversies with England, should not be bound by laws in which they have no voice or representation. The Puritan mentality reveals itself in the belief that all men would be tyrants if they could. Whether Adams means all human beings, or simply all males, is unclear. Either way, however, she is running close to the notion that power tends to corrupt, which owes much to the Calvinist view of human nature as thoroughly corrupted by original sin.

The checks and balances Adams sought to curb the tyrannical propensities of men showed up in the Constitution, though not with reference to "the Ladies." Once again the assumption was that power tends to corrupt, human nature tends to be selfish, and human beings must be constrained if they are to honor the common good. In distributing power among three separate branches of government, the writers of the Constitution drew on what they considered the best political experience

and theory. However, they were also expressing their recent experiences of tyranny and their sober if not cynical view of human nature, the roots of which owed a great deal to Puritan theology.

As is well known, religion most clearly appears in the Constitution in the first of the ten articles of amendment proposed in 1789 and enacted in 1791. That famous article reads: "Congress shall make no law respecting an establishment of religion, or prohibiting the free exercise thereof; or abridging the freedom of speech, or of the press; or the right of the people peacefully to assemble, and to petition the Government for a redress of grievances."[9] Each clause of this article has generated a spate of books, so it is by no means obvious what the seemingly innocent first phrases about religion were intended to convey.

Article VI of the Constitution had specified that no religious test should ever be required as a qualification for public office. That had proved insufficient to communicate the neutrality toward religion that the main framers of the Constitution desired. The first amendment therefore amounted to a compromise, offering both religionists and those who feared the influence of religion in state affairs something to stress.

Nonetheless it seems likely that the writers most wanted to ensure that there would never be an established church like that of England with political powers. They also wanted to ensure that all people would have the right to exercise their religious convictions without hindrance from either the government or people who disagreed with them. These two simple provisions were probably meant to establish a middle way, such that government would neither promote a particular religion nor allow any religion to be denied free exercise. Whether this meant government was to be indifferent to religion or simply impartial in supporting all varieties of it is highly debatable. The effect of the First

Amendment, however, is less debatable. Since the ratification of the Constitution, America has been religiously pluralistic not simply *de facto* but also *de jure*.

Thomas Jefferson

The last four decades of the 18th century, from the initial deterioration of relations with England to the election of Jefferson as the third president, involved four eventful phases in which the clergy and churches played significant roles. From 1760 to 1775 sentiment for independence grew, fueled by residual Puritan suspicions of the English crown. From 1775 to 1783 the colonies were waging war, reorganizing themselves after their victory, and forming states. The churches were divided in their loyalties and had to scramble to keep pace with the impact of both the war and its aftermath, but many ministers sanctioned the war as a righteous cause. They could point to the many grievances detailed in the Declaration of Independence as a solid warrant for opposing an unholy tyranny.

From 1783 to 1789, however, there was great debate about how the states were to confederate and considerable decline in Christian religion. Rationalism and religious apathy rose while traditional biblical religion waned. Historians tend to attribute this to postwar exhaustion and reorganization and to a reaction against the religious enthusiasm that had peaked during the Great Awakening. Whatever the causes, America moved even farther away from the Puritan ideal of making religion the soul of a virtuous new commonweal. During the federalist period (1789–1800) the churches had to begin to cope with the separation of church and state established by the Constitution and to rethink their existence in terms of completely voluntary membership. On the whole the congregational churches were better equipped to deal with these

changes than the Anglicans and the Methodists, who had been tied more closely to the prewar English patterns of establishment.[10]

Thomas Jefferson (1743–1826) was a major factor during this entire 40-year period, drafting the Declaration of Independence, governing and greatly influencing politics in Virginia, serving as the first secretary of state and the third president, establishing the University of Virginia, and generally gaining respect and influence as one of the thinkers most responsible for the shape of the new nation. Jefferson attended college at William and Mary, studying natural science and then the law, and by 1769 had begun a career in Virginia politics. Many Virginians were already opposed to British colonial policies, and by 1774 Jefferson had concluded that the British Parliament had no authority to legislate for the colonies—quite an avant-garde position. Jefferson impressed his colleagues sufficiently to be appointed to the Virginia delegation at the Second Continental Congress, where his affinities with the more radical group and his skills as a committeeman and writer brought him into the faction that proved most powerful. His draft of the Declaration of Independence was meant to express the mind of the American majority, but few historians doubt that it expressed his own mind as well.

Returning to Virginia Jefferson planned to reform his own state in accord with the new spirit expressed in the declaration. His plans included abolition of the laws of primogeniture (exclusive inheritance by the eldest son) to free property from the hands of a relative few and give more people the chance for a decent subsistence. A second target was educational change, based on his conviction that an ignorant people could not make rational decisions. His third reform aimed at establishing full religious liberty. After some years and considerable trouble, the first and third reforms went through, while the second reform achieved only partial success: the establishment of the University of Virginia. (Jefferson's plans for lower education were rejected.)

Jefferson served as governor of Virginia from 1779 to 1781, but when his conduct during the British invasion of 1780–1781 was criticized he determined to quit Virginia politics. The death of his wife compounded this period's darkness, which is reflected in his *Notes on Virginia*. Jefferson served a diplomatic mission in France from 1784 to 1789 and initially was enthusiastic for the forces that brought about the French Revolution. He was in favor of most of the articles of confederation drafted in Philadelphia in 1787, criticizing only its lack of a bill of rights and its failure to limit the tenure of the president. Accepting George Washington's request that he serve as secretary of state, Jefferson soon found himself embroiled in a wide-ranging disagreement with Alexander Hamilton, the secretary of the treasury. Jefferson championed what became the Democratic-Republican political party and platform while Hamilton led the Federalists. Perhaps the major difference lay in Jefferson's commitment to the rights of the individual citizen, which Hamilton was willing to subordinate to his dream of national grandeur. When Jefferson was elected president in 1800 he attempted to conciliate the Federalists, realizing that stability was vital to the new nation's survival. His engineering of the Louisiana Purchase and this example of moderation were high points of his presidency. Withdrawing after two terms, Jefferson returned to Virginia to pursue one last ambition: to establish an excellent university.

Jefferson was a man of many facets united by a first-rate mind. He knew Latin, Greek, French, Spanish, Italian, and Anglo-Saxon and was greatly interested in the science of his day. This dovetailed with his religious convictions, which were deistic, and included passionate commitment to the liberty of conscience and skepticism about claims of revelation. Like Franklin, Jefferson thought religion important for the support it furnished to ethics and public order but dangerous in its potential for curbing free inquiry and making people intolerant.[11]

For the inscription on his tombstone, Jefferson wanted three accomplishments noted: the Declaration of Independence, the University of Virginia, and the Virginia statute for religious freedom. The bill he wrote in 1779 finally passed the Virginia Assembly in 1786 after considerable controversy, but it was still a milestone in the new nation's translation into practical law of what John Adams called the spirit of the Revolution. The specific provisions of Jefferson's bill included ensuring that none

> be compelled to attend or support any religious worship, place, or ministry whatsoever, nor shall be enforced, restrained, molested, or burthened in his body or goods, nor shall otherwise suffer, on account of his religious opinions or belief; but that all men shall be free to profess, and by argument to maintain, their opinions in matters of religion, and that the same shall in no wise diminish, enlarge, or affect their civil capacities.[12]

The rationale supporting this view of religious liberty boiled down to Jefferson's commitment to enlightened religion. In his view belief rightly flowed only from evidence accepted by the mind. By making the mind free, God had implied that belief should never be compelled. The only rightful way for religion to press its claims was through reason. No civil punishments or rewards meant to promote religion befitted the Creator's way of designing the human person. All human beings were fallible, so it was no wonder that false religion had arisen from some having set themselves over others as directors of their faith. Indeed, compelling financial support for opinions people abhorred or simply did not hold was sinful and tyrannical, while linking religion and civil rights was as wrong as linking civil rights with people's opinions on physics or geometry.

Thus Jefferson consistently showed himself an individualist, a rationalist, and a fierce champion of the rights of conscience. This has made him something of a prototype of the distinctively American preference for freedom in all aspects of civil life, especially those closest to conscience.[13]

James Madison: "A Memorial and a Remonstrance"

James Madison (1751–1836) is best known as the fourth president and for his work in helping both to draft the Constitution and to get it ratified (largely by collaborating with Hamilton and Jay on *The Federalist Papers*). A member of the first House of Representatives, Madison sponsored the first ten amendments to the Constitution. He was secretary of state under Jefferson and during his own presidency oversaw U.S. fighting in the War of 1812.

Madison was born in the shadow of the Blue Ridge Mountains in Virginia and attended the College of New Jersey (soon to become Princeton University) partly because of its opposition to an episcopal church. Completing the four-year course in two years, Madison went on to study law. He was an early advocate of independence from England, denounced the imprisonment of Virginia dissenters from the established Anglican church, and in later life favored Unitarianism (without becoming a church member). During Virginia's revolutionary convention of 1776 he drafted the guarantee of religious freedom and helped Thomas Jefferson disestablish the church. At the Continental Congress he helped resolve disputes about claims to northwest territories by persuading Virginia to cede its chartered rights to the Congress. Madison stimulated the calling of the Constitutional Convention of 1787 and became known as the father of the Constitution. *The Federalist Papers,* which are regarded as the best commentary on the Constitution, were the principal reason for ratification.[14]

Madison is remembered for his fine mind, which oversaw the writing of the American Constitution and shaped the history of its interpretation through the Federalist Papers. (James Madison, C.W. Peale; Gilcrease Museum, Tulsa, Oklahoma)

Madison himself wrote 29 of the 85 papers, including two of the most influential, numbers 10 and 51. During his term in the House of Representatives he split with Hamilton (as Jefferson had) over the latter's subordination of individual rights to national priorities (specifically, how to fund the war debts). This turned Madison into a strict constructionist of the Constitution, for both tactical and philosophical reasons. Madison's tenure as secretary of state found him publicly subordinating his views to those of President Jefferson but in fact wielding great influence. The War of 1812 was the climax to long antagonism between America and Britain over British harassment of American shipping. Madison had to endure great criticism for his leadership during the war, but when he left office he was eulogized for having brought the nation success without infringing political, civil, or religious rights.

Like Jefferson, Madison was a firm believer in liberty of conscience and considered it the reason for most of the American political arrangements. In 1785 Madison had shown his colors regarding religious liberty by opposing a bill presented in the Virginia General Assembly by Patrick Henry. The bill did not intend the establishment of a particular Christian church, so it was not cast in the mold of old unions of church and state. Instead it sought general state support for all teachers of Christian religion— a middle way between establishment and nonestablishment. Madison's contrary response eventually passed the Assembly in 1786, along with Jefferson's bill establishing religious freedom. The two documents had a great impact on the Constitutional Convention that assembled in Philadelphia in 1787. It was no accident, then, that Madison introduced the first constitutional amendment, which included the clause on religion discussed earlier.

Henry's bill proposed making "the Christian religion" the established religion of the Virginia Commonwealth, with all denominations of Christians enjoying equal privileges, both civil and religious. Madison's "A Memorial and a Remonstrance" argued against this proposal on several grounds:

1. Because the obligations people owe their Creator can be carried out only by reason and conviction, Madison wrote, religion ought to be left to individual conscience. Madison considered this a natural and inalienable right. One's duties to one's Creator held priority over any civil duties and ought not to be abridged by institutions of civil society. Even if the majority held for given religious views, the rights of the minority were not to be trampled on.

2. If religion could not rightly be constrained by society at large, still less could it be constrained by a state legislature.

3. There was a rightful fear of a domino effect, if Henry's bill were enacted. If Christian religion in general could be established, why not a specific Christian church?

4. The bill could trample on the equality that all citizens ought to enjoy under the law: "Whilst we assert for ourselves a freedom to embrace, to profess and to observe the Religion which we believe to be of divine origin, we cannot deny an equal freedom to those whose minds have not yet yielded to the evidence which has convinced us. If this freedom be abused, it is an offence against God, not against man."[15]

Madison further criticized the notion that civil magistrates would be competent to judge whether certain churches were in fact complying with the requirements for receiving support, took exception to the assumption that Christianity needed state support for its survival or success, and argued that past instances of religious establishment had proven harmful to religion:

> During almost 15 centuries, has the legal establishment of Christianity been on trial. What have been its fruits? More or less in all places, pride and indolence in the Clergy; ignorance and servility in the laity; in both, superstition, bigotry, and persecution. Enquire of the Teachers of Christianity for the ages in which it appeared in its greatest lustre; those of every sect, point to the ages prior to its incorporation with Civil policy.[16]

In concluding Madison noted that government would do best to guarantee the free exercise of religion to all parties, that Henry's bill would reverse the tendency of persecuted citizens the world over to think of America as a land of liberty where they might live as their dissenting consciences dictated, that it would encourage emigration of Virginia's own citizens, that it would destroy traditions of moderation and revive old antagonisms, that it would harm the diffusion of Christianity, that it would weaken other laws (by proving unenforceable), that a bill of such magnitude ought to have the clear support of the majority of the citizenry (which would be hard to ascertain), and that since religion is such a fundamental right, abridging it in this way would endanger all other fundamental rights.

Madison's arguments resemble a Puritan sermon tidily advancing the divine truth. Their spirit is familiar from Jefferson's bill on religious liberty, and they show how these Founding Fathers were disturbed by any threat to the right of religious liberty. Madison called on his fellow Virginians to remember the history of established religion, both in Christendom as a whole and throughout 150 years of American experience. Like Roger Williams, he argued that to compel religious conscience in any way is directly to offend God. Madison had learned from Puritan excesses and the arguments of the Enlightenment philosophers to speak up for the negative aspects of religious liberty: the rights not only not to conform to a given church discipline but also not to believe. What had originally been a rather social issue—what church to join—had now become more individualistic: whether to believe and practice at all. The deistic translation of religion into rationalist terms did not forbid people's assembling in religious congregations, but it rendered such assemblying secondary if not unnecessary. Individual conscience was the key arena, and in the name of inalienable, Creator-given rights, Madison fought to safeguard individual conscience against any compulsion. The theological implication was that the individual conscience was more basic to Christianity than the Church.

Key Terms

Apocalyptic: a genre of religious literature found both in the Bible and in extrabiblical literature. Apocalyptic literature purports to be revelations from God about how history is going to unfold. The Book of Daniel in the Hebrew Bible and the Book of Revelation in the New Testament are both considered apocalyptic literature. Usually apocalyptic literature comes from a time when people are suffering oppression or feel their faith has not been rewarding them as they expected. The scenarios of God's coming to punish their enemies and reward their fidelity are meant to gladden believers' hearts and shore up their faith. In an extended sense, *apocalyptic* means cataclysmic or concerned with dreadful scenarios of the last day. People who are expecting woe, torment, and disaster can be said to exhibit an apocalyptic mentality, especially if they seriously think the end of the world is about to occur.

Typological exegesis: an interpretation (usually of Scripture) that focuses on how prior events or figures were fulfilled by later ones. For example, Christians argued that Jesus had fulfilled the messianic prophecies of the Old Testament. Indeed, they came to think that the entire Old Testament was a treasury of foreshadowings of Jesus. The apostle Paul had encouraged such a way of reading Scripture, seeing Christ as the Second Adam and Abraham as the prefiguring father of Christian faith. The Suffering Servant of Isaiah seemed to foretell the passion of Christ, while the ark that kept Noah safe during the flood seemed a prefiguring of the Church. Jewish rabbis used the biblical text similarly, speaking, for instance, of Jacob and Esau as prototypical Jews and Christians. The Puritan divines continued this way of treating

Scripture, trying to bring the biblical images into their own day and find God's purposes for America.

Discussion Questions

1. What does the sermon of Increase Mather have to do with the death of the two students by drowning?
2. How did typological exegesis allow Jonathan Edwards to think God was using New England to launch the latter days of glory?
3. Why did John Locke favor the light of reason over the light of revelation?
4. How did Deism encourage religious freedom?
5. What are the main differences between the deity mentioned in the Declaration of Independence and the biblical God?
6. What are the arguments for construing the First Amendment to the Constitution as making government indifferent to religion?
7. How did Jefferson's three major accomplishments—writing the Declaration of Independence, writing the statute of Virginia for religious liberty, and founding the University of Virginia—correlate?
8. How did Jefferson's views of religious conscience make him a prototype of American individualism?
9. How valid was Madison's argument that the history of established religion showed it to be a bad idea?
10. How had the notion of religious liberty changed from the time of Roger Williams to that of James Madison?

Notes

1. Increase Mather, "Man Knows Not His Time," in *The Puritans,* ed. Perry Miller and Thomas H. Johnson (Boston: Atlantic Books Company, 1938), pp. 345–346.

2. See Michael Wigglesworth, "God's Controversy with New England," in *God's New Israel,* ed. Conrad Cherry (Englewood Cliffs NJ: Prentice-Hall, 1971), pp. 44–54.

3. Cherry, p. 59. See also Edwin Scott Gaustad, *The Great Awakening in New England* (Chicago: Quadrangle Books, 1968) and Wesley M. Gewehr, *The Great Awakening in Virginia, 1740–1790* (Durham NC: Duke University Press, 1930).

4. John Locke, *Essay Concerning Human Understanding,* Book IV, Chapter XIX, in *Documents in the History of American Philosophy,* ed. Morton White (New York: Oxford University Press, 1972), pp. 27–28, 32–33.

5. Sydney E. Mead, "Christendom, Enlightenment, and the Revolution," in *Religion and the American Revolution,* ed. Jerald C. Brauer (Philadelphia: Fortress, 1976), pp. 48–49.

6. See Saul K. Padover, ed., *The Complete Jefferson* (New York: Duell, Sloan & Pearce, 1943), p. 945.

7. Richard B. Morris, ed., *Encyclopedia of American History* (New York: Harper & Row, 1976), pp. 563, 565, 566.

8. Alice S. Rossi, ed., *The Feminist Papers* (New York: Columbia University Press, 1973), pp. 10–11. For background see Rosemary Skinner Keller, "Women, Civil Religion, and the American Revolution," in *Women & Religion in America,* ed. Rosemary Radford Ruether and Rosemary Skinner Keller, vol. 2 (San Francisco: Harper & Row, 1983), pp. 368–408.

9. Morris, p. 575.

10. See Sydney E. Ahlstrom, *A Religious History of the American People* (New Haven CT: Yale University Press, 1972), pp. 360–384.

11. See "Jefferson," in *Encyclopedia Britannica,* vol. 22 (Chicago: Encyclopedia Britannica, 1987), pp. 349–353.

12. "Thomas Jefferson's Bill for Establishing Religious Freedom, 1779," in *A Documen-*

tary History of Religion in America, ed. Edwin S. Gaustad, vol. 1 (Grand Rapids MI: Eerdmans, 1982), p. 261.

13. On Jefferson as representative of adult virtues and the American character, see Erik H. Erikson, *Dimensions of a New Identity* (New York: W. W. Norton, 1974).

14. On Madison and the Federalist Papers, see Garry Wills, *Explaining America: The Federalist* (New York: Penguin Books, 1981).

15. James Madison, "A Memorial and a Remonstrance," in *Religious Issues in American History,* ed. Edwin Scott Gaustad (New York: Harper & Row, 1968), p. 74.

16. Ibid., p. 75.

CHAPTER 5

Evangelicals, Pioneers, and Sectarians

The Second Great Awakening

The deistic outlook of key framers of the American republic, which formed their ideas about religious liberty and the disestablishment of religion, was perhaps the most significant and distinctive result of the changeover from the colonial to the republican period. That is the thesis of Sidney Mead, whose lucid writings compel great respect. As Sydney Ahlstrom stressed the Puritan influence, Mead stressed the legacy of the Enlightenment.

However, the Puritan and enlightened religious emphases were never the whole story. Many Americans professed a more direct reliance on the biblical text. In examining the image of the United States as a biblical nation from 1776 to 1865 Mark A. Noll comments: "On the face of it, it would be hard to imagine a nation more thoroughly biblical than the United States between the American Revolution and the Civil War. The cadences of the Authorized Version informed the writing of the elite and the speech of the humble."[1] The elite included Jefferson and Franklin, whom we have depicted as rationalists. They did not scruple to use biblical imagery on public occasions, partly because such imagery was the coin of the linguistic realm, and partly because they considered religion a bulwark of civil morality. Indeed they regarded the Bible as a source of universal truths about the human condition that their deistic philosophical sources treated more rationally.

This way of regarding the Bible was one of the two quite different attitudes that shaped the public use of biblical literature between the Revolution and the Civil War:

> To come at the public use of Scripture from the inside is to recognize at once that the Bible represented two very different books. It was first a compendium of instruction for faith and practice, a source of universally valid insight about the human condition. At the deaths of Washington and Lincoln, for example, several ministers turned to the wisdom literature of the Old Testament to remind their congregations of verities ordained by God: that the Lord reigned sovereignly over the affairs of men and nations (Psalm 93:1), that a people will long remember its "righteous" men (Psalm 112:6), or even that godlike rulers must succumb to death with all humanity (Psalm 82:6–7). Used in this way the Bible that spoke to Americans was much the same as that which had spoken to Christians of all times and places.

Much more frequently, however, the Bible was not so much the truth above all truth as it was the story above all stories. On public occasions Scripture appeared regularly as a typical narrative imparting significance to the antitypical events, people, and situations of United States history. That is, ministers preached as if the stories of Scripture were being repeated, or could be repeated, in the unfolding life of the United States. This was as true for white Congregationalists and Presbyterians, decision-makers in American society, as it was for black Baptists and Methodists, who could express their opinions on public affairs only by indirection. Elite whites and slave blacks both looked, for instance, to the Pentateuch as a paradigm for American experience. Whites, at different times and places, saw the Exodus as the model for liberation from Great Britain or from the North; they regarded Moses as the archetype for the United States' own great lawgivers and friends of God. Blacks proclaimed Moses' cry to let his people go with entirely different intentions.[2]

We are familiar with typological exegesis from the preaching of Jonathan Edwards, the leading figure of the Great Awakening that swept through New England during the 1740s. In the rural South, Baptists and Methodists never dropped such a reading of the Bible, but in the middle states and the cities of the North religious fervor declined after the Revolution. A more liberal faith, based on reason and shying away from **evangelical** emotion, struck many educated people as more seemly. **Unitarianism** grew in New England, favored by those who found such traditional doctrines as the Trinity embarrassing or incredible. Nonetheless, at the turn of the century a Second Great Awakening got under way, with modest beginnings in New England and dramatic outbreaks of religious enthusiasm in Kentucky during camp meetings in 1800 and 1801. Thereafter **revivalism** was a regular feature of American Protestantism. In the years before the Civil War, evangelism was all the rage, but even in places where religion was more sober it shaped American culture. Thus the French observer Alexis de Tocqueville (whose work *Democracy in America* [1835] has become a standard reference when historians want an outsider's impressions) said that the religious aspect of the United States was the first thing that struck him. The longer he pondered American religious behavior, the more significant it seemed, because here religion and freedom pulled together, whereas in his native France they usually seemed at odds.

By the time Jonathan Edwards died in 1758, the first Great Awakening was also dead. The great preacher George Whitefield's tours kept sparks alive, but most of the country seemed to want a rest. In New England a group of Yale graduates tried to build on Edwards's work a "new divinity" that stressed regenerate church members and doctrinal orthodoxy, but they tended to bog down in distinctions and lose the spirit that had made his vision whole. Until the end of the 18th century most religious enthusiasm came from Baptists and Methodists, rather than from the Puritan resources of the Congregationalists. When the Second Great Awakening took hold, however, it worked mainly through the Congregationalist churches under the control of New Divinity pastors devoted to Calvinist orthodoxy. Yale University itself felt the inrush of the Holy Spirit in 1801, in good measure due to the earnest preaching of university president Timothy Dwight.

The "plain gospel truths" to which the Yale men attributed the palpable spiritual renewal running throughout the Connecticut Valley were three old-time verities:

1. The absolute sovereignty of God. Perhaps the American Revolution had somewhat prepared the ground for a reappreciation of this truth, by dramatically attacking English sovereignty over the colonies, but the main thrust was more traditional. What Calvin had so clearly yet profoundly appreciated, the implications of the doctrine of creation, once again took hold. All flesh was but grass. The grass withered, the flowers faded; only the Word of the Lord endured.

2. The doctrine of human depravity. If humans were but dust, as sinners they were abhorrent to the divine holiness. On their own, they were nothing but stinking heaps of foul deeds and foul intentions. Jonathan Edwards's famous sermon, "Sinners in the Hands of an Angry God," had developed this theme in classical fashion. Later cooler heads might say that such moral self-abasement had its psychological problems, but the religious payoff was a strongly felt need for repentance and conversion.

3. The atoning love of Christ. Christ had covered over the gap between divinity and humanity created by human dust and sinfulness. Christ had paid for humanity's sins, reopened the gates of heaven, and brought powers of regeneration. The new human being possible through the power of Christ's Spirit owed everything to divine grace, but such a person nonetheless was rightly considered a saint. As long as the Holy Spirit reigned in his or her heart, virtue was possible, and righteousness could flower.

The Second Great Awakening, like the revivalism that colored the westward expansion, focused people's hearts on the relief and joy that could flood them when they laid down their burdens of sin and guilt. Into lives that were often physically difficult and emotionally constrained, these religious movements brought recreation, hope, and a new sense of being alive.

Charles Grandison Finney (1792–1875) was the leading early exponent and theorist of revivalism. When Finney had a conversion experience in his late 20s he quit his law practice and took to the preaching trails. Although he had little formal education in theology, he got himself ordained. His fame came from the great success of the revivals he preached, which he attributed to his methodology. Using firm language, he preached and prayed very concretely, naming specific individuals and using a special bench for those anxious about their sins. His meetings often went on for hours, and his opponents criticized their emotionalism. Finney also arranged for lay leaders to run prayer sessions and for prayer sessions to be held at odd hours each day during a revival. A spectacularly successful revival in Rochester in 1831 and great successes in 1857 and 1858 were high moments in Finney's career. In the 1830s Finney published a book outlining his revivalist methods, *Lectures on Revivals of Religion*. He then assumed the presidency of Oberlin College, and in the years 1846–1847 his work *Lectures on Systematic Theology* made available a comprehensive revivalist theology.[3]

Religion in the Westward Expansion

The Methodist church was probably the most successful in stirring evangelical fervor among rural people and those moving west. Methodism arose from the reforms of John Wesley (1703–1791), who had been born in an Anglican parsonage, educated at Oxford, and ordained an Anglican priest in 1728. From the beginnings of his religious career Wesley stressed private study and devotion combined with corporate worship and service to the poor. He sought a spiritual home in Oxford and then in the mission fields of Georgia, but neither place satisfied him. A profound religious experience in 1738 gave him assurance of salvation, and he began to preach with great success about both the sufficiency of divine grace and the moral demands of the gospel. This put him in the midst of the evangelical fervor spearheaded by George Whitefield and other contemporary preachers of revival.

Wesley intended to work within the structures of the Anglican church, reaching out to those not normally touched by the establishment. Organizing interested people in study groups, and training lay preachers to spread the message and method, by 1747 Wesley's movement was making considerable impact throughout Britain. Methodism came to America in the 1760s, but during the Revolution its Anglican ties came under suspicion and it went into retreat. Most of the British missionaries went home, while Francis Asbury (1745–1816), who was to become the great apostle of Methodism in the United States, waited out the war as a political neutral in Delaware.

The movement picked up again after the war, but suffered from a lack of ordained ministers. When Wesley could not persuade the bishop of London to ordain Americans (who by then were citizens of a foreign realm), he decided to ordain them himself. The American Methodists organized themselves at a conference in Baltimore in 1784, Asbury becoming a superintendent (the Methodist equivalent of a bishop). The new church used a Sunday worship service and articles of faith that were created by Wesley from Anglican models. Its growth was rapid, and although Wesley himself remained within the established church, Methodism inevitably moved toward independence from Anglicanism. At the turn of the century it was characterized by evangelical fervor for preaching the Word, zeal for missionary activity, and concern for educating people in the spiritual life. Although numerous groups splintered off, Methodist numbers swelled, and by 1830 Methodists were the largest religious body in the United States.

The Methodists made much of their mark by carrying to the western frontier the sense of providential awakening that had broken out in New England and was reaffirming the long-held sense that God had great things in store for America. Where the Revolution in France had turned to godlessness, the American Revolution seemed to have opened the way to great gains in godliness.

William Clebsch has summarized this development and suggested how Methodist piety fitted into it:

> Hundreds of pulpits hurled condemnations at the French Revolution; the blood baths and the guillotine seemed signs that providential wrath turned secular forms of the new era into chaos. The gist of the messages was that a new Zion must indeed be a Zion if it were to be saved from new dimensions of human horror. For decades preachers all over America took up the cry, pointing to the contrast between France and America. However they came by the knowledge, they were sure that God fostered the new era only in the new world, and there only if a renewed and renewing Christianity flourished without constraint or restraint. The religious awakening in America at the turn of the century, commenced by Timothy Dwight (1752–1817) at Yale and then theologically grounded in the revised Calvinism of the New Haven school, proved the point. Theological reflection upon, and adjustment to, revivalism took

historical events as proofs of God's "Nay" to irreligious France and "Aye" to pious America . . . . When the quest for an open future took form in the westward movement, however, the hope for an ever new start in life found goals that were spatial, temporal, and material rather than universal, eternal, and spiritual. First the popular churches—Methodists then Baptists then Presbyterians—went out to suffuse the pioneer with piety . . . [their] tactics were modeled after the preachings of the Great Awakening, but when made into calculated devices with predictable results they became not awakenings of the spirit but resuscitations of the churches, not arousing courage and manly spirit for an unknown future but enlisting men into religious beliefs and behavior that leashed them to the traditions and stabilizing influences of the denominations. The spontaneity of a Francis Asbury (1745–1816) gave way to the competition of a Peter Cartwright (1785–1872), and the camp meeting became the revivalistic campaign.[4]

As Clebsch notes, apparently with some regret, the popular churches tended to try to organize the development of evangelical fervor and fit it to the service of their own denominational life. They also tended to combine spiritual awakening with rather conventional morality, so that the brothers and sisters who felt the Holy Spirit in the evening would comport themselves as model citizens during the day. The ethos that made Americanism a near candidate for god-

Just as the covered wagon became a common symbol of the pioneering American spirit, the railroad became a symbol of change and innovation. (On the Road, Thomas Otter; The Nelson-Atkins Museum of Art, Kansas City, Missouri [Nelson Fund])

liness helped them equate Christian living with the virtues of thrift, sobriety, and patriotism that the growing new nation needed. The demands of frontier life made great civic virtues of both trust in God and reliance on one's own strong arms.

In New England the Second Great Awakening had generally kept the people calm. However moved they felt by the Holy Spirit, they were not given to ecstatic cries or abnormal behavior. Things were somewhat different among the huge crowd (estimated at from 10,000 to 25,000) convened at Cane Ridge, Kentucky, in August 1801. Held under Presbyterian auspices, but drawing Baptists and Methodists as well, this meeting impressed some observers as a second Pentecost. Indeed it went beyond Pentecost in throwing people on the ground, jerking and screaming, and sending them into ecstatic dances and runs, fits of barks and laughing, and singing exercises. From Cane Ridge revivalism spread across Kentucky, Tennessee, and southern Ohio. The Baptists and Methodists looked more favorably on the dramatic effects of the Holy Spirit than the Presbyterians did, so they reaped the most denominational growth in the West. In fact the western successes had a rebound effect in the East, helping Methodists and Baptists grow there as well.

The Methodist growth was the most dramatic. In 1800 there were about 2700 members in the entire western conference. By 1812 there were about 31,000 members. In 1830 the one conference west of the Alleghanies had become eight conferences, and membership had risen to over 175,000, including more than 15,000 blacks and about 2000 natives. When the Methodist church divided into northern and southern branches in 1844, it had become the largest religious body in the country, numbering well over 1 million members. The main factor in this growth was the disciplined system of circuits and stations that the preachers rode and manned. The preachers kept up with the westward-mov-

ing population, serving them on the frontier they were constantly pushing back. All this was highly organized, and the camp meeting where people heard the word and declared their commitment to Christ became a staple feature of western life. The Methodists also prospered by stressing the common touch, favoring preachers who were more emotional than learned, more passionate than analytical. Peter Cartwright, the most famous of the down-to-earth circuit riders, once said that the educated preachers he had seen reminded him of lettuce growing under the shade of a peach tree—no doubt his ultimate picture of something dull and uninspiring.

Sectarians and Utopians

The waves of religious excitement that washed across the United States in the early decades of the 19th century left many people confused. With so many enthusiasts claiming visions or ecstatic experiences, where should they place their religious allegiance? Some Americans withdrew from religion in distaste, and in many periods the majority of Americans were not on the rolls of any of the churches. But few people could avoid the impact that evangelism and revivalism were making on popular culture. Religious experience and supposedly evangelical ethics were powerful factors in the typical small town. In some cases this simply begot new religious combinations, based on visions no doubt stimulated by the confusion of the times as well as personal need.

For example, in 1820 the young Joseph Smith received a vision to the effect that none of the options being urged on him by the different church groups was the right way. He would himself become the prophet of a newly revealed truth, with a new scripture and group identity. Smith founded the Mormons, the sect most vilified in the 19th century as having deviated from the true gospel (or common American-ism) and created an enclosed group suspicious of all outsiders.

The Mormons were far from alone in draw-ing animosity because they had turned away from the middle stream of Protestant piety. Catholics continued to be dismissed out of hand because their popish ways had kept them from entering that middle stream. Until immigration in the mid-19th century greatly increased the Catholic population, however, such dismissal was often more routine than venomous. The Seventh-Day Adventists, officially born in 1860, were another sectarian group stigmatized for their distinctive ideas and practices. The Adven-tists were prefigured by millennial sects (groups anticipating the thousand-year period when the just would reign with Christ) like the Millerites, which had arisen during the 1840s in New England. Even when the predicted year for the advent of the millennium (1843 in Miller's first preaching) had come and gone, adherents con-tinued to believe that the end was near, much to the scorn and unease of baffled outsiders. The decision to make Saturday (the Sabbath) their day of worship, rather than the Sunday favored by most Christians, further distin-guished the Adventists, who had come to think that only keeping the Sabbath in pure observ-ance would prepare them for the Second Coming.

Both the Mormons and the Seventh-Day Adventists sought a distinctive, separatist iden-tity while subscribing to many typically Amer-ican ideals. Both favored hard work, strong education, clean living, material prosperity, and close family and community ties. The Adven-tists sought a pure diet and were suspicious of modern medicine. The Mormons banned alco-hol, tobacco, and caffeine. Both groups mounted impressive missionary campaigns, their mem-bers accepting as a matter of course that they would spend at least part of their lives spread-ing the message.

The Christian Scientists formed by Mary Baker Eddy in the 19th century and the Jeho-vah's Witnesses created in the early 20th cen-tury bore many similarities to the Mormons and Adventists, although significant theological dif-ferences separated them. Themes of separation, purification, and attention to supposedly nat-ural food and medical practices were also found in such utopian groups as the Shakers and the Oneida Perfectionists, both of which flourished in the mid-19th century. The latter groups were communal, actually setting up idealistic socie-ties where they might have more control over all aspects of their daily life than was possible when they lived among outsiders. The Mor-mons, Adventists, and Christian Scientists held similar opinions even when they did not move out to remote areas to form their own enclosed communities. For them, too, the ideal was to fashion an environment purer, more intense, and more in keeping with the revelations granted their founding figures than was possible in American society at large.

The terminology regularly used to charac-terize these interesting, much abused, yet amazingly tough groups includes the words *sect* and *utopian*. *Sect* denotes something cut off or separated from a main body. Therefore the 19th-century sects were little different from the 16th- and 17th-century Puritan separationists, who cut themselves off from the parent Church of England to pursue a purer life. On the other hand, the Puritans remained in the mainstream of Calvinist theology, while the utopians intro-duced considerable novelty. Indeed, in the United States the Puritans/Congregationalists were a sufficiently mainstream group to make the term *sectarian* awkward. Similarly, the devotional groups—Methodists, Baptists—that quickly had great success in popularizing their sense of Prot-estant Christian life soon lost their original appearance of singularity and dissent. It was the fate of the Mormons, Adventists, Scientists, and Witnesses to remain sufficiently small during the 19th century to justify regarding them as idiosyncratic and willfully cut off from the common Protestant way. They themselves contributed to this impression (and sometimes seemed to glory in it) by their isolationist, us-against-them mentality and their distinctively purist practices.

Once again, however, closer analysis suggests that virtually all minority groups in the United States used an abused outsider's mentality to keep their ideals and their identity clear. Both Catholics and Jews, for example, fiercely protected their distinctive religious practices, even as they attempted to win entry to American business, political, and cultural life. Perhaps the antiquity of these two traditions kept them from seeming sects. No one could call them Johnny-come-latelies, and the revelations on which they depended were inseparable from biblical revelation itself. In contrast the disclosures claimed by such sectarians as Joseph Smith and Mary Baker Eddy were very recent and personal. Clearly Catholics and Jews could receive, and give back, as much animosity as any of the sectarian groups, but the sense of difference they created remained distinct from that generated by the groups that arose in the 19th century.

A utopia is a realm of perfection that exists not in space and time but in the mind or the spirit as an ideal. Utopian groups such as the Shakers, the Oneida Perfectionists, and some of the pietistic communities transported from Europe (Mennonites, Hutterites, and Amish, for example) were lured by an ideal of brotherly and sisterly love, cooperation, purity, and simplicity to set up rural ventures in self-help and holistic Christian living. The Shakers were founded by Ann Lee (1736–1784), who is profiled in the next section. They were unique in demanding celibacy of their members, and they established an appealing reputation for handicrafts, songs, and egalitarian living between the sexes based on their convictions about the bisexuality of the divinity. The Oneida community grew from revivalist roots under the direction of John Humphrey Noyes, who founded an Association of Perfectionists at Putney, Vermont, in 1842. Noyes advocated community of property and "complex" (communitarian) marriages, as expressions of equality and sharing in all areas of life. The Mennonites derived from the 16th century Dutch reformer Menno Simons and were **Anabaptists** and pacifists. Mennonite groups migrated to the United States in both the 17th and 19th centuries. The Amish were a branch of the Mennonites deriving from Jacob Amann, a 17th century Swiss dissenter. They emigrated to the United States in both the 18th and the 19th centuries, founding an especially strong community in eastern Pennsylvania. The Hutterites drew their name from Jacob Hutter, a 16th century Moravian Anabaptist leader who advocated a radical sharing of goods in self-sufficient communities. They came to the United States in the 19th century, but many moved to Canada during the First World War to avoid military conscription.

All these groups had suffered in Europe for their separatist positions, and several had briefly found refuge in Russia. Their communitarian views, along with their history of persecution, tended to make them suspicious of outsiders, and they preferred to live on their own, keeping their traditions of language, work, and religious observance untainted by the American mainstream.[5]

The Transcendentalists were 19th century New England writers and philosophers who favored a belief in the essential unity of all creation, in the innate goodness of human nature, and in the supremacy of insight for the revelation of the deepest truths. The Transcendentalists were electic, drawing from Western sources such as Coleridge and Plato, as well as from Indian and Chinese philosophy. They also admired the writings of European mystics such as Emanuel Swedenborg and Jakob Bohme. The

Stories of the virgin West triggered utopian images of an area where one might make a fresh start amidst unspoiled natural beauty. Native Americans inspired a mixed symbolism; some whites regarded them as representatives of unspoiled human nature. (Green River, Oregon, A. J. Miller; Gilcrease Museum, Tulsa, Oklahoma)

movement peaked between 1830 and 1855, when it was centered in Concord, Massachusetts, and attracted such figures as Ralph Waldo Emerson, Henry David Thoreau, Margaret Fuller, Orestes Brownson, and Bronson Alcott. From 1840 to 1844 the Transcendentalists published the magazine, *The Dial,* which influenced such other weighty writers as Walt Whitman, Herman Melville, and Nathaniel Hawthorne.

Ann Lee

The Shakers were founded by the Englishwoman Ann Lee (1736–1784), who had intense religious experiences from her childhood years in Manchester. She joined a group of enthusiasts that had broken away from English Quakers, endured a difficult marriage, and saw all four of her children die in infancy. Convinced that sexual intercourse was the root of all sin, in 1770 Lee had a vision of the Garden of Eden that convinced her that celibacy was the way to combat human sinfulness. The Shaking Quakers who followed her teaching got their name from their emotional religious practices. Moved by a further vision, Mother Ann, as she had come to be called, led a group of eight to America in 1774. The group settled in New York, waited out the American Revolution, and prepared themselves for the Second Coming.

The first generation of Shakers aroused considerable interest but even more suspicion and derision. In fact the Shakers occasionally suffered violence from inhospitable townsfolk, as illustrated by the following account of an incident in Petersham, New Hampshire, in 1781:

This being the first visit that Mother Ann and the Elders made in Petersham the inhabitants generally manifested a desire to see and hear for themselves, and as they pretended civility, they had full liberty. Accordingly, on Monday evening there came a considerable number of civil people, also a company of lewd fellows from the middle

of the town, who styled themselves the blackguard committee . . . entered three ruffians painted black and rushing forward, the foremost one seized hold of Mother, and, with the assistance of his comrades, attempted to drag her out, but Elizabeth Shattuck and several sisters instantly clinched hold of her, and held her, and Elizabeth being a large, heavy woman, and the passage narrow, the ruffians were not able to accomplish their purpose; and quitting their hold they suddenly fled out of the house . . . . Those who remained were about retiring to rest when Mother discovered, from the window, that her cruel persecutors were near, and made some attempts to conceal herself. The house was again assaulted by about thirty creatures in human shape; the doors being fastened, were burst open and broke, and these ruffians entered . . . . They seized firebrands, and searched the house, and at length found her in a bedroom; they immediately seized her by the feet, and inhumanly dragged her, feet foremost, out of the house, and threw her into a sleigh with as little ceremony as they would the dead carcase of a beast, and drove off, commiting, at the same time, acts of inhumanity and indecency which even savages would be ashamed of.[6]

The ruffians eventually became ashamed of themselves, and Mother Ann forgave them. The incident was remarkable, but the Shakers regularly aroused suspicion and resentment. People could not believe that their community was actually celibate and so castigated them as engaging in orgies and unnatural acts. Mother Ann's claim to be a revelation of God, the spouse of Jesus, agitated those concerned about theological orthodoxy. Many outsiders (especially patriarchal men) were offended by the freedom women enjoyed in the Shaker community and their equality with the men.

After the death of Ann Lee (due largely to a savage beating she received in Harvard, Massachusetts, in 1783), her followers developed her teachings by establishing a fully communitarian life. They organized themselves into "families" of celibates and celebrated a Father-Mother God. They held all property in common, shared work, and endeavored to create an atmosphere in which both work and prayer might unfold simply and beautifully. Sexual abstinence was a key doctrine, aimed at overcoming human sinfulness, and the concern for purity also penetrated their ideas of diet. They thought that a strong spiritual life would help them ward off physical disease, and their prayer rituals developed lovely songs and dances designed to strengthen the spirit. Shakers were pacifists, thinking violence and warfare signs of the degenerate times, and they hoped for the swift return of Jesus and Mother Ann.

The Shaker ritual dances acted out these interrelated beliefs. The bisexuality of the Shaker divinity, personalized by Jesus and Mother Ann, undergirded their sense of male-female complementarity in communal life, which the dances expressed. The dances began slowly and decorously, as the dancers worked their way into harmonious feelings they associated with the new, millennial age. Late in the night, however, many would spin their way into ecstatic union with Mother Ann and Jesus, anticipating the joy of paradise.

By the mid-19th century the Shakers had acquired a good reputation and begun to prosper. Throughout the years after her death, Mother Ann had continued to communicate with members of the community, through spiritual mediums. However, 60 years after Mother Ann's death, this contact declined, and the community shifted to artistic representations of its spiritual ties, above all through brilliant paintings. The Shakers began to lose members during the Civil War period. They maintained a few communities throughout the 20th century, but by the 1980s only two small groups remained, both in New England. That they had lasted 200 years was a great tribute to their practical shrewdness, as well as their spiritual depth, for they did well in their business dealings and made the products of Shaker crafts highly prized. Such fine work was in keeping with their spiritual convictions, since Mother Ann had taught that the heavenly light she received transformed the mundane into the extraordinary.[7]

While Ann Lee was perhaps the most original and successful of the women who helped shape the utopian groups in 19th century America, she was by no means the only remarkable one. Mary Baker Eddy founded the Christian Scientists, and the Ephrata Cloister founded the Dunkers (a German group) in Lancaster, Pennsylvania, in 1732. Like the Shakers the Dunkers advocated celibacy for both men and women (although they accepted married members). Many remarkable women followed their special rule for females known as the Rose Document. Moravian Brethren communities in nearby Bethlehem, Pennsylvania, offered women similar opportunities to live in an idealistic community, although the Moravians placed less stress on celibacy than on missionary activity. Jemima Wilkinson (1752–1819) outshone Ann Lee as a preacher. Raised a Quaker, she had religious experiences that led her to call herself the Universal Friend and tour New England proclaiming a message of repentance and winning hundreds of followers. In the 17th century, such Quaker women as Mary Fisher, Mary Dyer, and Elisabeth Hooten suffered for their convictions and won great respect.

Overall the sectarian and utopian groups offered many women more influence than they could find in the mainstream religious groups. Having already broken with portions of orthodoxy, the sectarians sometimes found it easier to create new, more egalitarian ways of regarding the sexes than mainstream Christianity provided.

On *The Book of Mormon*

The revelations that Joseph Smith received directed him to a spot where he discovered some golden plates. By translating them, he came into possession of *The Book of Mormon*, a supplement to the Bible. This new scripture told the story of the tribe of Joseph, one family of which God had led out of Jerusalem in 600 B.C.E. and transplanted to North America. After various trials and tribulations, some of which led to the formation of the Native American tribes, Mormon, a survivor of a massacre in 384 C.E., buried the plates that Joseph Smith found. The heavenly messenger who directed Smith to the plates was Moroni, the son of Mormon.

Joseph Smith continued to receive revelations throughout his life, as did the Mormon leaders who succeeded him, making Mormonism a religion enjoying ongoing disclosures from God. The wanderings Smith and his followers went through in the early years seemed to them like the wanderings of the children of Israel in the desert. Certainly they were no less painful. In Ohio, Missouri, and Illinois they met persecution and were wracked by internal dissent. Joseph Smith himself was jailed in Carthage, Illinois, in 1844 and killed by an angry mob. His successor, Brigham Young, led the community farther west until they reached the Great Salt Lake, where they stopped to establish their destined community, a new Zion in America.

The Mormons shared with other perfectionist groups the ideal of establishing a purified community. They also thought that America was God's chosen site for the inauguration of the final age and the New Jerusalem. Mormons stressed human industry and self-help, denying the Calvinist sense of human corruption that reigned in many Protestant churches. Mormons considered progress and material things to be good, and in Utah they organized themselves as a theocracy, developing a highly organized, effective church machinery that brought them considerable prosperity. The millennium they awaited would amount to a transformation of American life rather than the end of history.

Joseph Smith's account of the vision that led to his finding *The Book of Mormon* is prefaced to many editions of the work:

When I was thus in the act of calling upon God, I discovered a light appearing in my room, which continued to increase until the room was lighter than at noonday, when immediately a personage appeared at my bedside, standing in the air, for his feet did not touch the floor. He had on a loose robe of the most exquisite whiteness. It was a whiteness beyond anything earthly I had ever seen; nor do I believe that any earthly thing could be made to appear so exceedingly white and brilliant . . . . Not only was his robe exceedingly white, but his whole person was glorious beyond description, and his countenance truly like lightning. The room was exceedingly light, but not so very bright as immediately around his person. When I first looked upon him, I was afraid; but the fear soon left me. He called me by name, and said unto me that he was a messenger sent from the presence of God to me, and that his name was Moroni; that God had a work for me to do; and that my name should be had for good and evil among all nations, kindreds, and tongues, or that it should be both good and evil spoken among all people. He said there was a book deposited, written upon gold plates, giving an account of the former inhabitants of this continent, and the source from whence they sprang. He also said that the fulness of the everlasting Gospel was contained in it, as delivered by the Saviour to the ancient inhabitants.[8]

Several features of this portion of the account are worth noting:

1. The vision came to Joseph Smith when he was at prayer, and so it seemed an answer to his petitions, which at least implicitly must have been for knowledge of God's will and way for him.

2. Moroni bore similarities to the heavenly figure glimpsed by John of Patmos at the outset of the Book of Revelation: "one like a son of man, clothed with a long robe and with a golden girdle round his breast; his head and his hair were white as white wool, white as snow; his eyes were like a flame of fire . . . . When I saw him, I fell at his feet as though dead. But he laid his right

hand upon me, saying 'Fear not . . . .'" (Rev. 1:13–14, 17).

3. Moroni gave Joseph Smith precisely what he had sought: assurance that he would amount to something, that God had a significant mission in store for him. The divine work he would do would bring him both praise and blame, both love and hate, among the nations. From the outset, then, Smith was primed to be a stumbling block, a cause of division, and so a Christ figure.

4. The book that Moroni revealed to Joseph Smith, through the gold tablets, is significant on at least two grounds. It purports to describe the prehistory of America (something all Americans, presumably, would like to know), and it offers the "fullness" of the Gospels, which implies that without it the New Testament is incomplete. Moreover the Savior (Jesus?) gave this fuller gospel to the ancient inhabitants (of America).

The text of *The Book of Mormon* now in use collects various books composed by ancient historians of God's people in America—annals of the people who made the trek from Jerusalem to the New World. It states that Moroni was the last of these Nephite historians, and about 421 C.E. he hid the records in New York State. They were to be opened in the latter days, as God had told his prophets.

A small portion (also called the "Book of Mormon") of the work, suggests the style of the whole:

And it came to pass that I did speak unto my people, and did urge them with great energy, that they would stand boldly before the Lamanites and fight for their wives, and their children, and their houses, and their homes. And my words did arouse them somewhat to vigor, insomuch that they did not flee from before the Lamanites, but did stand with boldness against them. And it came to pass that we did contend with an army of thirty thousand against an army of fifty thousand. And it

came to pass that we did stand before them with such firmness that they did flee from before us. And it came to pass that when they had fled we did pursue them with our armies, and did meet them again, and did beat them; nevertheless the strength of the Lord was not with us; yea, we were left to ourselves, that the Spirit of the Lord did not abide in us; therefore we had become weak like unto our brethren. And my heart did sorrow because of this the great calamity of my people, because of their wickedness and their abominations. . . ."[9]

In style and content alike, the passage is reminiscent of many from the historical books of the Hebrew Bible. Warfare is the lot of the chosen people, who are forced to deal with wicked foes who seek their lives and fortunes. They fight well enough but don't win decisively because the Lord is not with them. Why is the Lord not with them? Why did the calamity occur? Because the people had been wicked, so the Spirit of the Lord could not abide in their midst. This is the kind of theology found in Joshua through 2 Kings. It reflects the ancient view of the Lord as the first warrior of the chosen people, the one who led them out of Egypt by his mighty arm. It suggests the problem of the charismatic leadership of the judges, who were effective only while the Spirit of the Lord was upon them. Indeed the first king, Saul, came to disaster when the Spirit of the Lord deserted him because of his disobedience and lack of faith. *The Book of Mormon* therefore puts itself in good company, making plausible its claim to be the supplement of Christian Scripture. Like Revelation, it narrates sacred history in terms of wickedness and punishment, goodness and grace.

Key Terms

Anabaptists: European groups of the 16th century who refused to allow their children to be baptized and made baptism an adult confession of faith. Hutterites, Swiss Brethren, and Mennonites fell into this category. The leading Protestant reformers—Luther, Zwingli, and Calvin—condemned the movement, holding for the validity and necessity of infant baptism, as did Roman Catholics. Anabaptists frequently suffered persecution and tens of thousands were put to death for their convictions.

Enthusiasm: claiming to be "filled with God," spiritually exalted, rapt in the Spirit. Our present connotation of the term is a pale remnant of this older meaning. Originally enthusiasts were people taken out of themselves by divine agency and rendered ecstatic. Gradually any churches that stirred up emotion, by singing, dancing, clapping, and the like came under the rubric "enthusiast." On the one hand, they merited praise for engaging both mind and heart with religious faith. On the other hand, they were always suspected of neglecting the rational, sober, prudential side of religion and immersing people in pure emotion. Pure emotion was sure to be short-lived. The apostle Paul's discussion (I Corinthians 12) of the various charismatic gifts already contained an implicit critique of enthusiasm, but the Enlightenment's stress on reason further clouded its image. Thus educated Americans of Jefferson's and Madison's generation were likely to have a low opinion of religious enthusiasm as something not only irrational but also bound to encourage an unbridled religious practice troublesome for a pluralistic society.

Evangelical: concerning the gospel or glad tidings (*euanggelion*). In the New Testament itself the word refers to the news that Jesus preached, and also to the news others preached about Jesus. Evangelical Christians are those who especially stress heralding this good news, proclaiming the gospel. Thus the Church of England's

Commission on Evangelism said: "To evangelize is to present Jesus Christ in the power of the Holy Spirit that [people] shall come to put their trust in God through him, to accept him as their Saviour, and serve him as their King in the fellowship of his Church." This emphasis came to the fore in the 18th century when effective preachers such as George Whitefield and John Wesley made proclaiming the good news the center of their ministerial effort. The Second Great Awakening added more fuel to this fire, and in its wake many Protestant churches supported great evangelists such as Charles Finney, Dwight Moody, Billy Sunday, and Billy Graham. Critics tend to find fault with the aggressive methods evangelicals sometimes employ and with their narrow view of personal salvation, which threatens to ignore social justice.

Revivalism: a concern with and a technique for quickening or reawakening faith. Some historians of the term and phenomenon in America see its beginnings in the ministry of Solomon Stoddard (1643–1729) in Northhampton, Massachusetts. His revivalism gave him leverage against Increase Mather, whose ministry in Boston was more intellectual and less geared to eliciting emotional arousal. The Great Awakening that occurred from the 1720s to the 1740s was the first peak of revivalism. This was carried from New England to the South and was taken up by many Methodists and Baptists. The Second Great Awakening early in the 19th century can also be considered a high point of revivalism, while its extension to the western frontier made the camp meeting and emotional sermon staples of pious efforts to keep the coals of faith glowing. Methodists, Baptists, and Disciples of Christ all favored a revivalist preaching style and theology. Revivalism overlaps evangelism, but usually it emphasizes stirring up the faith of believers rather than gaining new converts or preaching the gospel in virgin territory.

Unitarianism: In its American usage, the term refers to one of the groups that emerged from the demise of the Puritan sense of national covenant that had dominated New England in the early colonial days. The rational impulse brought forward by the Enlightenment and Deism contributed to the atmosphere in which believers (most of them educated) wanted to distance themselves from the Trinity and other strictly supernatural mysteries of traditional Christian faith. King's Chapel in Boston became the first Unitarian Church in 1785 and featured a worship service modified to accommodate this trend in faith. The Unitarians gained control of Harvard College in 1805 and were the moving spirits behind the establishment of Harvard Divinity School in 1816. In 1825 William Ellery Channing became head of a Unitarian Association that many previously congregationalist churches joined. Unitarians have generally stressed the goodness of human nature and the power of human reason, denying that human beings need a savior such as Jesus Christ. Instead they have seen Jesus as a moral example of what the love of God and one's fellow human beings should be like. Finally Unitarian thought has stressed the freedom of all people to believe as their consciences dictate and the priority of ethical uprightness over doctrinal orthodoxy.

Discussion Questions

1. Why were rationalists such as Jefferson and Franklin willing to use biblical language on public occasions?

2. How did the atoning love of Christ crown the plain gospel truths on which the Yale theologians based what became the Second Great Awakening?

3. What was John Wesley's method and why was it so successful?

4. Why did the Methodists experience such extraordinary growth in the first half of the 19th century?

5. Why did most sectarian and utopian groups of the 19th century arouse great animosity?

6. What themes did the sectarians and utopians tend to stress?

7. How was Ann Lee's view of God mirrored in the organization of the Shaker community?

8. What was the rationale and attraction of the celibacy advocated by several 19th century utopian groups?

9. What is the most striking feature in the account of Joseph Smith's reception of *The Book of Mormon?*

10. How does the similarity of *The Book of Mormon* to the Bible relate to Moroni's claim that it contained the fullness of the Gospel?

Notes

1. Mark A. Noll, "The Image of the United States as a Biblical Nation, 1776–1865," in *The Bible in America*, ed. Nathan O. Hatch and Mark A. Noll (New York: Oxford University Press, 1982), p. 39.

2. Ibid., pp. 40–41.

3. See Williston Walker, et al., *A History of the Christian Church*, 4th ed. (New York: Scribner's, 1985), pp. 653–654.

4. William A. Clebsch, *From Sacred to Profane America* (New York: Harper & Row, 1968), pp. 31–33. On the regular recurrence of evangelical upsurges, see William G. McLoughlin,

Revivals, Awakenings, and Reform (Chicago: University of Chicago Press, 1978).

5. See Catherine L. Albanese, *America: Religions and Religion* (Belmont CA: Wadsworth, 1981), pp. 137–161; R. Laurence Moore, *Religious Outsiders and the Making of Americans* (New York: Oxford University Press, 1986), pp. 25–47, 105–149.

6. Rosemary Radford Ruether and Catherine M. Prelinger, "Women in Sectarian and Utopian Groups," in *Women & Religion in America*, vol. 2, ed. Rosemary Radford Ruether and Rosemary Skinner Keller (San Francisco: Harper & Row, 1983), p. 310.

7. This sketch of Ann Lee is based on the work of Albanese, op. cit.

8. *The Book of Mormon* (Salt Lake City: The Church of Jesus Christ of the Latter Day Saints, 1963), p. xiv (unnumbered).

9. Ibid., p. 27.

CHAPTER 6

The Civil War Era

African-American Religion

The beginnings of a black population in the Americas can be traced to 1517 when the Spanish King Charles I began to import slaves from Africa to work on Spanish plantations in the New World. In 1619 black slaves arrived in Virginia on a Dutch ship to work on the developing tobacco, sugar, and cotton plantations. As the plantations grew, slave trading itself became a profitable business, and an elaborate network linked West Africa, the West Indies, and North America. Between 1681, when there were about 2000 slaves in Virginia, and the mid-18th century, when the colonies were about to go to war, the slave population grew to more than 4 million. The 18th-century European Enlightenment had moved some to a moral abhorrence of slavery, but this did American blacks little good until the 19th century.

In speaking of the religious legacy blacks brought from Africa, scholars tend to stress a positive view of both physical and human nature, a holistic worldview that kept body and spirit unified, a tendency to view fertility and vitality as the signs of divine blessing, openness to inspiration through dreams (where ancestors might speak), concern with spirits (both wicked and helpful), and the use of diviners and sacrificers to influence the spiritual world. The conditions in which they found themselves as slaves had much to say about how American blacks were able to retain and adapt their African heritage. Whereas slaves taken to Catholic areas such as Haiti, Cuba, and Brazil could express their traditional concern with spirits (or gods) through the Catholic cult of the saints, the Protestant piety of the English colonies in North America forced slaves either to maintain their traditions underground or reexpress them through biblical imagery. The slaves in North America also had the problem of being greatly outnumbered by the white citizens, whereas in Latin America they tended to be concentrated in areas where they outnumbered the white population and so could better control their own culture.

Still slaves in the North American colonies created some remarkable amalgamations of native African and new American traditions:

> Slaves in the American South reinterpreted Christian rituals, such as baptism, in terms of African initiation rites. They marched around their prayer houses counterclockwise in religious dances whose steps closely resembled those performed in Africa in honor of the gods; they emphasized possession by the spirit of the Christian god, just as Africans stressed possession by the gods; and they decorated graves in a manner that strongly suggested the funeral customs of people of the Kongo. The song styles and magical-medicinal practices of North American slaves also derived from Africa, as did naming practices, folk tales, and a host of other cultural customs that continued alongside Christianity.[1]

During the first generations of their presence, black slaves in the colonies experienced little pressure or invitation to convert to Christianity. Only in the early 18th century did whites become interested in Christianizing blacks. Not until the 1740s, when the Great Awakening sent shocks of revivalism through the colonies, did missions to blacks achieve much success. Revivalist religion was much more appealing to the slaves than the more sober, doctrine-centered religion of the Puritans and Anglicans. It encouraged an ecstatic behavior similar to that of their African traditions. It focused on conversion, a dramatic new beginning that might be likened to an African initiation. And revivalist religion made literacy less important, freeing illiterate blacks to pray and preach directly from experience.

Some white revivalists, seeing the impact of Christian spiritual experience on blacks, began to advocate the abolition of slavery. It would take nearly a century for abolition to become a strong movement, but blacks who heard Methodists or Baptists advocating their freedom were bound to think more favorably of those churches. The Baptists took the lead in organizing black churches in the South, and by the 1770s black preachers had gathered independent congregations (in keeping with the Baptist stress on the independence of local churches). In several Southern states, black Baptist churches came to outnumber white ones.

Richard Allen (1760–1831), a former slave, formed the first independent black church in the North. It was a black Methodist church organized in Philadelphia in 1794. Struggles with white Methodists over control of their churches led Allen and other blacks to form the African Methodist Episcopal Church in 1816. Black Episcopalians, Presbyterians, and Baptists also formed separate churches in the North in the first decades of the 19th century. Black Catholics, whose numbers were smaller, never formed independent churches, but they did organize two religious orders for black women. The Oblate Sisters of Providence began in Baltimore in 1829, while the Holy Family Sisters started in New Orleans in 1842.

Black churches have long been regarded as important beyond their strictly religious significance, because throughout American history they have been the institutions over which blacks have had greatest control. Thus the black

*Black slave labor was essential to the plantation system of the South, which defined the world for many African-Americans. (*Cotton Plantation on the Mississippi, *W. M. A. Walker; Gilcrease Museum, Tulsa, Oklahoma)*

churches have been at the heart of black American culture and community life, greatly influencing politics, social welfare, education, art, and the development of black leaders.

Early in the 19th century whites formed the American Colonization Society to forward the idea of black repatriation to Africa. The notion was a benign effort to solve racial problems and give blacks a better situation, but American black leaders criticized the idea on several scores. They feared it might lead to the forced emigration of blacks who opposed slavery. They also thought

it overlooked both the actual condition of American blacks, most of whom were generations removed from Africa, and the contributions blacks had made to fashioning the new nation. By that time most blacks thought of themselves as Americans, and some were moved to begin missionary ventures to Africa to share the riches they had found in Christianity.

Articulate black opposition to slavery also grew in the early 18th century, much of it led by black ministers. Many black abolitionists were also involved in the temperance, moral reform, and women's rights movements of the period. In 1830 Richard Allen convened a National Negro Convention in Philadelphia that considered the overall condition of African-Americans. In the South slavery continued to determine the condition of most blacks, and their religion was largely a response to the degradation they experienced on a daily basis. They tended to identify with the Israelites enslaved in Egypt and to picture Christian salvation as a liberation from their spiritual and physical bondage. While black religion was often rather otherworldly, looking to heaven for its freedom, it sometimes encouraged this-worldly revolts, and it nearly always helped blacks keep going.

Nat Turner, the son of an African slave, felt he had been called by God to lead his people from bondage. His short-lived revolt of 1831 in Virginia began with 7 followers and mustered a total of only 75, but in two days they killed 51 whites and terrorized the slave-holding population. The whites retaliated brutally, killing many innocent slaves, and repressive legislation soon followed, blocking black access to education and free assembly. But the rebellion destroyed the myth that blacks were content with their condition as slaves and fueled the bitter polemics between pro- and antislavery groups that hastened the Civil War.

Slavery in Cultural and Theological Perspective

The historical development of the United States centered industry in the Northern states and agriculture in the South. Because black slaves supplied most of the labor for this agricultural economy at cheap prices, slavery came to be assumed essential to the Southern way of life. That is not to say that all Southerners approved of slavery or thought black labor ideal. Charles Lyell, an English geologist touring the United

States in the 1840s, recorded Southern sentiments that suggest some of the cultural complexity:

Over a door in the principal street of New Orleans we read the inscription, "Negroes on sale here." It is natural that Southerners should not be aware how much a foreigner is shocked at this public mode of treating a large part of the population as mere chattels . . . . In a St. Louis paper, I read, in the narrative of a steamboat collision, the following passage: "We learn that the passengers, with few exceptions, lost all their effects; one gentleman in particular lost nine Negroes (who were on deck) and fourteen horses." Among the laws recently enacted in Louisiana, I was glad to see one to prevent persons of color exiled from other states, or transported for some offense, from becoming citizens. In spite of such statutes the Negro-exporting portions of the Union will always make the newer states play in some degree the part of penal settlements. Free blacks are allowed to be witnesses in the courts here, in cases where white men are concerned, a privilege they do not enjoy in some free states, as in Indiana; but they do not allow free blacks to come and settle here and say they have been compelled to adopt this precaution by the Abolitionists.

An intelligent Louisianian said to me, "Were we to emancipate our Negroes as suddenly as your government did the West Indians, they would be a doomed race; but there can be no doubt that white labor is more profitable even in this climate." "Then, why do you not encourage it?" I asked. "It must be the work of time," he replied; "The prejudices of owners have to be overcome, and the sugar and cotton crop is easily lost, if not taken in at once when ripe . . . . a planter, five miles below New Orleans, having resolved to dispense with slave labor, hired one hundred Irish and German emigrants at very high wages. In the middle of the harvest they struck for double pay. No others were to be had, and it was impossible to purchase slaves in a few days. In that short time he lost produce to the value of $10,000."[2]

These few observations and quotations from Lyell's letter touch on themes central to what slavery had become in Southern culture prior to the Civil War. The selling of blacks was a matter of course, as commonplace as selling horses. Indeed the account of the steamboat collision runs together the loss of blacks and the loss of horses—both were simply property. Northern opposition to slavery had infiltrated all congressional discussions of admitting new territories into the Union as states, for each new application occasioned a debate about whether the new state would be slaveholding or free. The question of what to do with runaway slaves had severely strained relations between Northern and Southern states. The Underground Railroad had siphoned tens of thousands of slaves out of the South, greatly irritating Southern slave owners. For a combination of reasons many Southerners had convinced themselves of two related propositions:

1. Slave labor was essential to their economy.
2. Black slaves were less human than whites and so did not suffer from their state the way that full human beings would have.

The second proposition could take the perhaps benevolent tone of the "intelligent Louisianian" quoted, who thought that rapid emancipation would leave most blacks helpless. But it was bolstered by the judgment that whites were more desirable laborers, if only they would be as docile as the blacks and not hold the plantation owners up for higher wages when the harvest came to its critical point.

When Southern churches took up the task of justifying slavery, they tended to try to make a biblical argument that slavery was an institution ordained by God. Benjamin Morgan Palmer, minister of the First Presbyterian Church in New Orleans, saw the election of the Republican presidential candidate, Abraham Lincoln, as a great threat to the institution of slavery and urged the Southern states to bind themselves to a sacred covenant to protect it. He also thought they should plan to fashion a separate existence for themselves, independent of the Northern states. If war followed, the Southerners could be sure they were defending the cause of God and religion against the atheistic Northerners. Moreover, by fighting to preserve the principle of self-government, the South would be carrying forward the manifest destiny God had given America.

More specifically Palmer used the popular biblical argument that blacks had descended from the race of Ham (or Canaan) that had been cursed into slavery (Genesis 9: 25–26). Indeed he believed that white influence on blacks had been benevolent, giving them employment, culture, and religion they would not have had otherwise. Northern sentiments against slavery were not necessarily more elevated than Southern defenses of slavery, and sermons preached on both sides of the divide risked both paternalism and turning blacks into pawns in the more broadly based competition between the two regions.

Southern churches came under theological attack for the treatment of slaves both in the South as a whole and in Southern slaveholding parishes in particular. Thus James Birney, himself a Southerner, in an address published in 1840 charged:

> Ministers and office-bearers and members of churches are slaveholders—buying and selling slaves (not as the regular slave trader but as their convenience or interest may from time to time require). As a general rule, the itinerant preachers in the Methodist church are not permitted to hold slaves, but there are frequent exceptions to the rule, especially of late. There are in the United States about 2,487,113 slaves and 386,069 free people of color. Of the slaves, 80,000 are members of the Methodist Church; 80,000 of the Baptist; and about 40,000 of other churches. These church members have no exemption from being sold by their owners as other slaves are. Instances are not rare of slaveholding members of churches selling slaves who are members of the same church with themselves. And members of churches have followed the business of slave auctioneers.[3]

Stephen S. Foster, vindicating in 1843 the strongly anticlerical language he had used when addressing an antislavery convention, repeated his view that the collusion of the clergy in slave-holding had made them into a brotherhood of thieves. Worse, it had led them to overlook such grave sins as adultery, which often accompanied slaveholding. Foster was convinced that slaveholders regularly used slave women for their own sexual pleasure, sometimes justifying this by referring to the women as "breeders" and to their offspring as "stock." The slave woman's body had become her master's property, to be used as he wished not only in the fields but also in the bedroom. The woman had little recourse, risking death if she resisted. Thus the slave-holder destroyed the marital bond—his own and that of the slave woman—and frequently was simply a rapist who deserved the death penalty. For the church to sanction such a stage of affairs, whether by its general support for slavery or by its failure to condemn the specific moral abuses to which slaveholding often led, brought religion into contempt. Obviously Foster was unpersuaded by references to the curse of Ham, or to Paul's letter to Philemon, which did not reject the institution of slavery (though it did commend freeing the runaway slave Onesimus).[4]

Abolitionism

The abolitionists, who were mainly North-erners, wanted to abolish slavery regardless of the cost to the Southern plantation system. A coalition of black and white abolitionists was responsible for turning the tide of opinion in the North against slavery. They also had some influence in the South, though perhaps their greater effect was to inflame Southern indignation at Northern interference in the Southern way of life. The abolitionists certainly did not root out the racism of Northerners, but they

did fill the press and lecture halls with articulate denunciations of slavery as immoral, degrading, and un-Christian.

Elijah Lovejoy (1802–1837) was one of several prominent martyrs to the abolitionist cause. A white Presbyterian minister and newspaper editor, he aroused great opposition by publishing a strongly abolitionist newspaper in St. Louis from 1833 to 1836. Forced to move across the Mississippi to Illinois, he found his antislavery essays as unpopular there as they had been in Missouri. Three times mobs destroyed his printing presses, and when Lovejoy stood guard over his presses to prevent a fourth destruction he was shot and killed.

Lovejoy made the first principle of abolitionism nothing less than the first lines of the Declaration of Independence: All people are created equal and are endowed by their Creator with certain inalienable rights, among which are life, liberty, and the pursuit of happiness. Stressing the equality of human beings as creatures of God, and their common right to liberty, the abolitionists found slavery repugnant to the principles on which the United States was founded. By turning other human beings into property, slavery directly contradicted the inalienable right of liberty. It tried to usurp the rights of God, who was the only lawful owner of human beings. Because it was both sinful and politically wrong, slavery would rapidly bring the destruction of America's most cherished religious and political institutions.[5]

The abolitionist cause engaged not just courageous male journalists but also equally courageous female writers and lecturers. Probably none was more influential than Harriet Beecher Stowe (1811–1896), author of *Uncle Tom's Cabin*. The daughter of an influential theologian, Lyman Beecher, Harriet was born in Connecticut and influenced by the abolitionist atmosphere of Lane Theological Seminary in Cincinnati during the 1830s. When she married a Lane professor of Scripture, she moved to Maine in 1850 and began writing her novel, inspired by the controversy over the fugitive slave acts. *Uncle Tom's Cabin*, subtitled *Life Among the Lowly*, appeared serially in an antislavery periodical, *National Era*, between June 1851 and April 1852. In book form it sold more than 300,000 copies in its first year, making Tom, Eliza, and the wicked Simon Legree household names in Europe as well as America. Southerners were enraged, so in 1853 Stowe published *The Key to Uncle Tom's Cabin*, a selection of documents designed to verify the accuracy of the conditions her novel had described. *Uncle Tom's Cabin* was undoubtedly the single most important piece of antislavery propaganda. When the Civil War broke out the book continued to be a source of support for President Lincoln and the Union cause. Stowe worked throughout the 1850s and 1860s for the abolitionist movement, writing, speaking, and traveling widely.

Sarah and Angelina Grimke, daughters of a distinguished South Carolina slaveholding family, became Quakers during the 1820s. Eventually they came to link antislavery with feminist views, but the beginnings of their idealism probably lay in their firsthand encounter with the cruelties of slavery. As one commentator has put it,

> slavery was particularly burdensome to the white women of the South because it was they who had the daily responsibility of oversight, especially of the house servants. Many white mistresses came to regard slaves as a trial, because of the difficult task of administration and care assigned to them. Many also came to see that as women they were in many ways as much in thrall to their husbands and brothers as the slaves were. Mary Chestnut said she never saw a true woman who was not an abolitionist even though it was rare for Southern women to act on this conviction.[6]

Angelina Grimke became increasingly strong in her opposition to slavery, and when challenged she would repeat Christ's golden rule: Do unto others as you would have them do unto you. Virtually all whites were unwilling to be slaves themselves. Therefore they had no basis for making slaves of blacks. By holding slaves the owners defaulted on their moral obligations to God and kept blacks underdeveloped morally. In Grimke's view neither sex nor color abrogated basic human rights. All people were equal under God.

Still the nation was far from agreeing with Grimke's understanding of Christianity. In 1857 Dred Scott, a slave from Missouri, sued for his freedom on the grounds that his master had taken him to Illinois and Wisconsin (free areas) before returning him to Missouri. The Missouri courts held that Scott was not a citizen, so the Supreme Court could have denied his case. But Chief Justice Taney wanted to deal with the issue of the restrictions on slavery. In doing so he declared not only that Scott was not a citizen but also that blacks had long been considered "so far inferior that they had no rights which the white man was bound to respect." The dissenting minority opinion of Justice Benjamin R. Curtis furnished Northern abolitionists, whom the decision outraged, with two key arguments: Free blacks were citizens, and the Congress was empowered by the Constitution (ART. 4, SEC. 3) to regulate slavery in the territories.

Perhaps the most radical of the abolitionists was William Lloyd Garrison (1805–1879), a journalist and lecturer. Born in Massachusetts, he was apprenticed at 13 to the editor of the Newburyport *Herald*. In 1826 he was appointed editor of the Newburyport *Free Press*, the failure of which sent him to Boston in 1828, where he became coeditor of the *National Philanthropist*. This journal was devoted to several reform causes and provided Garrison a good platform for his growing interest in abolitionism. Having met Benjamin Lundy, a Quaker journalist opposed to slavery, Garrison went to Baltimore in 1829 to coedit with Lundy *The Genius of Universal Emancipation*. But Garrison's unmeasured tirades in the pages of this journal did not sit well in slaveholding Maryland, and he was imprisoned in 1830. Back in Boston Garrison founded *The Liberator*, which from its first issue on January 1, 1831, declared a crusade against slavery and slaveholders. Garrison edited *The Liberator* until its last issue appeared 35 years later, when emancipation was finally proclaimed.

In contrast to various schemes for gradual emancipation, Garrison demanded immediate release of all slaves. He helped found the New England Antislavery Society in 1831 and the American Antislavery Society in 1833. Fellow Bostonians opposed to Garrison dragged him through the streets and nearly killed him in 1835. He continued to write that the North ought to withdraw from any compact with the South that sheltered slavery. Typical of his language was an 1843 resolution of the Massachusetts Antislavery Society that described the Constitution of the United States as "a covenant with death and an agreement with hell." In Framingham, Massachusetts, on July 4, 1854, Garrison publicly burned the Constitution, calling it a compromise with tyranny. As soon as President Lincoln issued the Emancipation Proclamation Garrison threw Lincoln his full support. His postwar years were spent promoting women's suffrage and prohibition. Whether Garrison generated more support than hatred for abolitionism is debatable, but he kept the cause in the headlines by his singleminded passion.

Frederick Douglass and Sojourner Truth

Frederick Douglass (1817–1895) was the black abolitionist who most eloquently advanced the cause of emancipation. Escaped from slavery in Maryland, Douglass went North and eventually became editor of the Rochester, New York, newspaper *North Star*. In addition to attacking slavery itself, Douglass strongly criticized Christians who appeared to tolerate slavery. His lectures took him across America and Britain, as he labored to bring all possible moral weight to bear against slavery.

At a speech in Boston's historic Faneuil Hall in 1842, Douglass addressed 4000 people, stirring them to an emotional response. First he told them that he stood before them as a slave—one who under the Constitution was the property of other people. Then he mentioned that his back was scarred from the lash of slaveholders, and that 2,500,000 other human beings continued to suffer such abuse and bondage. Though he had escaped, for which he thanked God, those others had no chance to speak out, being but goods and chattel, not human beings. Douglass noted that slaves were denied the rights of marriage and parenthood and had no share in the American heritage of liberty. Abolitionism was the cause that could save them from such misery, so Douglass blessed those gathered in Faneuil Hall in the name of abolitionism. They were being true to the cause of Christ, whose religion was being dreadfully mocked in the South.

Douglass did not exempt Northern Americans from his criticisms. Charging that many of the Southern preachers had learned their theology in the North, he described the way they would eviscerate the Scriptures by making Christ's Golden Rule apply only to slaveholders (saying, treat fellow slaveholders as you would have them treat you). Blacks, segregated in a different section of the Southern church, as they were segregated in many Northern churches, would hear only such texts as Ephesians 6:5: "Slaves, be obedient to those who are your earthly masters, with fear and trembling, in singleness of heart, as to Christ." The minister might then contrast the calloused hands of the slaves with the slender white hands of the masters, arguing that slaves manifestly had been created to do the working while masters had been created to do the thinking.[7]

In a speech in London's Finsbury Chapel in 1846 Douglass was even more graphic about the situation of slaves. Speaking of his native southern Maryland, he said that if a slave there struck his master the authorities could hang him, sever his head from his body, quarter his body, and display his head and quarters prominently in the neighborhood. A black woman attempting to defend her virtue by shielding herself from the attacks of her master could be killed on the spot. Worse, Southern Christianity supported this system. Ministers of religion, standing in the pulpit, regularly tortured the pages of Scripture to defend Southern slavery. For 200 hundred years slavery had depended on such connivance. The whips, chains, gags, and thumbscrews lay under the "droppings" of the sanctuary. Indeed the Anti-Slavery Society of America with which Douglass was working was often attacked as an infidel, godless body. But the real godlessness, to Douglass's mind, lay in the fact that Southern revivals and slaveholding went hand in hand. He himself loved the true religion of Christ, which was full of mercy and would bind up the wounds of those fallen among thieves. Too often, however, he found men sold to build churches, women sold to support missionaries, babies sold to buy bibles.[8]

Like Martin Luther King, Jr., slightly more than 100 years later, Douglass did not limit himself to the single issue of injustice to blacks. An editorial in the *North Star* in 1848 stingingly opposed the treaty ending the Mexican war, speaking for those who wanted no new territory gotten through an unjust conflict. By *peace* those enthusiastic for the treaty really meant *plunder.* Their delight in bloody victory glorified deeds of barbarous heroism by wicked men. To Douglass's mind the treaty simply robbed Mexico of some of her best lawful possessions. Bitterly he pronounced himself sick at the hypocrisy of the churches of Rochester thanking God for the victory and proclaiming it a triumph of Christianity. They ought rather to be craving

pardon for their crimes before the merciful God, he said.

Clearly Douglass was a powerful writer and speaker on fire with the need for Christian faith to show itself in passionate pursuit of justice. One might in fact see him as a forefather of the black liberation theology that developed in the middle of the 20th century.

Sojourner Truth (1797–1883), another leading black abolitionist, was a native of New York. She became a well-known speaker, at first attracting the curious but before long becoming recognized as a powerful leader in the abolitionist movement. While slavery was a primary focus of her work, she was opposed to all violations of human rights.

In Indiana in 1858 Truth was charged with being a consummate fraud. She had been recommended by Harriet Beecher Stowe, and those observing her had to admit that her knowledge and virtue were remarkable, all the more so since she had begun as a slave. Nonetheless, "ruffians" in Indiana had circulated the rumor that Truth was an impostor: a man in woman's clothing. They also suggested that she was a hireling of the Republican party (the political force most opposed to slavery). At one of her lectures some proslavery Democrats showed up to bait her. Voicing their doubt about her sex, they demanded that she show her breasts to some of the ladies in attendance. When Truth asked them the basis for their doubts, they mentioned her deep voice. Truth then told them that her breasts had suckled many a white baby to the neglect of her own offspring, and that the white children she had helped raise were far more manly than the accusers in front of her. Then she bared her bosom and asked them if they too wished to suck at her breast, saying that any shame involved in uncovering herself to the whole audience lay on their account, not hers.

For some white observers Sojourner Truth brought to life the heroic black character and fortitude described in *Uncle Tom's Cabin*. Her magnetic presence and powerful speaking voice riveted her audiences, and she seemed to combine both great courage and profound religious depths. Thus after one speaker had praised the Constitution, Truth rose and spoke about how her talks with God had led her to think about that document. She would walk the fields talking with God, she said. And one day, in a year when thousands of acres had been destroyed by weevils, she went over to some wheat that held up its head and looked fine, only to discover it was empty. So she asked God what was the matter with that wheat. He told her there was a little weasel in it. Talk about the Constitution reminded her of that experience, she said. She had heard all about its greatness, about the rights it granted human beings, but when she went up to it, searching its supposed fineness to find her rights, it was empty. So again she asked God what was the matter, and again God told her there was a weasel responsible.

Another time, having asked to hear some Scripture read (Truth was illiterate), she listened attentively to:

> For your hands are defiled with blood and your fingers with iniquity, your lips have spoken lies, and your tongue mutters wickedness. No one enters suit justly, no one goes to law honestly; they rely on empty pleas, they speak lies, they conceive mischief and bring forth iniquity. They hatch adders' eggs, they weave the spider's web; he who eats their eggs dies, and from one which is crushed a viper is hatched. (Isaiah 59: 3–5)

Truth then clapped her hands and asked whether that was in fact in the Bible. The reader assured her it was, whereupon she said that God had already told her that about the viper. Though she had never heard it aloud before, somehow she had already known it, so now she knew it double. The reader, narrating this incident, had no doubt she saw the viper as slavery, breaking out to bite those who had hatched it by their lies and injustice.

While Douglass and Truth were extraordinary spokespersons, ordinary blacks maintained effective religious lives before, during, and after the Civil War. Though some slaves attended white churches, others went to churches for blacks. Many participated in prayer meetings on their plantations, often in secret. The black interpretation of Christianity developed in these ways usually castigated slavery as opposed to God's will. Like the Israelites under the Egyptians, many blacks felt themselves the object of God's special concern and so hoped for deliverance. In their faith they also found reasons for feeling good about themselves and thinking that they were creatures of worth, even though much in the white world denied this.

After the war missionaries from the North, some of them blacks, tried to bring Southern slaves into the churches and improve their Christian education. They helped establish such black colleges as Fisk, Dillard, Hampton, and Tuskeegee. Some black Southerners gained political office during the Reconstruction and emancipation generally meant freedom for blacks to move out of the white churches and found their own groups. A gap grew between the more bookish religion of the educated and the more emotional religion of the illiterate, but after the failure of Reconstruction it was often the poor rural churches that best provided emotional solace and preserved continuity with the religion that many blacks had experienced while slaves.[10]

Writings of Abraham Lincoln

Abraham Lincoln (1809–1865), the 16th president of the United States, is known as the man who preserved the Union of the states and freed the slaves. Largely self-educated, Lincoln began his professional career as a lawyer in frontier Illinois in the 1830s and 1840s. He became highly successful and gained a reputa-

This mask made during Lincoln's life shows the gnarled features that became badges of martyrdom after his assassination. (*Abraham Lincoln Life Mask*, Leonard Volk; Gilcrease Museum, Tulsa, Oklahoma)

tion as a man who not only invariably grasped the essence of a legal case but also invariably was honest and fair. Lincoln served in Congress from 1847 to 1849, and he became nationally known through debates with Stephen Douglas during a senatorial campaign (that Douglas won). In those debates, Lincoln opposed the extension of slavery into the newly opening territories, arguing that eventually the nation would become either all slave or all free. Elected president in 1860, Lincoln immediately was preoccupied with the secession of the Southern states. He proclaimed the slaves in rebellious states free in 1863 and was assassinated in 1865 shortly after the Union victory.

Two of the many documents attesting to Lincoln's deeply religious view of the crisis of the Civil War are the proclamation he issued for March 30, 1863, when he established a National Day of Fasting, and his second inaugural address. The proclamation begins by noting the fact that the U.S. Senate had recognized the authority of God and asked the president to designate a day for national prayer and humiliation. Agreeing to this, Lincoln underscored the duty of nations to confess their sins and transgressions in humble sorrow, yet with the hope of receiving mercy and pardon. The sublime truth, Lincoln said, is that only those nations whose God is the Lord are blessed.

Reflecting further Lincoln asked whether it might not be that the awful calamity of civil war the nation was undergoing was a punishment for presumption, calculated to bring about the reformation of the whole people. Perhaps no other nation had received the blessings from God that America had received. But America had forgotten God, the source of its peace and riches. It had presumed to think its progress had come from its own human efforts. "Intoxicated with unbroken success, we have become too self-sufficient to feel the necessity of redeeming and preserving grace, too proud to pray to the God that made us."[11]

As an occasion for Americans to humble themselves before the deity, to confess their national sins, and to pray for forgiveness, the president designated April 30, 1863, as a day of national humiliation, fasting, and prayer. He asked all citizens to abstain from their ordinary pursuits, to unite in places of worship, and to keep the day holy to God. Having done that sincerely, the people might then hope that God would hear the cry of the nation on high, pardon the nation its sins, and restore it from its present suffering and division back to the unity and peace it had enjoyed before the war.

Note that Lincoln uses the older sense of *humiliation*, where the basic import is bowing low to God and reasserting the truths of one's lowliness before the Creator. Also notice the biblical accents of the theology, which is willing to ask whether misfortune and suffering do not announce some moral failures. Although much of the language is what we have seen in Enlightenment religion, Lincoln's style seems more traditionally biblical. Granting the need even in his century to avoid pieties peculiar to a given Christian tradition, it yet seems remarkable that he can speak of redeeming and preserving grace, a nice distinction favored by orthodox Christian theologians. The idea is that God must both carry people back from sin and preserve them in any righteousness they have.

Like redemption, preservation is a free gift. The public day that Lincoln proclaims is much like a Sabbath. People are to turn from their workaday concerns and expressly address themselves to God. It says much about the **civil religion** of the time that a president could expect people to consider prayer, fasting, and hallowing time for God appropriate responses to their troubles. Certainly, war—above all civil war—rouses people from their **secular** torpor and makes them more likely to consider their beginning and end. But Lincoln apparently feels no need to defend his religious assumptions. In his day most Americans still regarded God as their ever-present judge.

Lincoln's address at the inauguration of his second presidential term was delivered on March 4, 1865. The end of the Civil War was in sight, but so were the immense problems that reconstructing the Union would pose. In contrast to his first inaugural address, when the impending crisis was on the minds of all, the need now was to consider what the war had meant and where its end would leave the nation. In reviewing the cause of the war, Lincoln was singleminded: One-eighth of the entire national population had been black slaves in the South; the insurgents were willing to rend the Union to preserve the institution of slavery. In contrast, the government wanted only to restrict the spread of slavery into new territories. Both sides had expected the war to be brief, and both had prayed for God's aid.

The last half of Lincoln's brief address is explicitly religious.

> It may seem strange that any men should dare ask a just God's assistance in wringing their bread from the sweat of other men's faces, but let us judge not that we be not judged. The prayers of both could not be answered. That of neither has been answered fully. The Almighty has His own purposes. "Woe unto the world because of offenses! for it must needs be that offenses come; but woe to that man by whom the offense cometh."

If we shall suppose that American slavery is one of those offenses which, in the providence of God, must needs come, but which, having continued through his appointed time, He now wills to remove, and that He gives to both North and South this terrible war as the woe due to those by whom the offense came, shall we discern therein any departure from those divine attributes which the believers in a living God always ascribe to Him? Fondly do we hope, fervently do we pray, that this mighty scourge of war may speedily pass away.

Yet, if God wills that it continue until all the wealth piled up by the bondman's 250 years of unrequited toil shall be sunk, and until every drop of blood drawn with the lash shall be paid by another drawn with the sword, as was said 3000 years ago, so still it must be said, "the judgments of the Lord are true and righteous altogether."

With malice toward none, with charity for all, with firmness in the right as God gives us to see the right, let us strive on to finish the work we are in, to bind up the nation's wounds, to care for him who shall have borne the battle and for his widow and his orphan—to do all which may achieve a just and lasting peace among ourselves and with all nations.[12]

This is what one might call ethical religion, but with so resonant a biblical tone that the assumptions of divine judgment and mercy frankly intrude. Lincoln realizes both the depth of the wrongness that the war manifested and the forgiveness the end of the war would require. Superficial interpreters of wars seldom venture near the mysteries of Providence that wars reveal. Frankly religious interpreters often speak of sin and justice. But even theologically trained interpreters rarely linger over the only solution the Bible offers for gross sins and mutual recriminations. That is forgiveness—letting go of the past, burying both one's own guilt and the guilt of those who have sinned against oneself, and making a new start. Human beings find such letting go terribly difficult. They want vengeance, justice, retribution. Lincoln knew better, and in that knowledge lies much of his greatness.

Critics have claimed that Lincoln's own religion was superstitious, and that much of his motivation in opposing slavery was pragmatic. That does not remove the depth of insight in these passages. Of course, the states did not heed Lincoln's message, and one who could not bear Lincoln's sanity took his life shortly after this speech. But the message continues to sound in Lincoln's solemn cadences, and he was right to tell one who praised it, "I expect the latter [Second Inaugural] to wear as well as—perhaps better than—anything I have produced; but I believe it is not immediately popular. Men are not flattered by being shown that there has been a difference of purpose between the Almighty and them . . . . It is a truth which I thought needed to be told."[13]

Key Terms

Civil Religion: the fusion of culture, politics, and religion that makes it hard to separate who people are and how they defend their existence from their beliefs about ultimate reality. Prior to the American experiment in the separation of church and state, virtually all cultures aspired to a civil religion that would make their faith the soul of their national way of life. In ancient Rome, for example, religion was considered the bond of the Roman way of life, so that failure to acclaim the divinity of the emperor was considered seditious. In traditional China and Japan, it was hard to distinguish between religion and mores. With the disestablishment of religion in the United States, civil religion became less institutional, more nebulous. Scholars have tended to find it operating through holidays such as Thanksgiving and the Fourth of July when American prosperity was interpreted as God's blessing. Patriotism has frequently become so mixed with religion in many parts of American culture that to criticize government policies was tantamount to criticizing divine providence.

Secular: pertaining to the world of space and time, often to the neglect or denial of transcendent divine mystery. Secular culture proposes that work, play, politics, war, love, education, the arts, and other aspects of our common human life do not stretch beyond themselves for their fullest meaning but constitute a realm sufficient unto itself. Secularists tend to neglect such factors as death and injustice, which call the sufficiency of such an outlook radically into question. They also tend to neglect the highest aspirations and intentions of work, art, and love, which can make them ecstatic—occupations that carry people beyond themselves toward the mystery of existence.

Discussion Questions

1. What aspects of their native African religious culture did American slaves tend to retain?
2. Why did blacks respond better to the revivals that followed the Second Great Awakening than they had to the forms of Christianity they had first witnessed?
3. How significant was it to the debates about slavery that the New Testament had told slaves to obey their masters?
4. What were the main Christian arguments against slavery?
5. Why was *Uncle Tom's Cabin* so important to the abolitionist cause?
6. What was the view of blacks enshrined in the majority opinion in the Dred Scott decision?
7. Why did many antiabolitionists charge people like Stephen Douglass with atheism?
8. Explain Sojourner Truth's parable about the weeviled wheat.

9. What implications do you see in Lincoln's 1863 proclamation of a national day of fasting?
10. How realistic was Lincoln's Second Inaugural in speaking of forgiveness and "malice toward none?"

Notes

1. Albert J. Raboteau, "Afro-American Religions: An Overview," *The Encyclopedia of Religion*, vol. 1, ed. Mircea Eliade (New York: Macmillan, 1987), p. 96; and *Slave Religion* (New York: Oxford University Press, 1978).
2. Charles Lyell, "The Relative Merits of Negro and White Labor," in *The Annals of America*, vol. 7 (Chicago: Encyclopedia Britannica, 1976), pp. 516–517.
3. James G. Birney, "The Guilt of the Churches Supporting Slavery," in *The Annals of America*, p. 78.
4. See Barry Lee Eichler, "Slavery," in *Harper's Bible Dictionary*, ed. Paul J. Achtemeier (San Francisco: Harper & Row, 1985), p. 959.
5. See Edward S. Gaustad, ed., *A Documentary History of Religion in America*, vol. 1 (Grand Rapids, MI: Eerdmans, 1982), pp. 477–479.
6. Frank G. Kirkpatrick, "From Shackles to Liberation: Religion, The Grimke Sisters and Dissent," in *Women, Religion and Social Change*, ed. Yvonne Yazbeck Haddad and Ellison Banks Findley (Albany: State University of New York Press, 1985), p. 434.
7. See Gaustad, op. cit., pp. 472–473.
8. Ibid., pp. 474–475.
9. Ibid., pp. 475–477.
10. See Raboteau, "Afro-American Religions," pp. 97–98.
11. See Gaustad, p. 523.
12. Abraham Lincoln, "Second Inaugural Address," in *The Annals of America*, vol. 9 (Chicago: Encyclopedia Britannica, 1976), p. 556.
13. Ibid., p. 555.

7

The Era of Immigration

New Catholics

The century from 1820 to 1920 forever changed the character of the American people. Colonists, and then citizens, of non-English, non-Protestant stock were proportionately very few prior to 1820. That situation altered drastically after 1820, as floods of immigrants swelled the nation's population. A solid estimate is that over 33 million immigrants entered the country between 1820 and 1920. Their coming ended any possibility of changing the American option for nonestablished religion. Each new group further distanced the country from what in retrospect seemed the relatively homogeneous blend of ethnicity and religion that had prevailed before 1820. Both Catholics and Jews greatly multiplied their numbers, laying the foundations for a much more significant participation in American public life. Eastern Orthodox Christians and Asians also began to establish noteworthy communities.

At least ten ethnically different groups of Roman Catholics arrived during the century of immigration. All these people's native patrimony was an inseparate blend of religion and culture. Each group therefore had to face a radically new religious situation in pluralistic America. However much they might try to stay

The Great Depression hit hard at immigrants, who were mainly laborers and domestic servants. For most of these people, the Depression became psychological, compounding their sense of being second-class citizens. (20 South Street, Reginald Marsh; The Nelson-Atkins Museum of Art, Kansas City, Missouri [Gift of the Friends of Art])

in their own ghettoes and reproduce old-country ways, the Irish, the Italians, and all the other immigrant Catholic communities soon realized that their children and grandchildren would be both religiously and ethnically different from themselves. The flood of immigrants led the Catholic church as a whole to try to mediate a balanced entry of its people into the American mainstream—one that would make them full participants in the benefits of American prosperity while helping them retain their Catholic heritage. The ethnic diversity of Catholic faith became increasingly clear as the different groups realized (not without some tensions) that their faith was not homogeneous.

The Irish were the first Catholic immigrants to arrive in significant numbers (more than 260,000 between 1820 and 1840). However, the flood years were 1846–1851, when blight hit the potato crop and caused famine in Ireland. In that six-year period over 1 million people left Ireland, and more of them ended up in the United States than anyplace else. Between 1820 and 1920 about 4.3 million Irish became Americans; a large majority of them were Catholics. Because they were the first wave of Catholic immigrants, and also because most of them spoke English as their first or only language (Gaelic having declined steadily throughout the English occupation of Ireland), the Irish became the leaders of the American Catholic church, furnishing most of its bishops.

The Germans were the only other Catholic group to immigrate in significant numbers before the Civil War. About 1.5 million Germans entered the country before 1860, and another 3.5 million came between 1860 and 1900. A rough estimate places the Catholics at about 30 percent of the immigrant German population, so Catholics counted about 1.65 million immigrants by 1920. Where most of the Irish had been laborers and farm hands, many of the Germans were from the middle class. The **Kulturkampf** waged in Germany during the 1870s brought persecution to Catholicism, leading large numbers of nuns and priests to emigrate to the United States. The first German Catholic parish had been organized in Philadelphia in 1787, but by the end of the 19th century the main German Catholic presence was in the American Midwest.

The Italians did not enter the United States in large numbers until the last two decades of the 19th century, when about 1 million came. Between 1900 and 1920, however, over 3 million more arrived. The main reason was overpopulation in Italy, especially in the south. The typical pattern was for Italian males to come alone and later bring their families or fiancées. Many came with the idea of returning home as soon as they had made some money, and of the approximately 3.8 million Italians who came to the United States between 1899 and 1924, about 2.1 million did return to Italy.

Like the Italians Polish immigrants did not arrive in any great numbers before 1880. One estimate places the number of Poles in the United States in 1870 at only 50,000. By 1920, however, more than 2 million Poles had arrived, the vast majority of them Roman Catholics. They came from Germany, Austria, and Russia (Poland having been parceled out among various European powers), mainly for economic reasons: lack of land and opportunity in Europe.

Most newcomers were from the lower classes, men predominated over women, and perhaps 60 percent of them were unmarried.

French Canadians began immigrating after the American Civil War, and their numbers peaked in the last decades of the 19th century. By 1910 they numbered close to 1 million. As with all the other groups, they saw the United States as a land of economic opportunity.

In the American Southwest, following the Mexican-American War (1846–1848), about 80,000 people of Mexican heritage became residents of the United States through annexation of previously Mexican territory. Perhaps 60,000 of these people lived in what is now New Mexico. Immigration across the Mexican border was slow until the first decades of the 20th century, when over 200,000 Mexicans came. By 1916 about 550,000 Catholics belonged to Spanish-speaking parishes.

These six groups accounted for approximately 75 percent of the American Catholic population in 1916, when a religious census estimated the Catholic population at about 15.7 million. The remainder of the Catholic population came mainly from eastern European groups: Slovaks (about 400,000 Catholics immigrating between 1880 and 1920), Czechs or Bohemians (perhaps 300,000 Catholics coming prior to World War I, although many were indifferent to religion), Lithuanians (about 300,000 Catholics between 1870 and 1920), and Ukranians or Ruthenians (about 250,000 Catholics immigrating between 1880 and 1914, to make a total Catholic Ukranian population of about 500,000 in 1916).[1]

The American Catholic church responded heroically to the great challenge of caring for such a flood of new members. Often the church was the immigrants' major social and cultural as well as religious resource. Nuns especially did magnificent work in education and nursing.[2] The Vatican showed a special interest in the fate of Italian emigrants to America, sponsoring a corps of priests to serve them.[3] Still the Italians were but one of 28 language groups needing services from the church in 1920.

In 1905 a Hungarian bishop, Peter Vay, visited fellow countrymen in Chicago to consecrate a new church. As he described the experience,

> The workmen and their families awaited me at the entrance of the building. For the greatest part they were still dressed in their simple costume "from over the sea," and their whole demeanour showed that they had not long since arrived in these parts. Set adrift in that great city, without knowing the language, without friends or anyone to advise them, these poor folks are at the mercy of chance. And, in addition to all the other difficulties and problems which the municipal authorities have to face, we can well understand that this question of dealing with the foreign population of inferior civilisation is one of the greatest and hardest to solve. They have not only to be fed, they have also to be protected and educated. As long as the people will go to church and are willing to have their children brought up on religious principles there is nothing to fear. As long as they recognize their duty towards God they will also recognize and fulfill their duty towards their neighbour.[4]

Modern readers may blanche at Vay's term *inferior civilization*, but it probably reflected the way the municipal authorities felt about most of the new ethnic groups posing them so many problems. Vay is also typical of church leaders in thinking that if the newcomers could be helped to hold onto their faith, things eventually would turn out fine. Hard as conditions might be in their new home, the immigrants had opportunities the Old World could not match. If **nativism** and **know-nothingism** made life difficult for Catholic newcomers, those were simply bigotries that would have to be borne.[5] If their antagonistic neighbors seized on the untruths of sensationalists such as Maria Monk (an ex-nun who reported scandals in the convent), this, too, would just have to be borne. In time Catholics could show they were as good Americans as any other group, giving their blood in war and their sweat in the factories that made the nation grow.

New Jews

The Jewish population in the New World began modestly, although Luis de Torres, an interpreter traveling with Columbus, was a former Jew who had been baptized the day before Columbus' expedition set out. **Marranos** from the Iberian peninsula were quick to realize that the New World might offer them a wider range of action, and some accompanied Cortés in his invasion of Mexico. However, the **Inquisition** that had persecuted Jews in the Old World quickly reached its tentacles into New Spain, burning two Marranos as heretics in Mexico in 1528.

But Spanish and Portuguese Marranos continued to sail to the New World, and by the end of the 16th century they had settled in Central and South America in considerable numbers. There they secretly kept many of their Jewish ways and on the whole prospered. In keeping with the swing of rule in 17th century Brazil—from Portuguese to Dutch and then back to Portuguese sovereignty—Brazilian Marranos first lived cautiously, then openly declared themselves Jews, and then found their communities scattered. Many went to the Caribbean, where the Dutch and English ruled, and in 1654 a group set out for New Amsterdam, which was destined to become New York.

About the same time a group of Jewish settlers reached Newport, Rhode Island, and Jews also appeared sporadically at other English colonies. The majority were **Sephardim,** but soon **Ashkenazim** arrived from Amsterdam and London. Before the Revolution half a dozen Jewish communities existed in the British colonies, including one group in Montreal, and the total Jewish population was something like 2000. Jews experienced much more civil freedom and equality than had been the case in Europe, and such landmarks of religious liberty as the Virginia Bill of 1785 established Jewish emancipation from special restrictions for the first time in history. To the end of the 18th century immigration remain slow but steady, and the Ashkenazim had gained sufficient numbers to establish their first congregation in Philadelphia in 1795.

By 1900 there were perhaps 1.1 million Jews in the United States, out of a total population of about 76 million. In the first two-thirds of the 19th century perhaps 200,000 had arrived, most of them Ashkenazim from Germany who were fleeing persecution or seeking better economic opportunities. Largely due to the new sense of freedom they felt, the Reform movement that had begun in Europe flourished among them. Rabbi Isaac Mayer Wise of Cincinnati was the leading American figure in this movement. The first Reform synagogue was founded in 1825, and by 1880 all but 8 of the roughly 200 major Jewish synagogues were Reform. Jews fought on both sides during the Civil War, at which time their number was perhaps 150,000. The great period of Jewish immigration occurred soon after the Civil War. Persecution in Russia during the 1880s forced many to flee, and between 1881 and 1929 more than 2.3 million Jews arrived in the United States.

The arrival of so many immigrants from Russia and Eastern Europe complicated the life of the Jewish community. The first wave of newcomers had been largely Germans who felt quite emancipated from strict adherence to religious laws and favored the liberal outlook of the Reform movement. Reform theology stressed ethics and humanitarian values, in preference to the legal and mystical emphases of traditional **talmudic** Judaism, and Reform eased the accommodation of Jews to the pluralistic American way of life. The German community prospered in business and felt it was negotiating quite well the task of remaining Jewish while becoming American. The eastern European immigrants who arrived around the turn of the century were highly suspicious of such an accommodation. They preferred to establish their own, rather closed communities, where they might continue the ways they had long been used to in the old country. Thus they usually continued to speak Yiddish, wear sidelocks, keep the dietary and Sabbath laws, revere talmudic scholars as the guides for community life, and view interactions with Gentiles as disturbing if not defiling.[6]

Soon tensions arose between the Orthodox, as the traditionalists came to be called, and the Reformed, as well as between religious Jews of both stripes and the significant number of Jews who had become secularized—nonobserving and sometimes nonbelieving. The following incident from a Jewish adolescence lived in the mid-20th century suggests the personal pains such tensions between highly observant and more secularized Jews could produce.

We were all Jews at Camp Winsoki, most of us fleeing the heat and concrete of New York City, but among Jews who prayed three times each day and observed the Sabbath scrupulously and studied Torah and Talmud and Gemarrah after softball and basketball games, I felt ignorant and inadequate and impure, an outcast and a reject.

One summer, I fell in love with a wonderfully intelligent and beautiful dark-haired girl . . . and though I felt confident that she liked me as much as I liked her, I was tentative in my approaches to her, afraid to risk ruining a precious friendship by letting her know how I *really* felt. At socials, which took place in the canteen after the evening activity, I danced with her often, holding her as close as possible, loving the feel of her warm cheek next to mine, closing my eyes when her thumb would gently rub the back of my hand or her fingers would grace my neck. . . . Walking her back to her bunk one night in July, I ached too much not to take a chance and do what I had been longing to do—to kiss her, to tell her how much I liked her. But when I leaned toward her, she pushed me back firmly, and looked down, embarrassed. She liked me *very* much, she said—she wanted me to know that, and she didn't want to hurt my feelings—but, given where I came from, she just couldn't allow herself to become involved with me, no matter what she felt. Would I forgive her?

. . . What did she mean when she talked about where I came from? But of course I knew exactly what she meant and, her large brown eyes watering, she put my knowledge into words: it was just that her family would not approve of her going out with a boy who went to a public high school. "It's just"—she said—"it's that you're not Jewish enough for me."[7]

The pathos in this incident perhaps was sharper than what most American Jewish youth had experienced 50 years earlier, but only because 50 years earlier there would have been no contact at all between highly observant and more secularized Jews. Intellectually the battles were probably fiercer, traditionalists seeing Reform Jews and secularists as betrayers of what had preserved the Chosen People for over 2000 years and modernists charging the traditionalists with myth, superstition, and backwardness. The wonder, perhaps, is that so many secularists stayed as loyal to Jewish ethnicity as they did, refusing to let anyone inside or outside the Jewish community declare them non-Jews.

By the middle of the 20th century there were more than 5 million American Jews, and New York, with more than 2 million, was the greatest Jewish urban center the world had ever known. With the birth of the modern state of Israel in 1948, American Jews became the great financial support of the **Zionist** dream-become-reality. Whatever their tensions and differences of opinion, virtually all were thrilled that the people threatened with extinction in the Holocaust now had a state to call their own. Since 1948 the story of American Jews and Israelis has been intimately linked, and if such linkage has sometimes complicated the already difficult task of being both Jewish and American, it has also enriched it, giving many American Jews a very concrete reason to be proud of their roots and their biblical heritage.

Eastern Orthodox Christians

Prior to 1054, when eastern (Greek) and western (Roman) Christianity separated, the Catholic Church had suffered relatively few differences in doctrinal outlook. Certainly major heresies had come and gone, but East and West were equally concerned about orthodoxy and so equally repudiated **Gnosticism, Arianism,** and other threats to what the early church councils had declared to be traditional faith. Nonetheless the two realms of Christendom had developed two different religious styles, due to the two different cultures with which they were involved. The Eastern style assumed an emperor who had rights and responsibilities in the church, in contrast to the Western style that assumed a pope at the head of the religious realm and an emperor at the head of the civil order. For church administration, the East favored a collegial arrangement of bishops, while the West sought a hierarchical subordination of bishops to the pope. Eastern spirituality concentrated less on sin and more on the divine life conferred by grace. It pictured Christ as the Pantocrator, the "ruler of all" (everything in the cosmos). The Eastern liturgy grew to be a resplendent service of praise to this Pantocrator. Eastern spirituality also was markedly **trinitarian** and loved to honor Mary the Mother of God. Only monks could become bishops in the Eastern church, so the official spirituality was quite monastic, stressing asceticism. The heroes of the Eastern church were the great ascetics, who had learned how to pray to God constantly and cared nothing for the world.

Toward the end of the first millennium Eastern missionaries had established Christianity in eastern Europe and Russia, so when the Turks conquered Constantinople in 1453, the center of Eastern Orthodoxy shifted to Russia. Moscow came to think of itself as the third Rome, and Greek traditions were fully rooted in Russian culture. The first Eastern Orthodox priests on what is now American soil worked in Alaska when that area still belonged to Russia. After the sale of Alaska to the United States in 1867, the mission spread to other parts of the United States. In 1872 the center of the American Orthodox diocese shifted to San Francisco, and in 1905 it shifted again to New York. This diocese included all Orthodox Christians, Greeks as well as Russians.

The immigrations of the late 19th century brought to the United States members of Orthodox churches from what had been parts of the Austro-Hungarian empire (Galicia and Carpatho-Russia), as well as from Russia, the Ukraine, Greece, Serbia, Albania, Romania, Bulgaria, and Syria. All of these people theoretically were under the care of the one diocese, which in 1905 petitioned to become an autonomous church with the title "The American Church to the Holy Synod of St. Petersburg." However, the revolution of 1917 threw church-state relations in Russia into turmoil. By 1924 the original diocese had severed relations with Moscow and proclaimed itself independent. The crisis had come with a demand that the American Church declare itself loyal to the Soviet government, which it refused to do.

Meanwhile the non-Russian groups that had been under the jurisdiction of the original diocese centered in New York tended to go their own ways, establishing their own ethnic churches. Thus in 1922 Greek Orthodox Christians established their own diocese, which was related to the patriarch of Constantinople. Subsequently Rumanian, Albanian, Bulgarian, Mexican, Syrian, and other groups reworked their ecclesiastical affiliations. Presently the Russian, Greek, and Syrian-Lebanese Christians are the major American groups, the latter being affiliated with the patriarch of Antioch.

In 1986 the Orthodox Church in America, which embraces the Russian, Bulgarian, Albanian, and Mexican groups, numbered about 1 million adherents. It sponsors St. Vladimir's Seminary in New York, which not only prepares men for the priesthood but also runs a press that is a major outlet for Orthodox theology. The Orthodox Church in America also runs a seminary for training native Alaskan clergy and is a member of both the World Council of Churches and the National Council of Churches in the United States. About 400 parishes in the United States belong to this church; most of them use English in their worship services.

The Greek, Ukranian, Armenian, Coptic and other Orthodox Christian groups in the United States have ties with the historic centers of their people, but the Orthodox tradition of relative autonomy for local churches has allowed them to adapt to American ways. Their numbers vary greatly. In 1986 estimates placed Albanian Orthodox Christians in the United States at about 5,250, Carpatho-Russians at about 100,000, those affiliated with Antioch at about 300,000, the Orthodox Church in America (Russian) at about 1 million, and members of the Greek Orthodox Archdiocese of North and South America at nearly 2 million. The total Orthodox Christian membership in the United States currently is over 3 million and numbers about 1600 churches.[8]

For most American Orthodox people, the local church has been the cultural as well as the religious center of their lives. True to the traditions of the old country, where religion and culture had blended for hundreds of years, people did not know how to separate their faith from their ethnicity. Immigrant communities such as those of Greek Americans maintained close ties with their homeland whenever they could, and often people from the same area in the old country would emigrate to the same city in the United States. Thus in Wichita, Kansas, there are two Lebanese churches basically composed of people from two different towns in Lebanon. Obviously Orthodox people from areas behind the Iron Curtain have had more problems retaining ties with their native towns, but even Russians, Rumanians, Armenians, Bulgarians, Ukranians, and others have usually tried to keep some contact.

Nonetheless, as the first generation of immigrants has given way to second and third generations born in the United States, the Orthodox churches have had to struggle with the same problems of assimilation that Catholics, Jews, and Asian groups have faced. For example, what happens to the Greek community when young people go to public schools, mingle mainly with non-Greeks in business, and, above all, marry non-Greeks? The rise of Michael Dukakis to political prominence during the campaigns of 1988 offered an intriguing case study. Born of immigrant parents who ran a restaurant, Dukakis attended the originally Quaker Swarthmore College, married a Jewish woman, and continued to give his religious affiliation as Greek Orthodox. Fellow Greeks were an important part of his political organization, and his candidacy aroused great pride and interest not only in the Greek-American community but also in Greece itself. Thus newspapers in Athens followed his progress, considering it a major story.

As Irish-Americans who have returned to Ireland, Italian-Americans who have returned to Italy, and other recently Americanized ethnic groups have realized, the immigrations of the 19th century gave the United States a unique image around the world. So many different lands had sent people here that the word *America* was on the lips of millions of people who knew little English and had only the vaguest sense of American history or geography. That a son, a sister, or a cousin had gone to New York, Chi-

cago, or Atlanta was enough to focus interest on things American. It is another story to consider what the United States has made of this fund of good will, especially in its dealings with the Communist countries from which so many Orthodox Americans have come. But we would miss much of the pathos and resonance of the Orthodox story if we did not realize that freedom to worship, as well as freedom to prosper financially, has made many Eastern Christians deeply grateful to their new land, even though their traditional worship services imply strong criticisms of American secularism.

Cardinal Gibbons

James Gibbons (1834–1921) was the Archbishop of Baltimore for more than 40 years and had much to do with the assimilation of immigrant Catholics into the mainstream of American life. Gibbons was ordained a priest at the outbreak of the Civil War and spent the war serving as a chaplain to troops in the military hospitals of Baltimore. He was made a bishop in 1868 and assigned to North Carolina, which was missionary territory for Catholics. Gibbons attended the First Vatican Council in Rome (1869–1870), at which the doctrine of **papal infallibility** was defined. In 1872 he became bishop of Richmond, Virginia, and in 1877 he was moved to Baltimore and became archbishop of the country's mother diocese.

While working in Richmond, Gibbons realized the need for a clear and simple statement of Roman Catholic faith. To meet this need, he wrote *The Faith of Our Fathers*, published in 1876, which became the standard American work explaining Catholic faith and defending it against misrepresentations and attacks by outsiders. Pope Leo XIII made Gibbons a cardinal in 1886, confirming his status as one of the top leaders of the American Catholic church. Among Gibbons's major achievements was the establishment of the Catholic University of America in Washington, D.C., in 1889.

The last decades of the 19th century brought so many new Catholics to the United States that church leaders such as Gibbons had their hands full trying not only to help the newcomers adjust to American life but also to mediate their conflicts with other Catholics. These conflicts took many forms, but a regular motif was tension between Irish bishops and Catholics of other ethnic backgrounds over church power. The Italians, Polish, Germans and other non-Irish groups tended to want to retain autonomy over their own ethnic parishes. They also regularly wanted to hold their religious services and conduct their religious schools in Italian, Polish, German, or whatever else was their native language. The Irish favored minimizing ethic differences and encouraging all groups to move toward greater use of English. Gibbons generally went along with the Irish majority among the bishops but tried to lessen tensions among the various ethnic groups.

As cardinal archbishop of the diocese that historically had been at the heart of the American Catholic church Gibbons took the lead in representing American interests in Rome. His argument, typical of the majority of American bishops, was that the separation of church and state in America offered the Catholic church a splendid opportunity to grow. Gibbons and other leading American bishops were confident that the circumstances of free competition would work to the benefit of Catholicism, despite the anti-Catholic sentiments that broke out from time to time and the need for tactful dealings with both the government and other religious groups. Roman authorities reasoned differently; they thought that when Catholics were in the majority in a population Catholicism ought to be the established religion. They expected religious freedom for Catholics when they were in the minority, but their sense that only Catholicism was the true faith and church made

them reluctant either to grant full religious freedom to non-Catholic minority groups in Catholic lands or to countenance much contact between Catholics and Protestants.

Related to this difference of outlook was the desire of American church leaders to appoint their own bishops, make their own decisions, and so forth. Although the First Vatican Council had consolidated the primacy of the Bishop of Rome at the head of the Church, the question of how much autonomy the bishops of individual countries could have remained a matter for debate. In 1899 the American cause received a setback when Pope Leo XIII's encyclical *Testem Benevolentiae* criticized ideas supposed to be turning the Americans away from sound doctrine:

> Involved were such notions as the demand for relaxation of doctrine if converts were to be attracted in the modern age, depreciation of external spiritual guidance and increased reliance on direct inspiration, emphasis on active rather than passive virtues, and a lack of regard for the traditional vows taken in religious communities. The encyclical met with a predictably mixed reaction. No American bishop contested it . . . . William Halsey's comment comes [close to] the mark: they "were accused of heresy for espousing the activist individualism, self-confident mystique and optimistic idealism of American civilization."[9]

Despite this setback, Gibbons's overall effectiveness in representing the American church in Rome was noteworthy. For example, in 1887, while in Rome to receive the red hat that officially made him a cardinal, Gibbons took up the cause of the American labor movement. At the request of Archbishop Taschereau of Quebec, the Vatican had issued a ruling in 1884 that forbade Catholics to join the Knights of Labor, a forerunner of the unions that would arise later. Gibbons realized that most of the American Catholic church membership belonged to the working class and that often their working conditions and wages were oppressive and unjust.

The mines and factories that powered the rise of the United States to economic prosperity depended on the cheap labor largely supplied by immigrants from Europe. (*The Miner,* George Benjamin Luks. National Gallery of Art, Washington, D.C.; Chester Dale Collection)

Arguing for the right of workers to organize themselves and so better secure their own interests, Gibbons told Roman church officials that they were mistaken if they thought the struggle of the masses against the "mail-clad power" that often refused them their basic rights could advance without working people's organizing. Were the church to condemn the labor movement (which it feared because of the ties between labor and Communism in Europe), it would estrange the working class, turn public opinion against Catholicism, and cause a severe drop in church revenues.[10] Within two years the Vatican had lifted the ban.

On the home front, Gibbons faced the challenge of anti-Catholic feeling by arguing that Catholics of course could be, and wanted to be, loyal American citizens. American pluralism, as he understood it, kept particular religious views sufficiently apart from politics that the charges of critics that Catholics' loyalty to the pope made them untrustworthy were nonsense. In 1909 he noted that two synods of Protestant ministers had proclaimed that Catholics could not be trusted with political office. The ministers had further claimed that Catholics were kept ignorant of the church's true teachings and that they themselves were bringing these charges not out of religious antagonism but solely out of patriotism. Gibbons responded by noting that such charges had drawn little response and apparently had little support in the nation at large. He pointed to the illogic of arguing that Catholics could not uphold the Constitution when the Constitution itself said "no religious test shall ever be required as a qualification to any office or public trust under the United States." The Lutheran and Baptist synods would have had to amend the Constitution to make their views carry.

Gibbons went on to defend religious liberty in the sense detailed in the First Amendment and to rejoice that the nonsupport for the ministers' position suggested that the bigotries of the Know-Nothing days, when religious antag-

onism had flared into violence, seemed long gone. He made plain what he felt was the great loyalty of Catholic Americans to the principles of religious liberty and good citizenship, and he pledged that Catholicism would continue to be a bulwark of the moral virtues necessary for the nation's prosperity. The cardinal's clear, forceful style was very effective, and the two synods came away looking shabby on both religious and patriotic grounds. The fact that President William Howard Taft led the celebration for the golden jubilee of Gibbons's ordination in 1911, seemed to put the stamp of approval on American Catholicism.

The Pittsburgh Platform of Reform Judaism

Reform Judaism was the first of the reinterpretations of Judaism occasioned by the emancipation from special political and cultural restrictions that came to European Jews in the wake of the Enlightenment. The implications of Reform have varied from country to country, but certain common principles have obtained, including the view that change is legitimate in Judaism and the denial that any traditional formulation of Jewish belief or codification of Jewish law is eternal. Thus Reform Judaism has thought it proper, indeed desirable, to adapt and update Jewish traditions so that they might better serve Jews living in nontraditional circumstances. The stimulus to Reform was the advent of modernity to Europe in the form of new scientific and humanistic views.

The first proponents of Reform Judaism, working in the first decades of the 19th century, were laypeople concerned about the wholesale defections of Jews from the community because of the new opportunities emancipation gave Jews in European society. These first reformers focused on updating Jewish worship, adapting it to Western standards of aesthetics and decorum, in the hope that it would seem less foreign or antiquated. A generation later a group of rabbis who had studied at European universities as well as traditional Jewish schools took up the leadership of Reform. Having imbibed the critical historical and literary methods being used in the universities, they wanted to rethink Jewish worship and interpretation of scripture. Their ideological goal was a Judaism open to free, critical inquiry and not closed in on itself by dogmatic adherence to traditional teachings and methods. Meetings in Germany in the 1840s brought these rabbis together and made Reform a recognizable intellectual movement. Reform was eventually polarized between the views of Abraham Geiger, who valued tradition highly and thought of Reform as an evolution in keeping with the developmental character of Judaism throughout history, and the views of Samuel Holdheim, who thought of Reform as revolutionary. Holdheim thought that with the destruction of the Temple and Jewish state in 70 C.E. only the specifically religious aspects of Judaism—its monotheism and ethical tradition—retained their validity. The political and cultic aspects of the Jewish states could go, which amounted to jettisoning the whole of the "ceremonial law" that preoccupied rabbinic Judaism. The American branch of Reform Judaism tended to follow Holdheim, while most of Germany followed Geiger and tended to think of itself as "liberal Judaism."

Although Rabbi Isaac M. Wise, who led the development of the Reform movement in the United States, was himself rather moderate, by 1885 the more radical party predominated. Thus the Pittsburgh Platform of 1885 that enunciated the leading tenets of Reform represented a significant break with the rabbinic traditions of 1800 years.

The Pittsburgh Platform had eight main points:

1. Every religion is an attempt to grasp the Infinite, and every mode of revelation expresses the indwelling of God in human beings. Judaism is the highest conception of the idea of God, as taught by Scripture and the Jewish teachers in accordance with the development of their respective historical ages. Through all its struggles and trials, Judaism has preserved for humanity the idea of God as the central religious truth.

2. Although the Bible contains the record of the consecration of the Jewish people and is valuable for its religious and moral instruction, modern science is not antagonistic to the doctrines of Judaism, since the Bible clothed its (primitive) ideas in the (miraculous) terms of its own age.

3. "We recognize in the Mosaic legislation a system of training the Jewish people for its mission during its national life in Palestine, and today we accept as binding only the moral laws, and maintain only such ceremonies as elevate and sanctify our lives, but reject all such as are not adapted to the views and habits of modern civilization."[11]

4. The Mosaic and rabbinical laws regulating diet, priestly purity, and dress, because they originated in a distant time and fail to impress modern Jews, are more likely to obstruct than to further modern spiritual development.

5. Jews are a religious community rather than a nation and they have no expectation of a return to Palestine or the reestablishment of a sacrificial worship and a Jewish state.

6. Judaism is a progressive religion striving to be compatible with reason. Christianity and Islam are daughter religions of Judaism and have a providential role in spreading both monotheism and moral truth. Modern humanism is also an ally, inasmuch as it works for a reign of truth and righteousness.

7. The human soul, "which forever finds bliss in righteousness and misery in wickedness," is immortal but there are no bodily resurrection or Gehenna/Eden [Hell/Heaven] as places of everlasting punishment or reward.

8. It is the duty of Jews to participate in the great task of modern times, which is to remove social evils on the basis of justice and righteousness, in the spirit of the Mosaic legislation about the relations between rich and poor.

The Pittsburgh Platform broke with traditional Judaism in ways that may not be clear to the general reader. Traditional rabbinic Judaism had distinguished quite sharply between Jewish and gentile religion, keeping a place in God's affection for righteous Gentiles but not viewing other religions as positively as the platform did. The talmudic tradition might have agreed that monotheism was the key, but it gave much greater importance to the Mosaic legislation, as elaborated by the rabbis through the centuries, and it did not take the platform's progressive or evolutionary view of Jewish faith. For most of traditional Judaism the principles of faith could not change. They could only be reinterpreted, and the laws regarding worship and Jewish civil life could not be excised from the traditional core as the platform wished. Judaism was more than just a monotheism with an ethical program. Its cultic laws and aspirations for a full national life as a religious state were part of its essence.

Reform Judaism, therefore, is another instance of a religious people's struggle to come to terms with modernity. Certainly the conditions in Germany in the 19th century had stimulated this struggle, but Jews in the United States found conditions even more conducive to questioning how they ought to adapt their traditional ways. The breadth of opportunities afforded by a pluralistic culture in which Christianity theoretically had no special legal standing put pressure on Jews to rethink how they ought to live and present themselves. The German Jews who comprised the bulk of the first immigrant generations were primed by the movements in their homeland to consider the

Reform movement their answer. The eastern European immigrants who came at the end of the 19th century had stronger roots in the talmudic traditions and so were less attracted to Reform ideas about adaptation.

Key Terms

Arianism: a Christian heresy advanced by Arius of Alexandria in the fourth century. The Arians believed that the Logos (divine word) was not equal to the Father in possessing the divine nature but that "there was a time when he was not." The Council of Nicaea agreed with Athanasius of Alexandria that the Arian position violated traditional faith in the full divinity of Christ, the Logos incarnate, and so imperiled salvation.

Ashkenazim: The term has come to designate Jews of northern European origin, in contrast to the Sephardim, who originated in southern Europe (Iberia). Originally, however, it meant "German," and designated any of the Jews who lived in the Rhineland Valley or neighboring France before the Christian Crusades of the 11th to 13th centuries prompted them to move east into Slavic lands. Persecutions in eastern Europe in the 17th century caused many Ashkenazim to move back to western Europe. Eventually all Jews who adopted the synagogue ritual favored by this tradition were regarded as Ashkenazim. Until very recently most Ashkenazim used Yiddish as their common language, and today they account for about 80 percent of world Jewry.

Gnosticism: a generic name for views of salvation that contested with orthodox Christianity in the first through third centuries. The Gnostics got their name from the Greek word *gnosis* (knowledge). They claimed to possess secret knowledge that was the key to salvation. Generally this knowledge bore on how humanity had fallen into its current state of distance from God and debts to the flesh. The Gnostics tended to despise the flesh, sexuality, and marriage and either urge an extreme asceticism or allow licentious behavior because they considered fleshly matters insignificant. Some Gnostic groups gave women more authority than was possible in orthodox Christianity, and the Gnostic inclination to prize secret doctrines that would guarantee salvation continued in transmuted form throughout later Western history.

Inquisition: a papal commission charged with combatting heresy and religious deviance. Medieval and reform movements in the 11th and 12th centuries, especially the heretics known as the Cathari and Waldenses, moved Pope Gregory IX to institute the Inquisition in 1231. The commission was charged with seeking out heretics and punishing them. By 1252 the papacy had authorized the use of torture and death for convicted heretics who refused to recant. The Spanish Inquisition arose in 1478, after the reconquest of Spain from the Muslims, to purify Spain of lingering Muslim and Jewish influences. The Spanish government found the very severe policies of the Spanish Inquisition politically useful and resisted papal efforts to moderate the Spanish inquisitors. The first Grand Inquisitor, Tomas de Torquemada, used torture, had more than 2000 heretics burned at the stake, and made the auto-da-fé (the public ceremony at which sentences were pronounced) a major celebration.

Know-nothingism: an American political movement that flourished in the mid-1800s. It was a reaction to the waves of immigrants that were changing the character of the American population and soon gained an anti-Catholic edge. Know-nothingism centered in the East and mainly enlisted Protestants competing with the arriving Germans and Irish for jobs and political power. The movement got its name from the tendency of members to respond to questions about their organization by saying they knew nothing. Eventually they formed the American Party as a national political entity. Its goals included restrictions on immigration, the exclusion of the foreign-born from voting rights and holding public office, and a 21-year residency requirement for citizenship. By the 1855 Congress, the Know-Nothings had 43 seats in the House of Representatives. However, divisions over slavery prior to the Civil War split the party and thereafter its influence was small.

Kulturkampf: a German word meaning "struggle for civilization." The word represented the efforts of the German Chancellor Otto von Bismarck to subject Roman Catholicism to state controls during the 1870s. By 1873 those advocating such controls were trying to glorify their measures as a valiant battle on behalf of humanistic values. Bismarck's own Protestantism made him suspicious of Catholicism, and after the definition of papal infallibility at the First Vatican Council in 1870 he moved from suspicion to alarm. In 1871 he abolished the Catholic bureau in the Prussian ministry and forbade priests to speak about politics from the pulpit. In 1872 he made all religious schools subject to state inspection, excluded all religious teachers from the state schools, dissolved the Jesuit order in Germany, and severed diplomatic ties with the Vatican. Catholics resisted, and by 1887 things were back to normal, but these religious oppressions, along with economic considerations, stimulated many German Catholics to emigrate.

Marranos: Jews who converted to Christianity to escape persecution but continued to practice their Judaism secretly. The term is Spanish, of uncertain origin, and arose in the 14th century. Originally it was a term of abuse used by Christian detractors and applied to the descendants of those who originally had converted, to cast aspersions on their faith. Estimates are that at least 100,000 Spanish Jews converted to save themselves from fanatical Christian neighbors. By the mid-15th century the Marranos were a powerful community in Spain, influential in government, and the target of much wrath. Riots against Marranos in Cordoba in 1473 brought the Inquisition to take charge of the matter, and in 1480 more than 300 Marranos were burned and their property confiscated for the crown. Eventually the number of martyrs reached the tens of thousands. Continued opposition led to the expulsion of all Jews from Spain in 1492, and many went to the New World.

Nativism: the attitude or policy of favoring native inhabitants of a country against immigrants. The rise of this attitude in the mid-19th century in the United States produced the Know-Nothings and the American Party.

Papal infallibility: the Roman Catholic doctrine, defined at the First Vatican Council in 1870, that the pope, when speaking *ex cathedra* (formally, from his chair as official teacher) on matters of faith and morals, is protected by the Holy Spirit from error. The doctrine has generally been interpreted as having quite severe limitations (for example, the pope is expected to consult widely throughout the church) and to flow from the nature of both the Church (looked at as the flawless community of salvation) and the papacy (considered to be the institution unifying the Church). The existence of the doctrine has often been used to justify outsiders' fears that Catholics could not think for themselves and would be bound to follow any dictates of the pope (even those not limited to faith and morals).

Sephardim: Jews who lived in Spain and Portugal during the Middle Ages until their expulsion at the end of the 15th century. Most Sephardim then fled to North Africa and the Muslim world, thinking those areas safer than Christian realms. Eventually, however, they also settled in many other areas, including Holland, England, and Latin America. They differed from the Ashkenazim in preserving Babylonian rather than Palestinian ritual traditions, and in using Ladino rather than Yiddish. Sephardim now number about 4 percent of the worldwide Jewish population, about 750,000.

Talmudic: pertaining to the Talmud, the comprehensive collection of rabbinic teaching. The Talmud collects the Mishnah and the Gemarah (commentary on the Mishnah), which in turn is a collection of teachings, legal opinions, and stories about leading rabbis of the last centuries B.C.E. and the first centuries C.E. The Talmud exists in two main versions (one produced in Babylon and one in Palestine) dating from about 500 C.E. For Jewish theology, it gathers the traditional teachings about the oral law that has always accompanied Scripture. This oral law, which functions much as "tradition" has in Christian theology, goes back to Moses and primarily deals with how to appreciate and apply the Torah first granted on Mount Sinai, which in turn is understood as the blessed law or guidance expressing Israel's special covenant with God.

Trinitarian: pertaining to the Christian doctrine of God as Father-Son-Spirit. This doctrine claims biblical foundations and was clarified during the great Christian councils of the fourth and fifth centuries. The basic formula, "one God in three divine persons," has satisfied the orthodox throughout the centuries, but various groups have dissented, usually either by wanting to subordinate the Son to the Father or by arguing for a nontrinitarian, "unitarian" God. Orthodox theology has considered the Trinity a strict mystery and has structured the Christian liturgy in terms of addressing prayers above all to the Father, depending on the mediation of the Son, and thinking of the Spirit as moving in believers' hearts to raise them toward God.

Zionist: pertaining to a Jewish movement to reestablish a homeland for Jews in Palestine. In one sense Zionism is as old as the first expulsion of the Jews from Israel, during the Babylonian captivity of the sixth century B.C.E. and the Roman expulsions of the first century C.E. However, during the 16th and 17th centuries in Europe several messianic figures urged Jews to return to Palestine, while toward the end of the 19th century Theodor Herzl, an Austrian journalist, inspired a movement to make return a practical venture. A series of Zionist congresses at the turn of the century publicized this ideal, and in the first decades of the 20th century the pogroms in Russia sparked considerable emigration. By 1914 there were about 90,000 Jews in Palestine. The Balfour Declaration of 1917 pledged English support for a Jewish homeland, and Jewish numbers in Palestine steadily increased. The watershed came after the Second World War, when awareness of the Holocaust catalyzed both Jewish and non-Jewish sentiment, leading to the establishment of the modern state of Israel in 1948.

Discussion Questions

1. What were the main reasons for 19th-century Catholic immigration?

2. What were the principal tensions within the Catholic community, and why were Catholics hated by the Know-Nothings?

3. How did the Spanish Inquisition contribute to the arrival of Jews in North America?

4. What were the main differences between the German Jewish immigrants and those who came from eastern Europe?

5. What are the distinctive features of Eastern Orthodox Christianity?

6. Why has the Russian Orthodox Church played such a major role in the story of American Orthodoxy?

7. What were the main worries that Catholic officials in Rome had about American Catholicism?

8. What constitutional bases did Cardinal Gibbons have for arguing against those who questioned the patriotism of American Catholics?

9. What were the main reasons for the rise of Reform Judaism?

10. Evaluate the main propositions of the Pittsburgh Platform 100 years after its issuance.

Notes

1. See Jay P. Dolan, *The American Catholic Experience* (Garden City NY: Doubleday, 1985), pp. 127–135.

2. See Mary Ewens, O.P., "The Leadership of Nuns in Immigrant Catholicism," in *Women & Religion in America,* vol. 1, ed. Rosemary Ruether and Rosemary Keller (San Francisco: Harper & Row, 1981), pp. 101–149.

3. See the plea of Pope Leo XIII on behalf of the Italian immigrants, in John Tracy Ellis, ed., *Documents of American Catholic History,* vol. 2 (Wilmington DE: Michael Glazier, 1987), pp. 466–470.

4. Monsignor Vay de Voya, "Hungarian Immigrants in the United States," in *Documents of American Catholic History,* p. 557.

5. See Barbara Welter, "From Maria Monk to Paul Blanshard: A Century of Protestant Anti-Catholicism," in *Uncivil Religion*, ed. Robert N. Bellah and Frederick E. Greenspahn (New York: Crossroad, 1987), pp. 43–71.

6. See "America," *Encyclopedia Judaica*, vol. 2 (Jerusalem: Keter, 1972), pp. 808–816; R. Laurence Moore, *Religious Outsiders and the Making of Americans* (New York: Oxford University Press, 1986), pp. 72–101.

7. Jay Neugeboren, "A Samaritan at Camp Winsoki," in *Congregation: Contemporary Writers Read the Jewish Bible*, ed. David Rosenberg (New York: Harcourt Brace Jovanovich, 1987), pp. 457–458.

8. Mark S. Hoffman, ed., *The World Almanac 1987* (New York: World Almanac, 1987), p. 337. Other facts and figures come from "Orthodox Church in America," *The New Encyclopaedia Britannica*, vol. 8 (Chicago: Encyclopaedia Britannica, 1987), p. 1016.

9. James Hennessey, S.J., *American Catholics* (New York: Oxford University Press, 1981), pp. 202–203.

10. Dolan, op. cit., pp. 332–333.

11. "Pittsburgh Platform," in *The Encyclopedia Judaica*, vol. 13 (Jerusalem: Keter, 1972), p. 571. See also "Reform Judaism," in *The Encyclopedia Judaica*, vol. 14, pp. 23–28.

From Reconstruction to 1914

Urbanization and the Social Gospel

Although the second half of the 19th century brought into American life tens of millions of immigrants who were not Protestants, the years 1860 to 1900 were a time of great growth for the Protestant churches. The leading American families, whose wealth and influence most shaped national life, by and large were Anglo-Saxon, Scottish, or German Protestants. To many of them hard work and thrift had become the leading evangelical virtues, making wealth seem a rightful blessing from God—part of the "hundredfold" (Matt. 19:29, Mark 10:30) promised to the faithful disciple.

Despite the fact that secularization had taken hold strongly in Europe, American Protestantism continued to hew to a biblical morality, mostly due to the continuing evangelical influence. Throughout the land, revivals and voluntary religious groups fought secularism and kept biblical language and ideas predominant. Methodists, Baptists, Presbyterians, Disciples of Christ, and Congregationalists all united in promoting evangelical piety and ethics. Through a fully developed system of Sunday schools, denominational publications, support for missionary activities, groups that distributed bibles, moral crusades, and evangelical proselytizing, these mainstream Protestant churches largely shaped the general American character. In 1900 there were three times more members listed on Protestant church rolls than there had been in 1860, when the nation was on the brink of civil war. The wounds of the war had not completely healed, so many denominations were split between Southern and Northern branches, but there was much de facto agreement on the priority of biblical piety.

Nonetheless the beginnings of a severe challenge were clear by the last decades of the 19th century. The publication of Charles Darwin's *Origin of Species* in 1859 had given the world its first taste of scientific evolutionary theory. Parallel developments in geology had called into question the biblical picture of the Creation. In Germany a "higher criticism" had begun to subject the Bible to historical and literary analysis, on the assumption that it was as human a work as any other book and so could be investigated by humanistic methods. Thus educated people had several reasons for questioning the rather literal acceptance of the Bible that still prevailed in most popular Protestant churches. When this intellectual challenge joined with the social challenge posed by urbanization and industrialization, the unified world of 19th century mainstream Protestantism threatened to come apart.

That Protestantism had thrived in a small town culture, where people knew one another quite intimately, lived small-scale lives that could be dominated by the local church, and had a keen awareness of who was upholding the regulative mores and who was not. The shift of the patterns of American population from small, rural towns to large cities completely changed the religious situation. As the country neared the year 1900, more people lived in cities than in towns, and Henry Adams, a famous chronicler of the times, could say, "the American boy of 1854 stood nearer the year 1 than to the year 1900."[1]

Urbanization and secularization tended to go hand in hand because in the large, anonymous cities the predominant values seemed to be the pragmatic ones associated with labor and economics. However, religious and ethnic pluralism also were significant forces:

> The church crisis associated with massive urbanization was all the more difficult for Protestants because the new industrial workers crowding the cities were not just moving in from the countryside, but were coming largely from abroad. Most of these, moreover, now were coming from Catholic, and increasingly from non–English-speaking countries. So while between 1860 and 1900 the major Protestant churches tripled in membership (from 5 million to 16 million) the Catholic membership quadrupled (from 3 million to 12 million). Many Protestants saw this steady rise of Catholicism as a major threat to the national welfare. Catholics did not keep the Sabbath, they danced, being Europeans most of them drank, and since they were often poor, they were regarded as a threat to the stability and moral health of the nation generally. Nonetheless, there was little that Protestants could do but learn to live with Catholics, however mutually bitter the rivalries might be. The facts of the matter for Protestants were simple. In a nation with a large Catholic (and other non-Protestant) population, they could not simultaneously claim to believe in democracy and also claim that Protestant ideals and values should always rule. This logic, of course, did not prevent widespread anti-Catholic, anti-Jewish, and anti-"foreign" efforts. Nonetheless Protestants, especially in the cities, were faced with the fact that they would have to live with irreversible religious pluralism.[2]

By 1917 much Protestant theology had been influenced by "the social gospel" as a response to the human suffering caused by urbanization, industrialization, and the plight of the lower classes of poor people whom the dynamics of American society were creating. The term *social gospel* was introduced in a book by the German-American theologian Walter Rauschenbusch (1861–1918). Rauschenbusch was the son of Lutherans who had come to the United States to minister to German immigrants. Working as a Baptist minister in New York City in the 1880s he became well acquainted with the social problems caused by urbanization and was attracted to the social welfare platform proposed by the economist Henry George. With several other Baptist preachers, Rauschenbusch formed the Brotherhood of the Kingdom, a group dedicated to bringing the message of a Christian socialism to the working classes.

Rauschenbusch and his colleagues criticized the prevailing Protestantism of the day as too individualistic. By neglecting the social dimensions of the gospel, mainstream religion was allowing the forces that shaped most people's lives to go untouched by the gospel. As a cure these reformers proposed repentance for society's collective sins of greed, injustice, and carelessness to bring salvation to bear on the social sphere. They wanted theology to become more social minded and society to become more impregnated with evangelical ideas about justice and social responsibility.

The key concept in the theology of the social gospel was the Kingdom of God. Rauschenbusch and his friends understood this concept (which is prominent in the preaching of the **synoptic** Jesus) as the crux of the ethics that Jesus had taught. To their mind it was a collective notion, intending the common good of all people and opposing individualism, capitalism, and militarism (taken as expressions of isolation, greed, and aggression). Traditional theology failed to account for the collective notion of sin and evil and so was unable to provide the help needed by the millions who were suffering under unjust social structures. Seemingly condemned to poverty and second-class status by the going patterns, they cried out for relief. The churches had failed them badly by siding with the wealthy and failing to discourage the individualism and ambition driving the capitalistic system.

Needless to say, the proponents of the social gospel came in for great criticism, much as the proponents of **liberation theology** would nearly 100 years later. Many of the wealthy industrial barons were Protestant benefactors of great generosity—the Rockefellers and Carnegies, for example—and they tended to equate their prosperity with divine Providence or sanction for shrewd business dealing. They did not take well to the prophetic sting of the social gospel and their sympathizers in the churches were not slow to find the weak spots in the reformers' message, such as its assumption of an evolutionary model of human history, some kinship with Communist ideas, and a relative neglect of both personal prayer and the transcendence of divine grace. Nonetheless the proponents of the social gospel now tend to fare quite well in retrospective assessments of what they were trying to accomplish. They are seen as a powerful response to the social miseries created by the changing conditions of late 19th-century American society and as a valid translation of evangelical values into a more social key.

Missionary Idealism

Throughout the 19th century Europeans tended to continue to consider the United States missionary territory. As they sent millions emigrating to the New World, European church bodies regularly sent ministers along to care for the emigrants' religious needs. The religious situation in the United States only confirmed most churches' convictions about this policy, for zealous, aggressive evangelicals tended to draw into their folds Catholic, Lutheran, or Reformed immigrants who did not have a strong church circle of their own.

From the early decades of the 19th century, however, the well-established, English-speaking Protestant denominations had sent missionaries from the United States to labor abroad. By 1911 the Catholic Foreign Mission Society of America, known as Maryknoll, was doing the same. The social disruptions caused by the Civil War dampened the Protestant missionary venture, but by 1900 Baptists, Congregationalists, Disciples of Christ, Episcopalians, and Presbyterians all had significant missionary undertakings. During the Civil War and its aftermath, some of this missionary zeal was directed toward American blacks, who converted to Protestant Christianity in impressive numbers. Baptists and Methodists did the best, and by 1915 the black Protestants in the United States outnumbered all the Protestants in Africa and Asia.

The impetus to Christian missionary activity has no doubt always been complex, but the overriding conscious motive has usually been to spread the good news of Christ about salvation. Thus blacks who became Christians soon desired to send missionaries back to Africa, that they might enrich the land they had been forced to leave and somewhat redeem the horrors of slavery. Foreign missions have regularly had the overtones of a strong church body in a powerful land assuming parental responsibilities and begetting new churches abroad. Perhaps inevitably, the new churches were often considered colonies of the old, parental churches, and equally often the culture of the parental body mingled inextricably with the interpretation of the gospel it offered those it was missionizing. In the past generation missionaries have become highly self-critical and much more modest about their enterprises. Recognizing the evils of colonialism, and the ways that cultural bias can distort the good news of salvation, many missionaries (though not all) now bend over backward to keep their national heritage from misshaping the offer they are making. They work hard to develop native clergy and to help those they are missionizing work out what Christian faith means in their own cultural categories. The

global situation in which countries are mutually dependent and mutually aware of the limitations in any single culture has not taken away the impulse toward missionary activity, but it has made most churches more thoughtful.

In the 19th and early 20th centuries enthusiasm and confidence ran high. American culture as a whole was developing a self-confident attitude, and many religious leaders shared this spirit. After the Civil War, when Reconstruction seemed well under way, such diverse religious leaders as Rabbi Isaac M. Wise, Henry Ward Beecher, William Lawrence, and Washington Gladden all projected a grand future for the United States, confident that hard work would bring it both bounty and world leadership.[3] The individualistic ethic that the proponents of the social gospel would criticize a decade later was coming into full bloom, as the great industrial families made their huge fortunes in coal, railroads, banking, and the other enterprises that flourished from the mating of vast natural resources and cheap immigrant labor.

Thus missionaries tended to think they had a twofold gift to bestow. In addition to the power of the gospel to effect salvation they had the model of a Christian nation turning gospel values (translated into thrift and hard work) into material and cultural prosperity. Not all the missionaries were so uncritical, of course, but the self-confidence of the growing nation gave them much of the energy needed to set out to do good in foreign lands.

John R. Mott (1865–1955) was a leading representative of the American Protestant missionary movement. Born in New York, Mott was a Methodist layman who became deeply involved in international missions and church life through his work with the Young Men's Christian Association. In 1888 Mott had become student secretary of the International Committee of the YMCA, and he held that post until 1915. In 1895 he created the World's Student Christian

To native Americans of the West after the Civil War the locomotive symbolized both the amazing power of the whites and the destruction of traditional ways of life threatened by white culture. In this painting, a locomotive emerges on the far left of the horizon. (Advent of the Locomotive in Oregon, A. J. Miller; Gilcrease Museum, Tulsa, Oklahoma)

Federation, and he helped organize the World Missionary Conference held in Edinburgh in 1910, a meeting that many observers consider the beginning of the 20th century ecumenical movement that led to the formation of the World Council of Churches in 1948 and influenced the Second Vatican Council of 1962–1965. Mott served as chairman of the Student Volunteer Movement for Foreign Missions from 1915 to 1928 and of the International Missionary Council from 1921 to 1942. He was also president of the World's Alliance of YMCAs from 1926 to 1937. The peak of his career came in 1946 when his work for the international church and missionary movements brought him a share of the Nobel Prize for Peace.

In a book published in 1900 by the Student Volunteer Movement for Foreign Missions, Mott gave expression to his dream of evangelizing the whole world. The United States was becoming something of an empire, extending its influence throughout the world, and Mott wanted the Protestant ethos of the United States to embark on a similarly global career. He could already point to the fruits of the Student Volunteer Movement for Foreign Missions, which was enthroning Christ as king in both Northern and Southern hemispheres, both Orient and Occident, among all nations and races. Several countries were furnishing the students for this movement: the United States, Canada, Great Britain, and Ireland. The students were showing a holy impatience about the work, hoping to evangelize the whole world in their generation.

Reflecting on the basic task, which was to spread the word about Christ, Mott goes on to describe the manifold ways students were accomplishing it: in sermons and addresses in mission halls; in discussions in bazaars, street chapels, and inns; in house-to-house visits; in joining people at their festivals; in teaching Christian doctrine in schools; in circulating the Scriptures and Christian literature; in ministering to the sick; and in giving good example. "In all these and in other ways the Christian worker by voice and life, by pen and by printed page, in season and out of season, seeks to set forth those facts about Christ which in all lands have been found to be the power of God unto the salvation of every man that believeth."[4]

Two things stand out from this sample of John R. Mott's writing and career:

1. His writing translates rather standard evangelical views into an international idealism. Working with students, Mott paints them a picture of fields ripe for harvest and encourages them simply to let their energy and high hopes flower. With consummate confidence in the power of the gospel to improve any situation, whatever the culture, he sends his charges out on the best of missions: preaching God's word.
2. Mott's career suggests the organizational ability that the missionary enterprise and the increasing internationalization of the Protestant churches entailed. His many posts involved him in making worldwide contacts, managing staffs, overseeing publishing ventures, planning meetings, and much more. He became the friend of leaders in many different countries, and everywhere he tried to communicate to others his view of international peace, good-fellowship, and

religious harmony indebted to Christian missionary generosity.

Protestant Tensions

Writing of Protestant tensions, historian Martin Marty has said:

While trying to exclude nonwhites from participating in American life and while forcing tests of Americanization on non-Protestant whites, the keepers of the Protestant empire themselves faced four profound tests toward the end of the 19th century. How they faced them helped pose issues that have troubled the heirs of old-stock Protestantism ever since.[5]

The four tests were evolution, biblical authority, economic doctrines (labor/management tensions), and urbanization. The preceding discussion of urbanization and the social gospel has alluded to all four, but the tensions involved in the debates about biblical authority deserve more attention, since they have continued to be lively right down to the present day.

The central point in dispute involved the historical accuracy of the Bible. This point was taken up by Reform Judaism in the Pittsburgh Platform. There the Reform theologians made it axiomatic that all aspects of religion evolve. They had gotten this axiom from the European universities where they studied in the early decades of the 19th century. The same higher criticism that inspired Reform Judaism's views of inspiration and biblical authority inspired Christians who wished to analyze the Bible as a human work, a product of particular places and times. Most of those who wanted to apply higher criticism to the Bible did not doubt that the Bible expressed the Word of God. But they were intrigued by the human factors they thought they could see shaping individual books, and some of them no doubt hoped to ease some of the apparent conflicts between the way that

Genesis depicted the Creation and the way that evolutionary science explained it.

The uniqueness of the Bible in Christian life and the public perception that the Bible somehow lay at the foundations of the American national enterprise combined to make debates over the nature of biblical authority of more than scholarly interest. Since many Americans vaguely assumed a biblical warrant for their views that America was destined to lead the world, any explicit challenge to the notion that the Bible was a direct and fully explicit manifestation of the divine will was profoundly unsettling. Most Northern seminaries treated the Bible more as grist for preaching and prayer than as an object of scientific study, while in the South interest in finding texts that might support slavery had helped breed a biblical literalism. The evangelical tradition of favoring the heart over the head, even of distrusting learning (because it might inhibit emotional fervor for conversion and revival), also worked against cool, critical analysis. Just as in prior ages preachers had denounced the rationalism of Jefferson or the heresy of the Transcendentalists, who claimed God spoke to them directly, in the debates over biblical authority that raged at the end of the 19th century many preachers pictured the German professors responsible for higher criticism as soldiers in the army of the Antichrist.

Still the European views slowly made inroads. At Andover Seminary in Massachusetts, for example, professors began to admit the use of archeological and philological tools, finding no danger in admitting that Moses might not have written the entire Pentateuch or that Horeb and Sinai seemed to be the same mountain but might not be. However, a scholarly team at Princeton Seminary in New Jersey opposed this modest innovation. One of the Princeton professors, Charles Hodge, bragged that during his 58 years not one new idea had crept into Princeton or originated there.[6] Using the traditions of the Scottish school of "common sense" philosophy,

This New England church spire, typically dominating the village green, suggests the self-confidence and plain beauty of mainstream American Protestantism at its best. (Photo by J. T. Carmody)

which opposed the skepticism of Locke and Hume, the Princetonians argued quite neatly from the premise that the Bible had to be errorless because it had come directly from the errorless God.

Eventually the scholars employing higher criticism became much more radical in their analyses of the Bible than their forebears at Andover had allowed, while the Princeton position became the backbone of a widespread fundamentalism. Even denominations such as the Southern Baptists, who previously had prided themselves on their love and respect for religious freedom, began to impose standards of orthodox biblical interpretation, as the ouster of Professor Crawford H. Troy from the Southern Baptist Seminary in 1879 showed. Because his views on biblical **inspiration** diverged from those of most of his Baptist brethren, Troy (who had picked up many of his ideas in Berlin after the Civil War) was sent packing to Harvard University.

While the debates over the authority of the Bible proved to be the most significant causes of division among American Protestants, they were by no means the only conflicts. In addition to the proponents of the social gospel, Americans Protestants had to contend with such non-mainstream yet influential movements as Dispensationalism, the Holiness Movement, Pentecostalism, Christian Science, and the Jehovah's Witnesses.

Dispensationalism was a particular method of biblical interpretation designed for those who wanted to master the Bible as a whole, usually on their own or in nonacademic church groups. It proposed that the Bible as a whole was constituted according to an overall scheme. This viewpoint was originated by John Nelson Darby (1800–1882), one of the leaders of a group called the Plymouth Brethren, but it was greatly popularized by C. I. Scofield, through his Scofield Reference Bible (1902–1909). The main notion was that "God progressively dealt with man in seven dispensations, in each of which man was set a specific test, which continues as an abiding truth into subsequent dispensations."[7] The seven dispensations were innocence, related to the test of Eden; conscience, related to the Flood; government, related to civil authority up to Abraham; promise, related to Israel's stewardship of the divine truth given at Sinai; disciplinary correction, related to the death of Christ; the Church, which stands under the Spirit until Christ's return; and the Kingdom, which is to last 1000 years until eternity begins.

Many evangelical groups spread versions of this general dispensationalist scheme, which

tended to solidify commitment to the authority of the Bible as inspired by God and necessarily without error. If Dispensationalism was a reaction to the threats of higher criticism, the Holiness Movement was a reaction to the threats of liberalism or secularism in the ethical realm. Arguing that only the Holy Spirit could empower people to fulfill the moral law, Holiness preachers pushed their followers toward dramatic conversion experiences in the revivalist tradition and urged them to secure a "second blessing" in which the Spirit would free them from the power of sin. The Holiness Movement did best among poor people on the social margins who enjoyed dramatic religious experiences and were glad to discount material measures of success in favor of tokens of the Holy Spirit's cleansing and purification. John Wesley's Methodism had set the stage for this movement, but many other revivalist traditions contributed to the great appeal of the Holiness Movement.

Pentecostalism arose from the Holiness Movement after 1900. Pentecostalism laid greater stress on speaking in tongues and other emotional experiences attributed to the Holy Spirit. If liberals and secularists had stressed experience in humanistic terms, Pentecostalists would do the same in religious terms, stressing the sorts of signs associated with the Spirit's descent at Pentecost. Thus Pentecostals were like the Dispensationalists and members of the Holiness Movement in emphasizing the primacy of divine action, but they distinguished themselves by integrating the races long before integration had entered the Protestant mainstream. Perhaps the best representative of the Holiness Movement is the Church of the Nazarene, while the Assemblies of God exemplify Pentecostalism. Like the other groups just mentioned, Christian Science offered an interesting option outside the mainstream. In its case the lure was not so much a literal reading of the Bible or direct access to the Pentecostal Spirit (although Christian Scientists offered distinctive interpretations of the

Scriptures and spoke much about the spirit) as it was a means of self-help—a way to cure body and mind, apart from mainstream religion or medicine. Women especially found Christian Science an attractive outlet from the sometimes stifling religiosity of the second half of the 19th century, which often seemed to make them physically or psychologically ill.

The Jehovah's Witnesses originated in the scriptural interpretations of Charles Taze Russell (1852–1916). Convinced that Satan had infiltrated secular government and other churches, the **millennialist** Witnesses separated themselves from both. Witnesses generally refuse to salute the flag, enter military service, or take part in public elections. They think of themselves as existing to establish God's Kingdom, which they expect to arise after **Armageddon.** The biblical books of Daniel and Revelation serve them as God's revealed calculations of how and when the end is to come and the Kingdom is to be established. Witnesses are held to a strict moral code and are expected to proselytize actively. Thus it seems clear that they share much with the Dispensationalists and like them have embroidered the plain or commonsensible interpretations championed by the Princeton theologians and others inclined toward **fundamentalism.**

Dwight L. Moody

Dwight L. Moody (1837–1899) was probably the figure in whom the efforts of evangelicalism in the second half of the 19th century found happiest expression. Born in Northfield, Massachusetts, Moody left home at 17 to find work in Boston, where he was converted from Unitarianism to a fundamentalist version of evangelicalism. After working in Chicago as a shoe salesman, in 1860 he decided to devote himself to missionary work. Associating himself with the Chicago YMCA, Moody did church

work and helped run missions in the slums until 1870, when he began to collaborate with Ira Sankey, a writer of hymns, on evangelical tours. Twice they toured Britain, trying to revive people's faith by a simple, emotional appeal from the straightforward biblical text. Moody disliked sectarian disputes and turned aside from higher criticism of the Bible. He also rejected the social gospel movement and efforts to reconcile Christianity with evolution. He generally spoke of an old-fashioned gospel, which he preached in colorful, emotional terms. Taking the text quite literally, Moody looked forward to the return of Christ and urged his audiences to open themselves to repentance and salvation.

The main supporters of Moody's evangelical tours were American businessmen who favored his brand of piety and thought it would prove comforting to the poor. In contrast to the proponents of the social gospel, Moody taught that the best way to help the poor and renovate society was to bring individuals to God for the interior regeneration only the Holy Spirit could accomplish.

In 1879 Moody founded a seminary for girls in Northfield and conducted Bible conferences there each year thereafter. In 1889 he founded what is now the Moody Bible Institute in Chicago, which carries on his work of spreading the Scriptural word. Moody therefore stands as one of the leading exemplars of American evangelism, with Billy Sunday, Billy Graham, and other great popular preachers of the revivalist message.

What may distinguish Moody from the others is the electric atmosphere he and Sankey were able to create. To paraphrase an account of a revivalist meeting held in New York in 1875, preparations prior to the arrival of the crowd included the marshaling of the choir, the assembling of the ushers, the presence of the various workmen ready to throw switches and control the lighting. When the doors opened at the appointed time 5000 people rushed in and were deftly controlled by the ushers and seated in ten minutes. When both the floor and the galleries were filled, the doors were closed again. The people had to amuse themselves for the half-hour before Moody mounted the stage, but their anticipation eased any problems. They ran the gamut of ages and classes, but all expected something extraordinary.

About 15 minutes before the preaching was to start the choir began inviting the audience to join its hymn singing and then made lovely harmonies. The choir used the Moody-Sankey hymn book, which some observers of church singing have called the most effective work of its kind ever written. The hymns were composed of simple, positive words from the Gospels, stirring the crowd with such phrases as "safe in the arms of Jesus" and "I hear thy welcome voice."

During the evening service, Dwight L. Moody preached rather casually, concentrating on those who were not yet committed Christians. (In the afternoons he was more concerned to teach committed Christians, helping them fill out their faith.) At the end of his sermon he mentioned the various follow-up meetings that participants might attend on the spot, including an inquiry meeting for those seeking more information. Much of the efficiency of the meetings was owed to the businessmen who supported Moody's enterprise and helped him organize it. They convinced him that sound management principles could serve the salvation of souls as well as the conduct of a successful business. The spirit of the meetings, however, came from Moody's reliance on the Holy Spirit, the source of all the gifts that inspired people to feel the grace of God.

Those favorably inclined to Moody's project saw in the aftermath of his efforts a decline in crime and a general uplifting of public morals. Many who questioned the theology of the revival were satisfied that its practical effects out-

weighed any problems the theology could pose. Moody seemed to inspire respect, affection, confidence, and trust. Something genuine shone from his faith and sounded in his voice. He simply told others about his own inmost convictions, speaking from the heart about the good effects of the Spirit he felt and saw at first hand. His preaching urged study of the Bible and outreach to other people in need. It aimed at helping all people become whole, at peace with themselves, feeling reconciled with God and well-disposed toward all other people. Moody believed people should work hard at their faith, but with confidence and joy. Many nominal Christians fired by his preaching came to see his work as a rebuke to the torpor of the typical Christian church, where the inspiration of the Spirit and the power of the biblical word were far less plain. The simplicity of the surroundings at Moody's mission, as well as the simplicity and depth of his sermons, made many think that the ostentation of other churches, the great organs, soft cushions, and costly stained glass, were distractions. Such adornments might attract the rich, but the poor, who were the more natural population of God's kingdom, tended to be put off by them and stay away.

Such an account makes Dwight L. Moody a saint for his times. Insofar as large fractions of the late 19th century American population longed to hear a simple evangelical word that would pierce their hearts, assuring them of salvation and calling them to a better moral life, he was the right man with the right message. Evangelicals naturally tend to say that the Bible is always the right word, and that one need only preach it simply, from the heart, to witness effects similar to those achieved by Moody. The history of American religion, which seems to show that revivalism or great awakenings are a steady, perhaps cyclical occurrence, offers considerable evidence to back up this claim.[9] What that should mean for the academic study of the Bible is another question, but if one is interested in bringing consolation to simple people, the example of preachers such as Dwight L. Moody remains instructive, even though a Marxist analysis might stress how useful business interests could find it to have religion siphon off some of the discontent of the proletarian poor.

The Woman's Bible

Elizabeth Cady Stanton (1815–1902) is famous in American history for having formulated in 1848 the first organized demand for women's suffrage. Stanton's father was a U.S. congressman and later a judge on the Supreme Court of New York. While studying law in his office she learned of the legal discriminations against women and determined to overturn them. Her marriage in 1840 to Henry Brewster Stanton, also a lawyer, furthered her interest in legal reform, and with him she worked for the abolitionist cause. Her organizing work and petitions on behalf of women resulted in 1848 in a New York statute giving property rights to married women. With Lucretia Mott she organized the first women's rights convention in the United States at Seneca Falls and Rochester, New York, during the summer of 1848. Stanton drew up the convention's list of resolutions calling for improvements in the status of women, including the vote.

Stanton later collaborated with Susan B. Anthony in creating the National Woman Suffrage Association, doing much of the writing that laid out the arguments for women's rights to full citizenship. In later years she collaborated on a history of women's suffrage, edited *The Woman's Bible*, and published an autobiography entitled *Eighty Years and More*. Although it is important to realize that feminists such as the Grimke sisters had been paving the way toward women's suffrage since before the Civil War, Stanton's work certainly was a great leap forward.

As Stanton pondered the reasons for discrimination against women in law and general culture, she became more and more convinced that biases against women in the Bible were a major factor. American culture being so indebted and reverent toward the Bible, it was not surprising that the patriarchal slant of the Bible should influence American men and women alike to think of women as the daughters of Eve, the source of disorder, the unreliable half of the human race. Along with specific biblical teachings about men being the heads of women, men being the rightful rulers of the family, and warnings about sparing the rod and spoiling the child (which warnings were easily extended to not spoiling the wife), this general patriarchalism seemed to Stanton a great foe of women's struggle to achieve equality. She did not cast Christianity off completely, but she did become a sharp critic of those who wanted to grant the Bible unquestioned authority as the straightforward word of God. Stanton took naturally to the tenets of the higher critics, who were of the view that the Bible was a human work, and she came away convinced that one had to separate much chaff from the wheat if the Bible were to be viable for modern, equality-minded women.

The introduction Stanton wrote for the first edition of *The Woman's Bible* in 1895 shows her in fine form:

> From the Inauguration of the movement for woman's emancipation the Bible has been used to hold her in the "divinely ordained sphere," prescribed in the Old and New Testaments. The canon and civil law; church and state; priests and legislators; all political parties and religious denominations have alike taught that woman was made after man, of man, and for man, an inferior being subject to man. Creeds, codes, Scriptures and statutes, are all based on this idea. The fashions, forms, ceremonies and customs of society, church ordinances and discipline all grow out of this idea.

. . . The Bible teaches that woman brought sin and death into the world, that she precipitated the fall of the race, that she was arraigned before the judgment seat of Heaven, tried, condemned and sentenced. Marriage for her was to be a condition of bondage, maternity a period of suffering and anguish, and in silence and subjection, she was to play the role of a dependent on man's bounty for all her material wants, and for all the information she might desire on the vital questions of the hour, she was commanded to ask her husband at home. Here is the Bible position of woman briefly summed up.

. . . While their [women's] clergymen told them on the one hand, that they owed all the blessings and freedom they enjoyed to the Bible, on the other, they said it clearly marked out their circumscribed sphere of action: that the demands for political and civil rights were irreligious, dangerous to the stability of the home, the state and the church. Clerical appeals were circulated from time to time conjuring members of their churches to take no part in the antislavery or woman suffrage movements, as they were infidel in their tendencies, undermining the very foundations of society. No wonder the majority of women stood still, and with bowed heads, accepted the situation.[10]

Even those who argue that one cannot understand American history without paying close attention to how people were reading the Bible at given periods overlook the contribution of Elizabeth Cady Stanton and *The Woman's Bible*.[11] The different uses of the Bible during the debates about slavery are frequently mentioned, but the uses of feminists and antifeminists are passed by, perhaps because slavery as an issue is settled, while the place of women in either the Church or American culture at large is still at issue. Whatever the reason, it seems remarkable that nearly a century ago Elizabeth Cady Stanton and her suffragette sisters were advancing revisionist views of the Bible that differ little from what mainstream-to-liberal Christian theologians of most denominations are holding today. It is true that the number of women, let alone men, who accepted the arguments of *The Woman's Bible* in its day was very small. Nonetheless women's suffrage did come to the United States in 1920 with the passage of the 19th Amendment, and even though the Equal Rights Amendment pushed by feminists at the end of the 1970s did not secure ratification, the arguments Cady Stanton marshalled three-quarters of a century earlier remain instructive.

It is interesting to read historian Martin Marty's remarks about the Woman Suffrage movement, written close to 20 years ago in connection with his work on the Protestant experience in America, *Righteous Empire:*

In some forms, reformist groups had to oppose the churches in the name of their own professed ideals. A good example is the Woman Suffrage movement. The leaders of it found that they had been enslaved, as blacks had been, with justifications based on a literal view of Scripture. To free themselves, they found it worthwhile to publicize views of the higher criticism of the Bible; this only served to make them seem doubly dangerous to Protestants, even as it motivated them to enlarge their attacks on the churches. Elizabeth Cady Stanton went out of her way to denounce them, arguing in 1893 that "the most powerful influences against women's emancipation can be traced to religious superstitions." If subjugation of women was seen not to be based on divine mandate, men would not be able to sustain a religious base to their oppression. Wiser heads like Susan B. Anthony knew better than to take on the male clergy on their own ground: she wrote (in 1895), "*No*—I don't want my name on that Bible Committee—*You* fight that battle—and leave me to fight the secular—the political fellows." When Stanton's Bible Committee produced *The Woman's Bible,* the clergy responded. "It is the work of women and the devil." In time-honored fashion, Stanton claimed pure religion for her cause. The Devil had been too busy attending synods, general assemblies and conferences to study the languages and higher criticism. Her committee, she averred, had demonstrated greater reverence "for the great Spirit of All Good than does the Church."[12]

The lesson seems to be that it has never been easy to discern who has the true spirit of God, the correct interpretation of Scripture, or the best-formed religious conscience. When one adds the political questions about how best to promote one's ideas or religious interpretations, matters become impossibly tangled. In that case wiser heads do not necessarily refrain from taking on the clergy, but they do realize that misunderstanding goes with the territory of prophecy and reform, and they try to find deeper ground than political success in which to secure their peace of soul.

Key Terms

Armageddon: a term that occurs in Revelation 16:16, where it claims to be a Greek transliteration of a Hebrew term. (No such term occurs in Hebrew.) Armageddon apparently is the location of the final cosmic battle between good and evil. Apocalyptic literature such as Revelation tends to think in terms of such an ultimate showdown. Some scholars think the term is derived from Megiddo, a major pass in the Mount Carmel chain and the site of many battles in ancient Near Eastern days. By extension, Armageddon has come to symbolize doomsday, the final conflict in which God will definitively vindicate the good and punish evildoers.

Fundamentalism: the term comes from a series of booklets called *The Fundamentals* published in the United States between 1910 and 1915. The fundamentals were the basic teachings of Christianity: the divinity of Christ, the Second Coming, the inspiration and authority of the Bible, and the reality of heaven and hell. A Presbyterian general assembly of 1910, responding to controversy about the orthodoxy of some graduates of Union Theological Seminary in New York, said that the five essential doctrines were the inerrancy of Scripture, the Virgin Birth of Christ, Christ's substitutionary atonement for sins, Christ's resurrection, and the validity of Christ's miracles. All were understood rather literally, with little attention given to their symbolic or mysterious character. By extension the term *fundamentalist* came to be applied to those groups that stressed a doctrine of personal salvation and a literal interpretation of Scripture. Fundamentalism has the advantage of presenting a simple, powerful view of Christian faith that wastes little energy on ambiguities or complexities. It has the disadvantage of robbing Scripture and faith of their metaphoric character and so of diluting their value as ways into divine mystery.

Inspiration: the notion that Scripture derives from the inbreathing of divinity, which makes the text the body through which it would reveal itself. Inspiration may connote different amounts of divine dictation and control. In strong versions, such as those favored by fundamentalists, Scripture becomes a text God dictated or otherwise firmly controlled. It cannot err because of its complete dependence on divinity. In weaker versions, Scripture is a literary body in which divinity is frequently pleased to dwell, and scriptural images become privileged metaphors for the salvation God is offering in all times and places.

Liberation theology: a several-sided movement, strongest perhaps in Latin America but present also in Asian, African, European, and North American theologies, that emphasizes the economic, political, and ethical implications of salvation. The main thesis of the liberation theologians is that faith must result in works of justice, concern for the poor and marginalized, and resistance to structures that dehumanize people if it is to be worthy of the biblical God. Most liberation theologians do not deny the transcendent, otherworldly dimensions of Christian faith. But their greater interest is in liberating the oppressed—victims of poverty, racial discrimination, sexual discrimination, and the like—so that they can become full participants in the cultural life of their community. This, the liberation theologians say, is the first imperative of the gospel.

Millennialist: concerning belief that a thousand-year reign of Christ on earth will precede his Second Coming. During this period (millennium) Christ will reign in the midst of his saints, and at its conclusion he will take his saints with him to heaven. Millenialists were inspired by apocalyptic speculation in the Book of Daniel and by Chapter 20 of Revelation. Some early Christian heretics held this view, but so did such church fathers as Justin Martyr, Irenaeus, and Hippolytus. The great early teacher Origen condemned the idea, but it resurfaced in several medieval movements. Such early Protestant groups as the Anabaptists and Moravian Brethren were millenialists, while in the United States Mormons and Seventh Day Adventists have believed in the millennium.

Synoptic: referring to the first three of the New Testament gospels: Matthew, Mark, and Luke. The term comes from early efforts to set these three gospels side by side, that their likenesses and differences might be taken in "at a single glance." Current biblical scholarship tends to consider Mark the oldest gospel, and to make Mark a source for Matthew and Luke. The majority view postulates a second source for the things Matthew and Luke hold in common. The whole question of the relationship among the first three gospels is called "the synoptic problem" and continues to draw much attention from New Testament scholars.

Discussion Questions

1. What was the main threat that most American churchgoers perceived in Darwin's teachings about evolution?

2. What were the main tenets of the social gospel, and how did they respond to late 19th-century urbanization and industrialization?

3. How did the growth of America's self-confidence and sense of global destiny contribute to Protestant missionary idealism?

4. How realistic was John R. Mott's view of student missionaries?

5. On what grounds could one think it praiseworthy to have admitted no new ideas about the Bible for half a century?

6. What sort of a reading mentality is manifested in Dispensationalism?

7. Why was hymn singing so important a part of Dwight L. Moody's evangelical meetings?

8. What is the ideal relationship between the heart and the head in religious matters?

9. How valid was Elizabeth Cady Stanton's intuition that a literal reading of the Bible was a major stumbling block to women's emancipation?

10. What are the advantages and the disadvantages in the different tactical positions taken by Elizabeth Cady Stanton and Susan B. Anthony regarding how to deal with the religious enemy?

Notes

1. Quoted without citation in *Christianity in America: A Handbook,* ed. Mark A. Noll, Nathan O. Hatch, *et al.* (Grand Rapids MI: Eerdmans, 1983), p. 285.

2. Ibid., pp. 286–287.

3. See Conrad Cherry, ed., *God's New Israel* (Englewood Cliffs NJ: Prentice-Hall, 1971), pp. 211–270.

4. Edward S. Gaustad, ed., *A Documentary History of Religion in America,* vol. 2 (Grand Rapids MI: Eerdmans, 1983), p. 158.

5. Martin E. Marty, *Pilgrims in Their Own Land* (Boston: Little Brown, 1984), p. 297.

6. Ibid., p. 303.

7. J. C. O'Neill, "Dispensationalism," in *The Westminster Dictionary of Christian Theology,* ed. Alan Richardson and John Bowden (Philadelphia: Westminster, 1983), p. 158.

8. See Gaustad, op. cit., pp. 286–288.

9. See William G. McGloughlin, *Revivals, Awakenings, and Reform* (Chicago: University of Chicago Press, 1978).

10. Elizabeth Cady Stanton, *The Woman's Bible* (Salem NH: Ayer Company, 1986 Reprint Edition), pp. 7–9.

11. See, for example, Nathan O. Hatch and Mark A. Noll, eds., *The Bible in America* (New York: Oxford University Press, 1982).

12. Martin E. Marty, *Righteous Empire* (New York: Dial Press, 1970), pp. 203–204.

9

The Era of the World Wars

Destiny and War

Although one might argue that the rise of fundamentalism in its first decades was a major factor shaping 20th-century religion, the experience of the United States in two world wars dwarfs all other factors. Germany's precipitation of both wars put American ideas about national destiny and world responsibility to the test. When President Wilson set the nation's face for war, arguing that American principles of democracy and freedom required such a grave step, American clergy became leading proponents, gilding the war effort with a patina of righteousness. They nicely supported the government propaganda aimed at convincing U.S. citizens that Satan was guiding the German war machine, his hope being to obliterate freedom and Christian virtue. Thus the First World War became "the war to end all wars," an Armageddon where ultimate evil had to be countered by all who stood for righteousness.

To what extent government propagandists duped the American clergy is debatable. What seems surer is that many clergy were primed by their belief in America's providential role to resurrect biblical doctrines of holy warfare and picture opposition to Germany as a sacred duty. The pacifist option that would seem to be inherent in Christian ethics received little attention or support. Texts such as "I have not come to bring peace but a sword" (Matt. 10:34) were much preferred to "Put your sword back into its place; for all who take the sword will perish by the sword" (Matt. 26:52). The famous preacher Billy Sunday exemplified the cruder versions of this religious militarism when he said, "If you turn hell upside down, you will find 'Made in Germany' stamped on the bottom."[1] Catholic, Protestant, and Jewish leaders united behind the war effort, making the American cause a splendid fight for godliness, enlightenment, and freedom.

If we pause to reflect on so singular an instance of civil religion, several factors stand out, including the objective dangers posed by Germany and the historic ties between the United States and both England and France. But the maturing country had also been nurturing ambitions to world power. Despite the hesitancy that marked the American entry into both the First and the Second World Wars, once the argument was made that the free world required the full collaboration of its strongest, most noble representative, U.S. participation was certain.

It is hard not to be cynical about any country's war making at any time. In the history of war, the predominant motives so often have been territorial expansion, booty, power, and pride that the informed observer despairs of finding a just war, let alone a holy one. But many observers find that the two world wars of the 20th century fare better than their predecessors. The corruption of motives in the two world wars lies more in their conduct than in their purpose and goals. However inflated the depictions of the German menace, there were objective imperatives to checking Germany's imperial ambitions in the First World War and the even graver perils of Nazism in the Second World War.

America's attitudes toward the world wars are further illuminated by considering its patriotic propaganda against the background of the vast immigration that had recently occurred. The wars presented a golden opportunity for new Americans to prove their patriotism. If they were willing to shed their blood for their new homeland, would not the immigrant peoples be sure to be accounted full Americans? Of course the answer to that question was not a simple yes. Yet it would be hard to underestimate the hope of full acceptance that motivated many new Americans to serve in the two world wars. No doubt they loved their new country and could often point to concrete ways in which coming to it had proved a blessing. On the other hand, those looking beyond the wars were bound to think that having served with distinction might well prove the badge that would take them from the margins to the mainstream, maybe even to the inner sanctum. To some extent, their hopes and calculations proved correct, for after both wars, having been part of the successful effort was a leveling factor and common ground. Two generations after the Second World War, previously immigrant Jews, Irish, and Italians were among the wealthiest groups in the United States. They might still suffer some social handicaps, but compared to their full equality of opportunity such handicaps were few indeed.

In speaking about the First World War, after the treaty of Versailles and in the context of his hopes for the League of Nations, President Wilson cast the American war effort in such idealistic terms that he must be considered a shrewd translator of religious feelings into nationalistic pride. In Wilson's retrospective, the Allies were at a low ebb until American soldiers began to pour across the sea. In terms of both morale and physical strength, only the American contribution saved the day. The Americans' arrival checked the German advance toward Paris and thereafter the Germans were always on the defensive. The mere sight of the stalwart Americans had given Europeans back their heart. Wilson saw this American contribution as much more than simply fresh troops. He saw it as an outflow of the great ideals a free people carry within their hearts. In other words, Wilson's Americans had arrived to carry the banner of truth, justice, and the decent (Christian, truly idealistic) way of life. One might say they were a modern equivalent of the Puritan saints who fought for Christian freedom, or of the Crusaders who went off to crush the infidels and regain the Holy Land. Wilson might well have reddened to hear such comparisons, but, whether by calculation or honest belief, his view of the American contribution to Europe greatly profited from a quasi-religious view of both America and the war. The war was a contest between good and evil, which were contrasted in virtually **Manichean** terms. America was God's destined country, the land where freedom went hand in hand with material blessings and goodness of heart.

In describing the American presence at the Versailles Peace Conference, Wilson was no less idealistic about the role the other nations expected America to play. America had entered the war for no ulterior reasons, wanting only peace and freedom. Thus America was sought as an arbiter in many difficult disputes, as well as a source of the material aid that rebuilding would require. Those who had feared American expansions after its war with Spain had laid their fears to rest, and 21 years after that war America seemed truly at full majority, well ready to take up the burdens of international leadership. All of this had come about by the hand of God, so there was no turning back. The dreams that had come into the world with the nation's birth were now reaching fulfillment. Wilson's Puritan forebears could have been proud of his theology of election, though they might have wondered where their theology of human depravity had gone.

Religion in the Depression

The Great Depression that wracked America and Europe during the 1930s was the second part of a two-part interlude between the world wars, the first part being the giddy prosperity of the 1920s. Both prosperity and depression were internal affairs, but of course they could not help being related to American foreign policy. The success in the First World War helped fuel the confidence of the 1920s, while the depression made the Second World War economically attractive.

In writing about the cycles of American history, Arthur M. Schlesinger, Jr., has contrasted the pragmatism of the founding fathers with the idealism, if not outright ideology, of the Calvinist view of America's providential role in world affairs that drove Woodrow Wilson during the First World War and Secretary of State John Foster Dulles after the Second World War. The Founding Fathers had thought that states were bound to conduct foreign policy mainly from self-interest and that most of America's energy ought to go to keeping its own internal institutions strong. The Calvinist point of view tended to generate loftier rationales:

> The Calvinist mind pronounced America the redeemer nation—in the 18th century in Jonathan Edwards's theology of Providence, in the 19th century in Josiah Strong's theology of expansion, in the 20th century in Woodrow Wilson's gospel of world order and in John Foster Dulles's summons to a holy war against godless communism. . . . When America rejoined the big game in the 20th century, it did so with an exalted conviction of its destiny as the savior of the world, and no longer by example alone. The United States entered the First World War for balance of power reasons; but Woodrow Wilson could not bring himself to admit the national interest in preventing the whole force of Europe from being wielded by a single hand. Instead he made himself the prophet of a world beyond power politics where the bad old balance of power would give way to a radiant new community of power. The United States, Wilson said, had notified mankind at its birth: "We have come to redeem the world by giving it liberty and justice."[2]

Following the Russian Revolution of 1917, the Western world had what proved to be a powerful new ideology and nation in its game of power politics. Europe wondered what to make of the giant nation at its northeastern borders, as it wondered how to put its house together again after the First World War. France and England had assessed massive reparations against Germany, as much to punish Germany for starting the war as to compensate for damages the war had caused (though the manpower losses were terrible). France and England hoped to use these reparations to pay off their debts to the United States, but Germany refused to pay the $33 billion levied and the United States decided to provide loans and investments to Germany. By 1929 the American Stock Market had collapsed, bringing down both the European credit markets and the international banking system. Reparation payments ceased and the entire Western economy was ruined. In 1932 more than 30 million people were officially unemployed in the industrialized nations. While the United States tried to cope with its own economic problems, largely through Franklin Roosevelt's New Deal, Germany grew ripe for the Nazism that precipitated the next great European crisis.

In 1932 the American income, which had stood at $83 billion in 1929 before the crash had fallen to $40 billion. By early 1933 unemployment approached 15 million. Hunger, homelessness, fear, hopelessness, and violence all grew. The previously often mindless confidence in American business and automatic progress was devastated as the nation pondered its character and what it had become. The American churches that most profited from the depression included the Nazarenes, whose membership more than doubled between 1926 and 1936, and the Assemblies of God, whose membership more than tripled. The liberal, progressive churches were fair game for the fundamentalists, who could point to shattered hopes on every side. Among the mainstream Protestant churches there was a tendency to try to pull together and heal old wounds. Thus the Southern and Northern Methodists reunited in 1939, as did the Congregationalist and Christian churches in 1931 and the Reformed churches in 1946.

At the same time the tenets of the social gospel (many of them advocated by conservative evangelicals until the end of the First World War) seemed more relevant than ever. With or without them, many churches responded to the widespread needs of the unemployed, the homeless, and the poor by reviving the New Testament's call for practical charity and brotherly love. Matthew 25 was a classical text:

When the Son of man comes in his glory, and all the angels with him, then he will sit on his glorious throne. Before him will be gathered all the nations, and he will separate them one from another as a shepherd separates the sheep from the goats, and he will place the sheep at his right hand, but the goats at the left. Then the King will say to those at his right hand, "Come, O blessed of my Father, inherit the kingdom prepared for you from the foundation of the world; for I was hungry and you gave me food, I was thirsty and you gave me drink, I was a stranger and you welcomed me, I was naked and you clothed me, I was sick and you visited me, I was in prison and you came to me." Then the righteous will answer him, "Lord, when did we see thee hungry and feed thee, or thirsty and give thee drink? And when did we see thee a stranger and welcome thee, or naked and clothe thee? And when did we see thee sick or in prison and visit thee?" And the King will answer them, "Truly, I say to you, as you did it to one of the least of these my brethren, you did it to me" (Matt. 25:31–40).

On the other hand, the churches' efforts to respond to the mass sufferings accompanying the depression also produced a conservative backlash. American faith in free enterprise, private property, free competition, and individual rights died hard, and the wealthy classes were not about to admit responsibility for the depression or the poor. Charity for the poor, yes, but responsibility as a matter of strict jus-

This memorial to Helen Keller at Radcliffe College in Cambridge, Massachusetts, is a reminder of the status of women and disabled people in the first half of the 20th century. (Photo by J. T. Carmody)

ments as Moral Re-Armament appeared to try to revive ethics and retie evangelical mores to the attitudes that would make for prosperity, but they had only middling success. Right-wing demagogues flourished in several churches, among them Father Charles Coughlin, a vitriolic Roman Catholic critic of Roosevelt's New Deal. After 1936 the nation had to deal with such alarming foreign developments as the rise of imperialist regimes in Japan, Italy, and Germany. It became increasingly apparent that the United States would soon face critical decisions about how to check such tendencies, even though its own economic and social restoration was far from complete.

So the religious issues of the 1930s were brought into clearest relief by the social breakdown that had occurred. While one obvious response was to stress the social aspects of the gospel, another was to call the nation to moral reform. Like the deeper political analysts, however, the deeper theologians pondered the nature of modern humanity: how it differed from the humanity and political arrangements of prior eras, where it had gone wrong, and what it required if peace and prosperity were again to seem possible. The naiveté that Americans had indulged even through the First World War was badly bruised if not shattered. Certainly many people continued to think that a return to biblical fundamentals would quickly make things right, but more entertained sober thoughts about the profound problems of managing great power and the too real influence of **original sin.**

Neo-Orthodoxy

Prior to the First World War, European Protestant thought had been dominated by **theological liberalism.** The liberals were confident they could marry Christian faith to modern scientific culture, and they stressed such summary formulas as "the Fatherhood of God and the

tice, no. That seemed too close to godless communism.

The Protestant churches that had united to bring about Prohibition in 1920 suffered fits of anxiety between 1929 and 1933, as the corruptions associated with bootlegging finally swung public opinion against the amendment. With the repeal of Prohibition in 1933, some thought a major plank in the platform of American morality had come undone. Such move-

brotherhood of man," to show the compatibility between Christian idealism and that of benevolent humanists. Their Jesus was less the Son of God than the exemplary Son of Man, and in the teachings of Jesus ethics counted for more than theology proper or mysticism.

After the First World War Europe lay in shambles and a powerful reaction to liberalism set in. Theologians variously called Neo-Orthodox, Neo-Reform, Dialectical, and Critical strove to place more tension, more opposition, between Christian faith and secular culture or modernity. They especially wanted to stress the transcendence of divinity, which placed it far beyond any of the cultural containers religion might temporarily assume, as well as the sinfulness of human nature, which could do nothing good apart from God, and the crucial significance of Jesus Christ, who was humanity's only adequate revelation of the transcendent, gracious God. The landmark book that catalyzed this movement was the second edition of Swiss Calvinist theologian Karl Barth's *Commentary on Romans,* which appeared in 1919. Interpreting the Apostle Paul for his contemporaries in postwar Europe, Barth stressed the holiness and transcendence of the One revealed in Jesus Christ. Like such prior revivers of classical Reformation themes as Sören Kierkegaard (whose analysis of the distance of God from sinful human beings asserted the need for a leap of faith), Barth argued that for human beings to be drawn into contact with God they must encounter a profound crisis. By *crisis* he meant coming under a judgment that they could not pass on their own merits. Apart from faith and the merits of Christ, any interview with God, any significant reception of revelation, any genuine contact with God was bound to find human beings wanting.

Barth's theology struck a nerve in both Europe and the United States. Protestants on both sides of the Atlantic responded well to its powerful analyses of both humanity's sinfulness and the primacy of God's Word. Barth seemed to be recalling classical themes from the writings of Luther and Calvin that for some time had suffered neglect. He seemed to be restoring the solemnity of Scripture and the Reformers' doctrine of justification by faith alone. In giving all priority to God Barth challenged modern **humanism** head-on. Since humanistic thought seemed manifestly in disarray, as war torn as the bombed cities of Europe, the strict primacy of divinity came as a welcome change. Barth's biting message could be interpreted as just the searing the modern spirit needed.

By the 1930s Neo-Orthodoxy was the predominant theological school in many of the major Protestant theological centers of Europe, Britain, and the United States. Such leading theologians as Emil Brunner, Rudolf Bultmann, Friedrich Gogarten, Paul Tillich, C. H. Dodd, and Reinhold and H. Richard Niebuhr brought its influence to bear on doctrinal theology, scriptural studies, ethics, and cultural theology. Common to most such affiliates of Neo-Orthodoxy was a critical attitude toward both modern scientific culture and theological liberalism, an effort to reestablish Christian faith on the basis of revelation rather than reason, and a commitment to investigating biblical thought with modern research tools. Far from being fundamentalists, the Neo-Orthodox wanted to break open the strangeness of the Bible and set its untamed imagery into dialectical confrontation with current culture. Critics such as Rudolf Bultmann certainly borrowed much from contemporary philosophy and philology, but they subordinated these techniques to their primary conviction that the Word of God, as found in Scripture and rightful Church preaching, challenged all the products of modern intelligence. Most of the Neo-Orthodox also approved of the social ideals of the social gospel movement, although frequently they rejected the liberal theology associated with it. It was the lordship and judgment of God that they found compelling, not any hopes that humanity on its own could construct the kingdom of God on earth.

Neo-Orthodoxy had a special impact on Christology, the study and presentation of faith in Jesus Christ. Christ stood as the mediator between human sinfulness and the transcendent otherness of God. As Word he was the revelation that expressed the divine intent to save human beings from their alienation and sin. As Savior he was the one who had accomplished the work of redeeming humanity and bestowing on it the divine mercy and love. Thus Christ himself was both Judgment and Salvation. Human beings could never comprehend the absolute, definitive Word of God, so they had to accept it in fully obedient faith. The main work of the Church was to preach this Word and testify to it by a life of faith and service. But all priority remained with God, and without God's revealing initiatives humanity could know and do little of eternal worth.

The critics of Neo-Orthodoxy have usually found much to praise in its restoration of the classical themes of the 16th century Protestant reformers. On the other hand, many have felt that Barth placed God so far from human experience and took so low a view of natural reason and effort that his message simply urged blind faith. Granted the transcendence of God, what tools other than human imagination, reason, and love were available to make sense of divine revelation? Barth might denounce "religion" as a worthless human artifact, and he might thunder against doctrines of analogy, which taught that reason could say some trustworthy things about God, but what positive alternatives did human beings have, since neither Scripture nor the Creeds had popped out of heaven? Unless one were to become a literalist, reading the Bible with no thought to modern conditions, one was bound to have questions. Thus Paul Tillich and Rudolf Bultmann both backed away from Barth's rarefied claims for revelation, and the massive work of Barth's maturity, *Church Dogmatics,* itself offered more nuance.

In the United States Barth, Bultmann, Tillich, and the Niebuhrs injected a vigorous strain of intellectualism into what had recently been a rather flabby American theology. American philosophers interested in religion, such as William James and John Dewey, had provided solid intellectual fare, but neither had worked from Scripture or classical Christian tradition. In fact both had been highly critical of how religion and theology tended to work out in the individual personality and in the common culture. Using the massive evidence of the world wars, the Neo-Orthodox theologians challenged the pride and presumption of such naturalist thought. What country had been more cultured than modern Germany, and look where its art, science, and philosophy had led. Human genius, apart from the divine Word, simply put more power at the disposal of bent human wills and souls. In the name of realism, the Neo-Orthodox urged a repentance from naturalistic self-sufficiency, a return to the revelation of God that alone was the power and wisdom of Christ, the way to salvation.

Reinhold Niebuhr

Reinhold Niebuhr (1892–1971) grew up in a Lutheran manse and worked from 1915 to 1928 as a pastor in Detroit, where he observed firsthand the problems of American industrialization. That made him a strong critic of capitalism and inclined him toward a socialist view of economics and politics. In 1928 Niebuhr accepted an invitation to teach at Union Theological Seminary in New York City, where he was a major influence until his retirement in 1960. Although very active as a lecturer and a member of various social action committees, he saved time to write numerous books expressing a theological position that came to be known as "Christian realism." Niebuhrian realism meant never underestimating the presence of egotism, pride, and hypocrisy, which he saw afflicting humanity in all places and classes as the legacy of original sin. Niebuhr recalled both the classical Protestant reformers and the thought of the American Founding Fathers, who were at pains to curb the political effects of self-interest. Niebuhr was suspicious of claims to perfection or full purity of motive, regardless of who made them, and he joined with other Neo-Orthodox thinkers in attacking the liberal conviction that humanity was bound to evolve to higher states and progress to a more just or splendid culture. But Niebuhr balanced this pessimism with a deep faith that the image of God was never destroyed in human beings, and a belief that God gave grace everywhere, often quite outside explicitly Christian channels. If people would put aside their pretensions and simply work hard to make a more just society, such grace would help them achieve sufficiently good results to justify their labors. In addition to retrieving the legacy of the Reformation, Niebuhr was concerned to retrieve the riches of Renaissance thought. The two together might provide a self-critical yet hopeful view of cultural progress. Niebuhr was willing, often eager to work with non-Christians on projects of common interest, and he was one of the first Christian theologians to provide a theological justification for dialogue and collaboration between Christians and Jews.

Niebuhr's political evolution took him from an early alliance to radical socialism and pacifism to a later allegiance with liberal, anticommunist Democrats. He ran for political office while a Socialist and later served as chairman of the Americans for Democratic Action. Although during the 1930s he looked favorably on Marxism, he became critical of its ideological absolutism and denounced the tactics of Communists in both the United States and the Stalinist USSR.

At the advent of the Second World War, Niebuhr was a major influence against isolationism and pacifism, urging American participation in the war on the grounds that Hitler had to be thwarted. After the war he supported the cold war resistance to Soviet political expansion in Europe, and his notion of a self-critical yet firm use of power had considerable influence in the State Department. Niebuhr was as hard on American crusading and self-righteousness as he was on Communist ideology. He favored diplomatic recognition of mainland China and was an early opponent of the Vietnam war. No theologian of his era had more influence on government policy, and few if any were more respected preachers and lecturers. After 1952 his activities were curtailed by a stroke, but he continued to teach and write.

Robert McAfee Brown, a student of Niebuhr's at Union Theological Seminary and a continuer of Niebuhr's tradition of political activism, has recently edited a collection of Niebuhr's essays and addresses aimed at providing an overall view of his thought. A section from an essay entitled "Why the Christian Church is not Pacifist," written during the early years of the Second World War, conveys some of the flavor of Niebuhr's Christian realism. After agreeing that there is a valid sense in which one may speak of Christian faith as supporting pacifism, Niebuhr goes on to say,

> Yet most modern forms of Christian pacifism are heretical. Presumably inspired by the Christian gospel, they have really absorbed the Renaissance faith in the goodness of man, have rejected the Christian doctrine of original sin as an outmoded bit of pessimism, have reinterpreted the cross so that it is made to stand for the absurd idea that perfect love is guaranteed a simple victory over the world, and have rejected all other profound elements of the Christian gospel as "Pauline" accretions which must be stripped from the "simple gospel of Jesus." This form of pacifism is not only heretical when judged by the standards of the total gospel. It is equally heretical when judged by the facts of human existence. There are no historical realities which remotely conform to it. It is important to recognize this lack of conformity to the facts of experience as a criterion of heresy.[3]

Several items in this paragraph deserve comment. First, Niebuhr is not loathe to use the word *heresy,* which liberal theology tends to avoid. Social science recently has conditioned us to think that such terms as *heresy, evil, orthodoxy,* and *saintliness* are relative, the products of struggles within society to control opinion and worldview. Those who hold power and control popular opinion tend to brand deviants heretical and try to suppress their thought and organizations, which threaten the status quo. While one cannot deny that some such dynamics are at work in every society, such a characterization misses the point of the Christian usage on which Niebuhr draws. To his mind there is a certain objective order revealed throughout history and current experience. There is also a formative, doctrinal Christian faith, confirmed and guarded by the Church throughout the ages. Heresy is failure to honor the objective realities of either experience or Christian doctrinal tradition. The heretic develops a deficient, even a warped worldview, and the best intentions cannot remove the dangers to which that exposes both heretics themselves and those they influence. If one has faulty vision, one does not see what is really there, and so one stumbles and causes accidents.

What saves Niebuhr from dogmatism is the self-criticism built into his stress on human sinfulness. If one admits his theological emphasis, one ought immediately to challenge any pride or pretentiousness in one's own worldview or actions. To be sure, one has to avoid paralysis, develop a sense of humor, and plunge ahead, even as one affirms one's own liability to erring by either excess or deficiency. But, as in the case of evaluating pacifism, one must not allow idealism to obscure the historical record of people's inhumanities to one another. One cannot expect that love and well-meaning alone will be adequate tools for dealing with the Hitlers and Stalins of the world. The Christian understanding of the flaws in human nature will keep

one's feet on the ground. Human beings have "here," on earth, no lasting city (Heb. 13:14). Only in heaven (however one interprets that symbol) can they expect perfection. Here they have constantly to separate the wheat from the chaff. Here they must always keep a close watch on human motivation, their own as well as others'.

A few of Niebuhr's own lines about the meaning that human beings can find in the midst of life's mysteriousness make it plain that, far from taking away his delight in existence, his Christian realism made him profoundly grateful for his time in the passing city:

> The Christian faith is the right expression of the greatness and the weakness of man in relation to the mystery and meaning of life. It is an acknowledgment of human weakness, for, unlike "natural religion" and "natural theology," it does not regard the human mind as capable of resolving the enigma of existence, because it knows that human reason is itself involved in the enigma which it tries to comprehend. It is an acknowledgment of the greatness of the human spirit because it assumes that man is capable of apprehending clues to the divine mystery and accepting the disclosure of the purposes of God which He has made to us. It is a confession at once of both weakness and strength, because it recognizes that the disclosures of the divine are given to man, who is capable of apprehending them, when made, but is not capable of anticipating them.[4]

Writings of Franklin D. Roosevelt

Franklin Delano Roosevelt (1882–1945) is best remembered for leading the United States out of the depression and through the Second World War. Roosevelt attended Harvard College, married his distant cousin Eleanor Roosevelt in 1905, studied law at Columbia University, and began a legal career in New York. In 1910 he was elected to the New York Senate and in 1913 he became assistant secretary of the navy. Although he had been stricken with polio in 1921, in 1928 Roosevelt was elected governor of New York. From the beginning of his governorship he launched programs to help farmers and establish state relief agencies. When he was elected president in 1932, Roosevelt moved to combat the depression by establishing similar programs on a national scale. Congress quickly approved his sweeping plans for loans, creating jobs through federal work projects, and establishing social relief agencies, all of which became known as the New Deal. From Roosevelt, then, came the image of government as responsible for the basic material needs of its citizens.

Critics claimed that Roosevelt's programs were taking the country in a socialist direction, away from the minimalist view of government they associated with the Founding Fathers. Roosevelt replied that the times required government intervention. Typical of the programs he inaugurated were the Federal Emergency Relief Administration, which passed funds to state relief agencies for direct disbursement to needy individuals; the Civilian Conservation Corps, which put half a million young men to work on projects of reforestation and flood control; the Agricultural Adjustment Administration, which aimed at raising farm prices and increasing farmers' share of the national income; and the National Industrial Recovery Act, which appropriated over 3 billion dollars for public works and established an agency to set up and administer fair industrial practices, to regulate work hours and wages, to guarantee collective bargaining rights, and to abolish child labor in interstate commerce.

Elected to a second presidential term by a wide margin in 1936, Roosevelt moved to enact further recovery measures, though by that time he had firm opposition from both ends of the political spectrum, conservative businessmen arguing that he was introducing too much government control and suffering workers calling

for more radical measures. By 1937 Roosevelt had achieved a substantial national recovery from the depression, but when he tried to cut back on government spending the country tilted back into recession. By 1938 more massive projects were in place and the economy was again improving. Although there was now solid opposition to the New Deal, such projects as the Tennessee Valley Authority and the Works Progress Administration were well established.

Foreign affairs preoccupied Roosevelt from the end of his second term and throughout his unprecedented third term. He involved himself in currency and trade negotiations with European nations and established the Good Neighbor Policy, which eventually led to collective security and mutual defense agreements with several nations in the Western Hemisphere. By 1940 the United States was offering Britain all aid short of war, trying to stop Hitler without joining the armed conflict. The Lend-Lease Act of 1941 linked the United States more closely to the Allies, and the Atlantic Charter signed with Winston Churchill of Great Britain in August 1941 joined the two countries in a pledge to preserve freedom of the seas. In the Pacific Roosevelt began denying Japan supplies essential to the furtherance of its military alliance with Germany and Italy, and the Japanese attack on Pearl Harbor, Hawaii, on December 7, 1941, catapulted the United States into the war.

Roosevelt then presided over preparing the U.S. forces and supplies, orchestrating the wartime efforts of the Allies, and pushing for such a victory over the Axis (Germany-Italy-Japan) that there would be no repeat of what had happened at the end of the First World War, when the seeds of another war were left maturing. Roosevelt struck a deal with Stalin that helped the Allies gain victory, but the terms were insufficiently precise to check Russian ambitions after the war and prevent Soviet dominance of eastern Europe. Despite badly declining health,

Roosevelt won election to a fourth term in 1944 and managed to see the war through to its final phase. He died of a massive cerebral hemorrhage in April 1945.

In a speech to Congress on January 6, 1941, Roosevelt not only sought support for his Lend-Lease arrangements with Great Britain but also outlined the future he hoped the country could achieve after the war had ended. The speech is famous for the four freedoms Roosevelt mentioned. After detailing some of the personal sacrifices that helping the Allies would require, Roosevelt provided justification for them:

In the future days, which we seek to make secure, we look forward to a world founded upon four essential human freedoms. The first is freedom of speech and expression everywhere in the world. The second is the freedom of every person to worship God in his own way everywhere in the world. The third is freedom from want, which, translated into world terms, means economic understandings which will secure to every nation a healthy peacetime life for its inhabitants everywhere in the world. The fourth is freedom from fear—which, translated into world terms, means a worldwide reduction of armaments to such a point and in such a thorough fashion that no nation will be in a position to commit an act of physical aggression against any neighbor—anywhere in the world. . . . Since the beginning of our American history, we have been involved in change—in a perpetual peaceful revolution—a revolution which goes on steadily, quietly adjusting itself to changing conditions—without the concentration camp or the quicklime in the ditch. The world order which we seek is the cooperation of free countries, working together in a friendly, civilized society. This nation has placed its destiny in the hands and hearts of its millions of free men and women, and its faith in freedom under the guidance of God. Freedom means the supremacy of human rights everywhere. Our support goes to those who struggle to gain those rights or keep them. Our strength is in our unity of purpose. To that high concept there can be no end save victory.[5]

Roosevelt's annual address to Congress in January of 1942, after war had been declared, applied these general sentiments to the specific tasks at hand. The Allies would join together in a fight for freedom. No longer would the Axis have the luxury of attacking isolated nations one by one. The world was too small to accommodate both God and Hitler. The Nazi plan was to replace the Bible with Hitler's *Mein Kampf,* the cross with the swastika. Implicitly, therefore, the Allied war effort was a holy cause, God's own, waged against the forces threatening the end of human freedom.[6]

Reinhold Niebuhr praised the alliance between England and the United States that Roosevelt effected, seeing the destiny of those two Anglo-Saxon lands as the preservation of freedom at the present critical juncture.[7] Typically he also warned against the excesses, the pride, to which such a notion of destiny might lead. But he was one with Roosevelt in thinking that the Nazi threat to Western civilization (and to its Christian foundations) left no room for vacillating. Only a thorough military defeat would suppress the great evil and reopen the future.

The centuries through which ideals of freedom had matured in the United States thus came to a certain climax at the time of the Second World War. A present danger objective enough to warrant thinking of America's military mission as God's own capped the long-incubating sense of divine providence. The destiny for which America had been preparing now seemed nakedly manifest to politician and theologian alike. The only way to be faithful to American history or conscience was to fight Hitler and win the victory all the world's people deserved.

Key Terms

Humanism: for people of religious commitment who wish to use the term disparagingly, limiting one's interests, energies, and

The Boston Avenue Methodist Church in Tulsa,
Oklahoma, is famous for its art deco architecture and
represents some of the style of mainstream American
Protestantism during the period of the two World Wars.
(Photo by J. T. Carmody)

commitments to secular matters and not concerning oneself much with God or transcendent realities. *Humanity,* in such usage, therefore shrinks to what human beings experience and enact in their ordinary round of thoughts and activities. The depths of consciousness and conscience, where more than temporal or secular values can emerge, fall outside the humanist's pale, as do overt religious activities. Not accepting such a negative view of the term, some believers place an adjective such as *Christian* before their sort of humanism, meaning to imply that God's special sphere of activity can be precisely the realm of human affairs: politics, art, science, and even the ordinary interactions that keep human beings going, such as eating and making love. Humanists themselves often stress commitment to all people's well-being.

Manichean: concerning the views of Manes (215–275 C.E.), a Persian innovator who founded a religion based on a dualism of evil and good. Manicheanism derived from Zoroastrian dualism, but it differed from Zoroastrianism in making matter a principle of evil. Followers of Manes therefore were to be extremely ascetic and to keep themselves as untainted by the flesh (sex, food) as possible. Manicheanism enjoyed considerable popularity in the West during the fourth century. Prior to his Christian conversion, Augustine of Hippo was a Manichean, and some historians of Christian doctrine think that Augustine's pessimism about sexuality, the flesh, and human nature, which proved highly influential in Christian history, owed a great deal to his Manichean period. In broader usage, the term connotes any tendency to divide the world into two opposing camps of light and darkness, goodness and evil.

Original sin: a Christian doctrine, associated with St. Augustine, that tries to account for human disorder by postulating a mistake,

flaw, or sin at the foundations of the human race. The account of the disobedience of Adam and Eve in Genesis 3 was the prime biblical text cited, though Paul's teaching in Romans 5 was equally significant. The symbols and doctrine intended a warning about human nature: Experience showed that people regularly seek their own interest rather than the common good and sin from weakness, blindness, pride, and bondage to passion. Augustine's rather literal interpretation of Paul tied the transmission of original sin to sexual intercourse. It also made a person existing in an unbaptized state subject to Satan and hell. In such an interpretation, original sin was removed by baptism through the merits of Christ but remained in the unbaptized as something to be laid to their own account, making them guilty. Later theology has preferred to see original sin as "the sin of the world": the tilted, flawed situation all children enter and then somehow reaffirm. However conceived, the notion of original sin is opposed to a simple optimism about human nature and calls people to consider carefully the historical record of humanity's crimes and the tangle of human motivation.

Theological liberalism: a somewhat vague movement, influential in the 19th and early 20th centuries, especially among progressive Protestants. Liberal theologians generally claimed the freedom to reinterpret traditional Christian doctrines and embraced the new methods of textual criticism that subjected the Bible and church documents to the influences shaping all other human records. Behind the liberal theologians lay such developments as the Enlightenment and the Romantic movement, both of which emphasized human resources (intellectual or emotional) and raised serious questions about past traditions. Theological liberals tended to regard Christianity as more like than unlike other religions and to slough off the divinity of Jesus and his miracles.

Discussion Questions

1. What was Manichean in the American portrayal of the adversaries in the First World War?
2. What opportunities did the First World War offer immigrant Americans?
3. Why did the Calvinist mind pronounce America the redeemer nation?
4. What does the varied reaction of religious groups to the Depression suggest about the American religious mind?
5. What were the main tenets of Barthian Neo-Orthodoxy?
6. How was Neo-Orthodoxy a return to Reformation principles, and why did it achieve so great a success?
7. What does the activism of Reinhold Niebuhr suggest about Christian faith and theology?
8. Why did Niebuhr call most modern forms of pacifism heretical?
9. How did the New Deal compare with the social gospel?
10. To what extent were Roosevelt's four freedoms religious ideals?

Notes

1. Quoted without citation in Conrad Cherry, ed., *God's New Israel* (Englewood Cliffs NJ: Prentice-Hall, 1971), p. 273.

2. Arthur M. Schlesinger, Jr., *The Cycles of American History* (Boston: Houghton Mifflin, 1986), pp. 52, 54.

3. Reinhold Niebuhr, "Why the Christian Church is not Pacifist," in *The Essential Reinhold Niebuhr,* ed. Robert McAfee Brown (New Haven: Yale University Press, 1986), pp. 104–105.

4. Reinhold Niebuhr, "Mystery and Meaning," op. cit., p. 249.

5. Franklin D. Roosevelt, "The Four Freedoms," in *The Annals of America,* vol. 16 (Chicago: Encyclopaedia Britannica, 1976), p. 45.

6. See Cherry, op. cit., pp. 295–302.

7. See ibid., pp. 303–308.

PART TWO

Worldview in Religious America

Unlike the concept of the history of American religion, the concept of worldview requires substantial explanation, partly because of the concept itself, and partly because of the empirical bent of scholars of American religion, who tend to be better at history than at philosophy or theology.

The concept of worldview or *Weltanschaung* is not the clearest. The equivalent terms *outlook, sense of reality,* and *philosophy* do not quite capture the concept's essence. *Worldview* should connote not only one's orientation in the realm of space and time, geography and history, but also the values one spontaneously attributes to air and land, tribe and city, the self that is artistic and the self that is afflicted by what the philosopher Martin Heidegger called "everydayness." Indeed the term should include what one makes of the radical mysteriousness of life, the question marks that never fall away. This part explores how Americans talk to themselves about their human condition, how they give particular color and weight to the universal struggle to survive and find meaning. Such an exploration is bound to suffer many frustrations. Like all other peoples, Americans have been varied, inconsistent, and pluralistic. Indeed, some observers of American culture would stress individualism, and so diversity, as the primary American attribute. The term

The artist has transposed Rodin's classic sculpture of the thinker to suit America at the turn of the 20th century. (The Thinker: Portrait of Louis N. Kenton, Thomas Eakins. The Metropolitan Museum of Art, Kennedy Fund, 1917)

141

worldview therefore usually should be understood as *worldviews*—and not merely plural but hotly debated.

The interpretative position of this book is an attempt at balanced realism. The authors want to hold particulars and universals in dialectical tension, as traditional philosophy long has done and much postmodern philosophy aspires to do. Content to accept the suggestion of scholarly readers that a section on the American religious worldview or mindset ought to stress the diversity of outlooks the United States has accommodated, the authors still refuse to give up on sketching something that might distinguish American religiosity as a whole from the religiosity of the British, the French, or any other comparable people. It is salutary to keep asking whether something whole emerges from U.S. religious history, whether there is a holistic subject of which one can predicate various qualities. This whole keeps us seeking correlations, convergences, common characteristics.

Several further things must be mentioned. First, the authors are interested in wholes for pedagogical as well as philosophical reasons. In introductory, nonspecialist courses, students instinctively seek, and ought to get, an overview, some sense of the whole. Second, a brief word is needed about the relation between worldview and religion. Is there a worldview that is not religious? On the level of appearance, where one is simply describing how people seem to live, how they think, and what they say about their lives, the answer is yes. Many people can be described as configuring the world with so little positive reference to divinity or religious institutions that one has to call them secular, atheistic, or humanistic in ways that make those words antonyms of religion. Whether a teacher of religion can admit a worldview that disregards religion is a much more dubious question. One probably cannot separate religion from worldview when one tries to explain the existential structures and dynamics of human meaning. To put it concretely, probably no sketch or sense of reality worth considering can overlook the mysteriousness pushed in our faces by death, birth, creativity, natural change, mystical experience, suffering, love, insight, and the other factors one would mention when getting serious about defining humanity. That mysteriousness is the gist of any religion.

So this discussion of worldview in American religious history treats reality as having four irreducible aspects—nature, society, self, and divinity—and implies that nature, society, and self naturally depend on divinity (or ultimate mystery) for their full resonance. The three other themes—evil, salvation, and destiny—admit of nonreligious interpretations, but their best treatment, on both historical and philosophical grounds, associates what they have meant to Americans with the religious traditions that have flourished in the United States.

With these seven topics, the authors hope to suggest both the diversity and the congruence of American opinions about the basic structures of existence, which produce an American worldview that is both dialectical and religious.

The Land

A Physical Description of America

The two great determinants of the physical features of a country are its geology and its atmosphere. Beginning with gross geological features, the center of the coterminous 48 states is an interior lowland extending throughout North America from Canada to Mexico. Moving east and west from the center one encounters mountain ranges that separate the lowlands from the sea. In the East the Appalachians—a low, nearly unbroken range set well back from the ocean—divide the interior lowlands from a low coastal plain that stretches from New York City to the Mexican border. This coastal plain bends west in Georgia and Alabama, cutting off the Appalachians and swinging into south central Texas. West of the central lowlands the mountains are part of the Cordillera system ringing the Pacific basin. The easternmost part of this system, the Rocky Mountains, stretches from New Mexico to the Canadian border. Between the Rockies and the Pacific coastal mountains lie basins, ranges, and plateaus in a complex, intermountain area. Using the gross features of central lowlands, major mountain systems, plains, and intermountain areas, one can divide the United States into as many as 24 major subregions.

143

The features of the eastern United States, combined with the fact that the white settlers came from Europe, have caused some to think that indigenous white American culture, in contrast to imported European culture, began only when settlers moved west across the eastern mountains. In the vast expanses of the interior lowlands Americans could finally feel free of European constraints. The central lowlands are like a great saucer, depressed in the middle and sloping upward on the sides. The western lowlands or Great Plains run from Canada to Mexico in a swath at least 500 miles wide. Here was more than enough space for farming and ranching, for a system of small towns and highly individualized, self-reliant, life-styles. Between the Rockies and the Appalachians, the country developed an agricultural base to balance its coastal urbanity.

Human populations make such an impact on the environment that it is difficult to speak of the natural ecology of the continental United States. Scientists can observe lands that have reverted from human use to something approaching their presumably natural state, but the fauna of such lands never return as the flora tend to do. Among the main natural controls on the U.S. climate are the country's position in the middle latitudes, its central place in the North American continental landmass, the oceans at its eastern, western, and southern borders, and its geological pattern of mountains and lowlands.

Because the coterminous states lie entirely between the Tropic of Cancer and 50 degrees north latitude, only the high mountains have an arctic climate and only southernmost Florida is genuinely tropical. This median, temperate climatic positioning has much to do with the overall experience human beings have had on the American land. However, the middle latitudes admit great swings between their temperature extremes, especially in the central landmass. Thus while the mean temperatures for most American areas have been moderate, some areas have regularly experienced temperature variations over a range of 120 degrees Fahrenheit. Indeed North Dakota has ranged from 120°F to −60°F. In contrast, a city like San Francisco, whose climate is controlled by the Pacific ocean, has a relatively slight temperature differential between summer and winter.

In the West the Cordillera confines both Pacific temperatures and rainfall to the coastal regions. The main barriers are the Sierra Nevada and Cascade ranges, which eastward-moving weather must pass. West of them rain is abundant but on their eastern side the land is barren. Indeed the entire area between the Pacific and Rocky Mountains is largely dry, while the Great Plains are semiarid. East of the Great Plains moist air traveling north from the Gulf of Mexico increases the humidity. This gulf air produces more precipitation than the Atlantic and Pacific oceans together. The openness of the central lowlands, which allows air to travel rapidly from both south and north, often produces spectacularly violent weather: blizzards, tornadoes, hailstorms, and sudden drastic changes in temperature. If the landscape is less varied than that of either coast, the weather is more exciting, sometimes dangerously so.

There are three major bioclimatic regions in the United States. The East is a humid zone, the largest climatic area, and its character has profoundly influenced American history. It was the first environment the European settlers had to adapt to and tame. Heavily forested, it is divided into four zones.

1. The northernmost zone is subarctic forest, the southernmost fringe of the Canadian taiga. Here the main characteristics have been scrubby forest dominated by spruces and firs adapted to the harsh winters and short summers. While the average growing season is only about 120 days, there is

considerable variation. Thus Newberry, Michigan, has had growing seasons as short as 76 days and as long as 161 days. In this region farming is usually impractical.

2. The next area to the south is a humid microthermal zone offering milder winters and longer summers. Broadleaf trees replace the evergreens, and farming is possible.

3. The next climatic zone is described as humid subtropical and takes one into the Deep South. At its northern edge the growing season lengthens to nearly 200 days, the limit for cotton. Originally this area supported rich broadleaf forests and fauna, but overcutting, overcropping, and burning have reduced it to poor pines. Summers are long, hot, and uncomfortable.

4. The southernmost eastern zone is southern Florida, the only truly tropical area in the Unites States. Frost is virtually unknown and monsoon patterns of hot, rainy summers alternating with warm, drier winters prevail. Elevation is so slight that much of the area is swampy and difficult to farm.

The humid Pacific coast is a small zone, markedly different from its eastern counterpart. Because of the many coastal mountains, it has numerous microclimatic zones. The prevailing pattern overall is for winters to be rainy and summers dry, but the extent of the drought varies considerably from north to south. Where Washington averages only two months of summer drought, southern California averages five. In western Washington, Oregon, and northern California, winters are like those of northwestern Europe: raw, overcast, and drizzly. Summers tend to be cloudless, cool, and occasionally foggy. Central and southern coastal California enjoy a Mediterranean climate. Coastal temperatures tend to be cool, but the inland regions are very hot and dry in summer.

The third major climatic zone is that of the dry West, which includes the areas between the western mountain ranges and the Great Plains. Americans have found this the hardest area to tame, and everywhere water is the most precious commodity. Water determines the principal distinction in this region, which is between deserts and semiarid steppes. Only the Southwest is truly desert. Most of the other subareas are semiarid and will support ranching or judicious farming. The weather is often violent, and on occasion it can be devastating. During the 1930s, for example, western Oklahoma became a dust bowl.

While all of the climatic regions, like all of the geological regions, have worked a considerable influence on the people who have inhabited them, the most important transition has been from the humid eastern regions to the arid West. A subtle shift occurs between the 95th and 100th meridians, along a north-south axis from Texas to North Dakota. Originally prairies—a sea of tall grasses—this area has been tilled and planted in grains. West of this transition zone come the truly arid and desert areas and the irregular microclimates produced by the Rocky Mountains. East of it are the more humid zones of the central lowlands and the south, which extend to the Atlantic.[1]

This physical description of the United States bears no obvious implications for human character, let alone religion, and yet the area in which people live so subtly shapes their whole lives that one is not surprised to find southwestern art and religion perceptibly different from the art and religion of New England. Similarly, no one would mistake San Francisco for Boston or Chicago for New Orleans. Certainly history and ethnic mixture are large parts of the reason why, but so are geography and climate. The common human search for meaning and holiness is diversified by the habitats in which it takes place. In so vast and varied a country as the United States, it is not surprising that religion has gained so many different forms and faces.

Nature in American Piety

From the beginning of the colonial venture, nature stood before Americans as something to comprehend and transform through biblical categories. The many overtones to the land of promise in Old Testament narrative suggested that in their vast new homeland the settlers might make God's new Israel, a land flowing with milk, honey, and virtue. The biblical theme that God had espoused Israel in the wilderness, that the 40-year trek between Egypt and Canaan was a time of hard but virtuous religious living, suggested that the colonial time of establishing foundations might be privileged.

The imagery of Eden as a garden, lush and subservient to humanity's needs, played into the Puritan ideals of ascetic control and the new **Baconian** views of science, according to which knowledge was power to control nature and make it serve human welfare. Above all the newness of the opportunity fascinated the early American religious imagination. Those who had fled what they considered a decadent Europe looked on America as pristine and full of possibility. In terms of their intimacy with the God the Psalmist praised in all his wondrous works, as well as their hopes for better social relations and religious freedoms, the new settlers approached the virgin forests hopefully.

Jonathan Edwards (1703–1758), the first outstanding American theologian, was extremely interested in natural science as a boy and wrote exercise pieces on insects, the rainbow, and colors.[2] This training in science, combined with his philosophical studies of John Locke and his Calvinist theology, made Edwards a penetrating thinker. In maturity, Edwards regularly jotted down his reflections about various experiences and intellectual matters. Some of his thoughts about how nature offers images or shadows of divine things suggest his later religious use of his longstanding interest in the physical world.

It is very probable that the wonderful suitableness of green for the grass and plants, the blue of the skie, the white of the clouds, the colours of flowers, consists in a complicated proportion that these colours make one with another, either in their magnitude of the rays, the number of vibrations that are caused in the atmosphere, or some other way. So there is a great suitableness between the objects of different senses, as between sounds, colours, and smells; as between colours of the woods and flowers and the smells and the singing of birds, which it is probable consist in a certain proportion of the vibrations that are made in the different organs. So there are innumerable other agreeablenesses of motions, figures, etc. The gentle motions of waves, of the lily, etc., as it is agreeable to other things that represent calmness, gentleness, and benevolence, etc., the fields and woods seem to rejoice, and how joyfull do the birds seem to be in it. How much a resemblance is there of every grace in the field covered with plants and flowers when the sun shines serenely and undisturbedly upon them, how a resemblance, I say, of every grace and beautiful disposition of mind, of an inferiour towards a superior cause, preserver, benevolent benefactor, and a fountain of happiness. How great a resemblance of a holy and virtuous soul is a calm, serene day. What an infinite number of such like beauties is there in that one thing, the light, and how complicated an harmony and proportion it is probable belongs to it.[3]

In this mood, Edwards finds nature completely harmonious, and the close implication is that such harmony both comes from God and expresses the order of all divine things, including the virtuous soul. The long-standing Christian argument for the existence of God from the orderliness or design of nature plays in the background. The perfect complementarity of the colors and sounds of a lovely day cannot be accidental. Implied in their marvelous convergence is a complex series of causes or coordinations that had to come from the maker of heaven and earth. The faith Edwards has in the biblical God more supports his quasi-scientific estimate of natural harmony than fights with it. The religious import of this mood is not hard to imagine. One ought to praise the source of the beauty and harmony in nature. One ought to go and do likewise in human affairs, both those pertaining to one's own soul and those pertaining to social intercourse.

The simplicity and peace of nature have long offered people refuge from the frictions of social intercourse. Everywhere people have found solitude a way to refresh their souls. Nature is long and human life is short. Nature is vast and imperturbable, a welcome contrast to the pressure of human affairs, Edwards passes over the turbulences in nature itself. In this mood he has forgotten thunder and lightning, floods, and earthquakes. The destructions of nature, the calibrated depredations of life living on life, at best stand at the margins of his consciousness. He surely knows that nature is more than pleasant harmonies and that nature can seem cruel and wantonly destructive. In another mood he might meditate on the divine power, the wrath of God, that this side of nature foreshadows. But here the garden prevails over the wilderness. Here nature is the tame servant of God, the exemplary instructor of the human soul.

As the United States became industrialized, the aesthetic mood of Jonathan Edwards became more difficult to sustain. The same Bible that depicted a natural paradise and spoke glowingly of the promised land had put the earth into the charge of human beings. Whether the commission recorded in Genesis 1 was a license to exploit nature rather than a call for good stewardship of nature's bounty is a matter for biblical scholars to clarify. Regardless of how such a clarification might turn out, the bare biblical text was bound to make human beings think they were the overlords of nature and entitled to think of it largely in terms of the profit that subduing it might bring them.

Then God said, "Let us make man in our image, after our likeness, and let them have dominion over the fish of the sea, and over the birds of the air, and over the cattle, and over all the earth, and over every creeping thing that creeps upon the earth." So God created man in his own image, in the image of God he created him; male and female he created them. And God blessed them, and God said to them, "Be fruitful and multiply, and fill the earth and subdue it; and have dominion over the fish of the sea and over the birds of the air and over every living thing that moves upon the earth" (Gen. 1:26–28).

When it became clear that the mineral and other natural resources of the American continent could serve industrial production and expansion, the same religious instincts that equated material prospering with God's blessing stepped forward to anoint such development as a godly thing. Certainly some religious leaders spoke of the problems in such industrial development, citing the hardships suffered by the working classes, the strains put on the women and children exploited in the factories, the difficult lot of the miners, and the like. Certainly a few lamented the dirt and noise that were polluting the environment and seemed a shabby substitute for nature's grace and quiet. But the drive to produce, to earn good yield on the talents God had given Americans and not bury them in the ground, predictably got more attention. The ethic of responsibility, of earnest effort to be productive, of considering laziness the worst of sins, and of thinking that good works showed the presence of divine favor (a stunning reversal of classical Reformation theology) had won the day.

In light of such an ethic, nature was providential raw material, so bountiful in the New World that one need not worry about wearing it out, fouling its ecosystems, or offending against the divinity revealed in its harmonies. Second thoughts and recriminations would come much later, after the middle of the 20th century, when three-and-a-half centuries of treating nature almost entirely as the servant of human desires had created awful pollution. The American way of life built on Genesis 1:28 was then seen to be hostile to the good of nature and thus hostile to the good of posterity. The daily reports of chemical spills, polluted rivers and water tables, acid rain, the greenhouse effect, ozone depletion, soil erosion, and the like made it clear that the modern way of exploiting nature was a venture in geocide. Then the question became whether America had the spiritual resources to turn things around, to repent and be converted to ecological wisdom.

Errands and Frontiers

The westward expansion of the United States was perhaps the major drama of the period between the Revolution and the Civil War. Certainly early explorers such as Père Marquette had expanded the imagination of colonists and adventurers during the 17th and 18th centuries, but it was the likes of Lewis and Clark, with their overland expedition to the Pacific Northwest, who gave full flesh to the American wonder about the configuration of the continent on which the experiment of the United States would unfold. While private secretary to President Thomas Jefferson, Meriwether Lewis (1774–1809) prepared to fulfill Jefferson's hopes for a transcontinental expedition. One might view him as a prototype of the postrevolutionary American. Having gained their independence, the people of the United States naturally began to think more proprietarily and ambitiously about their place in the sun. Eventually they would buy, annex, and otherwise win the full width of the continent. In so doing they both extended the Puritans' sense of an errand in the wilderness of New England and etched in the American character a long-playing romance with the notion of the frontier.

The Puritans' sense of the errand in the wilderness was a charge to make a New Israel: a land and people covenanted to God in holiness, virtue, and prosperity. The sense of election running through the Old Testament merely shifted circuits to pass through a Calvinist system and emerge as a providential commission to develop the New World. Eventually this sense of election, providence, and destiny would take over early 20th-century American politics and lead to a national self-conception as leader of the free world and spearhead of the holy war against the godlessness first of Nazi Germany and then of the Soviet Union and the other Communist states. In the early colonial decades, however, the religious sense of election was both more intense and more modest. The plan and hope was to make a relatively small-scale city on a hill, whence American Indians and interested Europeans alike might see what fidelity to a biblical covenant with God could create.

By the time westward expansion got fully under way in the 19th century, the errand in the wilderness was more a pious memory than a present motivation. No doubt the preachers riding the frontier circuits felt they were bringing divine grace to needy, sinful areas, and no doubt some pioneers gave their homesteading ventures a religious rationale, as they thought about gaining their own land, their own homes, and freedom to control their own fate. But the Calvinist social covenant of the Puritans had yielded to the Baptists' and Methodists' more individualistic concern for personal salvation and regeneration. Revivalism was the pulse of the frontier as it passed through the Midwest. Jonathan Edwards would not have fit in at most camp meetings or riverside mass baptisms.

Perhaps the most interesting way to think of the religious implications of the western expansion is in terms of how the symbolism of the frontier provoked thoughts of God. In fact nature has historically lured given cultures toward an expanded sense of both their own possibilities and the divinity that might give order to their drives. For example, the oceanic expanse surrounding the islands of ancient Greece seems to have stimulated her people to expansion. The ever-receding horizon experienced by sailors was bound to extend the Greek mind. It is hard to say how directly this affected the Greeks' ability to differentiate the dynamics of consciousness and develop both a comprehensive metaphysics, ambitious to map the **ontology** of all of reality, and a sense that divinity itself was the mover of the human mind in such outgoings. But just as the wonderful light of the Greek islands tempts historians and psychologists to suggest an ecological basis for the Apollonian side of Greek culture (its interest in intellectual clarity and order), so the oceanic horizon may have worked on the Greeks to expand their intellectual horizons. Thus when Alexander the Great put together one of the first polycultural realms, the Greeks were already primed to take seriously the notion of an *oecumene*—an entire inhabited world making something whole.

One could develop a similar analogy from the desert experience of Israelite and Arab tribes. Both groups came to think of divinity as a single comprehensive field, transcending even the endless expanse of desert waste they could survey, and both became listeners for a Word of revelation. These Semitic people were more aural than visual and so leaned toward iconoclasm, letting nothing visual stand for God and insisting that the divine Word, unrepresented visually, be the only acceptable embodiment of the holy Lord of the Worlds. Both the Greek and the Semitic parallels prepare us to think of the ever-moving American western frontier as a similar prod to the expansion of consciousness associated with a transcendence that ultimately has to be correlated with God, the ultimate unbounded reality, the sole being fully infinite (without frontiers).

Insofar as Americans of the early 19th century encountered a nature that always seemed to offer more—another set of hills receding into the distance, more miles of waving grasses that stretched like the sea—they were bound to be both exhilarated and subdued. They were exhil-

arated by the novelty: new areas to explore, new things to learn, new ways to grow. They were subdued by the fatigue that set in when the new lands proved hard to bring under control and into production. All human beings know moments when the same novelty or vastness that excites them becomes overwhelming. As they realize they will never become the masters of their land, or their area of study, or the mysteriousness of their lives and world, they feel a world-weariness that is the downside of finitude. The human being is a peculiar creature both without boundaries (due to its spiritual aspirations) and completely fenced in (by its body and mortality). Any adventure such as the American westward trek was bound to stimulate both experiences of transcendence, in which imagination, will, and gratitude flowed out in an effort to match the endlessness of what was being revealed from sunrise to sunset, and experiences of finitude, in which the vastness of nature, like the endlessness of human folly, proved depressing.

Those who credit the westward expansion with stamping something permanently optimistic into the American character, along with such qualities as self-reliance and a fierce demand for individual freedoms, emphasize the exhilarating and testing aspects of frontier life. Probably they rightly consider the depressing aspects more idiosyncratic, private, and related to individual family circumstances (deaths, cripplings, disappointments) than the stuff of the common national character being forged. But Americans finally did run up against the end of the natural frontier, their population rose toward the limits of their continent's carrying capacity, and ecological pollution began to choke them. Then the sobering side of having their physical frontiers cease to recede became undeniable.

Nowadays, of course, all citizens of the earth should recognize that living on a globe by definition subjects one to both an ever-moving horizon and finite land and resources. The exploration of space has rekindled the old pioneer spirit in some, while for others scientific research and artistic creativity have become spiritual transformations of the previously physical forms of exploration and expedition.

Any estimate of the worldviews that have predominated in the United States has to underscore the expansive sense of nature created in those who settled the West. God had given the country great space. And while entrepreneurs might lick their chops mainly at the profits to be wrung from the mountains and valleys articulating America's space, many ordinary people took their perception of nature's bounty as a stimulus to thanksgiving, gratitude, and awe. They might not have stood before El Capitan in Yosemite Valley with the profound reverence typical of Native Americans, but most of them would have been stirred out of any purely pragmatic narrowness. The natural being, the physical existence, unfolded to those who traveled west tended also to unfurl their spirits. The world of Lewis and Clark was bigger than the world of a New England colonist 150 years earlier, if only because their eyes had seen so much more.

Smohalla

To personalize the issue of nature in the American worldview, it may be helpful to focus on Smohalla (ca. 1815–1895) an Indian prophet from the Upper Columbia river area of what is now eastern Washington. With several other Indian prophets of his time, he protested the threat to the Indian way of life presented by the encroachment of white settlers. Smohalla's response was to found a religious group, called the Dreamers, that stressed traditional Indian values and foresaw the demise of the whites. Around 1850, for example, he urged Indians to perform their traditional dances in honor of the dead as a way to incite the earth to a destruction and renewal that would both remove the

whites and restore the Indian dead. By 1872 Smohalla had a great following and his prophecies helped to inspire the Nez Perce war of 1877.

The road to such influence began in early maturity when Smohalla distinguished himself among his Wanapum people (a group related to the Nez Perce) as a warrior and medicine man. Because of conflict with a rival he left his native area and traveled south, staying away for several years. When he returned he claimed to have died and been resurrected and so to have been authorized to speak of what was to come between the Indians and the whites.

The problem of white encroachment into Indian areas of the Northwest had been exacerbated by the completion of the Northern Pacific Railway. The U.S. government wanted to move the Indians from their lands either to reservations or to homesteading areas where they could farm. This ran counter to the traditional Indian way of life, which had been based on hunting and fishing. Still, some Indians accepted the government's offer and decided to give agriculture a try. Smohalla opposed this capitulation, arguing that Indians were God's real people, created before the whites, blacks, and Chinese. (Both Indians and whites had to grapple with the question of how their senses of "god" related.) The later peoples had been created only because the Indians had forsaken their traditional ways and deserved God's punishment. The main requisite for the Indians to regain God's favor was for them to return to their traditional ways and neither plow the earth (take up agriculture) nor sign over their land to the U.S. government. Both such actions were contrary to nature.

Smohalla believed that the rituals of his Dreamer cult could return the Indians to what was their natural relation to God. The forces of nature invoked in the cult would rally to the Indians' side, as would the dead Indians who would be resurrected (as Smohalla himself had been). Together, all of these forces—nature, res-

While the buffalo represented sport to many Americans moving west, to some plains tribes of Native Americans the buffalo stood at the center of traditional culture. (Buffalos, George Catlin; Gilcrease Museum, Tulsa, Oklahoma)

urrected Indians, and God—would drive the whites from the Indians' land. The Dreamers believed that God's directives came to Smohalla and others in dreams, and that following such directions would put them in the right way, the way of power. Their rituals employed drumming, bells, and ecstatic dancing, all of which were calculated to bring on visions and an exalted state of mind.

When Smohalla gained the allegiance of Chief Joseph of the Nez Perce, his physical force increased considerably. The Indians united sufficiently to oppose the U.S. government's settlement policies and retard Indians' conversion to white ways. In 1855 the Nez Perce had signed a treaty creating a large reservation that preserved most of their traditional lands, but the discovery of gold in 1860 led the U.S. government to change the treaty in 1863 to reduce the Nez Perce lands to one-fourth of the original area. As more homesteaders came in, even these lands shrank. So in 1877 war broke out. Chief Joseph led an Indian army that resisted the white soldiers for five months, fleeing through Montana and Yellowstone Park. To subdue the rebellion the government promised the Nez Perce land in the Northwest but then transported them to areas in Oklahoma infected by malarial mosquitos. Smohalla's dark view of the whites was confirmed.

A famous quotation from Smohalla clarifies his attitudes toward nature and his rejection of the U.S. plan to make the northwestern Indians into farmers. To his mind farming was an attack on his mother the earth: "Shall I rip into the bosom of our mother the earth?" he said. The earth was a living relative, the source of all animals, plants, and human beings. Plowing desecrated the earth. It symbolized the white mentality, which was aggressive, destructive, alien to how Indians had lived with Mother Earth for generations. Naturally it had to be opposed, and naturally Smohalla could dream that the earth itself, and all those prior generations that had enjoyed good relations with the earth, would rise up to aid the opposition.

The point here is to contrast the mentality of the whites who moved west, first to homestead and then to mine and otherwise "develop" natural resources, with the Native American mentality. It is hard not to romanticize the native mentality because it seems such a pure contrast to the subjugating mentality of the whites. For the Native Americans, as for hunting and gathering peoples everywhere (and also for many early farming peoples), the earth was a sacred, living whole. The human tribe, let alone the human individual, was only a small factor in a holistic natural economy. The Grandfather Spirit and Mother Earth gave life in profusion wherever they passed. The stones under the ground were like the bones of Mother Earth. The grasses were like her hair. To dig into the earth was

unthinkable. In the spring, many Indian tribes removed their moccasins to walk softly on the earth, for then the Mother was pregnant with new life.

This mythic, colorful regard for Mother Earth could only flourish among nonliterate people who encountered nature directly and whose survival and prosperity depended on making nature the prime "book" they had to master. Overwhelmed by the power of nature, as well as their own sense of complete dependence, they learned to be sensitive to nature's every mood and fancy. Many Indians would speak to the plants and animals they had to kill for food, apologizing to them, thanking them for their donation of life. A complex system of taboos arose in many tribes to safeguard the venerability of animal life. Native American life had its dark sides, of course. But its different regard of nature told the few whites with ears to hear that the Bible had not exhausted the ways one might conceive of the relationships among humanity, nature, and divinity.

Brooke Medicine Eagle, the great-great-grandniece of Chief Joseph, recently has brought this Indian naturalism up to date. Reflecting on a vision given her by the Rainbow Woman, she has said,

In the philosophy of the true Indian people, Indian is an attitude, a state of mind; Indian is a state of being, the place of the heart. To allow the heart to be the distributor of energy on this planet; to allow your heart, your feelings, your emotions to distribute your energy; to pull that energy from the earth, from the sky; to pull it down and distribute it from your heart, the very center of your being—that is our purpose. Several traditions talk about four or five different worlds and say that the Creator made all these worlds with one simple law: that we shall be in harmony and in balance with all things, including the sun. And time and again people have destroyed that harmony; we have destroyed that harmony. And we have done it again needlessly. Unless we bring about that balance again, this is our last chance.[4]

Thoreau's *Walden*

Henry David Thoreau (1817–1862) is forever associated with the Transcendentalist movement, one of the most significant literary waves of 19th-century America. Thoreau grew up in Concord, Massachusetts, and went to Harvard College. His early interests were the Greek and Latin classics, natural history, and mathematics. In later years Thoreau said the greatest benefit he had received from Harvard had been access to its good library. Thoreau tried his hand at teaching but failed and so resigned himself to working in his father's pencil factory. Realizing that he felt most at home in the woods, Thoreau resolved to make his way as a poet of nature. By chance he became friendly with Ralph Waldo Emerson, who had settled in Concord and was beginning to have great success as a literary figure. Thoreau apprenticed himself to Emerson and gained his approval as a fine embodiment of the self-reliance that Emerson was preaching.

Under Emerson's leadership a sparkling literary group, the Transcendentalists, gathered in Concord and agreed to celebrate the individual, emotion, and nature in preference to the masses, reason, and humanity. Thoreau became a strong figure in this group, writing poems, essays, and regular entries in a journal that at his death had reached thousands of pages. Many of his early writings were published in the Transcendentalist magazine, *The Dial*, and he quickly became known as a remarkable nature writer.

Thoreau's greatest success came from his move to Walden Pond in 1845, where he stayed (on land owned by Emerson) for two years, living very simply and enjoying time to observe nature, reflect, read, and write. Two of his major writings came from this period. *A Week on the Concord and Merimmack Rivers* and *Walden, or Life in the Woods*. At that time he also spent a night in jail for refusing to pay his poll tax because he could not support a government that endorsed slavery and was engaged in an imperialist war with Mexico. Reflecting on his jail experience, Thoreau produced one of his most famous essays, "On Civil Disobedience."

In later years Thoreau was more a naturalist than a Transcendentalist philospher and spent more time in the family business than writing poetry. He also became a political activist, strongly supporting the abolitionist cause and helping the underground railroad. Only after his death did his reputation soar, as his principal ideas—the need to follow one's conscience, the superiority of the woods to the crowded streets, and the superiority of experiencing life to making a living—came to represent a stark challenge to thoughtless middle-class culture.

In the chapter of *Walden* entitled "Winter Animals," one finds the splendid descriptive powers for which Thoreau has long been celebrated. For example,

One night in the beginning of winter, before the pond froze over, about nine o'clock, I was startled by the loud honking of a goose, and, stepping to the door, heard the sound of their wings like a tempest in the woods as they flew low over my house. They passed over the pond toward Fair Haven, seemingly deterred from settling by my light, their commodore honking all the while with a regular beat. Suddenly an unmistakable cat-owl from very near me, with the most harsh and tremendous voice I ever heard from any inhabitant of the woods, responded at regular intervals to the goose, as if determined to expose and disgrace this intruder from Hudson's Bay by exhibiting a greater compass and volume of voice in a native, and *boo-hoo* him out of Concord horizon. What do you mean by alarming the citadel at this time of night consecrated to me? Do you think I am ever caught napping at such an hour, and that I have not got lungs and a larynx as well as yourself? *Boo-hoo, boo-hoo, boo-hoo!* It was one of the most thrilling discords I ever heard. And yet, if you had a discriminating ear, there were in it the elements of a concord such as these plains never saw nor heard.

I also heard the whooping of the ice in the pond, my great bedfellow in that part of Concord,

*The Shoshone Falls are a good example of the grand design that both Thoreau and Native Americans regularly found in nature. (*Shoshone Falls on the Snake River, *Thomas Moran; Gilcrease Museum, Tulsa, Oklahoma)*

as if it were restless in its bed and would fain turn over, were troubled with flatulency and bad dreams; or I was waked by the cracking of the ground by the frost, as if some one had driven a team against my door, and in the morning would find a crack in the earth a quarter of a mile long and a third of an inch wide.

Sometimes I heard the foxes as they ranged over the snow-crust, in moonlight nights, in search of a partridge or other game, barking raggedly and demoniacally like forest dogs, as if laboring with some anxiety, or seeking expression, struggling for light and to be dogs outright and run freely in the streets; for if we take the ages into our account, may there not be a civilization going on among brutes as well as men? They seemed to me to be rudimental, burrowing men, still standing on their defence, awaiting their transformation. Sometimes one came near to my window, attracted by my light, barked a vulpine curse at me, and then retreated.[5]

Thoreau's view of nature clearly bears some important similarities to those of Native Americans, and yet the differences between his sense of the woods and that of a typical Native American are equally instructive. He stands with the typical Indian in subordinating human affairs to the grander design of nature. During his Walden period Thoreau often ventured back into Concord society, but his psychic center lay in the woods. More times than not he was alone there, fitting into its patterns of light and sound, of trees swaying in the wind and squirrels husbanding nuts, rather than into the social patterns of Concord town life. In such isolation one's thought is free from the manipulations of ordinary conversation. Quiet frames one's inner words, making them stand out and seem more significant than they normally do. The particulars of physical existence take on sharper angles, more distinctive colors. One's spirit adjusts to the leisure of the woods and tends to become contemplative and poised, waiting for whatever revelations the day produces. The human focus inevitable in society vaporizes and drifts away, as though it had never been substantial. Something of the vastness of geological time presses on the imagination, shaping a new horizon from slowness and leisure.

Thoreau judged that such changes in the human personality made life in the woods better than life in the town. He found his time, his existence, better justified at Walden than it had ever been before. The spirituality lost in most workaday preoccupations was more easily retained. The distractions and lies of human intercourse slipped away. There was no reason to lie in the woods, and there was much opportunity to ponder, clarify, and sense the mind's natural desire to let what was be as it was without distortion. The less things had to be pulled into the orbit of human need and use, the less they had to be distorted.

But Thoreau remained very much the educated, refined, psychological white man throughout his time at Walden. The **anthropomorphism** that makes his descriptions of the cat-owl, the ice, and the foxes so winning could only have been written by a human being who could treasure the Harvard library. Thoreau's is an imagination stimulated by the woods to think about the human condition. It takes the animals and geology as tutors in how human beings ought to compose their souls. Certainly Thoreau does this without resorting to allegory. At Walden he wrote no bestiary. But he also wrote no ceremonials for the sweat lodge, or the rain dance, or the hallowing of Mother Earth in the spring. The best of white naturalism never entered into the **cosmological myth** characteristic of Native Americans and other precivilized peoples. Something in its cultural foundations, whether from the Bible or from classical literature, always kept the world under intellectual survey, stood aside as judge, if not master and engineer. Thoreau does not give himself to nature, is not immersed in nature's flow, as hunting and gathering peoples could be. He loved nature more for what it offers human beings, for how it gives perspective and detachment, than for its directly divine qualities. Nature is not the body of God to Thoreau, no matter how rhetorical the Transcendentalist nature poetry had become. So Thoreau is a congenial way station between the precivilized immersion in nature that American whites could never experience and the totally unattuned, unsympathetic attitudes of the worst developers, those who would ring Walden Pond with condominiums. As in his writing on civil disobedience, in *Walden* Thoreau remains a cautionary figure, more a magistrate than a prophet, telling us that we can judge our culture by what it considers profitable, how it compares spiritual freedom and financial or social gain.

Key Terms

Anthropomorphism: casting something nonhuman (for example, an animal) in human terms. Most ancient peoples have spoken of animals, plants, and forces of nature as though they had souls, minds, and wills. Most religions have pictured divinity on the model of human existence, speaking of intelligence, volition, and even passion as divine attributes. Human beings seem nearly condemned to anthropomorphism, inasmuch as we are always drawing from human experience and trying to render nonhuman beings intelligible in human terms. The danger in theology is to forget that anthropomorphic speech is always merely analogous and so take such figures as God's wrath or God's love as meaning what they would were God human.

Baconian: referring to the philosophy of Francis Bacon (1561–1626). Bacon proposed a new method, to supplant that of Aristotle, according to which human inquiry would become scientific by stressing induction. His ideal was a secular approach to the material world that would rid it of impractical symbolisms and bring nature into the service of human prosperity. While the particulars of Bacon's own theories provide for considerable nuance, generally he helped free natural science from religious contemplation and prepared the way for the technical approaches to nature illustrated by modern engineering.

Cosmological myth: the narrative understanding of reality that situates human existence within a cosmos taken to be fully alive and organically whole. Hunting and gathering peoples typically think of reality this way, telling themselves stories of how the world was born, how the sun and the moon quarreled, how death arose, why the animals no longer speak to human beings except in visions and dreams, and so forth. The cosmological myth keeps human beings closely tied to plant and animal life, encouraging a great sensitivity to the spiritual import such fellow citizens carry. It does not acknowledge a transcendent divinity who made the world from nothingness, and it does not differentiate such mental products as myths, mathematical formulas, philosophical theories, and mystical symbols.

Ontology: the study of being. While *metaphysics* suggests rather formalistic explorations of what lies beyond the physical, *ontology* suggests some wonder and ecstasy about the primordial fact that some things have stepped forth from the void of nothingness. Ontology therefore works at the roots of human language, trying to think about the most basic structures of reality: existence and essence, form and matter. Its great stimulus and continuing preoccupation, however, is being: the one ultimate quality and the many ways it is differently possessed.

Discussion Questions

1. How should the two great determinants of the physical features of a country figure in preliminary estimates of the worldview likely to develop in that country?

2. How does the transition zone between the 95th and 100th meridians help delineate the gross features of the U.S. climate?

3. What main biblical views of nature shaped the American colonists?

4. What role does divinity play in Jonathan Edwards' reflection on the harmonies of nature?

5. What were the main implications of the westward expansion for the religious psychology of Americans?

6. How was movement on the frontier different from the colonial errand in the wilderness?

7. Why did Smohalla so bitterly oppose agriculture and consider it an epitome of white waywardness?

8. What does the white treatment of the Nez Perce suggest about American views of the land in the 1870s?

9. What is the transformation that Thoreau's foxes await?
10. How does nature tend to work on the solitary human spirit?

Notes

1. See "United States of America: Physical and Human Geography," in *The New Encyclopaedia Britannica*, vol. 29 (Chicago: Encyclopaedia Britannica, 1987), pp. 154–167.

2. See Ola Elizabeth Winslow, ed., *Jonathan Edwards: Basic Writings* (New York: New American Library 1966), pp. 31–44.

3. Ibid., p. 252.

4. Joan Halifax, *Shamanic Voices: A Survey of Visionary Narratives* (New York: E.P. Dutton, 1979), p. 91.

5. Henry David Thoreau, *Walden* (New York: Milestone Editions, 1970), pp. 240–241.

The People

A Demographic Sketch of America

In any demographic overview of America, at least six different population groups deserve attention: Yankees, ethnics, blacks, Hispanics, Native Americans, and Orientals. Until about 1860, the nonnative population of the United States was overwhelmingly white, Anglo-Saxon, and Protestant (WASP). Most American citizens had come from Britain. The immigration of Irish and Germans somewhat diversified this pattern, but the Irish usually spoke English and the majority of the Germans were Protestants. So only the Roman Catholicism of the majority of the Irish and the fact that many of the Germans continued to prefer their native tongue put any significant cracks in the WASP mold. The 10 percent of the 5 million who immigrated between 1820 and 1860 and were not British, Irish, or German were absorbed rather easily.

This pattern changed dramatically between 1860 and 1920. Perhaps 30 million immigrants during that period came from areas that were neither English speaking nor Protestant: Italy, the Balkans, Poland, and Russia. They tended to establish their own neighborhoods, retain their native languages, develop social clubs, and publish newspapers geared to preserving much of what they had known in the Old World. Because of their numerical bulk and ethnic ways, the older settlers came to be considered non-immigrant, and "immigration" became a phenomenon of the late 19th century. Thus the Dutch and Scots-Irish are often associated more with English Americans than with the groups that came in the second half of the 19th century. The Yankee families, as the British stock is often called, continue to be a dominant force in the corporations and professions that shape our mainstream economy and culture.

If one considers the Yankees the first demographic group, the second would be the the so-called ethnics—Italians, Poles, etc.—most of whom settled in northern and midwestern cities. They were more Catholic than Protestant, and the majority were working class. They tended to cling to an ethic of hard work as the way to prosper in American society.

The other four groups that stand out in a demographic survey are blacks, Hispanics, Native Americans, and Orientals. Blacks have been trying since the Civil War to overcome the devastating effects of slavery. They won important gains with the civil rights legislation of the 1960s, and a generation later they had made significant economic and political progress. Nonetheless the black fraction of the population (currently about 12 percent) has long been afflicted by poverty and suffering out of proportion to its numbers. Recently the figures on unemployment and crime have dramatized the problems of inner city areas, where 60 percent of the black population now lives.

Hispanics, who make up about 6 percent of the current U.S. population, have generally settled in states close to Mexico, the country to which more than half of the Hispanic population traces its origin. Thus Arizona, California, New Mexico, Texas, and Colorado have the largest Hispanic populations. The 15 percent of the Hispanic population that comes from Puerto Rico is largely located in or near New York City,

Mrs. Iselin suggests the pride and strength of a Yankee matriarch, confident of her important place in the American scheme of things. (Mrs. Adrian Iselin, John Singer Sargent; National Gallery of Art, Washington, D.C.; Gift of Ernest Iselin)

while the 6 percent that is of Cuban origin is centered in Miami. Spanish continues to be the principal language of more than half the Hispanic population, and, like blacks, Hispanics still suffer more poverty, unemployment, and crime than their white neighbors. Both blacks and Hispanics have made economic and political progress recently by organizing to promote better jobs, housing, health care, and the like.

The Native American population remains the group least integrated into American society. The 1980 census set this population at slightly under 1.5 million with Arizona, Oklahoma, and New Mexico having the largest numbers. More than half of America's natives still live on reservations, which tend to be pockets of poverty and suffering. Education, health care, and housing are generally far below national standards. For example, Native Americans die of tuberculosis at six times the national rate, have much higher infant mortality rates, and have a significantly shorter average life span than the population at large. Life on most reservations has separated Native Americans from the general culture and prevented their entry into urban job markets.

Oriental Americans—mainly Japanese, Chinese, and Filipinos—are concentrated in the cities of California and Hawaii. Although they are less than 3 percent of the population, they have established sufficiently stable communities to begin making significant contributions to American life, especially through their success in higher education. More recently Koreans, Vietnamese, and Cambodians have been diversifying the profile of Oriental Americans.

The U.S. population is diversified regionally despite the tendency of mass communications and transportation to dilute regional differences. The South continues to think of itself as a distinct region, although it admits of considerable variety. The New England states are still a recognizably distinct area, even though one could argue that the coastal megalopolis from southern Maine to central Virginia has become equally significant. Nonetheless demographers are apt to speak of three traditional U.S. areas deriving from the original colonial occupations:

1. New England, now comprised of six states, was significant not only for what went on within its present borders but also for its impact on contiguous areas. Thus some would call New York; northern New Jersey and Pennsylvania; and much of the upper Midwest, from Ohio to the Dakotas, an extension of New England. New Englanders also had much to do with the development of the Pacific Northwest (Oregon and Washington) and Hawaii.

2. The South is the largest and most diffuse of the three original regions. Like New England and the Midlands, its original white settlers were predominantly British. The Chesapeake Bay area is the best candidate for the title "cultural hearth" of the South, while the eastern coast, from North Carolina to the border of Florida, has become self-consciously set apart. The slow entry of the South into industrialization kept it full of diverse subregions for much of its history. Still one can speak of a basic division between the Deep South, dominated by plantation culture, and the upland South, shaped by the Appalachian, Ozark, and other mountains. Blacks have been populous in the Deep South but the upland South has been strongly WASP. From Virginia to Texas the deep-upland distinction has been relatively plain. Some argue that Texas should be considered a major subregion, while others claim that distinction for Louisiana and Florida, because of their historic ties to France and Spain.

3. The third traditional geographic/demographic area is often called the Midlands (not to be confused with the Midwest). In this region are the Mid-Atlantic and upper Southern states: Pennsylvania, New Jersey, Delaware, and Maryland. Traditionally this has been an urban and highly ethnic area, with many different languages and subcultures.

Later population developments and movements created such further regional distinctions as the Midwest, running perhaps from Pittsburgh to Kansas (Colorado being the beginning of the West proper). The West is hard to define and quite various, since the culture of the Rocky Mountain regions differs significantly from those of the Pacific Coast. The Pacific Northwest, including northern California, thinks of itself as distinct from southern California, while the Southwest, beginning in western Oklahoma and Texas, is also culturally distinct, if only because of desert influences.[1]

Ethnicity in American Piety

This section deals briefly with what some have found to be a Jewish-American and a Mexican-American identity.

In Raskin's Fish Store, the clerks, all in yarmulkes, joked a lot with their customers. The fish was piled in huge heaps and the atmosphere evocative of an oriental bazaar. Most of the women had made the traditional Sabbath food, gefilte fish, the night before, but for those who had not had the time or the inclination, Raskin's sold its own gefilte fish, frozen. I saw no one buying less than five pounds of fish. In my neighborhood in Manhattan, at least half the late Friday afternoon customers were young working women buying the modest provisions for dinner with their boyfriends—two artichokes, two fillets of something, two candles, and so forth. There were obviously no intimate *soupers a deux* being planned here. The Books of Leviticus (Chapter 11) and Deuteronomy (Chapter 14:3–21) list the animals, fish, and fowl that are considered kosher, or fit to be eaten by Jews. Only sea creatures that have both fins and scales are considered kosher, so no lobster, clam, oyster, crab, or shrimp is ever seen in a kosher fish store. Other foods that are proscribed by Jewish law include meat from animals that do not both chew their cud and have cloven hooves, 24 kinds of birds (many of them birds of prey); insects, amphibian creatures or any creature that crawls "upon the belly"; any "winged swarming thing," rodent, or lizard; or any product that might come from these creatures, such as milk, eggs, or oil. Animals that are considered clean are cows, sheep, goat, deer, chickens, turkeys, geese, ducks, and doves. Other forbidden foods include pigs, camels, herons, storks, hawks, ravens, pelicans, ostriches, eels, snails, rattlesnakes, ants, and rock badgers. Eating kosher food and meats that have been slaughtered in the ritually prescribed manner is one of the basic disciplines of Jewish religious life.[2]

So basic a matter as diet therefore has distinguished observant Jews from the American cultural mainstream. For religious reasons, they have avoided the shellfish so popular on the coasts and, if they were exactly observant, foods not prepared according to kosher laws. The Hasidic community in New York that the author is describing favors large families that celebrate the Sabbath and the Jewish holidays with mass gatherings. It supports an intense synagogue life and such institutions as the *mikvah* (ritual bath), which also distinguish it from its gentile neighbors. The Jewish piety being displayed in such fidelity to religious traditions is more highly conscious of legal directives than American piety at large. *Torah*—divine instruction—is the heartbeat of traditional Jewish life, and in practice Torah means dozens of rules for the conduct of a sanctified life. Many of these rules deal with diet, as the quotation suggests, but many others deal with how to keep the Sabbath as a day of rest and religious observance. The general result is the endeavor to be mindful of God's favor in having fashioned a special covenant relationship. The Puritan colonists too were deeply concerned about their covenant with God, but theirs was an adaptation or reinterpretation of the original Mosaic covenant, which the Hasidic Jews of Brooklyn think they are still preserving. Obviously being American in such a traditional Jewish community has had special overtones. The ethnic has interacted with the American to produce a fascinating hybrid.

Moving from a Jewish-American setting to an Hispanic setting, consider the following story:

> Their daughter went to bed at the extraordinarily early hour of seven-thirty without having taken any supper at all. She slept late—until nine in the morning. Her mother began to think she was sick. What was wrong? What had happened? When the girl heard the questions, she burst into tears. She said that she didn't know what was wrong— even as she did indeed know that a lot was wrong. She asked her mother to leave for a while. She hoped against hope that she could entirely forget the previous day and resume the life she was living—for all the pain of joblessness. But she was still quite nervous because of the time she spent in the back room of the drugstore; more than that, she felt as if she had taken part in something "wrong," "bad," "sinful." She thought of going to the priest and talking with him. She thought of going to confession. She thought of seeking out a nun who had taught two of her younger brothers. The last alternative was the most pleasing to her, but she could not carry through her wish. When she thought of telling the nun what had happened in the drugstore, Teresa quickly abandoned the plan. She abandoned every plan, as a matter of fact, because in each case she could not possibly imagine herself sharing with anyone the strange story she had in mind.[3]

Here the locale is not New York but San Antonio, Texas, and the ethnic background is not Jewish but Hispanic. Teresa is a nice young girl looking for work, trying to help her family in its struggle against poverty. Going to a local drugstore to look for a job, she is told that she can indeed work there and earn money, if she will simply go into the back room, strip naked in front of a group of men, and be photographed. The prospect of this so unhinges her that she takes to her bed and then mopes about for several days. She feels so dirtied that she cannot tell her trouble to her parents, her priest, or even a nun she thinks of as sympathetic. The Hispanic Christianity bred into her both saves her from committing herself to the degrada-

tions of pornography and prevents her from working out her trauma. Purity has meant so much in her upbringing that she is paralyzed by such a gross attack on it.

It may be harder to think of a Hispanic girl in the Southwest understanding the kosher diet of a Hasidic girl in Brooklyn than it is to think of the Hasidic girl understanding the paralysis of the Hispanic girl, but even the latter understanding would take a considerable leap across cultural differences. The Jewish girl might have a relationship with her rabbi that approximated Teresa's relationship with her priest, but she would not have grown up with the practice of sacramental confession (as a focus for the Christian doctrine of sin) and she would not have had the Virgin Mary as her predominant role model. So the sympathy she could muster would be more female to female than religious person to religious person, although the two girls might share some notions about purity that would make pornography equally repulsive to both. Only by putting themselves out to learn about one another's religious traditions would they become religiously sympathetic, and since their traditions are a somewhat separatist Judaism with a vivid memory of Christian persecution and a historically anti-Semitic Christianity, they would have their work cut out for them.

One could no doubt find similar stories featuring Polish, Italian, Native American, or other subcultures outside the WASP mainstream. In most of them the religious factor would be important despite the inroads of secularism into most of ethnic America. Certainly the Catholicism of Polish and Italian Americans continues to be a significant factor, while the revivals of Native American culture regularly entail a return to traditional religious rituals. Certainly Jews who go back to their roots and rediscover their ethnicity find themselves contending with the Bible and the Talmud. Indeed one can argue that religion is usually the heart of a people's ethnic identity, because religion is where they have told themselves how their culture fits together, what it ultimately means. Jews celebrating the Sabbath meal inevitably have configured their Jewishness and Americanness in terms of a tradition associated with the creation account of Genesis and the liberation account of Exodus. Catholics going to confession or praying before the altar of the Blessed Virgin inevitably have configured their Polishness, Italianness, or Hispanicness, as well as their Americanness, in terms of the ideas about sin and purity such religious actions have renewed.

The Lively Experiment

In the eyes of the eminent historian of American religion Sidney E. Mead, the great accomplishment of the United States was to forge a union without an established, state-supported religion. This theme bears repeating in this treatment of the composition and religious variety of the nationalities comprising the American people. At the time of the American Constitution, the prevailing pattern throughout the whole world was for religion to be the heart of traditional culture. Thus it was thought natural for the king or leading powerholder to have sacred backing and equally natural for the church, synagogue, or mosque to be considered a support of national culture. Of course, many countries contained religious and ethnic minorities, but always at society's margins. At times they were allowed to practice their own faith freely, at other times they suffered persecution, or at least severe restrictions on the public character of their faith, their ability to proselytize, and so forth. The fate of the Jews in European history summarizes the thinking of Christianity prior to the American Constitution, while the status of non-Muslims in strict Muslim countries today shows that "establishment" is by no means merely a Christian or bygone notion.

The divisions that afflicted Christendom after the East-West schism of the 11th century and the Protestant Reformation of the 16th century did not radically alter the traditional outlook. Greeks and Romans, Protestants and Catholics, continued to expect that their brand of religion would fill every nook and cranny of popular culture and have a privileged status in the laws of the realm. Thus the Geneva ruled by John Calvin in the 16th century was as theocratic a regime as the pope might have desired for Rome.

The main reason for the nonestablishment of religion in the United States was pragmatic, although certainly such Founding Fathers as Franklin, Jefferson, and Madison agreed that nonestablishment was a good thing in its own right. The pragmatic reason was the inability of the different Protestant churches to agree on a single theology, church polity, sense of public mores, and so on. Congregationalists, Anglicans, Quakers, and the rest continued to think that where their numbers prevailed their religious ways ought to prevail. Indeed the different character of the early colonies derives in great part from the effort of most to form communities of people who would be congenial because they agreed on religious principles and had the same ethnic background. When it came to fighting a Revolution and then fashioning a country, however, the Founding Fathers found it obvious that no ideal of religious uniformity would ever be realized. If there were to be a union of the colonies, they would have to neutralize the potential for division always lurking in intense, if not fanatical, religious allegiances. So they proposed that no religion should have a privileged position in the United States—indeed that people should not be penalized for refusing to profess or exercise any religion at all.

The roots of the more idealistic side of the Founding Fathers' preference for nonestablishment lay in the European Enlightenment. Partly because of what they had witnessed in the religious wars that wracked Europe after the Ref-

The painter seems to lampoon the politicking of small
town America, where democracy settled into the fabric
of the nation's worldview. (Canvassing for a Vote,
George Caleb Bingham; The Nelson-Atkins
Museum of Art, Kansas City, Missouri [Nelson
Fund])

ormation, and partly because of their own revolt
against religious dogma and their insistence that
mature human beings would rely on reason
rather than faith, the leading Enlightenment
thinkers (especially the French) suggested an
ideal state in which people would rise above
religious divisiveness and conduct civic business on the basis of a reasonable legal system
open to all. In other words, common sense,
rather than a particular religious profession,
would be the basis of citizenship and public policies. As a dramatic sign of how deeply they felt

about this point of view and what it might entail,
many Europeans favored admitting Jews into
the mainstream of their nations' cultures and
dropping their centuries-old anti-Semitism.
Many Jews warmed to the possibilities laid out
by the Enlightenment (haskalah) and before long
came up with such revisions of Jewish exclu-
siveness as the Reform movement.

In the United States the federal legal code
and official philosophy about the separation of
church and state did not, of course, mean the
immediate end of religious contentiousness. The

tacit assumption remained that the new country would be a Protestant realm, and when the immigrations of the 19th century brought non-British, non-Protestant people into the country in significant numbers, nativist responses were not slow in developing. Catholics perhaps bore the major brunt of the resentment and bigotry that broke out, but others came in for their share of persecution. The persecution was seldom as bad as it had been in Europe, but on occasion it did lead to burnings and bloodshed. The Ku Klux Klan, with its doctrinaire hatred of blacks, Catholics, and Jews, has probably been the most odious expression of such nativism, but the fate of the Mormons throughout the 19th century suggests that any deviance from established WASP orthodoxy could rouse fierce passions. The Mormons were probably the most hated sect in the land during their formative days, and they returned good amounts of suspicion and anger, as did Catholics and Jews.

The problem the United States has negotiated—less perfectly than would have been ideal, but nonetheless admirably when one considers the overall history of religion—is the problem of election. Jews, Catholics, and Protestants have all thought of themselves as elect peoples, as have Mormons, "Moonies," and many other smaller groups. How does one live alongside people who are not elect, people who are deviant, heretical, even unclean? The United States has answered that one's religion, or lack of religion, ought to make no difference in civic life, and religious leaders have not been slow to see the advantages in this answer, as can be seen in Cardinal Gibbons's response to those who were questioning the patriotism of Catholics (see Chapter 7). But this answer has often failed to tame the deeper passions of religious faith, where the ideal of a holistic culture, based on a passionate love of God understood according to the orthodoxy of the group in question, has blazed ardently. Such latter-day groups as the Moral Majority, lead by the televangelist Jerry Fal-

well, amount to a rather tame, though no less politically provocative, version of the millennial religious hope that all citizens might share the same faith and mores. The strength of the resistance to the Moral Majority shows how thoroughly Americans have learned the lessons of nonestablishment and come to prize their traditions of religious liberty.

Indeed, at the Second Vatican Council, where Roman Catholicism tried to bring itself up to date and become effective in the modern world, the American experiment with religious liberty was accepted into official church doctrine. Largely through the scholarly work of the American Jesuit John Courtney Murray (1904–1967) the way had been prepared to show that genuine faith required respect for all people's consciences, and that consequently religious allegiance should never be imposed or made a condition for civil rights. Minorities and majorities ought to be equal under the law in their rights to worship, proselytize, or refrain from religious profession. The appeal of the Gospel, and by analogy the appeal of any other religious tradition, ought to go forward in freedom. Insofar as the United States had taught Catholics the benefits of a system in which religions could cooperate and compete as legal equals, the lively American experiment had converted one of the religious groups most distinguished by a dogmatic approach to doctrine and religious authority and a diligent guarding of the rights of the established church—no mean accomplishment.

Abraham Lincoln

It is quixotic to search for an individual American whose life might summarize and so adequately represent the character and aspirations of the American people as a whole, yet the search itself is illuminating, forcing one to refine one's intuitions about what the gravity of

Americanness has been, where the point of balance has lain, and what traits of character have been most distinctive. For example, one sometimes hears that William James (1842–1910), the most popular philosopher of **pragmatism,** had a quintessentially American mind—one that would never be mistaken for British or French—that conveyed insights and attitudes peculiar to the history and common philosophy of citizens of the United States. We shall see something of the mind of William James when we come to how selfhood has figured in American worldviews. But for now it is sufficient to note that while James's empirical temper—his concern to stay close to experience—and his interest in getting things done (or in calculating the effects of judging reality more by what is revealed through action than through speculative thought) do seem representatively American, his status as an intellectual and his family background as a privileged Yankee call his representativeness into question. For the purposes of this discussion Abraham Lincoln (1809–1865) seems more representative of America. His family origins were humbler; he lived closer to the midpoint of American history to date; he was more deeply involved in American public life; his thought patterns were more biblical; and he will forever be associated with the war that sought to sever the union of the American people and the victory that preserved that union.

Lincoln the martyr to the cause of preserving the union seems most apposite here. It is not that his life or ethnic background can stand duty for all Americans or that it was beyond reproach. Anyone who becomes president is rare, no matter how much his election may be read as the American people's choosing someone they think represents their collective convictions and aspirations. And clearly political elections are tilted, impure ways of canvassing American public opinion that often elevate impure candidates. But at such crucial junctures of a nation's life as its beginning and a crisis that threatens to sunder and prematurely end it, the presiding figures do gain larger-than-life status. Washington and Lincoln are now myths as much as men, and all the careful historical scholarship in the world is not likely to remove their mythic status. The story of national identity is always both mythic and religious, because it never gains much depth without entering into the mysteries of providence and destiny. At any rate, perhaps a sketch of Lincoln's life and thought will help reveal what taking him as a representative American suggests about the American people.

Lincoln was born in Kentucky in 1809, the son of a pioneer whose English forebears had come to Massachusetts in 1637. Abraham's mother, Nancy Hanks, may have been illegitimate and has been described as both sad and fervently religious. The Lincoln family was forced to move to southwestern Indiana in 1816, where they established themselves as squatters on public land, living in a crude log cabin. The boy helped clear the land, which the family later bought, and suffered through hard winters and a poverty exacerbated by the death of his mother in 1818. His father quickly remarried, and his stepmother, Sarah Johnston Lincoln, probably encouraged his love of reading, which began to compensate for the piecemeal formal education he received. In 1830, when Abraham was 21, the family moved to Illinois. By that time he was 6 feet, 4 inches tall, very strong, noted for his skill with an ax, and thought of as a moody but gifted storyteller.

After the move to Illinois Lincoln worked at various jobs, trying to find his niche. When he eventually became interested in politics and the law, he passed the bar and set up practice in 1836. Practicing in Springfield, Illinois, the state capital, Lincoln prospered by riding a wide circuit to handle small cases in county seats. His practice improved when he began representing railroad companies, but he also handled patent suits and criminal matters. After 20 years, Lincoln was numbered among the most successful lawyers in Illinois and began to receive national attention. In 1842, after some emotional ups and downs, he married Mary Todd, who came from a distinguished Kentucky family and bore him four sons, only one of whom survived to adulthood.

Lincoln attended Presbyterian church services while in Springfield and Washington but never joined a church. His early tendency toward freethinking yielded to a profound religiosity during the crisis of the Civil War, when he came to feel himself but a pawn in the workings of Providence. He was fond of the Bible and Shakespeare, both of which he knew well and used to good effect in his speeches. At his political beginnings Lincoln shared Andrew Jackson's devotion to the common people, but he thought government ought to concern itself more with the economic welfare of the common people than Jackson did. He admired Henry Clay and Daniel Webster and thought the main need of the West was for the federal government to build up the banking, tariffs, and transportation that might bring economic growth. As a member of the Illinois State Legislature, Lincoln worked for such development, especially better transportation. Although opposed to slavery, he thought abolitionists often did more harm than good. During his term in Congress (1847–1849), Lincoln condemned the war with Mexico and worked for the election of Zachary Taylor as president.

Not receiving from Taylor the political job he had expected, Lincoln virtually retired from politics for five years, until in 1854 Stephen Douglas maneuvered through Congress the Kansas-Nebraska Act that proposed opening the entire Louisiana Purchase to slavery. This led to the dissolution of the Whig Party, to which Lincoln had belonged, and the formation of the Republican Party. Lincoln and Douglas became dramatic opponents on the matter of opening the territories to slavery, and Lincoln used a ringing biblical quotation to argue that the country as a whole had to opt for slavery or against: "A house divided against itself cannot stand" (Matt. 12:25). Although Lincoln lost his senate race against Douglas, his eloquent analyses of the implications of slavery brought him national attention.

In 1860 Lincoln won the presidential election as the Republican candidate, despite the wholesale opposition of the Deep South. Before his inauguration South Carolina proclaimed its withdrawal from the Union. When Lincoln refused to countenance the division of territories between slave and free areas, six other states seceded and formed the Confederate States of America. The Confederate forces fired on Fort Sumter in Charlestown, South Carolina, initiating what became the Civil War. It took Lincoln until 1864 to find an effective war strategy, commanding general, and military staff, but he gradually created an effective high command and became more skillful at both statecraft and military direction. Gradually he also became more convinced of the need for abolition and finally in 1863 issued the Emancipation Proclamation (which, since it applied only to rebellious states holding slaves, was probably more important for its symbolism than for its immediate practical effect). During the winter of 1864–1865 he strengthened emancipation by securing an antislavery amendment to the Constitution. He managed to handle the many skirmishes with Congress stimulated by the wartime conditions, won reelection in 1864, and saw the Union forces prevail and so enable him to impose peace conditions the South had previously rejected. At first Lincoln supported a mild dominance of the South for reconstruction, but at his assassination in 1865 he may have been entertaining more radical views including military occupation.

Lincoln's assassination on Good Friday helped to cast him in a martyr's mantle. Two days later, Easter sermons throughout the land inevitably compared his sacrifice to that of Christ: a death for the many. Immediately revisionist biographies got under way, somewhat obscuring the fact that before his death Lincoln had begun to win widespread admiration for his good judgment and depth of insight. The great political question he had studied in bloody detail was whether a people could prove able to govern itself and maintain its territorial integrity against domestic foes.

For his status as a self-made man who overcame many adversities and possessed balanced judgment, resolution, and great patriotism, as well as wit, eloquence, shrewdness, and deep faith, Abraham Lincoln has entered the American treasury of heroes, standing below few if any of those considered builders of the nation and its people. Perhaps the most representative things about him were his commitment to the dignity of the individual human being and his determination to keep the United States a nation where the God-given value of each human being would be honored above all political or economic expediency. If so, the Americans who have given him such honor have been telling themselves that the nation's highest goal ought to be the antithesis of the slavery Lincoln so came to hate.

Alexis de Tocqueville's *Democracy in America*

The most prized outside evaluation of the American experiment has always been a study published by a young French political scientist in the years 1835–1840. Alexis de Tocqueville (1805–1859) was a liberal aristocrat considering a career in French politics when he journeyed through the United States for nine months during 1831 and 1832. He was most interested in the American understanding and practice of equality because he believed that it held the key to Europe's political future.

To de Tocqueville the preeminent characteristic of the social condition of Anglo-Americans was their democracy, which had been present in colonial days and grew ever stronger thereafter:

> In America the aristocratic element has always been feeble from its birth; and if at the present day it is not actually destroyed, it is at any rate so completely disabled that we can scarcely assign to it any degree of influence on the course of affairs. The democratic principle, on the contrary, has gained so much strength by time, by events, and by legislation, as to have become not only predominant, but all-powerful. No family or corporate authority can be perceived; very often one cannot even discover in it any very lasting individual influence. America, then, exhibits in her social state an extraordinary phenomenon. Men are there seen on a greater equality in point of fortune and intellect, or, in other words, more equal in their strength, than in any other country of the world, or in any age of which history has preserved the remembrance.[4]

This French aristocrat, accustomed to discriminating social status with a fine eye, found the relative classlessness of American society striking. De Tocqueville was writing just before the great waves of immigration started to change the features of American society. The population he had in view was Anglo-American as his terminology suggests. (However, he was also interested in the Catholicism he associated with the arrival of Irish settlers from the 1780s on). What he would have made of the later distinctions Americans made on the basis of economic status and ethnic origin is hard to say. Yet on the side of those who consider his remarks lastingly significant, one can note that the America he was observing had been in existence over 200 years, and that its Constitution was well into its third generation of citizens. One should note, however, that de Tocqueville's sense of the American people who shared the democratic freedoms he lauded was restricted by the biases of both the times and his own upbringing. Thus in speaking of "universal suffrage" he fails to mention that neither women nor blacks had the vote in America.[5]

De Tocqueville did, however, associate women with the influence he found religion exerting on the highly moral tone of American life. He perceptively noted what some scholars have called the feminization of American religion that occurred in the 19th century.

> I do not question that the great austerity of manners that is observable in the United States arises, in the first instance, from religious faith. Religion is often unable to restrain man from the numberless temptations which chance offers; nor can it check that passion for gain which everything contributes to arouse; but its influence over the mind of the woman is supreme, and women are the protectors of morals. There is certainly no country in the world where the tie of marriage is more respected than in America or where conjugal happiness is more highly or worthily appreciated. In Europe almost all the disturbances of society arise from the irregularities of domestic life. To despise the natural bonds and legitimate pleasures of home is to contract a taste for excesses, a restlessness of heart, and fluctuating desires. Agitated by the tumultuous passions that frequently disturb his dwelling, the European is galled by the obedience which the legislative powers of the state exact. But when the American retires from the turmoil of public life to the bosom of his family, he finds in it the image of order and peace.[6]

At times de Tocqueville sounds like Franklin and Jefferson, equating the significance of religion with what it contributes to the public morality that a democracy needs if it is to function well. On the other hand, his rather deistic outbursts tend to go more deeply into philosophical issues than theirs, as when he reflects on his dislike of **materialists:**

> If among the opinions of a democratic people any of those pernicious theories exist which tend to inculcate that all perishes with the body, let men by whom such theories are professed be marked as the natural foes of the whole people. The materialists are offensive to me in many respects; their doctrine I hold to be pernicious, and I am disgusted at their arrogance. If their system could be of any utility to man, it would seem to be by giving him a modest opinion of himself; but these reasoners show that it is not so; and when they think they have said enough to prove that they are brutes, they appear as proud as if they had demonstrated they are gods. Materialism, among all nations, is a dangerous disease of the human mind; but it is more especially to be dreaded among a democratic people because it readily amalgamates with that vice which is most familiar to the heart under such circumstances. Democracy encourages a taste for physical gratification; this taste, if it becomes excessive, soon disposes men to believe that all is matter only; and materialism, in its turn, hurries them on with mad impatience to these same delights; such is the fatal circle within which democratic nations are driven round. It were well that they should see the danger and hold back . . . . Do not seek to supersede the old religious opinions of men by new ones, lest in the passage from one faith to another, the soul being left for a while stripped of all belief, the love of physical gratifications should grow upon it and fill it wholly.[7]

It would be interesting to speculate on the relevance of this opinion to the rise of American prosperity after de Tocqueville.

Key Terms

Materialists: those who stress the physical, empirical side of human existence and reality as a whole, often disparaging spirituality or denying that there are spiritual entities such as God or an immortal human soul. Materialism can have a religious foundation and so take on the accommodated meaning of stressing the goodness of creation, as Genesis praises it, or stressing the incarnational character of Christian existence, as Jesus exemplifies it. In that case materialism tends to mean not the strict denial of spiritual realities but the conviction that the healthiest living concentrates on making the world a better place to live in. In de Tocqueville's view, materialism is rather crude, urging people to use the freedoms democracy offers to eat, drink, and be merry, grabbing what pleasure a body-bound existence can. He sees this as destructive of the self-sacrifice for the common good that democracy needs and so finds that the religions that show human beings a reality transcending the senses and the grave are powerful supports of democracy in the ideal sense.

Pragmatism: a concern with effects, results, actions, and deeds. As associated with William James, this viewpoint is subtle and realistic, a good extension of the common sense on which ordinary mental health, politics, and both business and personal life depend. Pragmatism can have the vicious connotation of being concerned only with results and so letting the end justify any means. It can also have the sophisticated connotation of thinking that human beings only know what is true and real when they are involved as participants.

Discussion Questions

1. What is the significance of a sketch of American demographics that makes Yankees and ethnics the two leading groups?
2. How ought one to connect blacks, Hispanics, Native Americans, and Orientals to the American mainstream?

3. What is the intended function of kosher laws and how does it compare to the impression made on outsiders?
4. How significant are such ethnically colored religious practices as confession of sins and prayers to the Virgin Mary?
5. What does the fact that nonestablishment mainly sprang from the inability of the early American Christian groups to agree on a common faith say about the state of Christianity in the 17th and 18th centuries?
6. How does the sense of election that many religious groups carry deep in their self-identity affect the American experiment in pluralism?
7. What features of Lincoln's life justify contemplating him as a representative American and what features make him unrepresentative?
8. How did Lincoln come to be considered a Christ figure and how valid is such a consideration?
9. Why was de Tocqueville so taken with American democracy, and why do you share, or not share, his high estimate?
10. What is the relation between de Tocqueville's disregard of women when it came to speaking of universal suffrage and his view of women as the main guardians of the nation's morals?

Notes

1. See "United States of America," in *The New Encyclopaedia Britannica*, vol. 29 (Chicago: Encyclopaedia Britannica, 1987), pp. 176–179.

2. Lis Harris, *Holy Days: The World of a Hasidic Family* (New York: Summit Books, 1985), pp. 57–58.

3. Robert Coles and Jane Hallowell Coles, *Women of Crisis: Lives of Struggle and Hope* (New

York: Delta/Seymour Lawrence, 1978), pp. 137–138.

4. Alexis de Tocqueville, *Democracy in America*, vol. 1 (New York: Alfred A. Knopf, 1963), pp. 52–53.

5. Ibid., p. 199.

6. Ibid., p. 304.

7. Alexis de Tocqueville, *Democracy in America*, vol. 2 (New York: Alfred A. Knopf, 1963), p. 145.

12

Theological Foundations

The God of the Early Colonists

In studying the origins of American colonial religion, William Warren Sweet has stressed the British desire to oppose Catholic Spain. From the time of Elizabeth, through the era of Cromwell, to the French and Indian War of the mid-18th century, this desire remained alive:

> The policy instituted by the crown in separating the English Church from the Papacy was eventually to mean that religion was to be a major motive in laying the foundations of empire. The call of the mission field and the conversion of the heathen were given lip service by all the early writers on colonization, but it produced little immediate fruit. The Elizabethan seamen were Protestants of the Protestants when it came to hating Roman Catholicism, but their personal religion was a strange compound of "fervid patriotism, a varied assortment of hates, a rough code of morals, and an unshaken trust in the providence of God. To the heathen, they brought not peace but a sword. To the Pope, whom they named with the Turk and the Devil, they wished destruction. For Queen and country they would go anywhere and attempt anything." The Spanish conquest of South and Central America has been called the last of the crusades and the Spanish *Conquistadores* the last of the crusaders. With equal appropriateness the Elizabethan Sea Dogs might be

termed Protestant crusaders. But instead of warring against the infidel, their crusading zeal was aimed primarily at Roman Catholicism and their particular venom was saved for Spanish Catholicism and all its works . . . . The same antipathy to Spain and Spanish Roman Catholicism, which the Elizabethan Sea Dogs and colonizers possessed to such a fanatical degree, is evidenced also as one of the powerful motives in determining Cromwell's colonial policy. He justified the attack upon the Spanish West Indies in 1655–1656 on the ground of Spanish outrages against English traders and colonists . . . . This anti-Spanish and anti-Catholic motive in colonization continued active down to the end of the Colonial period. The intercolonial wars covering nearly a century, from King William's War (1689–1697) through the French and Indian War (1756–1763) were in a sense a struggle between Protestantism and Roman Catholicism for empire in the New World. The British accused the Catholic missionaries of blessing "the Indian's tomahawk and scalping knife, and bade him God-speed in the work of destroying heretics." The English expedition against Spanish Florida in 1702 was justified not only on the ground of protecting the Carolinas against Spanish aggression, but also on the ground of religion, to protect Protestant truth from Catholic superstition.[1]

Our 400 years of hindsight make this aspect of colonial American religion seem barbaric and unedifying. It reminds us, however, that 16th and 17th century Christianity was more insular than it could be in the 20th century. Even with the discovery of the New World, and increasing knowledge of Asia, European Christians continued to think of their faith and worldview as normative. Consequently the differences between Protestants and Catholics were more important than their similarities as followers of Christ. No contact with pagans, Hindus, Buddhists, Confucians, or even Muslims and Jews gave Europeans pause to note how Catholics, Protestants, and Eastern Orthodox possessed the same Bible, the same conciliar creeds, and,

above all, the same God and Lord. The suspicion therefore is bound to arise that neither Protestants nor Catholics really grasped the fundamentals of their faith. Both were often inclined to fix on secondary matters and let political, military, and economic competition between their countries dress itself in religious garb and intensify their mutual animosity.

The second note that sounds strongly is the militant character in the background of colonial religion, which speaks volumes about many colonists' view of God. To justify their bellicose attitudes, the combatants had to call on the warrior deity of the Old Testament, or the Stern Judge demanding the strictest adherence to what the group in question considered genuine Christian faith. *Conquistadores*, privateers, and Cromwellian Puritan soldiers alike appointed themselves warriors in a sacred military adventure, cutting across the grain of virtually everything one finds on the lips of the evangelical Christ. From the outset of American colonial religion, therefore, one finds the biased interpretation of biblical texts familiar from other periods. It offers good evidence that recent scholars have been wise to stress **hermeneutics** and seek the prejudices that a given past age tended to bring to the biblical text. It is a reminder, as well, that Christians have made some progress in the 20th century, their ecumenical movement toward mutual tolerance being a noteworthy example.

The Puritan theology of the second generation of colonists transposed some of the fierceness of the English militants into attacks not so much on outside foes (though Indians and distant papists could come in for broadsides) as on backsliders in the colonial community itself. By the second generation the Puritans were isolated from England and feeling defensive.

This was reflected particularly in their fast day sermons. From the beginning, the Massachusetts Bay General Court had deemed days of collective humiliation important; the first pastors had taken such occasions to remind the people of their special covenant obligations and to enumerate and "improve" upon the various afflictions—storms, droughts, pestilence, shipwrecks and Indian raids— that God imposed on his Chosen People because of their lapses. The second generation clergy made this device of the fast day sermon a major weapon in resisting the "declension" [moral decline] of the Wilderness Zion, but altered the emphasis.

Instead of dwelling on the details of the disasters provoked by the Puritans' sins, the ministers treated the sins themselves as disasters; they examined directly the failings of the people. They took their doctrine from the prophets of the Old Testament, holding that the colony was being pursued for its sins because the inhabitants were falling away from their covenantal pledges. With less imagery and subtlety than their predecessors, the clergy outlined God's controversy with New England and

*The artist combines the biblical and naturalistic perspectives that shaped America's religious horizons before the Civil War. (*Elijah in the Desert, *Washington Allston; courtesy Museum of Fine Arts, Boston; Gift of Mrs. Samuel Hooper and Miss Alice Hooper.)*

offered for "uses" or applications, various plans of reformation. Pastoral skill was measured by the ability to evoke tears, arouse guilt and depict the judgments that might yet befall an unrepentant society. These lamentations were voiced increasingly on public occasions and were refined and stylized into a ritual with a definite literary form. This type of sermon has been called, after the prophet, a "jeremiad."[2]

It is interesting that this description of New England Puritan sermons focuses more on Old Testament themes than on themes of Jesus in the New Testament. Moreover, the theology of retribution for sins is only part of the Old Testament outlook, and the prophet Jeremiah is badly represented if one stresses only his castigation of Judah for her sins and overlooks his anticipations of a new covenant written on the heart and abounding in grace. The jeremiad was also used as a prod to reform and salvation. Perhaps the harshness of the first colonial years blended with the dour features of Calvinist thought to bring the Old Testament God of wrath to the fore. As will be seen in the next sections, the reactions against so grim a theology ranged from the Deists' retreat from biblical religion to the revivalists' stress on the possibilities for salvation and grace. But in the beginning American religious thought was a fierce thing, brimming with images of war and divine punishment.

Deism in American Piety

In speaking of the faith of the Founding Fathers of the United States—those who united the colonies, saw it through the Revolutionary War, and then got it on its feet as a new nation respected by Europe—Edwin Gaustad recently has described Benjamin Franklin and George Washington as "icons": sacred models. The irony is that both were reluctant religionists, Deists

quite minimal in their theology and more concerned with getting religion to support civic virtue than with such central Christian interests as imitating Christ to achieve salvation.

On the occasion of a commemoration of Franklin's death,

The Reverend Dr. William Smith, Anglican divine, College of Philadelphia provost, and frequent opponent of Franklin, delivered the lengthy eulogy. Not a time for stirring up old controversies or airing old grievances, this was a moment to bring the brand-new nation together, to heal, to "comfort ye, comfort ye, my people." It was a time to raise up for veneration a national icon, a cultic hero, and this is precisely what Dr. Smith was prepared to do. He presented to his earnest listeners a New World luminary, an Old Testament patriarch, a classical world Hercules, lawgiver, genius. In concluding Smith himself rose to Olympian heights: "Let all thy fellow citizens; let all thy compatriots; let every class of men with whom thou wert associated here on earth . . . let them consider thee as their guardian-genius, still present and presiding amongst them; and what they conceive thou wouldst advise to be DONE, let them advise and DO likewise—and they shall not greatly deviate from the path of virtue and glory!" One can only ask: If Franklin's enemies spoke this way, whatever would his friends say?

. . . . A civil religion centered on Washington is a more familiar story, but that familiarity must not blind us to the urgency and the fervor that an untried nation invested in the elevation of Washington to mythic status. Franklin was genius and mediator; Washington was creator and father. He caused the world, America's world, to be . . . . Like Moses, Washington led; like Moses, he was not a great speaker; like Moses, he won no reputation as a sophisticated theologian. His actions were his most eloquent words and his very presence his most forceful declaration. He wrote no treatise on military strategy, formulated no system of political theory, and composed no creed—not even of Franklin's modest and generalized kind.

Washington did talk about religion, but more in national than in private terms. An Anglican vestryman, he was baptized, married, and buried in the church of his childhood. But he wore denominational labels as lightly as theological ones. "In politics as in religion," he wrote in 1795, "my tenets are few and simple." That rare bit of introspection was directly on target. He did, of course, use the language of faith, but scarcely of any particular, readily identifiable faith. He acknowledged the all-powerful, if often inscrutable, Providence that governs human affairs and the destiny of nations. At the close of the American Revolution, he responded to a compliment by saying that "the praise is due to the *Grand Architect* of the Universe; who did not see fit to suffer his Superstructures and justice to be subjected to the ambition of the princes of the World, or to the rod of oppression, in the hands of any power upon Earth." That phrase, "Grand Architect," was wholly characteristic of Washington's many allusions to God: they all possessed a vaguely impersonal, broadly benign, calmly rational flavor. The "Governor of the Universe," "Higher Cause," "Great Ruler of Events," "All Wise Creator," "the Supreme Dispensor of all Good"—these and similar expressions constituted Washington's usual mode of religious discourse.[3]

No doubt Catholics, Lutherans, and Germans from the radical left-wing Reformation offered colonial America different religious expressions, but the Puritans and the Deists were more influential. The Great Awakening and subsequent American romance with revivalism also stirred more personal language about sin and salvation, the self and the Savior. But the public or civil religion of the new nation owed a great deal to the Washingtons and Franklins (the closest thing to an American aristocracy), whose personal preference for abstract, distant language about the deity, and greater interest in ethics than in theology fitted well with the needs of the new pluralistic country.

As early as the First Amendment depiction of the relations between religion and government (foreshadowed as we have seen in the writings of Jefferson and Madison that influenced the law in Virginia), the Founding Fathers' view of the utility of nonestablishment became canonized. Those who resisted the deistic theology of Franklin, Washington, and Jefferson logically enough resisted nonestablishment, but they could not make the case strongly enough to persuade their fellow Americans. The new nation plainly needed tolerance to keep it from flying apart, and many citizens realized, at least instinctively, that religious passions were among the most likely to enflame divisiveness.

By the end of the colonial period, the lesson of Catholic-Protestant and then intra-Protestant antagonism had begun to sink in. Certainly such antagonism would continue to flare up occasionally in each generation, especially when waves of immigrants seemed to threaten the long-standing Protestant dominance of civil religion. But those who would have promoted a crisp creed and shunned nonabiders had an impossible fight on their hands. The need to rally against a common tyrannical foe, as the revolutionaries saw it, and the interest of the common people in the economic and political aspects of the revolutionary struggle, determined that religion finally would go on the back burner.

The American Revolution was not clearly or principally a religious war (though many church pulpits raised support for it). That in itself may mark it as distinctly modern, so many prior wars having had religious overtones, especially in the post-Reformation generations. One part of the theology undergirding the revolutionary effort came from the Puritans, who thought King George had betrayed the new Israel. Another part was the view of God that worked for Washington (as the theology undergirding the Constitution was the view that worked for Jefferson and Franklin). That second theological part was deistic, in general imprint if not always in direct cause.

The prevalence of evangelical Christian theology in later American eras may make it difficult for some Americans to appreciate the appeal of deistic thought. Indeed Roman Catholics, Eastern Orthodox, Lutherans, Presbyterians, and others possessed of articulate theological traditions have spurned Deism as completely as have evangelicals, thinking Deism conceptually wooly and a pale substitute for the faith in the God-Man long handed down in Christian tradition. But to a period grown weary with religious conflict, disgusted with religious hatred and bigotry, deistic moves to a vague universal Ruler of the world could seem a blessed relief.

Throughout later American history, including our current generation, the narrowness of many confessional Christians (and, to a lesser extent, Jews and Muslims), has kept the deistic option alive. People not wanting to declare themselves atheists, convinced by upbringing or culture that reality better hangs together and conscience is better motivated if there is a Creator, have often joined groups that shunned doctrinal religion and focused on such common denominators as belief in a higher power, in the sanctity of individual conscience, in the dignity of the individual person, and in the need for common citizens to possess sources of self-sacrifice and civic virtue. Such people have frequently turned these convictions in the direction of a civil religion, making the prosperity of America (often idealized as the land of freedom, hard work, and natural virtue) the goal of their piety. This sort of civil religion certainly has differed from evangelical brands, yet it too has run the risk of forgetting the transcendence of God. There are deistic as well as biblical bases for limiting one's patriotism. For example, the universal concern of any true deistic Creator would have to embrace all nations. So the interesting historical question is what caused a given group or epoch to downplay such bases and make its deistic or evangelical convictions promote America as a uniquely religious nation?

The Theological and the Secular

Theology and secularity make strange bedfellows. On the one hand, theology usually delimits secular affairs, saying that what occurs in space and time is not the sum of existence. Because God transcends space and time and is the mysterious Other with whom human beings are fated to wrestle, theologians usually say that the meaning of existence does not stop at the grave. Indeed, throughout life such meaning is more a matter of what one is—how one composes one's soul—than of one's bank account, knowledge, or prestige in the community.

On the other hand, the biblical religions promote the notion of the world and human affairs blessed by God. Christianity raises the stakes, claiming that divinity actually took flesh and redeemed space and time to the core. Therefore nothing need be profane, everything can be holy. In such a perspective secular concerns such as politics and economics need not separate people from God. For those with eyes to see, hearts willing to open, laboring for a good common life and earning one's living can be paths to religious maturity.

Consider the various changes rung on the relations between the theological and the secular in just the historical movements indicated in the preceding sections. For the militant Protestants and Catholics who looked on the New World as a further extension of their interreligious battleground, establishing colonies in North America could be a sacred enterprise. Often it was not because the commercial interests were stronger than the religious interests. But when colonists needed a rationale, real or spurious, for their ventures, they spontaneously turned to religion. God willed it that their tradition prevail over their opponent's in the New World. Or God willed it that they themselves have the chance to exercise their faith free of political pressures. Or God willed it that the benighted natives of the New World have the chance to embrace Christianity and salvation. Those groups who equated financial prosperity with God's blessing could even say that God willed their busy efforts to create successful trading companies or lush plantations. When theology beds down with secular interests, God often becomes a member of the board, a commissioner of the work.

The Deists thought such a marriage of convenience unseemly, but they quickly worked out their own equivalent. Offended by the crudeness of the militant Christians and put off by the religious wars and self-serving invocations of God, the Deists avoided overt uses of biblical language and sanctions, feeling more comfortable with a God one might call Noble Spirit. Washington and Franklin were sophisticated about this, honoring both their own personal inclinations and what they perceived to be the political needs of the new country. The result was a shift of focus and interest, from the at times obsessive religiosity of the Puritans to the no-nonsense business of waging a war of liberation and founding a new political entity that might keep the former colonies pulling together enough to create a real country. So the religiosity of the Deists went into exercising and commending the virtues of hard work, integrity, honesty, dependability, and the like, which greatly helped them prosecute the business of the new country.

Still one could not call this deistic practicality a purely secular matter. Unless the Deists were hypocrites, they really believed that their abstract nomenclature for God honored the deity better than biblical specifics. They also believed that their theology did not conflict with the Bible but rendered the spirit of biblical theology in accents more acceptable to an enlightened age. Few of those who spoke this way wanted outright atheism. Most thought that human integrity and dignity required the ennobling influence of high ideas about God. However vague the Deists may have been about salvation, afterlife, and the need for divine grace to overturn

human sinfulness, they were not about to attack the traditional Christian views on such matters. If they contrived to make self-reliance and good character the hallmarks of the men Americans were to consider icons, enough passion attended this effort to tip us off that it was a religious venture. In their heart of hearts, the deistic Founding Fathers had a passion for the character they felt the new nation required. Their removed, nonpartisan deity who promoted good character was a pearl of great price.

The evangelicals who prospered in the wake of the Great Awakening and the revivalist movements on the western frontier worked still another series of changes on the relationship between theology and the secular. Biblical categories functioned very well for them, especially the categories concerned with sin, repentance, and spiritual renewal symbolizing salvation. One can exaggerate the number of people actually converted into steady churchgoers, but the impact of the revivalism under way at the end of the 18th century was certainly significant. Moreover, later revivalists renewed most of the biblical impulses throughout the 19th and 20th centuries. For most of them civic virtue depended on having one's heart warmed by the Spirit of Christ. Indeed the more extreme of the evangelicals wanted American culture to acknowledge its debts to biblical Christianity and be quite explicitly a Protestant Christian nation. The simplistic resort to 2000-year-old biblical categories doomed this movement to political problems, but both politicians and ordinary citizens regularly strove to put into law what they considered biblical ideals. Prohibition (very dubiously biblical) is a good example, as are the statutes of many states against adultery and sodomy. Some groups have targeted gambling, dancing, and sexual displays as condemned by the Holy Trinity, any good conscience, and the best of American tradition.

In this evangelical tradition, theology ought to preside over secular affairs, and decent behavior ought to result. How to square this ambition with the defense of personal liberty (especially in the realm of religious activity but also in secular matters) has been the evangelical bugaboo. On the one hand, evangelicals have been convinced that their God placed on them certain moral imperatives and that the country would be safe for their children, healthy in soul, and able to perform its providential role in world history only if they tried to make such moral imperatives the consensus of the land. On the other hand, evangelicals had no legal comeback when confronted with the right of other citizens to reject their set of moral imperatives, and the religious among such other citizens could mount a theological case for the primacy of conscience at least as good as the evangelicals' arguments on behalf of prohibition or antigambling statutes.

Much of the discussion among American groups trying to correlate theology and secular life has circled around the images of human nature the groups have presented. For those feeling that human nature is corrupt, secular affairs have been dark matters nearly bound to resist God's will. Separatist groups such as the Amish have been the most logical in living out such a theology. The evangelicals and Calvinists who have concluded that making money, taking sexual pleasure, and wielding power inevitably will be human beings' great obsessions have tended to make one of two different responses. Some have held themselves aloof, trying to participate in civil life only enough to survive without getting tainted. Others have damned the need to become tainted but rationalized it as the sinful way things are. Very few have taken the tack of challenging the theology of human corruption and saying that making money, taking sexual pleasure, and wielding power or influence are good in themselves (though easily distorted into idols). Thus the question how American religiosity best fits with American ideals of democratic politics and the flourishing of individual liberties remains an open one.[4]

Ralph Waldo Emerson

On the evening of July 15, 1838, Ralph Waldo Emerson addressed the senior class in Divinity College, Cambridge, Massachusetts. The opening paragraphs of this address from one theologian to aspiring others suggest the contributions of the Transcendentalists to the American sense of divinity.

In this refulgent summer, it has been a luxury to draw the breath of life. The grass grows, the buds burst, the meadow is spotted with fire and gold in the tint of flowers. The air is full of birds, and sweet with the breath of the pine, the balm-of-Gilead, and the new hay. Night brings no gloom to the heart with its welcome shade. Through the transparent darkness the stars pour their almost spiritual rays. Man under them seems a young child, and his huge globe a toy. The cool night bathes the world as with a river, and prepares his eyes again for the crimson dawn. The mystery of nature was never displayed more happily. The corn and the wine have been freely dealt to all creatures, and the never-broken silence with which the old bounty goes forward, has not yielded yet one word of explanation. One is constrainted to respect the perfection of this world, in which our senses converse. How wide; how rich; what invitation from every property it gives to every faculty of man! In its fruitful soils; in its navigable sea; in its mountains of metal and stone; in its forests of all woods; in its animals; in its chemical ingredients; in the powers and path of light, heat, attraction, and life, it is well worth the pith and heart of great men to subdue and enjoy it. The planters, the mechanics, the inventors, the astronomers, the builders of cities, and the captains, history delights to honor.

But when the mind opens, and reveals the laws which traverse the universe, and make things what they are, then shrinks the great world at once into a mere illustration and fable of the mind . . .

A more secret, sweet, and overpowering beauty appears to man when his heart and mind open to the sentiments of virtue. Then he is instructed in what is above him. Then he learns that his being is without bound; that, to the good, to the

Emerson and other naturalists, who knew the sea, unpopulated woods, mountains, and plains, retained a sensitivity to the fickleness of fate symbolized by unpredictable weather. (The Fog Warning, Winslow Homer; courtesy Museum of Fine Arts, Boston; Otis Norcross Fund)

perfect, he is born, low as he now lies in evil and weakness. That which he venerates is still his own, though he has not yet realized it. He *ought*. He knows the sense of that grand word, though his analysis fails entirely to render account of it. When in innocency, or when by intellectual perception, he attains to say,—"I love the Right; Truth is beautiful within and without, forever more. Virtue, I am thine: save me: use me: thee will I serve, day and night, in great, in small, that I may not be virtuous, but virtue;"—then is the end of the creation answered, and God is well pleased.[5]

The first paragraph displays a theme powerful in American religious history, the impact of physical nature. Emerson's poetic prose lingers lovingly over the beauties of nature, the harmonies, the sweetnesses. Yet his is a nature given to human beings for their spiritual instruction, a nature that most Platonists would find fitting. We get nothing of the evolutionary toil of nature, the wanton cruelties (to human perception), the gore, grime, and signs of godlessness. Does nature have any end, any meaning? Are its laws in fact open to human investigation? Has it any concern for humankind, or is ours but another of its endless sports, accidents, statistical improbabilities?

Yet Emerson writes so well, in an age when natural science had yet to discover the proportions of the universe we now confront, that the reader easily sits back for the entertaining ride. Indeed, even present-day readers can agree that nature is a storehouse of wonders, an object of contemplation we shall never exhaust. Present-day readers can also agree that those who conquer nature, whether intellectually or practically, are achieving something quintessentially human. The implication for American theology has been that scientific and entrepreneurial enterprise could be aspects of human greatness. Emerson does not tie this implication to biblical counsels. His only overt theological reference in our paragraphs is to a God well pleased when the human spirit opts to become virtuous. Some of his allusions to human evil leave open the question of what the ordinary interactions of human beings with nature are likely to produce: benefit or woe? Yet Emerson's spirit is so strong, so powerful a shaper of his perceptions of nature, that his overall position is clearly optimistic. Like Kant exulting about the starry heavens above and the moral law within, or Washington referring to the Grand Architect, Emerson wants a God both more dignified than what the Bible offers and more available as the source of nature and human inwardness.

For that is the upshot of the second and third paragraphs. Human intellectual activity and morality are more precious than human incursions into nature, however impressive and praiseworthy the latter may be. Emerson the spiritualist, the transcendentalist, is most enamored of the movements of the human mind and heart that not only allow our species to measure nature but also take us to a realm beyond nature, out of space and time, where something in us seems similar to divinity itself. This some-

thing is not the divine life praised by Eastern Orthodox Christianity as trinitarian love poured forth in our hearts by the Holy Spirit (Rom. 5:5) in virtue of Christ's death and resurrection. It is rather a natural human spirituality, the stuff of the human soul. It is more Greek than Hebraic, more deistic than evangelical. It has never become the mainstream of American religious thought, but it has borne affinities to American naturalists such as James and Dewey.[6]

An American Calvinist such as Jonathan Edwards could share with Emerson an enthusiasm for nature, perhaps could even wax eloquent about the presence of the divine Spirit in human spirituality. But Edwards was so concerned with the sinfulness of human nature that one would never mistake his diction for Emerson's. Both were heirs of the Enlightenment, but Edwards was also heir to the patristic and Reformed theological traditions. In contrast, Emerson often seems Oriental, a soul naturally Hindu or Buddhist.

Inasmuch as Emerson represents a highly educated, aesthetically refined personality, in contrast to the evangelical and pragmatic personalities who have predominated in American history, one could never present him or his thought as populist. Yet he has won admiration out of proportion to his representativeness, as has his friend Thoreau, as though in testimony to sentiments that Americans have more appreciated than embraced. One might say, then, that polar to the biblical concerns of American theology has been a sturdy naturalism in two senses. First, Americans have frequently honored nature, been intrigued by nature, and pictured religious consolation in terms of harmony with nature more than the biblical paradigms (concerned with separating Yahweh from the nature deities of Israel's neighbors) alone would allow. Second, Americans have had their own versions of the Enlightenment's stress on autonomous human reason, or even of the Eastern sense that the individual spirit is a microcosm of the universal worldspirit. Some Americans have wanted to consecrate the inner precincts of thought and conscience. Logically this could buttress the legal and cultural interest in individual liberties, and ironically it could reach some of the same conclusions about religious liberty that developed out of the Protestant stress on freedom of conscience. From time to time, therefore, Transcendentalists and Baptists were working the same furrows however different the tools they used and the crops they hoped to harvest.

Writings of Thomas Paine

Thomas Paine (1737–1809) was a Deist whose critiques of religion gave him the popular reputation of being an atheist. Paine's pamphlet "Common Sense" (1776) sold more than 500,000 copies and paved the way for the Declaration of Independence, arguing not just for an American revolt but for full independence. In theological matters Paine advocated studying the works of the Creator and inferring the Creator's qualities, rather than letting theologians intervene and muddy the waters.

So, for example, in an essay entitled "The Existence of God," Paine first noted that when people studied an impressive piece of machinery, they thought about the genius of its maker. When they studied geometry they thought of Euclid, and when they studied gravitation they thought of Newton.

> How then is it, that when we study the works of God in the creation, we stop short, and do not think of GOD? It is from the error of the schools in having taught those subjects as accomplishments only, and thereby separated the study of them from the *Being* who is the author of them.
>
> The Schools have made the study of theology to consist in the study of opinions in written or printed books; whereas theology should be studied in the works or books of creation. The study

of theology in books of opinions has often produced fanaticism, rancour, and cruelty of temper; and from hence have proceeded the numerous persecutions, the fanatical quarrels, the religious burnings and massacres, that have desolated Europe. But the study of theology in the works of the creation produces a direct contrary effect. The mind becomes at once enlightened and serene, a copy of the scene it beholds: information and adoration go hand in hand; and all the social faculties become enlarged.[7]

Here we see both the interest in nature mentioned in connection with Emerson and the Deist's aversion to traditional theology because traditional theology had seemed a source of religious warfare. Paine prefers **natural theology** to revelation, thinking the former better suited to the age of reason that dawned in his time. In Paine Deism represented the claims of conscience to abide by the truths generated through modern science and philosophy instead of the mythic depictions of God and reality enshrined in the Bible. What is peculiar to his position, however, is the insistence on experience. Theology that would mediate between the creature and the Creator takes people away from the right track. Contrary to the popular opinion of him, Paine was not an atheist. He had a deep desire to honor the power behind the wonders of creation. But his repudiation of established religion and the theology that he considered its tool made him abhorrent to people not willing to think as freely as he. Their charge of "atheism" should have been "irreligion" or, even more accurately, "opposition to established institutional religion."

The distinction is important, both in itself and for the history of American religion. Frequently those who dissented from the civil religion of popular American culture, which linked belief in a Supreme Being, attendance at church, and patriotism, were branded atheists or irreligious people. In fact, many such people devoutly honored the divine source of creation and strove mightily also to honor what they took to be imperatives of conscience. Ironically they were merely asking that the basic principles of the Protestant Reformation about the personal interpretation of Scripture and the sanctity of individual conscience be extended to include their own conscientious dissent from the orthodoxy of the predominant churches of the era. In so doing they prepared the way for the postmodern views of religion by favoring the dictates of individual conscience over dogma that one finds incredible.

In an essay entitled "Worship and Church Bells," Thomas Paine gave a more positive view of what he considered genuine religion to be. Note the stress on personal independence, care for the poor, and pursuit of the truth.

> No man ought to make a living by Religion. It is dishonest to do so. Religion is not an act that can be performed by proxy. One person cannot act religion for another. Every person must perform it for himself; and all that a priest can do is to take from him; he wants nothing but his money and then to riot in the spoil and laugh at his credulity.
>
> The only people who, as a professional sect of Christians provide for the poor of their society, are people known by the name Quakers. Those men have no priests. They assemble quietly in their places of meeting, and do not disturb their neighbors with shows and noise of bells. Religion does not unite itself to show and noise. True religion is without either. Where there is both there is no true religion.
>
> The first object for inquiry in all cases, more especially in matters of religious concern, is TRUTH. We ought to inquire into the truth of whatever we are taught to believe, and it is certain that the books called the Scriptures stand, in this respect, in more than a doubtful predicament. They have been held in existence, and in a sort of credit among the common class of people, by art, terror, and persecution. They have little or no credit among the enlightened part, but they have been made the means of encumbering the world with a numerous priesthood, who have fattened on the labour of the people, and consumed the sustenance that ought to be applied to the widows and the poor.[8]

In these paragraphs Paine is speaking for himself, voicing his own prejudices, which established religions could rebut quite easily. Regarding the attack on the priesthood it would suffice to point out that religions everywhere have enlisted mediators, people thought versed in religious truth or holy enough to encounter the divine without perishing. Certainly Paine is right that no one can alienate religious responsibility (taking care of one's own soul and conscience). But the history of religion, and indeed of human culture, does not bear out the individualism implied in these paragraphs. Paine was greatly influenced by the French Revolution, which became profoundly anticlerical, due in part to the abuses of Roman Catholicism, but due as well to the unwillingness of some revolutionaries to abide any constraints on the liberty of the individual. The general history of society, as well as idealistic considerations of the conditions in which people might best flourish, suggests that just as one employs an attorney, physician, or craftsman for tasks in which one is not skilled, one might call on a religious specialist to facilitate one's encounters with divinity.

Nonetheless, those who have encountered shady religious professionals may sympathize with Paine's call for self-reliance and criticism of religious profiteering. (On the other hand, the general history of religion reveals that the majority of religious professionals have lived rather spare lives, earning much less than industrialists and political worthies, because they thought spiritual riches more important.)

Paine's polemic against ceremonial, noisy show in religion is also idiosyncratic, though understandable granted his stress on one's personal responsibilities before the Creator. Once again the history of religions is against him, however, for it is replete with ceremonies, songs, dances, and other ways of engaging the whole person or community in worship. The most one can say is that such activity harbors the potential for being show rather than worship and should always be subject to careful critique.

The final paragraph, concerned with the pursuit of truth, pinpoints the bugaboo of the established churches in the modern era. Often they have seemed more concerned with defending past doctrines than with listening to what science or people's personal experience honestly represented as true. Paine's critique of the Scriptures suggests the problems educated people of the late 18th and early 19th centuries encountered, when they tried to correlate what they were told in the churches with the rest of what they thought true. Recent studies of biblical literature have removed many such difficulties, by showing the sort of literature the Bible contains and how such literature does not compete with natural science.

But Paine's general effort to protect intellectual integrity remains instructive. It represents the difficulties with received views of both God and the Bible that many Americans have experienced. In its passion for honesty (more than its biased views of religious experience as a whole) it remains relevant to present-day experience. Many Americans continue to struggle with church doctrines they find either incredible or irrelevant, while the churches that present Scripture as infallible or literally true in all details place great intellectual burdens on their educated members. However extreme he is, Thomas Paine stands for a solid fraction of Americans who through history have felt profound conflicts between official faith and intellectual honesty.

texts and other artifacts, concentrating on the assumptions interpreters tend to make and the process of communication between text and reader. Recently several theoretical schools have developed hermeneutical positions of considerable sophistication, speaking of the innate structures that govern human communication or the ways that interpreters may deconstruct texts and so liberate a wide range of possible meanings.

Natural theology: ways of reflecting on or speaking about God that purport to draw nothing determinative from Scripture but to derive from reason alone. Many natural theologies focus on the physical world, arguing that the being and order of nature bespeak an intelligent Creator. Other arguments, from human conscience and freedom, run to the conclusion that without a Creator and Judge human existence would be meaningless. To theologians who accept a biblical or other revelation from God, the problem with natural theology is its attempt at self-sufficiency. If God is more than what reason can fathom, limiting theology to the rational risks producing a tiny God, more limited than the attributes of God (even those that reason tends to produce) warrant. God then might not be a savior of human beings from sin, or the source of an existence beyond human sensing or conception. God then would tend to be but a projection of human intelligence, a mere image of humanity (rather than humanity's being a mere image of divinity).

Key Terms

Hermeneutics: the science or study of interpretation. Hermeneutics deals with the ways that human beings derive meaning from

Discussion Questions

1. Why have religious passions so frequently inspired warfare?
2. What is missing when the Old Testament God is presented as mainly a wrathful judge?

3. What were the advantages and the disadvantages of Washington's having only a few simple tenets in both politics and religion?

4. What did the Deists gain by speaking of God as the Grand Architect or the Great Ruler of Events?

5. How ought one to define the word *secular,* in light of mainstream American convictions that all nature and humanity alike have come from a divine Creator?

6. What are the problems with advocating the predominance of religious convictions in public affairs such as control of drinking and sexual relations?

7. What is Emerson's "above" that gives one instruction when one opens one's mind and heart to sentiments of virtue?

8. How does Emerson's description of nature accord with your experience of the physical world?

9. What is the perennial value in Paine's critique of established religion?

10. Why does the history of religion and human culture not bear out Paine's belief that true religion is quiet and private?

Notes

1. William Warren Sweet, *Religion in Colonial America* (New York: Charles Scribner's Sons, 1949), pp. 8–10.

2. Cedric B. Cowing, *The Great Awakening and the American Revolution* (Chicago: Rand McNally, 1971), pp. 12–13.

3. Edwin S. Gaustad, *Faith of Our Fathers* (San Francisco: Harper & Row, 1987), pp. 68–77. See also Herbert M. Morais, *Deism in Eighteenth Century America* (New York: Columbia University Press, 1934).

4. See Richard P. McBrien, *Caesar's Coin: Religion and Politics in America* (New York: Macmillan, 1987).

5. Ralph Waldo Emerson, *Essays & Lectures* (New York: The Library of America, 1983), pp. 75–76.

6. See William M. Shea, *The Naturalists and the Supernatural* (Macon, GA: Mercer University Press, 1984).

7. Moncure Daniel Conway, ed., *The Writings of Thomas Paine* (New York: AMS Press, 1967), p. 239.

8. Ibid., p. 250.

Selfhood

The Protestant Ethic

In dealing with doctrines of the self, two preoccupations regularly stand out: work and love. This section reflects on American attitudes toward work. The stereotype, stimulated by the German sociologist Max Weber, is that Calvinist ethics went hand in hand with the rise of capitalism. Since Calvinism probably was the systematic outlook most influential in the United States, to many Weber's thesis was the key to American drive and economic success. Criticism of Weber's views has shown matters to be more complicated, but it should be useful to begin by examining his thesis itself.

Weber found the source of the drive of modern capitalism (energetic application to making money) to lie in what he called "worldly asceticism." In contrast to the ascetical strivings of the medieval monks, who had left the world to concentrate on purifying their souls, the Protestant Reformers urged a devotional life compatible with worldly responsibilities. Their notion of vocation broadened the medieval notion and offered the possibility that all Christians might find the place where God called them to save their souls and improve the world.

Calvinists fully accepted the classical Reformation thesis that justification could not come through works, but as they thought about the significance of good works they began to see them as signs of election (God's favor, predestination to salvation). Thus Weber writes

. . . however useless good works might be as a means of attaining salvation, for even the elect remain beings of the flesh, and everything they do falls infinitely short of divine standards, nevertheless, they are indispensable as a sign of election. They are the technical means, not of purchasing salvation, but of getting rid of the fear of damnation . . . . In practice this means that God helps those who help themselves. Thus the Calvinist, as it is sometimes put, himself creates his own salvation, or, as would be more correct, the conviction of it. But this creation cannot, as in Catholicism, consist in a gradual accumulation of individual good works to one's credit, but rather in a systematic self-control which at every moment stands before the inexorable alternative, chosen or damned . . . . The God of Calvinism demanded of his believers not single good works, but a life of good works combined into a unified system. There was no place for the very human Catholic cycle of sin, repentance, atonement, release, followed by renewed sin. Nor was there any balance of merit for a life as a whole which could be adjusted by temporal punishments or the Churches' [sic] means of grace . . . . This active self-control . . . was also the most important practical ideal of Puritanism. In the deep contempt with which the cool reserve of its adherents is contrasted, in the reports of the trials of its martyrs, with the undisciplined blustering of the noble prelates and officials can be seen that respect for quiet self-control which still distinguishes the best type of English or American gentleman today . . . the end of this asceticism was to be able to lead an alert, intelligent life: the most urgent task the destruction of spontaneous, impulsive enjoyment, the most important means was to bring order into the conduct of its adherents.[1]

Weber's study dealt with more than Calvinism, but its main tenet of "rationalization"—

*Robert Fulton is famous for inventing the steam engine. His self-portrait suggests the confidence of an American impressed by the opportunities of the young 19th century. As a designer he bridged the worlds of art and commerce. (*Self Portrait, *attributed to Robert Fulton; The Nelson-Atkins Museum of Art, Kansas City, Missouri [Nelson Fund])*

suppressing emotion and bringing reason to bear on ordering business and political life as efficiently as possible—best applied to the British and American industrialists shaped by Puritan or Presbyterian religious ethics. No doubt such rationalization could be seen at work in modern science and technology, suggesting that religious motives interacted with several others. But the mystique with which Americans surrounded success in business made the notions of self-discipline, frugality, rectitude, prudent planning, and the like aspects of a worldly holiness. The likes of John D. Rockefeller and

Andrew Carnegie might later be stigmatized as profiteers on the backs of the poor working classes, but their success and wealth were so impressive that the average onlooker had to think they were doing many things correctly (or that God had especially blessed them). Moreover their philanthropies added the impression that they were not simply interested in making money but would generously share the fruits of their enterprise with the entire community. In a word, they were talented individuals who showed themselves good stewards of the wealth God had put into their hands. Their drive, discipline, and success therefore made them models one could set before any American child.

Indeed, their success contributed to an interpretation of Jesus ("The Gospel of Wealth") that joined with social Darwinism (the view that the fittest survive and prosper) to make worldly success a sign of God's blessing.

R. H. Tawney has approved Weber's linking the success of American capitalists such as Rockefeller and Carnegie to the new evaluation of business developed by Calvinist theology:

> Baptized in the bracing, if icy, waters of Calvinist theology, the life of business, once regarded as perilous to the soul . . . acquires a new sanctity. Labour is not merely an economic means: it is a spiritual end. Covetousness, if a danger to the soul, is a less formidable menace than sloth. So far from poverty being meritorious, it is a duty to choose the more profitable occupation. So far from there being an inevitable conflict between money-making and piety, they are natural allies, for the virtues incumbent on the elect—diligence, thrift, sobriety, prudence—are the most reliable passport to commercial prosperity. Thus the pursuit of riches, which had once been feared as the enemy of religion, was now welcomed as its ally.[2]

Those who dispute Weber's thesis tend to argue that the rise of modern capitalism was a more complex affair, and that one cannot draw from the writings of the major reformers any direct endorsement of the capitalistic system or spirit. As one commentator put it,

Calvin himself, who set severe limitations on usury and saw divine blessings as a trust to benefit one's neighbor, scarcely represents the spirit of capitalism. The revival of the OT [Old Testament] concept of "divine blessings" and the sense that we look to God in everything that we do, did, however, give a dignity to worldly activity as the sphere of our grateful obedience. Whether this justifies the Weber thesis is another matter.[3]

In recent years Americans have been rehashing the connections between worldview and work ethic, often under the stimulus of the economic successes of the Japanese or the academic successes of Asian-Americans. Commentators have shown the influence in those cases of Confucian notions such as the necessity of honoring one's parents by success. Once again, many other factors have been at work, but it is significant that working hard, seeking discipline and efficiency, and subordinating present enjoyments to future success do seem to relate to how people think of their time and what they believe they have been placed on earth to accomplish.

The Protestant ethic in fact has been broad enough to accommodate many different views of work, money, time, and social responsibility. For example, the social gospel promoted by Walter Rauschenbusch sharply criticized capitalism as oblivious to the harsh working conditions and other sufferings of the poor. And many Protestant scripture scholars have made it plain that Jesus' teachings about riches give little foundation for the Calvinist interpretation summarized by Tawney. Still, when one searches for the roots of the American view of the ideal self as hard working, disciplined, and financially successful, the notions that Weber brought forward remain instructive. If one could account financial success a sign of election, and if one could account worldly asceticism (helpful in business) a saintly achievement, the sky was the limit in applying one's drive to capitalistic enterprises. Later generations apparently lost the religious roots of this attitude and too often were driven simply by greed, but down to the present day many people who put heart and soul into their work think that they are doing something admirable. The workaholism that Catholicism in many ages would have branded a sin (as a species of idolatry) has seemed to many Americans the highest evidence of a commitment finally blessed by God.

Love in American Piety

The upshot of the American idealization of productive work was to spotlight the individual entrepreneur (until recently primarily male), spending himself for the sake of his business. The complementary image of love often idealized the wife and mother as the soul of the home, keeping it free of the corruption of the outside worlds of politics and business. Those who speak of the "feminization" of American culture and religion in the 19th century link women's domesticity with a shrinking of religion to the domestic sphere. Women were accounted more religious than men and religion became feminized, something that made typical men feel awkward. The sweet, if not sticky songs sung in Christian churches and the feminization of portraits and impressions of Jesus correlated with this movement. Yet such feminization did not staunch the tide of individualism. Indeed the tendency to separate love from questions of social justice helped shrink "charity" to the sphere of one-to-one benefactions, while the later drift of American individualism in the direction of what some sociologists have called "therapeutic" concerns (healing personal bruises) made personal commitments problematic.

The much-discussed recent book, *Habits of the Heart: Individualism and Commitment in American Life,* begins its report on love and individualism as follows:

> How Americans think about love is central to the ways we define the meaning of our lives in rela-

tion to the wider society. For most of us, the bond to spouse and children is our most fundamental social tie. The habits and modes of thought that govern intimate relationships are thus one of the central places where we may come to understand the cultural legacy with which we face the challenges of contemporary social life. Yet in spite of its great importance, love is also, increasingly, a source of insecurity, confusion, and uncertainty. The problems we have in thinking about love are an embodiment of the difficulty we have in thinking about social attachment in general.

A deeply ingrained individualism lies behind much contemporary understanding of love. The idea that people must take responsibility for deciding what they want and finding relationships that will meet their needs is widespread. In this sometimes somber utilitarianism, individuals may want lasting relationships, but such relationships are possible only so long as they meet the needs of the two people involved. All individuals can do is be clear about their own needs and avoid neurotic demands for such unrealizable goods as a lover who will give and ask nothing in return.[4]

It would be a complicated task to trace the historical evolution of this state of mind, but the limitations on love set by American individualism are worth considering. Certainly American religious thought has not neglected such matters as community and the common good. But the origins of American culture in colonial ventures forwarded by people who wanted to break free of old world patterns and the development of American culture through a century of westward expansion that put a premium on self-reliance (or the individualistic sense of grace stressed by the revivalists) tended to exalt the rights of the individual above the rights of the surrounding community.

We see remnants of such a traditional American tendency in the difficulties recently raised by the ecological crisis. The damage that American industry and consumerism have done to the environment suggests widespread changes in the American economic system and materialist life-style, but American political traditions seem ill-equipped to achieve such changes. Barry Commoner recently described the dilemma in the following terms:

> Perhaps the most profound question raised by environmental issues is to what extent the choice of production technologies should be determined by private economic considerations and to what extent by social concerns like environmental quality. These values are in sharp conflict. There appears to be a broad consensus that it is in the national interest to restore the quality of the environment, and the resultant legislation confirms the general impression that achieving this goal is a social, governmental responsibility. And, as we have seen, significant environmental improvement requires the proper choice of technologies and systems of production, so that this choice, too, becomes a social responsibility. Yet in our free-market economy the right to make such a choice is in private, not public, hands, and this is a right very few Americans would challenge.[5]

One could infer, then, that American piety has not produced a love of the earth equal to the American love of private enterprise. One could also infer from this that American religion has not been very successful in bringing people into communities that would both fulfill their desire for intimacy and purify it by linking them with greater public issues. The love of Jesus that many Christian devotions have encouraged has seldom directed Americans' thought about the political, economic, and technological systems they were developing. No doubt one could say the same of the piety developed in Europe, although individualistic accents have always been stronger in America. The result here, however, was often a love that seemed more romantic than realistic, more a private, if not escapist, emotion than a force capable of transforming culture.

The love of country toward which American religion often conspired flourished in time of war, but in ordinary times it was hard put to combat private greed.

Of course overcoming selfishness (individualism in the sense of concern narrowed to self-interest) has always been one of religion's greatest challenges. Whatever the special consideration necessary in the case of American women, many of whom (according to present-day feminist analysts) have suffered from a lack of the self-confidence and self-love necessary for strong individualism, the general judgment remains that the love nurtured in American piety has been considerably less self-transcending than what the biblical accounts of love (to which the majority of religious Americans looked for their norms) commended.[6]

At the end of a study of Martin Luther King, Jr., Frederick Downing has suggested the outreach that the most creative instances of love in American piety have achieved:

> The center of King's religious genius was the ability to identify with Christ to bring about his own "decentration" and thereby to deal creatively with his own shame. Though King was an extremely guilt-ridden man, typical of *homo religiosus*, his struggle with shame was even more primal and basic to his life-long wrestling match. Martin Luther King, Jr., took his own sense of shame and the shame of his country and placed it in the center of his mind and spirit. There, in an act of unusual courage, he attempted "to stare dauntingly at it." Shame is a painful experience of self-exposure. And when one is able to accept shame, it becomes an act of identification with Jesus, the crucified one. Late in his life King came to this type of understanding when he said to his worried friends who wanted him to stop marching, "I have to do this—to expose myself to bring this hate into the open." So he marched and he opened himself to the hostility of those around him. Yet, he continued to work nonviolently, knowing somehow that what he was about would bring a revelation of true selfhood and a vision of a more humane and just society. In his Atlanta church, he was able to confess his sins and to "expose" himself before God. In this way he continued his identification with Christ whose identity demanded that he love God above all others, including himself.[7]

Religious Sociability

In a sociological report published in 1970, Rodney Stark and Charles Y. Glock wrote:

> Examining the various denominations it is obvious that some resemble religious audiences while others come closer to the ideal of being religious communities. It is not possible to say absolutely just what proportion of a congregation ought to have how many friends from the congregation in order for the group to be called a true community or a primary group. Obviously it is not necessary that all be friends of all. But for the sake of comparison, we shall adopt several relatively arbitrary but reasonable standards. If we can consider a person to be imbedded in a religious community if at least two of his best five friends are members of his church, then it seems clear that the small Protestant sect groups come rather close to the ideal of being religious communities—80 percent of their members restrict their friendship to fellow congregants to this extent. Among the major denominations the Southern Baptists are the closest to this ideal with 60 percent of their members having at least two of their five best friends in their congregations. The Disciples of Christ, American Baptists, and Roman Catholics manage a bare majority of members who meet this standard of communal involvement. The least communally involved denomination is the Congregational Church with only 29 percent meeting our criterion of involvement. Thus, Christian churches range from religious audiences to religious communities and within all denominations the communal involvement of individual members varies greatly.[8]

Before reflecting on the implications this sketch might have for the American sense of selfhood, and for how Americans have felt liberated from their various oppressions through church membership, it may be instructive to examine some data about recent Jewish senses of community. In a study of the boundaries delineating the Orthodox Jewish community, Samuel Heilman recently surveyed non-Ortho-dox, nominally Orthodox, centrist Orthodox, and traditional Orthodox Jews about their ideas of friendship and the realities of friendship in their own lives.

Heilman's survey had four main questions.

1. He asked his interviewees to respond to the proposition, "An Orthodox Jew can be close friends with Jews of all degrees of observance." Of the non-Orthodox 33 percent strongly agreed with this statement and 45 percent agreed to some extent. Among the nominally Orthodox, 39 percent strongly agreed and 46 agreed to some extent. Centrist Orthodox Jews had 41 percent strongly agreeing and 47 percent agreeing to some extent. Of the traditional Orthodox Jews 24 percent strongly agreed and 46 percent agreed to some extent. The rhetoric, then, was that Orthodoxy need not keep one from establishing close ties with non-Orthodox Jews. Even the traditional Orthodox, whose beliefs made their lives quite distinctive in terms of diet and legal observance, were 70 percent confident of the proposition.

2. Next Heilman asked his interviewees whether their friends actually included Jews of all degrees of observance. Among the non-Orthodox, none said that all their close friends were Orthodox and only 3 percent said that most of their friends were Orthodox. Among the nominally Orthodox, 7 percent said that all of their close friends were Orthodox and 29 percent said that most of their close friends were Orthodox. Of the centrist Orthodox 13 percent said all their close friends were Orthodox and 62 percent said most of their close friends were Orthodox. Of the traditional Orthodox 46 percent reported that all their close friends were Orthodox and 50 percent said most were. Thus in practice the groups on both ends of the spectrum belied the rhet-

oric. The non-Orthodox in fact had few close friends who were Orthodox, while the traditional Orthodox had few close friends who were not Orthodox.

3. Heilman then asked for responses to the proposition, "An Orthodox Jew can be close friends with non-Jews." Of the non-Orthodox 22 percent strongly agreed and 43 percent agreed to some extent. Among the nominally Orthodox, 23 percent strongly agreed and 50 percent agreed to some extent. Centrist Orthodox checked in at 24 percent strongly agreeing and 46 percent agreeing to some extent, while the figures for the traditional Orthodox were 9 percent and 35 percent. Even the strictest Jews therefore were relatively optimistic about being close friends with non-Jews (44 percent), while nearly 70 percent of the others were optimistic.

4. Finally Heilman asked his interviewees about the actual composition of their circle of friends. In actual practice 27 percent of the non-Orthodox said that all their close friends were Jewish, 26 percent of the nominally Orthodox said that all their close friends were Jewish, 46 percent of the centrist Orthodox had all Jewish close friends, and 67 percent of the traditional Orthodox had all Jewish close friends.

In reflecting on the results of his survey, Heilman writes,

It is the optimism of the Orthodox that seems . . . surprising. They *know* they have relatively few close non-Jewish friends. After all, Orthodoxy—with its many restrictions on lifestyle and adherence to rituals that as part of their deep structure imply and foster segregation from the rest of the world—would seem to militate against openness. Nevertheless, beyond the traditionalist fringe, a majority of the other Orthodox (70 percent for the centrists and 73 percent

for the nominally Orthodox) agree in some way with the proposition that an Orthodox Jew can be close friends with non-Jews. But the centrists stand out particularly because although they share the same open attitude as those to their modernist left (including the non-Orthodox), in fact nearly half of them have no close friends who are not Jewish. Again they turn out to be divided and ambivalent.

And why? One might argue that their modern attitude of cosmopolitanism, a product of their being neither remote from nor untouched by contemporary America, encourages cultural contact while the realities and restraints of their Orthodoxy, along with the separation it fosters in domicile, eating habits, and worldview, discourage the very same cultural contact. A bit of that is true for the nominally Orthodox who nevertheless suffer less segregation by virtue of their minimal Orthodox practice. So their rhetoric more closely approaches the reality. But even the nominally Orthodox still have practices and life-styles that keep them, if not totally, at least very partially insulated from those who are unlike them. Hence, only about a quarter of them claim that they have close non-Jewish friends.[9]

When a group feels confident of its own identity and place in the surrounding American culture, it tends to be open to contacts with those outside the group, not seeing them as threats to what the group is about. When a group feels beleaguered, pushed to the margins of the surrounding culture and considered deviant, it tends to bar the doors and hunker down. The psychology of marginal groups suggests that they deal with persecution ambivalently, sometimes being objective about the fact that outsiders actually do hate them and sometimes provoking such hatred by aggressive displays of deviance from the cultural mainstream. Mormons, Seventh Day Adventists, and other religious outsiders have shown such a psychological profile.[10] Thinking the world a corrupt place, or feeling their convictions to be under attack by the outside culture, they regularly have internalized their outsider status and developed a suspicious cast of mind.

What may be different about the Jewish population Heilman surveyed is their long-standing tradition of being marginal to the mainstream of Christian cultures. In the measure that American culture has become more secular, religious affiliation has become less determinative of one's identity and so less a threat to the identities of others. Thus many Jews could think close friendship with non-Jews quite possible.

Still, for all religious groups, sociability or community remains an ideal. All groups long for experiences of worship, celebration, sharing trials, and the like that both disclose and nourish the traditions they share. All sense that the fullest individual identity emerges in community, not in splendid isolation. So for all American religious groups the negotiations necessitated by a pluralistic culture have been formidable. How were Protestants to relate to Catholics and Catholics to Protestants? How were Christians of any stripe to relate to Jews and Jews to Christians? What was any religious group to make of the nonreligious secularists or even atheists? The American experiment in nonestablished religion made answering these questions an important part of any religious person's sense of self as a Christian, Jew, or nonbeliever.

More recently, the same questions have impinged on Hindus, Buddhists, Muslims, and other religious groups who have established themselves in the United States. A century ago such questions had stronger ethnic tones, Italian Catholics having to negotiate relations with Irish Catholics or Polish Catholics, German Mennonites having to negotiate with Southern Baptists, and so on. Today relations between conservative, fundamentalist Protestants and liberal Protestants are equally complicated. How people fashion their religious groups and define them vis à vis the surrounding culture remains a fascinating phenomenon that says much about the sense of self possessed by members of a religious group.

Mary Baker Eddy

Mary Baker Eddy (1821–1910) grew up in a New England Congregationalist family. Plagued by ill health from childhood, she received little formal education. In 1843 she married, but her husband died before the birth of their son. Because Eddy's health continued to be poor, she had little contact with the boy, giving him to others to raise. Until well into her adulthood, Eddy experimented with various curative systems, seeking better health. Impressed by Phineas P. Quimby, a healer who avoided medicines, she thought he had rediscovered the spiritual powers shown by Jesus in his healings. When Quimby died, however, Baker's illness returned, and by 1866 she had come to consider herself hopeless. Still, in that year she read the New Testament assiduously and found herself restored. That experience marked the beginning of what she called Christian Science.

There followed years of working out her ideas about faith and health, and in 1875 she published *Science and Health,* her major work. With the Bible, it became the scripture of Christian Scientists. By 1879 Eddy and her followers had organized in Boston the First Church of Christ, Scientist. For ten years they also ran a Metaphysical College. By 1906 the impressive Mother Church was standing in Boston (it is still the headquarters of Christian Scientists) and the group was opening branch churches across the country. The founding of *The Christian Science Monitor* in 1908 gave Christian Science a highly respected daily newspaper, while numerous other literary organs, available in Christian Science reading rooms, promulgated Eddy's ideas. Eddy published several other books, and to her death she remained the leading figure in her organization.

The aspects of selfhood that Christian Science emphasizes may be inferred from its notions of healing and salvation:

> Salvation includes obedience to Jesus' command to heal the sick. Sickness is one expression of the fundamental error of the mortal mind that accepts existence as something separate from God. Healing, therefore, must be predicated on the action of the divine Mind or power outside of human thought. In Eddy's words, ". . . erring, finite, the human mind has an absolute need of something beyond itself for its redemption and healing." Healing is regarded not merely as a bodily change, but as a phase of full salvation from the flesh as well. It is the normalization of bodily function and formation through the divine government of the human mentality and of the bodily system that that mentality governs.[11]

Many commentators have remarked on the potentially stifling social conventions under which women labored in Eddy's day and the consequent plethora of psychosomatic illnesses they suffered. In finding her own way to mental and bodily health, Eddy produced an organization especially attractive to such women. They could accept the feminized, spiritualized conceptions of religion current in their culture, in effect going them one better by making bondage to the flesh a matter of illusion. The notion that a mind filled with divine power could prevail over sickly matter energized many women, and some men, while the outlets for their energy offered by church affairs frequently solidified their sense of restored health. Having a cause to which to dedicate themselves, something larger and more absorbing than their own ills, made it easy for many to feel whole and purposeful.

One may quarrel with various aspects of Christian Science, disputing whether it validly translates the healing methods of Jesus (which, as many American religious groups realized, had offered hope for both sick bodies and sick souls), or whether its metaphysics holds up to rigorous analysis, but it is hard to quarrel with the evidence Christian Science and many other systems offer that spiritual states of mind have an impact on bodily health. Indeed, anyone interested in salvation or liberation soon realizes that the self can require as much healing as unjust social structures. Buddhists have long made the case that one will do little good in society until one's own desires are rightly ordered (until grasping is extinguished). Christian Scientists work the same side of the street.

Other Christian groups tend to stress healing the human spirit from sin, or healing the mind from ignorance, but no reader of the New Testament can deny that Jesus' healing extended to physical illness (and mental disease). To heal the self is therefore a regular feature of religious programs, however obliquely their theological or psychological language may phrase their goals. Mary Baker Eddy stands in the history of American religious thought as one of numerous religious leaders who stressed such healing, unique only for her success as a propagandist and organizer. She made Christian Science a dignified, even staid affair, and if she never received much respect from mainstream Christianity, the impressive Mother Church and publications of her group gave it influence far beyond its relatively small membership. (Christian Scientists do not publish membership figures, but 250,000 might be a generous estimate.)

The status that Mary Baker Eddy gained in her organization is suggested by Article XXII of the *Manual of the Mother Church*:

> In the year eighteen hundred and ninety-five, loyal Christian Scientists had given to the author of their textbook, the Founder of Christian Science, the individual, endearing term of Mother. At first Mrs. Eddy objected to being called thus, but afterward consented on the ground that this appellative in the Church meant nothing more than a tender term such as sister or brother. In the year nineteen

hundred and three and after, owing to the public misunderstanding of this name, it is the duty of Christian Scientists to drop the word *mother* and to substitute Leader, already used in our periodicals . . . . If a member of this Church shall, mentally or otherwise, persist in working against the interests of another member, or the interests of our Pastor Emeritus [Eddy] and the accomplishment of what she understands is advantageous to this Church and to the cause of Christian Science, or shall influence others thus to act, upon her complaint or the complaint of a member for her or for himself, it shall be the duty of the Board of Directors immediately to call a meeting, and drop forever the name of the member guilty of this offense from the roll of Church membership . . . . If a member of this Church were to treat the author of our textbook disrespectfully and cruelly, upon her complaint that member should be excommunicated. If a member, without her having requested this information, shall trouble her on subjects unnecessarily and without her consent, it shall be considered an offense.[12]

No pope or patriarch, no leader of mainstream Protestant denominations, has claimed or received such privileges, and the document testifies to the upset that Eddy suffered in her later years, when she saw conspirators on every side trying to wreck her movement. It seems that mental health is always a fragile possession, something religious people have to safeguard, particularly when they immerse themselves intensely in systems claiming to cure all ills, mental and physical alike.

Writings of William James

William James (1842–1910) has been accounted by many observers the most rounded of the American philosophers and the one best representing the temper of the American mind. Various descriptions have attached themselves to James's thought. At times he has been described as a pragmatist, at other times as a radical empiricist (someone convinced that experience is the most important test of truth, and that experience shows reality to be pluralistic to its very foundations). Before he began to teach philosophy, at the age of 37, he had already established himself as a noteworthy psychologist. Perhaps his most famous works concerning religion were the Gifford Lectures he delivered in Edinburgh during the years 1901–1902, which were published as *The Varieties of Religious Experience*. In them James dealt with such matters as the healing of sick souls and the psychological foundations of mystical experience. Throughout he showed himself a sensitive, even sympathetic observer of religious phenomena.

Indeed the combination of a lasting interest in religion and a lasting willingness to defend religion from crude attacks, with a conviction that all truth claims had to submit to the test of experience, made James an original thinker regarding religion. Thus while he could find no evidence for survival after death, he found ample testimony to the existence of God. By the same experiential criteria, however, the divinity that James found was not the unified deity of the monotheistic faiths but a plurality of saving powers. James drew such further conclusions from his research into religious experience as that human beings do have a measure of freedom, and so of self-determination, and that the will one brings to belief or nonbelief is crucially important. When people want to find a power to heal them or direct their lives, they are more likely to do so.

In discussing how **pragmatism** might harmonize the empirical tendencies and demands of human beings with traditional religious aspirations, James criticized the **idealistic** pantheism of his day:

Affirming the Absolute Mind, which is [such pantheism's] substitute for God, to be the rational presupposition of all particulars of fact, whatever they may be, it remains supremely indifferent to what the particular facts of our world actually are. Be they what they may, the Absolute will father them . . . . He gives you indeed the assurance that all is well with *Him*, and for his eternal way of thinking; but thereupon he leaves you to be finitely saved by your own temporal devices.

Far be it from me to deny the majesty of this conception, or its capacity to yield religious comfort to a most respectable class of minds. But from the human point of view, no one can pretend that it doesn't suffer from the faults of remoteness and abstractness. It is eminently a product of what I have ventured to call the rationalistic temper. It disdains empiricism's needs. It substitutes a pallid outline for the real world's richness. It is dapper, it is noble in the bad sense, in the sense in which to be noble is to be inapt for humble service. In this real world of sweat and dirt, it seems to me that when a view of things is "noble," that ought to count as a presumption against its truth, and as a philosophic disqualification. The prince of darkness may be a gentleman, as we are told he is, but whatever the God of earth and heaven is, he can surely be no gentleman. His menial services are needed in the dust of our human trials, even more than his dignity is needed in the empyrean.[13]

In other writings, James contrasted two mental types, the tough-minded and the tender-minded, and implied that while he himself favored the tough-minded type, the tender-minded type had its rights, too. Among them was the need to feel a sense of security in the world and so to be religious. Thus James's regular empiricism was not so hard-headed, so scientific, that it ruled out the many experiences people reported of mystical union with something beyond ordinary human perception. If both tough-minded and tender-minded states of consciousness had data to which they could point—times, places, perceptions—the good pragmatist would take both into account.

The implication for James's sense of self was that truth might lead in any direction. One had only to assure that any truth claim had some

experiential, empirical basis and then follow the path it indicated. Inasmuch as that path proved fruitful, in the sense of expanding one's horizons or showing one how to improve one's condition, one ought to grant it respect. How absolute any truth claim ought to be depended on the evidence it could muster. The only claims that James ruled out were a priori, dogmatic claims that refused to tie themselves to experience.

It is interesting that James's sense of deity takes God apart from the "noble" and down into the sweat and dirt of daily life. Whether this is a vestige of Christian theology infiltrating his philosophy is hard to say, but it would fit the **kenotic** Christology suggested by the Apostle Paul in Philippians 2. More likely, James's predilection for down-to-earth ideas that could actually help people in their daily struggles came from his sense of where vigor resides in human affairs. He had beaten bouts of melancholy by finally choosing to believe there was meaning in daily existence, and with this victory went a regime of hikes and exercise designed to toughen the flesh and invigorate the spirit. James loved to deal with the particulars one could directly experience—the flowers of a given field, the ills of a particular person. He felt that speculation rooted in such particulars, trying to elaborate their significance, was valid, while speculation moving from generality to generality was suspect. The healthy self, one might infer, would be one that kept both feet on the ground and wanted its speculations to pay off in a better mastery of nature, more helpful contributions to society, and a personality both energetic and whole.

In a set of lectures entitled "A Pluralistic Universe," James concluded by again treating of religious experiences, defending their legitimacy, and suggesting the particularity that he wished them to retain.

There is a light in which all the naturally found and currently accepted distinctions, excellences,

Many of the sects that stressed mental health looked to the sea or the woods for a tranquillity hard to find in the press of human affairs. From this tranquillity they hoped the natural powers of the spirit might reassert themselves for healing. (Meditation by the Sea, Anonymous; courtesy Museum of Fine Arts, Boston; M. and M. Karolik Collection.)

and safeguards of our characters appear as utter childishness. Sincerely to give up one's conceit or hope of being good in one's own right is the only door to the universe's deeper reaches.

These deeper reaches are familiar to evangelical Christianity and to what is nowadays becoming known as "mind-cure" religion or "new thought." The phenomenon is that of new ranges of life succeeding on our most despairing moments. There are resources in us that naturalism with its literal and legal virtues never recks of, possibilities that take our breath away, of another kind of happiness and power, based on giving up our own will and letting something higher work for us, and these seem to show a world wider than either physics or philistine ethics can imagine. Here is a world in which all is well, in *spite* of certain forms of death, indeed *because* of certain forms of death— death of hope, death of strength, death of responsibility, of fear and worry, competency and desert, death of everything that paganism, naturalism, and legalism pin their faith on and tie their trust to.

Reason, operating on our other experiences, even our psychological experiences, would never have inferred these specifically religious experiences in advance of their actual coming. She could not suspect their existence, for they are discontinuous with the "natural" experiences they succeed upon and invert their values. But as they actually come and are given, creation widens to the view of their recipients. They suggest that our natural experience, our strictly moralistic and prudential experience, may be only a fragment of real human experience. They soften nature's outlines and open out the strangest possibilities and perspectives.

That is why it seems to me that the logical understanding, working in abstraction from such specifically religious experiences, will always omit something, and fail to reach completely adequate conclusions. Death and failure, it will always say, *are* death and failure simply, and can nevermore be one with life; so religious experience, peculiarly so called, needs, in my opinion, to be carefully considered and interpreted by anyone who aspires to reason out a more complete philosophy.[14]

For William James, therefore, the self is what its experiences suggest about it, and because the most provocative experiences are religious, one cannot estimate the self without taking religion deeply into account.

Key Terms

Idealistic: concerning the realm of pure thought, of ideas operating independently of sense experience. In some idealistic systems, only thought is accounted fully real. Both Hegelianism in the West and such Eastern systems as Hindu Vedanta and Buddhist Yogocara have espoused this position. The popular connotation of idealism as having to do with lofty aspirations,

high moral sentiments, can relate to this more metaphysical denotation, but it need not. Idealism as a metaphysical system does not solve the problem of evil but transposes it into a question of spiritual disorder.

Kenotic: concerned with self-emptying, self-sacrifice. The Pauline Christology sketched in Philippians 2 praises the Incarnate Word for having emptied himself of his heavenly status, assumed flesh, suffered, and died on human beings' behalf. This condescension was a mark of the divine goodness, and in Paul's eyes it ought to have led Christians to humility, self-sacrifice, and devotion to the needs of others. More generally, one may call kenotic any religious views that seek the improvement of human beings' flesh and blood condition and imply both an emptying of grandiose phrases and a will to stress experience and results.

Pragmatism: the philosophy of C.S. Peirce and William James, in which the test of truth and wisdom are practical effects and experiential foundations. James was not advocating a crude commitment to "what works," or intending to override ethical questions of the means to effective ends. He was impressed by the revelations of action, of what happened when people stayed close to their experience and struggled to let the yield of experience be their guide. Only by acting on their beliefs, by bringing their beliefs to the test of experience, would people finally know what their beliefs were worth.

Discussion Questions

1. How did Max Weber link Protestant worldly asceticism and capitalistic success?
2. What place did financial success play in the Calvinist sense of election?

3. How does the ecological crisis spotlight the need for religion to mediate between love of individual liberties and love of nature or the common good?

4. How does a therapeutic self-concern tend to make marital love complicated and dubious?

5. How valid a criterion of the quality of a religious group's communal life is members' having most of their close friends come from within the group?

6. What is valid in the proposition that individuals fully prosper only through communion with others?

7. How might the removal of 19th century American women from large areas of public life have contributed to their tendency toward frailness or illness?

8. What part does the mind play in physical sickness?

9. How did William James' stress on experience become a defense of religion?

10. What are the advantages and disadvantages of a pragmatic view of religious claims that asks them to pay off in terms of human healing?

Notes

1. Max Weber, *The Protestant Ethic and the Spirit of Capitalism* (New York: Charles Scribner's Sons, 1930), pp. 115–119.

2. R. H. Tawney, "Foreword," in Weber, pp. 2–3.

3. James A. Whyte, "Calvinist Ethics," in *The Westminster Dictionary of Christian Ethics*, ed. James F. Childress and John Macquarrie (Philadelphia: Westminster, 1986), p. 73.

4. Robert N. Bellah, Richard Madsen, William M. Sullivan, Ann Swidler, and Steven M. Tipton, *Habits of the Heart* (Berkeley: University of California Press, 1985), pp. 107–108.

5. Barry Commoner, "A Reporter at Large: The Environment," *The New Yorker,* 15 June, 1987, p. 57.

6. On love and justice in American religious thought, see Edwin S. Gaustad, ed., *A Documentary History of Religion in America*, vol. 2 (Grand Rapids, MI: Eerdmans, 1983), pp. 104–134.

7. Frederick L. Downing, *To See the Promised Land: The Faith Pilgrimage of Martin Luther King, Jr.* (Macon, GA: Mercer University Press, 1986), pp. 283–284.

8. Rodney Stark and Charles Y. Glock, *American Piety: The Nature of Religious Commitment* (Berkeley: University of California Press, 1970), pp. 167–168.

9. Samuel C. Heilman, "Orthodox Jews: An Open or Closed Group?" in *Uncivil Religion: Interreligious Hostility in America*, ed. Robert N. Bellah and Frederick E. Greenspahn (New York: Crossroad, 1987), pp. 125–126.

10. See R. Laurence Moore, *Religious Outsiders and the Making of Americans* (New York: Oxford University Press, 1986).

11. Stephen Gottschalk, "Christian Science," in *The Encyclopedia of Religion*, vol. 3, ed. Mircea Eliade (New York: Macmillan, 1987), p. 444.

12. Rosemary Radford Ruether and Rosemary Skinner Keller, eds., *Women & Religion in America*, vol. 1 (San Francisco: Harper & Row, 1981), pp. 81–82.

13. William James, "Pragmatism: 'A Happy Harmonizer,'" in *Documents in the History of American Philosophy*, ed. Morton White (New York: Oxford University Press, 1972), pp. 362–363.

14. William James, *Essays in Radical Empiricism and A Pluralistic Universe* (New York: Dutton, 1971), pp. 266–267.

CHAPTER **14**

American Views of Evil

Human Nature

All the religious, philosophical, and political rivulets that came to compose the mainstreams of American culture carried reflections about human nature. In thinking about people's ultimate responsibilities, what one might expect of one's fellow human beings, and how people might live together in peace and prosperity, those who contributed to American culture were bound to indicate what kind of animal (or spirit) they thought the typical human being was. Indeed, when they had to confront such challenging issues as slavery and war, Americans had to indicate just how evil or bent they thought human nature could be. There is no simple summary of how Americans have regarded human nature. There are prevailing opinions, however, and it is profitable to consider them.

Introducing a study of the concept of human nature in American thought, Merle Curti has written:

The transfer of ideas and values from the Old World, in the first century and a half of the settlement of the New, understandably included attitudes toward human nature. In the middle and southern colonies references to these involved little explicit and systematic analysis of the term itself. It was largely identified with Christian supernatural dualism and assimilated Aristotelian-medieval ideas and with proverbs and adages in the classical and Renaissance traditions. The phrase also involved a recognition of the influence of biology (including heredity), astrology, Special Providences, and the natural and social environment. As generally understood, human nature included a capacity for introspective probing of motives, both conscious and unconscious. Conflict between reason and the emotions and passions (including sex) was assumed to be an innate characteristic. The discussion of human nature likewise identified tension between selfishness and benevolence. On occasion, references to human nature touched on such matters as fixedness or malleability in the human condition and determination versus free will. The traditional uses of ideas about human nature included advisory maxims intended to help men and women resolve conflicts and meet sorrow. Moreover, the American environment accentuated older uses and even initiated new ones. These included some awareness of the stimulation provided by hitherto unheard and unseen wonders to the faculties of sensation and imagination, and the enlargement through the use of empirical science of man's ability to adapt himself to unusual circumstances and to transform inherent potentialities into new achievements. Even more important was the problem posed by the contrast between beggarly poverty in the Old World and self-sustenance of those who had known only impoverishment in England. The bounty and opportunities of the new land seemed, again, to expand human capacity. Also important was the need of justifying elites and social status in a relatively mobile society. Above all, attitudes toward human nature figured in questions raised by relations with Indians and Africans.[1]

In this summary American wrestling with the concept of human nature took a somewhat nuanced European heritage into the new circumstances of a vastly expanded theater for human initiative and emerged optimistic about the possibilities of removing poverty and expanding human capacity. One might add that

when the colonists contrasted their own culture with those of the Native Americans and Africans, they tended to think themselves fortunate for having received divine revelation and to wonder whether Native Americans and Africans weren't less than human. To be sure, there were exceptions to this tendency; some colonists found Native Americans or Africans healthier or nobler than the typical European. However, further experience showed that natives and blacks struggled with selfishness and conflict just as colonists did. Yet few Europeans had many doubts about the superiority of their culture, so few had many scruples about either supplanting natives or pressuring them to adopt European ways. More colonists worried about slavery, but even many of those who rejected slavery as immoral maintained a paternalistic view of blacks.

Curti's summary only hints at the suspicions of early Americans about the depravity of human nature. However, such depravity was a central theme in both classical Reformation thought and many of its American offspring. Luther and Calvin balanced their convictions about the necessity of divine grace for salvation with a reading of human nature that stressed the impotence of human works. Without faith, they thought, reason tended to produce prideful idols. Without grace, the human heart remained twisted and inclined to evil, while the human will remained weak. Puritan theology accepted this view of human nature as its basic heritage (though before long some Puritans had come to consider good works a necessary manifestation of sanctification, while others had begun to promote the notion that financial success was a sign of election). Perfectionist groups such as the Quakers rejected this pessimism, thinking that in the right circumstances (for example, wise child rearing) the seed of God planted in each person could overcome inclinations to evil and manifest the inclination of human nature toward peace, mutual trust, and tolerance.

Americans' struggles with evil often led them to project onto Native Americans and blacks the tangled emotions pent up in the white breast. (Cler-Mont, Chief of the Osages, George Catlin; Gilcrease Museum, Tulsa, Oklahoma)

Unitarians, following the lead of such luminaries as Ralph Waldo Emerson, tended to stress the kinship between the human spirit and divinity. This disturbed those Protestants sometimes called the Orthodox, who retained a strong sense of original sin. Trying to mediate between these two positions, Horace Bushnell (1802–1876) challenged the individualistic bias they shared, speaking of human beings' solidarity in both sin and redemption. As Claude Welch has said,

> Bushnell insisted that every child is truly born into a world of sin and bondage to sin . . . . Being "born" means much more than the physical act of generation; it is a social as much as a biological process . . . . Further, within this organic social

matrix the self comes to be itself only in a continuous process of gradual becoming . . . . There is no single moment at which a person becomes a moral agent, passing from "moral nullity" to independent moral agency. Only gradually does a child pass out from dependence in the sphere of his parents' moral agency to a proper responsibility of his own. Neither virtue nor sin, therefore, can be interpreted adequately as the product of separate and independent choice. The self is a social self, and virtue is a state rather than an act or a series of acts.[2]

Inasmuch as Christian education and church life might furnish a milieu of virtue, they could help the individual progress from the state of bondage to sin to the state of living by redemptive grace. Therefore 19th century American theology occasionally anticipated the impact of social science generated in the 20th century, when environment (people's social circumstances) got much attention.

The skeptical tradition passed down from the Founding Fathers influenced by Enlightenment thought never left the American scene, in good part because it was enshrined in the American political system of checks and balances. But the aspect of Jeffersonian democracy that stressed educating the common citizen toward political understanding and virtue combined with arguments from social science and Christian theology to make the American public school a focus of considerable hope. The Protestant character of mainstream American culture continued to counsel low expectations from human nature, but it supported the hope that hard work, discipline, and nourishing of the mind could keep natural depravity in check. Catholics, Jews, Eastern Orthodox, and others not formed by Protestant culture might bring forward theological objections, but in practice they agreed that an education combining intellectual and moral discipline was the best hope for forming the sort of character people needed to be good citizens and please God. Nonetheless, all of the

optimism American thinkers might generate about human nature was radically challenged by slavery and war.

Slavery

One can make the case that slavery symbolizes the depth to which American evil could go, when social movements, instead of curbing human selfishness or depravity, institutionalized the degradation of one group by another. The arguments among reformers over whether it was wise to try to legislate a better morality (regarding drink and violence as well as slavery) also show that different views of human nature could have quite practical consequences. However, even Marxist historians shy away from calling slavery simply evil, in part because that might sound theological and in part because they recognize that every political situation embodies a dialectical tension between rulers and ruled, both of whom are complex groups blending admirable and abhorrent traits.

Thus in speaking of the place of religion in the historical phenomenon of American slavery, Eugene Genovese has written:

We are told a great deal about the religious instruction of the slaves, by which is meant the attempt [to] inculcate a version of Protestant Christianity. Sometimes this instruction is interpreted as a good thing in itself and sometimes as a kind of brainwashing, but we may leave this question aside. Recently, Vincent Harding [a leading Black theologian], following the suggestive probing in Du Bois's pioneer work, has offered a different perspective and suggested that the slaves had their own way of taking up Christianity and forging it into a weapon of active resistance. Certainly, we must be struck by the appearance of one or another kind of messianic preacher in almost every slave revolt on record. Professor Harding therefore asks that we look at the slaves as active participants in their own religious experience and not merely as objects being worked on by slaveholding ideologues. This argument may be carried further to suggest that a distinctly black religion, at least in embryo, appeared in the quarters and played a role—the extent and precise content of which we have yet to evaluate—in shaping the daily lives of the slaves. In other words, quite apart from the problem of religion as a fact in overt resistance to slavery, we need to know how the slaves developed a religious life that enabled them to survive as autonomous human beings with a culture of their own within the white master's world.[3]

One may question Genovese's use of the word *autonomous* in reference to slaves, but the drift of his and Harding's position is a good reminder that even slavery begot shows of intelligence, will, heart, pride, imagination, sacrificial love, and the like that displayed a profound humanity, perhaps even a signal grace of God. Harding's own work has proposed the experience of black Americans as essential to the formation of a new America better able to fulfill the pledges made in its founding documents. In the case of black experience, where slavery is the most determining motif but other effects of racism also beg attention, Americans who wish can see the limits, the blindness, even the hypocrisy and bad faith that ate up their professed ideals of human equality and fairness from within. To focus on black Americans is to confess that white Americans have not really believed the rhetoric that all people are created equal and are endowed with inalienable rights. One might be moved to a similar confession by pondering the history of women or ethnic groups in the United States, but the history of the blacks is more compelling. On the other hand, those who defended slavery could bring forward biblical texts (e.g., *Philemon*); argue that some slaves were well cared for, that some slaves were not ready for emancipation, and that repudiating slavery would destroy the economy of the South; and in other ways make a plausible case for maintaining the status quo. Not all who argued in this way were

stupid, vicious, or self-serving. Slavery, and the arguments about it, became a very complicated matter—economically, politically, psychologically, and religiously. Whether it ever really became morally complicated is another question.

When one asks why the history of blacks is especially compelling, some paragraphs of Harding's on the black experience after the Civil War, during Reconstruction, come to mind:

> Often the spirit of black religious revivalism filled the Reconstruction political campaigns so that people could not tell whether they were going to a political campaign or to a revival meeting. Very often they were going to both. There was the hum of black religion on the edges of the constitutional conventions in the new legislatures that came into being all across the South. As one reads the documents of those black people, who met regularly to decide and declare what they wanted, you see them everywhere raising the issue of what we now call the common good. They lifted up the need for a society that would engage the gifts, the talents and the virtues of all its members. They asked for a society—and were willing to work for a society—which would benefit all of its people, where the strong would help the weak even if the weak could give no quid pro quo.
>
> To a large degree it was their white allies who betrayed their vision and helped another American vision prevail—the vision of expansion over the Indians, of moving out into the Pacific; the vision of railroads and factories, of American capitalism. That other vision prevailed over the humane visions that were being put forward in the post-Civil War period by black people when they spoke out of their best religious sense.
>
> As a result, black people had to endure the bitterness and the terror of the post-Reconstruction years. That was the period when the greatest task of all was the task of holding on to our humanity in the midst of a dehumanizing situation. That was the time when the greatest task was in many cases simply to hold on to our lives in the midst of the lynch mobs and the crowds who gathered to see us burned alive. That was the time when the greatest task was to hold on to

the vision that our own best gifts would one day be used to help build a new society in America. We had to hold on to these things, this vision, this understanding, this sense of ourselves; we had to hold on to them through a horrible period in our lives, because we knew that if we lost these things there was no hope for us, for our children, or for America. And in this period, the role of black religion was absolutely central in holding us up lest we should fall.[4]

As one can interpret slavery by focusing on the profit motive of the plantation owners, one can interpret the direction America took during Reconstruction by focusing on the drive for riches. Neither interpretation does justice to all the facts, but both have a solid claim to be taken seriously. Much evil occurs simply because some people want so badly to prosper that they will use others to this end. Thus they violate the maxim of many ethical systems that fellow human beings are not to be treated as means to one's own ends, ultimately because they are *fellow* human beings, one's equals in the possession of humanity. For some ethicists this equality is the end of the matter, while for others such equality bespeaks a common creaturehood under God, or even a common invitation to share the divine nature so that the image of God imprinted in creation might reach its full potential. Few black spokespersons expressed their hopes in such language, but many used biblical equivalents. For many the death of Jesus on behalf of all people gave all people a similar standing under God.

Indeed, the death of Jesus, along with the story of the exodus of the Hebrews from Egypt, served as a great paradigm for what slavery and continuing racism implied. If human beings had put to death the very Son of God, one could not be surprised at their mistreatment of their lesser sisters and brothers. On the other hand, if God had raised Jesus from the dead, as God had freed the Hebrews from slavery, hope could remain, could even flourish. Blacks clinging to

such biblical paradigms reenforced their sense of the wrongness in the treatment they were receiving, even as they sharpened their expectation that God one day would overturn the evil present order and set things right. Thus blacks often have given America excellent lessons in how to name, combat, and conquer evil by not letting hatred corrupt one's spirit.

To say this is not to deny the horrible effects of racism, let alone to imply that black virtue has redeemed the evils of racism. The drugs, crime, poverty, family suffering, and self-hatred scattered in the wake of American racism are too overwhelming to permit any sanitizing of what slavery has symbolized and helped effect. It is simply to say that just as slavery puts the perennial irrationality of sin, the perennial mysteriousness of iniquity, into American garb, so slavery also calls to mind the victories those suffering from slavery have won. Insofar as Americans reflected on such victories, they had to readjust their sense of human nature, providing not just for doing evil, for the sense of justice that prompts the punishment of evildoers, or for the way that evil can be mixed with good, but also for antidotes to evil—human resources for resuming the struggle, keeping going, or even, incredibly enough, forgiving the evildoer.

Issues Raised by Vietnam

A more recent symbol of American encounters with the dark side of the human psyche, with conflicts over public policy, and with the inertia of governmental decisions is the war waged in Vietnam. Two reflections—one illustrating how the egos of political leaders contribute to the misfiring of public policy and the other focusing on the influence of military leaders trained to think in terms of martial power—may stimulate further insight into how Americans have uncovered evil (or blundered into doing evil).

Where once he had argued the injustice of Vietnam being viewed as "his" war, Lyndon Johnson now brought to it a proprietary attitude. This should have been among the early warnings that LBJ would increasingly resist less than victory, no matter his periodic bombing halts or conciliatory statements inviting peace, because once he took a thing personally, his pride and vanity and ego knew no bounds. Always a man to put his brand on everything (he wore monogrammed shirts, boots, cuff links; flew his private LBJ flag when in residence at the LBJ ranch; saw to it that the names of Lynda Bird Johnson and Luci Baines Johnson and Lady Bird Johnson—not Claudia, as she had been named—had the magic initials LBJ), he now personalized and internalized the war. Troops became "my" boys, those were "my" helicopters, it was "my" pilots he prayed might return from their bombing missions as he paid nocturnal calls to the White House situation room to learn the latest from the battlefields; Walt Rostow became "my" intellectual because he was hawkish on LBJ's war. His machismo was mixed up in it now, his manhood. After a cabinet meeting in 1967 several staff aides and at least one cabinet member—Stewart Udall, Secretary of the Interior—remained behind for informal discussions; soon LBJ was waving his arms and fulminating about his war. Who the hell was Ho Chi Minh, anyway, that he thought he could push America around? Then the President did an astonishing thing: he unzipped his trousers, dangled a given appendage, and asked his shocked associates: "Has Ho Chi Minh got anything like that?"[5]

Arthur M. Schlesinger, Jr., has spotlighted the role of the military mind:

At every stage in the descent into the quagmire the military played a dominant role. First, they defined the Vietnam problem as a military problem, requiring a military solution. Then, at each point along the ghastly way, the generals promised that more military escalation would bring the victory so long sought and so steadily denied. The Pentagon not only succeeded in casting the problem in military terms; it cherished the war for its

own institutional reasons. Vietnam became an invaluable testing ground for new weapons and tactics as well as an indispensable place for on-the-job training and for promotions. "Civilians can scarcely understand," General Shoup, the admirable former commandant of the Marine Corps wrote, " . . . that many ambitious professionals truly yearn for wars and the opportunities for glory and distinction afforded only in combat." All the services, General Shoup said, wanted part of the action in Vietnam and competed for "the opportunity to practice their trade." . . . [The military] are driven by institutional self-interest to demand more men, more money, more weapons systems, more military involvement in policy and often (though not always) more military solutions. And they play on powerful sentiments of virility and patriotism.[6]

From the side of those who considered the American venture in Vietnam a defense of liberty against ruthless communism, one must note that the war soon developed into a complicated matter, blending many good intentions with many miscalculations. One might also point out that the Vietcong were no model of pure revolutionaries wanting only the liberation of the poor and the redress of social injustices. Both sin and grace, it seems, regularly weave their way through tangled events, human motives, chance occurrences, the interplay of biological, economic, and political factors.

Historically few wars have met the criteria of the traditional just war theory, which stipulated that one should be responding only to unjust aggression and that the actions one took should hold reasonable prospects of succeeding, of being proportionate to the evil they were trying to rebuff, and of doing more good than harm.

Philosophically, however, the argument that responding to violence with violence is necessary and is the best way to achieve justice is vulnerable on several grounds, not the least of which is the endless cycle of destruction and counterdestruction it tends to engender. Americans on the whole have been short on both historical perspective and philosophical detachment. We have been a pragmatic people, impressed by the newness of our national venture, little inclined to ponder the past because the present and future glittered with such fascinating possibilities. It is not surprising, therefore, that one of our presidents should know nothing about the mentality of Ho Chi Minh or that our general citizenry should find it hard to police our military establishment. Other new countries have shown similar tendencies, including the Communist states, where the proportion of the people in the military is more than twice that in non-Communist countries. When one adds a dose of American idealism and naiveté, defending democracy in Vietnam can seem to have begun in better moral shape than it ended. One can also see why many who served in Vietnam felt they were doing the patriotic thing.

Yet perhaps the most interesting result of the American experience in Vietnam was an end to the innocent view that the United States usually acted from pure motives and was rightly accounted the moral guardian of the world. Educated people have seldom enjoyed the innocence that much of the 20th-century American citizenry had. The apparent resurgence of such innocence in the 1980s, when Americans again voted for leaders who specialized in the roseate glow, suggests how painful the perspectives unveiled by the 1960s were. No people enjoys seeing its sins, its outright evils, stripped of their veneer of necessity or good intention. From the perspective of religious faith, however, such a stripping can seem both necessary and bearable. It can seem necessary because it is a condition of living in the light, of pursuing the truth. It can seem bearable because the human word or deed is never the final say. It would be ironic if the legacy of Vietnam called into question the religiosity of the nation calling itself the most religious in the world.

Martin Luther King, Jr.

Martin Luther King, Jr., came to oppose the American venture in Vietnam and to see it as an extension of the blindness responsible for racism. This judgment took some time to evolve, but in retrospect it seems the logical result of King's commitment to Christian faith and nonviolence. Indeed, as early as 1963 King had written:

> War is not the answer. Communism will never be defeated by the use of atomic bombs or nuclear weapons. Let us not join those who shout war and who through their misguided passions urge the United States to relinquish its participation in the United Nations. These are days when Christians must evince wise restraint and calm reasonableness. We must not call everyone a Communist or appeaser who recognizes that hate and hysteria are not the final answers to the problems of these turbulent days. We must not engage in a negative anticommunism, but rather in a positive thrust for democracy, realizing that our greatest defense against communism is to take offensive action in behalf of justice and righteousness. After our condemnation of the philosophy of communism has been eloquently expressed, we must with positive action seek to remove those conditions of poverty, insecurity, injustice, and racial discrimination which are the fertile soil in which the seed of communism grows and develops. Communism thrives only when the doors of opportunity are closed and human aspirations are stifled.[7]

When the Black Power movement arose in the United States, shortly before his death in 1968, King's first reaction was negative. He was put off by the anger he felt the movement exhibited and thought it exhibited more despair than hope. One can argue that a preacher is not necessarily a good politician and that the Kingdom of God may not inspire the political tactics necessary for dealing with either an establishment infected by racism or a Communist foe of the stature of Ho Chi Minh. Moreover, there is a long-standing argument about the transfer of principles individuals may choose for their personal response to evil and the principles leaders of a pluralistic nation may choose. And everywhere there is the ambiguity, tangled historical facts, social forces, and personal motives that complicate significant ventures such as war. On the other hand, without the idealism of preachers and such notions as the Kingdom of God human affairs sink toward the law of the jungle. Martin Luther King, Jr., eventually saw the point of the Black Power movement—the restoration of long-lacerated black pride—but to the end of his life he remained convinced that violence was a dangerous tactic, more likely to increase suffering in the long run than alleviate it.

How does one deal with an apparently unreasonable, implacable foe? What weight should one give to words, pledges, and promises in contrast to past and recent deeds? These questions dog all of a nation's foreign policy decisions, as they dog domestic decisions about economic policy, civil rights, and much more. The estimates one makes of human nature quickly become vastly significant. If the great thing is to defend one's manhood, a certain political style follows. If the great thing is to remove poverty, insecurity, injustice, and racial discrimination, a different political style follows. But even that is simplistic, because the same politician can both be obsessed with his manhood and sincerely want to fashion a great society of social and racial justice. Evil certainly does lodge in the human heart, but who has seen the human heart, sounded its depths, followed its twisting trails?

No one has ever produced a definitive map, but prophets and sages have produced valuable reports. The problem is that one has to muster some introspection, self-criticism, and education to appreciate what such scouts have to say. The Greek wisdom epitomized by the motto of the delphic oracle, "Know thyself," admits of no shortcuts. The biblical wisdom expressed in the prophetic literature and the parables of Jesus is similarly demanding. One can't live on the surface, merely float with the cultural tide, and become a strong foe of evil, a soldier well equipped to decide what "good fight" actually is.

The challenge put to the American character by such evil productions as slavery and much of the American involvement in Vietnam and Latin America seems to be to learn what in fact does oppose the brutalities of Communist dictatorships, the corruption responsible for much of the world's poverty, and the endless contempt of the rich and powerful for the poor who suffer in their wake. This is not a lesson easy to master, even when recent history seems to offer so many case studies in bad choices and wrong procedures. Indeed the difficulty of this lesson may be our best clue to the enormity of evil in human existence and so to the proportions of the task before American religion, as before all religions: the wrestling with ultimate matters.

To put the matter this way is to speak in biblical accents congenial to American Protestantism. It conjures up the insights of the Puritan divines who followed the Calvinists in meditating on the gratuity of salvation and the abysses of wickedness that salvation had to bridge. When the Calvinists said there is no health in human nature, they might have been writing the prologue to a lecture on the evil revealed in slavery and warfare. Other biblically based theologies (both Christian and Jewish) would require positive statements to balance the Calvinist reading of human nature. They argue that many human instincts move people toward the good and that one easily overlooks all that is beautiful in the world, goes well in society, or moves sensible people to bless the time they have been given. Still such other theologies would have to admit that human folly, weakness, and sin have produced terrible suffering. They would have to agree that like other peoples, Americans have often faced the winless situation of having to decide whether they were dealing with fools or knaves.

For Martin Luther King, Jr., this decision was a secondary matter. King learned quickly enough that knavery and foolishness collude. Shortly after coming to the age of reason, he learned that much in American society was twisted, slanted, a too-perfect illustration of original sin. Simply by being black and religious, he was plunged into the mysteries of oppression and absurdity. But he would never have become the leader he did if he had not refused to let such mysteries paralyze him. More important than wallowing in the metaphysics of evil was finding a basis for action and hope. As Eugene Genovese observed, most black movements for liberation depended on a prophetic preacher. One might further observe that such preachers did more than denounce injustice. By holding out visions of what individuals or America at large might become, could become if they wished, such preachers gave their audiences images of hope, symbols of what to work for.

Much in the American religious response to evil has validated the traditional analysis according to which evil is nothing positive. Real as the effects of evil may be, incontrovertible as its sufferings certainly are, one trying to oppose it soon finds that it depends on blindness (lack of vision), folly (lack of wisdom), and vice (lack of virtue, above all lack of justice and love) and so is nothing positive. Indeed, in combatting evil one finds that thinking of human nature as depraved threatens to lose the war before it has begun. Only if people do not really want injustice, violence, and suffering is fighting against the evils that cause such things psychologically possible. Only if most people are repulsed by evil, hate both its external effects and the corrosion of soul it creates, is life not absurd and political action not useless. True, the majority of political leaders and ordinary citizens alike are not reflective enough even to articulate this simple proposition. Most have not realized and taken to heart the principle that there is no practical alternative to hope. But most have realized in a commonsensical way that they have

no alternative to going out to work, dealing with their family problems, and finally surrendering themselves to an imperfect self and situation. Most have realized that the problem of evil is "solved" **ambulando,** by walking through it.

Writings of William Ellery Channing

William Ellery Channing (1780–1842) was famous in his day as a leading exponent of Christian morality. Channing's desire to formulate a rational expression of Christian faith that would appeal to all people of good will eventually brought him to Unitarianism. The great targets at which Channing took aim were slavery, drunkenness, poverty, and war. He earned the wrath of traditional Calvinists for slighting orthodox theology, but his sermons and writings made him highly influential. He believed that government could accomplish only minimal ends, such as maintaining public order. For the rest, religion had to advance the moral sensitivities of people, getting them to prefer justice to injustice, sobriety to drunkenness, and peace to war.

In 1842 in an address delivered at Lenox, Massachusetts, Channing celebrated the anniversary of the emancipation of slaves in the British West Indies. He had once wintered in the West Indies and observed at firsthand the sufferings visited on slaves when they passed from a benevolent owner to a cruel one. Although sympathetic to the abolitionists crying for the emancipation of American slaves, Channing had not joined their movement and wanted in his address merely to present his own opinion:

> On this day a few years ago, Eight Hundred Thousand human beings were set free from slavery; and to comprehend the greatness of the deliverance, a few words must first be said of the evil from which they were rescued . . . . Were I asked, what strikes me as the greatest evil inflicted by this system, I should say, it is the outrage offered

by slavery to human nature. Slavery does all that lies in human power to unmake men, to rob them of their humanity, to degrade men into brutes; and it does this by declaring them to be Property. Here is the master evil . . . That he may answer your end, that he may consent to be a slave, his spirit must be broken, his courage crushed; he must fear you. A feeling of his deep inferiority must be burnt into his soul. The idea of his rights must be quenched in him, by the blood of his lashed and lacerated body. Here is the damning evil of slavery. It destroys the spirit, the consciousness of a man. I care little in comparison for his hard outward lot, his poverty, his unfurnished house, his coarse fare; the terrible thing in slavery is the spirit of a slave, the extinction of the spirit of a man.[8]

The passion of Channing for what was right and against what was wrong extended to more than slavery, but one can sense that slavery summarized the worst outrages he had seen Americans commit. His address notes that the anniversary of West Indian emancipation was received coldly in the United States, because it brought American slavers no welcome message. One might question Channing's relative dismissal of the physical sufferings of slaves, and rather link the outrages of spiritual degradation to the poverty and neglect many slaves had to endure, but there is little doubt that he put his finger on the crux of slavery's evils. To his Unitarian mind, as to the mind of Emerson or Thoreau, spiritual freedom was the quintessence of human dignity. Consequently slavery was an utter abomination, the complete opposite of what human existence ought to be.

It is interesting that the individual liberty trumpeted throughout American cultural history can be invoked on both sides of the several great debates about justice that have absorbed Americans. Slavers, for example, could claim that they had the liberty to expand their holdings within a system they had not created and were not alone in finding unobjectionable. They could claim that the Bible manifestly did not condemn slavery, and that many slaves were better off than they would have been on their own.

These arguments failed to convince abolitionists and refined spirits such as Channing, for whom the rights of one group were always curtailed by the essential human needs of others. The slaver might have a general right to work his lands and negotiate ready labor, but this right had to cede to the more primordial right of any laborer to work voluntarily, as an act of free will. To be compelled to work at others' behest and for others' ends was to be violated, to have one's necessary autonomy ripped away. Such further compulsions as the frequent sexual abuse of female slaves only compounded the violation. On the whole the American sense of justice and the American legal system have come to agree with Channing, judging that individual liberty has definite boundaries. When the desires of some override the basic rights or spiritual needs of others, the result is evil or sin.

A similar tension attends the questions of how far the liberty of entrepreneurs should extend to developing the land; what limits the state ought to put on the rights of employers to dictate wages and working conditions of laborers; and how much liberty individuals ought to have to use alcohol, firearms, tobacco, drugs, abortifacients, pornographic materials, and many other things available in a consumer-driven society. The specific content of the tensions attending individual liberty may change from generation to generation, but the central value of human dignity spotlighted by Channing in the matter of slavery usually remains relevant. Of course slavery is an unusually clear case, at least in the hindsight of more than 350 years of American experience with it and its aftermath. How Channing's criteria would apply to the latter-day problems we have suggested is an intriguing question. The likelihood is that he would not have expected the state to control abuses of human liberty but would have urged

Penitents traditionally climb these steps at the shrine of St. Anne de Beaupré outside Quebec as an act of asceticism that may strengthen their petitions. (Photo by J. T. Carmody)

religious leaders and educators to do a better job of persuading people to better options than crime, drugs, pornography, abortion, and the rest.

In 1838 Channing delivered a lecture in Boston on Self-Culture. In it one may find his recipe for the improvement of both the individual and the commonwealth. Channing admits the place of intellectual development. He promotes education, especially when it includes a moral dimension and helps form character. But his most concrete writing is aroused by the need for temperance:

> To raise the moral and intellectual nature, we must put down the animal. Sensuality is the abyss in which very many souls are plunged and lost. Among the most prosperous classes, what a vast amount of intellectual life is drowned in luxurious excesses! It is one of the curses of wealth, that it is used to pamper the senses; and among the poorer classes, though luxury is wanting, yet a gross feeling often prevails, under which the spirit is overwhelmed. It is a sad sight to walk through our streets, and to see how many countenances bear marks of a lethargy and a brutal coarseness, induced by unrestrained indulgence. Whoever would cultivate the soul, must restrain the appetites. I am not an advocate for the doctrine, that animal food was not meant for man; but that this is used among us to excess; that as a people we should gain much in cheerfulness, activity, and buoyancy of mind, by less gross and stimulating food, I am strongly inclined to believe. Above all, let me urge on those, who would bring out and elevate their higher nature, to abstain from the use of spirituous liquors . . . . Of all the foes of the working class, this is the deadliest . . . . They ought to regard as their worst enemies (though unintentionally such), as the enemies of their rights, dignity, and influence, the men who desire to flood

city and country with distilled liquor . . . . I call on working men to take hold of the cause of temperance as peculiarly *their* cause.[9]

William Ellery Channing never narrowed morality to temperance, but he did have the soul of a reformer bent on ousting demon rum, and all the other chains shackling human dignity, so that people might truly flourish. Critics such as Orestes Brownson accused him of neglecting the social dimension of morality, and such criticism had some basis, since Channing by preference targeted the individual, whose self-cultivation he found the key to moral and social betterment. However dated some of Channing's examples and causes now sound, reading his lectures tends to elevate one's spirit. Here was a man intent on finding the causes of such gross social evils as slavery and stimulating people to embrace their cure. Here was a man convinced that human beings could make a decent life together, if they would bring order into their own souls and learn what a truly good human existence implied.

Key Terms

Ambulando: a Latin word meaning "by walking." The word usually occurs in the phrase, *solvitur ambulando,* meaning "it is solved by walking." The reference is to Zeno's paradox, where the problem was how to get across a distance if one can only travel half the way at a time and the distance is infinitely divisible into halves. Breaking out of the logical chains imposed by such a statement of the problem, practical people would say that one got across the distance by walking. In other words, many problems are revealed to be pseudoproblems when one stops worrying about the theoretical difficulties and gets on with the task of doing something practical about

them. From this experience, pragmatists have argued for the priority of doing over thinking, while people of common sense have learned not to take all intellectual difficulties seriously.

Discussion Questions

1. What reflections about human nature did contact with Native Americans and blacks tend to stimulate in colonial Americans?
2. How should one correlate the individual and the social aspects of human nature—for example, in assigning blame for an evil such as slavery?
3. What was the vision of Reconstructionist blacks that American expansionism betrayed?
4. What sort of autonomy was possible for slaves?
5. What does the influence of the institutional self-interest of the military in Vietnam suggest about the movement of original sin?
6. How do historical and philosophical studies tend to remove a dangerous innocence?
7. What links did civil rights leaders such as Martin Luther King, Jr., find between racism and the American venture in Vietnam?
8. Does communism flourish only in conditions of social injustice?
9. What is the relation between the human dignity William Ellery Channing saw slashed by slavery and the criterion for judging a people's social institutions?
10. What is the place of sensuality in both social decay and a fully human life?

Notes

1. Merle Curti, *Human Nature in American Thought* (Madison WI: University of Wisconsin Press, 1980), pp. 41–42.

2. Claude Welch, *Protestant Thought in the Nineteenth Century,* vol. 1 (New Haven: Yale University Press, 1972), p. 264.

3. Eugene D. Genovese, *In Red and Black: Marxian Explorations in Southern and Afro-American History* (Knoxville: University of Tennessee Press, 1984), pp. 106–107.

4. Vincent Harding, "Out of the Cauldron of Struggle: Black Religion and the Search for a New America," in *Religion: North American Style,* 2d ed., ed. Patrick H. McNamara (Belmont, CA: Wadsworth, 1984), pp. 258–259.

5. Larry L. King, "LBJ and Vietnam," in *A Sense of History,* ed. American Heritage (Boston: Houghton Mifflin, 1985), p. 799.

6. Arthur M. Schlesinger, Jr., *The Cycles of American History* (Boston: Houghton Mifflin, 1986), pp. 153–154.

7. Martin Luther King, Jr., *Strength to Love* (New York: Harper & Row, 1963), p. 100.

8. William Ellery Channing, *Selected Writings,* ed. David Robinson (New York: Paulist, 1985), p. 271.

9. Ibid., pp. 239–241.

Salvation

Justification by Faith

When Americans confronted evil, they had the span of reactions typical of people the world over. First they experienced incomprehension and anger; then they struggled to combat the evil, whether it was raids by Indians or oppressive taxes by the British; and finally the deeper among them wondered about the phenomenon of evil itself, drawing from their spiritual resources images that might bring evil somewhat under control. For those who wondered in this way, evil could become not just something external but a lodger in their own hearts, a blot on their own human nature.

Granted the English background of the majority of the colonists, Puritan and Anglican traditions supplied much of the material for reflection about the many ways that things were not as they should be. The crux of the Protestantism on which the early Americans tended to draw was that one could stand right before God—and so conquer evil, disorder, and sin—only through faith. On their own, apart from accepting the help God had made available in Christ, human beings were helpless.

Granted, 200 years after the Reformation launched by Luther and Calvin, Protestant the-

214

ology had reintroduced works, not as the source of justification but as its expression. However, this did not vitiate the religious instinct of the majority that God had to supply justification, righteousness, and grace. On its own human nature was corrupt, if not depraved. On its own human nature would more comply with tendencies toward evil than stand against them. Rationalists, influenced by the Enlightenment, might strip away such theological scaffolding, but their final estimates of human nature were quite similar. Ordinary citizens needed not only sound education but also legal checks and balances, if their government and social order were not to be destroyed by rampant self-interest.

The great awakenings and revivals dramatized this outlook. Jonathan Edwards's most famous sermon, "Sinners in the Hands of an Angry God," is far from being the whole of his theology, but anthologists have not been wrong to consider it representative of a powerful, foundational aspect of American religious thought. The main work or action required of human beings is repentance. The great sins to be overcome are forgetfulness of God, whose judgment always threatens, and self-reliance. As we have seen, William Ellery Channing and the Unitarians rejected this position, making *self-reliance* and *self-culture* honored words. Orthodox Calvinists in turn rejected such humanistic, **Pelagian** talk. To their mind Unitarianism compromised not only the central Christian doctrine of the Trinity but also the proper outlook on Christian ethics.

Seeking the solution to the fundamental problem of the human condition (why we do not do what reason and love suggest we should do) raises a fundamental question about that condition. Can people in fact be human on their own, from their apparently natural resources, or must they open themselves to superhuman powers to realize their potential? This question carries different overtones to different hearers. Those concerned about the **alienation** of

human responsibility to vague outside powers tend to hear in the question a call to immaturity. Atheists on the model of Ludwig Feuerbach, who greatly influenced Karl Marx, tend to react in this way. Pragmatists bent on mustering human imagination and will to improve the world often agree. Self-reliance, for individuals and groups alike, is their solution to the problems expressing disorder and evil. Such naysayers to justification by faith reject calling on God to plug the gaps in human meaning, to bail out people whose main problem has been their own folly.

Those less optimistic about human imagination and will, more persuaded by symbols, such as original sin, that suggest a radical impotence in human nature, think notions of self-reliance naive. Ironically, both those who reject justification by faith and those who reject its rejection consider their opponents unaware of the lessons of history, inexperienced in the workings of the human conscience.

A great deal in the difference between the two camps comes down to the horizons in which they set the data of history and conscience. For those upholding justification by faith, history shows generation after generation not achieving peace and justice, generation after generation spilling blood and wasting talent. Relatedly history shows us few saints, more villains, and a majority of people who would like to be good but cannot muster the wisdom or the strength. Unhappy people that history and conscience show us to be, who will rescue us from our plight? Where have the few heroes found the resources to be fully human, as all of us occasionally long to be? The mainstream of American religious thought has answered that only by opening themselves to God do people defeat the demons without and within. Only by letting God become the beginning and the beyond of their short existences can people grow wise or holy.

If asked where one might experience God, might feel justification take hold of their hearts

To many of the pioneers trying to establish themselves in territories such as Oklahoma, the mission complex represented saving grace reaching out to tame the wilderness of the fallen world. (*Dwight Mission Near Marble City, 1820,* Vinson Lackey; Gilcrease Museum, Tulsa, Oklahoma)

and invigorate their wills, the majority of American religionists would have pointed to rather dramatic encounters at camp meetings, revivals, sermons by fire-breathing preachers, or lonely vigils in the dead of night. There the biblical word and the Holy Spirit brought the person to feel the wretchedness of sin, the poverty of self-reliance, the hopelessness of venturing apart from God. There the heart took flame and one saw the questionable character of merely external religion, of relying on church attendance or ethical conformity to do the job of straightening one's bent spirit.

The variations on such themes that Catholicism offered its American adherents laid more stress on the work of the institutional church in mediating salvation, especially through the sacraments, but they did not fundamentally alter the main message. Christ was as necessary for salvation in Catholic as in Protestant churches. Catholic views of human nature did give more play to good works and were sometimes semi-Pelagian, but in the crunch they made divine grace as necessary for being fully human as Protestant theologies did.

Jewish views worked with different intellectual components, not having an incarnate savior and making more of religious law. Orthodox Jews saw fulfilling the Torah as the prime way of pleasing God and becoming what God wanted one to be, while Reform Jews were more concerned with an ethic one could explicate in terms of humanistic reason. But all American Jews found their tradition using biblical language about the loving-kindness of God, the graciousness of God on which their covenant stood. And all who confronted their tradition learned that one could not stay religious and define the human condition without reference to a transcendent God. The question then became whether this reference was credible, whether people did in fact become their best selves, make the most sense of their experience, and contribute most to the betterment of the world by drawing on the prophets and sages who had been lyric about the priority of loving God.

Humanists rejecting justification by faith, the need for grace if people were to realize their humanity, and similar theistic notions in fact were close to believers who stressed religious experience—whenever they were willing to consider the mysteries onto which both history and conscience opened. Thus William James, wanting to be thoroughly empiricist, had to confess that standing out among his empirical data were myriad testimonies to experiences of conversion, of desolation passing into consolation, of finding peace after the storm by saying yes to what one could not control, to what one had to suspect was the world's ordering by an Other.

The American conversation created by these voices, and so many others who spoke with shadings in between, has kept the great questions (how salvation comes, where healing can be found, and whether the great folly is irreligion or religion) alive and kicking down the decades. Does a person have to believe in God, have to find something transcendent, to become healed, whole, fully human? How can people best name such a transcendent something and induce experience of it? And if religion is the name for the generally positive response to this general question, how can one avoid pseudo-religion—hypocrisy, irrationality, alienation of responsibility, credulity, and immaturity? American justification by faith comes into focus only when it gathers to itself a host of queries.

Revivalism

Could Thomas Paine, the free-thinking pamphleteer of the American and French revolutions, have visited Broadway in 1865, he would have been amazed to find that the nation conceived in rational liberty was at last fulfilling its democratic promise in the power of evangelical faith. The emancipating glory of the great awakenings had made Christian liberty, Christian equality and Christian fraternity the passion of the land. The treasured gospel of the elect few passed into the hands of the baptized many. Common grace, not common sense, was the keynote of the age.

The Calvinist idea of foreordination, rejected as far as it concerned individuals, was now transferred to a grander object—the manifest destiny of a Christianized America. Men in all walks of life believed that the Sovereign Holy Spirit was endowing the nation with resources sufficient to convert and civilize the globe, to purge human society of all its evils, and to usher in Christ's reign on earth. Religious doctrines which Paine, in his book *The Age of Reason*, had discarded as the tattered vestment of an outworn aristocracy, became the wedding garb of a democratized church, bent on preparing men and institutions for a kind of proletarian marriage supper of the Lamb.[1]

No doubt some Americans walking on Broadway in 1865 would have thought the Civil War cause for sobriety in considering the destiny of the barely reunited states, but it is true that the age of reason Paine had prematurely announced enjoyed little popular favor. By 1865 the revolutionary period might have seemed the center of a sandwich, wrapped around by religious periods on both sides. Many Americans seemed unwilling to make do with the Deism of the Founding Fathers or the Unitarianism of leading thinkers of the early 19th century. The noble spirituality proposed by Emerson and Channing appealed to the upper classes in Boston and New York, but commoners throughout the country sought something earthier. Revivalism was not the only means through which a plainer, more emotional gospel swept through the land, but it captured what the quotation calls the democratic or proletarian character of the times. The liberty, equality, and fraternity proposed by the revivalists was rooted in a common experience of justification by faith. The common denominator opening vistas of a democratic church was the sense of having been lost but now being found, having been blind but now seeing through the power of the Christian gospel.

The revivalists, as their name implies, proposed that their work was simply renewing a faith grown weak. They suggested that America had always been a religious land, founded by people come in pursuit of religious liberty, blessed by the God who had created the land's wealth, and dependent for their virtues on the teaching of Christ, the power of the divine force in the human breast, the control of wayward passions available through Christian discipleship.

In historical fact, of course, the matter was more complicated. Early Americans in many periods were not signal churchgoers and Enlightenment rationalism captured many of early America's leading lights. Revivalists therefore had to pick and choose their precedents. They had greater success in stirring people to present experiences of the power of the gospel than in linking such experiences with the Declaration of Independence or the American Constitution. They had to skip over the angry debates about slavery, the complications being injected by foreign immigrants, and the challenges to American expansionism in Mexico to present to their audiences a posterity draped in Christian concord.

However, history was not the great interest of the common people. They wanted to feel compunction (regret over sin) rather than know its lineage. They wanted to dream dreams of an American mission to the pagan outer world, rather than to think hard about how their land was treating Native Americans and blacks. The religious imagination excited in 19th-century America was slow to project the complexity its heritage had found in the individual conscience onto the conscience and motivation of the nation as a whole. The social gospel movement had to force the enthusiasts to face the slums, the alcoholism, and the terrible working conditions that were ravaging the lives of many Americans. Proposing that such problems stemmed from systematic wrongs in the going economic and political orders was not a welcome message. Certainly some evangelicals were sensitive to social injustices, had linked themselves with abolitionism, and would link themselves to women's suffrage, but a theology of justification by faith allowed many preachers and mourning benchers alike to keep revival an affair of the heart.

An interesting case study from this period lies ready to hand in the Salvation Army, founded in England in 1865. The Army invaded the United States 15 years later, probably encouraged by the prevalence of revivalism there. Shortly after the arrival of the first contingent, a New York newspaper wished the Army well and editorialized:

> Its method differs widely from that of any other body of men and women who have given battle to Satan in this city; but the plans of a commander are entitled to respect until someone who has gone successfully over the same ground can be found to criticize them. If by marching through the streets, with colors flying, stopping on corners to sing and exhort, the Salvation Army can persuade any considerable number of men to stop lying, stealing and cheating and to lead upright lives in the future, no one has the slightest right to complain of the way in which the work is done. Clergymen of various denominations complain frequently that

there is a general lack of interest in religious affairs; perhaps if the Salvation Army gains some victories these gentlemen may gain a practical suggestion or two about the way of getting at the non-church-going class.[2]

The Salvation Army eventually developed many admirable social programs, including soup kitchens, shelters, and homes for unwed mothers. Taking aim at the saloons where it thought the Devil did his best work, the Army made it plain it intended to live and work with the most miserable classes, the people neglected by an America on the move. As a description of one early meeting put it:

A more motley, vice-smitten, pestilence-breeding congregation could seldom be found in a house of worship. There were negroes, dancing girls, prostitutes, and station house tramps sandwiched in between well-dressed visitors who had sauntered in merely out of curiosity. There were young men with canes and eyeglasses; seedy old pensioners with faded hair and stovepipe hats . . . walked in with catlike stillness and hid themselves in the corners, while glossy young negresses took prominent seats and stared at the modest English girls of the Salvation Army in an impudent way . . . . The floors were as clean as the deck of a man-of-war, but in a few minutes they were frescoed with tobacco juice, the stench became overpowering and a yellow fever pest house could not have been less attractive. It seemed as if the refuse of the Fourth ward dance cellars have been emptied for this occasion.[3]

In meetings such as this, there was no doubt that salvation had to come as a gift of God, through faith. There was no doubt that faith itself was a gift, nor that when faith came it could prove stronger than drink and vice. The Salvation Army was not fully representative of 19th-century American revivalism, and in many quarters it was not liked, but it dramatizes the strain of American piety that has produced some of the most vibrant church meetings and social movements. From Pentecostals to Catholic Workers, many Americans have thought a plain Christian faith both the answer to questions of life's meaning and a demonstration of what poor people most need. Again and again, *salvation* has brought to many Americans' minds feelings of repentance flooding the heart and soup kitchens serving the hungry.

Gracious Alternatives

For Jehovah's Witnesses, Seventh Day Adventists, Mormons, and other Protestant groups generally accounted separate from the mainstream, salvation tended to come through accepting the particular version of the gospel preached by the group. All three of these churches stressed the opposition between the fleshly life prevailing in the world and the spiritual life practiced by their people in separation from the world. Salvation therefore came in somewhat dualistic accents, reminiscent of the dichotomy between flesh and spirit stressed by the Johannine writings of the New Testament. Things became more complicated when such groups gained political or cultural power, as the Mormons did in Utah, but at the heart of these groups welcoming salvation had to mean risking being eccentric not just to the mainstream of American culture but also to the mainstream of American Christianity.

What is to be termed *mainstream* of course engenders considerable debate. Those who consider the term a dangerous fiction have data on their side, but it would play false to the general impression of most Americans through the last 200 years not to group the larger Protestant churches together in contrast to the unbelievers, Jews, Catholics, Eastern Orthodox, and sectarian Protestants. Thus Presbyterians, Lutherans, Methodists, Episcopalians, Congregationalists, and some Baptists have tended to stand for the American Christian mainstream. Matters shifted, of course, from place to place and time to time. The 52 million American

Catholics now constitute such a large bloc that one probably ought to count the majority of them in the mainstream. In eastern cities such as Boston and New York Catholics have sometimes been the largest plurality, if not the outright majority, and so have greatly colored what *mainstream* has conveyed to the local populace.

How did the American Christian mainstream, however defined, tend to shade the use of justification by faith dramatized by the revivalists? This discussion of "gracious alternatives," attempts to answer that question. First there is the implication that the mainstream was more decorous, not only abstaining from the shouts and jerks of the ecstatic revivalists but also holding back from the sorts of people evangelized by the Salvation Army. To the mind of the mainstream, *grace* connoted a certain propriety, as well as the free favor of God.

There was for Catholics, Orthodox, some Episcopalians, some Lutherans, and some Methodists the impress of what one can only call the catholic (with a small c) tradition, which wanted a different stress than the Calvinist understanding of human depravity and divine grace. Matters were often imprecise at this point, but suffice it to say that the catholic tradition called human nature more wounded than depraved and called grace the perfecting of nature rather than its replacement. Further, there was the sense that salvation could become intrinsic, rather than simply imputed to the saved person by virtue of Christ's works, and this sense led on to ways of thinking about grace as divinization that would have initially sounded strange to Calvinist ears.

Despite their differences in theological stress, which translated into different liturgical and moral sensibilities, along with different spiritualities, the mainstream churches supported culture, reason, and this-worldly ventures more than the revivalists could. The mainstream churches, after all, were part of the establishment and more or less comfortable with the powers ruling the politics, business, art, and education of the land. Partly in self-defense, and partly out of genuine conviction, they had to bless the many good things accomplished on American soil, the many achievements of what had begun as a humble errand in the wilderness. Salvation therefore was gracious in the sense of anointing American achievement and aspiration. It would be unfair to claim that mainstream Christianity lost its prophetic character and never criticized the going culture, but it would be untrue to make such prophecy the dominant characteristic. The Christ of the mainstream was not against American culture but would purify American culture of its omissions, its excesses, its many failures to be true to itself. Certainly "salvation" could be diluted in this process, and certainly all the mainstream churches were tempted to concentrate more on the individual than on stinging calls for social justice. Revivalism usually was equally individualistic, however, as were Catholic missions and retreats.

Black religion constituted a world unto itself, harboring considerable diversity and not greatly influencing the white mainstream. Black religion had to furnish from within itself both the revivalist strains that played on the edges of such mainstream organizations as the Methodist Church (and were a major factor in shaping the Baptist Church) and the establishmentarian strains that supported the going culture. Black Baptists, Pentecostals, Holiness groups and others tended to preach a salvation geared to helping people survive the injustices and sufferings perpetuated by American racism. They also tended to employ music and powerful preaching to achieve an emotional impact rarely sought or prized in the white mainstream.

Black Methodists, and to a greater extent black Catholics, probed their traditions convinced that grace could anoint culture and that sacramentality ought to color all one's readings of current events. Many black churches were forced to supply what social relief poor black communities could find, so the black understanding of salvation was seldom as individualistic as mainstream salvation was tempted to be. On the other hand, black religion could sustain an otherworldly focus, asking heaven to stand duty for the justice blacks knew should be part of daily life but had learned from painful experience was not likely to be this side of heaven.

The Jewish sense of creation as a great blessing from God, along with the sense of deferred messiahship that prevailed in most Jewish congregations, tended to produce an embrace of space and time more generous than that ruling most mainstream or sectarian Christian churches. Many Jews carried their expectations of immortality or resurrection lightly, transferring them to children and the family line. A zest for life bore many Jews into the centers of American finance, entertainment, the arts, sciences, education, and business, while the same zest for life caused Orthodox Jews to make communities closed to outsiders but humming with interactions among insiders.

"Gracious alternatives" perhaps suggests that mainstream American religion was more attractive than what flourished among ardent revivalists or sectarians, but any such attractiveness of course would have been in the eyes of the beholder. What the phrase should mainly call to mind, however, is the way that American religion domesticated salvation and the twofold result of such domestication. On the one hand, when salvation became gracious, it could lose its prophetic sting, its wild mien that was sometimes beautiful and sometimes ugly. On the other hand, when salvation became gracious, God more easily appeared to be "the soul of culture," as Paul Tillich's description of religion suggested God often should be. Then culture, for all its faults, held out the possibility of sacramentality: a series of times and places where divine life anointed human flesh and continued the incarnation of ultimate reality in human beings' midst.

Jonathan Edwards

Jonathan Edwards always stands at the foundations of American religious thought or philosophy. Blending Calvinist theology with the psychology (or philosophy) of John Locke, Edwards sought a middle course between a rationalism prevalent in his day that he found excessive and an emotionalism that he could not approve. His ideal was a religion of the heart, with a strong appreciation of how God works on the religious affections, that could engage the mind and emotion together. The beauty of God figured strongly in Edwards' theology, where people finally responded because of the lovely states of soul divine grace caused or the splendors of nature faith led them to appreciate as works of God.

In his studies of human nature, which the first Great Awakening helped to stimulate, Edwards deployed with great originality and skill the repertoire of theological concepts bequeathed him by Calvinism. Original sin bulked large in his estimates of human nature, yet he was convinced that one could speak meaningfully about human freedom. On their own people were mired in a sin or depravity that condemned them to hellfire. They still incurred blame, however, if they acted to procure sinful gains or pleasures. Somehow the decrees of God that bore on the committal of any person to hell never removed the justice with which that person's actual life came under sentence of hellfire.

Edwards finally justified his conclusions by reference to both the canonical (regulative) experience expressed in the Scriptures and the personal experience enjoyed by the saints, who manifested Christian holiness. Faith, grace, or religious experience transformed one's perceptions, opening out a new understanding of reality. On occasion Edwards associated such a new understanding of reality with the anointing from the Holy Spirit spoken of in 1 John 2: 20 ("But you have been anointed by the Holy One, and you all know."). To his mind the Holy Spirit gave spiritual understanding, and spiritual understanding could be described as a sense or taste of the moral beauty of divine things.

> Spiritual understanding primarily consists in this sense, or taste of the moral beauty of divine things; so that no knowledge can be called spiritual, any further than it arises from this, and has this in it. But secondarily, it includes all that discerning and knowledge of things of religion depends upon, and flows from such a sense. When the true beauty and amiableness of the holiness or true moral good that is in divine things, is discovered to the soul, it as it were opens a new world to its view. This shows the glory of all the perfections of God, and of everything appertaining to the divine being: for . . . the beauty of all arises from God's moral perfection. This shows the glory of all God's works, both of creation and providence: for 'tis the special glory of them, that God's holiness, righteousness, faithfulness and goodness are so manifested in them; and without these moral perfections, there would be no glory in that power and skill with which they are wrought.[4]

The implication here is that salvation shows itself in an appreciation of the perfections of God manifested in both nature and human creation. As such, the implication runs to the support of what we have called mainstream American Christianity and could undergird a wholesome American culture—science, aesthetics, and engagement with the world—to produce the economics and politics human societies require. In other places, Edwards has more to say about the downside of the human condition, the ravages of original sin. But here the prevailing note is graciousness, moral beauty. William A. Clebsch has argued that such an interest in beauty has been characteristic not only of Edwards but also of such other American religious thinkers as Emerson and William James.[5] Perhaps, then, it would be profitable to reflect on the connections one finds among salvation, beauty, and morality.

Inasmuch as salvation denotes healing, it connotes making well all the human faculties necessary for pleasing God. Salvation has also picked up other overtones but the prevailing sense in Western Christianity has been of having been healed of the blindness and distortion caused by sin and so of having been given back (or given for the first time) one's true self.

Morality suggests the actions of the true self, the real person who emerges after salvation. Morality is not so much a list of do's and don'ts as the proper, integral behavior of a person who is sound, whole, mature, and wise. For Christian faith, therefore, morality or ethical performance depends on salvation. People will not behave like whole human beings until they have been made whole. They may display certain virtues and avoid certain vices, but they will not be gracious in their dealings with other people, ordered in their dealings with nature, and peaceful in their hearts until they have experienced saving grace.

Beauty is the splendor that comes from harmony and intensity. It implies a light that takes one's breath away or an order or mode of presentation that collects one's spirit and elevates it. So both the sun glancing off the waters and the symmetry of a lovely face can rivet the eye, bring an intake of breath, and hush the spirit. One could say that significant encounters with beauty are peak experiences, telling human beings that for which they have been made. One could further say that the best theological intuitions about heaven have placed the appreciation of the divine beauty at its center.

All of this comes together in the term *moral beauty,* which dominates the quoted passage from Edwards. God is not a material being, so Edwards must speak beyond light glancing off waters, beyond even the blush or curve of a lovely human cheek. He is drawn to the goodness, the holiness, of God and transmutes these potentially abstract notions into something nearly sensible, nearly sensuous. The moral beauty of

The simple grace of this reconstructed early American house at Fruitlands in Harvard, Massachusetts, represents an instinct that beauty and virtue ought to be functional. (Photo by J. T. Carmody)

God is the riveting appeal holiness should make in our souls, because genuine holiness is not a tidy propriety but the outward form of intrinsic goodness, the expression of purest love. Salvation then becomes the entry to a new world, the world of divinity still veiled but somehow more expressive, more communicative of its incomprehensible goodness. Edwards is at the verge of the mystical language of the saints, who stammer before the divine goodness and beauty. He is in the tracks of the parables that make God's goodness incommensurate with justice on a human scale, bound to travel on to forgiveness and largess. Edwards would not deny the propriety of the rush of tears down the cheeks of the alcoholic or prostitute saved in the slum mission, but he would suggest that as salvation penetrates one's being it moves one away from self-concern to concern for what God is doing everywhere, indeed to what God always and everywhere is.

Writings of Charles Grandison Finney

Charles Grandison Finney (1792–1875) was the first of the professional evangelists. Born in Connecticut, he studied law but turned to revivalism after undergoing a religious conversion in his late 20s. His work in upstate New York was licensed by the Presbyterians, won him significant success, and drew considerable criticism from such Presbyterians as Lyman Beecher, who found his methods crude. During the early 1830s Finney conducted ongoing revivals at the Second Free Presbyterian Church and the Broadway Tabernacle in New York City.

In 1835 he became a professor of theology in Oberlin, Ohio, and the minister at Oberlin's First Congregational Church. From 1851 to 1866 he was the president of Oberlin College.

Finney's revivalism depended on his convictions about the efficacy of common sense, the Bible, and humanity's ability to reform itself (with the help of conversion and saving grace). In a lecture entitled "How to Promote a Revival," Finney stressed a figure from Hosea (10:12): breaking up fallow ground. His lecture proceeded in two parts. First, in answer to the question, "What is it to break up the fallow ground," he explained:

> To break up the fallow ground, is to break up your hearts—to prepare your minds to bring forth fruit unto God. The mind of man is often compared in the Bible to ground, and the word of God to seed sown in it, and the fruit represents the actions and affections of those who receive it. To break up the fallow ground, therefore, is to bring the mind into such a state, that it is fitted to receive the word of God. Sometimes your hearts get matted down hard and dry, and all run to waste, till there is no such thing as getting fruit from them till they are all broken up, and mellowed down, and fitted to receive the word of God. It is this softening of the heart, so as to make it feel the truth, which the prophet calls breaking up your fallow ground.[6]

While Finney did not deny the necessity of the word of God to accomplish conversion and salvation, his stress usually fell on the contribution of the preacher and the listener. He was convinced that mere emotion would not do the job, but that when people were helped to examine their souls, to learn what in fact lay on their consciences, they could prepare themselves for a grace that would be efficacious.

Thus when it came to the second of his topics, how the fallow ground was to be broken up, Finney began by ruling out direct efforts to make people feel compunction.

> People run into a mistake on this subject, from not making the laws of the mind the object of thought. There are great errors on the subject of the laws which govern the mind. People talk about religious feeling, as if they thought they could, by direct effort, call forth emotion. But this is not the way the mind acts. No man can make himself feel in this way, merely by trying to feel. The emotions of the mind are not directly under our control. We cannot by willing, or by direct volition, call up our emotions. We might as well think to call spirits up from the deep. The emotions are purely involuntary states of mind . . . So if a man thinks of God, and fastens his mind on any parts of God's character, he will feel—emotions will come up, by the very laws of the mind. If he is a friend of God, let him contemplate God as a gracious and holy being, and he will have emotions of friendship kindled in his mind. If he is an enemy of God, only let him get the true character of God before his mind, and look at it, and fasten his attention on it, and his enmity will rise against God.[7]

Finney's convictions about the priority of attending to God and people's state of soul led him to propose detailed examinations of conscience. Thus he wanted people to consider such sins of omission as ingratitude, want of love of God, neglect of the Bible, unbelief, and neglect of prayer. Then he wanted them to consider such sins of commission as worldly mindedness, pride, envy, censoriousness, slander, levity, and robbing God. On this last point he noted:

> Instances in which you have misspent your time and squandered hours which God gave you to serve him and save souls, in vain amusements or foolish conversation, reading novels, or doing nothing; cases where you have misapplied your talents and powers of mind; where you have squandered money on your lusts, or spent it for things you did not need, and which neither contributed to your health, comfort or usefulness. Perhaps some of you who are here tonight have laid out God's money for TOBACCO. I will not speak of rum, for I presume there is no professor of religion here tonight that would drink rum. I hope there is no one that uses that filthy poison, tobacco. Think of a professor of religion, using God's money to poison himself with tobacco![8]

One can see that despite a veneer of biblicism, Finney stressed moralism: amending one's character. Following in a good Calvinist line (though criticized by many Calvinists) he urged people to get their heads straight, survey their souls, and be moved by the disorders they saw to change their ways. His points come neatly outlined. He undergirds his views with references to the psychology of the day, which owed much to Scottish common sense (as has much other fundamentalism). He has the good preacher's and teacher's knack for bringing in apt examples to illustrate his views.

Finney somewhat complicates the stereotype of revivalism held in many quarters. He was not an enthusiast, trying to get people to roll in the aisles. He was a moralist, wanting to change people's minds and thereby change their behavior. Like W. E. Channing, he offered little from the poetic, mystical side of religion, and little that one might call profound biblical theology. Much of his appeal lay in the pragmatism and common sense esteemed by his audiences. When he put to them very clearly how they might change their lives and please God, they sat up and took notice.

The criticism American religion of this sort has regularly drawn is several sided:

1. It tends to deal mainly, if not exclusively, with what medieval Christianity called the purgative way: the first stage in a devout life. After the purgative way came the illuminative and unitative ways, where moralism was beside the point because people were solidly in love with God. Apt as Finney's sermons might be for beginners, they tended to leave mature Christians cold.
2. It risks Pelagianism—overstressing what common sense and will power can achieve. Salvation is not a matter of a neat examination of conscience. Sin is a more formidable enemy than spiritual indolence or inefficiency. Until people have been taken over by the Spirit of God their religion will not make them the sharers in divinity that the New Testament proposes they can be.
3. Finney also risks puritanism and failing to appreciate the implications of the incarnation. Tobacco and alcohol are creatures (things ultimately made by God) that any sensible person uses carefully, mindful of their dangers. But neither is the Devil incarnate, and people less moralistic than Finney tend to find more of God in creation, more reasons to praise God for his abundant gifts.

Thus the lawyerly mind Finney brought to many of his sermons could shortchange revivalism and salvation, not delving deeply enough into either sin or salvation to go below moralism and find the sacramentality of the divine love.

Key Terms

Alienation: making foreign, giving over to someone else. For humanists religion is something that does not fit their convictions and so is foreign. Moreover, religion is something they believe causes people to give over to God responsibilities they themselves ought to assume. Thus the classical Marxist critique of religion makes it an opiate keeping people from striving for social justice. In the case of Feuerbach, the argument was that "God" is a dangerous projection of human ideals, causing people to place in "heaven" energy they ought to apply to this-worldly tasks of securing justice, peace, the flourishing of culture, and so forth.

Pelagian: referring to the supposed teachings of an Irish monk, Pelagius, who died about 419 and was an opponent of St. Augustine. The Pelagian position stressed human freedom and responsibility in the work of salvation. The Augustinian position stressed the gratuity of salvation and humanity's dependence on God. Orthodox Christianity favored Augustine, though when proper nuance is applied the two positions may not be irreconcilable. Still the stereotype became that moralistic types, bent on having people scour their consciences and bootstrap their way to salvation, were heretical on the model of Pelagius.

Discussion Questions

1. Can people in fact become fully human on their own, or do they require the grace of a transcendent divinity?
2. How does salvation relate to images of human nature as sick or broken?
3. What is the meaning of the phrase "a kind of proletarian marriage supper of the Lamb"?
4. What is the image of blacks in the second quotation about the Salvation Army?
5. How did the Christian mainstream adjust the meaning of justification by faith so that it supported American culture?
6. How has the Jewish sense of creation colored Jewish approaches to American culture?
7. Why was Jonathan Edwards so enamored of the moral beauty of God?
8. How might spiritual understanding recast one's sense of creation and salvation?
9. What is revealed in C. G. Finney's references to tobacco?
10. What are the benefits and limits of moralistic approaches to salvation?

Notes

1. Timothy L. Smith, *Revivalism and Social Reform in Mid-Nineteenth Century America* (New York: Abingdon, 1957), p. 7.

2. Herbert A. Wisbey, Jr., *Soldiers Without Swords: A History of the Salvation Army in the United States* (New York: Macmillan, 1956), p. 3.

3. Ibid., p. 6.

4. Jonathan Edwards, "The Sense of the Heart," in *Documents in the History of American Philosophy*, ed. Morton White (New York: Oxford University Press, 1972), pp 46–47. See Jonathan Edwards, *Religious Affections*, ed. John E. Smith (New Haven: Yale University Press, 1959), pp. 270–75.

5. William A. Clebsch, *American Religious Thought: A History* (Chicago: University of Chicago Press, 1973).

6. Charles Grandison Finney, *Lectures on Revivals of Religion* (Cambridge, MA: Belknap/Harvard University Press, 1960), pp. 38–39.

7. Ibid., p. 39.

8. Ibid., p. 47.

Destiny

God's New Israel

When we think about the self-conception that Americans have forged, about how they tend to think of their nation, it becomes clear that the colonial beginnings have maintained a strong inertia throughout later history. We have seen that those colonial beginnings were ripe with hopes that in the virgin New World a people would arise worthy of the holy covenants God had offered. Because the theme of covenant was so much richer in the Old Testament than in the New Testament and because of the similarity in many colonists' minds between ancient Israel, which was both a nation and a people, and the new American nation and people, the habit arose of likening the American people to a New Israel.

Implicit in this conception was the Christian assumption that Judaism had been passed by because many New Testament passages interpreted the followers of Jesus as the successors of Israel in being God's people. As Jesus had fulfilled what the New Testament authors took to be messianic prophecies, so the followers of Jesus had inherited the covenantal relationship previously enjoyed by Jesus's old people, his fellow Jews. Certainly conflicts between Jews

*The early colonists' "errand in the wilderness" took on the aura of a holy war when Washington rode out at the head of the colonial troops during the revolutionary era. (*Washington and Lafayette at the Battle of Brandywine, *John Vanderlyn; Gilcrease Museum, Tulsa, Oklahoma)*

who became Christians and Jews who refused to become Christians contributed to the harsh language (which some have called anti-Semitic) in which some New Testament passages express the Christian sense of supercession. Certainly the theology of Paul was complicated if not confused on the matter (Romans 9–11 being the most relevant passage). But the fact remains that from the New Testament period

Christians designated themselves the new Chosen People, and when Christianity became the established religion of the Roman Empire and Christians began to outnumber Jews, this designation entered into the Christian psyche as a given. Thus the colonists setting forth for the New World or reflecting on the potential of the beginnings they had made could summon the figure of the New Israel with no qualm of conscience. They saw the future as theirs, much as Israel had contemplated Canaan and dreamed of establishing there a land whose prosperity would express God's blessings.

Early American writers as diverse as John Winthrop, Jonathan Edwards, and Nicholas Street employed this imagery.[1] It tended to associate the colonists and pioneers with a small people possessed of God's blessing but surrounded by many trials. If groups such as the Puritans could think of themselves as having escaped Pharaoh, all the new Americans could think of themselves as sojourning in the wilderness, in search of a cloud by day and a pillar of fire by night that might guide their way. Not all the early Americans were so intensely religious that they used the Bible as a map or guidebook. But analogies to Israel's trials in the wilderness easily came to mind, as analogies to Israel's covenants with God came to mind when the colonies set about writing their laws and compacts. The influence was less on the letter of such agreements than on the spirit. Inasmuch as religion still commanded the back, if not the front, of colonial leaders' minds, what the people were doing in fashioning their contracts and making their joint plans likened them to Israel's tribes because of their common relation to God.

The New Israelites often conceived their future in terms of the theology one finds in the history of the Old Testament (Joshua through Kings), where the theme is that Israel sinned in the sight of the Lord and so knew hard times as punishment. That is to say, an equation was regularly made between virtue and blessing, vice and misfortune. Other portions of the Old Testament, passages in the New Testament, and centuries of relatively sophisticated Christian speculation about the meaning of history had loosened any rigid joining of virtue and prosperity, of sin and worldly failure. The problem classically set by the Book of Job, that the good frequently suffer while the wicked flourish, remained highly visible. Yet the newness of the American venture tended to brush aside or dilute the sophistication developed in the Old World, where the Machiavellian complexities of political or economic success were well known. By the time it had second and third generations America had assumed a naiveté about the wilderness. The wilderness could symbolize untamed human nature, fallen potential in need of hard work to become a garden of virtue, but the stronger symbolism ran to the conclusion that the New World was a fresh opportunity, an unprecedented chance to find Eden and not be unworthy of it. The corruptions of Europe might be avoided. If vision were clear and will strong from the outset, a new Jerusalem might arise to center the New Israel.

This conception of new possibilities carried in its train new responsibilities. The clearest responsibilities were to be faithful to God, who had placed the colonists in such an advantageous position. More tacit yet still influential were such charges as converting the Native Americans (or at least shaping them for the better); besting the papists who threatened to pollute the virgin wilderness in the North, South, and Southwest; and showing the Old World, indeed any nations with eyes to see, that Protestant Christianity could produce the most virtuous and prosperous realm yet known to human history.

The first two of these tacit or collateral responsibilities (converting the native and besting the papists) shifted, waned, or became causes for shame as the decades went by. The third responsibility (producing virtue and prosperity) was less subject to empirical test and grew to mythic proportions, as Conrad Cherry has noted. By the time of the Civil War, Americans had plenty of data available to chasten their sense of having been given a mission to be the city on a hill meant to illumine the rest of the world. Yet this mythical imperative continued strong through the Second World War, and some observers would say it came to grief only in Vietnam. Other observers would say it remained

The traders and trappers who explored the central waterways were an advance guard of the waves of Americans who set out in high excitement to tame the western wilderness. (Fur Traders Descending the Missouri, *George Caleb Bingham; The Metropolitan Museum of Art, Morris K. Jesup Fund, 1933 [33.61])*

potent through the 1980s, explaining much in American policy toward Latin America and the Soviet Union.

Indeed the American myth of having been destined to display to the whole world the good effects of a special relation to God can seem to have virtually required a shadow self, a dark counterplayer, such as the Soviet Union or international communism. Like Israel and Canaan, or even Christ and Satan, American democracy and Soviet communism would neatly separate as goodness and evil, light and dark-

ness. The "evil empire" President Reagan castigated comes from such a lexicon. It may owe more to Manichean principles than to Christianity or the Hebrew Bible, but it depended for its resonance on a long history of separating people into elect and outsiders, chosen and unchosen, clean and unclean.

In some minds that history alone was enough to discredit such a dualism and to bring to consciousness the self-criticism championed by the Israelite prophets. Where was the parallel self-criticism keeping the American myth of special destiny tame? Robert Bellah and others have pointed out that America has had its prophets to keep its civil religion from pure chauvinism, but in the measure that the American self-conception as God's New Israel has been mythic, it has evaded most of such prophecy or has called it unpatriotic.[2] The potent imagery of the New Israel continues to exist.

God's Old Israel

Jews were not present in significant numbers in America until the late 19th century, when pogroms in eastern Europe brought millions of Jewish immigrants in a few decades. The German Jews who had come earlier by and large were sympathetic to Reform Judaism and so accepted the pluralism and secularism of American culture and law. The more Orthodox eastern European populations who came later profited from American pluralism and religious liberty, which legally, and to some extent culturally, freed them to create an introverted life in their own ghettoes. But they feared the secularism of American culture, as had all prior religious groups centered in a profound sense of the sacred and the ideal wholeness of life under God.

Jews naturally could not accept the Christian theology of Americans as God's newly covenanted people, but they could and did accept the optimism of their new country, its sense of limitless possibility, and its democratic inclination to base success on ability. Despite the American rhetoric about equal opportunity, Jews experienced considerable discrimination and prejudice. Yet in comparison to what they had suffered in Christian Europe, the slights Americans imposed seemed minor. On the whole, material life and culture were flourishing in the United States. Jews made their way in business, the arts, education, the sciences, and eventually even politics. After a few generations during

which poverty, working at small businesses, and learning both a new language and a new cultural situation were the main preoccupations, successes began to pour in. The more the United States became ethnically and religiously diverse and the more the unofficial Protestant orthodoxy was diluted in sensibility and style by various Catholic subcultures, Asians, and other immigrant groups, the more anti-Semitism faded or went underground.

The major Jewish contribution to the American sense of destiny has focused on secular interpretations, though frequently these have been highly idealistic about social justice. Jews in the labor, socialist, and even communist movements have seemed to translate an ancient prophetic energy into a passion for this-worldly justice: helping the poor, educating the ignorant, healing the sick. Jewish convictions about the goodness of creation, as previously noted, have counterbalanced Christian pessimism about human nature, leading to many affirmations that things can change, that the lot of the poor can be improved, and that education can become excellent and effective. For their own part, Jews have had centuries of suffering to provide them ballast against naiveté.

Rabbi Isaac Mayer Wise, the father of American Reform Judaism, came to the United States in 1846 from Bohemia. He had two dollars in his pocket when he began, but he ended as the founder of Hebrew Union College in Cincinnati, the leading intellectual center of American Reform Jewry. In 1869 Wise delivered a lecture entitled "Our Country's Place in History" before the Theological and Religious Library Association of Cincinnati. The lecture shows that he had become quite the American.

Among the major topics and highlights of Wise's talk were a conception of history as Providence realized (God's will working itself out); a rejection of fatalism (arguing that nations can seize their providential roles or reject them); a conviction that progress is the criterion by which one can judge whether a nation has been fulfilling its destiny; a negative judgment on the period that closed the 15th century (and prepared for the explorations of the 16th century that created America); damning references to the Inquisition and the sufferings of the Jews thrown out of Spain; references to the birth of new knowledge during the Renaissance and to the travails of the birth of colonial America; a dark reading of the Spanish colonial expeditions in Mexico and South America; allusions to the Protestant Reformation as both offering Jews some shelter from southern European persecutions and sundering Europe with war; praise for the Puritans and first colonists as people championing common sense and freedom; even higher praise for Washington and the revolutionaries; a conviction that the 13 colonies were wise in the extreme not to attempt to fashion a new kingdom (Washington, like the biblical Gideon, was too good a man to be a king); admiration for the American Constitution; a conviction that the Constitution had given America its destined place in history, making it like Greece in sending out beacons of light; and an appeal to his fellow Americans to guard their traditions of liberty so that their destined place in history might long continue, progressing ever forward. Only wickedness, leading to a desertion of liberty, could stop American progress.[3]

Rabbi Wise's lecture is a stimulating invitation to reflect, not so much on his rapid-fire interpretation of America's place in world history, as on his chosen emphases, which were presumably based on his Jewish convictions. Liberty emerges as the American emblem, the great American achievement. The American establishment of liberty, enshrined in the Constitution, was the culmination of prior history and the realization of a special providential mission. One cannot help reading the allusions to the fate of Spanish Jewry in 1492 as the backdrop of Wise's interpretation of the colonial venture that led to the United States. The first colonists were bent on achieving a religious liberty denied them in England or other European countries, but Jews had suffered much greater denials, and for much longer periods.

It is peculiar that a lecture given in 1869 would make no reference to the Civil War or slavery, two related phenomena likely to give anyone reflecting on American destiny considerable pause. It is perhaps more understandable, yet also interesting, that Wise says relatively little about analogies between the destiny of the United States and the destiny of biblical Israel. Either he knew little of this theme in American intellectual history or he considered it too dangerous. Yet perhaps his chosen stress on liberty subtly covered both the Civil War and the destiny of biblical Israel. For the great ideological battle in the Civil War was over the right of some people to discount the liberty of other people and make them slaves, while the history of biblical Israel could be read as the struggle to find freedom in right relationship to God (and the history of postbiblical Israel could be read as the struggle to retain the freedom to practice the things that made Jews Jewish).

Despite the obvious economic, political, and regional factors that contributed to the Civil War, the military conflict became a showplace for different conceptions of human nature. And although biblical Israel tolerated slaves, Jewish thought—under the influence of both the paradigm of the Exodus, when God took Israel from slavery, and the historical experience of being downtrodden in Christian Europe and the Muslim lands—had become extremely sensitive to human rights. Thus the rabbis had elaborated many safeguards for human dignity, while many Jewish intellectuals had become enthusiastic for the Enlightenment precisely because it offered the hope that Jews could become full citizens of cultures based on reason rather than religious prejudice.

One should not stuff all later Jewish interest in socialism and human betterment under the label of liberty, but liberty is a good focus for much of what the Old Israel, in its recent forms, has offered American culture. Liberty, the child and condition of justice, rang out in the American Revolution and Constitution. Therefore, Jewish immigrants such as Isaac Mayer Wise could easily and gladly speak of "our country's" place in history and call themselves American Jews or Jewish Americans.

American Catholicism

Much the same could be said of American Catholics or Catholic Americans. For while the few Catholic colonists suffered some discriminations, and the 19th century immigrants often saw signs such as "No Irish Need Apply," on the whole Catholics, like Jews, found their new country more encouraging than discouraging, a cause more for enthusiasm than for complaint. Irish who had left their native land because of famine, Germans eager for expanded religious or economic opportunity, Italians desperate for work—all looked on America as a land of new beginnings and limitless horizons.

No doubt harsh living and working conditions, and poverty in New York, Boston, Chicago, and even the rural Midwest chastened the mythic enthusiasm of the 19th-century Catholic emigrants from Europe, as it has chastened the enthusiasm of the Hispanics who have immigrated in the 20th century. The streets of America were not paved with gold, and Americans were not vice-free, uncorrupted by Old World prejudices about religion, class, sex, and race. Still, the patterns of prejudice were less fixed than they had been in Europe, and the economic opportunities were frequently much better. The Irish were freer of English domination, Italians were freer of the constraints of the Church, and those Germans who were intensely religious warmed to the American tradition of religious liberty, breathing a sigh of relief that in America there was no *Kulturkampf.*

Indeed, the enthusiasm that most American Catholics generated bothered their ecclesiastical

superiors, both in the United States and in Rome. Official Catholic views of American destiny were soberer than what the immigrant enthusiasts tended to produce, even though American Catholic bishops as early as John Carroll had sensed that the nonestablishment of religion in America could be a great boon. Some American bishops (most of them foreign born) remained suspicious of the Protestant culture controlling the American mainstream. Others feared the dilution of Catholic faith in the solvents of American pluralism. But most American Catholic church leaders nonetheless urged their people to become good citizens and strove to open such crucial American establishments as education and politics to Catholic membership. Roman authorities long remained considerably more dubious, suspecting the American Catholic church of a desire for independence that did not fit Roman traditions of a monarchical papal authority. The tensions between Roman authoritarianism and American independence have persisted to the present day, complicating relations between Pope John Paul II and the American Catholic bishops.

Ultimately Catholic theology could not uncritically bless America as a unique providence of God, any more than profound Protestant or Jewish theology could. Any monotheistic faith must point out the dangers of chauvinism and idolatry lurking close to the linkage of patriotism and religion. The next chapter deals with recent discussions about civil religion, the amalgamation of patriotism and faith. Here it is necessary only to note that while the sociological and theological analysis of civil religion may be a phenomenon of the last quarter century, the reality of the phenomenon, and some attention to it on the part of religious leaders, is far from new. When Pope Leo XIII condemned "Americanism," he was attacking the danger of too closely joining faith and commitment to one's national culture. Many commentators believe that what Leo condemned was little held by the American Catholic church, but the fact remains that the warning about blind patriotism has virtually always been relevant.

From the Israelite prophets concerned with a reliance on power politics that seemed to vitiate the Mosaic and Davidic covenants, to the early Christians who could not call Caesar Lord, the tension between church and state, religion and politics, has always forced religious leaders to put a damper on secular, national, and ethnic loyalties. Unless one had a more profound loyalty to God, any of these other loyalties could twist personalities and cultures out of shape. The Nazi phenomenon is perhaps the most glaring case in point, and the example of the Protestant German Confessing Church that opposed Nazism is one of the heroic points of recent church history. Indeed many have criticized Pope Pius XII for not condemning Nazism and the Holocaust more vigorously. In countries such as Spain and Portugal, many have seen a Catholic version of civil religion in the pejorative sense, a Catholic instance of faith and patriotism joining too closely to the detriment of both. So the same theology that warranted warnings to American Catholics not to let their enthusiasm about American culture and America's place in history run away with them has also warranted warnings to other portions of the Catholic community, including Rome itself.

In the American case, however, the peculiar wrinkle was working out a Catholic approach to the destiny America had started to see for itself in colonial times. How should Catholics think about sharing in the formation of God's new Israel? What Catholic overtones ought to emerge when talk turned to America's role as the guardian of morality and justice, as the great foe of Nazism and Communism? These were interesting questions, even though few American Catholics dealt with them explicitly.

The general Catholic response to such questions was to make some distinctions. Catholic natural law theory offered a basis for speaking to any person of reason and good will apart from convictions peculiar to religious faith, so

Catholics could enter into debates about national priorities and virtues. They might not gravitate to the biblical language favored by many Protestants, but they could agree that American traditions of religious liberty, defense of individual rights, democratic institutions, and the like were both precious and exemplary. Catholics who had immigrated from lands where such traditions did not prevail had vivid memories from which to draw enthusiasm for American ways. They could agree that the lively experiment under way in the United States ought to become a model for all modern societies and an example to the British, the French, the Italians, and nations much farther afield. Nothing in their faith prohibited American Catholics from arguing that American traditions fitted the gospel or the historical unfolding of Christian humanism better than the traditions of European or other Catholics. Such an argument would go down hard in Rome, Paris, or other venerable centers of Catholic culture, but theologically American Catholics had every right to have such an argument taken seriously.

The only bugaboo, instantly perceived by Protestant Americans, was the fidelity to the Pope expected of all Catholics. Could Americans pledge such fidelity, or would pledging it violate American patriotism by making a foreign power more central than the law and traditions of their own country? Catholic leaders such as Cardinal Gibbons argued skillfully, on the grounds of the First Amendment, that the question should never have been raised. They argued that because the amendment guaranteed free exercise of religion and proper separation of church and state those who would put a special burden on Catholics to show their patriotism might be suspected of simple bigotry. Nonetheless, many Catholics went to war, from the Civil War onward, and served their country in other self-sacrificing ways, in part to prove that the sort of allegiance they gave the Pope need not detract from their American patriotism. Despite their many sacrifices, however, the

Protestant bias, or fear of Catholic disloyalty, was fully exorcized only with the election of John F. Kennedy as president in 1960. Only after that could American Catholics and non-Catholics alike think that the destiny of the United States could apply to Catholics, and be forwarded by Catholics, as easily as by any other religious group.

John Dewey

John Dewey (1859–1952) is best known for his theories of education, but those theories dovetailed with his convictions about the "common faith" that ought to unite Americans, and so they bore on the destiny Dewey thought Americans ought to share. Indeed Dewey thought of the classroom as the laboratory in which to inculcate the experience of a pluralistic democracy (and so he opposed parochial schools). Dewey himself grew up in Burlington, Vermont, the third of four children in a middle-class, white, Anglo-Saxon, Protestant family. Such families composed half of the Burlington community, while foreign-born Irish and Canadian Catholics composed the other half. From boyhood, then, Dewey experienced the religious and ethnic roots of the pluralism of American culture. As a senior at the University of Vermont he warmed to the general studies designed to cap his undergraduate education, and he graduated with an abiding interest in large philosophical, political, economic, and religious questions.

During his graduate studies at Johns Hopkins University, Dewey became a neo-Hegelian, enthusiastic about both that spiritual synthesis and its alternatives to the puritanical view of religion and morality enforced in his home by his mother. After receiving his doctorate in philosophy, he taught at the University of Michigan for ten years and found himself attracted to such psychologists as William James. Gradually he became convinced that American education was

not taking into account the latest findings of philosophy and psychology, so he began working on a new philosophy of education. Married and possessed of a large family, he left Michigan in 1896 to become head of a department at the University of Chicago that combined philosophy, psychology, and education—precisely his own mixture of interests.

Influenced by the evolutionary science that was taking hold, Dewey abandoned his Hegelian sympathies and began to apply an instrumentalist or pragmatic theory of knowledge to education. The enthusiasm of William James for the work of Dewey and his Chicago colleagues gave them a big boost, while educators were increasingly influenced by such Deweyian tenets as the need to build on the interests of the child, the need for schooling to mix thinking and doing, the ideals that the school be a miniature of the wider community and the teacher a collaborator with the student rather than a taskmaster, and the notion that the general aim of education should be simply the growth of the child. Many of these theories have become part of American educational orthodoxy, but when they were first advanced considerable uproar ensued. Because of these theories and the Laboratory Schools designed to test them, the Deweyians became the leaders of a "progressive" educational movement aimed at thorough-going reform. Work with immigrant and minority groups in Chicago only extended this impression.

In 1904 Dewey moved to Columbia University in New York City, where he reigned for 47 years as first a professor and then a professor emeritus of philosophy. A prolific writer, he was soon recognized as the leading American philosopher of his day, making major contributions in such diverse areas as cognitive theory, psychology, educational theory, social philosophy, religion, and fine arts. Through articles in *The New Republic,* Dewey extended his influence beyond academe and gained the status of a leading interpreter of both domestic and foreign affairs. Among his practical achievements were helping to draft the Kellogg-Briand Pact (which sought to outlaw future wars) after the First World War, to create the American Association of University Professors, to fashion the first teachers' union in New York City, and to develop the New School for Social Research. Dewey also participated in the American Civil Liberties Union and traveled the globe lecturing and studying social change. He remained active until shortly before his death at the age of 93, having lived to see progressive education severely criticized but quite ably defending it.

In the course of his Terry Lectures at Yale University, published in 1934, John Dewey discoursed on the function of religion in society. His views reflect not only his own philosophical convictions but also his experience as a member of an American pluralistic culture in which no one religion could hold sway. To his mind this stood out as a remarkably novel state of affairs, when one surveyed the prior history of culture and religion.

> But the thing new in history, the thing once unheard of, is that the [religious] organization in question is a *special* institution within a secular community. Even where there are established churches, they are constituted by the state and may be unmade by the state. Not only the national state but other forms of organization among groups have grown in power and influence at the expense of organizations built upon and about a religion. The correlate of this fact is that membership in associations of the latter type is more and more a matter of the voluntary choice of individuals, who may tend to accept responsibilities imposed by the church but who accept them of their own volition . . . . The shift in what I have called the social center of gravity accompanies the enormous expansion of associations formed for educational, philanthropic and scientific purposes, which have occurred independently of any religion. These social modes have grown so much that they exercise the greater hold upon the thought and interest of most persons, even of those holding membership in churches. This positive extension of

interests which, from the standpoint of a religion, are non-religious, is so great that in comparison with it the direct effect of science upon the creeds of religion seems to me of secondary importance.[4]

In the more than 50 years since Dewey's Terry Lectures, conditions have certainly changed, in both the United States and the world at large, requiring some nuance about his analysis. Yet much of what he proposed remains valid. Despite the surges of fundamentalist religions that seek to reestablish religion at the center of culture, secularism dominates in many areas and has good credentials as the typically modern or postmodern cultural standard. Religion struggles for a clear correlation with politics, social thought, and economics, such as it had in most phases of premodern history, while individual rights, on the model of the United States, have increasingly conspired to make religious allegiance a matter of personal choice rather than a cultural given.

Dewey vigorously applauded this historical development and saw it as the condition for applying the undoubted energy available in religious commitment to the secular tasks facing humankind. One might say that his scenario for the realization of American destiny depended on a domestication of religious faith that would make it better serve the humanistic common good.

> The ideal ends to which we attach our faith are not shadowy and wavering. They assume concrete form in our understanding of our relations to one another and the values contained in these relations. We who now live are parts of a humanity that extends into the remote past, a humanity that has interacted with nature. The things in civilization we most prize are not of ourselves. They exist by grace of the doings and sufferings of the continuous human community in which we are a link. Ours is the responsibility of conserving, transmitting, rectifying and expanding the heritage of values we have received that those who come after us may receive it more solid and secure, more widely accessible and more generously shared

than we have received it. Here are all the elements for a religious faith that shall not be confined to sect, class, or race. Such a faith has always been implicitly the common faith of mankind. It remains to make it explicit and militant.[5]

This interpretation of the destiny of religion in America's future no doubt would win applause from Founding Fathers like Jefferson and Franklin. Whether it does justice to the facts of religious experience, as exposed by William James, or to the needs of human beings for myths, rituals, and doctrines that explain the mysteries of existence, is another question. But what stands beyond question is the power and influence John Dewey exerted in fashioning a humanistic interpretation of the American social project and gathering to it many admirable ideals.

Writings of Reinhold Niebuhr

Chapter 9 dealt with Reinhold Niebuhr (1892–1971), drawing on his theology in the context of the world wars that shaped American history during the 20th century. Here he comes to mind as an ironic interpreter of American views of destiny. From his Christian faith and learned reading of history, Niebuhr derived a balanced view of both human nature and American experience. On the one hand, he scorned the atheistic humanists who tried to repose virtue and a glorious future in human nature, using both the data of the past and Christian views of original sin to brand such a position naive. On the other hand, he felt compelled to be hopeful about the future, if only because he believed God could do more good than human beings could do evil. His patriotic feelings about American history led him to think that, whatever its failings, the United States had gained the responsibility of carrying the torch of freedom in the world.

In analyzing Marxist schemes, Niebuhr came to speak of a "secularized providence," mean-

ing a conviction that history unfolds according to determined patterns, which is derived not from faith in a transcendent God but from historical forces such as class warfare or economic determinism. As he thought about such a conviction, Niebuhr realized that it differed little from the religious belief that a revealed scenario of the future was available for those who vouchsafed faith. On further reflection, Niebuhr judged the Marxist version of such a view of the future to pivot on the hope that humankind could remove its ambiguities and become the master of its own destiny: "That hope is that man may be delivered from his ambiguous position of being both creature and creator of the historical process and become unequivocally the master of his own destiny."[6]

Precise as the Marxist version of this hope may be, it does not differ substantially from the vaguer liberal version of the same longing. The classical liberals (many of whose ideas were quite different from the ideas of those called liberals during the second half of the 20th century) also reposed their hopes in a human nature freed of religious shackles and able to express its innate goodness or perfectibility. In the American case such a notion blended with long-standing ideas about the destined place of the country in history. Still experience showed the limitations in America's ability to realize such a destiny.

Our dream of the universal good is sufficiently valid to bring us in voluntary alliance with many peoples, who have similar conceptions of the good life. But neither their conceptions of the good, nor their interests, which are always compounded with ideals, are identical with our own. In this situation it is natural that many of our people should fail to perceive that historical destiny may be beguiled, deflected and transfigured by human policy, but that it cannot be coerced. They become impatient and want to use the atomic bomb (symbol of the technical efficiency upon which our world authority rests) not only to put an end to the recalcitrance of our foes but to eliminate the equivocal attitudes of the Asian and other peoples, who are not as clearly our allies as we should like them to be. Yet on the whole, we have as a nation learned the lesson of history tolerably well. We have heeded the warning "let not the wise man glory in his wisdom, let not the mighty man glory in his strength." Though we are not without vainglorious delusions in regard to our power, we are saved by a certain grace inherent in our common sense rather than in abstract theories from attempting to cut through the vast ambiguities of our historic situation and thereby bringing our destiny to a tragic conclusion by seeking to bring it to a neat and logical one.[7]

Only a little exposure to Reinhold Neibuhr therefore teaches the reader that from him one will get few simple prescriptions, few easy reductions of history or theology to tidy formulas. Perhaps the greatest virtue of his thought and political commentary is the dialectical, complicated sense of ambiguity he always retained. Above all Niebuhr abhorred theological or political oversimplification. Were a Communist to present him with an ideological interpretation of history, neat as a proposition out of Euclid, he would scoff at its naiveté. Equally, however, he would scoff at oversimplification in American garb, including that of cynics who rejected all pretension of finding meaning or direction in history.

For Niebuhr the truth lay in a more skeptical, self-critical attitude and reading. Compared to the butcheries of the Communists, the great foe during the Cold War era when Niebuhr was most influential politically, the American political system and philosophical outlook seemed quite good. Compared to the purity of heart that willed only one thing, obedience to the (admittedly often hard to discern) will of God, American motivation demanded constant scrutiny and criticism. Niebuhr had cut his theological teeth on the biblical prophets, learning that much human moving and shaking is faithless folly. He had taken to heart the Reformation themes of humanity's inability to justify

itself and the need for the church (or the nation) always to be reformed. On top of this heritage, study of the Nazi movement in Europe prior to the Second World War convinced him that pacifism was not realistic or faithful to Christian doctrine. Related studies of ideological movements (Nazi, Soviet, and Liberal alike) convinced him that ideas not chastening themselves by constant reference to what in fact has happened in human history were a menace. (In this he was much like Eric Voegelin, who branded the modern ideologies gnosticisms—systems out of touch with actual human experience and drawn astray by the symmetry of unhistorical systems of ideas.[8])

So Niebuhr found many ironies in American history and political thought, many ways in which self-conceptions proved superficial and best ideals were betrayed by ignorance either of what Americans in fact had experienced in history or of what a balanced view of human nature was bound to conclude.

In Niebuhr's view, the United States was fated, or forced by a rational interpretation of history, to seek ways to use its vast powers responsibly in relation to the events actually shaping the increasingly global political arena. Thus in reflecting on the isolationist temptations that some Americans had indulged during the 20th century (temptations that would have kept America from entering either world war) Niebuhr wrote:

It was a rather unique historical phenomenon that a nation with our potentialities should have been tempted to isolationism and withdrawal from world responsibilities. Various factors contributed to the persuasiveness of the temptation. We were so strong and our continental security seemed so impregnable (on cursory glance at least) that we were encouraged in the illusion that we could live our own life without too much regard for a harassed world. Our sense of superior virtue over the alleged evils of European civilization and our fear of losing our innocence if we braved the tumults of world politics, added spiritual vanity to ignoble prudence as a second cause of our irresponsibility. We thought we might keep ourselves free of the evils of a warring world and thus preserve a healthy civilization amidst the expected doom of a decrepit one. This hope of furnishing the seed-corn for a new beginning persuaded moral idealists to combine with cynical realists in propounding the policy of power without responsibility.[9]

What, then, should Americans do? How should we think about our destiny? In Niebuhrian categories, the answer seems to be to develop a moral realism—a principled look at the world and action in the world that does not ignore the facts of evil or the responsibility of good people to oppose evil but also does not consider our nation a simon-pure agent of goodness or an unlimited power capable of shaping history to our own ends. For such a moral realism, we would finally have to go where Niebuhr himself went, to the Bible and other repositories of the wise view that human beings are only weak and sinful creatures of a day and must always take their true hopes from a God who transcends their ambiguities and sinfulness.

Discussion Questions

1. Why did early Americans make more of the Israelite covenant with God in their political self-conceptions than of the new covenant discussed in the New Testament?
2. How did the American use of symbols like "New Israel" tend toward a self-serving Manicheanism?
3. Why have Jewish American interpretations of the destiny of the United States tended to focus on secular matters?
4. Why did Rabbi Wise probably decide not to comment on either the Civil War or the theme of God's New Israel?
5. What were the main benefits that Catholic immigrants found in the United States?
6. What in the international character of Roman Catholicism tended to dampen high rhetoric about the providential destiny of the United States?
7. Why has the educational thought of John Dewey come under attack from recent "back to the basics" movements?
8. What are the advantages, and the disadvantages, of Dewey's secularist redirection of religious energies in terms of a "common faith"?
9. What in Reinhold Niebuhr's Christian allegiance was bound to make him reject the Communist understanding of humanity's possible mastery of historical destiny?
10. What would a moral realism suggest about American foreign policy in areas such as Latin America?

Notes

1. See Conrad Cherry, ed. *God's New Israel: Religious Interpretations of American Destiny* (Englewood Cliffs NJ: Prentice-Hall, 1971).

2. See Robert N. Bellah, *The Broken Covenant* (New York: Seabury, 1975).

3. Isaac M. Wise, "Our Country's Place in History," in *God's New Israel,* pp. 218–228.

4. John Dewey, *A Common Faith* (New Haven CT: Yale University Press, 1934), pp. 61–62.

5. Ibid., p. 87.

6. Reinhold Niebuhr, *The Irony of American History* (New York: Charles Scribner's Sons, 1952), pp. 66–67.

7. Ibid., p. 75.

8. See Eric Voegelin, *Science, Politics, and Gnosticism* (Chicago: Henry Regnery, 1968).

9. Niebuhr, *The Irony of American History,* p. 131.

PART Three

Recent Interests and Trends

The issue of securing peace for a world threatened by awesome destructive powers increasingly defines our estimates of contemporary cultural movements. (Peace on Earth, Jacques Lipchitz; the Nelson-Atkins Museum of Art, Kansas City, Missouri [Acquired through the Elmer F. Pierson Foundation])

This book so far has surveyed the history of American religion and the American religious worldview. It remains to bring the story up to date by suggesting the issues that have been most important during the past generation. Just as the historical survey had to be concise, and the presentation of the American worldview had to be a sketch, so this part can give only indications of recent developments on the American religious scene. Still the report should prove interesting when one sets it against the prior two parts as background, and reporting on recent developments provides another opportunity to assess what religion and American culture have done to one another through their interactions.

241

The Critique of Civil Religion

The Concept of Civil Religion

The central referent in discussions of American civil religion over the past two decades has been an essay by Robert N. Bellah, a leading sociologist of religion. This essay, "Civil Religion in America," appeared in the Winter 1967 issue of *Daedalus,* the quarterly journal of the American Academy of Arts and Sciences.

Bellah's essay begins with a reference to the inaugural speech of President Kennedy, given January 20, 1961, noting that it had three references to God (two early on and one near the end) that framed its central treatment of secular matters. After suggesting that this usage has been virtually customary for American presidents, and that critics or cynics might say that such usage shows the impotence of religion in American life, Bellah entered his own demurs:

> Considering the separation of church and state, how is a president justified in using the word *God* at all? The answer is that the separation of church and state has not denied the political realm a religious dimension. Although matters of personal religious belief, worship, and association are considered to be strictly private affairs, there are, at

the same time, certain common elements of religious orientation that the great majority of Americans share. These have played a crucial role in the development of American institutions and still provide a religious dimension for the whole fabric of American life, including the political sphere. This public religious dimension is expressed in a set of beliefs, symbols, and rituals that I am calling the American civil religion. The inauguration of a president is an important ceremonial event in this religion. It reaffirms, among other things, the religious legitimation of the highest political authority.[1]

Bellah went on to spell out the significance of the beliefs, symbols, and rituals that he found constituting American civil religion. As with the popular American motto, "In God we trust," the references of presidents such as Kennedy to divine power as the ultimate witness and sanction of both their oath-taking and their execution of their presidential responsibilities gave a boundary to the political authority vested in the American people. As a democratic realm, America has made the will of the people the source of practical political power, that is, election to office. Nonetheless, by regularly referring to divinity as the witness of its political processes, America has reminded itself that the will of human beings, which can be various and inconstant, is not the ultimate judge of right and wrong. However one defines *God* or the conscience that makes God its final judge, the references to divinity that one regularly finds in American political discourse have freed the spirits of all American citizens. The ultimate criterion of success or failure could not be the vagaries of political history. It had to be something less corruptible, something better answering the needs of the soul for genuine justice, for the occurrence of what ought to be (and would be were human existence fair).

American references to God as the ultimate source of human rights and political authority brim with overtones of the country's revolu-

tionary beginnings. When they rose up against the English monarchy, the American colonists appealed to a higher authority than the crown. The Declaration of Independence makes this plain. There can arise times, circumstances, historical crises when one has to oppose human law and authority, if one is to be faithful to conscience and higher, heavenly standards of justice. The Kennedy inaugural, like similar speeches of his predecessors, invoked this tradition, reaffirming its venerable delineation of the American sense of political conscience.

When Kennedy ended his inaugural address with the words, "here on earth God's work must truly be our own," to Bellah's mind he added to the notion that divine authority is the ultimate sanction of human politics the further notion that the political process has a goal transcending purely temporal concerns. Kennedy's words, with Bellah's commentary, offer another illustration of the thesis of Bellah's seminal study.

> Now the trumpet summons us again—not as a call to bear arms, though arms we need—not as a call to battle, though embattled we are—but as a call to bear the burden of a long twilight struggle, year in and year out, "rejoicing in hope, patient in tribulation"—a struggle against the common enemies of man: tyranny, poverty, disease, and war itself.[2]

Note how Bellah's exegesis of these lines brings them close to the theme of destiny elaborated in the last chapter.

> The whole address can be understood as only the most recent statement of a theme that lies very deep in the American tradition, namely the obligation, both collective and individual, to carry out God's will on earth. This was the motivating spirit of those who founded America, and it has been present in every generation since. Just below the surface throughout Kennedy's inaugural address, it becomes explicit in the closing statement that God's work must be our own. That this very activist and noncontemplative conception of the fundamental religious obligation, which has been

historically associated with the Protestant position, should be enunciated so clearly in the first major statement of the first Catholic president seems to underline how deeply established it is in the American outlook.[3]

Bellah enlarged his exposition of the historical forebears of Kennedy's remarks and the fuller implications of the concept of both past and contemporary civil religion. But it is sufficient to say that he argued that Kennedy's words represented a long-standing tradition, discernible in such Founding Fathers as Franklin, Washington, and Jefferson; that the experience of the Civil War wrought significant changes on the sense that the Revolution had given to civil religion; and that events of the 1960s had brought the entire matter up for review again, constituting a third trial of the viability of American civil religion.

Bellah could not take up such matters as the calculation that entered into Kennedy's, or any prior American politician's, use of religious language on civil occasions; the liabilities in understanding one's nation to have been commissioned to make God's work on earth its own; the limitations in making civil religion something activist and noncontemplative; the problems of working with an intrinsically nebulous conception of God and God's relations to politics; or the great advantages in fashioning a pluralistic culture. In part because of these further issues, many treatments of American civil religion are more dismissive than laudatory. Theologians tend to find civil religion like near beer, tepid and tame. Political and cultural analysts tend to find civil religion but a grace note, a bow tied to a secular package of willfulness and infighting. For philosophers like Reinhold Niebuhr, however, American civil religion was not so unworthy of respect. In the course of history, the span of world empires, what the Founding Fathers worked out for this nation can seem truly extraordinary. To John Courtney Murray, coming not from the Protestant tradition that nourished Niebuhr and most of the civil religionists but from Kennedy's Catholic tradition, civil religion could express something natural but God given and God supported, something validly the basis for political and civil cooperation and so considerably to be praised. Indeed, for Sidney Mead, civil religion has stood in counterpoint with the American decision to have no established church—a decision Mead considered as monumental as the establishment of the Church under Constantine in the fourth century.

Church-State Relations

Civil religion, of course, is related to the way that a given nation or culture handles the interactions between its politics and its religion. Until modern times, most cultures had a hard time separating religion and politics. For example, ancient India relied on the myth of the division of the primal man into four parts to legitimate its caste system, ancient China considered Confucianism the interpretation of a tradition antedating history and grounded in the sacred rhythms of the cosmos, ancient Rome joined the offices of the emperor and the priest as two overlapping sites of the holy authority running the world, and ancient Egypt considered the Pharaoh the prime mediator of *maat*, cosmic law. Even ancient Israel, the biblical people of God, considered the king sacred, as revealed by David's references to the holiness of the person of Saul. Christianity broke with this pattern in challenging the divinity of the Roman emperor and opening the church to all nations, but the emperors anointed in Christendom carried a priestly authority, while the monarchical style that developed in the papacy, and the popes' interest in wielding secular influence, show that Catholic Christianity felt many urges to keep church and state unified.

It does not matter, at this point, that Christianity traditionally claimed to be a revealed religion, unique in its rights and truth. In fact Christians often lived under pagan or Muslim rulers, as in recent times they have lived under militantly atheistic regimes. Moreover, the divisions among Christians produced at least the forerunners of the modern debates about religious pluralism, most vehemently so in the wake of the 16th-century Protestant Reformation. The civil religion envisioned by the American Founding Fathers was more negative than positive—more a veto on the establishment of a particular Christian church as the religious authority of the land than a constructive effort to develop a faith based on something transcending all denominational differences. Indeed the usual criticism of civil religion one hears from theologians is that it is based on the least common denominators, the sort of doctrines proposed by Rousseau (the originator of the term *civil religion*): belief in the existence of God, afterlife, reward for virtue and punishment for vice, and tolerance of others' views.

At any rate the civil religion of a given regime clearly will be what its churches and state work together to make the common ground that all citizens can be presumed to share. What can both political and religious leaders reasonably assume that Americans traditionally believe about the ultimate matters orienting their culture? Inasmuch as American leaders have assumed that most Americans believe in a divinity transcending the world and providing judgment on human actions, they have referred to such a divinity in their speeches and perhaps have taken such a divinity into account when they have made their political calculations.

No one church or theological tradition has monopolized the language or symbols used in American civil religion, though clearly biblical language and symbols have been prominent and Christian faith (largely Protestant) has been at least tacitly assumed the most appropriate

This classical American Protestant church reminds us of the fusion of Christian piety and patriotism that has shaped American civil religion. (Photo by J. T. Carmody)

interpretation. Many American politicians have been more interested in morality than in theology proper, thinking the main utility of religion its influence on citizens' behavior. Indeed, there could be no theological orthodoxy in the case of American civil religion or in the cases of the civil religions of other countries espousing religious pluralism and nonestablishment. One of the principal dogmas of civil religion, in fact, was that religious dogma (especially on the model of Roman Catholic utterances) did not fit the American religious scene, where tolerance was both a practical necessity and, increasingly, a good in its own right.

In his recent study of religion and politics in America, Richard McBrien has found it necessary to devote his opening chapters to clarifying terms and laying out connections that apply to the church-state discussion. Having noted that religion and morality are not the same thing, McBrien moves on to note that religion should not be confused with church.

> If morality has been confused with religion, so has religion been confused with church. Again and again, participants in the debate about religion in U.S. public life have cast the discussion in church-state terms, as if religion were identical with Christianity. This has been true not only of politicians and journalists but of religious leaders as well, some of whom believe that the United States of America is a Christian nation or at least one founded on so-called Judeo-Christian principles.
>
> The confusion has not been limited to the morality/religion/church side of the dialectic. State and society have also been collapsed into one. The separation of church and *state* has been understood as the separation of church and *society,* even though the state is only a part of society. The church-and-state relationship is of a much more limited kind. It governs the juridical relationship of the institution of the church and the institution of the state. . . .
>
> We take it as a matter of constitutional principle that Christians in the United States have as much right as any other citizens to participate

fully in the public life of the nation and in U.S. society generally. We also take it as a matter of constitutional principle that the church in the United States has as much right as any other voluntary association to participate fully in the public life of the nation and in U.S. society generally.[4]

McBrien is trying to break through the unthinking coalescence of notions that frequently obscures the analysis of church-state issues. In his lexicon, the separation of church and state does not mean the separation of either morality or religion from public life, nor the separation of church and society. Only when one has a church, a body institutionalizing religion, attempting to dominate the state, the official political arm of society, does one have a violation of the separate church-state relationship enshrined in the Constitution. Similarly, only when one has the state trying to infringe individual or collective religious liberty does one have the constitutional relationship wronged from the other end. Consequently there is great room for religious, moral, and church activity in society, while there is also great room for state interest in religion, morality, and church life.

Our traditions of free speech and lobbying allow religious citizens to make their views known and bring them to bear on the political process, just as they allow nonreligious citizens to do so. The only problem comes when a religious body, a church, synagogue, mosque, or atheistic equivalent, would attempt to control state (secular) policy, or when the state would interfere with the liberty of private citizens to practice their religious faith. Problems of definition and practice still remain. For example, is prohibiting blood transfusions a legitimate expression of religious belief, or can, or should, the state so regulate medical practice as to override claims to such a prohibition based on religious grounds? But McBrien has in fact delineated the main paths.

It remains to be said that by accepting civil religion on the model of Bellah's description, Americans have let themselves in for many legal,

American religious thinkers have always worried that prosperity (considered as a sign of divine favor) might become an end in itself and that comfort might overly domesticate the tough temper of biblical religion. (Bedroom, ca 1830; The Nelson-Atkins Museum of Art, Kansas City, Missouri [Nelson Fund])

philosophical, political, and theological battles over how precisely to work out an allowance, even an encouragement, of religion (as part of the country's basic patrimony and cultural conviction) that will be evenhanded toward particular religionists and will not discriminate against nonreligionists. That has been the price Americans have been willing to pay to honor the general religious convictions at their historical and cultural wellsprings, the individual's freedom to practice or not practice a given religion, and the tolerance necessary in a pluralistic society.

Secularism

There has always been secularism in the American civil religion. From the first a few Americans were unbelievers, many Americans were unchurched, and leading American politicians were more interested in the this-worldly uses of religion than in religion's transcendent truths. If we define *secularism* as concentrating most of one's time and energy on this-worldly affairs and giving little thought to the transcendent truths (or claims) of religion, it is clear that American culture in general has long had a substantial secular component. It is less clear how that component has affected American civil religion. A first impression might be that much American civil religion has been sufficiently vague and nonthreatening (weak in its claims for transcendent truths) to allow religious or unreligious secularists to tolerate it without qualm. For example, the references to God and religious duties that have run through the typical American celebration of the Fourth of July, Memorial Day, Labor Day, and even Thanksgiving usually have been innocuous enough to cause little pain to people focused on this-worldly business and uneasy with concerns about transcendent meaning. Even the inauguration speeches of presidents could be passed off as customary, a set of code words for high-mindedness, a bow of reverence to the symbols from which American culture arose but which recent generations had left far behind.

During the same 1960s that witnessed debates about American civil religion, there were perhaps more vigorous debates about secularism: what it was; whether it was compatible with religious faith; whether it was required by biblical faith (as some argued); what it meant for dialogue with Marxists, scientists, and atheists; how it related to the spirituality proper to people "come of age"; whether theologians such as Dietrich Bonhoeffer, who spoke of the need to live "as if God were not given," had not signaled the beginning of a time when religion would turn away from transcendence. The book that collected many of these currents and catalyzed discussion in the United States was Harvey Cox's *The Secular City*. Cox argued that secularization was both a fact of modern culture and good for Christianity, something that theologians and laity alike would ideally combine with urbanization to make the wave of the religious future. By concentrating on this-worldly matters of social justice, politics, and (by extension) culture generally, Christians might be truer to such mandates from the Bible as the need to fill

the earth and subdue it, the need to incarnate the love of God in love of brothers and sisters (especially the poor and suffering), and the need to revamp a Western religious heritage rightly criticized since the Enlightenment as tending to alienate people from themselves and the earth.

The result of this debate and discussion, as one might have predicted, was a significant acceptance of the importance of making religion respectable in this-worldly terms but a rejection of any all-out advocacy of secularization that would deny the traditional sense that divinity had values, rights, and purposes beyond human concerns and ken. In short the debate called forth many contemplative spirits who refused to give up on prayer, liturgy, consecrated religious life, and other familiar expressions of the nonpragmatic, otherworldly side of faith. Indeed, within a few years Cox himself was writing about play and celebration, in an effort to balance the one-sided stress on the secular and political that his blockbuster book had featured.

But the fact that theologians on the whole have sorted out the implications of secularization quite well has not lessened the phenomenon, nor has it lessened the urgency of analyzing how secularization has been changing traditional American ideas about national destiny and civil religion. The phenomenon of secularization has many causes but the outstanding factors seem to be the technology and science that have allowed human beings increasingly to master nature and communications that have shrunk the globe and enticed many people into predominantly instrumentalist (technical) ways of thinking (to the detriment of the holistic, contemplative ways that nourish a sense of divine mystery). Some analysts of American secularization would add urbanization and consumerism as other contributing factors. Each of the aforementioned factors has tended to immerse people in this-worldly concerns and weakened the hold of transcendent images, concerns for experiences of God, or other ecstatic experiences that might call the adequacy of this-worldly concerns into question.

Whatever one points to as the sources of secularization, the fact seems to be that in recent decades transcendence has become a less familiar notion than it would have been a century ago, let alone in the days when Jonathan Edwards was preaching in western Massachusetts. On the other hand, though the old language may not sit well with the typical middle-class, reasonably well-educated American today, some analysts argue that certain features of the life cycle and ordinary human fate keep the old questions about transcendence alive and kicking. Death and suffering continue to make many Americans face the question of what their lives are about and what they want to concentrate their small vial of time on. Profound experiences of love, beauty, creativity, and an unearthly harmony signaling the divine continue to convince many that money, banking, pleasure, politics, sports, and even family responsibilities—the typical preoccupations emphasized by secularization—cannot be the be-all and end-all of life.

Critics of secularization have said that peak experiences, whether of pain or of joy, still challenge the flat, rather two-dimensional world induced by secularization. Whether one labels the transcendence carried in such a challenge religious or humanistic (the upper reaches of human potential, but not requiring a God radically other than the human realm), it can stop the flow of secularization and bring back into focus the unanswerable but crucial questions that have always defined the human being: Where have we come from? Where are we going? For what ought we to live? For what should we be willing to die? What can save us from our twistedness? What does our thirst for immortality, justice, and holiness mean?

Those who see the American traditions of civil religion as simply a veneer for secularism

take such questions as a radical challenge to American civil religion. Usually they ask that American culture not continue to define *tolerance* as the avoidance of deep questions about faith and its passions. They are convinced that such passions are necessary if one is to honor the radical questions implied in being fully human and need not precipitate unholy war. Those who consider the American traditions of civil religion handsome achievements, perhaps especially in their enablement of civility in American debates about deeper matters, tend to view secularization more benignly. Many of the latter, in fact, think that religion continues to do its best work by organizing human beings as Kennedy's inaugural suggested: to fight tyranny, poverty, disease, and war. (Note that tyranny comes first, as though in tacit tribute to the priority Americans have placed on liberty and individual freedoms, not the least of which have concerned religion.)

Secularism, with its implication of dismissing traditional religion, tends to find only a few militant supporters nowadays. The style of John Dewey has passed from mainstream popularity because more experience of human potential has shaken our confidence that we can manage our might to the betterment of either humankind or Mother Earth. Thus civil religion, like all religion, is beset by challenges on many sides to show its utility, to prove that it makes a difference. Therefore secularization continues to be a refining fire urging those who clarify its implications and effects to ask quite pointedly what any people ought to be living for.

Reassessing the Past: Lyman Beecher

A representative figure from the past may prove a good case study in which to find both positive and negative potential in American civil religion. Lyman Beecher (1775–1863) lived almost precisely the span from the American Revolution to the Civil War. Graduating from Yale in 1797, Beecher held Presbyterian pastorates in Connecticut and Boston, distinguishing himself for his opposition to rationalism, Catholicism, and liquor. In his later career he became an eloquent advocate of the interests of the western frontier, working at Lane Theological Seminary in Cincinnati. Among the 13 children of his three marriages, Henry Ward Beecher and Harriet Beecher Stowe now stand out, but several others were influential educators, feminists, and religious leaders.

Lyman Beecher's entries into controversy included his attacks on Catholic convents and potential Catholic influence in the expanding West. To his mind the civility of American religion reposed in its Protestant traditions, so he was loathe to witness the influx of Catholic immigrants that began with the Irish fleeing from famine before the Civil War. In Beecher the attitudes of the Puritan colonists remained strong. Not only did he think of the United States as a nation formed by people fleeing religious oppression, but also he frequently specified such oppression as signally represented by the dogmatisms of Rome, popish superstitions, and the like. Thus convents were abominations because they symbolized the way the Catholic church wanted to keep young women in thrall, while Catholic influence on the western frontier would have blunted, if not perverted, the extension of the holy errand in the wilderness that had consecrated colonial New England. The West was the vanguard of American destiny, so in his plea that America care for western expansion Beecher definitely subscribed to the myth of America's providential role in the world and tried to forward it.

In August of 1834 a Protestant mob burned the Ursuline convent in Charlestown, Massachusetts. Some observers tried to link this attack to a sermon that Lyman Beecher had preached just before it, though there is little evidence that any in the mob had heard him speak. While making his "Plea for the West," Beecher had described popery as a despotism having hostile designs on America. The burning of the convent caused such an uproar among the increasingly strong Catholic population of Boston that Catholic priests had to help restore order and blunt the threat of counterviolence.

Beecher's further views appear in the following paragraph describing the situation, and they illustrate where what in retrospect we might call American civil religion (the conception of how religion related to Americanism) stood 40 years after the establishment of a constitution guaranteeing religious liberty and the equality of all faiths under the law.

> For what was the city of Boston for five nights under arms—her military upon the alert—her citizens enrolled, and a body of five hundred men constantly patrolling the streets? Why were the accustomed lectures for public worship, and other public secular meetings, suspended? Why were the citizens, at the sound of bell, convened at midday in Fanueil Hall?—to hear Catholicism eulogized, and thanksgivings offered to his reverence the bishop for his merciful protection of the children of the Pilgrims? And why by the cradle of liberty, and under the shadow of Bunker's Hill, did men turn pale, and whisper, and look over their shoulders and around to ascertain whether it were safe to speak aloud, or meet to worship God? Has it come to this, that the capital of New England has been thrown into consternation by the threats of a Catholic mob, and that her temples and mansions stand only through the forbearance of a Catholic bishop? There can be no liberty in the presence of such masses of dark mind, and of such despotic power over it in a single man. Safety on such terms is not the protection of law, but of single-handed despotism. Will our great cities consent to receive protection from the Catholic priesthood, dependent on the Catholic powers of Europe, and favored by his Holiness, who is himself governed by the bayonets of Austria? . . . The Catholic effervescence, though it obstructed for the moment, aided us on the whole. It was a

favourable providence, which called me back to speak in undaunted tones, when, without someone to explain, and take correct ground, and inspire courage, all were likely to quail and be carried away. Before I left the tide turned, and Catholicism forever in New England must row up stream, carefully watched, and increasingly understood and obstructed by public sentiment.[5]

The paragraph does Beecher no credit by today's ecumenical standards; a phrase such as "such masses of dark mind" carries an ugly bigotry. Yet biographers of Beecher laud his overall largeness of mind,[6] and one must remember the historical context (a New England both fearful of Catholic newcomers and thrown back by their presence on a prideful reassertion of New England's Protestant contributions to the Revolution that founded the United States) as well as the whole history of mutual bigotry among different religious groups in the United States.[7]

What this provides in the consideration of civil religion is an antidote to any saccharine view of civic religion as all sweet tolerance and cooperation. Just as American ideals of civil liberty failed of achievement in such signal areas as the treatment of slaves, Native Americans, women, and many immigrant groups (perhaps especially Latin Americans and Asians, many of whom might claim that prejudice remains strong to this day), so American ideals of religious liberty and civility frequently failed and Catholics, Jews, Mormons, and various sectarian groups frequently suffered as a result. In their turn some groups who experienced prejudice and were not treated equally because of bias against their religious traditions both gave reason for Protestant fears, at least on occasion, and could return dislike for dislike.

The positive side of civil religion, its virtuous contributions to American pluralism and peace, should not blind us to its failures. It has often been assumed that American religion was a generalized version of Protestant Christianity and those who did not subscribe to this view of

American religion were (in contravention of the First Amendment of the Constitution) treated as second-class citizens. Whatever the merits of the intervention of the American Civil Liberties Union in recent legal cases, the historical record shows that there were ample reasons why such an organization needed to come into being. The historical record also shows that immigrant groups were wise to found their labor unions and gain collective representation to bargain with business management, even though on occasion such labor unions themselves caused problems, even helping to divide the country along ethnic, racial, and religious lines. Lyman Beecher was simply being a man of his day, a captive of the prejudices of his day, when he expressed his limited understanding of American civil religion. To the present day all sorts of religious and secular groups show themselves similarly limited in their understanding of how America ought both to honor the religious instinct of its majority and to avoid infringing the equality it promises all its citizens under the law.

Writings of John Courtney Murray

John Courtney Murray (1904–1967) was a Jesuit priest, for many years the editor of the most influential American Catholic journal of theology, *Theological Studies,* and the principal architect of the Vatican II Decree on Religious Liberty. Throughout his career, Murray was stimulated by his admiration for the American achievement to reflect on traditional Catholic teaching about the religious rights of majorities and minorities in pluralistic cultural situations. The Catholic position prior to Vatican II had stressed religious freedom for Catholics when they were a minority but privileges for Catholics, if not outright establishment, when Catholics were a majority. The rationale for this position was that Catholicism was the truest faith—

the version of God's own revealed religion, Christianity, that best comported with Scripture and tradition.

From his extensive reading in American history and wide contacts with Protestant Americans Murray knew how offensive this Catholic position was. Through studies in the history of Catholic thought on relations between the ecclesiastical and secular realms, he found more flexibility than the theology of his Roman superiors granted. Murray published his findings in *Theological Studies* but ran afoul of the Vatican and was told to cease airing his views. He complied with the letter of this command but continued to research the topic and converse with American intellectuals.

The *Decree on Religious Liberty* of the Second Vatican Council vindicated Murray's position. Indeed Murray wrote much of the draft of the decree. By that time Catholic authorities had become convinced that the religious pluralism of modern states was not entirely bad. They had also become convinced that freedom of conscience was a God-given right, and that to abridge it, especially in the matter of religious observance, was offensive to God. Few Catholic authorities acknowledged the debt they owed Protestantism for this insight, but many Catholic theologians did. They specifically recognized that the American experiment in religious pluralism, undertaken under Protestant auspices, had been the laboratory in which the political consequences of religious liberty had been clarified.

When John Courtney Murray represented his Catholic tradition at American discussions of church-state relations, he drew not only on specifically theological notions of the movement of God in the human conscience but also on the natural law theory highly developed by the medieval scholastic thinkers Catholicism revered. Natural law offered a basis for discussion that did not appeal to special revelation or religious tradition. Supposedly any person could follow

the rationale of a natural law argument, because supposedly its only appeal was to common human experience and reason. Recently many commentators have suggested that natural law theory usually did assume theological foundations and scaffolding, but exponents such as Murray could invite those of other faiths or no faith to discuss matters such as church-state relations and religious liberty apart from theology.

Defending natural law theory against the modern liberal thinkers who had derided it, Murray offered a sophisticated interpretation of both the balance and the history that such theory should have implied:

> First, natural-law theory does not pretend to do more than it can, which is to give a philosophical account of the moral experience of humanity and to lay down a charter of essential humanism. It does not show the individual the way to sainthood, but only to manhood. It does not promise to transform society into the City of God on earth, but only to prescribe, for the purposes of law and social custom, that minimum of morality which must be observed by the members of a society, if the social environment is to be human and habitable. At that, for a man to be reasonably human, and for a society to be essentially civil—these are no mean achievements. The ideal of the reasonable man, who does his duty to God, to others, and to himself, is not an ignoble one. In fact, it puts such a challenge to the inertness and perversity which are part of the human stuff, that Christian doctrine from the day of St. Augustine has taught the necessity of divine grace for this integral fulfillment of the natural law.
>
> ... The Christian call is to transcend nature, notably to transcend what is noblest in nature, the faculty of reason. But it is not a call to escape from nature, or to dismantle nature's own structure, and least of all to deny that man is intelligent, that nature is intelligible, and that nature's intelligibilities are laws for the mind that grasps them. Insofar as they touch the moral life, the energies of grace, which are the action of the Holy Spirit, quicken to new and fuller life the dyna-

misms of nature, which are resident in reason. Were it otherwise, grace would not be supernatural but only miraculous. . . .

At about the turn of the century it was rather generally believed in professional circles that the Scholastic idea of natural law, as an operative concept in the fields of ethics, political theory, and law and jurisprudence was dead. In other words, it was generally assumed that the great 19th-century attack on natural law [much of it launched in the name either of a more historical understanding of human nature or of an atheism denying any creator of human nature] had been successful. In this respect, of course, the 19th century exhibited those extensive powers of learned misunderstanding which it possessed to an astonishing degree. In its extraordinary ignorance of philosophical and legal history, it supposed that the "law of nature" of the Age of the Enlightenment was the *jus naturale* of an earlier and in many ways more enlightened age. It supposed therefore that in doing away with the former, it had likewise done away with the latter. This was by no means the case. The theory of the "law of nature" that was the creature of the Enlightenment was as fragile, time-conditioned, and transitory a phenomenon as the Enlightenment itself. But the ancient idea of the natural law is as inherently perennial as the *philosophia prerennis* of which it is an integral part. Its reappearance after its widely attended funeral is one of the interesting intellectual phenomena of our generation.[8]

Murray's articulation of the relation between nature and grace is classically Catholic, arguing for their junction in the proposition that grace builds on nature (to preserve and fulfill nature). It rejects the attempt of much Protestant theology to leap over nature and deal only with gospel imperatives of love. In terms of political ramifications, it offers a basis on which all people of good will might discuss their common problems and cooperate to solve them. Murray's own view of human nature yields little to Reinhold Niebuhr in minimalism: Irrationality and wickedness are strewn across the historical record. He agrees that people cannot be fully

human unless they open themselves to transhuman powers. But he does not deprecate human reason or will, and he is more hopeful about the capacity of human beings to bracket their special allegiances, including those of religion, and discuss what their common nature and citizenship require of them if they are jointly to promote the common good.

On the precise question of civil religion, which was not Murray's particular interest, the inference might be that natural law furnishes a respectable version of the orientation of human beings to a power beyond themselves. This power is indeed the ultimate sanction for political authority and the ultimate judge of how well such authority has been exercised. Only a fool would deny the historical influence of Christianity (more precisely Protestant Christianity) in the formation of American traditions of citizenship and patriotism. But no single interpretation of humanity's responsibilities to God ought to have a privileged place in a pluralistic society, command the schools or courts, or in any other way ride roughshod over the rights of religious minorities and nonreligious citizens. In short neither Lyman Beecher nor Cardinal Ottaviani (the head of the Holy Office in Rome that tried to quash Murray's work on church-state relations and retain the traditional Catholic claims to privileged treatment) would be a good interpreter of the relations between secular and religious realms in a pluralistic society on the American model.

Key Terms

Natural Law: what can be inferred about the rights and obligations incumbent on all human beings, on the basis of historical experience and rational analysis. Natural law theory assumes that God, the source of creation, has worked rationally and so encoded in all creatures "laws" governing their actions. Human beings are the peculiar creatures endowed with reason and freedom, so the laws special to them pertain to moral rather than physical actions. The most general moral law encoded in human nature is that people are to do good and avoid evil. The more one descends from this general law to particular situations and obligations, the more one has to consult experience, on-the-spot analyses, and the virtue of prudence. Proponents of natural law theory have tended to think that human beings able to agree that God has made an intelligible creation ought to be able to reach sufficient agreement about the basic nature of humankind and the basic ends of society to nurture the ongoing discussion and collaboration necessary for promoting the common weal, avoiding war, and prosecuting prosperity (decent material living and the flourishing of higher culture).

Discussion Questions

1. Explain Bellah's sentence, "This public religious dimension is expressed in a set of beliefs, symbols, and rituals that I am calling the American civil religion."
2. How does the American notion that the political process has a goal transcending purely temporal concerns relate to American views of national destiny?
3. How efficacious have Rousseau's elements of a civil religion (belief in the existence of God, afterlife, reward and punishment, and tolerance) been in American history?
4. Why does Richard McBrien want to limit the church-and-state relationship to something less than the relation between religion and society?
5. What is the relation between technology and secularization?

6. How does secularism currently vitiate American traditions of civil religion?
7. What aspects of traditional Catholicism gave Lyman Beecher legitimate pause about its fitness for the American pluralistic scene?
8. What do the many unofficial enfringements on religious liberty throughout American history suggest about the need to temper Christian assumptions and promote the appreciation of other religious traditions?
9. How does John Courtney Murray's Catholic sense of the relations between nature and grace differ from those of traditional Protestantism?
10. What are the main problems with thinking about civil religion in terms of natural law?

Notes

1. Robert N. Bellah, "Civil Religion in America," in *Religion in America,* ed. William G. McLoughlin and Robert N. Bellah (Boston: Houghton Mifflin, 1968), pp. 5–6.

2. Ibid., p. 7.

3. Ibid., p. 7.

4. Richard P. McBrien, *Caesar's Coin: Religion and Politics in America* (New York: Macmillan, 1987), pp. 42–43.

5. Barbara M. Cross, ed., *The Autobiography of Lyman Beecher,* vol. 2 (Cambridge MA: Belknap/Harvard, 1961), pp. 251–252.

6. See, for example, Stuart Henry, *Unvanquished Puritan: A Portrait of Lyman Beecher* (Grand Rapids MI: Eerdmans, 1973).

7. See Robert N. Bellah and Frederick E. Greenspahn, eds., *Uncivil Religion: Interreligious Hostility in America* (New York: Crossroad, 1987).

8. John Courtney Murray, S.J.: *We Hold These Truths: Catholic Reflections on the American Proposition* (New York: Sheed and Ward, 1960), pp. 297–299.

18

Ecumenism

The Protestant Ecumenical Movement

American civil religion both sponsored a tendency among Americans to seek common religious and patriotic ground, where their denominational differences might recede into the background, and tolerated considerable incivility or hostility among different religious groups. After the Second World War many Americans were affected by a worldwide ecumenical movement among Christians. The word *ecumenical* comes from a Greek word meaning "the entire inhabited world." Christian tradition had employed *ecumenical* when referring to the early Church councils that had gathered bishops from many areas and produced doctrinal decisions considered binding on the entire Church.

However, the various **schisms** and **heresies** that had sundered Christianity had somewhat mocked the Church's ideal of worldwide catholicity and unity. The worst of these ecclesiastical fractures were the sundering of East and West in 1054 and the further sundering of the western Church during the 16th-century Protestant Reformation. In the early 20th century—

partly as a response to the experience of missionaries in Africa and Asia, who saw with fresh eyes the damage done to Christian credibility by competition and antagonism among the different churches—some European Protestants conceived the idea of working to reunite the sisters and brothers who had been separated for many centuries.

> In 1910, a number of missionary societies held a conference in Edinburgh, Scotland, that by common consent is described as the birth of the modern ecumenical movement. The purpose of the conference was to develop a common missionary strategy that would not only avoid the scandal of the past but provide for a more creative and collaborative use of resources in the future.[1]

In addition to this missionary impetus, there were two other developments in the ecumenical movement. The first was a series of pan-Protestant conferences on life and work held in Stockholm (1925) and Oxford (1937) that drew delegates from many different countries. The second was a series of faith and order conferences held in Lausanne (1927) and Edinburgh (1937), which included both Protestant and Eastern Orthodox representatives.

The 1937 conferences took place under the advancing shadow of Hitler and the Second World War, but before war broke out the life and work group had merged with the faith and order group and met in Utrecht (1938) to work out a proposal for a world council of churches. After the war the World Council of Churches became a reality at Amsterdam in 1948. The initial organization was essentially a fusion of the churches that had participated in the life and work and faith and order conferences, but in 1961 they were joined by the churches that had been active in the International Missionary Council.

> Some 146 churches—Protestant, Anglican, and Orthodox—were the original members of the World Council of Churches. During World War II,

a skeleton staff in Geneva engaged in refugee relief and found various ways for Christians to communicate across the national barriers created by the war. The person most responsible during these interim years, W. A. Visser 't Hooft, a Dutch lay theologian, was elected the first general secretary of the World Council of Churches, and permanent headquarters were established in Geneva. At the time of its creation, the World Council of Churches defined itself as "composed of churches which acknowledge Jesus Christ as God and Savior." From the beginning the WCC has made clear (despite misunderstanding by outsiders) that its task is "to serve the churches," not to become a superchurch itself or to be a Protestant/Orthodox counterpart to the Vatican.[2]

In 1950 American Protestants, following the lead of the World Council of Churches, formed the National Council of Churches of Christ in the United States. At the outset this body was formed by merging 12 national interdenominational agencies already in existence. Like the World Council of Churches, the National Council of Churches conceived of itself as a service agency, not a superchurch. Its purpose was to offer an organized structure through which member churches could express their common faith and cooperate on practical programs. The ecumenical activities sponsored by the National Council have included study of the faith and order of the church; work on revising the English Bible; development of materials on evangelism, religious education, and family life; promotion of religious and moral values in the communications media; encouragement of such women's organizations as Church Women United; and sponsorship of prayer and observances for Christian unity. The National Council has been a clearinghouse for materials from overseas, as well as a source of contact with overseas churches. It has channeled funds collected in response to overseas emergencies and sponsored programs to fight such domestic and foreign evils as illiteracy, disease, hunger, and overpopulation. The National Council has also produced critiques of American economic, social, and foreign policies, sometimes to the dismay of its more conservative members or churches not willing to become members. In the 1970s it reorganized its work in terms of four major programs: Christian Life and Mission, Overseas Ministries, Christian Education, and Christian Unity. Membership rolls in the mid-1980s counted 32 Protestant and Eastern Orthodox churches as full members, while more than 40 other churches, including conservative Protestants and Roman Catholics, cooperated with some National Council programs.

A major tension in Protestant ecumenism during the past decade and a half has focused on the World Council of Churches' Program to Combat Racism, which has assigned money each year to groups around the world working to oppose racism and repression. This program has been abhorrent to some conservative churches, which believe it encourages violent protests in third world countries, especially Africa. Overall, however, the Protestant ecumenical movement has brought to center stage the question of the Church's unity and need for concerted action in its witness to the gospel.

Theologians have made considerable progress in resolving doctrinal tensions between different Protestant traditions, some of which go back to shortly after the Lutheran and Calvinistic reformations. Cooperation on practical programs, especially those for social relief, has also helped to lower historic barriers. The impetus throughout has been not simply to make Protestant Christianity more effective in its inner communion or outer missions but, perhaps more profoundly, to bring the churches face to face with what all have agreed is a divine imperative: Christ's will (expressed in such biblical passages as John 17) that his followers be one.

In the gospel of John the unity of Christ's followers is intimately tied to the unity of the trinitarian persons. The unity within the godhead ought to find a reflection in the unity among the members of Christ, who are like branches to his vine. Moreover, the unity of Christ's followers ought to be the great sign to the world that the Father sent the Son (for salvation) and that the Father loves the world as He loves the Son. Knowing of such love, feeling it in the Holy Spirit, seeing its good effects in the union among Christ's believers, the world might embrace the salvation God offers it.

Ecumenical reunion therefore has been nothing gimmicky or cosmetic. Reading the Bible seriously, most Protestant ecumenical theologians have found church unity to be of the essence of their faith, an elemental component of their sense of how both the being and the mission of the church were constituted. This conviction has been the glue keeping the Protestant ecumenical movement together despite the inevitable wrangles and disagreements among the member churches.

Vatican II

The initial Roman Catholic response to the Protestant ecumenical movement was at best hesitant and frequently rather negative. Because of Roman Catholic convictions about the schismatic or heretical character of the Protestant churches, the Roman Catholic Church did not join the World Council of Churches. Indeed it did not even send observers to the first assemblies at Amsterdam (1948) and Evanston (1954).

Nonetheless, some Catholic theologians, mainly in Europe, developed contacts with Protestants (in some cases extending collaborations vital during the war years), and by 1961, Pope John XXIII was permitting Catholic observers at the third World Council of Churches assembly in New Delhi. In turn John XXIII invited Protestant churches to send observers to the Second Vatican Council (1962–1965), where a new era of Protestant-Catholic relations dawned.

Among the main strides immediately made by the council (often called Vatican II) were its affirmation of the long-standing sense of Protestants that the church is always in need of reform, its introduction of Catholic matters to the mainstream of Protestant church life by inviting Protestant observers, its development of many warm personal relations that broke down traditional barriers, its attention to missionary bishops who had collaborated with Protestants and knew the price church division extracted in missionary territories, and its production of documents on both church life and ecumenism that took new account of Protestant doctrinal positions and realities.

For example, in its decree on missionary activity (#15), the council said

> To the extent that their beliefs are common, they [Catholics and Noncatholics] can make before the nations a common profession of faith in God and in Jesus Christ. They can collaborate in social and in technical projects as well as in cultural and religious ones. Let them work together especially for the sake of Christ, their common Lord. Let His Name be the bond that unites them! This cooperation should be undertaken not only among private persons, but also, according to the judgment of the local Ordinary [bishop], among Churches or ecclesial Communities and their enterprises.[3]

In its decree on Ecumenism, the council praised the ecumenical movement, urged Catholics to pray for their "separated brethren," allowed for joint prayer on special occasions, and urged that ecumenism become an important component of theological studies, including those forming bishops, priests, and missionaries.

Perhaps the most significant ecumenical progress achieved by the council, however, came when it granted church status to Protestant bodies and began dealing with them as true churches. In other words, the council went beyond affirming that individual separated brethren might possess good faith and do good works, and began to speak positively about churches not in communion with Rome. Thus its decree on ecumenism (#3) said

> The brethren divided from us also carry out many of the sacred actions of the Christian religion. Undoubtedly, in ways that vary according to the condition of each Church or Community, these actions can truly engender a life of grace, and can be rightly described as capable of providing access to the community of salvation. It follows that these separated Churches and Communities, though we believe they suffer from defects already mentioned, have by no means been deprived of significance and importance in the mystery of salvation.[4]

The council was a venture in compromise between progressive and conservative factions within Roman Catholicism. On many matters, including ecumenism, its documents were at pains both to open new avenues of thought and to reaffirm traditional Catholic convictions. Thus the writers of the decree on ecumenism, which praised the separated brethren as providing access to the community of salvation (surely the major function of any church), felt obliged to say (#19): "One should recognize that between these Churches and Communities, on the one hand, and the Catholic Church on the other, there are very weighty differences not only of a historical, sociological, psychological, and cultural nature, but especially in the interpretation of revealed truth."[5] Thus in 1965 there was Catholic-Protestant ecumenical progress, but the road to reunion still seemed a long one.

To indicate where American Catholic theology has gone with the initiatives of Vatican II, and to suggest where the thorniest issues remain, it may be helpful to consider the question of intercommunion. Intercommunion denotes sharing the eucharist or Lord's Supper across denominational lines. It conjures up images of Orthodox and Anglicans, or Catholics and Lutherans, celebrating one eucharist at which

The Episcopal Divinity School in Cambridge,
Massachusetts, a member of the Boston Theological
Institute, is typical of the church institutions that have
joined larger, ecumenical ventures. (Photo by J. T.
Carmody)

members of both churches take the sacrament
("commune"). Richard P. McBrien, who was
quoted on church-state relations in Chapter 17,
is a leading American Catholic theologian who,
in a large work on Catholicism, approaches the
issue of intercommunion as follows:

> It is not clear what finally determines the possi-
> bility of eucharistic sharing. Some churches within
> the Body of Christ [the community formed by all
> Christian believers]—e.g., Catholic, Anglican,
> Orthodox, and to a lesser extent Lutheran—already
> agree in principle on most, if not practically all,
> major matters of faith, including even the Real
> Presence of Christ [in the eucharist] and the sac-

rificial nature of the Eucharist. What, then, keeps
these churches from formal intercommunion?

> It would seem that, while common faith is a
> necessary condition for intercommunion, some-
> thing is required beyond common faith, namely,
> a recognition that the other party or community
> really is a member of one's Christian family and
> should permanently be welcome to enjoy table
> fellowship with us. There is a mystery of recon-
> ciliation here which has its secular analogue in
> the reconciliation of friends or of relatives who
> have fallen out of favor with one another. Only
> time and some generous and gracious gestures
> can heal the wounds. A precipitous or prema-
> turely arranged "reconciliation" can do more harm

than good. Such an occasion can be painful, or at least awkward and uncomfortable, for both sides. The same situation apparently obtains in the Body of Christ today.[6]

One might add several background or contextual comments.

1. Many Christians consider the eucharist the peak of Christian sacramental faith, the place where the mysteries Christians confess come to their most acute focus: the symbolic reception of the salvation and divine life, the personal intimacy of love, that Christ offers the believer.

2. The analogy of the family table raises the question: If churches feel unable to share communion, are they members of the same (most comprehensive) family, the same Body of Christ?

3. What changes are wrought on the traditional intra-Christian sense of historical separations when one resets Christian church life in the context of today's global situation? Christians clearly are a minority not only among the members of the world community but also among the religious members. Islam, Hinduism, Buddhism, Judaism, and other religious groups collectively outnumber Christians. In such a context, do the historical divergences among Christians shrink considerably in significance? Does the Christians' common confession of faith in Christ bulk larger and so suggest they might more readily commune together in Christ's sacrament of unity?

4. Without denying that the eucharist demands a common faith, if Christians are to share it in good conscience, what impact should the unifying activity and symbolism of the eucharist have on practical policies about intercommunion? To what extent does eucharistic communion *create* ecclesiastical unity, and so to what extent does Christ's will for the unity of his followers encour-

age, perhaps even command, sacramental intercommunion?

As more American Catholic and Protestant ecumenical theologians consider these questions, more radically unifying possibilities may emerge. Indeed some European theologians think the major Christian churches already possess sufficient unity to consider themselves one Church and so should both declare ecumenical reunion substantially achieved and move to a phase of learning, by living out such a declaration, what remains to be done for the Church to show itself to the world as one.[7]

Ecumenical Expansions

The ecumenical interest and desire that began with some European Protestants, drew in a significant Orthodox participation, and leaped to another level when Roman Catholics joined the game, has continued to extend its influence. Although new, significantly different questions arose when what had been an intra-Christian movement sent out extra-Christian tendrils, a certain religious logic brought Christians into new dialogues with Jews, Muslims, and Asian religionists, both sides now seeking common ground. Having learned that dialogue could import better feelings into what were potentially hostile, volatile relationships, during the 1970s and 1980s Christians and others promoted open discussion of similarities and differences across what previously had been wide religious divides.

Curiously this extension of ecumenical interest to non-Christian religions took flame after the mid-1970s, when a decade of hopes for major Protestant-Catholic-Orthodox reunions had come up with few practical results. Veteran ecumenists knew that substantial progress was bound to be slow, but even they were discouraged by the foot-dragging among lead-

The Unitarianism associated with Harvard University's main church anticipated the recent interest in dialogue among the major world religions. Because it downplayed traditional Christian doctrine, Unitarianism was freer than most church groups to applaud the wisdom and sensitivity of Eastern religions. (Photo by J. T. Carmody)

ers of the different institutional churches. Although theologians had achieved substantial agreement on previously divisive doctrinal points, popes, bishops, and leaders of nonhierarchical churches struck no deals and worked out few mergers (though Lutherans, Congregationalists, and other previously divided Protestant groups did accomplish some significant church unions). Perhaps the fields seemed greener outside the explicitly Christian pasturage.

More likely, however, Christian theologians simply came to a belated recognition of the solidarity of the present world's five billion inhabitants and the common need to solve such problems as the proliferation of nuclear weapons, the pollution of the environment, the widening gap between rich and poor nations, a creaky international monetary system, and great international debt. Clearly, Muslim, Jewish, Christian, Hindu, Buddhist, and Marxist ideological convictions could play significant roles in dealing with such global problems. The more religious leaders could do to promote understanding across religious and cultural barriers, the better they would serve the now international goals of peace and justice.

Thus various documents of the World Council of Churches and the Vatican promoted interreligious dialogue and many ventures in bilateral understanding got under way. Especially poignant were Jewish-Christian exchanges, where the two sides attempted to come to grips with 2000 years of estrangement. Christian-Muslim discussions were slower to develop, but the massive numbers of people potentially involved (perhaps 2 billion, about 40 percent of the world's population) made that dialogue portentous. Christian-Buddhist discussions often focused on meditation and philosophy, because many Westerners had come to admire Zen or other Buddhist schools. Discussions with Marxists usually took the participants into deep considerations of belief and unbelief, as well as of political and sociological matters. Insofar as the label *ecumenism* was sometimes affixed to any or all such discussions, it became a woolly term, virtually indistinguishable from *outreach* or *transtraditional contact*. But benign observers tended to think that almost any contact, discussion, sharing, and mutual learning among groups that previously had stood apart from one another in fear and dislike ought to be accounted progress.

Americans were helped in both intra- and extra-Christian ecumenical endeavors by their traditions of civil religion and religious liberty. They were used to thinking of pluralism as tolerable, perhaps even desirable. In their background lay many religious groups that had longed for a culture fully permeated by creedal

convictions. But when Americans remembered such groups, they could sympathize with Muslims who had yet to separate the secular and religious realms or to admit pluralism into their national codes. Jews reflecting on their experience in the United States, somewhat in contrast to their experience in other nations, tended to promote pluralism and a high estimate of diversity, because both suited their needs as a minority in the midst of a vaguely Christian mainstream. Catholics gradually shook loose from the dogmatism of their pre-Vatican II tradition and learned to hold back from premature declarations either of accord or of heretical separation. On the other hand, very conservative Protestants, Catholics, and Jews tended to oppose ecumenism and abhor the murkiness of American religious pluralism, longing for black and white lines of right and wrong, of faith and unbelief.

Newcomers to the American scene, such as Muslims, Hindus, and Buddhists, tended to be bewildered by Americans' wish for both diversity, which encouraged freedom, and dialogue, which sometimes seemed to imply unity, even uniformity. The first generations of new Asian-Americans typically kept their religious convictions apart from their work and politics, but as Buddhists and Hindu communities became established, they saw that dialogue could serve their own purposes by making them appear less strange to their neighbors, more plausibly people who might add to the American treasury.

Thus a several-sided discussion among different religious groups has replaced the early implications of ecumenism, leading to a growing conviction that mutual understanding, tolerance, and education have to become parts of the American, indeed the global, way of life. On the other hand, those who participate in serious ecumenical dialogues tend to come away sobered by their experience. Sharing hot dogs and a ball game is not the same as sharing convictions about karma, sin, or revelation. The need to produce sufficient mutual understanding and respect to enable people to work together, live alongside one another, and combat such common problems as drugs, teenage pregnancy, and illiteracy has pressured people to put aside doctrinal, even behavioral differences, and agree on common, nonsectarian judgments and behavior patterns. On the other hand, such pressure has only sharpened many people's sense that how one views the world, whether one looks first to Christ or Buddha, to Muhammad or Moses, makes an enormous difference in one's understanding of American citizenship.[8]

Consider the city of Tulsa in 1985, celebrating the 20th anniversary of the Vatican II declaration on the relationship between the Church and non-Christian religions, *Nostra Aetate*. Amid a glow of mutual understanding and good will, with good principal speeches and helpful educational workshops, Christians and Jews (few non-Christians other than Jews participated, largely because Tulsa had few non-Christians other than Jews) stumbled through an evening of community sharing. The celebration was quintessentially American in its civility, pluralism, and relative superficiality. As the French philosopher Albert Camus said about human beings generally, there was much more to admire than despise. Still a great poignancy prevailed, at least for people with any training in Christian theology, world religions, or American history.

The Vatican II declaration, in its day, was a fine bit of progress for Catholics, marking the first time the Catholic church had officially shown much admiration for non-Christian ways to salvation or full humanity. But the declaration's day was 20 years past, and since its day the world had grown more lethal with conflicts between Irish Catholics and Irish Protestants, Arabs and Jews, Sikhs and Hindus, Buddhists and Hindus, Muslims and Christians. Tolerance on the pattern of American civil religion certainly offered a useful model, but much of the world was rejecting traditional American civility.

Few theologians seemed to be exercising the self-criticism, the radical reassessment of their own traditions, necessary to tear out by the roots their tradition's claims to chosenness, special distinction in God's eyes, reasons by which to exalt itself above other nations or traditions, reasons for avoiding a theology in which one would be only as good as one's ethical performance, as one's justice and love. So in the Tulsa of 1985 ecumenism at the grassroots could mean only a praiseworthy diminution of bigotry. The eradication of bigotry by the relinquishment of claims to existential superiority was too bold an idea to bring to table and share around like bread and wine, even though it might mold people into a sister-and-brotherhood sharper and deeper than bland neighborliness.

Robert McAfee Brown

Robert McAfee Brown (1920–) is a leading Protestant ecumenical theologian and a good example of where fidelity to ecumenical instincts could take a 20th century American.[9] As a student at Union Theological Seminary in New York, Brown came under the influence of Reinhold Niebuhr and passed from pacifism to a measured participation in the Second World War (as a naval chaplain). Having established himself as a constructive theologian (one concerned with the construction, or intellectual building, of Christian faith), Brown entered the ecumenical discussions that became more significant on the American religious scene after the mid-1950s. With the Catholic ecumenist Gustave Weigel, he produced in 1960 a key book, *An American Dialogue*, subtitled: "A Protestant Looks at Catholicism and a Catholic Looks at Protestantism." Brown's look was more conciliatory than Weigel's but both men found much to admire in the other's version of Christianity, as well as many things to criticize. Ecumenical dialogue had entered a phase of frank discussion, of getting out perceptions (some of which proved to be misperceptions), fears, and occasionally admirations that had long lived underground and sometimes festered. The momentum started by the World Council of Churches was reaching out to Roman Catholicism, potentially the most dramatic partner for ecumenical discussion aimed at eventual church reunion. For ecumenists, the 1960s were heady days.

This was even more the case when Protestant ecumenists such as Brown attended the Second Vatican Council as observers, learning at firsthand the political ways and means of Roman Catholicism, forging friendships and alliances that, sometimes with amazing speed, broke down presumed theological barriers and revealed mutual longings for union and mutual pain that so much hurt had occurred in the past. Brown came home from Vatican II confirmed in the catholicity of his Protestantism, gifted with new friends and a new sense of how rich an ecumenically united Church might be. Until the end of the 1960s, when Vietnam came to preoccupy his conscience, he worked hard at forwarding the Protestant-Catholic advances established at the council.

But Vietnam, the plight of migrant farm workers in California (where Brown had moved early in the 1960s), and other political matters demanded attention, and in responding Brown found a new sort of ecumenism. Not only did he meet Catholics and fellow Protestants on the picket lines, he met many agnostics, professed atheists, and secular humanists (as they later would be called), whose commitment and brains he also had to admire. He also met Jews, ripe with biblical, talmudic, **hasidic,** and secular wisdom. Indeed, he, Catholic theologian Michael Novak, and Jewish theologian Abraham Heschel collaborated on a book that displayed an ecumenical opposition to the Vietnam war, a religious critique moving across the biblical and traditional Western board.

By the time that thought about Vietnam; travel to third world sites for ecumenical gatherings; and firsthand experience of Vietnam, Eastern Europe, South Africa, and Latin America had worked their influence, the Robert McAfee Brown of the mid- and late 1970s had become a liberation theologian. Liberation theology was at first mainly associated with Latin America but quickly spread to many other parts of the world, as well as to black and feminist Americans. It stressed the priority of social justice on theology's proper agenda. It urged a clear declaration that any religion worth its salt would strive mightily to influence its times so that economic fairness, political participation, cultural development, and the like would reach those most in need.

At the same time, Brown, who had returned to Union Theological, was involved with Jewish theological reflections on the Holocaust. Soon he could sense a virtually seamless web linking the ecumenism trying to reform the Church; the liberation theology trying to reform the nations' systems of warmaking, discrimination, and oppression; and the Jewish-Christian condemnation of the heart of darkness from which the Holocaust sprang. It is symbolic that whereas Brown had earlier popularized the work of the Swiss Calvinist theologian Karl Barth, in his later career he popularized the work of the Latin American Catholic liberation theologian Gustavo Gutierrez and the Jewish novelist Elie Wiesel.

To Robert McAfee Brown *ecumenism* has come to collect to itself all species of right-mindedness and right commitment, but this has occurred only because of his central, abiding commitment to the grace of redemption disclosed in Christ. Writing about how to say the proper yeses and noes to Caesar, about the unexpectedly liberating news the Bible carries when it is read from the perspective of the poor, and about the link between political commitment and spirituality in liberation theology, Brown has rounded out a vision emblematic of the progressive movements of his theological lifetime. The interesting thing is that new insights, convictions, and commitments have not so much replaced old ones as taken them up into a higher viewpoint. For example, Brown is no less a Christian (Protestant genus, Presbyterian species) than he was when he began teaching theology in the 1950s. He is no less friendly with Roman Catholics than he was during the days of *An American Dialogue* and his work as an observer at Vatican II. His political commitments, always strong but brought to a boil by Vietnam, have kept pace with U.S. involvement in Latin America. His ties with Gutierrez and the other Latin American liberation theologians have remained strong, as have his contributions, largely from a liberationist perspective, to the World Council of Churches. He has continued to stay in touch with Jewish theology, serving on the national committee to establish an American memorial to the Holocaust and journeying to Oslo to be with Wiesel when he received the Nobel Prize for Peace.

The Muslim, Buddhist, and other aspects of ecumenism, only lately beginning to assemble themselves, remain largely outside Brown's ecumenical theology, although not outside his awareness. Feminist, black, and gay liberations have also caught his attention, working themselves into his writings and activist contributions when appropriate. The result has been something so organic that it might seem natural or fated, could one not sense the many concrete decisions (to go to Rome for Vatican II, to go to jail for antisegregationist marches, to go to Cuba to witness conditions, to go to World Council of Churches meetings and plead for third world representation, to go to Nicaragua to witness conditions, to go to Heschel and Wiesel for Jewish wisdom, to go back to Union Theological from Stanford the better to serve the Church, and so on).

In Robert McAfee Brown's life, which he would blush to hear called paradigmatic, each yes to new demands, each willingness to be stretched and grow, led to another ascent to a higher viewpoint, a stronger feeling of kinship with human beings in need. Inasmuch as he represents recent American ecumenism, Brown suggests how important such outreach could be, how powerful an antidote to the isolationism, chauvinism, and arrogance always tempting a powerful nation. Like his mentor Reinhold Niebuhr, Brown has kept verifying the Protestant proposition that the church (and the state) are always in need of reform, because only God is without flaw.

Writings of Abraham Joshua Heschel

Abraham Joshua Heschel (1907–1972) made his mark during a 25-year career as professor of Jewish ethics and mysticism at Jewish Theological Seminary in New York. Born in Warsaw, he received a traditional talmudic education, capped by studies at the University of Berlin. He then taught in various Jewish institutions in Germany, before being deported by the Nazis in 1938. He taught in London and at Hebrew Union College in Cincinnati, before moving to Jewish Theological Seminary in 1945.

Heschel combined an affinity for the religious experience nourished by prophetic, talmudic, and hasidic sources with a commitment to issues of social justice such as rejecting racism and militarism. In elaborating from Jewish sources a contemporary philosophy of religion, strong on the experience of encounter with God, he offered his own tradition a renovation of its personal foundations. In joining with people concerned about social justice to bring the moral resources of religion to bear on political dysfunctions (places where American culture was not honoring its pledges of equality and rationality) he took his tradition into the marketplace of ethical influence and made it highly respectable. It was typical of Heschel to write (originally in German) a substantial work on the biblical prophets that probed the foundations of the prophetic experience. It was equally typical of him to join with Robert McAfee Brown and Michael Novak to produce an ecumenical attack on American policies during the Vietnam war. Heschel's ecumenism therefore was an admirable blend of deep roots in his own tradition and great openness to others seeking God or social justice along different paths. The American traditions of religious liberty, civil religion, and free debate served him well, and he responded by making a huge contribution to the dialogue between American Jews and Christians.

The introduction to a posthumous edition of essays Heschel had written on Hasidism (the Jewish line from which his family came) may indicate the stature he attained in both American religious life at large and the Jewish community.

> The loss occasioned by the death of Rabbi Abraham Joshua Heschel in 1972 has been felt with increasing poignancy. Time has not served its customary conciliatory function. The passing years have only emphasized the immensity of the void and the unique stature of the man.
>
> For the Christian world, what Reinhold Niebuhr once described as a "commanding and authoritative voice . . . in the religious life of America" has been silenced. Both Catholics and Protestants sought out Heschel's opinions on theological and social issues, because they believed these opinions represented an authentic Jewish perception expressed by one whose wisdom, piety, and integrity they esteemed. This fraternity with the Christian community manifested itself, for example, in Heschel's persuasive presence at the Second Vatican Council and in his close bonds with leading figures of the Protestant church. It had its basis in the prophetic call for a just society and in what Heschel described as "Depth Theology"—those underpinnings of religion, such as humility, compassion, faith, and awe, which

characterize the community of all true men of spirit.

> For the Jewish world, the death of Abraham Heschel has, of course, been an incomparably greater blow. Jewry has lost a scholar, a thinker, a poet, and a social reformer of the first rank. One of Heschel's unusual qualities was the universality of his concern. His interests were not limited to any single epoch or subject but embraced the totality of Jewish experience . . . . It was this mastery of virtually the entire Jewish creative experience which contributed to the richness of Heschel's own thinking. If his scholarship moved readily across the vertical dimension from the Bible to contemporary thought, his Jewish concern was just as remarkably horizontal. By this I mean his understanding of, sympathy for, and acceptance by almost the entire spectrum of Jewish life— from the Zionists and the Hebraists to the Yiddishists, and from the Reform and Conservative to the Orthodox and the Hasidim.[10]

Thus Heschel gave a personal example of ecumenical largeness of spirit, much as Robert McAfee Brown has done. Samuel Dresner, author of the quoted description of Heschel, believes this largeness of spirit comes from Heschel's Hasidic background. Heschel himself considered Hasidism the most significant achievement of European Judaism.

Two selections from Heschel's study of Rabbi Nahman of Kosow indicate how his Hasidic background would have primed him to bring to his own theological and political work both humor and a sense of the diversity of the paths to God. Rabbi Nahman, a somewhat reluctant follower of the Baal Shem Tov (the founder of modern Hasidism), was a crusty character who was convinced that human beings need to be browbeaten into virtue and longed to die and go to God lest he sin and fail his Lord. Heschel's study ponders the traditions about Rabbi Nahman, bringing out the peculiar version of typically Hasidic ardor that Nahman developed.

> R. Nahman apparently possessed the gift of song. The impact of his musical talents is reflected in the

following tale. Once, on the morning of the Sabbath, R. Nahman and one of his intimates(?), R. Yudel, went to the bathhouse next to the house of study. "R. Nahman went about his business very quickly, but R. Yudel followed a more leisurely pace. While the latter was removing his clothes in the *mikveh* [bath], R. Nahman (had already finished, departed, and had commenced) leading the congregation in worship. When R. Yudel emerged from the *mikveh,* he heard R. Nahman singing. . . . This inflamed him so that he raced to the house of study while still in his undergarments and danced there for some two hours!"

. . . While the Besht [Baal Shem Tov] faced the world with love, with joy, and with compassion, R. Nahman approached it with tension, bitterness, and revulsion. The Besht's demeanor was pleasantness. R. Nahman used to be harsh and authoritative with his disciples, as if he had come to pronounce judgment. The Besht was patient, sought to understand the way of each man, loved peace, and preached it; R. Nahman was short-tempered, waging a constant war for the conquest of men's hearts. Greater, he believed, is the power of opposition than that of conciliation.[11]

A tradition that can embrace such diverse masters as the Besht and Rabbi Nahman prepares people to endure the ambiguities of religion and so to live well in a pluralistic culture. Abraham Joshua Heschel no doubt learned many new things living in Germany and the United States, many things beyond the horizon of his native Polish Jewry. Yet he probably could have found equivalents to many of the new situations he encountered simply by returning to the wellsprings of his own spiritual formation. Human nature is colored by new social circumstances, but it retains many similarities across cultural boundaries.

The genius, if one may call it that, of the American cultural venture has been its willingness to invite such a great variety of originally foreign traditions to take root on American soil. Thus Abraham Joshua Heschel came to represent not only his own personal sense of Jewish existence but also the traditions of hundreds of thousands of American Jews, whose energetic participation in American public life brought both many of them, and many of the non-Jews with whom they dealt, to desire a spokesman for such traditions. Because Heschel was by temperament less partisan than universalist, his interpretation of both Hasidism in particular and Judaism in general related it well to the American mainstream. He did this especially well by applying Jewish values to current American social problems, but also by making appealing presentations of Jewish fervor for prayer, mystical experience, and exaltation—qualities signal among the leading Hasidim but well-known in other religions traditions as well. From the depths of particularity (Hasidism), therefore, Heschel drew forth general, universal principles and conclusions, anticipating latter-day ecumenicists, who have come to realize that one can profitably meet serious adherents of another religious tradition only if one's own religious adherence has deeply penetrated the divine mystery.

Key Terms

Hasidic: pertaining to the religious movement begun in eastern Europe by Israel ben Eliezer (1700–1760), known as the Baal Shem Tov (the Master of the Good Name, abbreviated to Besht). The term *Hasidim* was much older, having long designated the "pious" people zealous for the observance of the law. In the modern movement, followers of the Besht stressed the joy of communing with God, the transports of prayer, the power of spiritual purification, and the ability of religious fervor to bring people through the persecutions regularly visited on European Jewry. Hasidim conceived of their lives as an opportunity to help God redeem the world, and outstand-

ing rabbis such as Besht and Rabbi Nahman gave this conception power and spice.

Heresies: deviations from orthodoxy, departures from right doctrine. Although heresies stress the intellectual component of
faith, they take their importance from the
overall effect religious bodies have associated with them. To think wrongly about
faith, and so to construe reality wrongly,
has been abhorrent, because it has been
considered certain to lead people to false
worship and morality. Pluralistic cultures
have had to temper this judgment, proposing to traditional religionists that disagreements about doctrinal matters, even
disagreements about the nature of God and
what God demands of people, ought not
to sunder the social fabric, ought to be
amenable to civil negotiations that would
let religiously differing groups live in peace.
In fact living in pluralistic cultures has
tended to make religionists downplay or
privatize doctrinal purity, which raises a
question about when tolerance becomes
indifference.

Schisms: separations of religious groups based
on disputes about authority and political
arrangements. For example, the separation
of the eastern and western branches of
Christendom that became official in 1054
resulted more from disputes about the
powers of the Bishop of Rome than from
doctrinal disagreements. Certainly East and
West had come to have different doctrinal,
liturgical, and disciplinary traditions, but
the greater bone of contention was whether
the monarchical political tradition of the
West would prevail over the collegial tradition of the East. Similarly, many intra-
Protestant church separations have been
more schismatic than heretical (though all
differences in political understanding of
religion tend to have theological implications).

Discussion Questions

1. What was the influence of missionary
   experience in the rise of Protestant
   ecumenism?
2. Why has the National Council of Churches
   not wanted to be considered a superchurch?
3. Why has the Roman Catholic Church not
   joined the World Council of Churches?
4. What is the symbolic significance of intercommunion?
5. What principles developed in Christian
   ecumenism would not apply to dialogue
   with people of non-Christian faiths?
6. How adequate a focus for dialogue among
   the world religions would be a discussion
   of the ideal product of each tradition's
   ministries—the sort of people Buddhists,
   Christians, Jews, Muslims, would each like
   to produce?
7. What does the image of upward progress
   suggest about the development of Robert
   McAfee Brown's ecumenism?
8. Why has Brown written books on Gutierrez and Wiesel?
9. What does the influence of Abraham Joshua
   Heschel on his American contemporaries
   suggest about Jewish contributions to
   ecumenism?
10. How valid is the principle that ecumenical
    dialogue best flourishes when the parties
    are all strong adherents of a deep tradition
    (such as Hasidism)?

Notes

1. Robert McAfee Brown, "Ecumenical
Movement," in *The Encyclopedia of Religion*, vol.
5, ed. Mircea Eliade (New York: Macmillan,
1987), p. 18.

2. Ibid., p. 20.

3. J. Deretz and A. Nocent, eds., *Dictionary of the Council* (Washington DC: Corpus, 1968), p. 152.

4. Ibid.

5. Ibid., p. 87.

6. Richard P. McBrien, *Catholicism*, vol. 2 (Minneapolis: Winston, 1980), p. 855.

7. See Heinrich Fries and Karl Rahner, *Unity of the Churches: An Actual Possibility* (New York: Paulist, 1985).

8. See Hans Küng, *Christianity and the World Religions* (Garden City NY: Doubleday, 1986).

9. The best overview of Brown's career is his own autobiographical *Creative Dislocation* (Nashville TN: Abingdon, 1980).

10. Samuel H. Dresner, "Introduction: Heschel as a Hasidic Scholar," in Abraham Joshua Heschel, *The Circle of the Baal Shem Tov: Studies in Hasidism*, ed. Samuel H. Dresner (Chicago: University of Chicago Press, 1985), pp. vii–viii.

11. Abraham Joshua Heschel, "Rabbi Nahman of Kosow: Companion of the Baal Shem Tov," ibid., pp. 135, 145–146.

19

Fundamentalists and Evangelicals

Biblical Interpretation

By some estimates the United States is now home to perhaps 50 million evangelical Christians—a fifth of the population. Within this bloc are the fundamentalists, for whom the Bible is the inspired, literally infallible word of God. Fundamentalists also base their religious lives on other propositions, but their understanding of the Bible is the key. Evangelicals—a broader designation—are Christians for whom the gospel, as expressed in the Bible, is the be-all-and-end-all of life.

To get a start on understanding American fundamentalists, consider the following from a recent article:

Historically, fundamentalism first emerged among American Protestant evangelicals in the latter part of the 19th century in response to the spread of theological modernism in the northern churches, especially the Baptist and Presbyterian denominations. Fundamentalism was not, initially, a distinct movement, but part of a broad wave of conservative Protestant discontent with liberal theology. The movement first became prominent in late 19th century premillennial prophetic and biblical conferences [those organized by churches expecting the thousand-year reign of Christ] that stressed the literal interpretation of scripture. In 1910, the Presbyterian General Assembly, responding to questions raised about the orthodoxy of graduates of Union Theological Seminary, adopted a five-point declaration of "essential" doctrines: (1) the inerrancy of scripture, (2) the Virgin Birth of Christ, (3) his substitutionary atonement, (4) his bodily resurrection, and (5) the authenticity of the miracles. Because of their parallels with other fundamentalist short creeds, these articles became the basis of the "five points of fundamentalism." They were also promoted in a series of small volumes entitled *The Fundamentals: A Testimony to the Truth* published between 1905 and 1915. These booklets, financed and promoted by two southern California oil millionaires, Milton and Lyman Stewart, were written by various authors in defense of the inerrancy of scripture against higher criticism, Darwinism, the Social Gospel, and other thought patterns associated with modernism. Over three million copies of *The Fundamentals* were eventually distributed. In 1919, William B. Riley founded the World's Christian Fundamentals Association. This initiative brought heightened visibility and organizational coherency to fundamentalism and marked a new, more active political phase of the movement.[1]

Popular analyses of fundamentalism (considered as a tendency occurring in many religions) usually speak of its arising during times when social consensus has broken apart and culture has lost its coherence. They also stress its character as an obviously successful way of picturing reality and coping with it. Some of these analyses suggest ties between fundamentalism and authoritarian personalities, which demand clear doctrinal lines and strict moral principles. The recent Roman Catholic equivalent to Protestant fundamentalism has been the Traditionalist movement led by French Archbishop Marcel Lefebvre, whose rallying cry has been to go back to the Latin Mass. In the wake of Vatican II there has been considerable debate among Catholics about the path the church ought to take; the Traditionalists have offered a clear, simple alternative.

One can find obvious parallels to these Christian instances of fundamentalism in branches of Judaism and Islam (and no doubt in other religions as well). The common denominator seems to be a rejection of the confusions attendant on social and intellectual change, a search for secure moorings in simple, supposedly indisputable basic notions, and a reverence for both the past and scriptural authority.

The controversies over teaching evolution in the American schools during the 1920s became a bugaboo of American fundamentalists because all members of the movement were tainted by the ridicule Clarence Darrow heaped on William Jennings Bryant during the Scopes trial in Tennessee in 1925. Fundamentalism retreated to the sidelines of American public life during the 1930s and 1940s. After the Second World War, however, it made a comeback, first allying itself with anti-Communist forces and then gaining an influential voice in the electronic media. Today it is again influential politically, promoting an agenda focused on family issues, opposition to communism, abortion, homosexuality, and drugs, and it remains rooted in a literalist approach to the Bible. Evangelicalism often promotes a similarly conservative social agenda, but usually it is not so literal about biblical inspiration and infallibility. Some evangelicals (for example, those associated with the periodical *Sojourners*) also find that the Bible requires a special concern for the poor and social justice.

The problems with a literalist approach to the Bible are such that fundamentalism gets little sympathy from academic theology and religious studies. Only a small amount of biblical study is necessary to reveal immense problems regarding original texts, translations, mythology, and other features of a literary corpus whose roots are at least 3000 years old. To take every

The prayer tower at Oral Roberts University, Tulsa, Oklahoma, dominates a university campus dedicated to conservative, antiliberal Christian education. (Photo by J. T. Carmody)

Reflecting on the benefits of a unified worldview that offers firm assurances about basic matters also helps make the fundamentalist phenomenon intelligible. For example, many of the world's great works of art have sprung from cultures whose sense of wherefrom and whereto was compelling. From the medieval cathedrals to literary products such as the Talmud, certain fundamentals have held sway in the background. However, the characteristic of most such great works of art was that their cultural milieux allowed, even promoted, vigorous intellectual searching. Medieval Christian theology, defined as faith seeking understanding, spotlighted questioning, realizing that by raising questions people could pursue the blazing divine light. The Jewish theology exhibited in the Talmud reveals much the same: Faith loosened the imagination and sharpened the intellect.

Both these theologies, however, and the architecture, music, literature, science, and painting with which they were allied, reposed in some fundamental convictions. Such convictions themselves could become objects of inquiry, even of challenge. But on the whole talmudic Jews, like medieval Christians, did not doubt the authenticity, truth, or wisdom of their biblical sources. On the whole, they lived within a reality framed by biblical symbols, conceptions of human nature, and pictures of how the world began and humankind arose. Thus even the art of Michelangelo (well after the Middle Ages) comes to its most dazzling achievements in his sculptures of David and the Pietà, and in his paintings of the creation of Adam.

So "biblical interpretation" has been a weighty factor in many prior periods of Christian history. On the other hand, the Bible no longer inspires the whole of American culture, though the roots of American culture continue to be unintelligible without a knowledge of the Bible. Fundamentalists trace this recent state of affairs to the beginning of the 20th century, when historical criticism began to invade biblical stud-

word of the Bible as virtually dictated by God is to make the Bible supernatural in a sense close to superstition or credulity. Consequently many evangelicals accommodate the sense in which the Bible is believed to be God's revelation, speaking of the adequacy of the biblical message concerning everything necessary for salvation, rather than of the Bible's competence in matters of science or history.

One can muster considerable sympathy for people desperately in need of clear answers.

ies. But whether it makes ours an age of Antichrist is open for debate. Perhaps the most interesting issue would be the assumptions any partners would bring to such a debate.

In analyzing the ties between American fundamentalism and millennialist movements (those focused on the second coming of Christ), Ernest R. Sandeen argued that one should not lean overmuch on the five doctrinal points mentioned earlier but should think of fundamentalism as having been shaped by a group (the millennialists) that had members in many different Protestant denominations and slowly became strong enough to spearhead the reaction against liberal theology: "When seen in this light, millenarian leaders did come close to success during the last decade of the 19th and the first decade of the 20th century. In their campaign against Liberalism they felt they had at least partially dammed the tide of infidelity."[2] Fundamentalists—and some conservative evangelicals—have continued to persevere at this task, opposing Darwinism, communism, the "sexual revolution," and what they have considered other manifestations of infidelity to the biblical foundations of America's greatness.

Rural Religion

Stereotypical fundamentalism has thrived in rural America, apart from the sophistication (or degeneracy) of urban life. The success of fundamentalist and evangelical groups in American cities has overturned that stereotype, but it remains worth analyzing. The stereotype suggested that among poor, badly educated, often supposedly simple people who eked out a living from the land or the industry (for example, mining) that dominated their area, ministers could preach the Bible with no adornment save a rollicking style and perhaps some stirring singing. The truth was usually more compli-

cated. For example, consider the following advice offered those contemplating a rural ministry:

> Do you ever think of country folks as "hicks" and "hayseeds"? Then in God's name, go! You are not worthy to be a rural preacher. Do you ever think of going from country to city as "getting back to civilization"? Then in God's name, go! What good can you do to a people you are longing to leave, and to places which you despise? Do you feel that the city has more advantages to offer, under any circumstances whatever, than the country? Then in God's name, go! You do not know what it is all about. You do not know the country at all—no, though you are born and reared there. You have no marriage with nature. Your eyes have not seen the glory of the shining of the Lord.
>
> But if, deep in your heart, you really feel how cheaply inferior are Riverside Church and St. Peter's of the Vatican to any cathedral forest where the thrushes are singing evensong; if you can understand how positively dull is Radio City compared with any winter landscape where the evergreen trees droop under burdens of new snow sparkling with diamonds, while the blue mountains stand high against the sunset—then maybe you are rural-hearted. If every urban sojourn sets your soul singing "My heart's in the highlands, my heart is not here," and every rural absence soon begins to stab you with throbbing homesickness, then maybe you are rural-hearted, and maybe you will do.[3]

The ecological sensitivity that came relatively late to most American religionists often has been in rural America for generations. Whatever its deficiencies in scientific understanding, rural ministries on the model suggested in the quotation would never have sanctioned polluting nature, defacing the forest cathedrals or blue mountains. There may be a parallel address for urban ministers, of course, that makes love of the teeming city a prerequisite for good work there. Or a treatise on parishioners, the people to be served in either the country or the city, might undercut much of the concern for locale exhibited in either address. Still, considering the positive attractions of rural America begins to complicate the picture of poor people, bent in back and simple in mind, taking to a Bible-centered religion like ducks to water. It begins to humanize both rural religion and evangelicalism, making both a matter of people like oneself, embedded in a given locale and struggling to find meaning, happiness, fulfillment there.

A Catholic example will help dislodge the rural stereotype still further. Interviewing some aged people of New Mexico, Robert Coles discovered that their outwardly simple lives had occasioned much religious wisdom. One old man disclosed to Coles what he had learned about the differences between men and women.

> We [he and his wife] are both old, so I guess we both think more of death. "Do you think of death?" my sons will ask me. They mean no harm. They worry about us, and know we have little time left. I tell them no, not too much. But how much is too much? I don't know. I swear, until I was 70 I never thought of death at all. Then all the celebration: my 70th birthday. And soon we were married 50 years. I turned to my wife one day and asked her—I hesitated a good long time before I dared to speak—whether she worried about dying. No, she said. But she must have known what was on my mind, because she said she had been thinking a lot about death, lately—asking herself what it would be like after the heart stops and one is no longer among the living. I asked her when she'd first had her thoughts of that kind, and she said many years ago—perhaps when she was carrying our first son, and even before that, too. I was dumbfounded. I thought she was joking. No, she wasn't, though. We had a long talk. I had never before that day realized what it is to be a man, what it is to be a woman. There are some joys to old age, but none greater than realizing that finally you are learning about the really important things. Perhaps God reveals some of His mysteries to us at the very end before He receives us into His Kingdom—or tells us no, we do not merit it.
> . . . After we lost a child—he would have been another son—my wife told me she wasn't sleeping well; for a month or more it lasted, though I

can't say I knew much about what it was like for her at night. She did tell me once that she wasn't feeling well, and the pain kept her up. Only now do I know that it was her sadness; she would sit and wonder what kind of boy we might have had. I had told her we already had three, and best to be grateful for them, rather than feel sorry for too long that we had lost one. But for a mother each child is precious; and she carried the boy, not me! I don't think a man can put himself in a woman's shoes; but I think a woman is always putting herself in everyone else's shoes—her children's, her husband's, her neighbor's. It is only these recent days, when we both know that soon we are to go, that we share our lives with each other in words. To be old is to be given time to remember; and if you are blessed with good health, as we are, there is also energy to share memories with one another, and with the children and grandchildren.[4]

The man quoted had spent most of his life working for Anglos. He had been formed by a rather strict Hispanic Catholicism, in which heaven and hell predominated as two very real destinies but the Bible was not paramount. The outward frame of his life had been simple and poor. He had not been blessed with great educational opportunities or chances to experience "higher" culture. Yet he loved the music associated with church, and he loved the majestic countryside, the brilliant light, the mountains, and the snows. Through reflections such as his, Coles tracked what the "old ones" of New Mexico had experienced in such a habitat, how the rhythms of nature had influenced their sense of the life cycle, the unfolding of lifetime. Some of what Coles discovered one no doubt would also hear from urban old people, because it comes from somewhat commonplace reflections about sickness, loss, and memories. But much is specified by the rural milieu in which the old ones have lived 70 or 80 years. Much seems simplified and intensified into what one can only call wisdom, perhaps because the sometimes breathtaking physical landscape constantly offers perspective, keeping human affairs to proper scale.

The faith of the old man just quoted was not fundamentalist or evangelical in the sense of a Protestant understanding of biblical authority, but it was simple, basic, and relatively unquestioned. The main precepts of faith and morals that guided his life came from the clergy like missives from God. That is not to say the old ones had not raised many a question and struggled with many a teaching. It is to say that God was as real in their lives as their children and the constantly moving skies and that their times, traditions, and rural context had made their religion like the air they breathed and the food they ate. The novel and movie, *The Milagro Bean Field War,* captures some of this religious flavor in its treatment of the old visionary's sense of the saints. One suspects there would be moving parallels in the lives of old people in Appalachia or the deep South, where for the saints one might substitute beloved texts from the Bible or gospel songs. In our rush to remove the physical poverty of rural areas or lend them our sociological sympathies we sometimes overlook such riches.

The Electronic Church

Every Sunday morning, nearly 130 million Americans . . . tune their radio and television sets to the "electric church." The term refers to commercial religious programs produced for television and radio by evangelical and usually fundamentalist organizations . . . the electric church is far more than a "religious gathering." It is a significant organizational development comprising five religious broadcast networks, more than 60 syndicated television programs, and an ever-expanding number of television and radio stations owned by religious groups. Moreover, this phenomenon has become a major sociopolitical movement of our time . . . . There is no doubt that this Sunday-morning gathering plays a key role in the social and political agenda of the New Right and was instrumental in the election of Ronald Reagan as president. Its influence continues in the policies of the Reagan administration and in the Republican congressional leadership.[5]

In the several years since the publication of the book from which this quotation came, Americans have witnessed such further developments as publicity about the sexual adventures of Pentecostal preachers Jim Bakker and Jimmy Swaggart and Pat Robertson's unsuccessful bid for the Republican presidential nomination. While such developments have wounded the image of the "televangelists" and cast doubt on their political clout, they have not eliminated the large Sunday audience. True, preachers such as the evangelical healer Oral Roberts reported a drastic decline in donations in 1988 (probably due not only to the publicity generated by Bakker and Swaggart but also to Roberts's own claim that God would take his life if he did not raise great sums), but their enterprises by no means closed shop. Whether the majority of those who watch the Sunday programs seek entertainment or inspiration, a great many televisions and radios remain turned on. The electronic church shows no signs of quitting the American scene in the near future.

Most treatments of televangelism link it with the revivalist tradition of Charles Grandison Finney, Dwight Moody, and Billy Sunday, who stirred great numbers of people in their day. By taking advantage of modern communications media, pioneer televangelists such as Billy Graham greatly multiplied their audiences. But only with the development of regular programs and then evangelical networks did analysts have to consider a qualitatively new phenomenon. While many who watched or listened to the regular programming no doubt considered it a supplement to their active membership in a local church, analysts had to deal with the fact that such groups as the PTL club were creating their own regular constituency, perhaps their own religious community or church. If regular financial contributions were the criterion of solid church membership, one had to say that mil-

This sculpture of praying hands stands outside the hospital at Oral Roberts University, where medicine and spiritual healing seek a healthy partnership. (Photo by J. T. Carmody)

lions of Americans were members of electronic churches. Convinced that they were supporting prayer ministries, and in some cases overseas missionary efforts, they looked upon leaders such as Jim Bakker, Jerry Falwell, and Oral Roberts as great religious personalities doing signal work for God.

The link between the electronic church and a narrow interpretation of scripture is not hard to make, though one should not assume that all the standout electronic ministers have preached the same message. Jerry Falwell, for example, rejects the concern with healing that

is so important to Oral Roberts. But what virtually all the electronic ministers and healers share is a relatively literal, unsophisticated, uncritical understanding of the Bible as the Word of God. Whether they are Baptists or Pentecostals, virtually all think that the scriptural Word is linked with the Holy Spirit and is the primary font of truth (a power that can change minds, hearts, and bodies) and the obvious font of the morality Americans ought to espouse. Whether or not they subscribe to the five doctrinal points important to fundamentalism, they make the Bible the cornerstone of their preaching, worldview, and interpretation of American civil religion.

What marks the electronic church as a contemporary phenomenon is its immersion in both recent technology and the business mentality often accompanying such technology in American culture at large.

> The overriding ethos of industrial society—a cost-accounting mentality and the urge to build and control institutions—helps explain both the ethos of urban revivalism and the ethos of religious television . . . the ethos of religious television and the notion of God's technology fit neatly into the post-industrial era, in which technology will "solve" all our social problems. As part of the business and entrepreneurial tradition, televangelists are businessmen for the Lord. They are eager to seize available opportunities to sell the gospel through mass communications. They pursue their goals of winning souls and building teleministries without hesitation, never questioning the appropriateness of using television to do so. Neither are they encumbered by denominational deliberations. Rather, their concern is how to use television effectively. Schooled in pragmatism, televangelists know how to reach the individual Christian, offering hope and love to ameliorate fear and anxiety and, perhaps more importantly, offering membership in their television communities as a means of acknowledging the viewers' importance to them.[6]

The amelioration of fear and anxiety probably accounts for most of the success of the electronic church, for rarely have television's religious communities embarked on social programs targeting relief for the hungry and the homeless. One should not overlook the political ambitions of preachers such as Falwell and Robertson, who want to link their religious communities with a conservative philosophy and agenda. Nonetheless, the same charge of privatism, if not narcissism, that mainstream churches have frequently hurled at fundamentalists and revivalists of past eras has often been hurled at the electronic ministers. Few televangelists have attacked the economic and political systems enmeshed in such American social problems as poverty, homelessness, ecological ruin, drugs, teenage pregnancy, huge budget deficits, illiteracy, and the like. Most have contented themselves with moral exhortation, refusing to criticize the spirit of free enterprise and capitalism powering the American way of life.

A good representative of the psychological orientation implied in many television ministries, though perhaps more explicit and honest than most, is Robert H. Schuller's promotion of self-esteem. For while Schuller admits social failures, the new reformation he seeks focuses on self-love:

> The "will to self-love" is the deepest of all human desires. Because the human being is created in the image of God, the will to dignity is the irreducible, psychological, and spiritual nucleus around which the life of the human soul revolves and evolves. The need for dignity, self-worth, self-respect, and self-esteem is the deepest of all human needs. If our need for dignity is assaulted or ignored by the church, then truly we are "lost sinners." Unsaved and unfulfilled, we will be naturally led down a destructive road of ego-tripping. Unsatisfied, we will be restless, bored, and drawn to launch dangerous adventures—wars included. Unsatiated, our drive for pride as a prince or princess of heaven will drive us to destructive power and dishonest manipulations. An immense, complex tangle of negative emotions will be woven around our poor lost souls . . . all the problems facing the church will find healing answers if we start with and do not get distracted at any time from meeting every person's deepest need—his hunger for self-esteem, self-worth, and personal dignity. This means that human dignity becomes the ultimate human value. It is the indivisible cell, the nonnegotiable need, the uncompromising quality of humanity. When persons lose their dignity, they lose their humanity. A person can survive without power and pleasure, but he cannot survive if he loses all pride in being a person! So the self-esteem of every human soul must become the healthy core of our humanity-helping religion.[7]

Most critics of such a theological position (which owes more to psychology than to fundamentalist theology) admit that faith ought to heal people and convince them of their great worth. On the other hand, critics also tend to charge that Schuller neglects something more basic in the preaching of Jesus and the traditions of Christian, Jewish, and Muslim biblical religion. That is the love of God, with whole mind, heart, soul, and strength, and the love of neighbor as oneself. In the famous words of St. Augustine, the authority so often invoked during the old Reformation, "You have made us for yourself, O Lord, and our hearts are restless til they rest in You." If self-esteem is substituting for the love of God, then Schuller, and others in the electronic church who similarly promote self-love, have made radical changes in biblical tradition. Where Jesus preached the Kingdom of God, they are preaching a psychology with little apparent concern for social justice.

Billy Graham

One would not classify Billy Graham as a psychological reductionist, but many critics of his early career (he has evolved) charged that he neglected the social dimensions of the gospel by concentrating overly on personal experiences of conversion. In response to these charges, Graham broadened his theological outreach somewhat. But he remains associated with the traditional revivalist stress on one-time, dramatic confession of sin and acceptance of Christ as savior and lord.

William Franklin ("Billy") Graham, Jr., was born in 1918 in Charlotte, North Carolina, the son of a prosperous dairy farmer. At age 16 he made a profession of faith, a decision for Christ, at a revival meeting. His subsequent schooling occurred at Bob Jones College and the Florida Bible Institute, both fundamentalist institutions, and at age 21 he was ordained a Southern Baptist minister. Later he took a bachelor's degree in anthropology at Wheaton College in Illinois.

Billy Graham made his reputation after the Second World War as a radio preacher, tent revivalist, and participant in various "Youth for Christ" rallies. By 1950 he had become the best known spokesman for evangelism. He established the Billy Graham Evangelistic Association, published various books, developed a syndicated newspaper column, and traveled the world conducting crusades, many of which were televised. Through personal friendships with a string of presidents—Eisenhower, Johnson, and Nixon—he was credited with considerable political influence, as though his theology fitted the civil religion those presidents wished to encourage.

Something of the flavor of Graham's work, and its increasingly international scope, appears in the following description from a highly admiring biography:

He preached in Baptist, Roman Catholic, and Lutheran churches in Warsaw, all crowded to the doors; and in the open air outside the Baptist church in the industrial city of Bialystok, near the Soviet border. He was brilliantly interpreted throughout the tour by Dr. Zdzislaw Pawlik, general secretary of the Polish Ecumenical Council. At Poznan, in Western Poland, the church of the Dominican order overflowed with 3000 men and women of all ages, including many hundreds of students. The people stood shoulder to shoulder, for these great churches do not contain many seats; they stood in side chapels, the churchyard, or wherever they could hear, with priests and seminarians doing all they could to assist. "We have met here in the Holy Spirit," said the rector, opening the service, "and He will unite us and hold us together." The Warsaw and Bialystok Baptist choirs led the singing . . . . Busloads of people came from other Communist Eastern European countries. The total of men, women, and children who heard Billy Graham preach in Poland was estimated at around 60,000. Far greater were the numbers— approximately 110 million in Poland and beyond its borders in the Ukraine and elsewhere—who, understanding Polish, could hear the sermons on tape or read them in print: a new dimension of great potential for Billy's ministry in Communist countries.[8]

There is no denying the massive numbers Billy Graham has reached around the world, and one cannot deprecate the sincerity of those who have found him a mouthpiece of God. Whether hearers such as the Catholic Poles would finally accept his theory of biblical interpretation is another question, often bracketable on the occasion of a crusade but likely to surface in the aftermath. Graham's vigor and charisma, along with the lyric words of the Bible he often invokes, explain why so often he receives an enthusiastic hearing. Moreover, those who associate the success of fundamentalism and televangelism with the spiritual hunger of present-day people have good arguments on their side. Those who find similarities between Graham's preaching and the style of Jesus or the ministry of the early Church may also have a strong case. However, Graham's crusades leave unanswered such questions as what happens after the enthusiasm goes away, how does biblical preaching stimulate social justice and political reform, and how can one square literalism with present-day scriptural scholarship.

Another nagging question concerns the financial probity of many televangelists. Both American religious history and the history of religion in other cultures suggests that enthusiastic faith can become a profitable business allowing some evangelists to live high on the hog. These matters may not apply to Billy Graham himself, but they do apply to televangelism as a whole, and they should also beget analogous queries about how mainstream churches handle their finances. The necessity for such questions was revealed by the scandals concerning Vatican banking practices in the 1980s.

A sample of Billy Graham's own writings can suggest how he regularly interprets the Bible.

For instance, in treating of "Lucifer and the Angelic Rebellion," Graham writes:

> Few people realize the profound part angelic forces play in human events. It is Daniel who most dramatically reveals the constant and bitter conflict between the holy angels faithful to God and the angels of darkness allied with Satan (Daniel 10: 11–14). This Satan, or the devil, was once called "Lucifer, the son of the morning." Along with Michael he may have been one of the two archangels, but he was cast from heaven with his rebel forces, and continues to fight. Satan may appear to be winning the war because sometimes he wins important battles, but the final outcome is certain. One day he will be defeated and stripped of his powers eternally. God will shatter the powers of darkness . . . . Satan and his demons are known by the discord they promote, the wars they start, the hatred they engender, the murders they initiate, the opposition to God and His commandments. They are dedicated to the spirit of destruction. On the other hand the holy angels obey their Creator. No discordant note sounds among the angels of heaven . . . . Could it be that God wanted to be sure that men would not question the existence of Satan and his demon-hosts? Perhaps He had this in mind when He inspired the writing of Ezekiel 28, which sets forth the typology of Satan in the earthly sense . . . . We live in a perpetual battlefield—the great War of the Ages continues to rage. The lines of battle press in ever more tightly about God's own people. The wars among nations on earth are merely popgun affairs compared to the fierceness of battle in the spiritual, unseen world. This invisible spiritual conflict is waged around us incessantly and unremittingly.[9]

By combining a rather literal reading of scriptural texts with present times, and concentrating on unempirical assertions hard to verify or falsify on historical grounds, Graham weaves a plausible spiritual interpretation of good and evil. As A. G. Mojtabai's recent book on the literalist mentality in Amarillo, Texas, shows, such plausibility is more than enough to send many Americans streaming out of their churches with visions of Satanic overtones to the military and political struggles between the Soviet Union and the United States.[10]

Writings of Jerry Falwell

By 1980 the independent Baptist minister Jerry Falwell had developed the leading syndicated program in religious television, "The Old Time Gospel Hour," emanating from his church in Lynchburg, Virginia. He is more famous, however, for having organized the Moral Majority, a group dedicated to restoring what they take to be traditional American moral values in public, political life. Falwell is a fundamentalist, taking his cue from a literal reading of biblical texts. His moral agenda includes keeping America strong against communism, turning the tide against drugs and feminism, and restoring what he considers Christian family values. Some of his comments on the equal rights amendment, up for consideration at the time of his first important book, *Listen, America!*, suggest how he combined biblical literalism and conservative politics.

> The Equal Rights Amendment strikes at the foundation of our entire social structure. If passed, this amendment would accomplish exactly the opposite of its outward claims. By mandating an absolute equality under the law, it will actually take away many of the special rights women now enjoy. A definite violation of holy Scripture, ERA defies the mandate that "the husband is the head of the wife, even as Christ is the head of the church" (Ep. 5:23). In 1 Peter 3:7 we read that husbands are to give their wives honor as unto the weaker vessel, that they are both heirs together of the grace of life. Because a woman is weaker does not mean that she is less important . . . .
>
> ERA proponents voted down and eliminated all clauses that would have preserved women's exemption from the military, draft, and wartime combat duty; that would have preserved the rights of wives, mothers, and widows to be financially supported by their husbands' benefits; that would have preserved the right of privacy in school and public restrooms, hospitals, and prisons; that would have preserved the rights of legislatures to pass laws against abortion, and homosexual and lesbian privileges.[11]

On the one hand, Falwell is concerned about doctrines, such as feminism, that he thinks violate biblical standards. To his mind the Bible mandates the subjection of wives to husbands. Because it flies in the face of this mandate, feminism must be an abomination. On the other hand, Falwell reads into the ERA a basketful of repugnant legal consequences, many of which supporters of the amendment denied. Some of the consequences (for example, abortion and homosexuality) violate his sense of morality. Others, such as drafting women into military service and removing the privacy of separate bathrooms for women and men violate his sense of American custom or taste.

More Americans than just the members of his Moral Majority were likely to agree with Falwell in rejecting such consequences. His presentation against the ERA skillfully blended theological, ethical, and cultural claims, making a simple yet powerful package. How much presentations such as his had to do with depicting Ronald Reagan and other conservative political candidates as defenders of traditional American values against rampant radicalism, hedonism, and paganism is hard to say, but all political analysts agreed that religious conservatives greatly contributed to the 1980 Republican victory.

One finds in Falwell's writings an alternative to liberal social agendas, but only as a secondary matter. The primary matter is the attack on movements in favor of feminism, gay rights, abortion rights, progressive education, free expression (extending even to pornography), and socialism or communism. Falwell assumes that he can call on American history to depict these movements as antitraditional and repugnant to the American mainstream. He also assumes that anything superficially contradicting the Bible will be similarly repugnant to the American majority.

In response, Falwell's critics have asked, What about the claims of blacks, Native Americans, women, and other marginal groups that America needs drastic changes if it is to honor its best traditions? What about the homeless, the jobless, the hungry, the victims of domestic violence, the pregnant teenagers, the drug addicts, the dent made in the federal budget by military arms, the harm wreaked on the environment by unbridled development? The general answer one finds in fundamentalist conservatives such as Falwell is that if the country would return to biblical values, most such problems would solve themselves. What will not work, they are sure, is big government, social engineering. What must be ruled out of court is **secular humanism,** that is, any criticism of traditional religion or the linkage between biblical morality (as the fundamentalists interpret it) and American traditions. Compared to the threats of communism and other ideologies opposed to the American way of life, American social problems must take a back seat. It is more important to preserve the status quo, whatever its social injustices, than to risk liberal programs that might sap the country's religious vigor.

Because many fundamentalists follow Falwell in linking what they take to be biblical verities with a conservative-to-radical-right-wing political outlook on everything from military policy to abortion, the question of church-state relations or, more precisely, of the relations between religion and politics, has become complex and muddied. (One might say the same about the consequences of left-wing, liberal religionists pushing a political agenda regularly in conflict with that of the fundamentalists.) For while most commentators agree that religious people should suffer no diminution of their civil or political rights because their views derive from their religious convictions, many commentators also agree that the doctrinaire linking of political programs with religious orthodoxies is dangerously in conflict with the American ideal of separating the secular and religious realms so that no religious bodies have overriding political influence either *de jure* or *de facto*.

The substance in the fears of those who worry about linking religion and politics may appear in some remarks Falwell has made about Israel in which he seems to move quickly from his fundamentalist exegesis of biblical texts to conclusions for American foreign policy:

The last book of the Bible, the Book of Revelation, contains prophecy regarding future events. Israel plays a significant role in that prophecy. This tiny nation will once again be attacked by her enemies, led by the great Russian armies and her Arab allies, but as the prophet Ezekiel prophesied in Ezekiel 38 and 39, Russia will be defeated and Israel once again will be spared by the hand of God. If the Russians would only read what God has in store for them and believe it, they may find themselves falling on their knees, forsaking their godlessness, and crying unto the God of Israel for forgiveness. No, God is not finished with the nation Israel . . . . Every nation that has ever stood with the Jews has felt the hand of God's blessing on them. I firmly believe God has blessed America because America has blessed the Jew. If this nation wants her fields to remain white with grain, her scientific achievements to remain notable, and her freedom to remain intact, America must continue to stand with Israel.

There are some very distressing developments presently in American-Israeli relations. I see a growing willingness to accept as reputable and civilized the murderers of the PLO. There is an increasing tendency to allow our need for oil to blind us to our greater need for God's continued blessing. If America allows herself to be blackmailed by the oil cartel and trades her allegiance to Israel for a petroleum "mess of pottage," she will also trade her position of world leadership for a place in the history books alongside of Rome. We cannot allow that to happen.

The Jews are returning to their land of unbelief. They are spiritually blind and desperately in need of their Messiah and Savior. Yet they are God's people, and in the world today Bible-believing Christians in America are the best friends the nation of Israel has. We must remain so.[12]

From his reading of Israel's place in God's scheme for saving the world, Falwell would make the United States a staunch defender of Israel. That is a melding of religion and foreign policy that frightens many Christians, as well as most politicians.

Key Terms

Secular Humanism: a term usually employed by fundamentalist Christians to denote those who deny the validity of religious claims in the realms of either ultimate truth or practical politics. Secular humanists therefore are those who are agnostics or atheists, who concentrate on this-worldly matters, and whose main concern is that human beings flourish. Whether a Christian or Jew can be a secular humanist is an interesting question in the abstract, apart from fundamentalist assumptions, but in the fundamentalist camp the notion is ludicrous. Indeed, sometimes virtually all opponents of the fundamentalist political agenda—feminists, socialists, gay rights advocates, pacifists, and progressive educators—are swept together and labeled secular humanists, because they do not make the Bible their operative authority in all aspects of daily life.

Discussion Questions

1. How many of the famous five fundamentals can be derived from a commitment to biblical inerrancy?

2. Why were evolution in particular and modernism in general so abhorrent to many biblical religionists?
3. Does the passage on the qualities requisite for a good rural minister romanticize rural living?
4. How might living in rural New Mexico have contributed to the insights of the old man Robert Coles interviewed?
5. What has been the link in televangelism between fundamentalism and entrepreneurship?
6. Why have the televangelists been weak on social justice?
7. What are the ecumenical implications of the description of Billy Graham's crusade in Poland?
8. What does Billy Graham's interpretation of angels suggest about literalist exegesis and theology?
9. How should a passage such as Ephesians 5:23 figure in American political controversies such as the one surrounding the Equal Rights Amendment?
10. What does Jerry Falwell's reading of biblical prophecy regarding Israel suggest about fundamentalist approaches to American foreign policy?

Notes

1. William Dinges, "Fundamentalism," in *The New Dictionary of Theology*, ed. Joseph A. Komonchak, Mary Collins, and Dermot A. Lane (Wilmington DE: Michael Glazier, 1987), pp. 411–412.

2. Ernest R. Sandeen, *The Roots of Fundamentalism* (Chicago: University of Chicago Press, 1970), p. xvii; also George Marsden, *Fundamentalism and American Culture* (New York: Harper & Row, 1980); David F. Wells and John D. Woodbridge, eds., *The Evangelicals*, rev. ed. (Grand Rapids MI: Baker House, 1975).

3.   Arthur Wentworth Hewitt, *Highland Shepherds* (Chicago: Willet, Clarke & Company, 1939), pp. 2–3.

4.   Robert Coles, *The Old Ones of New Mexico* (Albuquerque: University of New Mexico Press, 1973), pp. 47–48.

5.   Razelle Frankl, *Televangelism: The Marketing of Popular Religion* (Carbondale: Southern Illinois University Press, 1987), pp. 3–4.

6.   Ibid., pp. 147–148.

7.   Robert H. Schuller, *Self Esteem: The New Reformation* (Waco TX: Word Books, 1982), pp. 33–35.

8.   John Pollock, *Billy Graham: Evangelist to the World* (New York: Harper & Row, 1979), pp. 310–311.

9.   Billy Graham, *Angels: God's Secret Agents* (Garden City NY: Doubleday, 1975), pp. 59, 65–66.

10.   See A. G. Mojtabai, *Blessed Assurance* (Boston: Houghton Mifflin, 1986).

11.   Jerry Falwell, *Listen, America!* (Garden City NY: Doubleday, 1980), pp. 151, 157.

12.   Ibid., pp. 112–113.

20 Eastern Religions

The point in this chapter is to suggest how Americans recently have been responding to religious traditions outside the American mainstream (Judeo-Christian traditions). Some adherents of these traditions have been in the United States for several generations, but only since the 1960s have they gained wide interest and significant numbers of converts.

Hinduism

Hinduism is the ancient parent religion of India, an umbrella of beliefs unifying the many different theistic sects that flourish on the Indian subcontinent. In the opinion of many scholars, Hinduism arose from the fusion of beliefs of the peoples native to the subcontinent with the beliefs of Aryan peoples who invaded around 1500 B.C.E. Most influential among such beliefs were the significance of **karma** and **dharma.** The doctrine of karma taught virtually all Indians (Buddhists and Jains as well as Hindus) that they would be trapped in a cycle of deaths and rebirths until they cleansed themselves of desire. The doctrine of dharma clarified the responsibilities peculiar to one's status in the caste structure of Indian society. A further important factor in Hinduism has been the continuance of fertility interests (concern for the flourishing of both nature and the human species) that predated the Aryan invasions. Modern Hinduism has been influenced by encounters with Islam and Christianity. The first Muslim empire was established in India in 1175, while British influence became strong early in the 18th century. In 1893, as part of a World's Fair celebrating the 400th anniversary of the discovery of America, representatives of various world religions assembled in Chicago for a World's Parliament of Religions. One of the stars of this Parliament was Swami Vivekananda, a spokesman for Vedanta, perhaps the most prestigious school of Hindu philosophy. Vedanta teaches the essential unity of all phenomena, including the identity of the deepest self with the ground of all reality. This teaching goes back to Shankara (788–820), the founder of Vedantic "nondualism," but Swami Vivekananda had also been influenced by the saint Ramakrishna (1836–1886), who had stressed an eclectic theism based on emotional love (*bhakti*). Vivekananda added commitments to serving the poor, making the Vedanta societies he established in the United States at the turn of the 20th century comprehensive blends of metaphysics, devotionalism, and social action. What drew most attention to the Vedanta societies, however, were the lectures on Indian philosophy that stressed the unity of all things and urged purification of the spiritual self.

The Vedantists worked out a worship service quite like that of the typical Protestant church, so that Americans' first impressions of Hinduism were of a relatively tame, spiritualist venture, perhaps not wholly different from Unitarianism, Quakerism, Shakerism, or Christian Science. Only Americans who visited India or read about Indian culture had much contact with the full, rich, and at times exotic religious life of the whole subcontinent. Only they learned about the massive Hindu mythology, the wealth of religious rituals, the varieties of Indian gods and goddesses.

Mohandas Gandhi (1869–1948), the next Indian to make a great impact on American consciousness, was distinctive for combining religious idealism with savvy politics. Gandhi had trained as a British lawyer and appropriated much of the teachings of Jesus. His God was the Truth one could find in all cultures, especially when one sought it with a pure conscience and was dedicated to social justice. To champion Indian independence from British colonial rule, Gandhi worked out a philosophy of nonviolent resistance to unjust laws and policies. Gradually he mobilized India to strikes and marches that finally forced the British to grant home rule. First Indians, and then much of the Western world, came to regard Gandhi as a *mahatma*, a great soul. Drawing on **yogic** traditions, especially those dealing with purifying work, Gandhi made his movement a spiritual path, a way to the liberation from karma that most Hindus considered the prime religious task.

Through his influence on Martin Luther King, Jr., Gandhi was a factor in the debates about nonviolent resistance that punctuated American culture during the 1960s and 1970s. Americans as diverse as Erik H. Erikson, the leading interpreter of the psychological tasks built into the life cycle, and Thomas Merton, a Trappist monk widely respected for his spiritual writings, found Gandhi well worth studying.[1]

Merton interpreted Gandhi's views of nonviolence as follows:

Ahimsa (nonviolence) is for Gandhi the basic law of our being. That is why it can be used as the most effective principle for social action, since it is in deep accord with the truth of man's nature and corresponds to his innate desire for peace, justice, order, freedom, and personal dignity. Since *himsa* (violence) degrades and corrupts man, to meet force with force and hatred only increases man's progressive degeneration. Nonviolence, on the contrary, heals and restores man's nature, while giving him a means to restore social order and justice. *Ahimsa* is not a policy for the seizure of power. It is a way of transforming relationships so as to bring about a peaceful transfer of power, effected freely and without compulsion by all concerned, because all have come to recognize it as right. Since *ahimsa* is in man's nature itself, it can be learned by all, though Gandhi is careful to state that he does not expect everyone to practice it perfectly. However, all men should be willing to engage in the risk and wager of *ahimsa* because violent policies have not only proved bankrupt but threaten man with extinction.[2]

More organized than Gandhiites in recent American history have been the followers of Swami Yogananda, the founder of the Self-Realization Fellowship; the followers of the Maharishi Mahesh Yogi, the founder of the Transcendental Meditation movement; and the followers of A. C. Bhaktivedanta, founder of the International Society for Krishna Consciousness (the Hare Krishnas). Yogananda popularized yogic meditation and, indirectly, the yogas (disciplines) concerned with toning the body. The Maharishi popularized transcendental meditation, an easy form of mental relaxation and purification. The colorfully clad Hare Krishnas popularized devotional love to Krishna, the leading Indian god. The group got a reputation as a cult, however, which to the lay American meant an idiosyncratic religious group inclined to brainwash young people into spiritual idealism and generate large sums of money for its leaders.

Noting that Hare Krishna communities in the United States grew from 30 to 50 in the years 1975–1983, and that even greater growth was occurring in other parts of the world, most notably Latin America (from 8 to 40 groups in the same period), E. Burke Rochford has spoken of the group's future as follows:

> The history of Hare Krishna in America has been one of change and adaptation . . . . [Its] ability to

adapt to what have often been the most adverse circumstances points to the flexibility and ultimate resiliency of the movement. It is these qualities, combined with the deep faith and commitment of the devotees themselves, which will be the Krishna movement's greatest assets as it approaches the 21st century . . . the nature of the modern world virtually assures that conditions favorable to the Krishna movement and other new religions will arise again and again in the future, again to encourage their growth and increase their overall influence.[3]

According to the 1988 *Britannica Book of the Year,* there were in 1987 about 810,000 Hindus living in the United States and Canada. The majority of them were probably immigrants from India, or from Indian communities in other parts of the world, but a few were converts. While their number leaves Hindus still a tiny minority in a Northern American population of about 268 million, it will be interesting to see whether an Americanized Hinduism (or Buddhism or Islam) can develop on this continent. American traditions of religious liberty leave the door open, but much in traditional Hinduism (spiritualism and caste structure, for example) is quite foreign to the American mainstream (though not without some analogies). If Hinduism does prosper in the United States, we can expect to hear more about meditation, yoga, reincarnation, vegetarianism, and nonviolence than we have in the past.

Buddhism

The prevailing dates for Gautama, the Indian prince whose enlightenment brought him the title of Buddha (enlightened one) are 536–476 B.C.E. The Buddha accepted much of the Hindu orthodoxy of his day but broke with the contemporary stress on ritualistic sacrifice. He also denied the existence of an independent self (the *atman* important in Hinduism; an unchanging core identity) and formulated the fruits of his enlightenment in terms of his famous Four Noble Truths: All life is suffering; the cause of suffering is desire; if one removes desire, one can remove suffering; and the way to remove desire is to follow the noble eightfold path of right views, right intention, right speech, right action, right livelihood, right effort, right mindfulness, and right concentration. Summarized, the Buddhist program traditionally has stressed meditation, wisdom, and morality, and the great treasures to which the followers of Gautama have clung have been the Buddha himself, the Dharma (Teaching), and the Sangha (religious community).

Buddhism eventually died out in India, but not before it had taken root in East Asia, dominating Sri Lanka, Burma, Thailand, Tibet, Cambodia, Laos, Vietnam, China, and Japan. It had competition from native traditions in those countries, most notably from Confucian ethics, but everywhere it made a deep impression, especially in philosophy and aesthetics. The two major branches of Buddhism, Theravada and Mahayana, both supported monks and nuns (the core of the Sangha) and agreed on such basic ethical precepts as the prohibition of murder, theft, lying, unchastity, and taking intoxicants. Like Hindus, Buddhists favor nonviolence and vegetarianism. They believe celibacy is useful to spiritual progress and seek escape from the cycle of death and rebirth.

Chinese, Japanese, Korean, Vietnamese, Cambodian, Laotian, Thai, and Tibetan immigrants to the United States have tended to bring their various Buddhist traditions. Often these have been practiced in the home and ethnic community without much attention to how they might assume an institutional structure in the new country.

The first wave of Asian immigration was made up of Chinese who came to California during the Gold Rush; by 1860 they numbered 60,000. The first Chinese temple was built in San Francisco in 1853, and there were eight by 1875. These were the characteristically syncretistic temples of Chinese

popular religion, combining Buddhist, Taoist, and Confucian features. But Buddhist priests were early present among the population, and eventually more purely Buddhist centers were established. These include Buddha's Universal Church (San Francisco, 1963), a modern reconstruction of Buddhism, and the "orthodox" . . . Sino-American Buddhist Association (San Francisco, 1959) . . . . Although they traveled to Hawaii when it was not yet a U.S. possession, Japanese immigrants did not arrive on the mainland in large numbers until the end of the 19th century and the beginning of the 20th century. As in its homeland, Japanese-American Buddhism took a much more structured form than Chinese. As a result . . . the Buddhist Church of America (BCA) was founded in San Francisco in 1899. Adapting its worship to a somewhat Protestant format and working diligently to serve the Japanese community, the BCA has been the preponderant Japanese Buddhist institution, with over 100 churches and missions operating by the 1980s.[4]

The Buddhist sect most successful in the United States has been Zen, a branch developed in China and transplanted to Japan that stresses meditation. The first Americans interested in Japan and Buddhism came under the influence of Zen teachers, most notably D. T. Suzuki, whose writings generated a widespread interest. In recent decades Americans have formed their own Zen institutions, usually still under Japanese influence, and have begun to develop their own *roshis* (teachers). One of the best known is Philip Kapleau, head of a Zen Center in Rochester, New York. Kapleau has worked hard to translate Zen into American idioms, patiently dealing in his conferences with such matters as, "If Americans spend their time meditating, energetic societies will out produce us and even 'bury' us," and "Can I practice Zen and be a good Jew (or Catholic)?"

To answer the first worry, Kapleau drew on personal experience:

In 1966, when I was leaving Japan after 13 years of training there, a farewell party was given me by a group of Japanese Zen friends. At one point a businessman, the owner of a large factory, came up to me and whispered confidentially, "Kapleau-san, if you go to Washington and see your President Johnson, tell him that we Japanese have a secret weapon that will enable us to out produce the United States." "Really? What is it?" "Zen!" This man's firm, like many Japanese corporations today, was regularly sending its employees into Zen monasteries. The purpose is not only to develop in them greater self-discipline and awareness, but also to teach them that whether work is dreary or rewarding depends not on the work itself but on their mind state while doing it.[5]

In dealing with the second matter, Kapleau told his audience to transcend selfhood, asking what they were before they were Jewish or Catholic.

Question yourself day and night with the yearning to know and the conviction that you can know. Learn to live the way a fish swims or a bird flies—unself-consciously. Let go of ambition—it leads to aggression. Be aware and responsive. In whatever your right hand finds to do involve also your left. Avoid unnecessary judgments. Be modest and unassuming; offer your opinion only when it is asked for. Forget your good deeds and confess your bad ones. And never fail to relate every effect to the cause that produced it . . . . To practice Zen Buddhism means to transcend your self, and to transcend your self means to forget your self. When that happens, you are neither a good Catholic nor a good Zen Buddhist.[6]

Another prominent Japanese-American Buddhist group is Nichiren Shoshu of America, which is associated with the teachings and organization of the medieval Japanese religious teacher Nichiren (1222–1282). Nichiren's followers stress the Lotus Sutra, a famous Mahayana Buddhist scripture depicting the Pure Land to which the devout may expect to go. By placing their faith in the Lotus Sutra (taken as heavenly revelation), the devout hope to escape suffering and rebirth. Their outlook leads them to stress harmony: Subject and object are not two; cause and effect are simultaneous; mind and

body are not two; and society and religion form a single unity.

The practices of Nichiren Shoshu are twofold: Gongyo and Daimoku. Gongyo involves reciting the liturgy of Nichiren Shoshu five times in the morning and three times in the evening. The liturgy includes part of the second and all of the sixteenth chapter of the Lotus Sutra. The chanting is performed entirely in Japanese, in a clear voice, with concentration focused on the Gohonzon (the central portion of the home altar, containing a rectangular paper scroll inscribed with the Japanese characters of the names of the Buddhas and Bodhisattvas in the Lotus Sutra). For the individual, the Gohonzon represents his own Buddha-nature, clear and pure. The practice of Gongyo is followed by the chanting of the well-known Daimoku. Incumbent on all followers of "True Buddhism," this mantric formula of Nam Myoho Renge Kyo is the highest practical expression of the law of simultaneous cause and effect, resulting in the attainment of harmony with the universe for its reciters.[7]

The 1988 *Britannica Book of the Year* estimates that in 1987 there were 190,000 Buddhists in Canada and the United States. Largely because of the influence of Zen, these 190,000 seem to have made a greater intellectual impact than their Hindu counterparts, who outnumber them about four to one. As insights such as Kapleau's into the influence of Zen on Japanese productivity become better known, that influence may only widen.[8]

Islam

Islam is the originally Near Eastern religion founded by the prophet Muhammad (570–632 C.E.). The words *Islam* and *Muslim* both refer to the submission to Allah incumbent on true believers. The collection of revelations Allah gave to Muhammad is called the Qur'an and is the chief scripture of Islam, while the example of the Prophet is the closest thing to a Muslim paradigm. Muslims have divided into two main groups, Sunnis and Shiites, due to a dispute over succession to Muhammad in rule of the community. (Sunnis say succession did not follow Muhammad's blood line; Shiites say it did.) But in most matters of faith and legal (ethical) practice the two groups remain close. The "five pillars" customarily used to summarize Muslim faith are indicative propositions: One must profess the core faith that there is no God but Allah and that Muhammad is His prophet; one must pray five times a day; one must fast during the month of Ramadan; one should make a pilgrimage to Mecca at least once during one's lifetime; and one must give alms for the support of the poor. Muslims stress the strict monotheism taught by Muhammad, which makes submission of oneself to Allah the great virtue and idolatry the great vice. They also underscore the Judgment that Muhammad and the Qur'an promised will separate believers from unbelievers, consigning the former to the Garden and the latter to the Fire.

Shortly after the death of Muhammad in 632, Islam spread like wildfire, becoming the greatest force in the Middle East and the Mediterranean world within two centuries. Until 1492, when the Muslims were defeated in Spain, Islam had a strong influence in all of Southern Europe. Today it not only predominates in the Middle East and Indonesia (at 175 million the fifth largest nation in the world) but also greatly influences the Indian subcontinent (Pakistan and Bangledesh are Muslim nations), some African countries, and parts of the Soviet Union. There are also Muslims in China, the United States, and Europe.

Some scholars think Muslim adventurers from Spain and North Africa may have explored the Americas before Columbus. A Spanish edict in 1543 expelling Muslims from overseas Spanish territories suggests that Islam had some presence there. Perhaps 15 to 20 percent of the slaves brought to the Americas from West Africa between 1530 and 1850 were Muslims, some educated and literate in Arabic. Most of their Muslim traditions died out in the New World, but some enclaves practiced Islam secretly. Prior to the Civil War, Islam had a small visibility in the American South. The Muslim presence was much stronger in the Caribbean, especially in Guyana, where about 15 percent of the imported labor (about 250,000 East Indians brought by the British between 1835 and 1917) were Muslims.

In the late 19th and early 20th centuries some Muslim immigrants from the Ottoman empire came to the United States, along with people from Morocco, the Sudan, and Yemen.

The overwhelming majority were uneducated village men, 14 to 40 years of age, who hoped to return to their homeland after making a fortune in America. Many began their careers as wholesale traders for Arab Christian merchants who had settled in New York City, Boston, and Philadelphia about 20 years earlier. Arab Muslims dispersed throughout the Dakotas, Minnesota, Montana, Alberta, and Manitoba. After World War I, many purchased small farms, but others were drawn to the factories of Chicago, Gary, Pittsburgh, and Detroit, where an enterprising few opened grocery stores, restaurants, coffee houses, barber shops, and funeral parlors. The majority of the men never married, violating the ideals of Islam. They feared American Christian brides would not embrace Islam or adjust well to life in the old country when they returned. Men who had married before they emigrated often never saw their wives and children again, although they sent them money regularly. Of the handful who did marry, three quarters either found Muslim brides in the United States or managed to import brides from abroad, and the rest wed North American Christian women. Many mixed and unmixed marriages were troubled, and some ended in divorce. Lacking access to a proper Islamic education, most of the tiny second generation converted to Christianity and were assimilated into the U.S. or Canadian mainstream.[9]

Between 1900 and 1925, some 40,000 Turks, Kurds, Albanians, and Bosnians who were Sunni

This huge mosque in Delhi, India, is a reminder of the grandeur of the historical Muslim empire and the millions of believers Islam continues to enroll. (Photo by J. T. Carmody)

Muslims emigrated from the Balkans to the United States, most finally settling in the industrial cities of the eastern seaboard and the Great Lakes. Detroit is an example of how a Sunni community grew. The Detroit community was founded in 1903 by a Turkish immigrant. During the 1920s and 1930s Turks and Kurds swelled the community to about 2,000. They kept themselves apart from a small community of Lebanese Shiite Muslims who arrived during the 1920s, preserving the sectarian divisions of the old world. Funeral and charitable organizations helped preserve the community, but there were frictions between Turks and Kurds. The first imam (religious leader) was an Arab who arrived in Detroit in 1912 and held religious services in his home.

Early in the 20th century Muslims from Russia, Poland, and the Crimea arrived in the United States in small numbers, tending to cluster near

New York City. By the 1940s the Sunni community of New York numbered several thousand, held highly visible celebrations of holy days, and fostered intermarriage among different ethnic groups within the Muslim community, including Afro-American converts. When possible Muslims built mosques, but they generally kept a low profile and nurtured their faith rather privately.

> North American Muslims are ethnically diversified on the basis of national origin, language, and religious sect. Arabic-speaking Muslims form the biggest and most differentiated Muslim group in the United States (although only 10 percent of Arab-Americans are Muslims); they include Yemeni migrant farmworkers in California, factory workers from Lebanon, Palestine, and the two Yemens, prosperous Lebanese and Palestinian businessmen, and highly trained professionals of all Arab nationalities. Other large Muslim nationality groups in the United States are the Iranians (90,000), who cluster primarily in California, and the Turks (85,000).[10]

Black Muslims derive from a peddler who appeared in a Detroit ghetto in 1930. Claiming to be from the holy city Mecca, he taught that American blacks are members of a tribe (Shabazz) whose religion before their enslavement in the United States was Islam. One convert, a former Baptist named Elijah Poole (who became Elijah Muhammad on giving up his "slave" name), took charge of the movement in 1934 and moved it to Chicago. From the outset it was controversial, because it charged white society with injustice and urged separation of the races. The Black Muslims demanded a separate state and recruited many of their members from prisons.

> Elijah Muhammad's version of Islam differed from [orthodox Islam] at crucial points. He claimed that Allah is the Supreme Black Man, sharing his divinity with all black men . . . . Moreover, W. D. Fard [the first founder] was said to be Allah incarnate [idolatrous to orthodox Muslims] . . . . Elijah

Muhammad claimed to be the messenger and prophet of Fard. Islam teaches there are no prophets after Muhammad. As for judgment, Elijah held that it is rendered in this world, not in the world to come. There is no heaven or hell. Temporal judgment will soon be rendered on the white man in particular. Blacks should separate themselves from whites racially, socially, and economically as well as religiously . . . all humans derive originally from the black race, the white man coming into existence as a result of a genetic experiment by a black scientist that went wrong, resulting unfortunately in "blue-eyed devils" without true humanity.[11]

In 1987 Muslims in Canada and the United States numbered about 2,682,000. Because of their diverse ethnic character, they have seldom presented themselves as a unified community. Generally, however, devotion to Allah, Muhammad, the Qur'an, and such basic precepts as the Five Pillars have both separated them from the cultural mainstream and given them some coherence. Every likelihood is that Islam will become more important in the United States. Demographers predict that by the year 2000 U.S. Muslims will outnumber U.S. Jews.

Malcolm X

Malcolm X (1925–1965) was born Malcolm Little in Omaha, Nebraska. He grew up in Lansing, Michigan, and saw his house burned down by Ku Klux Klanners. While in prison for burglary, he joined the Black Muslims in 1946. After serving seven years in jail, he went to Chicago and joined Elijah Muhammad. Having proved himself an effective speaker, Malcolm X was assigned to Mosque Seven in New York City. He inflamed white antagonism by his invective against white exploitation, and outraged many by judging the assassination of President Kennedy a case of the chickens having come home to roost. Suspended by Elijah Muhammad for this statement, Malcolm X decided in 1964 to form his own organization. He went on a pilgrimage to Mecca, converted to Orthodox Islam, and renounced his previous racism, affirming the possibility of world brother-and-sisterhood. Hostility continued between his followers and those of Elijah Muhammad, however, and he was killed at a rally in Harlem in 1965. Because he had long advocated violence (for self-defense) most of the civil rights leadership had repudiated him. Nonetheless, his final conversion, and the publication of his autobiography in 1965, made him a powerful symbol for American blacks.

At the end of his pilgrimage to Mecca in 1964, Malcolm X wrote to some friends describing his experience:

> Never have I witnessed such sincere hospitality and overwhelming spirit of true brotherhood as is practiced by people of all colors and races here in this Ancient Holy Land, the home of Abraham, Muhammad, and all the other prophets of the Holy Scriptures. For the past week, I have been utterly speechless and spellbound by the graciousness I see displayed all around me by people *of all colors* . . . . There were tens of thousands of pilgrims, from all over the world. They were of all colors, from blue-eyed blonds to black-skinned Africans. But we were all participating in the same ritual, displaying a spirit of unity and brotherhood that my experience in America had led me to believe could never exist between the white and the nonwhite. America needs to understand Islam because it is the one religion that erases from its society the race problem . . . . I have never before seen *sincere* and *true* brotherhood practiced by all colors together, irrespective of their color.[12]

Such sentiments allowed Malcolm X to shake hands with other black leaders such as Martin Luther King, Jr., and caused his assassination to be seen as a great loss to the whole black movement. Prior to his conversion to orthodoxy and a potentially universalist vision of Islam, however, Malcolm X had made his mark

by preaching eloquently the doctrine developed by Elijah Muhammad's Black Muslims. The following quotation from his autobiography reflects the sermons he gave while coming to prominence as a Black Muslim:

> Original Man was black, in the continent called Africa where the human race had emerged on the planet Earth. The black man, original man, built great empires and civilizations and cultures while the white man was still living on all fours in caves. "The devil white man," down through history, out of his devilish nature, had pillaged, murdered, raped, and exploited every race of man not white.
>
> Human history's greatest crime was the traffic in black flesh when the devil white man went into Africa and murdered and kidnapped to bring to the West in chains, in slave ships, millions of black men, women, and children who were worked and beaten and tortured as slaves . . . . And where the religion of every other people on earth taught its believers of a God with whom they could identify, a God who at least looked like one of their own kind, the slavemaster injected his Christian religion into this "Negro." This "Negro" was taught to worship an alien God having the same blond hair, pale skin, and blue eyes as the slavemaster. This religion taught the "Negro" that black was a curse. It taught him to hate everything black, including himself. It taught him that everything white was good, to be admired, respected, and loved . . . . The white man's Christian religion further deceived and brainwashed this "Negro" to always turn the other cheek, and grin, and scrape, and bow, and be humble, and to sing, and to pray, and to take whatever was dished out by the devilish white man, and to look for his pie in the sky, and for his heaven in the hereafter, while right here on earth the slavemaster white man enjoyed *his* heaven.[13]

The critique of white religion suggested here differs only slightly from what one finds in Marxist and other analyses that find religion alienating (keeping human beings from working to improve conditions on earth by directing their energies to heaven). The special twist in the rhetoric of Malcolm X is his reference to the price white Christianity extracted from black pride. By moving blacks to internalize the slavery of their external conditions and truly consider themselves inferior, white Christians taught blacks to feel second in the divine scheme of things. Abolitionists and others fighting racist interpretations of the scriptures sensed some of this internalized alienation, but it took the Black Power movement of the 1960s to bring the matter to clear consciousness. One may interpret the Black Muslim ideology as a somewhat deliberate attempt to create a history, mythology, and psychology that might heal some of the psychic wounds inflicted by racism and so restore black self-esteem.

Until Malcolm X experienced the pilgrimage in Mecca, with its harmonious blend of many different races, he had no basis for thinking that whites and blacks might cooperate, might live peacefully. It is possible, but probably pointless, to argue that such a basis existed in many parts of American society, and that he was simply blind to it. The fact is that prior to the pilgrimage he thought highly critical, if need be violent, responses were what fit the American situation, and afterward he was committed to reforms worked across racial lines. The Christianity that some would say in principle is not racist had not been as demonstrative of racial equality, to say the least, as the Islam that Malcolm X met in Mecca. So he judged by an empirical test, in the best tradition of William James or John Dewey, reasoning in a very American fashion.

Was Malcolm X a prophet? Many (by no means all of them blacks or Muslims) have thought he was. Prophets are those who hold up the signs of the times and call their contemporaries to account. Prophets possess a vision of how things ought to be, and in the light of that vision they denounce what is not right. Sometimes it takes prophets many years before they learn to balance the negative and positive portions of their preaching. In the case of Mal-colm X, as in the cases of the prophets who worked at the time of Israel's exile to Babylon, the first instinct was that things were out of joint, that people had sinned. Only later did the intimations of grace and hope come forth based on a perception of God's love and fidelity.

Negative prophecy predominated in the preaching of Malcolm X, but at the end of his life he was perhaps turning a corner, beginning to suspect a more positive program. The tragedy is that, like Martin Luther King, Jr., he lost the time to develop this program. Both King and Malcolm X died young, only halfway through their natural life span. Both lost the years when greater experience would in all likelihood have matured their wisdom and deepened their prophetic authority. But they also gained the martyr's mantle because their followers, and many others, saw that they had given their lives for what they believed. In the light of his murder, Malcolm X has gained the authority of one whose last words, recorded in his autobiography, ring with a special resonance. Like King, he could not know that he was soon to be killed, but he could suspect he might well be. Therefore, his sense of hope becomes all the more impressive, all the richer a legacy.

Writings of Shunryu Suzuki

Shunryu Suzuki (1905–1971) was a master of the Soto Zen school who came to the United States in 1958 and founded several Zen groups in California, mostly notably the Zen Center in San Francisco and the Zen Mountain Center at Tassajara Springs, near Carmel. The Soto Zen school stresses how enlightenment ought to pervade everyday life. It opposes all dualism and focuses on the here and now. In contrast to the more dramatic Rinzai Zen school, it does not seek sudden enlightenment, stress teasing koans (enigmatic sayings), or clout people to stir their spirits.

Those trying to Americanize Asian traditions have sometimes approached Native American spirituality as a potential mediator between Asian and white ways. (Jol-Lee, George Catlin; Gilcrease Museum, Tulsa, Oklahoma)

If D. T. Suzuki was the pioneer who brought Rinzai Zen to American consciousness, Shunryu Suzuki's was the quiet voice that made Soto convictions persuasive to many. In his work one can find epitomized the efforts at cross-cultural translation that all the Eastern traditions have faced when they decided to set up shop in the United States. Thousands of Americans have applauded Shunryu Suzuki's elucidation of what they needed to regain vision and inner peace.

Suzuki made most of his impact through somewhat informal conferences he gave to those interested in *zazen* (meditation). After his death, a group he used to visit in Los Altos, California, assembled some of these conferences and edited them into a book. The result, *Zen Mind, Beginner's Mind,* is one of the most charming introductions to Zen one could imagine. Consider the prologue to this little book, which begins with a dictum on the beginner's mind itself and then starts the orientation:

> "In the beginner's mind there are many possibilities, but in the expert's mind there are few." People say that practicing Zen is difficult, but there is a misunderstanding as to why. It is not difficult because it is hard to sit in the cross-legged posture, or to attain enlightenment. It is difficult because it is hard to keep our mind pure and our practice pure in its fundamental sense . . . . The goal of practice is always to keep our beginner's mind . . . . For Zen students the most important thing is not to be dualistic. Our "original mind" includes everything within itself. It is always rich and sufficient within itself. You should not lose your self-sufficient state of mind. This does not mean a closed mind, but actually an empty mind and a ready mind. If your mind is empty, it is always ready for anything; it is open to everything. In the beginner's mind there are many possibilities; in the expert's mind there are few.[14]

Assumed in this orientation are some basic convictions of Mahayana Buddhism. First there is the notion that all people have a buddha mind, a basic consciousness that of itself is pure, good, even perfect. Without downplaying the usefulness of the historical Buddha (Gautama), many Mahayana schools have concentrated more on the buddha mind within each individual. All of us are potentially Buddhas. But while some Mahayana schools have concentrated on wisdom (penetrating philosophy, usually directed toward key sutras, or scriptures, such as the Prajna-paramita, or Wisdom-That-Has-Gone Beyond), and others have concentrated on devotions (such as the Nichiren chants), Zen has concentrated on "meditation," meaning the mental effort to discover (the Rinzai stress) or to express (the Soto stress) one's innate buddhahood. Thus Zen has located the key to successful living in the mind, the consciousness. As one's mind is, so will one's person and life be.

Second, because of its focus on mind, Zen has made much of the experience of original light, awareness, and self-possession. The mind is where one realizes that one is a knower, that one's spirit is attuned to whatever exists, and that everything is intelligible and assimilable to the self. But while Western philosophy has tended to be dualistic, setting mind and world against one another, Zen has striven to undercut such dualism. In the beginning, when the mind is pure, self and other are not antagonistic. For the beginner's mind that Suzuki is cultivating, all is fresh and full of light, nothing is to be despised, fought, or judged evil.

In the epilogue to this collection of Suzuki's conferences, the topic is Zen Mind.

"Before the rain stops we can hear a bird. Even under the heavy snow we see snowdrops and some new growth." Here in America we cannot define Zen Buddhists the same way we do in Japan. American students are not priests and yet not completely laymen. I understand it this way: that you are not priests is an easy matter, but that you are not exactly laymen is more difficult. I think you are special people and want some special practice that is not exactly a priest's practice and not exactly a layman's practice. You are on your way to discovering some appropriate way of life. I think that is our Zen community, our group.

But we must also know what our undivided original way is and what Dogen's [the founder of Soto Zen's] practice is. Dogen-zenji said that some may attain enlightenment and some may not. This is a point I am very much interested in. Although we all have the same fundamental practice which we carry out in the same way, some may attain enlightenment and some may not. It means that even if we have no experience of enlightenment, if we sit in the proper way with the right attitude and understanding of practice, then that is Zen. The main point is to practice seriously, and the important attitude is to understand and have confidence in big mind.[15]

The opening dictum is a typical bit of Zen poetry, making its impact more visually than conceptually. The point seems to be the interconnection of cyclic phases: The bird sings before the rain stops; raining and clearing are on a continuum, are not radically separate. The snow falls but new growth under the snow suggests that snowing, stopping, and growing are more related than separate, more phases of a single process than discrete moments or processes. Spring is within winter, and perhaps winter continues in spring.

Why these images triggered Suzuki's remarks on adapting Zen to America, or why they came to mind as an emblem of his remarks, is not hard to imagine. He had discovered that distinctions or attitudes traditional in Japan, such as the differences between priests and laity, did not work well here. So he adapted, and in adapting he was supported by Dogen's relativizing of enlightenment. Whereas it is fine to be flooded with light like the Buddha, too much concentration on enlightenment can obscure the deeper matter of right practice. In Soto Zen one's practice assumes one's fundamentally enlightened nature and expresses it. One must have confidence in the big mind, the lightsomeness of reality as a whole. One must not get lost in words or evaluations.

In conference after conference, Suzuki urged people to live in the present, stop dichotomizing, pay attention, go with the flow of their lives. He made it plain that Zen is a general method but also a product of Buddhism (a particular set of convictions that the method well serves). Theoretically, one might practice Zen and develop a Zen mind (which is a beginner's mind) and still work as an artist or a businesswoman, play as an athlete or a pianist, perhaps even worship as a Christian or a Jew. The point throughout would be the same: purifying one's mind, being whole, avoiding dualism.

Key Terms

Dharma: teaching, especially teaching that details the obligations of one's state in life. The term can have metaphysical implications—the Teaching by which reality stands or which shows the Way to escape the cycle of deaths and rebirths. When it refers to social obligations, it suggests the Hindu caste system and the particular responsibilities of priests, warriors, merchants/farmers, and laborers. While Hinduism considers pleasure and profit legitimate life goals, dharma and release (*moksha*) are its more noble aims.

Karma: the influence of one's moral acts on one's state of being. Indians generally assume that people are immersed in a process of deaths and rebirths. How people manage, whether they advance toward release or recede deeper into the process, depends on what they have done in their previous lives. Karma is not fatalistic, but it does suggest that much of what one presently is has been preconditioned by one's past lives. Similarly, what one will be in future lives depends on how one responds to moral challenges now. Inasmuch as it denotes action or work, karma can become an object of discipline. By detachment from the fruits (success or failure) of action, one can live in the world and not accrue more attachment or karma.

Yogic: pertaining to discipline, method—especially that concerned with gaining release from the cycle of deaths and rebirths. The classical yoga of Patanjali concentrates on purifying consciousness, with the goal of reaching a state below ordinary awareness, even below sleep, in which one would be pure consciousness, without attachment to anything (aware of nothing in particular). Other yogas have fixed on philosophical study, purifying work (karma-yoga), or emotional love. Each such yoga could be a pathway to salvation, and a wise guru would help a striver decide which yoga best fit his or her personality.

Discussion Questions

1. How might the Vedanta teachings about the nondual character of reality quench desire and advance liberation?
2. Explain the appeal of Gandhian nonviolence.
3. What sort of personality are the five basic Buddhist ethical precepts geared to produce?
4. How could chanting a mantric formula convince Nichiren Buddhists of their harmony with the universe?
5. How did Black Muslim theology change the tenets of orthodox Islam?
6. What sort of personality are the five pillars of Islam geared to produce?
7. Why did his pilgrimage to Mecca have such an effect on Malcolm X?
8. What are the main requisites for admirable prophecy?
9. How are Americans primed to regard the beginner's mind?
10. What are the prospects for Soto Zen outside California?

Notes

1. See Erik H. Erikson, *Gandhi's Truth* (New York: W. W. Norton, 1969), and Thomas Merton, *Gandhi on Non-Violence* (New York: New Directions, 1965).

2. Merton, p. 23.

3. E. Burke Rochford, Jr., *Hare Krishna in America* (New Brunswick NJ: Rutgers University Press, 1985), p. 281.

4. Robert S. Ellwood, "Buddhism in the West," in *The Encyclopedia of Religion*, vol. 2, ed.

Mircea Eliade (New York: Macmillan, 1987), p. 438.

5. Philip Kapleau, *Zen: Dawn in the West* (Garden City NY: Doubleday/Anchor, 1980), pp. 10–11.

6. Ibid., p. 40.

7. Charles S. Prebish, *American Buddhism* (North Scituate MA: Duxbury Press, 1979), p. 78.

8. See William Ouchi, *Theory Z* (Reading MA: Addison-Wesley, 1981).

9. Barbara J. Bilge, "Islam in America," in *The Encyclopedia of Religion*, vol. 7, p. 427.

10. Ibid., p. 429.

11. Robert S. Ellwood and Harry B. Partin, *Religious and Spiritual Groups in Modern America*, 2d ed. (Englewood Cliffs NJ: Prentice-Hall, 1988), pp. 294–295.

12. Malcolm X, *The Autobiography of Malcolm X* (New York: Grove Press, 1966), pp. 339–340.

13. Ibid., pp. 163–164.

14. Shunryu Suzuki, *Zen Mind, Beginner's Mind* (New York: Weatherhill, 1975), p. 21.

15. Ibid., p. 133.

21

Liberation Theology

The issue of social justice pressing on the conscience of religious Americans has made liberation theology a powerful influence. American theologians and laity alike have felt a strong pressure from Latin American, black, and feminist camps to rethink traditional positions. This chapter surveys some of the elements of what *liberation theology* has come to connote in the United States.

General Themes

The various black, Latin American, feminist, and other liberation theologians share a conviction that religion ought to promote social justice. If there is a single crucial plank in the liberationist platform, that is it: God wants justice. Convinced of this, liberation theologians frequently claim the Israelite prophets as progenitors. In saying that justice ought to roll down like a mighty stream, that religious rituals mean less than caring for the widow and the orphan, and that mercy is more important than sacrifice, the prophets focused biblical faith on the power of God to free people from the oppressions crippling their lives. Much as they were convinced that idolatrous worship would lead to Israel's ruin, they were perhaps more strongly convinced that right faith would show itself in fair dealing, kindness, and compassion, especially toward the least fortunate members of a given society.

When it comes to New Testament sources, the liberation theologians tend to cite Matthew 25. There Jesus distinguishes between the sheep and the goats, saying that those who have shown mercy and kindness toward the needy—the sick, the imprisoned, the hungry—will do well before the heavenly king at judgment time, while those who have neglected their needy neighbors will fare badly. Indeed Jesus identifies himself with such needy people, saying that he will take any act of kindness done to them as done to himself.

Another New Testament text favored by the liberation theologians is 1 John 4:20–21: "If any one says, 'I love God,' and hates his brother, he is a liar; for he who does not love his brother whom he has seen, cannot love God whom he has not seen. And this commandment we have from him, that he who loves God should love his brother also." To the mind of the liberation theologians, this linkage of neighborly love with love of God implies a host of social responsibilities. One does not love God and is not on the path to salvation as long as one is unconcerned about the poor and suffering in one's midst. Until those who profess to be religious set about improving their societies, their religious profession will be blurred, if not bogus.

Commitment to some version of this insistence on social justice cuts across the spectrum of liberation theologians. Latin Americans trying to overturn repressive right-wing military regimes, blacks trying to bring American religiosity to bear on cleaning up the ghettos, Asians trying to deal with the poverty and indifference to suffering that scores their societies, Africans trying to overcome the lingering effects of colonialism and the distortions of apartheid, women fighting sexism, and gays fighting discrimination or homophobia—all who take up the cud-

gels of liberation theology seek to have faith make a difference in how people are treated, where society puts its money and energy, whether justice and mercy will prevail over greed and indifference.

Those who expect liberation theology to be politically minded are quite correct, but interest in politics has not meant a neglect of spirituality. Despite the charges of their critics that they are nothing more than warmed-over social workers, or baptized radicals, most of the liberation theologians in fact are hungry for God to appear as Jesus indicated God should appear. When he was starting his ministry at the synagogue in Nazareth, Jesus borrowed from the prophet Isaiah: "The Spirit of the Lord is upon me, because he has anointed me to preach good news to the poor. He has sent me to proclaim release to the captives and recovering of sight to the blind, to set at liberty those who are oppressed, to proclaim the acceptable year of the Lord" (Luke 4:18–19). In her Magnificat, woven from the song of Hannah, Mary, the mother of Jesus, spoke equally directly of liberation: "He has shown strength with his arm, he has scattered the proud in the imagination of their hearts, he has put down the mighty from their thrones, and exalted those of low degree; he has filled the hungry with good things, and the rich he has sent empty away" (Luke 1:51–53).

Admittedly the state of the poor in the United States is nothing like that in Sao Paolo, Calcutta, eastern Africa, and so on. But American liberation theologians insist that such matters as rendering justice to those denied the American dream and caring for the helpless and downtrodden are the messages the churches and synagogues should be preaching. Their theology has stayed close to the example of Jesus and to the preachings of the prophets, perhaps especially Amos and Isaiah. Thus American liberation theologians have noted that Jesus consorted with the outcasts of his day: the

Liberation theologians usually stress the dignity that individuals can feel when they are allowed to think well of their traditional cultural roots. (*Gaw-Zaw-Que-Dung*, George Catlin; Gilcrease Museum, Tulsa, Oklahoma)

The site of Thoreau's cabin at Walden Pond in Concord, Massachusetts, suggests the roots of independent thinking and civil disobedience upon which an American liberation theology might draw. However, Thoreau was more individualistic than liberation theologians generally think desirable. (Photo by J. T. Carmody)

prostitutes, taxgatherers, and poor. He flayed the religious professionals who did nothing to relieve the burdens of the poor, and he called blessed those who made God their great treasure. In Jesus' eyes money was at best a neutral but more often a negative influence. If it was easier for a camel to pass through the eye of a needle than for a rich person to enter the Kingdom of God, where were those who concentrated their whole lives on accumulating money and power likely to end up? How could God bless a people caring more for money than for compassion, worrying more about their bank accounts or the Dow Jones average than about the homeless and the hungry?

In one of the richest countries of the world, millions of people live on the street, are malnourished, or can offer their children no decent future. Meanwhile, billions of dollars buy deadly arms and drugs and support corrupt foreign regimes. Is this not a great perversion of biblical values, of right order as original Judaism and Christianity presented it to be? This is how American liberation theologians have been reasoning over the past two decades. It is the instinct behind their call for redress of the sufferings of the poor, the victims of racism and sexism, Native Americans, the elderly, and the handicapped. Until Americans become converted from their guns, creature comforts, distractions, and apathy, the liberation theologians cannot account them justified before God.

While each group of liberation theologians has risked excesses and loss of perspective, the general drift of American liberation theology has been quite clear and influential. Certainly the mainstream Protestant churches and the Catholic bishops have heeded the cry, for both have sharpened their calls for peacemaking, a fairer distribution of the goods flowing from the American economy, a change of heart that would make the needs of the many take priority over the wants of the few, and a more responsible foreign policy that would keep America from being a friend of torturers and a foe of freedom.

Many Blacks, feminists, and gays have thrown off mainstream religion, thinking it part of the establishment they consider their problem, yet American liberation theologians have retained ties to all such groups, often working with them on particular campaigns. The sense of the liberation theologians that being religious in present-day America means being countercultural has sometimes seemed a nostalgic throwback to the 1960s, yet it also has solid biblical roots. Inasmuch as the "world" that often is the enemy of the biblical God and his spokespersons continues strong in popular American value judgments, the liberation theologians have felt privileged to be countercultural, enemies of the status quo.

Latin American Influences

Perhaps the most systematic, thoroughgoing liberation theology has come out of Latin America in response to the terrible poverty and repressive governments of that area. It is no accident that several ministers in the Sandinista government that arose from the ouster of the Nicaraguan dictator Anastasio Somoza have been Catholic priests. Despite the wishes of the Vatican that priests and nuns not take political office,

many have argued that the critical nature of the times, the extraordinary circumstances created by revolutionary change, have made their political service necessary.

Since 1968—when the Conference of Latin American bishops meeting at Medellin, Columbia, placed the church on the side of the poor—many clergy and simple faithful alike have been vigorous opponents of the right-wing military dictatorships that have predominated in Latin America. In taking such a stance believers have both risked their lives, many in fact being murdered or "disappeared," and challenged the facile equation of liberation and communism made by both the dictatorships and their supporters in the United States. The stories of murder, torture, degradation, and corruption coming from Latin America are too well known to require documentation here.[1] Suffice it to say that leading Latin American liberation theologians such as Gustavo Gutierrez and José Miranda have argued that such perversion is precisely what happens when people turn away from the imperative calls of conscience and Scripture and refuse to honor God by rendering their neighbors justice. The result has been a twistedness, a horrible dimming of spiritual light, and a rush into nihilism all too similar to what flourished in the Nazi camps and Soviet gulags, the worst features of Maoist China, South African apartheid, and the other infamies that have expressed diabolical evil in this century. People become haters of God, fleeing from the light of elemental humanity because their deeds are evil.

Amazingly, however, most Latin American liberation theologians have urged resisting such evil as nonviolently as possible. The few who have sanctioned taking up arms, often by arguing that the *violencia blanca* (white violence) of systematic poverty, illiteracy, and degradation will be overturned only by physical force, have received disproportionate attention in the United States. But the majority have kept contrasting the gospel's call for conversion and forgiveness to the evil ways of the people responsible for the horrors in their societies. Especially valiant have been the women—most of them the mothers, wives, and sisters of "disappeared" men who have shown up regularly in the plazas of the capital cities to protest the butchery. Their simple presence and continuing witness would long ago have shamed people possessing a religious conscience.

Situations such as those in Central American and South American countries whose anti-Communist regimes the United States has long supported easily call forth unbridled rhetoric. It is hard to know how best to convey the magnitude of the affronts the human spirit receives when it contemplates murder and torture become business as usual and cynical sermonizing about threats to national security used to justify the horrors. The same applies when the perversions are committed by leftist regimes, of course. None of the respectable liberation theologians makes crimes committed by socialists better than crimes committed by fascists. For leading theologians such as Gustavo Gutierrez, Jon Sobrino, and Leonardo Boff ideology of either the right or the left is noxious. What matters is what is happening to people who are poor and have few prospects. What matters is whether the benefits and burdens of a society are being shared fairly, whether all members are being invited to participate in the governmental structures directing their fate, whether membership in the society nourishes one's basic humanity or twists it out of shape.

Much of the message that Latin American liberation theologians have been exporting to the United States is summarized in the following sentences:

> Theologians of liberation must be read not in the ivory towers of certain departments of theology (to borrow an image from Pope John Paul II), but in the slums, in the miserable neighborhoods of the destitute, in the factories, on the plantations—wherever an oppressed people live, suffer, strug-

gle, and die. To pretend to "discuss liberation theology" *without seeing the poor* is to miss the whole point, for one fails to see the central problem of the theology being discussed. For the kernel and core of liberation theology is not theology, but liberation. It is not the theologian but the poor who count in this theology . . . . For many persons, a living, direct experience of poverty and of the people's struggle with poverty will be required of them before they will be able to understand this theology. Cardinal Daneels, Archbishop of Brussels, on his return from a visit to Brazil, grasped this very clearly: " . . . . Liberation theology begins with a very acute, very profound sensitivity to poverty. We see this poverty every day on television. It is another matter, however, to see it on the spot—to allow it to penetrate all five senses, to let ourselves be touched by the suffering of the poor, to feel their anguish, to experience the filth of the slums sticking to our skin."[2]

Robert McAfee Brown, who was referred to earlier, has worked steadily to appropriate the insights of Latin American theology and apply them to the United States. In a recent book linking spirituality and liberation, he has argued that a great lesson from Latin America is the coincidence of the things we do to improve the world and the things we do to praise God. How sharp an edge this thesis can gain becomes clear when Brown concretizes it:

> Without denying the importance of the words we speak directly to God in prayer, either in public or in private, we can begin to see from our new perspective how deeds themselves can be forms of prayer. A prayer of intercession may be a trip to the city jail to provide bail for someone wrongly arrested because of having the wrong skin color; an act of praise of God may be the affirmation of a Laotian child's success in the English as a Second Language program; an act of contrition may be persuading a Congressional representative to vote against aid to the Nicaraguan *contras;* a Hail Mary may be involvement in a political group trying to implement the concern for the poor that is celebrated in the Magnificat; a choral response may be joining in the cheers at a rally to reverse the

arms race; a blessing may be the gift of time and money that enables a woman victimized by sexual harassment to secure legal help; a prayer of adoration may be the formation of a political coalition to fight a specific injustice at city hall.

Conversely, a word spoken to God in private may be the condition for a deed done for a victim in public; an inner impulse, empowered by grace, may generate a political conviction; a meditation on scripture may inspire an act of civil disobedience; hearing a sermon about Nathan challenging David may focus the need to challenge the Immigration Service or the State Department. *Laborare est orare*—to work is to pray—was how the medieval monks put it. We are only beginning to catch up with them.[3]

From Latin American sources, both Catholic and Protestant, Brown has sharpened his sense of what religious profession ought to mean in his own country. Accepting the liberation theologians' stress on doing, he has worked out a spirituality that makes prayer and political involvement move back and forth like the intake and output of one's breath. In that way faith becomes as whole as life itself, dissolving most of the tensions between interior and exterior, private and social, love of God and love of neighbor. In that way the point is not so much imagining the poor of Latin America as seeing the poor of one's own country and the influence of one's own country on the poverty of Latin America and then trying to do something about both.

Marxist Influences

The great criticism of liberation theology, both outside and inside the church, has been that it draws on Marxist philosophy and so must be tainted by godlessness and hatred. Critics have specifically charged that Marxist atheism; materialism; and views of class conflict, religion, and ideology are bound to poison any theology influenced by them. Some critics have also argued that one cannot pick and choose when dealing with Marxism. At one point Vatican officials, trying to correct what they took to be abuses in Latin American liberation theology, flatly stated that any borrowings from Marxism left one vulnerable to swallowing, or being swallowed by, the whole.

It may be helpful to consider several of the Marxist viewpoints that liberation theologians claim to have appropriated and bent to their own uses. For example, the Marxist critique of religion has charged that religion tends to alienate people from the earth and their social responsibilities, making them fixate on otherworldly treasures. Liberation theologians have tended to say, "yes and no." In saying yes, they agree that sometimes religion has made people unduly otherworldly. Indeed they have confessed the complicity of the Catholic church in Latin America's shabby past history, showing that often the church supported regimes in which only a few wealthy people profited and many poor people lived miserable lives by taking the edge off potentially revolutionary anger and preaching the primacy of heaven or the necessity of carrying one's cross in this life.

Liberation theologians have also tended to accept some of what Marxists have proposed about materialism, arguing that the genuine God of the Bible is a God influential in history and concerned about the material well-being of all people. The living God is not abstract, remote, unconcerned, and willing to let anyone try to distance love of God from love of neighbor. Most liberation theologians have abhorred class struggle in principle but noted that rich and poor often are at odds because often the operative economic and sociological systems are discriminatory, serving not the common good but the desires of the privileged few. Not to fight against such social distortions would be to condone the great sufferings, from poor health to poor education, of millions of ordinary people.

Many liberation theologians claim to have learned much from the Marxist insight that people regularly put forward worldviews and philosophies calculated to defend their own interests. Thus the haves of a given society are by and large conservative, admiring and defending the status quo, while the have-nots are open to change and hunger for better justice and opportunity. Not to know the relation between one's ideology, which includes one's religious views (theistic or atheistic), is to fail the test of self-knowledge in a highly significant way politically. Thus both radicals and conservatives should hear from religious leaders a strong challenge to their assumptions about how authorities ought to distribute the goods of a society, how the needs of the many relate to the wants of the few, why God has given human beings time and made them mutually dependent, where money and power ought to rank compared to prayer and social service.

Finally the liberation theologians have tended to deny the proposition that one cannot pick and choose when trying to learn from a philosophy such as Marxism. Certainly they would agree that one has to consider what Marxism or capitalism has in fact led to in history—what political, economic, and religious consequences have flowed when people formed by given ideas have come to power. But the history of Christianity, as just one example, has shown that theologians and church leaders have always borrowed from outside sources, using Plato and Aristotle or Confucius and Lao Tzu as their cultural circumstances or missionary needs dictated. In those prior cases church leaders made the gospel the criterion and control of both what they borrowed and how they integrated what they borrowed into the Christian message. Why should matters have to be different with Marxism? Marxists seem to have discovered some important things about how labor functions in a society, how religion can be alienating, how ideology relates to people's places on the socioeconomic ladder, and how people can organize themselves in small cells for effective political action. Why cannot religious people take such insights to heart, purifying them, if need be, by

the standard of Christ's teaching and practice and by what Christianity has learned through the ages? Indeed, can one not argue that religious people, who presumably think (as Gandhi did) that all truth is a gift of God, have an obligation to take to heart and use whatever apparently valid insights anyone, believer or atheist, turns up? Is this obligation not implied in Paul's parting advice to the Philippians:

> Finally, brethren, whatever is true, whatever is honorable, whatever is just, whatever is pure, whatever is lovely, whatever is gracious, if there is any excellence, if there is anything worthy of praise, think about these things. What you have learned and received and heard and seen in me, do; and the God of peace will be with you. (Phil. 4:8–9).

In illustrating how some Marxist notions seem to have proven beneficial in the analyses of Latin American theologians, the American liberation theologian Phillip Berryman, who worked as a missionary in Guatemala, has written:

> A comparison might illustrate what they [Latin American liberation theologians using Marxist tools] mean. Brazil has a higher per capita income than Cuba and a far more sophisticated level of industrialization. Yet in Cuba there is none of the hunger that is widespread in Brazil. Some might grudgingly admit that perhaps there is a trade-off between satisfying people's material needs and establishing democratic freedoms. What these writers are saying, however, is that for most people in Brazil, what the dominant ideology calls freedom is an illusion. Cuba and other socialist countries, even though they do not have political parties that compete in elections, might have forms of participation that are genuine. Moreover, it may be that needed revolutionary changes can be brought about only through what some will call authoritarian rule.[4]

One might add that Pope John Paul II's 1988 encyclical on social justice (*Sollicitudo Rei Socialis*) criticizes both totalitarian and capitalist regimes and teaches that Christian faith does not sanction any particular economic system but judges all by their fruits (which include human rights as well as material welfare).

One of the strongest criticisms of liberation theology has been advanced by Michael Novak, who argues that democratic capitalism, as best represented by the United States, has been the most effective means the world has found for reducing poverty and hunger, as well as for honoring the basic dignity of human beings. Novak underscores three principal heritages from the Bible—its notions of sin, creation, and community—that he thinks were decisive in fashioning the liberal institutions of the West and are threatened by Marxist ideas. In short, Novak charges the liberation theologians with being utopian, focused on an ideal society that never has been rather than working with the best system (democratic capitalism) that actual experience has so far produced.

> There are two approaches to the theology of political economy, the utopian and the realistic. The utopian approach, frankly recommended by such liberation theologians as Juan Luis Segundo, S.J., argues from abstractions about a future that has never been. Permit me to take an example from Bishop Tutu of South Africa, speaking of the liberation of South Africa. Asked by a journalist whether he is a socialist, Bishop Tutu unambiguously replies, "absolutely, yes." Asked then to specify the concrete socialist model he would like South Africa to follow, the bishop demurs. We have not yet seen, he says, "the kind of society" he would recommend. And he adds: "But then we are visionaries. We hope we are visionaries. And we leave it to others to try and put flesh to the things we try to dream." A better description of the utopian approach is hard to find. One encounters it frequently in socialist and Marxist writings. Grand moral principles are asserted. Bishop Tutu says: "And all I long for is a society that will be compassionate, sharing, and caring." He leaves the institutional questions—those that "put flesh to" his dreams—to others. This is one approach.
>
> The other—the realistic approach . . . is concerned with concrete realities, proximate next steps,

and comparisons based upon actual existents . . . it takes care to use as its proximate standard of measurement the simple question: *Compared to what?* "The goal of liberation theology is a non-capitalist, socialist society," some will say; to which the realist asks: "Like what? Bulgaria? Cuba? Sweden? Identify your nearest concrete model."[5]

Novak asks good questions, but Berryman suggests that liberation theologians other than Segundo and Tutu have been grappling with them for some time. Many Latin American theologians would be quite capable of saying what they prefer in the Cuban system and what they reject in the Brazilian. And while the utopian imagination certainly can be misleading if people do not keep their feet on the ground, it remains intimately tied to religious instincts about how things ought to be in human society. Thus Jesus was fully utopian when speaking about the Kingdom of God, but few Christian theologians, conservative or liberationist, have been willing to say that Jesus was not realistic in assessing what God wanted to happen in human beings' midst.

James Cone

James Cone (1938–) has become the most prominent black American liberation theologian. A professor of systematic theology at Union Theological Seminary in New York, Cone produced one of the first black theologies of liberation, arguing that the black experience in the United States, starting with slave days and continuing into present times, furnished this country its starkest challenge. On biblical grounds, Cone believed, the situation of blacks revealed the racist sin at the heart of American culture and so cried out to all people of judgment and faith for radical change. Since launching his liberation theology in the late 1960s, Cone has filled in its background with historical studies in the black American experience and has connected black theology with liberation theologies developing in the third world, especially Africa.

Like Robert McAfee Brown, Cone has recently been at pains to relate liberation to spirituality, trying to overcome the disparity that some would establish between devotional faith and political faith. In so doing he has stressed the distinctive character of black worship, due to the distinctive situation in which most American blacks have found themselves. He has written:

> Black worship has been wrought out of the experience of slavery, lynching, ghettoes and police brutality. We have "been buked and scorned" and "talked about sho's you borned." In worship, we try to say something about ourselves other than what has been said about us in the white church and the society it justifies. Through sermon, prayer and song, we transcend societal humiliation and degradation and explore heavenly mysteries with starry crowns and gospel shoes. Our church is the only place we can go with tears in our eyes without anyone asking, "What are you crying about?" We can preach, shout, and sing the songs of Zion according to the rhythm of the pain and joy of life, without being subjected to the dehumanizing observations of white intellectuals—sociologists, psychologists and theologians. In worship we can be who we are as defined by our struggle to be something other than the society says we are. Accordingly, our gathering for worship is dictated by an *historical* and *theological* necessity that is related to the dialectic of oppression and liberation. Apart from the historical reality of oppression and our attempt to liberate ourselves from it, we should have no reason to sing, "My soul looks back and wonders how I got over." To understand the interplay of the past, present, and future as these are expressed in black worship, it is necessary to examine the historical context that created its unique style.[6]

Cone's convictions about the historical circumstances that begot Black faith in the United States have led him to study such black creations as spirituals and the blues. Similarly, his convictions about the central place of racism in American history have led him to approach theologians in South Africa and other distant lands to discuss similarities and differences between his experiences and theirs. Cone has consistently joined theology and work for political change. Without denying the need for a social, political, and economic agenda, he has spent considerable time on worship, as the quotation suggests.

With many other analysts of the American black experience, Cone has noted that the black church has been the only institution that American blacks themselves have controlled. It has fostered black oratory, scholarship, and political involvement. It has been the main social welfare agency in the black community and the repository of the majority of black hopes. So while a Marxist critique of the otherworldliness to which churchgoing can lead remains relevant, Cone tends to focus on the strength that blacks have drawn from going to church. To have a place where one could let one's tears flow, cry out one's pain, and find one's judgments and hopes reaffirmed has been crucial to black survival. In the stories of the Exodus and the Resurrection, many American blacks have found the strength to keep going in their own oppressive situations. James Cone certainly is impressed by what the black church was able to accomplish, so he certainly is not going to swallow whole any critique that would call churchgoing completely alienating.

In making this judgment Cone agrees with the Latin American liberation theologians who have studied what they call "popular religion," that is, the religion on which the poor, often illiterate masses have relied. In the Latin American case, popular religion has blended a strong cult of Mary and the saints with traditional Catholic doctrine (and sometimes with pre-Christian Indian traditions). In the black case, Americans have modified African traditions and worked out new amalgamations of biblical materials under the influence of their conditions as slaves or ghettoized people.

Liberation theology therefore admits of many different strands, nuances, and modes of expression. The common denominator is an insistence that faith focus on freeing people from the forces crushing or limiting their humanity and twisting their daily lives out of shape. But precisely what overtones "oppression" or "liberation" ought to carry can be quite different in Brazil and Cuba, in black churches and Hispanic churches, in the United States and South Africa, in Latin America and Asia. What does not change is the conviction that any God worth worshiping cares about people's sufferings and energizes them to remove what sources of suffering they can.

Most human suffering comes from human sources. Some sicknesses and natural disasters are "acts of God," but the great sources of poverty, illness, hunger, illiteracy, addiction, and the like are evil individuals and dysfunctional social systems. Nature has proven it can provide sufficient bounty to feed a controlled earthly population. Human industry can produce enough wealth to clothe, educate, and inspire to admirable cultures the vast majority. The problem is the greed and violence resident in the human heart and expressed in economic systems that care more about military arms than about children's schooling, more about the luxuries of the few than about the basic needs of the many. That is how James Cone and the other liberation theologians see the problem.

Writings of the American Catholic Bishops

Prior to their issuance of two blockbuster pastoral letters during the 1980s, the American Catholic bishops were not identified with liberation theology. However, their letters on the nuclear arms race and the American economy changed that, much to the chagrin of critics such as Michael Novak. Indeed the American bishops and Pope John Paul II seem to have been dancing an interesting minuet, the bishops initially taking their lead from papal statements about peacemaking and labor, and John Paul II then extending the bishops' economic views in his encyclical on social matters.

On May 3, 1983, the American Catholic bishops issued their letter entitled "The Challenge of Peace: God's Promise and Our Response," which drew great attention for its treatment of nuclear arms policies. On the one hand, the bishops' letter was complex and ambiguous:

> We believe work to develop nonviolent means of fending off aggression and resolving conflict best reflects the call of Jesus both to love and to justice. Indeed, each increase in the potential destructiveness of weapons and therefore of war serves to underline the rightness of the way Jesus mandated to his followers. But, on the other hand, the fact of aggression, oppression and injustice in our world also serves to legitimate the resort to weapons and armed force in defense of justice. We must recognize the reality of the paradox we face as Christians living in the context of the world as it presently exists; we must continue to articulate our belief that love is possible and the only real hope for all human relations, and yet accept that force, even deadly force, is sometimes justified and that nations must provide for their defense.[7]

This is the recent Catholic version of realism about the human condition. Peace is the ideal, and love is the only force capable of fulfilling human relations, yet sin and human disorder make aggression, destruction, and violence a sorry fact. In view of that sorry fact, nations and individuals alike have the right to defend themselves, to preserve their lives from unjust aggression. Traditional theory about the conditions for a **just war** laid down some guidelines, the most significant of which curbed reactions so that counterforce would be proportionate to the aggression in question and would not create more damage than good.

The question in latter days, however, has become whether nuclear arms, in the awesome degree to which the superpowers now possess them, haven't changed the entire situation and called into question the use of any aggressive or reactive force that would seriously imperil huge populations or even the whole ecosphere.

In responding to this new situation, the bishops allowed the possession of nuclear arms as a deterrent, as long as their possession was viewed as merely an interim stage on the way to negotiations for a more stable situation and the reduction of the arms arsenals. This allowance was grudging, granted the destructive potential in the arms currently possessed, the chance that political instabilities would trigger the use of such arms, and the moral ambiguity in using as threats weapons whose destructive potential caused many to argue for their absolute prohibition (on the grounds that no evil to be combatted could exceed the evil to which the large-scale use of nuclear weapons would lead).

The bishops' letter was published before the scenarios for "nuclear winter" (the dust of nuclear explosions blotting out the sun and so imperiling all life) became widely known and escalated the cries for an absolute condemnation of any substantial use of nuclear weapons. Some critics have argued that one may not in good conscience threaten what one may not actually do, and so more have concluded that policies of deterrence based on the threat to use nuclear weapons are themselves immoral.

What is liberating about this teaching of the Catholic bishops is the entry of religious principles, both biblical and traditional, into the debate about American military policy. For while a few critics have charged the bishops with not having the competence to pass judgment on military matters, more have welcomed their voice, thinking that the basic questions finally are more moral than technical and that the wide consultation that preceded the bishops' letter made it clear that they did their best to inform themselves about the data essential to passing moral judgments.

The bishops went through similar consultations before releasing their letter on the American economy, entitled "Economic Justice for All," on November 18, 1986. Once again there had been meetings at which experts from various points along the spectrum of political and philosophical opinion had given their views, and once again the final document appeared only after several drafts had been published to solicit a wide range of reactions. In this second letter the impact of liberation theology was plainer than it had been in the letter on peacemaking.

After indicating some of the many positive items to mention about the recent state of the economy in the United States and the mood of hardworking Americans, the bishops tackled the negative indices, sounding much like their counterparts in Latin America:

> These signs of hope are not the whole story. There have been failures—some of them massive and ugly: Poor and homeless people sleep in community shelters and in our church basements; the hungry line up in soup lines. Unemployment gnaws at the self-respect of both middle-aged persons who have lost jobs and the young who cannot find them. Hardworking men and women wonder if the system of enterprise that helped them yesterday might destroy their jobs and communities tomorrow. Families confront major new challenges: dwindling social supports for family stability; economic pressures that force both parents of young children to work outside the home; a driven pace of life among the successful that can sap love and commitment; lack of hope among those who have less or nothing at all. Very different kinds of families bear different burdens of our economic system. Farmers face the loss of their land and way of life; young people find it difficult to choose farming as a vocation; farming communities are threatened; migrant farmworkers break their backs in serflike conditions for disgracefully low wages. And beyond our shores, the reality of 800 million people living in absolute poverty and 450 million malnourished or facing starvation casts an ominous shadow over all these hopes and problems at home.[8]

In criticizing the prevailing capitalist system in the United States, the bishops are generous with praise for the initiative it has sponsored, but they do not withhold negative comments on the selfishness and lack of concern for the poor that it has tolerated. In the bishops' eyes the poor, both at home and abroad, deserve the highest priority. Behind this lies the basic criterion to which the bishops recur for judging all economic matters: What happens to ordinary people, to the common good?

In the bishops' view, individual freedoms do not have absolute priority over the common good. Indeed rights to private property and entrepreneurial initiatives that wound the common good and increase poverty require sharp challenge. The goods of the earth exist for all the earth's people. In light of the gratuity of creation, no one has the right to luxuries while anyone else lacks necessities. Insofar as American economics does not honor these basic judgments, it runs afoul of the bishops' Christian instincts and so merits a prophetic rebuke. Traditions of individual freedom cannot justify a system catering to greed and unbridled money-making. The commandment to love one's neighbor as oneself requires that economics, like politics and military policy, bow to the overall welfare of all the citizenry, especially the poor, whom Jesus made the first citizens of the Kingdom of Heaven. One sees, then, that even so traditionally middle-of-the-road a group as the leaders of a large institutional church have been moved by the times and the impact of liberation theology to reread the Bible with more prophetic eyes.

Key Terms

Just War: one that would meet the basic requirements of conscience and honor the essential equality of all human beings in the sight of God. Traditionally, a just war was hard to find. A just war had to be a response to unjust aggression with a reasonable hope of success, to safeguard the rights of noncombatants, and to use no more destructive force than was necessary to gain victory. Overall one had to have good grounds for thinking that going to war would bring more good than harm. War therefore was seen as a last resort, after negotiations had broken down and the evils inflicted by one's enemy had become intolerable. Clearly the Western nations rarely listened to this traditional Christian teaching, but it remained a pressure to solve international problems by negotiation rather than violence.

Discussion Questions

1. How valid is the liberation theologians' general assumption that religion ought to promote social justice?

2. How does liberation theology tend to evaluate money?

3. How valid is the Latin American assertion that systematic poverty, malnutrition, illiteracy, and the like constitute a "white violence"?

4. Why has the option of many Latin American churches to take the side of the poor resulted in the killing of priests, nuns, and laity?

5. How valid is the Marxist position that ideology tends to be self-serving and is usually related to one's position on the economic or social ladder?

6. May one pick and choose from an alien philosophy, for example, discarding its atheism and using its social analyses?

7. What are the strengths in Michael Novak's position that one ought to speak concretely

about the political or social regime one is trying to bring about?

8. What is the dialectic of oppression and liberation that James Cone finds crucial to understanding black worship?

9. What are the special overtones introduced by a theology of liberation highly mindful of racism?

10. How valid is the position of the Catholic bishops that nuclear arms can be tolerated as a temporary stage on the road to a stable peace?

11. Should the needs of the poor in American society take precedence over the wants of the entrepreneurial class?

Notes

1. See, for example, James LeMoyne, "Testifying to Torture," *The New York Times Magazine*, June 5, 1988, pp. 44–48, 62–66, on the situation in Honduras. For general background on American involvement in Latin America, see Penny Lernoux, *Cry of the People* (Garden City NY: Doubleday, 1980).

2. Leonardo Boff and Clodovis Boff, *Liberation Theology: From Confrontation to Dialogue* (San Francisco: Harper & Row, 1986), pp. 10–11.

3. Robert McAfee Brown, *Spirituality and Liberation* (Philadelphia: Westminster, 1988), pp. 134–135.

4. Phillip Berryman, *Liberation Theology* (Philadelphia: Temple University Press, 1987), p. 142.

5. Michael Novak, *Will It Liberate: Questions about Liberation Theology* (New York: Paulist, 1986), pp. 53–54.

6. James Cone, "Black Worship," in *The Study of Spirituality*, ed. Cheslyn Jones, Geoffrey Wainwright, and Edward Yarnold (New York: Oxford University Press, 1986), p. 482.

7. The American Catholic Bishops, "The Challenge of Peace," in *Documents of American Catholic History*, vol. 3, ed. John Tracy Ellis (Wilmington DE: Michael Glazier, 1987), p. 811.

8. The American Catholic Bishops, "Economic Justice for All," ibid., pp. 992–993.

22 | # Feminism

Across a full spectrum of political and religious convictions, in the past three decades American women, and men, have become much more articulate about both sexism and women's distinct contributions to American culture. This chapter samples some representative concerns.

Historical Perspectives

While there are indications that prehistoric women sometimes lived in cultures that considered the sex roles polar but equal, the history of women's existence shows a basic pattern of male dominance. Curiously, perhaps, the leading early deity seems to have been female, a goddess figure associated with the mysteries of birthing, but this seldom made women the chief tribal authorities. Gerda Lerner has presented interesting hypotheses about the origin of patriarchy in the ancient Near East and the connections between the subordination of women and slavery.[1] Most surveys of women's experience with the world religions find women regularly to have been the second sex, prized mainly for fertility and compliance. Women have lived with a more ambiguous self-image than men, usually being both more exalted and more degraded. Male leaders have set the social tone, making masculinity "normal," and femininity "other," even abnormal or deviant.[2]

The biblical traditions on which American religion drew so strongly repeated this general pattern, though with specifically Jewish or Christian nuance. The Protestant Christianity that predominated in the establishment of American culture tended to take New Testament texts as its first authority and so consider women subordinate to men. Women played Eve to men's Adam, carrying the stigma of being the weaker sex, the one that had first succumbed to temptation. Men were the "heads" of women, as Christ was the head of the church. Ministers could claim New Testament precedent (1 Tim. 2:11–12) for women to be silent in church and not presume to teach others. As men were to work out their salvation by the sweat of their brows, so women were to seek justification through childbearing.

Of course many churches did not directly translate the New Testament texts about women into precepts for everyday life, but the primacy of men (patriarchy) was assumed, even though egalitarian texts such as Galatians 3:28 were available as a counterweight. In most churches' view, the fact that Jesus treated women well did not overbalance his choosing only men for his inner core of disciples. The fact that he made Mary Magdalene the first witness to his resurrection did not make her equal to Peter, James, and John. Both Luther and Calvin interpreted Scripture so that women were subordinate to men in the Christian scheme of things, and few American churches disagreed. The Shakers were an egregious exception, although some left-wing Protestant churches have opened the ministry to women.

Catholic and Jewish motifs more verified this general pattern in early American religion than challenged it. Catholics paid more attention to Mary, the mother of Jesus, than Protestants did, which placed a feminine component close to the heart of popular Catholic religion. But Catholics and Orthodox Christians did not allow women to be ordained priests, although Catholic nuns had a great influence in the parochial school systems and hospitals and provided great help during the decades when immigrants arrived in huge numbers. Jewish women could not become rabbis (although recently Reform and Conservative Judaism have admitted women to the rabbinate), and talmudic tradition made official religion a male preserve. Thus Jewish women were held to only 3 of the 613 commandments whose observance is the gist of Orthodox faith, while many rabbinic texts, following in the wake of the Hebrew Bible, expressed worries about female human nature. The result was the ambiguous self-image mentioned previously: Jewish women were both exalted and suspected more than Jewish men.

Despite these liabilities in the legacy they received from the past, many American women made signal contributions to both civic and religious life. This book has mentioned Anne Lee, Mary Baker Eddy, the Grimké sisters, and Elizabeth Cady Stanton. Mother Cabrini and Aimee Semple McPherson are both worthy of comment, contributing as they did to the upbuilding of the American Catholic community and Protestant fundamentalism. Women have been preachers, healers, teachers, abolitionists, founders of both religious communities and businesses, and, recently, both professors and liberation theologians. The three volumes edited by Rosemary Ruether and Rosemary Keller provide ample witness to the variety of roles women have played in American religious history.[3] No one familiar with this history could doubt that American religion would have been much different had women not asserted themselves regularly and effectively.

Nonetheless most women throughout American history have made their religious contributions through the role of wife or mother. This is true of women the world over throughout history. Emancipation, suffrage, and full access to the worlds of work, politics, and higher culture are recent phenomena. Recent feminism, taken as a self-conscious, articulate, and politically powerful movement to promote women's full equality with men, is a historical novelty. Researchers going back to mine the experience of American women in the 17th, 18th, 19th, and even early 20th centuries need to walk a fine line. On the one hand, they have to use the stimulus of today's feminist sensibilities to find, appreciate, and perhaps present to

Mary Cassatt combined the independent skills of a premiere artist with the domestic themes traditionally associated with women. (Mother Feeding Her Child; The Metropolitan Museum of Art; from the collection of James Stillman, gift of Dr. Ernest G. Stillman, 1922 [22.16.22])

official (scholarly) consciousness for the first time the creativity and power women in fact developed in many past situations. On the other hand, they have to avoid the temptation of thinking that such achievements meant in the past what they would mean today.

On the whole creative American women of past centuries tended to make their contributions and wield their power somewhat obliquely. On occasion women certainly were owners, artists, and figures able to shape American mores. Generally, however, they had to work within the limits and through the stereotypes imposed by their association with the domestic sphere. Thus in the 19th century, when religion and women both tended to be excluded from the worlds of business and politics, women generally had to start with the common expectation that their job was to elevate the moral tone, refine manners, and resist the drag of sensuality.

Women seldom seized power and commanded the fate of the politics, church order, art, science, or public opinion of their day. The usual pattern was for women to contribute either by modifying or redirecting going patterns, or by proposing somewhat offbeat alternatives. So, for example, Anne Lee and Mary Baker Eddy, two of America's female religious founders, both proposed religious systems virtually bound to be marginal to the Christian mainstream. Lee's bisexual deity and celibate community life contributed to a Shaker spirituality much admired both by some contemporaries and by many historians, but its impact was meager compared to the revivalism promoted by the patriarchal Baptists and Methodists. Eddy's Christian Science appealed to 19th century American/Victorian women subject to "the vapors," but it always retained the image of a quirky, if not cranky, movement on the fringe. One could say analogous things about the influence of Madame Blavatsky's **theosophy** and Aimee Semple McPherson's Church of the Foursquare Gospel. They are only footnotes to the main story told in standard histories of American religion

such as that of Sydney Ahlstrom. Even when one accepts the feminist proposition that patriarchy has infected the standard histories, leaving many women outside the "canon" from the beginning, any attempt to give such female religious leaders the status of Jonathan Edwards, William Penn, Lyman Beecher, or even Billy Graham would be a dubious enterprise.

Theological Emphases

When feminists now treat of religious matters, whether those pertaining to American history or those best located in the province of the world religions, they tend to separate into two camps. Some feminists, perhaps the predominant force in the recent development of feminist theory, tend to deprecate religion, viewing it as a primary tool of the oppressor. They believe that all religious establishments have supported patriarchal structures and made patriarchy an essential ingredient in their worldviews. This antireligious outlook finds religion to have been alienating for women, inhibiting their growth and abetting their subordination.

The other feminist group includes those who either find religion to have generated some good things for women in the past or who insist that, whatever its historical failings, religion can be a source of hope and empowerment nowadays. Concerning past history, the fact seems to be that, whatever the patriarchal overlords of the established or prevailing religions intended, in fact the Scriptures gave women ammunition for their fight to be heard. Thus the biblical message so influential in American history presented role models (Sarah, Deborah, Esther, Mary, the Magdalene) that later women of spirit could cite. The Beatitudes, which formed the core of Jesus's preaching, could easily seem more applicable to the typical woman than to the typical man. And the later history of the biblically generated religions furnished numerous other role models and texts that could arm egalitarian-minded women such as Joan of Arc, Catherine of Siena, Teresa of Avila, Abigail Adams, Elizabeth Cady Stanton, and Sojourner Truth for battle.

Perhaps the most important argument in the arsenal of the religious feminists, however, has come from experience. Many simply have found the notions of God and salvation essential to their construction of the universe, their sense of self-worth, and their hopes for redress from cultures that refused to treat them fairly. If there were no God to whom they could appeal, they would feel the most pitiable of all human beings. Like many black slaves, they have felt they needed images of heaven and symbols of divine judgment as therapy for their souls, reminders that power-politics and the judgment of men are not the last word.

This chapter will not join the debates about the liabilities and utilities of religion. It will concentrate on the positive proposals of religious feminists that have made an enormous impact on American religious life in the past two decades. Moreover it will note the thorough-going reconstruction of both community life and theology in the strict sense (the study of God) that religious feminists have proposed.

Feminist theologians (female and male) have recently scoured the scriptures and found female imagery for God which, along with more speculative analyses and arguments, has led them to propose depatriarchalizing the deity. As the early Mary Daly put it, feminist convictions about the equal humanity of men and women make it necessary to go beyond God the Father and find new images, either androgynous or transsexual, that correct the historically predominant impression that the deity is male. Because of patriarchal cultural biases, this impression sprang naturally from the cultural soil in which both Judaism and Christianity were nourished. Both biblical Israel and the Hellenistic world assumed a patriarchal mindset, so it was natural for the theologies they developed to picture the deity as male. Nonetheless, the foundational writers were not wholly consistent on this point. Prophets such as Isaiah and Jeremiah sometimes used feminine imagery for God and the philosophical theology stimulated by Hellenistic culture tended to place God beyond any of the delimitations implied by sex.

Present-day feminist theologians usually exploit some version of the biblical doctrine that human beings have been created in the image of God to ask for proper representation of femininity in the deity. In effect this means that all predication about God ought to avoid literalism, so that God turn out no more "really" male than female. If God is beyond all human conceptualization, there is no basis for considering God more male than female, less a woman than a man.

On the other hand, because theology ought to be not merely negative but also positive or affirmative (kataphatic), some feminist theologians realize that there are advantages in developing feminine images for divinity. Just as millions have profited from approaching God as their Father, so millions might profit from approaching God as their Mother. Indeed the cultural jolt involved could be salutary, inviting people to realize that all language about God is conditioned and limited, while (as many women report) considering God to be as much maternal as paternal might do wonders for women's self-image. If Christian and Jewish religious groups then recast their liturgies, catechisms, ordinary preaching, and teaching to honor this bisexuality in the reconsidered God, many benefits to women might ensue.

Another front on which religious feminists have been working has been to incorporate women as full equals in religious community life. This has been the theological rationale, for example, behind the movements to make women eligible for ordination to the priesthood, the ministry (in the Protestant churches that have not yet ordained women), and the rabbinate. Charging their historic communities with sexism, however inadvertent, proponents of women's ordination have argued that making women eligible to share with men the authority and service at the heart of biblical religion is the great symbol women need if they are to find their religious community credible. For example, Roman Catholic feminists have rejected the argument put forth by Pope Paul VI that women cannot be ordained priests because priests represent Christ and Christ was a man. Christ was also Jewish, probably in his 30s, and probably bearded. By the Pope's logic, some feminists have argued, perhaps only a million people in the world nowadays could represent Christ physically and most Catholic priests would not qualify.

A more freighted focus for the religious feminist cause has been reproductive freedom, where sisterhood has found the going hard. Some of the divisions within the ranks of religious feminists have been deep and bitter, one side abhorring abortion as the murder of innocent life and the other side abhorring restrictions on women's right to control their sexuality (indeed, often accounting them the inmost reach of patriarchal tyranny). The theological implications have been assessed differently by the different sides, as have the philosophical assumptions and the biological data. (What is a human person? When is prenatal life viable?) Still, apart from fierce partisans on the extremes, most religious women have managed a civil discussion, agreeing that two values worth prizing seem to be in conflict and wondering how to correlate or prioritize them so that each gets its due.[4]

It must be admitted that, because of evangelical convictions, convictions about the sanctity of prenatal life, or other factors, many religious women have rejected the term *feminism* and dissociated themselves from the feminist movement. For them feminism is unladylike, conjuring up images of strident Amazons. In response, most moderate feminists ask: What's in a name? They point out that they are merely advocating the equal humanity of women with men and women's right to fair, equal treatment in all phases of American culture. It remains to be seen what American religious feminism will finally become, but the large percentage of women in America's religious congregations, and the cogency of their arguments, both historical and theological, seem to ensure that the spotlight now focused on the status of women in many churches and synagogues is not likely to dim for some while.

Feminist Spirituality

Feminist theologians are characteristically opposed to dualism. On the whole they argue against the matter/spirit, body/mind, object/subject dichotomies that have had great influence in Western religious thought. Indeed many feminist theologians favor holism: the connections between ecology and economics, prayer and politics, ethics and doctrinal theology. They also tend to argue for collaboration rather than competition, for the linking of selves into a circle rather than the distinction of selves across a bargaining table. Racism, sexism, poverty, and militarism more flow together, according to feminist theory, than drift apart. Reality is a matter of wheels within wheels, similar patterns running in many different directions. *Spirituality* is a good word to use when naming the elevation of mind and heart needed to appreciate such interconnectedness and relate it to the mystery of God. Spirituality implies the living faith and experience that bring religion into what actually shapes people's ideas and biographies.

A good example of the religious holism advanced recently by feminist theologies occurs in an article by Susan Thistlethwaite entitled "God and Her Survival in a Nuclear Age":

> Yet [Mary Daly] and other white feminists who understand the significance of claiming the earth and bodily process in divinity need to hear the

difference race makes. From black women writers, I hear that history is to be taken as the location of struggle, of survival, of life and death. Yes, the survival of God is the survival of nature: the earth and all its splendors, including but not limited to human beings. Surely the wanton destruction of the basis of life would be an irreparable rending of the worship relationship that is the content of religion's use of the term God. But survival is not mere persistence in being nor is it the idea of progressive material success as defined in the West. God and her survival are threatened both by the otherworldly spirituality of nuclear fundamentalists that makes this earth of penultimate concern *and* by their companion capitalist materiality that measures all life for its monetary values. Survival is the fullness of life, the solidarity between the ancestry of the planet and the race to come. And you cannot find that vision in Plato or his heirs.[5]

If the correlation and fusion of different aspects of reality is one hallmark of feminist spirituality, a stress on women's need for self-affirmation is another. Indeed it has become accepted as standard doctrine among American feminists that women have suffered severe hindrances in their strivings to develop the self-confidence and self-worth necessary for effective political or religious action. When classical Western theology has focused on pride as the archetypal sin, it has neglected the more regular failing of women: lack of courage and confidence to be, to take a stand, and to shoulder the burdens of history. Saying "I will not serve" has been more typical of men than of women. Women have tended either to serve too much, becoming diffused and resentful in the process, or to shy away with excuses, saying, "I cannot serve, I have nothing to offer."

In introducing a recent collection of studies on women's spirituality, Joann Wolski Conn places this characterization in psychological and religious context:

For women the possibilities for mature humanity/spirituality are restricted. Models of human development universally recognize that movement away from conformity and predetermined role expectations and toward greater autonomy (i.e., self-direction, self-affirmation, self-reliance) is necessary for maturity. Yet women's experience shows that most women are socialized into conformity to subordinate roles or are arrested at the threshold of autonomy. To make matters worse, the most prevalent psychological models of human development stop at autonomy, at a notion of maturity as differentiation from others, as independence, as taking control of one's life. Yet women's experience also convinces them that maturity must include not only autonomy but also relationship. It must value not only independence but also belonging. That is, women's experience makes them suspicious of autonomy as the goal of human maturity, while it makes them struggle against social pressures even to reach as far as that ambiguous goal.

. . . Christian teaching and practice, instead of promoting women's maturity, has significantly contributed to its restriction. Women have consistently been taught to value only one type of religious development—self-denial and sacrifice of one's own needs for the sake of others. Whereas men have been taught to couple self-denial with prophetic courage to resist unjust authority, women have been taught to see all male authority as God-given and to judge that assertion of their own desires was a sign of selfishness and pride. The problem lies not so much with the model of religious development as with its application. For example, to encourage self-denial without attention to the way in which women are prevented from having a self (i.e., sufficient self-direction, autonomy) is, in effect, simply to promote conformity to a male-approved role.[6]

In searching for sources that might nourish the self, promote a proper autonomy, and value relationships, some American feminists recently have gravitated toward a positive witchcraft and goddess religion. Such religious feminists have generally put aside the Christian or Jewish tradition in which they were raised and deliberately cast their spiritual lot with neo-paganism. The witchcraft and goddess religion most have favored derive from pre-Christian European traditions and stress the fertility of nature; the possibility of gaining harmony with the earth; the powers latent in the psyche that chanting, dancing, and the release of sexual inhibitions can raise; the centrality of women's sensuality, fertility, and periodicity in the maintenance of life and psychic health; and opposition to the death-dealing present in militarism, ecological destruction, and political or economic systems that concentrate more on power and profits than on people. While some adherents of the new witchcraft and goddess religion are serious to the point of being grim, it is more typical of witches (and the few warlocks who accompany them) to be relaxed, playful, and rather fey.

Witches vary considerably in their beliefs and personality traits, but portions of a 1976 interview with an Irish witch, Sharon Devlin, convey some of the background, ideas, and spirit one might call typical:

> I am a hereditary Witch, but this does *not* mean that I have a direct lineage from mother to daughter, although [laughter] I did allege this as a neurotic teenager. What it does mean is that I am from a Witch family. My great-great-grandmother on my father's side was named Mary MacGoll. She was a fat, little, pudgy, browneyed woman of Scots descent (whom I am supposed to resemble). She was a local midwife and healer, basically a faith healer. I doubt she would have described herself as a Pagan. She was raised as a Presbyterian and she remained a devout Christian, but her Christianity was of the peasant variety; it was centered on the Virgin Mary. She got her power from the Tuatha De Danaan. Most people call them the Gentry or the Sidhe or the Shining Ones. And there are many stories about the fairies that are associated with her . . . . The peak of my "convent period" was when I was about 15. I entered a convent for a brief time—about six weeks—and then was forcibly removed by my parents. My mother went to bed and simply refused to get up unless my father removed me. My father told the Mother Superior that he didn't want my tits to dry up on me as hers had. So I was spirited from

my spiritual refuge and back into the world. . . . What I actually am is an offshoot of Paganism and early Irish Christianity. I follow beliefs which formed the basis of the Culdee Church. The Culdee Church was the only true union of Paganism and the real teachings of Christ; it was brutally stamped out by the papacy. The Culdee Church continued to believe in the ancient Celtic gods. It continued to believe in the Danu and the Dagda and it considered all the ancient heroes and heroines of Ireland to be saints. They had women clergy. They did not believe that sexual intercourse was sinful and, as a matter of fact, on all the church doors was a big portrait of the Great Mother giving birth with her clitoris exposed and her labia pulled wide and her mouth open because she is in birth ecstasy.[7]

While most witches would not follow Sharon Devlin in joining Christianity with witchcraft, they would acknowledge the mixed nature that Celtic religion long had after the advent of Christianity, and many would not mind such **syncretism,** arguing that all religious symbols come from the human psyche and may (or may not) prove serviceable.

Rosemary Ruether

When one looks for an American feminist theologian to represent the vitality and influence that such theology has achieved in the past two decades, Rosemary Ruether, Georgia Harkness Professor of Applied Theology at Garret-Evangelical Theological Seminary in Evanston, Illinois, is sure to come to mind. Trained at the Claremont Graduate School as a specialist in early Christianity, since the mid-1960s Ruether has published articles and books on a wide range of subjects, including history, politics, socialism, feminism, ecology, anti-Semitism, and doctrinal theology. She has lectured all over the world, promoting feminist liberation theology, and her many works on the history and theory of women's religious experience have been main sources of the religious women's movement (especially during the 1970s, when such sources were hard to find). For the first generation of religious feminists, Rosemary Ruether was both the researcher and the role model who made a feminist theology seem possible.

In the preface to a work she edited in 1974, which served many feminists as their first comprehensive source on the topic of religion and sexism, Ruether disclosed her own beliefs:

> The essays in this volume have been written to fill a growing need for a more exact idea of the role of religion, specifically the Judeo-Christian tradition, in shaping the traditional cultural images that have degraded and suppressed women. To what extent did Judaism and Christianity contribute directly to and promote this heritage of misogyny? To what extent, as is often argued, were they responsible for combatting an earlier denigration of women and contributing to woman's gradual rise to a more respected position in modern times? Much of the current literature in the woman's movement has been written by women who are alienated from religion and who, although perhaps occasionally indicating a recognition of the role of the Church in this history of repression, have little historical or doctrinal information about this process. This leaves a serious gap in the understanding of the dilemma of woman's liberation, for religion has been not only a contributing factor, it is undoubtedly the single most important shaper and enforcer of the image and role of women in culture and society. If one takes either a more Marxist or a more psychological view and assumes that the real "cause" of misogyny lies on the level of the economic power struggle or on the level of an immature adolescent psyche in the male struggling for freedom from the mother, it still remains that it has been religion that has been the ideological reflection of this sexual domination and subjugation. And it has been religion, as a social institution, that has been its cultural sanctioner.[8]

Ruether developed her own feminist theology in the decade between the book from which we have quoted and her work *Sexism and God-Talk: Toward a Feminist Theology*. This latter work is one of the fullest constructive theologies yet to appear from feminists, and it probably commands the centrist position among American religious feminists. On the one hand, Ruether wants to update traditional (largely Christian) theology in view of the feminist critiques of past Western religion, but on the other hand, she has not gone over to the new witchcraft and does not judge biblical religion intrinsically nonviable for women. She has been influenced by the interest of feminist theoreticians in language, so that in her view reforming one's language for God, one's theological discourse proper, is an important revisionist task. And she has continued to pursue a political agenda, in keeping with her socialist convictions, so that her language for God constantly bears on liberating the oppressed from the powers and oversights crippling their lives.

The flavor of Ruether's own theology appears in the following passage:

> We need to start with language for the Divine as redeemer, as liberator, as one who fosters full personhood and, in that context, speak of God/ess as creator, as source of being. Patriarchal theologies of "hope" or liberation affirm the God of Exodus, the God who uproots us from present historical systems and puts us on the road to new possibilities. But they typically do this in negation of God/ess as Matrix, as source and ground of our being. They make the fundamental mistake of identifying the ground of creation with the foundations of existing social systems. Being, matter, and nature become the ontocratic base for the evil system of what is. Liberation is liberation out of or against nature into spirit. This identification of matter, nature, and being with mother makes such patriarchal theology hostile to women as symbols of all that "drags us down" from freedom. The hostility of males to any symbol of God/ess as female is rooted in this identification of mother with the negation of liberated spirit. God/ess as Matrix is thought of as "static" immanence. A static, devouring, death-dealing matter is imaged, with horror, as extinguishing the free flight

Willem de Kooning's painting suggests the ambivalence, perhaps even violence, that modern consciousness has revealed in the way women have been treated and regarded. (Woman IV; The Nelson-Atkins Museum of Art, Kansas City, Missouri [Gift of Mr. William Inge])

of transcendent consciousness. The dualism of nature and transcendence, matter and spirit as female against male is basic to male typology. Feminist theology must fundamentally reject this dualism of nature and spirit. . . . The God/ess who is the foundation (at one and the same time) of our being and our new being embraces both the roots of the material substratum of our existence (matter) and also the endlessly new creative potential (spirit). The God/ess who is the foundation of our being-new being does not lead us back to a stifled, dependent self or uproot us in a spirit-trip outside the earth. Rather it leads us to the converted center, the harmonization of self and body, self and other, self and world. It is the *Shalom* of our being.[9]

The dichotomies latent in the theology of hope that Ruether attacks reflect largely European thought indebted to Hegel's view that history unfolds through dialectical conflicts. Ruether therefore is perhaps as much American as feminist in finding them unsuitable. Still, in her desire to keep matter and spirit together, to associate being and becoming, and to honor the maternal matrix as well as paternal energies of liberation, she shows herself a balanced interpreter of mainstream-to-liberal feminist theology. A biblical scholar such as Elisabeth Schüssler Fiorenza might pay more attention to the roles of women in the New Testament and might make more of how the teaching of Jesus broke stereotypes, was egalitarian, and stressed incorporating all ranks of people into the Kingdom of God.[10] But Ruether has had few peers in laying out the conceptual renovations that a constructive feminist theology requires.

Since the work just quoted was published, leaders of American feminist theology have paid considerable attention to racism and lesbianism. In some ways this has simply filled out the agenda implied from the beginning, when feminist theology first began to articulate the experiences of women who felt neglected or degraded by traditional theology. In other ways it has applied pressure both for a more radical critique of traditional Western religion and for a more separatist theological context (women-identified women taking the lead and women's experience greatly overbalancing any requirement to make theology a renovation of its classical sources, including most prominently the Scriptures).

Writings of Mary Daly

Mary Daly is a professor of theology at Boston College and perhaps the leading radical feminist theologian. (Indeed in some places Daly urges women to separate themselves from men as much as possible.) Her passage from mainstream Christian faith to a repudiation of such faith in the name of feminism shows where the dynamics of radical feminism are likely to lodge and lead. After gaining doctorates in philosophy and theology in Europe (Freibourg), Daly came to American notice with a book entitled *The Church and the Second Sex*. The notion of women being the second sex came from Simone de Beauvoir, whose study of women's place in Western culture and social conditioning many feminists consider a classic. Daly's contribution was to apply some of de Beauvoir's ideas to the existence of Christian women and show that women had suffered both historical and theological discrimination in Christianity. Recent contributions from black, gay, and other women on the social margin have only reinforced this verdict, sometimes indicting mainstream feminism as itself blind to many oppressions in which it connives.

Following that work, Daly published *Beyond God the Father*, a book that drew on her familiarity with the theology of Paul Tillich to associate divinity with God as a verb form. In other words, for Daly God was less a patriarchal superhero than an active form of being that had none of the intrinsic limitations of sexuality. God was transsexual, and all the cultural limitations imposed on women in the name, or under the influence, of the patriarchal God lost their religious legitimation.

In writing *Gyn/Ecology: The Metaethics of Radical Feminism* (1978) Daly left the Christian camp and established herself as a powerful critic of Christianity and theoretician of radical feminism. Such subsequent books as *Pure Lust* (1984) built on the foundations laid in *Gyn/Ecology* and consolidated Daly's reputation in feminist circles. *Gyn/Ecology* stands out as the book in which Daly accomplished her rite of passage, and it behooves us to study some of its achievements and claims.

The most impressive portion of *Gyn/Ecology* is the second part, where Daly deals with various egregious examples of the sufferings inflicted on women in patriarchal societies. To her mind such disparate yet cognate cultural phenomena as the burning of widows practiced in India, Chinese foot binding, African clitoridectomy, European witch burning, and American gynecological practice have followed the pattern of a primal murder of the Goddess, the symbol and reality of women's divine status. As patriarchy arose on the bones of the goddess religion, so patriarchy continued to murder women and their sense of divinity in diverse ways, most notably in such atrocities as widow burning and foot binding.

Critics have taken issue with the figures and descriptions Daly offered for each of her case studies, yet, even if one ignores them, the main lines of her argument remain clear and impressive. Again and again patriarchal cultures have not scrupled to slay or slash at women, expressing the ambivalence or outright hatred that women's otherness has frequently occasioned in men. One might bring Daly's list of examples up to date by speaking of wife abuse in present-day American society: In tens of thousands of Americans homes, men regularly visit upon women a pent-up frustration and wrath that can only be called hatred.

In Daly's interpretation the abuse of the women considered witches in Christian Europe during the 16th and 17th centuries was a product of psychic sickness. Generalizing about the treatment of witches—the investigations, interrogations, and punishments—she writes:

> It is clear that the witches were physically and mentally mutilated and dismembered by their persecutors. A witch was forced to relieve her torture by confessing that she acted out the sexual fantasies of her male judges as they described these to her. The judges achieved erotic gratification from her torture, from the sight of her being stripped and gang raped, from seeing her mangled body, from forcing her to "admit" acting out *their* erotic fantasies, from her spiritual and physical slow death. These disturbing and sadistic men were creating the delusion of devils other than themselves—projecting their own evil intent onto these "devils" which were mirror images of themselves—much as sadistic psychiatrists today, influenced by myth, media, and professional training, fantasy themselves as sought-after healers of the "sickness" which they themselves invent.[11]

One of the problems with Daly's book is the hyperbolic language, often clever and punning, that controls her analyses throughout. What in some ways purport to be historical studies are clearly driven by powerful prejudgments, the goal of which is to name and condemn the masculinity that Daly judges has been murderous toward women throughout recorded history. While such rhetoric wins much applause from those already sharing Daly's position, it tends to rebuff even mainstream feminists, who find it excessive and distorting. Nonetheless, the phenomena in question have their own objective power, which Daly's possible excesses cannot mute. Widow burning, foot binding, genital mutilation, and witch burning did occur. They were historical movements with no parallel tortures inflicted by women on men. On even a restrained interpretation, they do seem to have been a conduit for male ambivalence and hatred toward females. Thus they do give plausibility to the radical feminist claim that women should separate themselves from men to preserve their lives and mother the sane forces on which the preservation of planetary life depends.

If one is able to indict Hinduism, Chinese culture, African culture (both tribal and Muslim), and European Christianity with high crimes against women—and it seems warranted on the basis of a sober reading of the historical record—patriarchy has proved to be more than benign head patting. It has proved to be (at least on significant occasions) an expression of male regret that humanity is two-sexed, of male envy at female generativity (the genital focus of much male sadism is significant), and of male destructiveness (the downside of testosterone?) that radical feminists quickly label the cause of both history's military carnage and contemporary technological ventures in ecocide.

Virtually deaf to the counterpropositions that God made humanity male as well as female, that many heterosexual encounters bring delight and mutual flourishing, that male children should not be burdened with the sins of their fathers, and that separatism tends to work few significant cultural changes, Mary Daly becomes obsessed with her good case about the lethal potential in maleness and so leaves heterosexual women, or lesbian women who have had decent experiences with men, nowhere to go. As one reads through the footnotes of *Gyn/Ecology*, it becomes clear that any male writer is going to fail Daly's (unarticulated) tests for credibility, and that either personal pain or an understandable recoil at the horrors in women's history have determined many of Daly's theological positions. Many readers come away conflicted and resentful, perhaps admiring the brilliance and power of the writing and argument, but doubting the balance.

Rebounding from the horrors of male-female failure, Daly can write lyrically of women's love for other women:

Women loving women do not seek to lose our identity, but to express it, discover it, create it. A Spinster/Lesbian can be and often is a deeply loving friend to another woman without being her "lover," but it is impossible to be female-identified lovers without being friends and sisters. The Presence of Enspiriting Female Selves to each other is a creative gynergetic flow that may assume different shapes and colors. The sparking of ideas and the flaming of physical passion emerge from the same source. The bonding of woman-loving women survives its transformations because its source is the Sister-Self. It survives because the very meaning of this bonding is Surviving, that is, Super-living. It is biophilic bonding.[12]

For every reader who finds such a passage a key to personal discovery, an expression of personal seeking, there probably would be (were readers drawn from across the board of American citizenry) ten who would be put off. That does not diminish the power of Daly's vision, though it may diminish its claim to universality. From pain (whether personal or scholarly/historical) behind and vision ahead, radical feminism has presented traditional religion some dramatic alternatives and imperatives. The imperatives include the demand that all religious agencies, indeed all cultural agencies, show themselves genuinely loving and nurturing toward women and that they forthrightly denounce the injuries done to women through the institutions and mindsets of patriarchal religion.

Key Terms

Syncretism: a running together of different intellectual, ritual, or cultural systems that creates a hybrid. In pluralistic cultures such as the Hellenistic world of the early centuries C.E., ordinary citizens frequently drew from various pagan mystery religions, Eastern (e.g., Egyptian) sources, and Christianity to fashion an amalgamation of religious notions, a potpourri. Few syncretistic religious systems have survived and prospered (Sikhism, blending Hinduism and Islam in a new Indian synthesis, may be an exception), but many cultures have tolerated different religious streams, with the result that many ordinary believers have not cared much about doctrinal purity. Thus many Indians could consider Buddhism a subset of Hinduism, or of a generalized Indian religion, and make the Buddha but another manifestation of the Hindu god Vishnu, while many Japanese gladly ran together Buddhist and Shinto notions, little distinguishing between Shinto gods (kami) and Buddhists saints (bodhisattvas).

Theosophy: a system of thought proposing privileged wisdom about God, the cosmos, the individual, and salvation. Usually theosophists depend on the direct perceptions of supposedly gifted individuals and rate such perceptions a higher wisdom than what either the historical religions or the empirical sciences can establish. Theosophy has obvious affinities to gnosticism, hermeticism, and other traditions based on secret, intuitive lore, and usually it perches on the border where philosophy, mysticism, and magic draw together. Recent American theosophists have taken inspiration from such diverse sources as Oriental (Vedanta) thought and the writings of Jakob Boehme and Emanuel Swedenborg.

Discussion Questions

1. To what extent are the foundations of Christianity and Judaism patriarchal?

2. Why have female American religious innovators tended to produce marginal movements?

3. What is the prevailing view of religion among secular feminists?

4. How important are the feminist revisions of language about God?

5. Why have religious feminists tended to favor a holistic spirituality?

6. What are the problems with the feminist spiritual ideal of achieving both autonomy and relationship?

7. What does Ruether mean when she suggests that religion has been the ideological reflection of sexual domination and subjugation?

8. How attractive and viable did you find Ruether's God/ess?

9. What pathologies have been exhibited in witch and widow burning, foot binding, and clitoridectomy?

10. What are the revelations and limitations in Daly's sketch of women loving women?

Notes

1. See Gerda Lerner, *The Creation of Patriarchy* (New York: Oxford University Press, 1986).

2. See Arvind Sharma, ed., *Women in World Religions* (Albany: State University of New York Press, 1987); Denise Lardner Carmody, *Women and World Religions*, 2d ed. (Englewood Cliffs NJ: Prentice-Hall, 1988).

3. See Rosemary Radford Ruether and Rosemary Skinner Keller, eds., *Women & Religion in America*, 3 vols. (San Francisco: Harper & Row, 1981).

4. See Denise Lardner Carmody, *The Double Cross: Ordination, Abortion and Catholic Feminism* (New York: Crossroad, 1986).

5. Susan B. Thistlethwaite, "God and Her Survival in a Nuclear Age," *Journal of Feminist Studies in Religion*, vol. 4, no. 1 (1988): 87-88.

6. Joann Wolski Conn, ed., *Women's Spirituality: Resources for Christian Development* (New York: Paulist, 1986), pp. 3–4.

7. Margot Adler, *Drawing Down the Moon*, rev. ed. (Boston: Beacon Press, 1986), pp. 136–137, 139. See also Starhawk, *The Spiral Dance* (San Francisco: Harper & Row, 1979).

8. Rosemary Radford Ruether, ed., *Religion and Sexism* (New York: Simon and Schuster, 1974) p. iv.

9. Rosemary Radford Ruether, *Sexism and God-Talk: Toward a Feminist Theology* (Boston: Beacon Press, 1983), pp. 70–71.

10. Elisabeth Schüssler Fiorenza, *In Memory of Her* (New York: Crossroad, 1983).

11. Mary Daly, *Gyn/Ecology* (Boston: Beacon Press, 1978), p. 214.

12. Ibid., p. 373.

23 Spirituality

In an effort to respond to the increased psychological sensitivities of many contemporary Americans, as well as their concerns about values and social justice, many religious authorities have focused on "spirituality": religion as personally meaningful, God as experiential. This chapter sketches some of the major preoccupations of the recent interest in spirituality.

Prayer

Spirituality suggests religious doctrine and practice that have been personalized, made a vehicle for people's existential searches for God, ultimate meaning, and healing. Two cautions that appear regularly in recent American writings on spirituality are that the term should not connote any contempt for matter or the flesh, and that "spiritualism," in the sense of dealing with the occult, has never entered the mainstream of American religious life (though often it has had an intriguing existence on the margins).[1]

Central to mainstream Christian and Jewish interpretations of spirituality have been certain understandings and promotions of prayer. Perhaps the simplest definition of prayer is "the lifting of the mind and heart to God." Whether one can pray without possessing a God admits of discussion. Is Buddhist or Hindu meditation prayer? Is Buddhist or Hindu devotionalism—petition of saintly figures such as Kuan-yin (the Goddess of Mercy revered throughout East Asia) or Krishna (the god prominent in much Hindu **bhakti**)—radically different from Christian or Jewish prayer? The key is whether the outreach carries the person's or community's whole being (mind, will, and affection), at least implicitly placing them in the hands (to use a personalist figure) of the ultimacy toward which they stretch. Thus traditional Christian and Jewish worship clearly qualify as prayer, as does most Native American religious address of the ultimate powers. Confucian address or remembrance of the ancestors is a more complicated question, as is the midnight rumination of the supposedly secular person who finds peace by surrendering to whoever or whatever may be running the universe.

The ecumenism of recent decades has brought a fresh interest not just in spirituality generally but also in prayer as a specific spiritual focus. Seminars on centering prayer, the Jesus prayer, zazen (Zen meditation), yoga, **Sufi** techniques, and many other approaches to communion with the divine mystery dot the listings of retreat houses, conference centers, and summer schools. In part as a reaction against the technology and secularism that seem to be choking the contemplative side of the American psyche, feminists, ecologists, and some previously stuffy theologians lately have agreed that cultural healing and deepening require quiet, introspection, and a better tapping of the wellsprings of imagination, creativity, and love.

The article on prayer in *The Westminster Dictionary of Christian Spirituality*, a representative recent handbook, has five subtopics: Adoration, Confession, Intercession, Petition, and Thanksgiving. While the distinctions among these different aspects of prayer are far from

ironclad, they remind the reader that *prayer* is a generic term. In other words, one can lift the mind and heart to God for several purposes, in several different moods or modes.

Some passing descriptions of these subspecies of prayer may indicate the range that address of God traditionally has encompassed.[2] First, concerning adoration:

> Adoration is a form of prayer which lies at the very heart of religion. The word which seems to characterize adoration most aptly is *absolute*. On the one hand, there is the sense of the absolute claim of God. It is indeed this claim which initiates and calls forth the prayer of adoration. God is unique in his absoluteness, and so he is different from everything created and finite. That is why adoration may be offered to God alone.

A second feature of adoration is the absolute self-surrender of the person doing the adoring.

Second, concerning confession: "Confession is the acknowledgment of our sins, the honest recognition that we fail and fail and fail again. It brings sin out into the open instead of burying it in our deep minds and is intended to save us from despair. There is forgiveness, new life and eternal hope."

Third, concerning intercession: "Intercession is prayer with, for and on behalf of another person, group of people or even the world, which is undertaken by an individual or group. For true intercession, the intercessor must be in solidarity with God, that is trying to live out faith faithfully."

Fourth, concerning petition:

> Petition is the prayer of asking. It is often regarded as a "low level" of prayer like the mewing of a cat for milk, and it may be selfish . . . . Petition [better] means that we recognize our entire dependence on God and that the earth is his and we should ask his permission before we take anything, even a crust of bread. It demands the recognition that we are not lone individuals but members of a family and that my request may have to be denied for the sake of others. It is the

prayer of faith and may not be the simplest and easiest stage of prayer, but one which requires great spiritual maturity. Fundamental is the belief that God waits for us to ask not only to try our faith, but because he wants the whole of our life to be in relation to him, every need, hope and fear binding us to himself.

Fifth, concerning thanksgiving:

It is sometimes said that Christians praise God for what he is and thank him for what he has done. But those concepts interpenetrate, for it is hard to separate gratitude for what God has done from joy that he is what he is. In the Old Testament praise is directed toward the Name of God which means his revealed character which is ever the same. But as it is in his acts in history that his name is made known, the praise of his name is mingled with thanksgiving for his acts. Nowhere is this seen more vividly than in the last six psalms in the Psalter.

The changes one might want to enter, the better to accommodate the non-Christian theistic prayer that has flourished in America in the past or is being promoted today, would be relatively minor. The qualifications that a Buddhist master such as Shunryu Suzuki would want to place probably would head in the direction of denying any divinity apart from the flux of natural and psychological experience, and so of suggesting that the point to prayer is centering oneself in the here and now, coming to know one's intrinsic (buddha) nature and the nondual character of all reality.

Prayer furnishes an invaluable entryway for correlating American religion with personal liberation. All Americans who have prayed have sought liberation—freedom from what was binding them as individuals or groups, an expansion of their horizons and hopes. Thus one can study the rockings of Hasidic Jews; the Way of the Cross prayed by pious Catholics; the gospel songs of ecstatic Pentecostals; the formal, sober prayers of the deistic Founding Fathers; and the chants of Native American

healers. In these and many other ways Americans have adored, confessed, interceded, petitioned, or thanked their deity as habits of their religious hearts. These are the methods they tried for resting their spirits; wiping away their tears; pouring out their gratitude; and demanding that their lives make sense, show a purpose, and create more blessing than pain.

Mormons, Jehovah's Witnesses, Nichiren Buddhists, Seventh Day Adventists, and Shakers, as well as Methodists, Baptists, Presbyterians, Catholics, and Greek Orthodox have all, in their various ways, sought through prayer a spirituality that would save them from the everyday pressures of business, fatigue, and doubt that called into question the worth of going on. The recent excursions of Americans in search of new spiritual forms have only expressed a similar search in different words or practices. Little substantial has changed, probably because the final source of both spirituality and prayer is the human condition itself: the need all men and women at least occasionally feel for reassurance that their time is significant, that their work and love are neither casual nor useless.

Wholeness

As we saw when considering feminism, many who have recently been searching for a new spirituality have recognized the interconnections among the different aspects of their lives and so come to speak of "ecological" or "holistic" horizons. In their case, *ecology* has meant less the systems of a given natural habitat or the need to fight pollution than the interconnected nature of human or natural reality. Moreover, the desire powering the ecological probings one finds in recent American spirituality has regularly increased people's sense of wholeness. As such, it inevitably has dealt with healing the bruised spirits that have kept people from integrity, health, and joy.

The link between wholeness and love emerges in the following lines from a recent work on holistic spirituality:

> In loving God heart to heart, the traditional Christian of simpler ages found a center, a still point of the turning world. The love of God, with whole mind, heart, soul, and strength, was Jesus' first commandment, and like to it was Jesus' second commandment, the love of neighbor as oneself. Conjoined, these loves were like the hub of a wheel, a center from which all other duties or preoccupations could radiate like spokes. Because they had a common reference point, the same central source, the spokes could be ordered and cooperative. If each bore its load, the person's time would turn steadily, carrying him forward, making for genuine progress. So one talked of Christian faith as "the way," or one read Bonaventure on the itinerary of the mind's ascent to God, or Bunyan's *Pilgrim's Progress* graced the center of one's bookcase. Traditionally, wholeness and progress were thought equally possible, joint ingredients in religious living. The task for us, in a more complicated time, is to keep the flames of such hope leaping. How can we, with all the assaults on our consciousness, all the importunings of our time and money, find a path, an outlook, a regimen that will integrate our lives sufficiently to give us a sense of a growing wholeness, an increasing peace? That is the tall question a holistic spirituality sets out to answer.[3]

The connections between holism and healing emerge more clearly in spiritualities that begin with human brokenness or sin. Such a beginning is not hard to find, being amply available in both classical texts from the world religions and the data of any historical period. Considering the latter first, one would note the economic, political, and psychological signs of brokenness that pepper the pages of the daily newspaper. Crime and confusion, grief and pain are so prevalent that one is tempted to expect most "news" to be bad. And even when one gets a salutary reminder that the vast majority of the time the telephones work, the mail comes through, the paycheck arrives, the kids are healthy, and the sun gives enough light to show us the way, it remains sobering how much evil human beings do, how much pain human systems cause by excluding so many from their services.

A theology centered in certain texts of St. Paul, St. John, the Buddha, or Confucius is not surprised by such pain. The first of the Buddha's Noble Truths, "All life is suffering," suggests that the news will never be otherwise. The skepticism of Master Kung about human goodness (*jen*), that is, his sense that few of his fellow Chinese had attained a signal measure of it, suggested the same to traditional China. Inasmuch as they followed Luther or Calvin, Americans thought of human nature as corrupted by sin, as needing the grace of Christ to supply enough wholeness to make either private or public life possible. Jews, Catholics, Native Americans, and others in the United States thought somewhat differently, but none of their traditions could blink the facts of human twistedness, brokenness, suffering.

In gazing steadfastly at this prominent dimension of human existence, recent American writers on spirituality have tried to bring political (public) and personal (private) matters together, denying that work for liberation is different from spirituality. Robert McAfee Brown's writings on this theme draw on the leading Latin American liberation theologian, Gustavo Gutierrez, and there are a dozen other writers bringing forth similar messages.

If we return to the thesis that the force to which Christians traditionally looked for wholeness was love, does it follow that love is also the basic source of the healing that human brokenness postulates? Can wholeness in the two senses of integration and repair be mainly a matter of love? Probably the majority of those swept up by the recent American interest in

Spirituality typically underscores the ambiguity of material possessions and the dangers of drowning in a surfeit of creature comforts. (Still Life #24, Tom Wesselmann; The Nelson-Atkins Museum of Art, Kansas City, Missouri [Gift of the Guild of the Friends of Art])

spirituality would say yes, though many would want to say more about what "love" ought to imply. Probably both the psychologists (those initially drawn to focus on the individual person) and the sociologists (those initially drawn to focus on political or cultural problems) would agree that after one has dealt with rational analyses and strategies, the key task still remains: providing the inspiration, motivation, and power to embrace what reason suggests. One cannot legislate morality, let alone compassion and sacrifice. There is a cognate notion that the letter kills but the spirit quickens. And there is the experience, fortunately widespread, that individuals bloom only when they fall in love with another person or a great work, and that communities flourish only when the bonds creating them are cords of affection, ties of friendship.

So the holistic spiritualities probably win and merit most applause when they rivet their analyses to love and test the long-standing proposition that God is love. The proposition seems to imply that God's part in personal or political liberation has to be through works of love. How one then deals with such horrors as the Holocaust, the birth of a defective child, or any other instance where evil seems naked, evolution seems cruel, and nature and history seem senseless of course remains the great burden of **theodicy.** To say that God is love, or to postulate that in all its doings divinity is loving, does not remove the data marking human perversion or nature's caprice. It merely sharpens the edge of the questions about good and evil, justice and absurdity, God and nothingness.

Holistic spiritualities remind us that love, however blessed an indication of where healing and integrity reside, does not remove the need for faith. Theists have no monopoly on faith, of course, since Marxists and secularists also have to go beyond the data of history and the stock market, if they are to work with bright hopes. But theists, or religionists in general, have the special burden of finding a way to write God or the universe a blank check. Any responsible way, most holistic spiritualities would say, cannot encourage intellectual suicide, because most holistic spiritualities speak up for the rights of the mind as well as the heart. But in the final analysis faith goes beyond what the mind can know with certainty. Just as one spouse can never prove the fidelity of the other beyond the shadow of a doubt, so the religious believer can never prove the fidelity of the other beyond the shadow of a doubt, so the religious believer can never finally prove that the universe is benevolent or that God is holy and good. The witness themselves whether it makes sense to expect the sun to rise again and the next day to be worth living.

Ecological Sensitivities

The wholeness for which recent American spirituality has been searching has often included a desire for better connections with the earth. Such diverse influences as feminism, Native American spirituality, and a retrieval of the cre-ation-centered theology of medieval mystics such as Hildegard of Bingen and Mechthilde of Magdeburg have all caused many spiritual writers to reject the dualism passed down from Hellenistic times and boldly affirm the goodness of both the earth and the human body. The devastations wrought by our pollutions of air, water, and earth have raised a consciousness of the price that modern technology exacts first from the ecosystem and then from the human spirit, which no longer appreciates its kinship with the lilies of the field, the birds of the air, the wonders of the mountains, the everchanging tides of the seas.

This attraction to ecology directly ties into holism and healing, for how can creatures drawn from the dust of the earth, as Genesis puts it, be whole or healed unless they feel at home with the earth, at one with creation? The proportions of what modern Westerners have lost becomes clear only when one considers Native American spirituality, grounded in the kinship of all creatures, or when one thinks about Japanese Buddhism, for which nature is a better symbol of ultimacy than anything human ever could be, because nature is spontaneous, unreflective, perfect without striving or having to learn.

To be sure advantages have come with the reflection that makes human beings a unique species, with the technology that has made modernity a new age in history. And it is risky, though tempting, to link the unprecedent carnage of the 20th century with humanity's increasing urbanization, distance from the cycles of nature, and diminution of the sense of awe that used to keep our kind humble (as one realizes when reading the 38th chapter of the Book of Job, where God finally speaks, from the whirlwind, and stops Job's mouth, because Job was not present when the foundations of the earth were laid, so Job cannot possess the wisdom into which human fates must fit themselves).

The priority of inner freedom, sensitivity to nature, and religious wisdom in Native American cultural goals has attracted some Americans seeking an antidote to consumerism and secularism. (His-Oo-San-Chees, George Catlin; Gilcrease Museum, Tulsa, Oklahoma)

A strong stand of naturalism in traditional American piety might have nourished the recent American interest in making ecological sensitivities a high priority in the spirituality necessary for the 21st century, but it is doubtful that many recent American theologians have consciously drawn on this strand. Some no doubt have nourished themselves with Thoreau or Jonathan Edwards, but more have listened to Eastern or Native American wisdom, the reflections of John Muir, the poetries of Annie Dillard at Tinker Creek, or the eloquent pleas of Jonathan Schell that the earth not be fated for nuclear holocaust. Such secular sources as the wise, graceful writings of Lewis Thomas about the lives of a cell; the compassionate, poignant writings of Oliver Sacks about neurology; the challenging evolutionary writings of Stephen Jay Gould and Richard Dawkins to the effect that nature has no teleology, no purpose; and the brilliant yet bleak writings of Stephen Hawking about the first milliseconds of creation and their aftermath have suggested the inexhaustible wonders of creation, the boundless physical context that any spirituality ignores at peril of seeming trivial or contributing to the murder of the earth. Theologians certainly may be charged with insularity, keeping only to their own kind, but enough of them have been interested in the wider streams of American culture, including what might be called the streams of humanistic science, to make it plain to theology in general and spirituality in particular that the earth, the ecosphere, and the cosmos provide prime data for questions about the designs of God, the patterns of salvation, and the requirements for human health.

What, then, should a contemporary spiritual writer aware of even a few of these trends do? What import do such trends carry, when one gets down to cases and tries to imagine the prayer or the political action that the 21st century will demand? Perhaps first one learns to bless and take nourishment from the sources where better relations with the earth have been limned. Second, one turns to the sacramental liturgies that take the human spirit into the grand chorus of praise faith is bound to think rises from the whole of creation. These would include Jewish and Christian liturgies using the Psalms of natural praise, where everything that breathes praises the Lord, and the Orthodox Christian liturgy, where Christ is the Pantocrator, the Lord of All, and the Spirit moving throughout creation makes the whole divine.

To these liturgies one could add Native American ceremonies in which all the directions human beings can face, all the elements entering into the rituals of the sweatlodge, all the birds and flowers of a given habitat stand with the two-leggeds to praise the Grandfather or the Holy Spirit to whom they are responsible and in whose sight they are but diverse citizens of one earthly economy and polity.[4] One could also add such cultural gems as the products of Zen in Japan: the tea ceremony, floral arrangement, and haiku poetry.

Any such creations feed the imagination with alternatives to telephone wires, mine shafts, and oil rigs in the bay. Any such religious or aesthetic achievements contest the developers who assume nature has no rights; the noisemakers who rape the night and make time wholly babble; and the advertisers who would keep the spirit so itchy, so acquisitive, that it would never learn how less can be more, how asceticism is the sine qua non for meeting God.

As such language may suggest, ecological sensibilities, taken as grist for the mills of American spirituality, tend to nurture poetry, imagination, and mysticism. All three stand up to be counted against the thinning of the spirit, the glut of the soul, the denaturing of humanity being worked by technology and mass communications. Most spiritual writers acknowledge that technology and communications are neutral, no more positive or negative in their spiritual potential than silence, which can drive those unprepared into madness, or asceticism, which can feed demons of repression. But technology and communications, computers and VCRs, driven by the profit motive and submissive to the mass market, have become major foes of spirituality and major impediments to wisdom and maturity. One cannot possess one's soul in the impatience, the constant movement, of the cinema or the video. Even freezes and replays will not do. One has to recollect emotion in tranquility if there is to be poetry. One has to go far from the madding crowd, if there is to be mystical converse with God.

Two-dimensional humanity, fostered by bad education, bad preaching, and surfeits of lowest common denominator advertising and communications, plays into the hands of the demagogues and mavens of profitability. As the recent spiritual theologians mournfully discover, one cannot leap over what the centuries of reflection on holiness have shown: the loss of sensate, superficial life goes before the gain of real, spiritual life. One had to lose the world, control the flesh, reject the devils of mammon and pride, if one is to gain heavenly life.

Ecological considerations have sparked such reflections because the depredations manifestly being visited on nature—the acid rain, greenhouse effect, hole in the ozone layer, extinction of species, and so on—shows us the results of the contemporary will to power. In their mirror we see how what has been controlling the human spirit looks when it is projected on the virginity of the Amazon forest, the vast deserts, and the Arctic tundra.[5] The mirror is not kind, does not easily forgive. In what we have been doing to nature, what we have been missing about creation, we have shown ourselves fools saying in our hearts that there is no Creator and there will be no rendering of account. So, at least, have intoned the more rigorous of the ecologically minded theologians and religious writers who retain the Platonic conviction that humankind is not the measure, that

what we have not created we have no right to destroy.[6]

Thomas Merton

Thomas Merton (1915–1968) was a Trappist monk from whose silence and solitude issued a stream of writings that made him one of the most influential American spiritual guides of his century. Brought up in France by bohemian parents, Merton moved from atheism to Catholicism while a student at Columbia University and then joined the Trappists, a later branch of the Benedictine family known for the severity of its monastic regime. He spent the bulk of his adult years in a community at Gethsemane, Kentucky, but in 1948 the publication of his autobiography, *The Seven Storey Mountain*, made him famous. Anything that he wrote thereafter went forth into a public prepared to consider him a striking anomaly and witness to a troubled age. At first Merton wrote rather traditional reflections on prayer or studies in religious history, but gradually he turned his pen to social, political, artistic, and interreligious topics, becoming in the 1960s a leading Catholic voice on such diverse topics as racial justice, the involvement of the United States in Vietnam, and dialogue with Buddhists. Rather ironically Merton died by accidental electrocution while attending a conference in Bangkok that dealt with correlations between Buddhist and Christian spirituality. In his person he seemed to sum up the forces changing the face not only of his church (he was at the peak of his prominence during the Second Vatican Council) but also of his country.

Merton won much of his popularity because of his limpid, clear, and moving style. He was hungry to find spiritual nourishment wherever he could, and the directions his hunger took him say much about where American spirituality had gone by 1968. For example, Merton had returned to the spirituality of the desert fathers, the monks who had gone apart from the cultural centers of Christianity during its early days (especially after the establishment of Christianity as the official religion of the Roman Empire) in search of stark encounters with God. Consider, for example, the following summary of the monk's life, something obviously of professional interest to Merton but also relevant to anyone seeking the essentials of righteousness:

> An Elder said: Here is the monk's life-work, obedience, meditation, not judging others, not reviling, not complaining. For it is written: You who love the Lord, hate evil. So this is the monk's life— not to walk in agreement with the unjust man, nor to look with his eyes upon evil, nor to go about being curious, and neither to examine nor to listen to the business of others. Not to take anything with his hands, but rather to give to others. Not to be proud in his heart, nor to malign others in his thoughts. Not to fill his stomach, but in all things to behave with discretion. Behold, in all this you have the monk.[7]

Notice how little theory there is in this description. Practice is all. The mind receives enough information to stimulate images of men living a simple, pure life, but nothing to spark prurience about the spiritual life, no peeking into mystical transports, nothing sexy like temptations to pleasure or pride. All is understated, commonplace, nearly moralistic. Little, in fact, is specifically Christian. More is simply what comes from reflections on the essentials of the spiritual life, the practice that may justify one before the divine mystery. The desert fathers do not go in for descriptions of the chariot of God, for heavenly scenes with the cherubim singing and the seraphim unfolding their dazzling wings. In their writing, like the landscape they preferred, rocks and bare patches predominate over luxurious vegetation. That does not mean vegetation is evil, art is forbidden, and barrenness is the only way. It does mean that solid virtue is not gimmicky or dramatic, that

hype is the enemy of the real. Thomas Merton, himself a rather dramatic personality, obviously took both nourishment and chastening from the spare ways of the desert fathers. When he later betook himself to Taoist and Zen sources, he delighted in finding a stripped, cranky spirit similar to what he had found in the Thebaid, the Egyptian outback where so many of the desert fathers flourished.

One of Merton's last writings was a journal published posthumously. In it he had recorded many of his impressions during his journey to Bangkok and, more substantially, to the inner precincts of Buddhist monasticism, where he felt quite at home. Indeed, the entire compass of humanity's spiritual venturings had become Merton's home, as one of his essays on the Bhagavad-Gita (the Hindu Scripture) suggests. The topic is violence and war making, and Merton obviously brings to his reading of this most influential Hindu text not only the richness of his own Christian spiritual tradition but also the signs of his nuclear times.

> But the *Gita* presents a problem to some who read it in the present context of violence and war which mark the crisis of the West. The *Gita* appears to accept and to justify war. Arjuna is exhorted to submit his will to Krishna by going to war against his enemies, who are also his own kin, because war is his duty as a prince and warrior. Here we are uneasily reminded of the fact that in Hinduism as well as in Judaism, Islam, and Christianity, there is a concept of a "holy war" which is "willed by God," and we are furthermore reminded of the fact that, historically, this concept has been secularized and inflated beyond measure. It has now "escalated" to the point where slaughter, violence, revolution, the annihilation of enemies, the extermination of entire populations and even genocide *have become a way of life*. There is hardly a nation on earth today that is not to some extent committed to a philosophy or to a mystique of violence. One way or other, whether on the left or on the right, whether in defense of a bloated establishment or of an improvised guerilla gov-

ernment in the jungle, whether in terms of a police state or in terms of a ghetto revolution, the human race is polarizing itself into camps armed with everything from Molotov cocktails to the most sophisticated technological instruments of death. At such a time, the doctrine that "war is the will of God" can be disastrous if it is not handled with extreme care. For *everyone* seems in practice to be thinking along some such lines with the exception of a few sensitive and well-meaning souls (mostly the kind of people who will read this book). The *Gita* is not a justification for war nor does it propound a war-making mystique.[8]

For Thomas Merton, contemporary civilization had made the globe, the whole earth, one's teacher and charge. One must use whatever wisdom, East or West, could bring the earth into perspective and stir the energies necessary to preserve the life come from God. While Merton's globalism and catholicity made him uncharacteristic in his own day, since then, and in good measure because of his example, American spiritual writers increasingly have reached out to any source of guidance that offered perspective on the lethal weapons developed in the 20th century, the genocidal convulsions associated with Hitler, Stalin, Mao, and the despots bloodying the villages of Asia and Africa before their names slipped into oblivion: Pol Pot, Idi Amin, and too many others. For Thomas Merton spirituality seldom went on holiday. If it retreated to the desert to learn elementary monasticism, it charged back into the current political fray convinced that what was happening to poor people, blacks, and both those who made nuclear weapons and those at whom they were aimed was what one had to amend if one was to please God.

Writings of Elie Wiesel

Elie Wiesel (1928–) is a Nobel Laureate for Peace and the leading voice forcing the world to remember the horrors of the Holocaust.

Growing up in Romania, Wiesel became deeply immersed in Hasidic piety, including works of the **Kabbalah.** In 1944 the Nazis deported all the Jews of his town to Auschwitz, where most of his family died. He himself survived both Auschwitz and Buchenwald. After the war he studied in France and then went to the United States, where he became a naturalized citizen in 1963. His first novel, a semiautobiographical account of his experiences in Auschwitz, was written in Yiddish but its French version made him famous. The English version, *Night* (1960), pushed him into even greater prominence.

Wiesel has continued to produce a steady stream of novels and articles, most of them focused on either the Holocaust or the spiritual plight of humanity after Auschwitz. Since 1976 he has been a professor at Boston University, though he has continued to live in New York and travel widely to lecture. He served as the head of the committee to erect a memorial to the Holocaust in the United States, and his Nobel Peace Prize publicized the heroic efforts he has made to ask the world to learn the lessons of the Holocaust, so that similar atrocities may never again occur.

Two brief samples from Wiesel's work and one from Robert McAfee Brown may suggest the character of his writing and contribution to recent spirituality. The first comes from *Night* and is typical of the spiritual revolt the young Wiesel experienced from his years in the camps. The time is Rosh Hashanah, the end of the old year and the beginning of the new, a solemn Jewish holy day.

> Ten thousand men had come to attend the solemn service, heads of the blocks, Kapos, functionaries of death.
> "Bless the Eternal . . ." The voice of the officiant had just made itself heard. I thought at first it was the wind. "Blessed be the Name of the Eternal!" Thousands of voices repeated the benediction; thousands of men prostrated themselves like trees before a tempest. "Blessed be the Name of the Eternal!"

Why, but why should I bless Him? In every fiber I rebelled. Because He had had thousands of children burned in His pits? Because He kept six crematories working night and day, on Sundays and feast days? Because in His great might He had created Auschwitz, Birkenau, Buna, and so many factories of death? How could I say to Him: "Blessed art Thou, Eternal, Master of the Universe, Who chose us from among the races to be tortured day and night, to see our fathers, our mothers, our brothers end in the crematory? Praise be Thy Holy Name, Thou Who hast chosen us to be butchered on Thine altar?"[9]

The tension builds between what Wiesel has been brought up to believe, God's lordship over creation, and his own daily experience of living in hell, witnessing a degradation any just or good God would have to condemn. When a boy is hanged, Wiesel feels God dying, faith evaporating. By the book's end, the reader has made a full tour of hell and come away well aware that atheism may be a viable option, even an imperative for conscience.

Yet the novel does not settle the issue, and Wiesel's later works have kept him clinging to God, a God he must condemn yet cannot leave, if only because retaining his Jewish identity, and so denying the Nazis the victory they sought, requires grappling with the God of his ancestors. Wiesel cannot absolve God. He will not accept the simple proposition that God made human beings free and tolerates their abuses of freedom for the sake of the love and creativity that cannot flourish in compulsion. The God of his tradition has been so exalted that sun and moon do not rise without Him, time and tide move only by His will. Thus genocide and mad hatred come under God's providence and must be laid to God's account. When Wiesel tallies God's account—somewhat aware that a creature never can, yet persuaded that each human being must speak out the judgments experience has fostered—he finds God guilty of horrible crimes. Only Satan would say otherwise, would speak up for God and try to blot out the record.

But then, most remarkably, Wiesel makes life move on. Having judged God guilty of war crimes, he joins the chorus of those who for centuries have begun their prayers, "Blessed art Thou, Lord God of the Universe." God is guilty, responsible, to be condemned, yet Jews, indeed all human beings, must continue to call on God, bless the divine name, and grapple with the divine lordship.

When one seeks the roots of this illogic or superlogic, this amazing both/and (both condemnation and prayer), Wiesel's Hasidic background steps to the fore. The rabbis who have played in Wiesel's imagination as paragons of wisdom and faith may not have traversed so fiery a furnace as the Holocaust, but their existence in eastern Europe was filled with trials. The Nazis were merely the most recent, most efficient, and maddest in a line of anti-Semites. So rabbis such as the Baal Shem Tov, the Maggid of Mezeritch, and Nahman of Bratzlav became expert in handling paradoxes, skilled at voyaging on the waters of absurdity, the seas of nihilism. Courageously they became saints of a blazing realism: evil is nigh, powerful, bestial, yet God is also nigh, perhaps more powerful (one must believe), perhaps willing to send angels to subdue the beasts and comfort the faithful.

As a poetic preface of sorts to a collection of studies of Hasidic masters, Wiesel once wrote: "My father, an enlightened spirit, believed in man. My grandfather, a fervent Hasid, believed in God. The one taught me to speak, the other to sing. Both loved stories. And when I tell mine, I hear their voices. Whispering from beyond the silenced storm, they are what links the survivor to their memory."[10]

Note the progression. Wiesel's father had dared to hope that the Enlightenment (Haskalah) would bring Jews into the mainstream of European culture and bring their tradition up to date, by transferring what had been an otherworldly focus to the affairs of human beings. His grandfather, more representative of a thousand years of talmudic Judaism, had made God the center of his life, the substance of his soul. Both had formed the boy Eleazer, and a bond between them was their love of stories. So that boy, grown and burned by the Holocaust and now a teller of tales, realizes that his work salvages their memory and preserves the tradition they were trying to hand down. The whispers coming from the far side of the Holocaust, serving as his muse, make his family alive, in all the poignancy of the worlds that used to be, the worlds in which faith in God and humanity were possible. The implication may well be that only by telling his stories, returning to the wellspring of his memory, where something antedates the Holocaust, has Wiesel been able to keep going, to find the strength not to let the night, the no, of Auschwitz be the last word.

Toward the end of his study of Wiesel's work, Robert McAfee Brown, groping for the light in Wiesel's world, the forces denying that reality is all night, emphasizes Wiesel's Hasidic background and suggests what Hasidic celebration has meant to Wiesel's spirituality (and what it perhaps could mean to all spirituality struggling after Auschwitz).

First of all, remembering Wiesel's acknowledgement that whatever he has, he has received, we note that the trait is characteristically Hasidic. The *zaddikim* [Hasidic saints] counseled joy for others, whether they attained it themselves or not. It is not inconsequential that the French title of Wiesel's initial collection of Hasidic tales is *Célébration hassidique*. The Hasidic message of celebration is strongly communal, but even if a Jew is isolated, the affirmation rings true. Wiesel reminds such a one: "Your experience is not meaningless, it is part of an entity that takes it into account. Know that eternity is present in every moment; that every table may become altar and every man high priest. Know that there is more than one path leading to God, but that the surest goes through joy and not through tears. Know that God does not like suffering and sadness and least of all those you deliberately inflict upon yourself. God is not that complicated; He is not jealous of your happiness nor

of the kindness that you show to others. On the contrary: the road to God goes through man."[11]

Key Terms

Bhakti: an Indian term for devotional love, one of the pathways for gaining release from the cycle of death and rebirth. If people place their trust in a deity such as Krishna, making him the center of their emotional lives, they can hope to accomplish what yogins accomplish through trance or philosophers accomplish through study. Bhakti has been the most popular religious pathway in India, because it seems open to all. Women, who seldom have been eligible for religious study or formal asceticism, have gravitated toward bhakti, and the various theistic cults dominating the religion of the subcontinent more often than not have depended on bhakti for their appeal (in some cults, however, such as those of Shiva or Kali, love has been mingled with fear).

Kabbalah: a medieval Jewish mystical movement that sought the inner meaning of the Torah and frequently became rather gnostic. The Kabbalists took their fervor and imagination to the sacred pages, convinced that the Master of the Universe had left there the keys to nature and history, as well as to the self. By such stratagems as assigning numerical values to the different letters of the Hebrew alphabet, they would calculate the secret message of a line from Genesis or a chapter of Exodus. They also developed complicated theories of how divinity had diffused itself through creation and what was necessary if redemption were to bring back to God the fallen away parts of creation. The Hasidim often steeped themselves in Kabbalistic lore and thought it their task to carry sparks of divinity into the world or bring the unredeemed back through their joy.

Sufi: pertaining to the mystical dimension of Islam. The Sufis arose when Islam was becoming a prosperous, this-worldly power dominating the Middle East. In part they were an ascetic movement protesting the corruptions threatened by this-worldly power. But the Sufi movement was also like early Christian monasticism and later Jewish Hasidism an outlet for those who wanted more ardor and introspection than formal orthodoxy, regulated by Muslim law (*Shariah*), tended to develop. The great Sufis claimed to be faithful to the Qur'an, the example of Muhammad, and the intents of the Shariah, but Muslim lawyers remained suspicious of Sufi ecstaticism and the liberty of spirit some Sufis manifested.

Theodicy: the task of defending the divine justice and showing that God's dealings with the world have been honorable. When taken as a function of philosophy, and so a matter of reasoning to the divine justice in the face of great evil in the world, theodicy has fared badly. Phenomena such as the Holocaust, the extermination of Armenians by Turks or Chinese by Japanese, or even the death of a single innocent child, throw up walls many find impossible to scale. When taken as a subtask of theology, of faith seeking understanding, theodicy has stayed closer to the mysteriousness of all God's doings, from making the world from nothingness to redeeming the world by self-spending love. Such mysteriousness does not remove the need to protest injustice and evil, but it may shift the focus of the inquiry more to human perversions of God's will or to the statistical probabilities of a world running by evolutionary chance. Indeed for some theologians God is a fellow sufferer and protester, fighting evil alongside human beings.

Discussion Questions

1. What are the places of adoration and confession in prayer?
2. How has the prayer of Americans tended to serve their quests for personal liberation?
3. How does love help people gain wholeness?
4. What are the main healings that wholeness demands nowadays?
5. How do traditional spiritualities such as those of Native Americans spotlight ecological values?
6. To what extent does human beings' treatment of nature offer a mirror showing their prevailing spiritual states?
7. How universal are the virtues that Thomas Merton found to be the crux of the desert fathers' monastic life?
8. Why could Merton assume that the teachings of the Bhagavad-Gita were relevant to his fellow Americans?
9. How has Elie Wiesel been able both to reject God and urge living before God joyously?
10. To what extent does any contemporary American spirituality worth its salt have to grapple with the revelations of the Holocaust?

Notes

1. See Catherine L. Albanese, *America: Religions and Religion* (Belmont CA: Wadsworth, 1981), pp. 163–188.

2. See John Macquarrie et al., "Prayer," in *The Westminster Dictionary of Christian Spirituality,* ed. Gordon S. Wakefield (Philadelphia: Westminster, 1983), pp. 307–313.

3. John Carmody, *Holistic Spirituality* (New York: Paulist, 1983), p. 5.

4. See Joseph Epes Brown, *The Spiritual Legacy of the American Indian* (New York: Crossroad, 1982).

5. See, for example, Barry Lopez, *Arctic Dreams* (New York: Charles Scribner's Sons, 1986).

6. See John Carmody, *Ecology and Religion* (New York: Paulist, 1983).

7. Thomas Merton, *The Wisdom of the Desert* (New York: New Directions, 1960), pp. 28–29.

8. Thomas Merton, *The Asian Journal of Thomas Merton* (New York: New Directions, 1975), pp. 350–351.

9. Elie Wiesel, *Night* (New York: Avon, 1960), pp. 77–78.

10. Elie Wiesel, *Souls on Fire* (New York: Vintage Books, 1973), p. 1.

11. Robert McAfee Brown, *Elie Wiesel: Messenger to All Humanity* (Notre Dame IN: University of Notre Dame Press, 1983), pp. 219–220. The quotation from Wiesel comes from *Souls on Fire*, p. 208.

CHAPTER 24

Conclusion

American religion is no easier to summarize than it is to introduce. Even though the nearly 500 years of European presence in North America are a short time compared to European civilization itself, they are enough to defeat anyone seeking tidy evolutionary formulas. Even more daunting is the range of the population that has come to inhabit the United States: now a quarter of a billion, through the centuries significantly more. Still it is the business of introductory texts to sketch main lines, dissect basic patterns, and hope that further studies will absolve the half-truths and overgeneralizations that such efforts necessarily involve. To that end this chapter offers some overall impressions, the most general of which concern the significance of the Protestant Christian dominance of American culture, the shadings introduced by the large population usually considered minority or marginal to the dominant Protestantism, and the upshot for the average American: a noteworthy individualism.

The Protestant Dominance

Here the subject matter is the Protestant dominance presented by the foregoing studies in American religious history and worldview.

342

The fact is that colonial America was a refuge for Protestant groups, of quite varying hue, who wanted a new beginning. If the New England Puritans rightly attract most of the attention because of their cultural influence, much of the profile they etched was repeated, with a somewhat looser mien, in the other colonies. The centrality of the Bible; the tension between an original Reformation bias in favor of individual interpretation of the Bible and a second- or third-generation Protestant orthodoxy threatening that bias; the moralism that expected civic life to follow biblical edicts; the sense of election, errand, and destiny all proved portentous in American history.

Certainly one may argue that Enlightenment rationalism, Deism, or a potentially secularist bias toward the primacy of public affairs and the disestablishment of religion formed a fruitful, dialectical tension with such generative religious instincts. The generation of the rather rationalistic Founding Fathers was crucial. But even the Founding Fathers had to bow to the generative religious instincts on public occasions, producing at least a facsimile of biblical piety and moralism, and after the Founding Fathers the revivals of biblicism proved potent indeed.

Thus Grant Wacker, ruminating about the central thesis of a study entitled "The Demise of Biblical Civilization," cannot quite believe there was a demise:

I am uneasy with the title of this essay. The shadows that crossed the biblical civilization of the late 19th century were not, as many contemporaries believed, the signs of impending winter. A long and genial Indian summer of biblical authority has persisted into the 1980s, and it may turn out that it is not an Indian summer at all, but the beginnings of a new spring. Nonetheless, no student of modern American culture could say, as did English traveler James Bryce in 1888, that Americans are basically a religious people . . . scholars such as Winthrop S. Hudson, Robert T.

Handy and Edwin S. Gaustad—historians who have made it their business to see American religion in the long perspective—have similarly concluded that the 1920s and 1930s were a watershed. The average person did not disavow the Bible so much as simply abandon it. By the end of the 1930s, to borrow a phrase from Conrad Wright, Americans had grown accustomed to using "a secular rather than a theological vocabulary when issues really seem[ed] worth arguing about."[1]

It may be that periods of American history during the 16th, 17th, and 18th centuries would have shown the average American less wedded to the Bible than was the case in the 19th century, but it is more certain that during the 20th century biblical literalism came unglued. And even though biblical literalism persists among an impressive fraction of present-day Americans, the revival of biblicism in both mainstream Protestantism and Roman Catholicism is qualitatively different from what one would have experienced in 1889. Nowadays those critical yet enthusiastic about the Bible seem more moved by the Bible's mythology, poetry, and humanistic insight than by the conviction that all ultimately significant wisdom reposes in its pages. Secularism now rules the policies of the government, the authoritative interpretations of the law of the land, and the ethos of business.

Still Protestant convictions about the lay vocation, holy worldliness, and righteousness expressing itself in hard work begetting prosperity underlie many of the propensities of present-day American secularism. If one traces the historical evolution of the ambitions ruling the white American majority nowadays, one is bound to run into the "Protestant ethic," even though one is likely to realize that so simple an equation as "industry is godliness" never existed. So, by several analytical routes, one concludes that the American versions of the 16th-century Reformers' main theses were formidably central to the construction of American culture.

Whatever nuance feminist, ethnic, and minority studies rightly could demand one place on such a thesis, it still seems valid in principle.

This Protestant dominance has not only worked itself out as a demographic prevalence, a matter of more people representing themselves as Protestant Christians than as adherents of any other religious (or irreligious) tradition. It had also entered the fabric of constitutional philosophy, been part and parcel of the example and rhetoric deemed classically American: how Washington comported himself; how Jefferson wrote; how Lincoln spoke; and how William James, Nathaniel Hawthorne, Herman Melville, William Faulkner, and other giants of American letters construed the world. Even when they put aside their Protestant upbringing and the biblical phrases or starched moralism imbibed from nursery days, such exemplars retained a skepticism about human nature and government, a commitment to activist or this-worldly evaluative standards, best understood by studying the relations between classical Protestantism and 18th-century Enlightenment thought.

Of course this interpretation puts aside the emotionalism prominent in much evangelical Protestantism. It hews more to the Calvinist line of Protestant theology than to the Episcopalian, Lutheran, Baptist, or Methodist, let alone to the Pentecostal or Mormon. But while it may be vulnerable on demographic grounds (which place the Protestant majority outside the Calvinist camp), it seems more than defensible on the grounds of cultural influence. Calvinism-cum-Enlightenment thought definitely seems to provide the basic articulation of American public culture and civil religion. The elite few who have been most responsible for casting the institutional structures forming the democratic many without doubt have been more Calvinist and Enlightened than Baptist or Lutheran, let alone Catholic or Jewish. The steel in the American spine, the cut in the American skepticism, and the self-anointing in the American sense of destiny all derive from these traditions. And while certainly one ought to distinguish, even separate, these two traditions as originally quite disparate, in American practice they often fused. The reason promoted by the Enlightenment, or translated by its Scottish descendents into common sense, seemed a worthy bearer of biblical election, vocation, and duty to praise God by good stewardship.

Minority Colorings

The minority colorings in American religion, which other interpreters might well consider pluralistic emphases strongly challenging the Calvinist-Enlightenment predominance, are many and diverse. In the measure that we consider fundamentalist and evangelical infusions of literalism, emotionalism, and antiintellectualism significant, we qualify the representativeness of the image presented to the world by the leading American statesmen, scientists, and people of letters. In the measure that we scan the impact of the 19th-century or latter 20th-century immigrations, we have to ask whether the United States hasn't become quite a different country and culture since the Civil War, the influence of its formative years notwithstanding.

Both immigrations, the one largely European and the other more Latin American and Asian, have put into the public consciousness alternatives not only to Calvinist reflexes but also to Protestantism as a whole. Both immigrations have also challenged Enlightenment verities, even as Enlightenment verities and Protestant assumptions have worked on the immigrant populations, acculturating them to American disciplines and dreams. If there is no melting pot, as recent assessments of such acculturation have suggested, neither are there simply ethnic enclaves untouched by the combined secularism and piety that dominated the nation by the Civil War.

In the freshness of a Sierra Nevada morning many of the preoccupations and upsets of both contemporary and traditional American culture fade away, exposing the radical mystery of existence from which all authentic religious renewal springs. (*Sierra Nevada Morning,* Albert Bierstadt; Gilcrease Museum, Tulsa, Oklahoma)

The tolerance, civil religion, and overall pluralism hailed in many quarters as the great American achievement have certainly prevailed in sufficient force to allow the historian to speak of a typical American pattern, according to which the third generation of immigrant groups usually finds itself sufficiently accepted, acclimated, and educated to compete quite well in American business and politics. They remain ethnic through the fourth and fifth generations, but dilution seems stronger than resurgence of ethnic pride. Irish, Italian, Polish, and other representatives of immigrant Roman Catholicism offer good case studies in wholesale though incomplete assimilation. Jews and Greeks offer more good case studies. Hispanics and Asians are interesting for the new twists they seem to be working on the standard pattern, though much in that pattern continues for those who manage to escape the ghettos and enter mainstream education.

The great exceptions to this pattern have been blacks and Native Americans, in good part because they were minorities from the beginning, conceived from colonial times as outsiders, even when the country or the productive work in fact was theirs. Both groups have assimilated somewhat in recent generations; some of their number have certainly become middle class in outlook as well as financial standing. But the roots of difference, the reasons for nonassimilation (to the admittedly vague consensus of the white mainstream), go deep, and the more blacks discover such roots, the more complicated becomes their passage. Like other ethnic groups, blacks realize their rich heritage should not be surrendered. But also, unlike American Jews or Catholics, blacks can find the American experience so warped, so poisoned by slavery, that they become ambivalent about claiming this land and culture as their own.

Consider, for example, one of the paradigms of black wisdom that Toni Morrison creates in her splendid novel *Beloved*. Baby Suggs is a self-developed, self-anointed preacher, enjoying a phase of powerful largeheartedness before she dies convinced that whites have broken her heartstrings.

> "Here," she said, "in this here place, we flesh; flesh that weeps, laughs; flesh that dances on bare feet in grass. Love it. Love it hard. Yonder they do not love your flesh. They despise it. They don't love your eyes; they'd just as soon pick em out. No more do they love the skin on your back. Yonder they flay it. And O my people they do not love your hands. Those they only use, tie, bind, chop off and leave empty. Love your hands! Love them. Raise them up and kiss them. Touch others with them, pat them together, stroke them on your face 'cause they don't love that either. *You* got to love it, *you*! And no, they ain't in love with your mouth.

Yonder, out there, they will see it broken and break it again. What you say out of it they will not heed. What you scream from it they do not hear. What you put into it to nourish your body they will snatch away and give you leavins instead. No, they don't love your mouth. *You* got to love it. This is flesh I'm talking about here. Flesh that needs to be loved. Feet that need to rest and to dance; backs that need support; shoulders that need arms, strong arms I'm telling you. And O my people, out yonder, hear me, they do not love your neck unnoosed and straight. So love your neck; put a hand on it, grace it, stroke it and hold it up. And all your inside parts that they'd just as soon slop for hogs, you got to love them. The dark, dark liver—love it, love it, and the beat and beating heart, love that too. More than eyes or feet. More than lungs that have yet to draw free air. More than your life-holding womb and your life-giving private parts, hear me now, love your heart. For this is the prize." Saying no more, she stood up then and danced with her twisted hip the rest of what her heart had to say while the others opened their mouths and gave her the music. Long notes held until the four-part harmony was perfect enough for their deeply loved flesh.[2]

One can note and praise many good preachments of white American culture, but urging such a moving love of human flesh (especially black flesh) is not one of them. And in sensing that white culture largely omitted or never knew such a love, one finds much that is wrong in the American mainstream coming into clear focus. Certainly the love reflected in holistic spirituality moves to the same drummer. And certainly black culture doesn't solve all its problems, let alone all the problems of American culture at large, simply by taking a Baby Suggs to its bosom. But those who would decry any orthodox history of American culture or religion (on the grounds that millions, including many Protestants, never accepted the dominant Protestant ideals) could find in Baby Suggs a literary-religious argument for demurring on deeper grounds.

Like the battle over the literary canon defining the great books Americans ought to read,[3] the battles over the standard lines of American culture head into philosophical questions about standards and criteria of excellence. A canon is, etymologically, a ruler. But how long should it be, what markings should it carry, to what should it be applied? One can answer these questions, and derive reasoned arguments for one's admission of some books or people into the standard list and one's exclusion of others, but the venture is as perilous as it is necessary.

If what in fact apparently shaped the ideals and ideas of past generations is a powerful criterion, so is what should have shaped them, what would have shaped them had prejudice and exclusion not ousted many contenders from the battle before they could fire a shot. Surprisingly, though, one of the results of thinking about such canonical battles is the reaffirmation of American convictions about pluralism and rights of conscience to which it leads. Inasmuch as such convictions came from what we have called the dominant Protestant outlook and were the occasion for the success of originally immigrant majorities, they show that the instincts launching American culture may well have implied many of the correctives demanded by those now arguing for a wider range in American normativeness. One could claim that such correctives were sanctioned from the beginning.

Liberty and Individualism

The American ideal, and achievement, has been to build a country on the principle of maximum personal freedom. However much social realities have hedged this principle, putting controls on the powerful and limiting the poor, the ideal has remained. Individual initiative, free enterprise, and freedom of speech have all

remained precious, central aspects of the American dream that few citizens would disparage. The same is true of religious liberty, that is, the freedom to worship as one's conscience dictates and to publicize one's faith and invite others to join in. None of these rights has been unlimited. All have suffered checks and balances, legal or social, that have restrained much of their potential abuse. But the ideal has burned brightly, and the reality has matched the ideal sufficiently to keep cynicism at bay.

The United States has been a country where people could worship as they wished. Jews, Catholics, Mormons, Seventh Day Adventists, and other minorities have suffered for their faith. They have learned about discrimination and prejudice, in ways usually subtle and occasionally gross. But on the whole Americans have repudiated the Ku Klux Klan, the Know Nothings, and the neo-Nazis who would have overturned the traditions of religious liberty and the right to be different. On the whole, the burden of proof has lain with those who would restrict freedom of speech and worship, heinous exceptions regarding blacks notwithstanding.

Perhaps that has been the main lesson of the American experience: Pluralism is viable; individual freedoms can make a country thrive. The question now seems to be, What price has the American option for personal liberties exacted, and how should the option proceed in the 21st century, if the American tricentennial is to be happy?

Looking to the past, revisionist historians have shown the many ways in which the country welshed on the deal supposedly struck in the Constitution. If one judges Native Americans, blacks, women, and ethnic latecomers to have gotten less than a fair share of the pie, the lofty rhetoric about individual freedoms and equal opportunity has to come down a few pegs. The barrios, reservations, ghettos, and "men only" clubs stand as sobering calls to reconsider. Add to these the government corruptions lately called to mind by such terms as *Watergate*, *Irangate*, and *Contras*, which were preceded throughout history by many cousins and multiplied by follies in Vietnam, the Philippines, and other areas where *anti-Communism* became a code word for corrupt dictatorship. Of course there are good reasons for continuing to maintain that the American experiment has generally been an astounding success. But there are also good reasons to pause, take stock, and go humbly. Americans who cannot abide such reasons, who think it unpatriotic or irreligious to sponsor self-criticism, now seem a theological problem.

Another way of putting the question of where the American experiment in freedom should go is to ask what habits religion and the other potent shapers of American culture should now be trying to establish in people's hearts. Robert Bellah and his colleagues at the University of California recently pursued this question, trying first to determine the habits presently prevailing and then to reflect on how viable they seemed to be.[4] The results were not comforting. In Bellah's reading—which of course reflects long-standing convictions he has expressed about American civil religion and the compact Americans should have been making with one another—the traditions of personal liberty have now spawned a dangerous individualism. Few Americans now seem comfortable making commitments, and few enjoy vibrant, supportive communities, perhaps because such communities flourish only from commitment. Religious communities are no exception to this pattern, which may be the most telling revelation about recent American habits. Perhaps the best way to illustrate the point, and end this study on a positive note, would be to describe a religious American behaving contrary to individualistic patterns and showing thereby how a primary commitment to the common good can develop community. Along the way, he will suggest the need to go beyond personal comfort

and enter the mysteries of what the New Testament calls **kenosis** (self-emptying).

Joe Greer, a priest in Boston, made a few decisions during the middle 1970s, when Boston was at the height of its racial tension.

At the time, Father Greer was serving (as he always had served) in an all-white parish—St. Mark's in Dorchester, a section of Boston at the epicenter of the integration upheaval. A small number of Boston priests were fervently committed to civil rights, but Father Greer was not among them. He harbored memories from his youth of blacks and Irish nightly trading taunts, fists, rocks, and bottles up at Roxbury Crossing. "Look, I don't love blacks as much as I love my own Irish people," he told me. "But God made us all, and He didn't make any garbage. We'd boxed the blacks into Roxbury, and that had to stop. I was ordained to help people, and right then the blacks needed help. But, believe me, I wasn't enthusiastic about it." . . . The parishoners of St. Mark's were incensed by Father Greer's involvement in carrying out the court's decision. Some of his fellow priests were so angry that they lined up with the protestors as he rode into South Boston on those charged mornings. The buses were pelted with rocks and splattered with refuse. One kindly looking older lady held a rosary in one hand and greeted the buses with the extended middle finger of the other. Father Greer was regularly spit at as he ushered his charges into their new schools. At a restaurant in Dorchester one evening, following a television appearance in which he had appealed for calm, an enraged waitress threw a salad in his face. Threatening and abusive calls were daily occurrences at the rectory, and the bitterness lingered; a number of his parishoners felt that he had abandoned them.[5]

Father Greer might well have agreed that he had abandoned them, at least the part of them unwilling to change for the sake of justice and peace. Without enthusiasm, but with determination, he insisted on doing his bit to keep the violence down and gain time, room, for negotiations. At a given juncture he realized that what might please him or his own ethnic community was not serving the common good, the people at large. He made the theological judgment that the common good was more important in God's sight and so was where his own conscience had to lodge. Certainly he was not alone in his judgment, and certainly many nonreligious people reached the same conclusion. But perhaps he was a hero, a patriot, and a bit of a saint. Perhaps he was a model of what America has depended on to keep its traditions of personal liberty from spawning a vicious individualism, a selfishness bound to wound civility and encourage "everyone for himself" or "dog eat dog."

How can individuals fixated on their liberties and particularist groups be moved to higher viewpoints? What do we need to realize the great potential husbanded through the American centuries? Certainly no single answer, no panacea, leaps from the pages of American religious history. But an analysis of honorable people, such as those singled out in this book, suggests that one goes widest in one's affection, sympathy, and understanding by deeply penetrating one's own religious tradition. At the depths of the traditions most significant in American history one finds all people condemned to ignorance, mortality, and suffering. Thus Jews, Christians, and all other Americans who get down to basics can find that all of us are simply people whose lives are short, who have never seen God, who are not privy to the ultimate design of the universe. Consequently all of us have reason to back away from self-promotion and self-concern, the numerous ways we try to make ourselves the center of the universe. Now and then all of us can glimpse humble ways to help our country deliver on its constitutional promises. For Joe Greer, the way was riding a bus and taking flak. For us authors and for you readers it probably will be similarly simple and unglamorous. But there it will be, asking us to choose. Godspeed.

Key Terms

Kenosis: self-emptying. The term appears in Philippians 2, where Paul is describing the incarnation and sacrifice of Christ. It has entered Christian theology as a provocation to think hard about the sacrifices entailed in the work of redemption. Extended to religious discourse in general, it appears in discussions of how to combat evil and what part forgiveness, reconciliation, and new beginnings play in establishing community. It poses some of the most fundamental challenges to civil discourse: When does liberty become vicious individualism? What kinds of sacrifice are not foolish but admirable, not outside the basic business of civility but central to forming a people, avoiding a bloodbath, and preserving the third, spiritual dimension without which culture may be merely materialistic fodder?

Discussion Questions

1. How much has the Protestant dominance of American religious history been tied to the influence of the Bible?
2. What has been the prevailing American view of human nature?
3. What is the significance of the fact that those who shaped American culture are now numerically a minority?
4. How true and significant is the charge that American culture on the whole has failed to love human flesh properly?
5. How central to the American tradition of defending personal freedoms has religious liberty been?
6. What does the example of Joe Greer suggest about future American religion and foreign policy?

Notes

1. Grant Wacker, "The Demise of Biblical Civilization," in *The Bible in America*, ed. Nathan O. Hatch and Mark A. Noll (New York: Oxford University Press, 1982), pp. 121–122.

2. Toni Morrison, *Beloved* (New York: Alfred A. Knopf, 1987), pp. 88–89.

3. See James Atlas, "The Battle of the Books," *The New York Times Magazine*, June 5, 1988, pp. 24–27, 72–75, 85, 94.

4. See Robert N. Bellah, et al., *Habits of the Heart* (Berkeley: University of California Press, 1985).

5. Paul Wilkes, "Profiles (Father Joseph Greer)," *The New Yorker*, June 13, 1988, pp. 59–60.

Appendix

Approximate Membership Data on Major American Religious Groups (1985)

Adventists, Seventh-Day	623,000
Baptists	30,000,000
Buddhists	250,000
Christian Church (Disciples of Christ)	1,157,000
Christian Churches and Churches of Christ	1,041,000
Church of the Nazarene	500,000
Churches of Christ	1,250,000
Eastern Orthodox Churches	4,000,000
Episcopalians	2,768,000
Friends United Meeting (Quakers)	57,500
Jehovah's Witnesses	697,660
Jewish Congregations	5,817,000
Latter-Day Saints (Mormons)	3,602,000
Lutherans	8,500,000
Mennonites	90,000
Methodists	13,000,000
Pentecostals	3,300,000
Presbyterians	3,300,000
Roman Catholics	52,000,000
Salvation Army	420,000
United Universalist Association	175,000
United Churches of Christ	1,700,000

Sources: Constance H. Jacquet, Jr., ed., *Yearbook of American and Canadian Churches 1986* (Nashville: Abingdon, 1986), and Frank S. Mead and Samuel S. Hill, *Handbook of Denominations in the United States,* new 8th ed. (Nashville: Abingdon, 1985).

From *Christianity: An Introduction,* 2d ed., by Denise Lardner Carmody and John Tully Carmody, © 1989, 1983 by Wadsworth Publishing Company. Reprinted by permission of the publisher.

Glossary

Alienation: making foreign, giving over to someone else. For atheists religion is something that does not fit their convictions and so is foreign. Moreover, religion is something they believe causes people to give over to God responsibilities they themselves ought to assume. Thus the classical Marxist critique of religion makes it an opiate keeping people from striving for social justice. In the case of Feuerbach, the argument was that "God" is a dangerous projection of human ideals, causing people to place in "heaven" energy they ought to apply to this-worldly tasks of securing justice, peace, the flourishing of culture, and so forth.

Ambulando: a Latin word meaning "by walking." The word usually occurs in the phrase, *solvitur ambulando*, meaning "it is solved by walking." The reference is to Zeno's paradox, where the problem was how to get across a distance if one can only travel half the way at a time and the distance is infinitely divisible into halves. Breaking out of the logical chains imposed by such a statement of the problem, practical people would say that one got across the distance by walking. In other words, many problems are revealed to be pseudoproblems when one stops worrying about the theoretical difficulties and gets on with the task of doing something practical about them. From this experience, pragma-

tists have argued for the priority of doing over thinking, while people of common sense have learned not to take all intellectual difficulties seriously.

Anabaptists: European groups of the 16th century who refused to allow their children to be baptized and made baptism an adult confession of faith. Hutterites, Swiss Brethren, and Mennonites fell into this category. The leading Protestant reformers—Luther, Zwingli, and Calvin—condemned the movement, holding for the validity and necessity of infant baptism, as did Roman Catholics. Anabaptists frequently suffered persecution and tens of thousands were put to death for their convictions.

Anthropomorphism: casting something non-human (for example, an animal) in human terms. Most ancient peoples have spoken of animals, plants, and forces of nature as though they had souls, minds, and wills. Most religions have pictured divinity on the model of human existence, speaking of intelligence, volition, and even passion as divine attributes. Human beings seem nearly condemned to anthropomorphism, inasmuch as we are always drawing from human experience and trying to render nonhuman beings intelligible in human terms. The danger in theology is to forget that anthropomorphic speech is always merely analogous and so take such figures as God's wrath or God's love as meaning what they would were God human.

Apocalyptic: a genre of religious literature found both in the Bible and in extrabiblical literature. Apocalyptic literature purports to be revelations from God about how history is going to unfold. The Book of Daniel in the Hebrew Bible and the Book of Revelation in the New Testament are both considered apocalyptic literature. Usually apocalyptic literature comes from a time when people are suffering oppression or feel their faith has not been rewarding them as they expected. The scenarios of God's coming to punish their enemies and reward their fidelity are meant to gladden believers' hearts and shore up their faith. In an extended sense, *apocalyptic* means cataclysmic or concerned with dreadful scenarios of the last day. People who are expecting woe, torment, and disaster can be said to exhibit an apocalyptic mentality, especially if they seriously think the end of the world is about to occur.

Arianism: a Christian heresy advanced by Arius of Alexandria in the fourth century. The Arians believed that the Logos (Divine Word) was not equal to the Father in possessing the divine nature but that "there was a time when he was not." The Council of Nicaea agreed with Athanasius of Alexandria that the Arian position violated traditional faith in the full divinity of Christ, the Logos incarnate, and so imperiled salvation.

Armageddon: a term that occurs in Revelation 16:16, where it claims to be a Greek transliteration of a Hebrew term. (No such term occurs in Hebrew.) Armageddon apparently is the location of the final cosmic battle between good and evil. Apocalyptic literature such as Revelation tends to think in terms of such an ultimate showdown. Some scholars think the term is derived from Megio, a major pass in the Mount Carmel chain and the site of many battles in ancient Near Eastern days. By extension, Armageddon has come to symbolize doomsday, the final conflict in which God will definitively vindicate the good and punish evildoers.

Ashkenazim: the term has come to designate Jews of northern European origin, in contrast to the Sephardim, who originated in southern Europe (Iberia). Originally, however, it meant "German" and designated any of the Jews who lived in the Rhineland Valley or neighboring France before the Christian Crusades of the 11th to 13th century prompted them to move east into Slavic lands. Persecutions in eastern Europe in the 17th century caused many Ashkenazim to move back to western Europe. Eventually all Jews who adopted the synagogue ritual favored by this tradition were regarded as Ashkenazim. Until very recently most Ashkenazim used Yiddish as their common language, and today they account for about 80 percent of world Jewry.

Baconian: referring to the philosophy of Francis Bacon (1561–1626). Bacon proposed a new method, to supplant that of Aristotle, according to which human inquiry would become scientific by stressing induction. His ideal was a secular approach to the material world that would rid it of impractical symbolisms and bring nature into the service of human prosperity. While the particulars of Bacon's own theories provide for considerable nuance, his thought generally helped free natural science from religious contemplation and prepare the way for the technical approaches to nature illustrated by modern engineering.

Baptist: pertaining to churches that arose out of English Congregationalism in the 17th century. The first Baptists were Puritan congregations that had withdrawn from the Church of England to achieve a purer church life free of civil control. Their leader was John Smyth, a clergyman who had left the Anglican church about 1606 to minister to a separatist congregation at Gainsborough on Trent. This congregation emigrated to Amsterdam in 1608 to escape persecution. In Amsterdam Smyth rejected infant baptism as unscriptural and a hinderance to forming a pure church. The influence for this position may have come from the Mennonites he encountered in Amsterdam. Other early Baptists then backed away from the Mennonites, returned to England, and established a church opposed to infant baptism. Another group of Baptists emerged in England in 1638. This group established baptism by immersion. Baptists grew in numbers in the mid-17th century, when Puritanism was gaining power, but after the restoration of the crown they were subject to discrimination. In the United States Roger Williams founded the first Baptist church in Rhode Island in 1639.

Bhakti: an Indian term for devotional love, one of the pathways for gaining release from the cycle of death and rebirth. If people place their trust in a deity such as Krishna, making him the center of their emotional lives, they can hope to accomplish what yogins accomplish through trance or philosophers accomplish through study. Bhakti has been the most popular religious pathway in India, because it seems open to all. Women, who seldom have been eligible for religious study or formal asceticism, have gravitated toward bhakti, and the various theistic cults dominating the religion of the subcontinent more often than not have depended on bhakti for their appeal (in some cults, however, such as those of Shiva or Kali, love has been mingled with fear).

Civil Religion: the fusion of culture, politics, and religion that makes it hard to separate who people are and how they defend their existence from their beliefs about ultimate reality. Prior to the American experiment in the separation of church and state, virtually all cultures aspired to a civil religion that would make their faith the soul of their national way of life. In ancient Rome, for example, religion was considered the bond of the Roman way of life, so that failure to acclaim the divinity of the emperor was considered seditious. In traditional China and Japan, it was hard to distinguish between religion and mores. With the disestablishment of religion in the United States, civil religion became less institutional, more nebulous. Scholars have tended to find it operating through holidays such as Thanksgiving and the Fourth of July, when American prosperity was interpreted as God's blessing. Patriotism has frequently become so mixed with religion in many parts of American culture that to criticize government policies was tantamount to critcizing divine providence.

Congregationalists: in 16th century English terminology *Congregationalist* was often synonymous with *Separatist* because most of the churches separating from the established Church of England favored a political order in which power was vested democratically in the congregation as a whole. The congregation as a whole had a covenant with God, who had gathered (congregated) them as his people. Calvinist theology generally prevailed in the Congregational churches. In American terminology, both the Plymouth Pilgrims and the Massachusetts Puritans were congregationalists; they stressed a Calvinist theology of covenant, stood separate from the Anglican church, and made the community as a whole the locus of church power.

Cosmological myth: the narrative understanding of reality that situates human existence within a cosmos taken to be fully alive and organically whole. Hunting and gathering peoples typically think of reality this way, telling themselves stories of how the world was born, how the sun and the moon quarreled, how death arose, why the animals no longer speak to human beings except in visions and dreams, and so forth. The cosmological myth keeps human beings closely tied to plant and animal life, encouraging a great sensitivity to the spiritual import such fellow citizens carry. It does not acknowledge a transcendent divinity who made the world from nothingness, and it does not differentiate such mental products as myths, mathematical formulas, philosophical theories, and mystical symbols.

Dharma: teaching, especially teaching that details the obligations of one's state in life. The term can have metaphysical implications—the Teaching by which reality stands or which shows the Way to escape the cycle of deaths and rebirths. When it refers to social obligations, it suggests the Hindu caste system and the particular responsibilities of priests, warriors, merchants/farmers, and laborers. While Hinduism considers pleasure and profit legitimate life goals, dharma and release (moksha) are its more noble aims.

Divination: efforts to discern the future, find the will of the holy powers, or determine a cause of sickness. Most tribal peoples have developed religious functionaries who carry out divination by going into a trance, being taken over by a helping spirit, or reading the signs of such "systems" as cracks in a tortoise shell, the flight of birds in the sky, the pattern of chits shaken out of a basket, or the entrails of animals. Divination sometimes became a protoscience, attributing order to natural elements and seeking the correlation between this order and human affairs. Usually diviners were shrewd about the psychosomatic causes of illness and the psychosocial causes of disputes, aberrant behavior, and other problems that brought families or tribes into crisis (times for reconsideration and decision).

Enlightenment: a European movement of the 17th and 18th centuries that urged people to cast aside traditional religious authority, including that of the Bible, and think for themselves. Enlightenment thinkers such as Hume, Voltaire, and Kant doubted the reality of miracles, distrusted ecclesiastical influences, and were repulsed by religious wars and bigotries. They considered humanity sufficiently mature to manage its own affairs without outside, "supernatural," influences, and they especially prized the autonomy of the individual conscience.

Enthusiasm: claiming to be "filled with God," spiritually exalted, rapt in the Spirit. Our present connotation of the term is a pale remnant of this older meaning. Originally enthusiasts were people taken out of themselves by divine agency and rendered ecstatic. Gradually any churches that stirred up emotion, by singing, dancing, clapping, and the like came under the rubric "enthusiast." On the one hand, they merited praise for engaging both mind and heart with religious faith. On the other hand, they were always suspected of neglecting the rational, sober, prudential side of religion and immersing people in pure emotion. Pure emotion was sure to be short-lived. The apostle Paul's discussion (I Corinthians 12) of the various charismatic gifts already contained an implicit critique of enthusiasm, but the Enlightenment's stress on reason further clouded its image. Thus educated Americans of Jefferson's and Madison's generation

were likely to have a low opinion of religious enthusiasm as something not only irrational but also bound to encourage an unbridled religious practice troublesome for a pluralistic society.

Evangelical: concerning the gospel or glad tidings (*euanggelion*). In the New Testament itself the word refers to the news that Jesus preached, and also to the news others preached about Jesus. Evangelical Christians are those who especially stress heralding this good news, proclaiming the gospel. Thus the Church of England's Commission on Evangelism said: "To evangelize is to present Jesus Christ in the power of the Holy Spirit that [people] shall come to put their trust in God through him, to accept him as their Saviour, and serve him as their King in the fellowship of his Church." This emphasis came to the fore in the 18th century when effective preachers such as George Whitefield and John Wesley made proclaiming the good news the center of their ministerial effort. The Second Great Awakening added more fuel to this fire, and in its wake many Protestant churches supported great evangelists such as Charles Finney, Dwight Moody, Billy Sunday, and Billy Graham. Critics tend to find fault with the aggressive methods evangelicals sometimes employ and with their narrow view of personal salvation, which threatens to ignore social justice.

Fundamentalism: the term comes from a series of booklets called *The Fundamentals* published in the United States between 1910 and 1915. The fundamentals were the basic teachings of Christianity: the divinity of Christ, the Second Coming, the inspiration and authority of the Bible, and the reality of heaven and hell. (A Presbyterian general assembly of 1910, responding to controversy about the orthodoxy of some graduates of Union Theological Seminary in New York, said that the five essential doctrines were the inerrancy of Scripture, the Virgin Birth of Christ, Christ's substitutionary atonement for sins, Christ's resurrection, and the validity of Christ's miracles.) All were understood rather literally, with little attention given to their symbolic or mysterious character. By extension the term fundamentalism came to be applied to those groups that stressed a doctrine of personal salvation and a literal interpretation of Scriptures. Fundamentalism has the advantage of presenting a simple, powerful view of Christian faith that wastes little energy on ambiguities or complexities. It has the disadvantage of robbing Scripture and faith of their metaphoric character and so of diluting their value as ways into divine mystery.

Gnostic: one who claims secret, privileged knowledge, usually purporting to bring salvation. One of the earliest doctrinal battles the early Christian church fought was with various Gnostic groups, most of whom downplayed the centrality of faith in Christ for salvation and condemned works of the flesh—eating, procreating, and celebrating—as the main ways people were trapped apart from God. More broadly, Gnostics have been those elitist groups that claimed to possess a superior insight or spiritual regime not available to the hoi polloi and exempted themselves from the ordinary laws of Christian morality. Because of this they have generally been repudiated by both church authorities and the Christian "sense of the faithful," which has confessed the narrow way of Christ to be the only sure way to salvation.

Gnosticism: a generic name for views of salvation that contested with orthodox Christianity in the first through third centuries. The Gnostics got their name from the Greek word *gnosis* (knowledge). They claimed to possess secret knowledge that was the key to salvation. Generally this knowledge bore on how humanity had fallen into its current state of distance from God and debts to the flesh. The Gnostics tended to despise the flesh, sexuality, and marriage, and either urge an extreme asceticism or allow licentious behavior because they considered fleshly matters insignificant. Some Gnostic groups gave women more authority than was possible in orthodox Christianity, and the Gnostic inclination to prize secret doctrines that would guarantee salvation continued in transmuted form throughout later Western history.

Hasidic: pertaining to the religious movement begun in eastern Europe by Israel ben Eliezer (1700–1760), known as the Baal Shem Tov

(the Master of the Good Name, abbreviated to Besht). The term *Hasidim* was much older, having long designated the "pious" people zealous for the observance of the law. In the modern movement, followers of the Besht stressed the joy of communing with God, the transports of prayer, the power of spiritual purification, and the ability of religious fervor to bring people through the persecutions regularly visited on European Jewry. Hasidim conceived of their lives as an opportunity to help God redeem the world, and outstanding rabbis such as the Besht and Rabbi Nahman gave this conception power and spice.

Heresies: deviations from orthodoxy, departures from right doctrine. Although heresies stress the intellectual component of faith, they take their importance from the overall effect religious bodies have associated with them. To think wrongly about faith, and so to construe reality wrongly, has been abhorrent, because it has been considered certain to lead people to false worship and morality. Pluralistic cultures have had to temper this judgment, proposing to traditional religionists that disagreements about doctrinal matters, even disagreements about the nature of God and what God demands of people, ought not to sunder the social fabric, ought to be amenable to civil negotiations that would let religiously differing groups live in peace. In fact living in pluralistic cultures has tended to make religionists downplay or privatize doctrinal purity, which raises a question about when tolerance becomes indifference.

Hermeneutics: the science or study of interpretation. Hermeneutics deals with the ways that human beings derive meaning from texts and other artifacts, concentrating on the assumptions interpreters tend to make and the process of communication between text and reader. Recently several theoretical schools have developed hermeneutical positions of considerable sophistication, speaking of the innate structures that govern human communication or the ways that interpreters may deconstruct texts and so liberate a wide range of possible meanings.

Humanism: for people of religious commitment who wish to use the term disparagingly, limiting one's interests, energies, and commitments to secular matters and not concerning oneself much with God or transcendent realities. *Humanity*, in such usage, therefore shrinks to what human beings experience and enact in their ordinary round of thoughts and activities. The depths of consciousness and conscience, where more than temporal or secular values can emerge, fall outside the humanist's pale, as do overt religious activities. Not accepting such a negative view of the term, some believers place an adjective such as *Christian* before their sort of humanism, meaning to imply that God's special sphere of activity can be precisely the realm of human affairs: politics, art, science, and even the ordinary interactions that keep humanbeings going, such as eating and making love. Humanists themselves often stress commitment to all people's well-being.

Idealistic: concerning the realm of pure thought, of ideas operating independently of sense experience. In some idealistic systems, only thought is accounted fully real. Both Hegelianism in the west and such Eastern systems as Hindu Vedanta and Buddhist Yogacara have espoused this position. The popular connotation of idealism as having to do with lofty aspirations, high moral sentiments, can relate to this more metaphysical denotation, but it need not. Idealism as a metaphysical system does not solve the problem of evil but transposes it into a question of spiritual disorder.

Inquisition: a papal commission charged with combatting heresy and religious deviance. Medieval and reform movements in the 11th and 12th centuries, especially the heretics known as the Cathari and Waldenses, moved Pope Gregory IX to institute the Inquisition in 1231. The commission was charged with seeking out heretics and punishing them. By 1252 the papacy had authorized the use of torture and death for convicted heretics who refused to recant. The Spanish Inquisition arose in 1478, after the reconquest of Spain from the Muslims, to purify Spain of lingering Muslim and Jewish influences. The Spanish government found the very severe policies of the Spanish Inquisition politically useful and resisted papal efforts to moder-

ate the Spanish inquisitors. The first Grand Inquisitor, Tomas de Torquemada, used torture, had more than 2000 heretics burned at the stake, and made the auto-da-fé (the public ceremony at which sentences were pronounced) a major celebration.

Inspiration: the notion that Scripture derives from the inbreathing of divinity, which makes the text the body through which divinity would reveal itself. Inspiration may connote different amounts of divine dictation and control. In strong versions, such as those favored by fundamentalists, Scripture becomes a text God dictated or otherwise firmly controlled. It cannot err because of its complete dependence on divinity. In weaker versions, Scripture is a literary body in which divinity is frequently pleased to dwell, and scriptural images become privileged metaphors for the salvation God is offering in all times and places.

Just War: one that would meet the basic requirements of conscience and honor the essential equality of all human beings in the sight of God. Traditionally, a just war was hard to find. A just war had to be a response to unjust aggression with a reasonable hope of success, to safeguard the rights of noncombatants, and to use no more destructive force than was necessary to gain victory. Overall one had to have good grounds for thinking that going to war would bring more good than harm. War therefore was seen as a last resort, after negotiations had broken down and the evils inflicted by one's enemy had become intolerable. Clearly the Western nations rarely listened to this traditional Christian teaching, but it remained a pressure to solve international problems by negotiation rather than violence.

Kabbalah: a medieval Jewish mystical movement that sought the inner meaning of the Torah and frequently became rather gnostic. The Kabbalists took their fervor and imagination to the sacred pages, convinced that the Master of the Universe had left there the keys to nature and history, as to the self. By such stratagems as assigning numerical values to the different letters of the Hebrew alphabet, they would calculate the secret message of a line from Genesis or a chapter of Exodus. They also developed complicated theories of how divinity had diffused itself through creation and what was necessary if redemption were to bring back to God the fallen away parts of creation. The Hasidim often steeped themselves in Kabbalistic lore and thought it their task to carry sparks of divinity into the world or bring the unredeemed back through their joy.

Karma: the influence of one's moral acts on one's state of being. Indians generally assume that people are immersed in a process of deaths and rebirths. How people manage, whether they advance toward release or recede deeper into the process, depends on what they have done in their previous lives. Karma is not fatalistic, but it does suggest that much of what one presently is has been preconditioned by one's past lives. Similarly, what one will be in future lives depends on how one responds to moral challenges now. Inasmuch as it denotes action or work, karma can become an object of discipline. By detachment from the fruits (success or failure) of action, one can live in the world and not accrue more attachment or karma.

Kenosis: self-emptying. The term appears in Philippians 2, where Paul is describing the incarnation and sacrifice of Christ. It has entered Christian theology as a provocation to think hard about the sacrifices entailed in the work of redemption. Extended to religious discourse in general, it appears in discussions of how to combat evil and what part forgiveness, reconciliation, and new beginnings play in establishing community. It poses some of the most fundamental challenges to civil discourse: When does liberty become vicious individualism? What kinds of sacrifice are not foolish but admirable, not outside the basic business of civility but central to forming a people, avoiding a bloodbath, and preserving the third, spiritual dimension without which culture may be merely materialistic fodder?

Kenotic: concerned with self-emptying, self-sacrifice. The Pauline Christology sketched in Philippians 2 praises the incarnate word for having emptied himself of his heavenly status, assumed flesh, suffered, and died on human beings'

behalf. This condescension was a mark of the divine goodness, and in Paul's eyes it ought to have led Christians to humility, self-sacrifice, and devotion to the needs of others. More generally, one may call kenotic any religious views that seek the improvement of human beings' flesh and blood condition and imply both an emptying of grandiose phrases and a will to stress experience and results.

Know-nothingism: an American political movement that flourished in the mid-1800s. It was a reaction to the waves of immigrants that were changing the character of the American population and soon gained an anti-Catholic edge. Know-nothingism centered in the east and mainly enlisted Protestants competing with the arriving Germans and Irish for jobs and political power. The movement got its name from the tendency of members to respond to questions about their organization by saying they knew nothing. Eventually they formed the American Party as a national political entity. Its goals included restrictions on immigration, the exclusion of the foreign-born from voting rights and holding public office, and a 21-year residency requirement for citizenship. By the 1855 Congress, the Know-Nothings had 43 seats in the House of Representatives. However, divisions over slavery prior to the Civil War split the party and thereafter its influence was small.

Kulturkampf: a German word meaning "struggle for civilization." The word represented the efforts of the German Chancellor Otto von Bismarck to subject Roman Catholicism to state controls during the 1870s. By 1873 those advocating such controls were trying to glorify their measures as a valiant battle on behalf of humanistic values. Bismarck's own Protestantism made him suspicious of Catholicism, and after the definition of papal infallibility at the First Vatican Council in 1870 he moved from suspicion to alarm. In 1871 he abolished the Catholic bureau in the Prussian ministry and forbade priests to speak about politics from the pulpit. In 1872 he made all religious schools subject to state inspection, excluded all religious teachers from the state schools, dissolved the Jesuit order in Germany, and severed diplomatic ties with the Vatican. Catholics resisted, and by 1887 things were back to normal, but these religious oppressions, along with economic considerations, stimulated many German Catholics to emigrate.

Liberation theology: a several-sided movement, strongest perhaps in Latin America but present also in Asian, African, European, and North American theologies, that emphasizes the economic, political, and ethical implications of salvation. The main thesis of the liberation theologians is that faith must result in works of justice, concern for the poor and marginalized, and resistance to structures that dehumanize people if it is to be worthy of the biblical God. Most liberation theologians do not deny the transcendent, otherworldly dimensions of Christian faith. But their greater interest is in liberating the oppressed—victims of poverty, racial discrimination, sexual discrimination, and the like—so that they can become full participants in the cultural life of their community. This, the liberation theologians say, is the first imperative of the gospel.

Manichean: concerning the views of Manes (215–275 C.E.), a Persian innovator who founded a religion based on a dualism of evil and good. Manicheanism derived from Zoroastrian dualism, but it differed from Zoroastrianism in making matter a principle of evil. Followers of Manes therefore, were to be extremely ascetic and to keep themselves as untainted by the flesh (sex, food) as possible. Manicheanism enjoyed considerable popularity in the West during the fourth century. Prior to his Christian conversion, Augustine of Hippo was a Manichean, and some historians of Christian doctrine think that Augustine's pessimism about sexuality, the flesh, and human nature, which proved highly influential in Christian history, owed a great deal to his Manichean period. In broader usage, the term connotes any tendency to divide the world into two opposing camps of light and darkness, goodness and evil.

Marranos: Jews who converted to Christianity to escape persecution but continued to practice their Judaism secretly. The term is Spanish, of uncertain origin, and arose in the 14th century.

Originally it was a term of abuse used by Christian detractors and applied to the descendants of those who originally had converted, to cast aspersions on their faith. Estimates are that at least 100,000 Spanish Jews converted to save themselves from fanatical Christian neighbors. By the mid-15th century the Marranos were a powerful community in Spain, influential in government, and the target of much wrath. Riots against Marranos in Cordoba in 1473 brought the Inquisition to take charge of the matter, and in 1480 more than 300 Marranos were burned and their property confiscated for the crown. Eventually the number of martyrs reached the tens of thousands. Continued opposition led to the expulsion of all Jews from Spain in 1492, and many went to the New World.

Materialists: those who stress the physical, empirical side of human existence and reality as a whole, often disparaging spirituality or denying that there are spiritual entities such as God or an immortal human soul. Materialism can have a religious foundation and so take on the accommodated meaning of stressing the goodness of creation, as Genesis praises it, or stressing the incarnational character of Christian existence, as Jesus exemplifies it. In that case materialism tends to mean not the strict denial of spiritual realities but the conviction that the healthiest living concentrates on making the world a better place to live in. In de Tocqueville's view, materialism is rather crude, urging people to use the freedoms democracy offers to eat, drink, and be merry, grabbing what pleasure a body-bound existence can. He sees this as destructive of the self-sacrifice for the common good that democracy needs and so finds that the religions that show human beings a reality transcending the senses and the grave are powerful supports of democracy in the ideal sense.

Millennialist: one who expects the millennium, the thousand-year reign of Christ. Millennialists come in different garbs and with different sub-theories, but common to them all is an expectation that history will soon stop (often at the end of a thousand-year period) and God will intervene to set things right. Millennialism draws on the more orthodox notion of Christ's second coming to render judgment and bring the saved to heaven. It has ties with both gnosticism and apocalyptic literature (that claiming to have been disclosed by God because Christ will soon return), and throughout Christian history it has spiced many reform movements. In the United States such groups as The Seventh Day Adventists and the Jehovah's Witnesses have been shaped by Millennialism.

Nativism: the attitude or policy of favoring native inhabitants of a country against immigrants. The rise of this attitude in the mid-19th century in the United States produced the Know-Nothings and the American Party.

Natural Law: what can be inferred about the rights and obligations incumbent on all human beings, on the basis of historical experience and rational analysis. Natural law theory assumes that God, the source of creation, has worked rationally and so encoded in all creatures "laws" governing their actions. Human beings are the peculiar creatures endowed with reason and freedom, so the laws special to them pertain to moral rather than physical actions. The most general moral law encoded in human nature is that people are to do good and avoid evil. The more one descends from this general law to particular situations and obligations, the more one has to consult experience, on-the-spot analyses, and the virtue of prudence. Proponents of natural law theory have tended to think that human beings able to agree that God has made an intelligible creation ought to be able to reach sufficient agreement about the basic nature of humankind and the basic ends of society to nurture the ongoing discussion and collaboration necessary for promoting the common weal, avoiding war, and prosecuting prosperity (decent material living and the flourishing of higher culture).

Natural theology: ways of reflecting on God or speaking about God that at least purport to draw nothing determinative from Scripture but rather to derive from reason alone. Many natural theologies focus on the physical world, arguing that the being and order of nature bespeak an intelligent Creator. Other arguments, from

human conscience and freedom, run to the conclusion that without a Creator and Judge human existence would be meaningless. To theologians who accept a biblical or other revelation from God, the problem with natural theology is its attempt at self-sufficiency. If God is more than what reason can fathom, limiting theology to the rational is risking producing a tiny God, more limited than the attributes of God (even those that reason tends to produce) warrant. God then might not be a savior of human beings from sin, or the source of an existence beyond what eye has seen, ear has heard, it has entered the human heart to conceive. God then would tend to be but a projection of human intelligence, but an image of humanity (rather than vice versa, humanity being a mere image of divinity).

Ontology: the study of being. While *metaphysics* suggests rather formalistic explorations of what lies beyond the physical, *ontology* suggests some wonder and ecstasy about the primordial fact that some things have stepped forth from the void of nothingness. Ontology therefore works at the roots of human language, trying to think about the most basic structures of reality: existence and essence, form and matter. Its great stimulus and continuing preoccupation, however, is being: the one ultimate quality and the many ways it is differently possessed.

Original sin: a Christian doctrine, associated with St. Augustine, that tries to account for human disorder by postulating a mistake, flaw, or sin at the foundations of the human race. The account of the disobedience of Adam and Eve in Genesis 3 was the prime biblical text cited, though Paul's teaching in Romans 5 was equally significant. The symbols and doctrine intended a warning about human nature: Experience showed that people regularly seek their own interest rather than the common good and sin from weakness, blindness, pride, and bondage to passion. Augustine's rather literal interpretation of Paul tied the transmission of original sin to sexual intercourse. It also made a person existing in an unbaptized state subject to Satan and hell. In such an interpretation, original sin was removed by baptism through the merits of

Christ but remained in the unbaptized as something to be laid to their own account, making them guilty. Later theology has preferred to see original sin as "the sin of the world": the tilted, flawed situation all children enter and then somehow reaffirm. However conceived, the notion of original sin is opposed to a simple optimism about human nature and calls people to consider carefully the historical record of humanity's crimes and the tangle of human motivation.

Papal Infallibility: the Roman Catholic doctrine, defined at the First Vatican Council in 1870, that the pope, when speaking *ex cathedra* (formally, from his chair as official teacher) on matters of faith and morals, is protected by the Holy Spirit from error. The doctrine has generally been interpreted as having quite severe limitations (for example, the pope is expected to consult widely throughout the church) and to flow from the nature of both the Church (looked at as the everlasting community of salvation) and the papacy (considered to be the institution unifying the Church). The existence of the doctrine has often been used to justify outsiders' fears that Catholics could not think for themselves and would be bound to follow any dictates of the pope (even those not limited to faith and morals).

Pelagian: referring to the supposed teachings of an Irish monk, Pelagius, who died about 419 and was an opponent of St. Augustine. The Pelagian position stressed human freedom and responsibility in the work of salvation. The Augustinian position stressed the gratuity of salvation and humanity's dependence on God. Orthodox Christianity favored Augustine, though when proper nuance is applied, the two positions may not be irreconcilable. The stereotype became that moralistic types, bent on having people scour their consciences and bootstrap their way to salvation, were heretical on the model of Pelagius. Precisely how to correlate divine grace and human freedom remains mysterious, but mainstream Christianity has held for both the priority of God's love and the necessity of human cooperation.

Pragmatism: the philosophy of C.S. Peirce and

William James, in which the test of truth and wisdom was practical effects and experiential foundations. James was not advocating a crude commitment to "what works" or intending to override ethical questions of the means to effective ends. He was impressed by the revelations of action, of what happened when people stayed close to their experience and struggled to let the yield of experience be their guide. Only by acting on their beliefs, by bringing their beliefs to the test of experience, would people finally know what their beliefs were worth.

Presbytery: the council of elders charged with running a church. Presbyterian churches tend to deny the distinction of bishops from elders that Episcopalian churches find in the New Testament. Their elders are of two main kinds: teachers (ministers) and rulers elected by the congregations. Presbyterian churches claim Calvinist roots, their system of government having first been developed in Calvin's Geneva. The Scottish church, under John Knox, stressed presbyterianism and exported it to the New World. Although the 17th century Massachusetts Puritan churches spoke of elders, they are usually considered to have been more congregational than presbyterian. Insofar as any congregation elects presbyters and has some rights over the presbyterian council, however, the distinction between the two forms of church government can be narrow.

Puritans: the current connotations of prudishness and repression of sensuality distort the historical reality of the groups who first carried this name. The origins of these groups lay in their objection to the adornment of worship promoted by the Book of Common Prayer issued under Queen Elizabeth I. Those who so objected were called Puritans because they wanted a simpler form of worship, closer to what they thought was the spirit of the Bible (as interpreted by the Protestant Reformers, especially Calvin). Other Puritans opposed the appointment of bishops in the English church because they felt that such a move was contrary to the pure biblical faith they hoped the English Reformation would achieve. The Puritan movement stressed conversion, a strict moral code, austerity, and hard work, for all of which it usually assumed scriptural foundations.

Regeneration: a term meaning rebirth, mentioned by such New Testament texts as Titus 3:5, John 3:5, and Matthew 19:28. In early Christian theological reflection, a question arose about the relation between the rebirth accomplished in baptism and the need for Christians to pray for forgiveness: Is not the work of the Holy Spirit in baptism, where the person is reborn to divine life, sufficient to grant forgiveness? Augustine distinguished between the washing away of sins in baptism and the need for the regenerate person to resist the infirmity that leads to sin. By the time of John Wesley and the Methodist reform this distinction had broadened. Wesley denied that baptism was more than an external work and argued that true or full rebirth would be an internal work. Other Protestant groups thinking this way demanded a confession of rebirth or a testimony to God's action in the person's soul as a condition for adult participation in church life. Some churches equated regeneration with a vivid, adult experience of the Holy Spirit that usually included striking gifts such as the ability to speak in tongues.

Revivalism: a concern with and a technique for quickening or reawakening faith. Some historians of the term and phenomenon in America see its beginnings in the ministry of Solomon Stoddard (1643–1729) in Northhampton, Massachusetts that gave him leverage against Increase Mather, whose ministry in Boston was more intellectual and less geared to eliciting emotional arousal. The Great Awakening that occurred from the 1720s to the 1740s was the first peak of revivalism. This was carried from New England to the South and was taken up by many Methodists and Baptists. The Second Great Awakening early in the 19th century can also be considered a high point of revivalism, while its extension to the western frontier made the camp meeting and emotional sermon staples of pious efforts to keep the coals of faith glowing. Methodists, Baptists, and Disciples of Christ all favored a revivalist preaching style and theology. Revivalism overlaps evangelism, but usually it emphasizes stirring up the faith of believers rather than gaining new converts or preaching the gospel in virgin territory.

Schisms: separations of religious groups based on disputes about authority and political arrangements. For example, the separation of the eastern and western branches of Christendom that became official in 1054 resulted more from disputes about the powers of the Bishop of Rome than from doctrinal disagreements. Certainly East and West had come to have different doctrinal, liturgical, and disciplinary traditions, but the greater bone of contention was whether the monarchical political tradition of the West would prevail over the collegial tradition of the East. Similarly, many intra-Protestant church separations have been more schismatic than heretical (though all differences in political understanding of religion tend to have theological implications).

Secular: pertaining to the world of space and time, often to the neglect or denial of transcendent divine mystery. Secular culture proposes that work, play, politics, war, love, education, the arts, and other aspects of our common human life do not stretch beyond themselves for their fullest meaning but constitute a realm sufficient unto itself. Secularists tend to neglect such factors as death and injustice, which call the sufficiency of such an outlook radically into question. They also tend to neglect the highest aspirations and intentions of work, art, and love, which can make them ecstatic—occupations that carry people beyond themselves toward the mystery of existence.

Secular Humanism: a term usually employed by fundamentalist Christians to denote those who deny the validity of religious claims in the realms of either ultimate truth or practical politics. Secular humanists therefore are those who are agnostics or atheists, who concentrate on this-worldly matters, and whose main concern is that human beings flourish. Whether a Christian or Jew can be a secular humanist is an interesting question in the abstract, apart from fundamentalist assumptions, but in the fundamentalist camp the notion is ludicrous. Indeed, sometimes virtually all opponents of the fundamentalist political agenda—feminists, socialists, gay rights advocates, pacifists, and progressive educators—are swept together and labeled secular humanists, because they do not make the Bible their operative authority in all aspects of daily life.

Sephardim: Jews who lived in Spain and Portugal during the Middle Ages until their expulsion at the end of the 15th century. Most Sephardim then fled to North Africa and the Muslim world, thinking those areas safer than Christian realms. Eventually, however, they also settled in many other areas, including Holland, England, and Latin America. They differed from the Ashkenazim in preserving Babylonian rather than Palestinian ritual traditions, and in using Ladino rather than Yiddish. Sephardim now number about 4 percent of the worldwide Jewish population, about 750,000.

Shamanism: archaic techniques for gaining ecstasy. This definition, which owes much to Mircea Eliade, one of the pioneer students of the phenomenon of shamanism across many different religious complexes, points to both the mechanics of shamans and some of their motivation. By dancing, ingesting tobacco or hallucinogens, staring hypnotically at a skull, fasting, retreating into solitude, letting themselves be mesmerized by the beating of a drum, singing, and other preparatory and suggestive techniques, shamans gained the ability to inhabit two different realms of consciousness. In addition to normal consciousness, they could "travel" to arealm in which they encountered the gods or spirits responsible for crucial factors in the life of their people (the movement of the game, for example). They could also speak with animals, guide the souls of the dead, or fight with the malignant spirits responsible for an illness. The shamanic tribes relied on their visionaries to heal a community dispute; find where the absent game had gone; cure illnesses; determine where the tribe ought to travel; and placate the spirits responsible for disease, flood, or famine—that is, to deal with all crises requiring communications with the powers holding their fate. In time the ecstatic experience itself moved many shamans to sing or dance as a personal need. They had become positively addicted to

their flights and enraptured by the expanded consciousness to which their shamanizing took them.

Sufi: pertaining to the mystical dimension of Islam. The Sufis arose when Islam was becoming a prosperous, this-worldly power dominating the Middle East. In part they were an ascetic movement protesting the corruptions threatened by this-worldly power. But the Sufi movement was also like early Christian monasticism and later Jewish Hasidism in offering an outlet for those who wanted more ardor and introspection than formal orthodoxy, regulated by Muslim law (*Shariah*), tended to develop. The great Sufis claimed to be faithful to the Qur'an, the example of Muhammad, and the intents of the Shariah, but Muslim lawyers remained suspicious of Sufi ecstaticism and the liberty of spirit some Sufis manifested.

Syncretism: a running together of different intellectual, ritual, or cultural systems that creates a hybrid. In pluralistic cultures such as the Hellenistic world of the early centuries B.C.E., ordinary citizens frequently drew from various pagan mystery religions, Eastern (e.g., Egyptian) sources, and Christianity to fashion an amalgamation of religious notions, a potpourri. Few syncretistic religious systems have survived and prospered (Sikhism, blending Hinduism and Islam in a new Indian synthesis, may be an exception), but many cultures have tolerated different religious streams, with the result that many ordinary believers have not cared much about doctrinal purity. Thus many Indians could consider Buddhism a subset of Hinduism, or of a generalized Indian religion, and make the Buddha but another manifestation of the Hindu god Vishnu, while many Japanese gladly ran together Buddhist and Shinto notions, little distinguishing between Shinto gods (kami) and Buddhists saints (bodhisattvas).

Synoptic: referring to the first three of the New Testament gospels, Matthew, Mark, and Luke. The term comes from early efforts to set these three gospels side by side, that their likenesses and differences might be taken in "at a single glance." Current biblical scholarship tends to consider Mark the oldest gospel, and to make

Mark a source for Matthew and Luke. The majority view postulates a second source for the things Matthew and Luke hold in common. The whole question of the relationship among the first three gospels is called "the synoptic problem" and continues to draw much attention from New Testament scholars.

Talmudic: pertaining to the Talmud, the comprehensive collection of rabbinic teaching. The Talmud collects the Mishnah and the Gemarah (commentary on the Mishnah), which in turn is a collection of teachings, legal opinions, and stories about leading rabbis of the last centuries B.C.E. and the first centuries C.E. The Talmud exists in two main versions (one produced in Babylon and one in Palestine) dating from about 500 C.E. For Jewish theology, it gathers the traditional teachings about the oral law that has always accompanied Scripture. This oral law, which functions much as "tradition" has in Christian theology, goes back to Moses and primarily deals with how to appreciate and apply the Torah first granted on Mount Sinai, which in turn is understood as the blessed law or guidance expressing Israel's special covenant with God.

Theocracy: political rule by religious leaders. Theocracies usually deny much separation between civil and religious realms, arguing that God is Lord of all creation. Most traditional religions have been theocratic. Classical Hindu, Buddhist, Muslim, Christian, and Jewish cultures all were holistic fusions of what we now call secular and sacred concerns. The advantages of theocratic regimes include the possibility of a holistic culture and the probability that religious and ethical questions will be considered very important for civic life. The disadvantages of theocracies include the probability that the religious leaders will shortchange secular competencies and that they will try to regulate the morals of other citizens.

Theodicy: the task of defending the divine justice and showing that God's dealings with the world have been honorable. When taken as a function of philosophy, and so a matter of reasoning to the divine justice in the face of great evil in the world, theodicy has fared badly. Phenomena such as the Holocaust, the extermination of

Armenians by Turks or Chinese by Japanese, or even the death of a single innocent child, throw up walls many find impossible to scale. When taken as a subtask of theology, of faith seeking understanding, theodicy has stayed closer to the mysteriousness of all God's doings, from making the world from nothingness to redeeming the world by self-spending love. Such mysteriousness does not remove the need to protest injustice and evil, but it may shift the focus of the inquiry more to human perversions of God's will or to the statistical probabilities of a world running by evolutionary chance. Indeed for some theologians God is a fellow sufferer and protester, fighting evil alongside human beings.

Theological liberalism: a somewhat vague movement, influential in the 19th and early 20th centuries, especially among progressive Protestants. Liberal theologians generally claimed the freedom to reinterpret traditional Christian doctrines and embraced the new methods of textural criticism that subjected the Bible and church documents to the influences shaping all other human records. Behind the liberal theologians lay such developments as the Enlightenment and the Romantic movement, both of which emphasized human resources (intellectual or emotional) and raised serious questions about past traditions. Theological liberals tended to regard Christianity as more like than unlike other religions and to slough off the divinity of Jesus and his miracles.

Theosophy: a system of thought proposing privileged wisdom about God, the cosmos, the individual, and salvation. Usually theosophists depend on the direct perceptions of supposedly gifted individuals and rate such perceptions a higher wisdom than what either the historical religions or the empirical sciences can establish. Theosophy has obvious affinities to gnosticism, hermeticism, and other traditions based on secret, intuitive lore, and usually it perches on the border where philosophy, mysticism, and magic draw together. Recent American theosophists have taken inspiration from such diverse sources as Oriental (Vedanta) thought and the writings of Jakob Boehme and Emanuel Swedenborg.

Tradition: past practice and understanding of a

culture or faith that is considered a living mentor. Etymologically tradition is what is "handed on." It holds the danger of becoming merely a sterile repetition of what was done in the past, but it is also inevitable: No age starts completely anew; every age is bound to be shaped by prior ages, even when it rebels against them. Church officials often argue about who should guide and clarify tradition and how tradition should be shaped. In periods when individual conscience came into clear focus, tradition could be set against private interpretation, whether concerning the Bible or Christian doctrine and morality. Every new cultural era has the difficult task of trying to translate tradition afresh, for study soon shows that one cannot simply repeat past formulas or practices. To do so in changed circumstances would not hand on the original message but cause it to miscarry.

Trinitarian: pertaining to the Christian doctrine of God as Father-Son-Spirit. This doctrine claims biblical foundations and was clarified during the great Christian councils of the fourth and fifth centuries. The basic formula, "one God in three divine persons," has satisfied the orthodox throughout the centuries, but various groups have dissented, usually either by wanting to subordinate the Son to the Father or by arguing for a nontrinitarian, "unitarian" God. Orthodox theology has considered the Trinity a strict mystery and has structured the Christian liturgy in terms of addressing prayers above all to the Father, depending on the mediation of the Son, and thinking of the Spirit as moving in believers' hearts to raise them toward God.

Typological exegesis: an interpretation (usually of Scripture) that focuses on how prior events or figures were fulfilled by later ones. For example, Christians argued that Jesus had fulfilled the messianic prophecies of the Old Testament. Indeed, they came to think that the entire Old Testament was a treasury of foreshadowings of Jesus. The apostle Paul had encouraged such a way of reading Scripture, seeing Christ as the Second Adam and Abraham as the prefiguring father of Christian faith. The Suffering Servant of Isaiah seemed to foretell the passion of Christ, while the ark that kept Noah safe during the flood seemed a prefiguring of the Church.

Jewish rabbis used the biblical text similarly, speaking, for instance, of Jacob and Esau as prototypical Jews and Christians. The Puritan divines continued this way of treating Scripture, trying to bring the biblical images into their own day and find God's purposes for America.

Unitarianism: in its American usage, the term refers to one of the groups that emerged from the demise of the Puritan sense of national covenant that had dominated New England in the early colonial days. The rational impulse brought forward by the Enlightenment and Deism contributed to the atmosphere in which believers (most of them educated) wanted to distance themselves from the Trinity and other strictly supernatural mysteries of traditional Christian faith. King's Chapel in Boston became the first Unitarian Church in 1785 and featured a worship service modified to accommodate this trend in faith. The Unitarians gained control of Harvard College in 1805 and were the moving spirits behind the establishment of Harvard Divinity School in 1816. In 1825 William Ellery Channing became head of a Unitarian Association that many previously Congregationalist churches joined. Unitarians have generally stressed the goodness of human nature and the power of human reason, denying that human beings need a savior such as Jesus Christ. Instead they have seen Jesus as a moral example of what the love of God and one's fellow human beings should be like. Finally Unitarian thought has stressed the freedom of all people to believe as their consciences dictate and the priority of ethical uprightness over doctrinal orthodoxy.

Yogic: pertaining to discipline, method—especially that concerned with gaining release from the cycle of deaths and rebirths. The classical yoga of Patanjali concentrates on purifying consiousness, with the goal of reaching a state below ordinary awareness, even below sleep, in which one would be pure consciousness, without attachment to anything (aware of nothing in particular). Other yogas have fixed on philosophical study, purifying work (karma-yoga), or emotional love. Each such yoga could be a pathway to salvation, and a wise guru would help a striver decide which yoga best fit his or her personality.

Zionist: pertaining to a Jewish movement to reestablish a homeland for Jews in Palestine. In one sense Zionism is as old as the first expulsion of the Jews from Israel, during the Babylonian captivity of the sixth century B.C.E. and the Roman expulsions of the first century C.E. However, during the 16th and 17th centuries in Europe several messianic figures urged Jews to return to Palestine, while toward the end of the 19th century Theodor Herzl, an Austrian journalist, inspired a movement to make return a practical venture. A series of Zionist congresses at the turn of the century publicized this ideal, and in the first decades of the 20th century the pograms in Russia sparked considerable emigration. By 1914 there were about 90,000 Jews in Palestine. The Balfour Declaration of 1917 pledged English support for a Jewish homeland, and Jewish numbers in Palestine steadily increased. The watershed came after the Second World War, when awareness of the Holocaust catalyzed both Jewish and non-Jewish sentiment, leading to the establishment of the modern state of Israel in 1948.

Bibliography

Ahlstrom, Sydney E. *A Religious History of the American People*. New Haven CT: Yale University Press, 1972.

Ahlstrom, Sydney E., ed. *Theology in America: The Major Protestant Voices from Puritanism to Neo-Orthodoxy*. Indianapolis IN: Bobbs-Merrill, 1967.

Bercovitch, Sacvan. *The Puritan Origins of the American Self*. New Haven CT: Yale University Press, 1975.

Bellah, Robert N., Richard Madsen, William M. Sullivan, Ann Swidler, and Steven M. Tipton, *Habits of the Heart*. Berkeley: University of California Press, 1985.

Bellah, Robert N., *The Broken Covenant: American Civil Religion in Time of Trial*. New York: Seabury, 1975.

Bellah, Robert N., and Frederick E. Greenspahn. *Uncivil Religion: Interreligious Hostility in America*. New York: Crossroad, 1987.

Brauer, Jerald C., ed. *Religion and the American Revolution*. Philadelphia PA: Fortress, 1976.

Cherry, Conrad, ed. *God's New Israel: Religious Interpretations of American Destiny*. New York: Prentice-Hall, 1971.

Clebsch, William A. *American Religious Thought*. Chicago: University of Chicago Press, 1975.

Clebsch, William A. *From Sacred to Profane America: The Role of Religion in American History*. New York: Harper & Row, 1968.

Coleman, John A. *An American Strategic Theology*. New York: Paulist, 1982.

Degler, Carl. *At Odds: Women and the Family in America from the Revolution to the Present*. New York: Oxford University Press, 1980.

Dolan, Jay P. *The American Catholic Experience*. Garden City NY: Doubleday, 1985.

Ellis, John T., ed. *Documents of American Catholic History*. Wilmington, DE: Michael Glazier, 1987.

Gaustad, Edwin S., ed. *A Documentary History of Religion in America*. Grand Rapids MI: Eerdmans, 1982.

Gaustad, Edwin S. *Historical Atlas of Religion in America*. New York: Harper & Row, 1962.

Gaustad, Edwin S. *The Great Awakening in New England*. Chicago: Quadrangle Books, 1968.

Greven, Philip. *The Protestant Temperament*. New York: Alfred A. Knopf, 1977.

Hall, Peter D. *The Organization of American Culture, 1700–1900*. New York: New York University Press, 1982.

Handlin, Oscar. *Adventure in Freedom: Three Hundred Years of Jewish Life in America*. New York: McGraw-Hill, 1954.

Handlin, Oscar. *The Uprooted: The Epic Story of the Great Migrations that Made the American People*. New York: Grosset & Dunlap, 1951.

Hatch, Nathan O., and Mark A. Noll, eds. *The Bible*

in America. New York: Oxford University Press, 1982.

Hennessey, James. *American Catholics*. New York: Oxford University Press, 1981.

Highman, John, and Paul K. Conkin, eds. *New Directions in American Intellectual History*. Baltimore MD: Johns Hopkins, 1979.

Hofstadter, Richard. *Anti-Intellectualism in American Life*. New York: Alfred A. Knopf, 1963.

Karp, Abraham J., ed. *The Jewish Experience in America*. New York: KTAV, 1969.

MacIntyre, Alasdair. *After Virtue*. Notre Dame IN: University of Notre Dame Press, 1981.

Marty, Martin E. *Righteous Empire: The Protestant Experience in America*. New York: Dial Press, 1970.

Marty, Martin E. *The Public Church*. New York: Crossroad, 1981.

McFadden, Thomas M., ed. *America in Theological Perspective*. New York: Seabury, 1976.

McLoughlin, William G. *Revivals, Awakenings, and Reform*. Chicago: University of Chicago Press, 1978.

McNamara, Patrick H. *Religion: American Style*, 2d ed. Belmont CA: Wadsworth, 1984.

Mead, Sidney E. *The Lively Experiment: The Shaping of Christianity in America*. New York: Harper & Row, 1963.

Mojtabai, A. G. *Blessed Assurance: At Home with the Bomb in Amarillo, Texas*. Boston: Houghton Mifflin, 1986.

Moore, R. Laurence. *Religious Outsiders and the Making of Americans*. New York: Oxford University Press, 1986.

Palmer, Parker J. *The Company of Strangers: Christians and the Renewal of America's Public Life*. New York: Crossroad, 1981.

Parsons, Elsie C. *American Indian Life*. Lincoln: University of Nebraska Press/Bison, 1967.

Ruether, Rosemary R., and Rosemary S. Keller, eds. *Women & Religion in America*. San Francisco: Harper & Row, 1981.

Silberman, Charles. *A Certain People: American Jews and Their Lives Today*. New York: Summit Books, 1985.

Tocqueville, Alexis de. *Democracy in America*. Garden City NY: Doubleday, 1969.

Wells, David F., and John D. Woodbridge. eds. *The Evangelicals*, rev. ed. Grand Rapids MI: Baker House, 1977.

White, Morton, ed. *Science & Sentiment in America*. New York: Oxford University Press, 1972.

Wilmore, Gayraud S., and James H. Cone, eds. *Black Theology: A Documentary History, 1966–1979*. Maryknoll NY: Orbis, 1979.

Index

Boldface numbers indicate pages on which key terms are defined.